CRIMINOLOGY TODAY

FRANK SCHMALLEGER, PH.D.
The Justice Research Association

PRENTICE HALL, ENGLEWOOD CLIFFS, NEW JERSEY 07632

Library of Congress Cataloging-in-Publication Data
Schmalleger, Frank,
Criminology today/ Frank Schmalleger.
P. cm.
Includes bibliographical references and index.
ISBN 0-13-291824-2
1. Criminology. 2. Criminology—United States. I. Title.
HV6025.S346 1996 95-15801
364—dc20 CIP

Director of manufacturing & production: *Bruce Johnson*
Project manager: *Janet M. McGillicuddy*
Acquisitions editor: *Robin Baliszewski*
Manufacturing buyer: *Ed O'Dougherty*
Editorial assistant: *Rose Mary Florio*
Photo research: *Chris Pullo*
Electronic art: *Mark LaSalle*
Formatting/page make-up: *Janet M. McGillicuddy*
Template creation: *Steven Hartner*
Cover design: *Bruce Kenselaer*
Interior design: *Patrice Sheridan*
Cover art: *John Marin* (1870–1953), *City Movement, Downtown Manhattan #2,* watercolor & ink; 1936, Hunter Museum of American Art, Chattanooga, Tennessee, Gift of the Benwood Foundation

A Simon & Schuster Company
Englewood Cliffs, New Jersey 07632

*ChapterOpeningPhotoCredits:*1-Pool/SabaPressPhotos,Inc.;2-USAToday;3-BohdanHyrnewych/StockBoston;4-The Granger Collection; 5-Ian Turner/Spooner/Gamma-Liaison, Inc.; 6-Photofest; 7-Stephen Shames/Matric International; 8-AP/Wide World Photos; 9-Photofest; 10-Joel Stettenheim/SABA Press Photos, Inc.; 11-Mark Yankus; 12-Anthony Barboza; 13-McNamee/Bettmann; 14-Photofest

Printed in the United States of America

10 9 8 7 6 5 4 3 2 1

ISBN 0-13-291824-2

Prentice-Hall International (UK) Limited, *London*
Prentice-Hall of Australia Pty. Limited, *Sydney*
Prentice-Hall Canada Inc., *Toronto*
Prentice-Hall Hispanoamericana, S.A., *Mexico*
Prentice-Hall of India Private Limited, *New Delhi*
Prentice-Hall of Japan, Inc., *Tokyo*
Simon & Schuster Asia Pte. Ltd., *Singapore*
Editora Prentice-Hall do Brasil, Ltda., *Rio de Janeiro*

To my wife, Harmonie,

whose loving spirit and close friendship

have been my constant inspiration.

And to my daughter, Nicole, whom I will always cherish.

CONTENTS

FOREWARD

The United States is currently witnessing an unprecedented level of violent crime. Not only do the rates of criminal violence exceed anything in our history, but the acts have become more random, more brutal, and targeted toward more vulnerable victims, for example, children and innocent bystanders.

Unfortunately, experts predict another crime wave by the year 2000 because of a projected increase in the number of teenagers in America, who are twice as violent as adults. The next generation of children is also more likely to be born to a single mother, to experience poverty, and to be unemployed than previous generations—all factors known to relate to later criminality. When James Q. Wilson, a foremost authority on crime, wrote recently about what advice he would give to Americans struggling with the crime problem, he offered just two words: "Get ready."[1]

It is this sense of urgency that creates a daunting challenge for today's criminology students. Students must, above all, learn criminology so that they can contribute to it's solutions. In short, *criminology students must seek to become relevant.* We have become too detached from applied criminology, and as a result, current crime policies are overly bureaucratic and highly political. We must strive to change the perception that "criminologists...are insular and detached types who fiddle with equations while the cities burn."[2]

Criminology is the only academic discipline devoted exclusively to the scientific study of crime causation and control. When the public pressures government officials to "do something" about the crime problem, surely criminologists have an obligation to assist in identifying key issues, proposing policy and program solutions, and evaluating the consequences.

But learning criminology is not easy. In fact, it is hard to imagine a more difficult subject matter than criminology. At its core, criminology requires an understanding of the vagaries of human behavior, with an appreciation of their biological, cultural, and sociological foundations. Each of these contributes a partial explanation for crime, but none is comprehensive and all are fraught with controversy. Understanding crime is made even more complex because the behavior is defined and controlled by a justice system comprised of many diverse organizations, such as the police and corrections, and each of them is governed by a separate system of complex laws and philosophies. How is one to make sense of all these competing theories and contradictory data?

Thank goodness for Frank Schmalleger's new book, *Criminology Today*! In writing it, he has done most of the hard work for us. He succeeds in making this complex social problem clearly understandable. He begins by describing, in an easy-to-understand manner, the nature and diversity of the crime problem today. He critically reviews the nation's divergent crime indicators, and suggests what recent patterns portend about the crime problem—ever changing, ever more threatening. He then advances our understanding of the causes of crime by synthesizing criminology's most salient theories, grounding his review in current as well as historical traditions. Students can flounder in crime data and theory without a good and objective guide. Dr. Schmalleger serves as an authoritative and compassionate guide.

The uniqueness of this book and its biggest strength, derives from Schmalleger's orientation: it is always practical and socially relevant. He teaches the student how to relate criminology facts and theories to the everyday world in which we live. Discussions of the death penalty, for example, are illustrated with newspaper stories of recent executions. And the material covered in the text is particularly up-to-date. Events such as the use of DNA evidence in the O.J. Simpson murder trial, the recent federal Crime Bill, and the Oklahoma City bombing, are all discussed. Including such material not only makes the connection between academic criminology and real-world practice patently obvious, it provides an immediate attention getter for students, who are more likely to become fully engaged by such timely material. In a sense, it makes criminology come alive.

This book synthesizes and interprets the best available evidence on crime and crime control, but it goes still further. In his final chapter, Schmalleger encourages us to consider our future and work towards promoting better crime prevention and control practices. In the end, mastering the material in *Criminology Today* should enable us to do much more than simply sit passively and "get ready" for the next crime wave. For what we understand, we can often change. Schmalleger's text provides an excellent road map for increasing that understanding.

Joan Petersilia, Ph.D.
Professor of Criminology, Law & Society
University of California, Irvine
and former President
The American Society of Criminology

1. James Q. Wilson and Joan Petersilia, *Crime*, Institute for Contemporary Studies, San Francisco, 1995.
2. Currie, Elliott, "Shifting the Balance: On Social Action and the Future of Criminological Research," *Journal of Research in Crime and Delinquency*, Vol. 30, no. 4, 1993.

PREFACE

More than a quarter century ago the great criminologist Austin Turk, began the preface to his book *Criminality and Legal Order* with these words:[1]

> Embarrassment provided much of the initial push that led to the writing of this book. I was embarrassed at my lack of good answers when confronted by students who wondered, somewhat irreverently, why criminology is 'such a confused mish-mash.'... Some of these students were especially bothered by the 'unreality' of criminological studies, by which they meant the lack of sustained attention to connections between the theories and statistics about crime, and what they heard every day about relations among social conflicts, political maneuvers, and law violation and enforcement.

Much has changed since Turk's time, yet much remains the same. Far more criminological studies have been proposed and conducted. The Law Enforcement Assistance Administration, funded under President Johnson, which made many millions of dollars available in the fight against crime, has come and gone. The Clinton administration's $30 billion crime bill has become reality, with agencies everywhere scrambling for a part of the financial pie it represents.

Yet crime is still with us, and while crime statistics may actually be showing some decline (although not necessarily because of the Violent Crime Control and Law Enforcement Act of 1994, since such decline was evident before the bill's passage), fear of crime continues to run high among wide segments of the American population. Recent public opinion polls conducted by *USA Today*, CNN, and Gallup interviewers all show that crime outranks the economy, health care, foreign policy, and other social issues as the primary concern of the American public today.

Such heightening of concern, while new to many of today's students, appears to follow something of a cyclical pattern. For a long while concerns over individ-

1. Austin Turk, *Criminality and Legal Order* (Chicago: Rand McNally, 1969), p. vii.

ual rights have swung the proverbial social and legislative pendulums in what has now come to be seen by many as an overly permissive direction—one in which criminal offenders are coddled and shielded from accountability. Contemporary policy-makers now find themselves awash in calls to reverse the pendulums' direction in order to protect the law-abiding public, to ensure the swift and certain punishment of criminal predators, to unshackle agents of law enforcement, and to make certain that individual offenders are held firmly responsible for their actions.

Because of the ever-increasing interest in crime and its causation, today's textbook market is flooded with introductory criminology books. What makes *Criminology Today* different from all the other available texts which deal with the same subject matter? The following list highlights what I see as the important differences:

- *Criminology Today* is up-to-date. It addresses the latest social issues and discusses innovative criminological perspectives within a well-grounded and traditional theoretical framework
- *Criminology Today* is socially relevant. It contrasts contemporary issues of crime and social order with existing and proposed crime-control policies.
- *Criminology Today* is interesting and easy to read. It is written for today's student, and makes use of attention-getting stories, news briefs, images, and graphical outlines to capture student attention.
- *Criminology Today* is policy oriented. Unlike most existing texts, *Criminology Today* stresses the consequences of criminological thought for social policy, and describes the practical issues associated with understanding and controlling crime. Social policies focusing upon prevention, treatment, rehabilitation, and victim restoration are all discussed.
- Finally, *Criminology Today* is thematic. It builds upon the divergence between the social problems viewpoint and the social responsibility perspective. In so doing, it highlights the central issue facing criminologists today: whether crime should be addressed as a matter of individual responsibility and accountability, or treated as a symptom of a dysfunctional society.

The thematic approach of *Criminology Today* presents the social problem perspective as one which holds that crime is a manifestation of underlying cultural issues such as poverty, discrimination, and the breakdown of traditional social institutions. The social responsibility perspective, on the other hand, claims that individuals are fundamentally responsible for their own behavior, and maintains that they choose crime over other, more law-abiding, courses of action. The thematic difference is an important one. Few of today's books provide students with a useful framework for integrating the voluminous material contained within the field. Contrasting the two perspectives, as this book does, provides fertile ground for a dialectical process whereby readers can better understand the central issues defining contemporary criminology and come to their own conclusions about the value of criminological theorizing.

As an author I have tried to ensure that today's students will find *Criminology Today* relevant, interesting, and informative. It is my fondest hope that this book will assist them in drawing their own conclusions about the American crime problem, that it will help prepare them for the future, and that it will allow them to make informed decisions about public policy in the crime-control area. For one day it is they who will forge public policy, and it is they who will soon be writing books like this one.

Frank Schmalleger, Ph. D., Director
The Justice Research Association

ACKNOWLEDGMENTS

A book like *Criminology Today* draws upon the talents and resources of many people, and is the end result of much previous effort. This text could not have been written without the groundwork laid by previous criminologists, academicians, and researchers. Hence, a hearty "thank you" is due everyone who has contributed to the development of the field of criminology throughout the years, and especially those theorists, authors, and social commentators who are cited in this book. Without their work the field would be that much poorer. I would like to thank, as well, all the adopters—professors and students alike—of my previous textbooks, for they have given me the encouragement and fostered the steadfastness required to write *Criminology Today.*

The Prentice Hall team whom I have come to know so well, and which has worked so professionally with me on this and other projects deserves a special thanks. The team includes: Robin Baliszewski, Janet McGillicuddy, Rose Mary Florio, Judy Casillo, Fred Hamden, Sally Ann Bailey and Chris Pullo. My thanks also to cover designer, Bruce Kenselaer, and interior designer Patrice Sheridan, whose efforts have helped make *Criminology Today* both attractive and visually appealing.

Manuscript reviewers Michael P. Brown, Ph.D., Ball State University; Mark L. Dantzker, Ph.D., Loyola University; Joan Luxenburg, Ed. D., University of Central Oklahoma; Glen E. Sapp, Central Carolina Community College; Dianne Carmody, Ph.D., Western Washington University; Martin E. Heischmidt, Rend Lake College; and Anthony W. Zumpetta, Ed. D., West Chester University, are due a special "thank you" for helping me stick to important themes when I might otherwise have strayed, and for their guidance in matters of detail. I am especially thankful to supplements author Michael Brown for the quality products he has created, and for his exceptional ability to intuitively build upon concepts in the text.

This book has benefited greatly from the quick availability of information and other resources which are available through on-line services such as America-on-Line and Compuserve, and in various locations on the Internet's World Wide Web. I am grateful to the many information providers who, although they must remain anonymous, have helped establish such useful resources.

I am thankful as well for the assistance of Bill Tafoya and Nancy Carnes, both with the FBI; David Beatty, Director of Public Affairs with the National Victim Center; Chris Rose Crisafulli at the National Criminal Justice Reference Service; and Barbara Maxwell at *USA Today.*

Last, but by no means least, I wish to thank my family—my wife, Harmonie; daughter, Nicole; and mother, Margaret—for their very personal help and encouragement.

ABOUT THE AUTHOR

Frank Schmalleger, Ph.D., is Director of The Justice Research Association, a private consulting firm and "think-tank" focusing on issues of crime and justice. The Justice Research Association, which is based in Hilton Head Island, South Carolina, serves the needs of the nation's civil and criminal justice planners and administrators through workshops, conferences, and grant-writing and program evaluation support.

Dr. Schmalleger holds degrees from the University of Notre Dame and the Ohio State University, having earned both a master's (1970) and doctorate in sociology (1974) from Ohio State University with a special emphasis in criminology. From 1976-1994 he taught criminal justice courses at Pembroke State University, a campus of the University of North Carolina. For the last 16 of those years he chaired the university's Department of Sociology, Social Work, and Criminal Justice. As an adjunct professor with Webster University in St. Louis, Missouri, Schmalleger helped develop the university's graduate program in security administration and loss prevention. He taught courses in that curriculum for more than a decade. Schmalleger has also taught in the New School for Social Research's online graduate program, helping to build the world's first electronic classrooms in support of distance learning through computer telecommunications.

Frank Schmalleger is the author of numerous articles and many books, including the widely used *Criminal Justice Today: An Introductory Text for the 21st Century* (Prentice Hall), now in its third edition; *Criminal Justice: A Brief Introduction* (Prentice Hall, 1994); *Computers in Criminal Justice* (Wyndham Hall Press, 1991); *Career Paths: A Guide to Jobs in Federal Law Enforcement* (Regents/Prentice Hall, 1994); *Criminal Justice Ethics* (Greenwood Press, 1991); *Finding Criminal Justice in the Library* (Wyndham Hall Press, 1991); *Ethics in Criminal Justice* (Wyndham Hall Press, 1990); *A History of Corrections* (Foundations Press of Notre Dame, 1983); and *The Social Basis of Criminal Justice* (University Press of America, 1981).

Schmalleger is also founding editor of the journal *The Justice Professional.* He serves as editor for the Prentice Hall series *Criminal Justice in the Twenty-First Century,* and as Imprint Advisor for Greenwood Publishing Group's criminal justice reference series. His most recent project involves development of an encyclopedia on crime and justice for Greenwood Publishing Group, for which he has been asked to serve as editor-in-chief.

Schmalleger's philosophy of both teaching and writing can be summed up in these words: "In order to communicate knowledge we must first catch, then hold, a person's interest—be it student, colleague, or policy-maker. Our writing, our speaking, and our teaching must be relevant to the problems facing people today, and they must—in some way—help solve those problems."

P A R T   O N E

THE CRIME PICTURE

I'm the big man, I got the gun. Why does she have this attitude?

—Statement made to police by a 16-year-old boy charged with killing 38-year-old Christine Schweiger with a sawed-off shotgun while her 10-year-old daughter watched. Ms. Schweiger told the boy she had no money.

...if you wish to make a big difference in crime, you must make fundamental changes in society.

—James Q. Wilson[1]

CHAPTER 1

WHAT IS CRIMINOLOGY?

Crime is the only way to get ahead, Duke—You'll never have anything if you live your life within the law.

—*Dialog from the NBC-TV movie Beyond Suspicion*[2]

Violence is tearing the heart out of our country.

—*President Clinton*

Much is already known about the phenomenon of crime. Further development in theoretical criminology will result primarily from making sense out of what we already know.

—*George B. Vold and Thomas J. Bernard*[3]

IMPORTANT TERMS

- crime
- civil law
- criminal law
- administrative law
- deviance
- phenomenology
- criminologist
- criminology
- criminal justice
- theory
- unicausal
- criminal justice system
- social policies
- social problem perspective
- social relativity
- social responsibility perspective

INTRODUCTION

In an event which has since reached legendary status, former football superstar turned actor Orenthal James (better known as "O.J.") Simpson was arrested on June 17, 1994, and charged with double murder. Dead were Simpson's estranged wife, Nicole, and Nicole's handsome male friend, young Los Angeles waiter Ronald Goldman. The murders, which occurred in the exclusive Brentwood section of West Los Angeles, were especially grisly. Both victims suffered multiple stab wounds. One veteran police officer called to investigate said, "It was the bloodiest crime scene I have ever seen."

At first Simpson seemed an unlikely suspect. Friends said he appeared very much in love with Nicole, even though their marriage hadn't worked out, and an alibi placed him on the way to the airport at the time of the killings. Simpson attended Nicole's funeral, looking quite bereaved. Soon, however, evidence against Simpson began to mount. A man living in a guest cottage at the Simpson estate reported hearing someone he thought was Simpson returning hurriedly home around the time of the murders. Police found blood stains on Simpson's white Ford Bronco, and a bloody glove discovered at Simpson's home matched one found at the murder scene. As Simpson's alibi grew shaky, critical DNA evidence based upon blood samples linked Simpson to the murder scene.

Public opinion shifted against Simpson soon after a warrant was issued for his arrest. What appeared as an attempt to flee the country was captured on television as Simpson and a friend, former Buffalo Bills star Al Cowlings, drove along Los Angeles freeways—their location revealed to authorities by the cellular phone in Simpson's vehicle. In the car detectives discovered a loaded gun, passports, and $10,000 in cash. It was later learned that previous incidents on file with Los Angeles police had shown Simpson to be what some called an "insanely jealous" and sometimes abusive husband. Past calls made by a frantic Nicole to 911 operators were played on national television and radio. In the background Simpson could be heard breaking things and screaming at her.

The O. J. Simpson case is just one of many involving celebrities. The public, it seems, is enthralled by crime—especially sensational crimes and those involving media figures and other well-known personalities. Over the last two decades allegations of criminal activity against celebrities making the headlines have included charges of attempted murder against Danish socialite Claus von Bulow, whose

The nature of criminal activity is changing rapidly, with an increasing number of serious crimes being committed by young people. *Mike Bonnicksen/ The Wenatchee World.*

initial conviction of attempting to kill his wealthy wife via hypodermic injection was overturned in a second trial; the imprisonment of World Heavyweight boxing champion Michael Tyson for the rape of a Miss Black America contestant; socialite Jean Harris's release from prison after serving 12 years for the murder of the Scarsdale Diet Doctor Herman Tarnower, after Tarnower spurned her (Harris later published her prison memoirs in the book *They Always Call Us Ladies*); the imprisonment of New York Hotel Queen Leona Helmsley, convicted of tax evasion charges; evangelist Jim Bakker's conviction on charges of misusing financial contributions made to his ministry; and allegations of child sexual molestation against rock superstar Michael Jackson.

An ongoing investigation into claims of child sex abuse against Jackson was curtailed in 1994 after the singer agreed to pay an estimated $10 to $24 million (details of the amount were never made public) to settle charges by a young boy that he was sexually molested by Jackson. The boy, who had originally charged that Jackson seduced and fondled him throughout the course of a four-month relationship, refused to provide prosecutors with additional evidence after the settlement was reached.[4] Jackson denied any wrongdoing, contending that he was the victim of a failed extortion plot by the boy's father, a wealthy Beverly Hills dentist.[5]

Cult figures have also appeared prominent in the media spotlight on criminal activity. The murder-suicide of 85 Branch Davidian followers of David Koresh in Waco, Texas, in 1993; the more than 900 deaths by cyanide-laced Kool Aid of Jim Jones's People's Temple members in Jonestown, Guyana, in 1978; and the October 1994 murder-suicide of 53 Canadian, Swiss, and Australian mem-

Michael Jackson kissing Lisa Marie Presley shortly after their ill-fated wedding. In 1994 the superstar paid an estimated $10 to $24 million to settle charges by a young boy that he was sexually molested by Jackson. *Mark Cardwell/Reuters/Bettmann.*

bers of the Order of the Solar Temple will be remembered by most.[6] The 1995 bombing of the Alfred P. Murrah Federal Building in Oklahoma City, in which nearly 200 people died (and which is discussed in more detail in Chapter 9) provides a horrific example of the potential held by zealots bent on wreaking havoc and creating soical disorder.

Other instances of well-publicized criminal activity in past years have included spectacular personal assaults such as the vicious attack on Olympic figure skater Nancy Kerrigan by a jealous rival's hired thug, and Lorena Bobbitt's 1994 acquittal on charges of malicious wounding after she admittedly cut off her husband's penis with a kitchen knife as he slept. Recent episodes of serial killing—also much in the public eye—are almost too numerous to list, although Jeffrey Dahmer's gruesome homosexual dismemberment slayings of at least fifteen young men are hard to forget.

Criminal activity appears as ceaseless as it is pervasive. The year 1995 opened with intense media focus on abortion-clinic killings by right-to-life activists Paul Hill and John Salvi, the on-going O.J. Simpson trial, and a series of attacks on White House property. Also in the news were the legal appeals of convicted "Hollywood Madam," Heidi Fleiss; the "terrorism trial" of Sheik Omar Abdel-Rahman and eleven others accused of the 1993 World Trade Center bombing; a spectacular if inept defense offered by Colin Ferguson, who acted as his own attorney while being tried on charges of shooting into a crowded Long Island Rail Road commuter train—killing six people and wounding nineteen in 1993; and political wrangling over possible modifications to the Violent Crime Control and Law Enforcement Act of 1994.

WHAT IS CRIME?

Americans and the American mass media display an unabashed penchant for closely following spectacular crimes and thoroughly documenting the alleged misdeeds of celebrities. Of course, not all misdeeds are crimes. **Crime,** simply put, is behavior in violation of the criminal laws of a state, the federal government, or of a local jurisdiction that has the power to make such laws. Without a law that circumscribes a particular form of behavior, there can be no crime, no matter how deviant or socially repugnant the behavior in question may be.

Crime behavior in violation of the criminal laws of a state, the federal government, or a local jurisdiction that has the power to make such laws.

This notion of crime as behavior that violates the law derives from earlier work by criminologists, such as Paul Tappan,[7] who defined crime as "an intentional act in violation of the criminal law...committed without defense or excuse, and penalized by the state as a felony or misdemeanor." Edwin Sutherland,[8] regarded by many as a founding figure in American criminology, said of crime that its "essential characteristic...is that it is behavior which is prohibited by the State as an injury to the State and against which the State may react...by punishment."

In the study of criminology three major contemporary forms of the law must be distinguished: civil, criminal, and administrative. **Civil law** deals with arrangements between individuals, such as contracts and claims to property. Civil law exists primarily for the purpose of enforcing private rights. In contrast, **criminal law** regulates those actions which have the potential to harm interests of the state or of the federal government. Because the state is made up of citizens, acts which are harmful to citizens of the state are fundamentally criminal in nature. Hence, while serious crimes with identifiable victims like murder and rape are clearly criminal, offenses that have no obvious victims such as drug use, gambling, and prostitution may be regulated by the criminal law because they detract from the quality of life or decrease social order. Serious criminal offenses are referred to as felonies, while other, less serious crimes are termed misdemeanors. A third category of criminal law violation, the ticketable offense, includes a variety of minor regulated behaviors, including jay walking, some motor vehicle law violations, and—in a few jurisdictions—minor incursions of the law regulating the use and possession of controlled substances. In addition to civil and criminal laws, a third category of law—administrative—can be identified. **Administrative law** regulates many daily business activities, and violations of such regulations generally result in warnings or fines, depending upon their adjudged severity.

Civil law that body of laws which regulates arrangements between individuals, such as contracts and claims to property.

Criminal law that body of law which regulates those actions which have the potential to harm interests of the state or the federal government.

Administrative law regulates many daily business activities, and violations of such regulations generally result in warnings or fines, depending upon their adjudged severity.

Although the legalistic approach to crime—which sees crime as a violation of the criminal law—is useful in the study of criminology, it is also limiting. Not recognized by any legalistic definition of crime are fundamentally immoral forms of behavior by individuals who are powerful enough to influence the making of laws and the imposition of criminal definitions on lawbreakers. By making their own laws, powerful but immoral individuals may escape the label "criminal." Hence, in a later chapter we will also focus on the process of criminalization—that is, the method by which some forms of behavior are made illegal while others are not.

Likewise, our somewhat narrow definition suffers from the fact that formalized laws have not always existed. Undoubtedly, much immoral behavior occurred even in dimly remembered historical epochs, and contemporary laws probably now regulate most such behavior. Similarly, while certain forms of behavior are currently circumscribed by law, it may be that laws pertaining to them have only recently been enacted.

In the near future we may find laws changing further still, perhaps even legitimizing former "crimes" or recognizing that fundamentally moral forms of behavior have been unduly criminalized. Over the last few years, for example, states and members of the public have debated the virtues of euthanasia. Dr. Jack Kevorkian, perhaps the best known pro-euthanasia spokesperson, has been waging a crusade to legalize doctor-assisted suicide for terminally ill individuals. Now, inspired by a growing "right to die" movement, some jurisdictions appear ready to lift the ban. In November 1994 Oregon became the first state to legalize doctor-assisted suicide under prescribed conditions. Although a judge later blocked the Oregon law from taking immediate effect,[9] the new statute represented a complete about-face in the legal status of medically assisted suicide.

Practical considerations are also forcing a reevaluation of existing laws. Recently, for example, former U.S. Surgeon General Joycelyn Elders suggested that drug legalization could reduce the rate of other crimes. "I do think it would likely reduce the crime rate if drugs were legalized,"[10] Elders remarked in a speech to the National Press Club. Other countries that have legalized drugs, Elders said, have seen a drop in violence. She suggested that studies are needed to determine whether the legalization in the United States of controlled substances such as heroin, cocaine, and marijuana could reduce the incidence of criminal violence.

CRIME AND DEVIANCE

Deviance behavior that violates social norms or which is statistically different from the "average."

From the popular point of view, most crimes are regarded as deviant forms of behavior—that is, as behavior which is in some way abnormal. Abnormality, **deviance,** and crime, however, are concepts that do not always easily mesh. Some forms of deviance are not criminal, and the reverse is equally true. Deviant styles of dress, for example, while perhaps outlandish to the majority, are not circumscribed by criminal law unless, perhaps, decency statutes are violated by a lack of clothing. Even in such cases, laws are subject to interpretation and may be modified as social norms change over time.

In November 1991, for example, Patricia Marks, a New York county judge, overturned the convictions of ten women who had been arrested for publicly displaying their breasts. The women, known as the Topfree Ten, had originally been arrested in 1989 after baring their chests during a picnic in a city park. New York law forbids women from displaying their breasts in public—unless they are breastfeeding or performing on stage. Judge Marks, in reversing the convictions, ruled that the New York law was sexist and gender-biased because "male and female breasts are physiologically similar except for lactation capability."[11] The judge relied in part on the tes-

Deviance is relevant to the social context within which it occurs, as these bathers on an Italian nude beach show. *Lucas/The Image Works.*

timony of experts who articulated their belief "that community standards have changed and women's breasts are no longer considered a private or intimate part of the body." This case holds special interest for students of criminology because it highlights the role that societal interpretation plays in defining a criminal offense. Even if Judge Marks is right, and there is no noteworthy physiological difference between the breasts of men and women, American society nonetheless appears to have turned relatively minor differences of size and shape into a major distinguishing factor between the sexes. In other words, a relatively insignificant biological difference has been endowed with great social significance—and laws have evolved based upon subjective perceptions rather than objective considerations.

Some forms of behavior, while quite common, are still against the law. Speeding on interstate highways, for example, while probably something that most motorists engage in at one time or another, is illegal. Complicating matters still further is the fact that some forms of behavior are illegal in some jurisdictions but not so in others. Adult homosexual behavior, for example, is regarded as a matter of personal choice in many states, but is considered a criminal offense in others.

IN MINNESOTA, A CRIME OF COVER-UP

Police Say Muslim's Dress Breaks the Law

Can a mode of dress be against the law in the United States—even when it almost completely covers the body? As the story in this box shows, styles of dress may be more than just a matter of individual choice.

Minneapolis—As a Muslim, Tayyibah Amatullah chooses to cover her entire body with layers of clothing, leaving only her eyes visible to the outside world.

To her, it's a matter of religious freedom.

To St. Paul police, it's breaking the law.

Amatullah, 21, of Minneapolis says she was shopping in a downtown St. Paul mall when five police officers ticketed her for concealing her identity.

Because of three bank robberies, thefts and other mall crime, police have stepped up enforcement of a seldom-used law that prevents people from hiding their identity "by means of a robe, mask or other disguise."

Police say they've ticketed people wearing ski masks and gang members wearing bandannas over their faces.

Police say Amatullah didn't look like the traditional Muslim women they've seen.

Her clothes were dirty and tattered. She wore gloves. Her face was hidden. When they asked her to remove her veil, she refused.

The citation upsets Muslims here—about 25,000 live in the Twin Cities area. They say the case is an infringement of their religious and human rights.

"We're angry," says Magda Saikali, an activist who organized protests over Amatullah's treatment. "We are harassed all the time because of our clothes.... But this is really too much."

Across the USA, religious groups are increasingly winning the battle for rights. A federal bill enacted last November made it more difficult for officials to interfere with religious practices.

"It's not for [St. Paul police] to define what they think a Muslim should dress like," says Ibrahim Hooper of the Council on American-Islamic Relations in Washington, D.C. The group is considering legal action, including a discrimination claim, against the police department.

"We have to make it possible for a Muslim woman who wants to wear a face veil to walk the streets of Minnesota," Hooper says.

Police spokesman Paul Adelmann says, "Procedure is not to tag everybody." But when officers stopped Amatullah to question her, she "was belligerent" and refused to show her face. "They didn't know if it was a man or a woman or what."

Amatullah denies her clothes were tattered. She says the officers told her "you can't run around dressed like that in public."

She also says she was told to either leave the mall or take off the veil. When she refused, she says she was taken to a room where police forced her to remove it.

"I felt degraded," says Amatullah, who converted to Islam two years ago. "It's just like somebody pulling down your underwear in public."

To add to the controversy, police released reports that Amatullah had been arrested three years ago for shoplifting and again nine months ago, in similar dress, for writing a bad check.

Amatullah says she was caught shoplifting on her 18th birthday, but says that was before she converted to Islam. She says the charge was eventually reduced in court.

She denies writing bad checks but says she was arrested on an outstanding ticket for not having car insurance. She says she is still paying off the $550 fine.

For Saikali and other Twin Cities Muslims, Amatullah's record is irrelevant.

Amatullah is scheduled to appear in court on Monday.

St. Paul's assistant city attorney, Theodore Leon, is reviewing the charge, which could bring a maximum $700 fine and 90 days in jail.

"I didn't do anything to hurt anybody," says Amatullah. "Why is it that people can walk around half naked and nobody will say anything? I choose to cover up and people have a problem with it."

Religion vs. Local Laws

- School officials in Livingston, California, banned Sikh students from wearing ***kirpans***, sheathed blades worn next to the skin that are considered sacred, citing a no-weapons policy. A federal appeals court ruled the policy violates religious freedom.

"We're Angry": From left, Magda Saikali, Adrianna Sutherland, and Amatullah Bantely protest the ticketing of Tayyibah Amatullah. The women spoke at the University of Minnesota. *Cheryl Meyer/Star Tribune.*

- The Supreme Court upheld Oregon's refusal to pay unemployment to a Native American fired for using peyote, a drug outlawed as hallucinogenic but part of tribal religious rituals since before Columbus.
- Amish leaders persuaded Minnesota's Supreme Court to overturn a requirement that they affix orange warning signals to their slow-moving black vehicles. They objected to the bright color on religious grounds.
- Cubans in Florida ran into a law banning the ritual sacrifice of chickens required by Santeria, a religion with African roots. The Supreme Court overturned it.
- A Rhode Island medical examiner performed an autopsy on a Laotian immigrant, overriding Hmong refugees who say autopsies mutilate the body and prevent the spirit from being set free.

—Gary Fields

Source: Carolyn Pesce, "In Minn., A Crime of Cover-up," *USA Today*, October 5, 1994, p. 3A.

QUESTIONS

1. What is the difference between crime and deviance? Why might certain modes of dress be considered deviant? How can deviant modes of dress be criminalized?
2. Should the way in which a person dresses be controlled by law? If so, what limits should the law specify?
3. Do you believe that religious dress codes should be especially protected by the courts? Why or why not?

Criminologist one who is trained in the field of criminology. Also, one who studies crime, criminals, and criminal behavior.

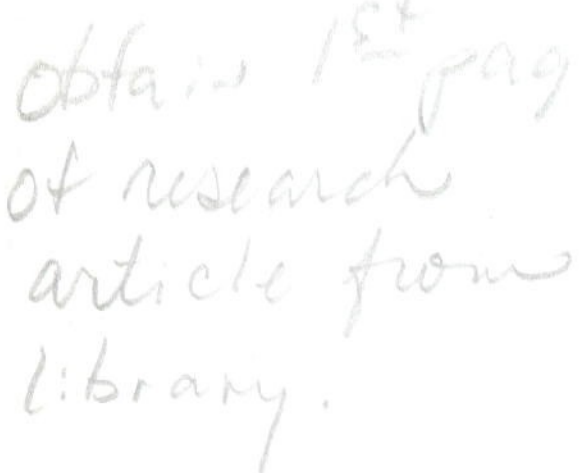

WHAT DO CRIMINOLOGISTS DO?

A typical dictionary definition of **criminologist** is "one who studies crime, criminals, and criminal behavior."[12] People who have doctoral degrees (Ph.D.s) in the field of criminology or criminal justice from accredited universities often refer to themselves as criminologists. Most Ph.D. criminologists either teach criminology or criminology-related subjects in institutions of higher learning, including universities and two- and four-year colleges. Nearly all criminology professors are involved in research or writing projects by which they strive to advance criminological knowledge. Some Ph.D. criminologists are strictly researchers and work for federal agencies such as the National Institute of Justice and the National Criminal Justice Reference Service or for private (albeit often government-funded) organizations with names like RAND Corporation, the Search Group, Inc., and so forth. The results of criminological research in the United States are generally published in journals such as *Criminology* (the official publication of the American Society of Criminology), *Justice Quarterly* (the Academy of Criminal Justice Sciences), and the *American Journal of Criminal Justice* (the Southern Criminal Justice Association). International journals are numerous and include the *Canadian Journal of Criminology* and the *British Journal of Criminology.*

The term "criminologist" may also be properly applied to persons who have earned master's of arts, master's of science, and bachelor's degrees in the field. Degrees such as these often provide entree into police investigative or support work, probation and parole agencies, court-support activities, and correctional (prison) work. Forensics laboratory technicians, ballistics experts, computer crime investigators, polygraph operators, crime scene photographers, and prison program directors provide examples of a few of the kinds of jobs available to criminologists. Criminologists also work for many government agencies interested in the development of effective social policies intended to deter or combat crime. Many criminologists at the master's level teach at two- and four-year colleges and schools.

Private security provides another career track for individuals interested in criminology. The number of personnel employed by private security agencies today is twice that of public law enforcement agencies, and the gap is widening. Many upper- and midlevel private managers working for private security firms today are holders of criminology or criminal justice degrees. The same will soon be true for the majority of law enforcement personnel.

Of course, individual criminologists do many other things. Quite a few persons with undergraduate degrees in criminology or criminal justice go on to law school. Some teach high school, others become private investigators, many provide civic organizations (like victims' assistance and justice advocacy groups) with much needed expertise, a few work for politicians and legislative bodies, while some appear on talk shows to debate the pros and cons of various kinds of social policies designed to "fight" crime. Some even write books such as this one!

WHAT IS CRIMINOLOGY?

As our earlier discussion of the nature of crime and deviance indicates, criminologists not only must deal with a difficult subject matter—consisting of a broad

Criminology examines the causes of crime and seeks ways to prevent or control it. Criminal justice examines the criminal justice system, including police, courts, and corrections. *D. Greco/The Image Works.*

range of circumscribed forms of behavior—they must also manage their work under changing conditions mandated by capricious laws and by historical revision of those law, all of which leads to considerable difficulties in defining the subject matter under study.

The attempt to understand crime predates written history. Prehistoric evidence, including skeletal remains showing signs of primitive cranial surgery, seem to indicate that preliterate people explained deviant behavior via reference to spirit possession. Surgery was an attempt to release unwanted spiritual influences. In the thousands of years since, many other theoretical perspectives on crime have been advanced. This book describes a wide variety of criminological theories and covers some of the more popular ones in detail. Before we can begin any discussion of criminology, however, it is necessary to define a few terms. Definitions of **criminology** abound. Edwin Sutherland, one of the best-known criminologists of this century, suggested that criminology consists of three "principal divisions":[13] (1) the sociology of law, (2) scientific analysis of the causes of crime, and (3) crime control. Another well-known criminologist, Clarence Ray Jeffery, similarly sees three components of the field: (1) detection (of the offender), (2) treatment, and (3) explaining crime and criminal behavior.[14]

Criminology the scientific study of crime and criminal behavior, including their form, causes, legal aspects, and control.

For our purposes, we will use a somewhat broader definition, which says that criminology is the scientific study of crime and criminal behavior, including their manifestations, causes, legal aspects, and control. Criminology includes considerations of possible solutions to the problem of crime. Hence, this text details treatment strategies and social policy considerations that have grown out of the existing array of theoretical explanations for crime. Our definition is in keeping with the work of Jack Gibbs, one of the outstanding criminologists of the present century, who has written that the purpose of criminology is to offer well-researched and objective answers to four basic questions:[15] (1) "Why do crime rates vary?" (2) "Why do individuals differ as to criminality?" (3) "Why is there variation in reactions to crime?" and (4) "What are the possible means of controlling criminality?"

Criminology, at least in its present form, is primarily a social science that builds upon sociological and psychological foundations. It also draws upon the biological sciences and makes use of rigorous methodological techniques developed by other "physical" sciences. Criminology contributes to the discipline of **criminal justice,** which emphasizes application of the criminal law as well as study of the components of the justice system, including the police, courts, and corrections.

Criminal justice the scientific study of crime, the criminal law, and components of the criminal justice system, including the police, courts, and corrections.

While criminologists are generally concerned with uncovering the motivation behind criminal activity, they may look to many other disciplines for clues to what they seek. Hence, biology, sociology, political science, economics, medicine, and numerous other fields all have something to offer the student of criminology, as do the tools provided by statistics, computer science, and other forms of scientific analysis. Contemporary criminologists recognize that their field is interdisciplinary—that is, it draws upon other disciplines to provide an integrated approach to understanding the problem of crime in contemporary society and to advancing solutions to the problems crime creates. However, just as physicists today are seeking a unified field theory to explain the wide variety of observable forms of matter and energy, criminologists have yet to develop an integrated interdisciplinary approach to crime and criminal behavior that can explain crime while also leading to effective social policies in the area of crime control. The attempt to construct criminological theories of relevance is made all the more difficult because, as we have discussed earlier, the phenomenon under study—crime—is subject to arbitrary and sometimes unpredictable legalistic and definitional changes.

Not only must a criminology of relevance integrate the various theoretical perspectives of biology, medicine, psychology, sociology, economics, and other disciplines—it must also blend the requirements of the law with emotional and rational calls for morality and justice. Is the death penalty, for example, justified? If so, on what basis? Because it is a type of vengeance, and therefore deserved? Can we say that it is unjustified because many studies have shown that it does little to reduce the rate of serious crime such as murder? Just what do we mean by justice, and what can criminological studies tell us—if anything—about what is just and what is unjust?

Theoretical Criminology

Theoretical criminology, a subfield of general criminology, is the variety of criminology most often found in colleges and universities. Theoretical criminology, rather than just describing crime and its occurrence, posits explanations for criminal behavior. As Edwin Sutherland put it, "[t]he problem in criminology is to explain the criminality of behavior.... However, an explanation of criminal behavior should be a specific part of [a] general theory of behavior and its task should be to differentiate criminal from noncriminal behavior."

To explain and understand crime, criminologists have built many theories. **Theories,** at least in their ideal form, are composed of clearly stated propositions that posit relationships, often of a causal sort, between events and things under study. An old Roman theory, for example, proposed that insanity was caused by the influence of the moon, and may even have followed its cycles—hence the term "lunacy."

Theory a series of interrelated propositions that attempt to describe, explain, predict, and ultimately to control some class of events. A theory gains explanatory power from inherent logical consistency and is "tested" by how well it describes and predicts reality.

Theories, in effect, attempt to provide us with explanatory power and help us to understand the phenomenon under study. The more applicable a theory is found to be, the more generalizable it is from one specific instance to others—in other words, the more it can be applied to other situations. Unfortunately, as Don Gottfredson observes, "[t]heories in criminology tend to be unclear and lacking in justifiable generality."[16] When we consider the wide range of behaviors regarded as criminal, however—from murder, through drug use, to white-collar crime—it seems difficult to imagine one theory that can explain them all, or which might even explain the same type of behavior under varying circumstances. Yet, many past theoretical approaches to crime causation were **unicausal** and all inclusive. That is, they posited a single, identifiable, source for all serious deviant and criminal behavior.

Unicausal having one cause. Theories that are unicausal posit only one source for all that they attempt to explain.

Today, generally accepted research designs, coupled with careful data-gathering strategies and elaborate statistical techniques for data analysis (all of which are discussed in more detail in Chapter 3), have yielded considerable confidence in certain explanations for crime, while at the same time tending to disprove others. Most modern theories of criminal behavior, however, remain nearly unicausal, often because modern quantitative research techniques permit only a testing of narrowly defined causal propositions.

While we will use the word "theory" in describing the many explanations for crime covered by this book, it should be recognized that the word is only loosely applicable to some of the perspectives we will discuss. Many social scientists insist that to be considered "theories," explanations must consist of sets of clearly stated, logically interrelated, and measurable propositions. The fact that only a few of the "theories" which this book contains rise above the level of organized conjecture—and that those that do offer only limited generalizability—is one of the greatest failures of criminology today.

SOCIAL POLICY AND CRIME

Of potentially greater significance than theory testing itself are **social policies** based upon research findings. A little over a year ago, for example, the U.S. Senate heard testimony from Attorney General Janet Reno, Senator Paul Simon, and television studio executives over the claim that television is responsible for encouraging violent acts among young people. The hearing grew, in part, from an Ohio mother's claim that a Music Television (MTV) cartoon, "Beavis and Butt-Head," led her 5-year-old son to set a fire that killed his 2-year-old sister. The show had featured one of the lead characters intoning "fire is good." As the investigation revealed, experts who study televised cartoons have found that violent episodes average nearly 1 every 2 minutes.[17]

Social policies government initiatives, programs, and plans intended to address problems in society. The "War on Crime," for example, is a kind of generic (large-scale) social policy—one consisting of many smaller programs.

In a recent report[18] presented to Attorney General Reno, the Citizens Task Force on TV Violence recommended, among other things, restricting violence on television between 6 A.M. and 10 P.M.—the time when children are most likely to be watching. The task force told Reno that networks and cable companies should voluntarily agree to the restrictive period or face regulation through government action.

Copycat violence has also been attributed to films. Touchstone Pictures, for example, reedited the movie *The Program,* cutting scenes in which drunken football players test their nerve by lying end to end in the middle of a highway. Several young men who apparently copied the stunt were either killed or critically injured. Commenting on the incidents, a Touchstone spokesperson said, "[w]hile the scene in the movie in no way advocates this irresponsible activity, it is impossible for us to ignore that someone may have recklessly chosen to imitate it...."[19] While the jury (and the Senate) is still out on TV violence, legislation can soon be expected to regulate programming if the television industry does not do more to regulate itself. In the words of Senator Simon, "TV is a powerful sales medium, and too often what it sells is violence."[20]

Professional criminologists are themselves acutely aware of the need to link sound social policy to the objective findings of well conducted criminological research. A recent meeting of the American Society of Criminology (ASC), for example, focused on the need to forge just such a link. At the meeting, ASC president Alfred Blumstein, of Carnegie Mellon University, told criminologists gathered there that "an important mission of the ASC and its members involves the generation of knowledge that is useful in dealing with crime and the operation of the criminal justice system, and then helping public officials to use that knowledge intelligently and effectively."[21] Blumstein added that "[s]o little is known about the causes of crime and about the effects of criminal justice policy on crime that new insights about the criminal justice system can often be extremely revealing and can eventually change the way people think about the crime problem or about the criminal justice system."[22]

Social Policy and the Fear of Crime

The fear of crime is pervasive in contemporary America. Two decades ago crime was the number one concern of Americans voicing opinions in public polls. In the interim, concern over crime came to be replaced with cold war and, later, economic worries. Following a spate of seemingly random violence, however, including well-publicized shootings of foreign tourists in Florida, cult-based violence in Texas and elsewhere, gang-related drive-by shootings, terrorist bombings, and highly visible inner-city violence, fear of crime once again moved to the forefront of national concerns.

As a box in this chapter shows, a CNN/*USA Today*/Gallup poll recently found that 38% of people polled often worry about being sexually assaulted, 35% often worry about being burglarized, and 90% of all respondents felt safe when alone at night only by staying home. Almost half of those polled have had special locks installed for residential security, and nearly a third have purchased guns. In some areas guns have proliferated to the extent that citizens who don't carry them may be in the minority. Fear of crime appears to be greatest in inner-city areas. In the CNN poll only 33% of respondents reported feeling safe when using public transportation by themselves at night, and nearly the same percentage admitted to carrying a weapon for personal protection. Another 10% carried whistles to attract attention in the event of attack.

More telling than the statistics alone is the fact that respondents in every category reported greater fear today than fifteen years ago (in 1981). Nearly twice as many people (19%) reported frequently fearing for their lives as in 1981 (11%). The survey also revealed fast-growing concern over personal and sexual assault.

Another survey of American voters, the 1994 Battleground Survey,[23] found that crime topped the list of citizens' concerns. In the words of the pollsters, "Americans say crime is the No. 1 problem facing the country today...."[24] Crime was reported to be the respondents "top concern" by 26% of all those participating in the survey—easily outdistancing reported concerns over the economy (9%), jobs (7%), unemployment (7%), and drugs (6%). Interestingly, respondents to the Battleground Survey, which attempts to identify "hot" political issues, appeared to separate drug-related crimes from the threat of more personal crimes such as murder, rape, and robbery. An independent *Washington Post* poll, conducted shortly after the Battleground Survey confirmed the survey's findings, showing that 21% of Americans were more concerned about crime than about any other issue.[25]

A final study, conducted at about the same time as the CNN survey, found that workplace homicide is the fastest-growing type of murder in the United States today, and that it is the leading cause of workplace death for women.[26] Experts explained the rise in on-the-job homicides as the outgrowth of the recession years of the early 1990s which led to corporate downsizing and increased job-related stresses.[27] Substance abuse and the ready availability of guns were cited as other contributing factors. Robbery is another. Of all workers, taxi drivers are most at risk of being murdered on the job. A recent National Institute for Occupational Safety and Health study showed that, during the past decade, 26.9 of every 100,000 taxi drivers and dispatchers were murdered on the job—nearly 40 times the overall 0.7 per 100,000 job-related homicide rate for all workers.[28]

Fear of crime is not necessarily directly related to the actual incidence of crime (crime rates are discussed in Chapter 2). It is, however, an important indicator of social concern—one that can easily translate into the development of public policy agendas designed to ameliorate the issues so identified.

Social policy initiatives predicated upon the fear of crime can be telling. In 1993, for example, responding to voters' fears of rampant interpersonal violence among city residents, District of Columbia Mayor Sharon Pratt Kelly drew international attention by asking President Clinton to assign national guard units to patrol the streets of the nation's capitol. After the president refused, Fred Thomas, the city's police chief, declared a crime emergency. Under the declaration, Thomas increased police patrols in high-crime areas. The federal government responded by assisting with the creation of a specialized task force of local and federal officers, and stiffer penalties targeting the city's juvenile offenders were passed. Even the New York City Transit Police Department joined the city's effort to combat crime by surveying its officers to see how many would volunteer for patrol duty in the District during their days off.

CRIME FIGHTERS ON THE MARCH

Neighbors Taking Back Their Streets

When government crime-control policies fail, citizens sometimes take matters into their own hands. As this story describes, Jackson, Tennessee, residents have decided to take their streets back from criminals and drug dealers, and are not waiting for police or government intervention.

For Shirlene Mercer, it was the empty feeling of watching young boys die that drove her to the streets.

A year later, the Jackson, Tenn., woman has rallied a town into action. And her weekly anti-crime marches—leading between 50 and 350 residents into crime-battered neighborhoods—are credited in part for murders in Jackson falling from 19 in 1993 to only four so far this year.

"What we have come to understand is when the community comes together, black and white, rich and poor, everybody gets together and unites to speak out against the violence, drug dealing and all the things destroying our community," she says. "I think it could work anywhere."

Crime experts say it is.

Across the country, grass-roots efforts to stop the violence are blooming into a national attack on crime.

Marches and vigils lead to petition drives, tougher laws and community policing programs with bite:

- Grieving wife in Flint, Mich., leads thousands in a fight that brings about state-wide sentencing reform.
- A councilman who watches gang members buy arm-loads of ammunition fights to ban bullet sales in Chicago.
- A Dallas woman who lost her son to a gang bullet leads marches to counter the Southern state's pro-gun mentality.
- A Seattle computer consultant leads volunteers in planting 10,000 daffodils to remember a slain Japanese student.
- Pittsburgh police hunt for illegal guns based on anonymous tips to a new hot line set up by local businesses.
- Angry Milwaukee residents, scared by soaring murder rates, go door-to-door seeking to ban handguns.

"It's the only way" to fight crime, says Andrew Chisom, director of a University of South Carolina anti-violence program that helps 10 Southern states design prevention programs. "We still think federal bucks can do away with these problems. They cannot."

He says the efforts "have certainly proven volunteerism is the best interdiction policy we could have in America because it recruits average Joe Blow citizens."

An estimated 100 million Americans have been affected by violent crime. Some suffer silently—others want to act.

"It's therapeutic, but it's also exhausting," says Julia Cooper, whose son was pulled from his car and fatally shot in the head by a gang member two years ago. Cooper, of Texans Against Violence, says going against gun owners in the Lone Star State often leaves her "so tired and emotionally drained."

But "it can only do good," she says. "People say we're not changing the world, and we're not. But one small step at a time is a step in the right direction. I think this is the way we start." Crime fighters agree.

Attorney General Janet Reno urged local residents to find their own solutions—create their own battle plans against crime—when she detailed how the Justice Department will enact the new, sweeping federal crime laws.

Pittsburgh Police Chief Earl Buford says everyone can help.

"It's absolutely critical that the extra eyes and ears are out there to help," says Buford. "If there is one thing we've learned in law enforcement, it's that we can't do the job by ourselves. We all have a stake in this."

Dave Brown, 34, of Boise, Idaho, once walked across the country to raise awareness of crimes against children. Now he has launched a national magazine called Wanted by the Law: America's Monthly Crime Report! The magazine tells stories of heroics by both citizens and police officers. And it's filled with pictures of the nation's most wanted. "People want to know who their neighbors are now," Brown says. "Crimes are so heinous." And, he says, people across the nation are linked by a need to stop violence. "People are just fed up, but they don't know where to begin."

Next month, people from across the nation will gather at a Washington, D.C., conference to learn how to mount grass-roots attacks on gun violence.

The toughest part of the fight, some activists say, is battling the gun lobby. "On any level, once you get going you're going to run up against the NRA," says Desmond Riley of the Educational Fund to End Handgun Violence.

"People don't want to be boycotted by gun owners," Riley says. "They don't want massive mailings sent to them."

But the National Rifle Association promises not to quit fighting to protect gun owners.

"It's finally very clear that this fight is about them wanting to take every gun from every American," says NRA chief Wayne LaPierre. "We're not going to let that happen." He says cities where guns are banned are not safer.

And, he echoes the NRA call to reform the criminal justice system in an attempt to keep violent offenders off the streets.

The NRA's goals are similar to Linda Clark's, who often finds people unwilling to help out of fear of the gun lobby.

"A lot of times there are doors that are closed, but you just have to turn and go the other way," says Clark, a Flint, Mich., woman who worked for sentencing reform after her husband was killed in a convenience store holdup. Kevin Clark had stopped to buy treats for his two children.

"We sometimes forget that we the people are the government," his wife says. "We have a mandate to say how it's run."

Chisom says programs that work key on kids not much younger than the people accused of killing Clark's husband. "I don't want to sound mushy, but when youngsters see that people care, they respond to that care," he says.

Shirlene Mercer says involving kids made Jackson safer. "That's why we put the children on the front line of our marches," says Jackson.

"We have to teach children that they have to be sensitive about what's going on around them. As a mama, you care about your children."

Source: Robert Davis, "Crime Fighters on the March," *USA Today*, September 30, 1994, p. 9A. Copyright 1994, *USA Today*. Reprinted with permission.

QUESTIONS

1. Do you believe that citizens should take an active role in crime prevention, such as that described in this article? Why or why not?

2. What kinds of citizen involvement in crime prevention can you envision that are not discussed in this article?
3. What kinds of government policies might further the role of citizen involvement in crime prevention? How might such policies be crafted so as to ensure meaningful cooperation between citizen volunteers and formal agencies of justice?

Social Policy Legislation

While Mayor Kelly's concerns focused on the city of Washington, D.C., a far more widespread social policy initiative can be found in federal anticrime efforts, often called the "war on crime." The war on crime began in the 1960s as rising urban violence fueled increasing national concern over crime. The presidential Commission on Law Enforcement and Administration of Justice issued a series of reports in 1965 calling for increased professionalism within the ranks of criminal justice practitioners, and citing various social ills, such as poverty and unemployment, as contributing to the problem of crime. A second presidential commission on the Causes and Prevention of Violence was appointed by President Lyndon Johnson in 1968. The report of the 1968 commission called for increased federal spending on police activities and enhanced social welfare programs.

As some writers have observed, the first phase of the federal war on crime was based upon a social philosophy that attempted to address underlying cultural and social conditions which fed crime. Unfortunately, however, even as massive federal funding infused social welfare programs, crime continued to rise. Social programs themselves faced growing criticism that they tended to perpetuate the very problems they were intended to address. The first phase in the war on crime ended around 1981 with the election of President Ronald Reagan. Characteristic of the second phase, new emphasis came to be placed on fighting criminals rather than the causes of crime. The war on crime became a "war on criminals."[29] In keeping with the times, the 1984 Comprehensive Crime Control Act abolished parole at the federal level, mandated new sentencing guidelines for federal judges, limited use of the insanity defense, and enacted sweeping punishments, including property forfeitures for persons involved with drugs. In a few years the major emphasis in the ever-widening war on crime focused on a specific battle—the war on drugs. Under President Bush a cabinet-level "drug czar" position was created and William Bennett, former Education Secretary in the Reagan administration, was appointed to lead the nation's efforts against illegal drugs.

Illicit drugs, and the vast profits to be reaped from their importation and sale, came to be identified as the source of much of the crime inundating the nation. Drug dealers, because of the apparent ease with which they accumulated wealth, rapidly acquired the status of demigods in inner-city areas and served as role models for an entire generation of young Americans. Widespread and seemingly senseless violence grew out of the efforts of dealers to protect their turf, and juvenile gangs flourished as they, too, became involved in drug-related activities. Illegal

Fear of crime is the American public's top concern. *H. Darr Beisner/USA Today.*

weapons, including those of mass destruction, proliferated—funded by drug proceeds. Drug crime became organized and violent.

The war on drugs was well supported throughout the early 1990s by federal and state tax dollars. In 1991 alone government agencies nationwide spent nearly $24 billion[30] to fight the drugs war, with most of the money going to criminal justice efforts—and very little to rehabilitation or counseling initiatives outside of the system. Seventy-nine percent of all monies spent to combat drugs went to criminal justice agencies, while only 21% reached agencies focused on rehabilitation and educational activities. State and local governments spent a total of $15.9 billion on criminal justice activities such as incarcerating prisoners and paying for police, according to a report by the Office of National Drug Control Policy. States paid $6.8 billion in 1991 to support their prisons and local jails, with an additional $4.2 billion in state monies going to fund police services. Judicial and legal services cost states $1.5 billion. Per capita spending on antidrug efforts varied greatly, ranging from only $13 per citizen per year in South Dakota to over $154 per person per year in Alaska. Average per capita spending by state and local governments was $63.08. Even with the aid of such massive expenditures, the war on drugs had little immediate result other than grossly overworked criminal justice agencies and intolerably overcrowded jails and prisons.

The most notable recent development in the federal war on crime is the 1994 federal Violent Crime Control and Enforcement Act (discussed in more detail in Chapter 13), signed into law by President Clinton on September 13, 1994. The new legislation makes it illegal to manufacture, possess, or transfer ownership of 19 types of semiautomatic assault weapons; adds 60 new crimes to the federal death penalty list; and calls for a sentence of life in prison for those who commit serious violent felonies for a third time. The act also provides more than $13.4 billion to enhance the activities of local, state, and federal law enforcement agencies, including $8.8 billion to hire 100,000 additional police officers. Another $1.6 billion is allocated to fight violence against women, and $9.9 billion is made available for prison expansion. Immediately before passage of the Violent Crime Control and

Enforcement Act, the Brady Bill became law. The Brady Handgun Violence Prevention Act established a five-day waiting period for handgun purchasers, created a national instant criminal background checking system that can be accessed by licensed gun retailers, and placed added restrictions on gun dealers nationwide.

The United States is not the only country fighting crime with strict new legal mandates. Indeed, a growing conservatism in many other countries, coupled with new concerns about crime, have led a number of nations to recently enact legislation designed to curb crime. In 1994, for example, the British parliament passed the Criminal Justice and Police Bill, marking the return to a get-tough English crime policy. British Home Secretary Michael Howard called the legislation "the most comprehensive attempt to tackle crime [in England] in more than three decades."[31] The degree to which British social policy shifted with passage of the bill can be easily seen in one feature of the bill, which removed a suspect's right to silence. According to Howard, "the right of silence, [is] an age-old feature of Britain's justice system that has been copied in many countries, [but which] was a charter for terrorists and professional criminals." Prior to the bill's passage suspects were told that they had a right to remain silent under police questioning, and that anything they might say could be taken down and be used as evidence against them. The bill mandates that suspects now be told only that failure to mention relevant information during questioning at the police station may damage their case. Another feature of the new statute gives courts wider powers to sentence persistent offenders aged 12 to 14 and doubles the maximum permissible sentence in institutions for youthful offenders. These changes in British law have been condemned by many civil rights advocates.

THE THEME OF THIS BOOK

This book builds upon a social policy theme by contrasting two operative perspectives now popular in American society, and in much of the rest of the world. One point of view, termed the **social problems perspective,** holds that crime is a manifestation of underlying social problems such as poverty, discrimination, the breakdown of traditional social institutions, the poor quality of formal education available to some, pervasive family violence experienced during the formative years, and inadequate socialization practices that leave young people without the fundamental values necessary to contribute meaningfully to the society in which they live. Advocates of the social problems perspective, while generally agreeing that crime and violence have reached epidemic proportions, advance solutions based upon what is, in effect, a public health model which says that crime needs to be addressed much like a public health concern.

Social problems perspective the belief that crime is a manifestation of underlying social problems, such as poverty, discrimination, pervasive family violence, inadequate socialization practices, and the breakdown of traditional social institutions.

Proponents of this perspective typically foresee solutions to the crime problem as coming in the form of large-scale government expenditures in support of social programs designed to address the issues that lie at the root of crime. Recently, for example, Health and Human Services Secretary Donna Shalala, commenting on a shooting rampage that occurred on a Long Island, New York, commuter train, told a gathering of the nation's mayors that "[v]iolence affects all of us. It must be thought of as a public health crisis that requires public health solutions like polio in the 1950s and AIDS today."[32] Shalala called violence "not just a criminal justice but also a public health problem because it's preventable."

Those who advocate a social problems perspective often look to legislatively enhanced social, educational, occupational, and other opportunities as offering programmatic solutions to the problem of crime. The social problems approach to crime is characteristic of what social scientists term a *macro* approach because it portrays instances of individual behavior (crimes) as arising out of widespread and contributory social conditions which enmesh the unwitting individual in a causal nexus of social forces transcending his or her ability to control. In December 1993, in response to growing national concerns about crime and violence, President Clinton appointed a federal task force to study the issues involved. Commenting on the president's initiative, Health and Human Services Secretary Shalala concluded, "[r]ebuilding civil society is very much a part of what we need to talk about. It's a complex issue that requires a very comprehensive solution.... We're going to see what the government can do. It may be laws. It may simply be inspiring different parts of our society to take their own responsibilities. In the end, it will be communities organizing, community by community, neighborhood by neighborhood."[33]

A contrasting perspective lays the cause of crime at the feet of individual perpetrators. This point of view holds that individuals are fundamentally responsible for their own behavior, and maintains that they choose crime over other, more law-abiding, courses of action. Perpetrators may choose crime, advocates of this perspective say, because it is exciting, it offers illicit pleasures and the companionship of like-minded thrill-seekers, or because it is simply less demanding than conformity. This viewpoint, which we shall call the **social responsibility perspective,** tends to become increasingly popular in times when the fear of crime rises. Advocates of the social responsibility perspective, with their emphasis on individual choice, tend to believe that social programs do little to solve the problem of crime because, they say, a certain number of crime-prone individuals, for a variety of personalized reasons, will always make irresponsible choices. Hence, advocates of the social responsibility approach suggest crime reduction strategies based upon firm punishments, imprisonment, individualized rehabilitation, increased security, and a wider use of police powers. The social responsibility perspective characteristically emphasizes a form of *micro* analysis that tends to focus on the individual offender and his or her biology, psychology, background, and immediate life experiences. A note about wording is in order: although this perspective might also be termed the "individual responsibility perspective" since it stresses individual responsibility above all else, we've chosen to call it the "social responsibility perspective" instead, since it holds that individuals must be ultimately responsible to their social group and that they should be held accountable by group standards if they are not.

Social responsibility perspective a viewpoint which holds that individuals are fundamentally responsible for their own behavior and which maintains that they choose crime over other, more law-abiding, courses of action.

In recent years the social responsibility perspective has come to the forefront of national thinking. Examples of a new conservatism in our nation's approach to criminals abound. In 1993, for example, the U.S. Senate, in sending its version of the crime bill to the House of Representatives, called for expansion of the federal death penalty from a handful of offenses to fifty-two crimes.[34] Similarly, California

POLL: MORE FEAR BEING MURDERED

Nearly twice as many Americans worry about being murdered now than in 1981, and many are arming themselves. A *USA Today*/CNN/Gallup Poll shows 30% have bought a gun for protection and only 33% feel safe alone at night on public transportation.

More than 20,000 people are slain in the United States annually. "If that happened all at once, maybe we would put the effort into solving the problem," says Christine Edmunds of the National Victim Center.

A Justice Department survey says crime cost $19.1 billion in 1991. Contributing: saving the kids who are shot. Their advanced care averages $14,434, says a survey by the National Association of Children's Hospitals and Related Institutions. Fifteen youths a day were killed by gunfire in 1991.

Mental costs also are high. Survivors are haunted by losses, especially when the holidays bring "an empty plate, and empty place," says Lula M. Redmond, author of *Surviving When Someone You Love Was Murdered*.

In Largo, Florida, Teri Peters, 38, still lights a holiday candle for her father, who was shot and killed 18 years ago.

Source: "Poll: More Fear Being Murdered," *USA Today*, November 26–28, 1993, pp. A1 and A8.

Governor Pete Wilson announced his support for state legislation that would repeal the state's sweeping "Inmate Bill of Rights." Governor Wilson focused extensively on ending conjugal visits for California inmates, a practice whereby incarcerated individuals are allowed sexual contact with their spouses inside of the prison environment. California's Inmate Bill of Rights became law in 1975 and granted sweeping civil liberties to inmates, including conjugal visits and the right to challenge any visitation regulations. It also prevented officials from enforcing grooming standards or blocking inmates from receiving any literature, including pornography. In an attitude reflective of today's growing conservatism, Wilson said, "It is outrageous that we cannot prevent convicted child molesters and other sex offenders from receiving hard-core pornographic material."[35]

THE SOCIAL CONTEXT OF CRIME

Crime does not occur in a vacuum. Every crime has a quasi-unique set of causes, consequences, and participants. Crime affects some people more than others, having a special impact on those who are direct participants in the act itself—offenders, victims, police officers, bystanders, and so on. Crime, in general, provokes reactions—from the individuals it victimizes, from concerned groups of citizens, from the criminal justice system, and sometimes from society as a whole, which manifests its concerns via the creation of social policy. Reactions to crime, from the everyday to the precedent setting, may color the course of future criminal events.

In this book we shall attempt to identify and examine some of the many social, psychological, economic, biological, and other causes of crime, while simulta-

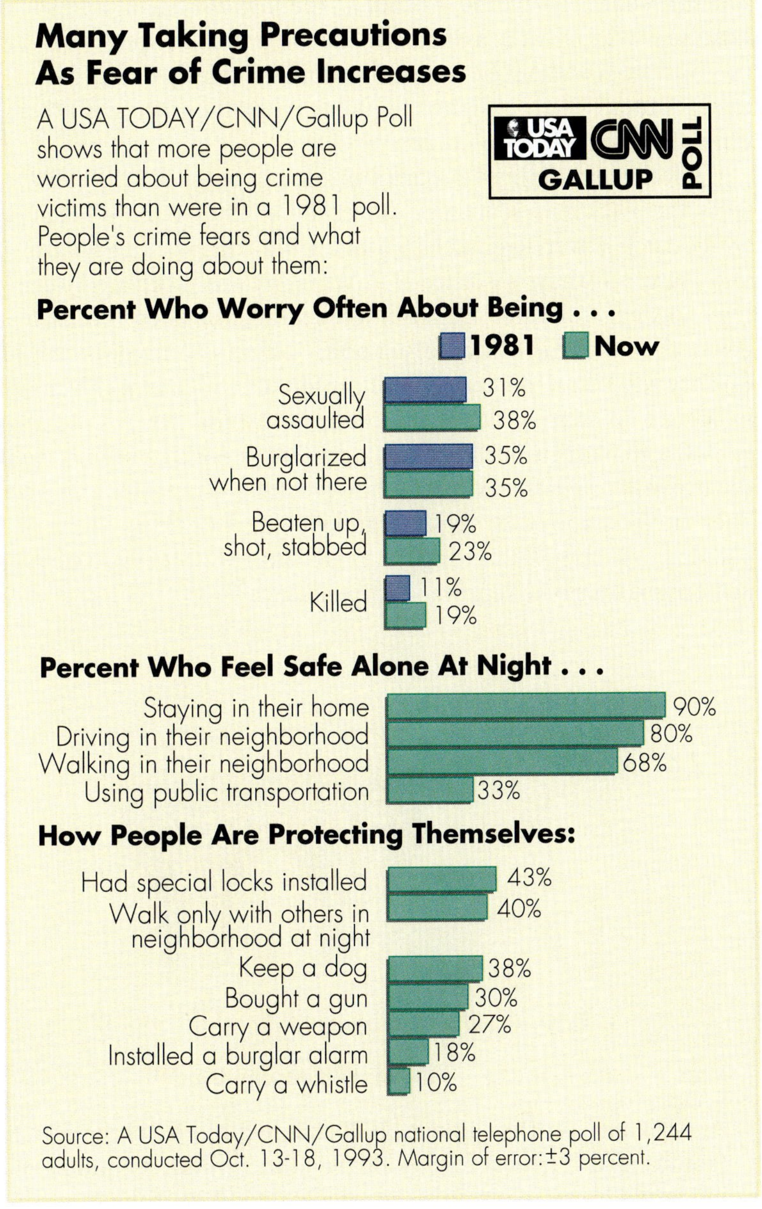

neously expounding upon the many differing perspectives that have been advanced to explain both crime and criminality. An example of differing perspectives can be found in an upcoming box in this chapter entitled "The Murder of John Lennon." The box provides insight into the motivation of Mark David Chapman (Lennon's killer) and shows that the assumptions we, as outsiders to the event itself, make about the genesis of criminal purpose are not always correct. As the box reveals, popular conceptions of criminal motivation are typically shaped by media portrayals of offender motivation, which often fail to take into consideration the felt experiences of the law violator. As we identify and study this diversity of perspectives on criminality, we will discover that there is a characteristic disjuncture between victims, offenders, the justice system, and society as to the significance which each assigns to the behavior in question—and, often, to its motivation. It will not be unusual to find, for example, that sociological or psychological initiatives are assigned to offenders by theorists and others, with which the offenders themselves do not identify.

Another example of misattribution can be seen in the case of Damian Williams, the black man sentenced in December 1993 to ten years in prison for beating white truck driver Reginald Denny during the Los Angeles riots. Most reporters and many attorneys assumed that Williams was motivated during the beating by his knowledge of verdicts of innocence that had been returned earlier that same day in the state trial of California police officers accused of beating black motorist Rodney King—an incident whose capture on videotape galvanized the nation. An infuriated Williams, the media supposed (and reported), attacked Denny in response to frustrations he felt at a justice system that seemed to protect whites at the expense of blacks. Williams, however, told a reporter at his sentencing that he knew nothing about the verdicts, and was just caught up in the riots. "Maybe other people knew about [the King verdicts], but I wasn't aware of it until later...I was just caught up in the rapture," Williams said.[36]

26-CB

THEORY VERSUS REALITY

The Murder of John Lennon

At 10:50 P.M. on December 8, 1980, 25-year-old Mark David Chapman killed famous musician and former Beatle John Lennon. Lennon, who was returning home from a recording session with his wife, Yoko Ono, died in a hail of bullets fired from Chapman's .38-caliber pistol. As a musical luminary, John Lennon was well known to the world. Even his private life—from his residence in the exclusive Dakota Apartments in New York City to his dietary preferences and investment portfolios—was the subject of popular news stories and media exposés.

Following Lennon's death, the public generally assumed that Chapman had chosen his murderous course of action due to innate, albeit perverted, needs fed by a twisted rationale—specifically, to become famous by killing a celebrity. In similar assassination attempts involving Gerald Ford, Ronald Reagan, and others, the media has assumed much the same type of motivation. News stories have communicated to the public the image of would-be assassins sparked by the desire to make headlines and see their names become household words. To assign such motivation to the killers of famous people is understandable from the media perspective. Many of the people encountered by newscasters and writers in daily work have an obvious interest in seeing their names in print. Constant experiences with such people do much to convince by-line authors and narrators that the drive for glory is a major motivator of human behavior.

Such "pop psychology," however, probably does not provide an accurate assessment of the motivation of most assassins. We know from recent conversations with Mark David Chapman that he, at least, was driven by a different mind-set. In an interview ten years after the killing (the first one he gave since the shooting), Chapman related a story of twisted emotions and evil whisperings inside his own head. Just before the shooting, the unemployed Chapman, living in Hawaii, had gotten married. Faced with a difficult financial situation and rising debts, he became enraged by what he perceived as Lennon's "phoniness." Lennon, he reasoned, had become rich singing about the virtues of the common person—yet Lennon himself lived in luxury made possible by wealth far beyond the reach of Chapman and others like him. According to Chapman, "He [Lennon] had told us to imagine.... He had told us not to be greedy. And I had believed!" In effect, Chapman shifted responsibility for his own failure onto Lennon. For that, he reasoned, Lennon must pay. In preparation for the killing, Chapman would record his own voice over Lennon's songs—screaming things like, "John Lennon must die! John Lennon is a phony." Once a born-again Christian, Chapman turned to Satanism, and prayed for demons to enter his body so that he could have the strength to carry out the mission he had set for himself.

Today, says Chapman, he has changed. Much of his time behind bars is spent writing religious tracts and other stories, with inspiration drawn from verses Lennon made famous. Chapman will be eligible for parole in the year 2000.

QUESTIONS

1. Why did Chapman kill Lennon? Will we ever be sure of his true motivation? How can we be certain we have uncovered it?
2. Was Chapman "insane" at the time of the killing? What does "insanity" mean in this context? How can it be determined?
3. Should Chapman be released from custody? Why or why not?

Reference: Jack Jones, "Decade Later, Killer Prays to be Forgiven," *USA Today*, December 3, 1990, p. 1A.

Making Sense of Crime: The Causes and Consequences of the Criminal Event

This book is built around the idea that criminal activity is diversely created and variously interpreted. That is, while a given instance of criminal behavior has many causes it simultaneously holds different levels of significance—at least one for offenders and another (generally quite different, of course) for victims. Similarly, a plethora of social interest groups, from criminal rights advocates, through victim's assistance networks, and politically active organizations, all interpret law-breaking behavior from unique points of view. For this reason, we have chosen to apply the concept of **social relativity** to the study of criminality. Social relativity refers to the fact that social events are differently interpreted according to the cultural experiences and personal interests of the initiator, the observer, or the recipient of that behavior.

Social relativity the notion that social events are differently interpreted according to the cultural experiences and personal interests of the initiator, the observer, or the recipient of that behavior.

Figure 1.1 depicts the causes and consequences of crime in rudimentary diagrammatic form. A glance at the figure shows that the criminal event (as central to the diagram as it is to this book) is ultimately a consequence of the coming together of "inputs" provided by the:

- offender
- victim
- society
- justice system

The offender brings with him or with her personal life experiences, a peculiar biology (insofar as he or she is a unique organism), a personality, motivation, intent, values and beliefs, and various kinds of knowledge (some of which may be useful in the commission of crime). Recent research, for example, has tended to cement the link between child-rearing practices and criminality in later life. Joan McCord,[37] reporting on a thirty-year study of family relationships and crime, found that self-confident, nonpunitive, and affectionate mothers tend to insulate their male children from delinquency and, consequently, later criminal activity. Difficulties associated with the birthing process have also been linked to crime in adulthood.[38] Birth trauma and "negative" familial relationships are but two of the literally thousands of kinds of experiences individuals may have. Whether or not the individual who undergoes trauma at birth and is deprived of positive maternal experiences will turn to crime depends upon many other things—including his or her own mixture of other experiences and characteristics, the appearance of a suitable victim, failure of the justice system to prevent crime, and the evolution of a social environment in which criminal behavior is somehow encouraged.

Some crimes are especially difficult to understand. In 1995, for example, the town of Union, South Carolina, was devastated by the trial of Susan Smith. Smith, who originally claimed a carjacker had forced her from her car and drove off with her two young sons still in the vehicle, confessed to the murders of both Alex, 1, and Michael, 3. Smith said she drove the car, with her sons still strapped into child safety seats, off a pier and into a nearby lake. An exhaustive ten-day-long nation-wide search for the boys had failed to turn up any significant leads, and the case might have gone unsolved until investigators discovered a letter from Smith's lover saying that he felt unable to accept both her and the children. An autopsy revealed that the children were still alive as the car went into the lake, but that both drowned as the car flipped onto its roof and sunk.

Criminal justice system the various agencies of "justice," especially police, courts, and corrections, whose goal it is to apprehend, convict, punish, and rehabilitate law violators.

Like the offender, the **criminal justice system** also contributes to the criminal event, albeit unwillingly, through its failure to adequately identify and treat dan-

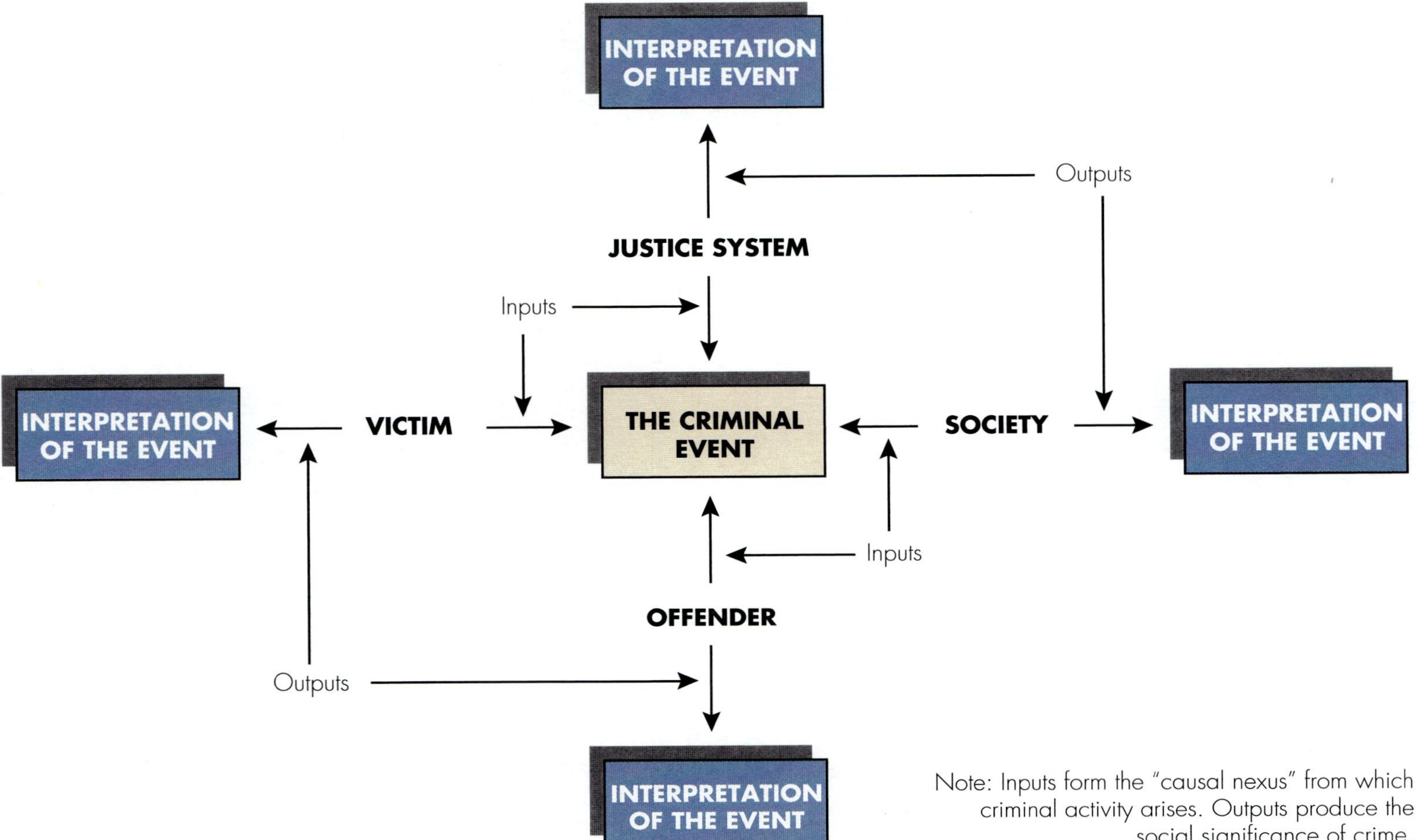

FIGURE 1.1 The Causes and Consequences of Crime. *Source*: Frank Schmalleger and Ted Alleman, "The Collective Reality of Crime: An Integrative Approach to the Causes and Consequences of the Criminal Event," in Gregg Barak (ed.), *Varieties of Criminology: Readings from a Dynamic Discipline* (Westport: Praeger, 1994), p. 120.

gerous potential offenders, and via the early release of convicted criminals who later become repeat offenders. Prison itself may be a "school for crime," fostering anger against society, and a propensity for continued criminality in inmates who have been "turned out." Similarly, the failure of system-sponsored crime prevention programs—ranging from the patrol activities of local police departments to educational and diversionary programs intended to redirect budding offenders—all help to set the stage for the criminal event. Of course, proper system response may reduce crime. A recent study by Carol W. Kohfeld and John Sprague,[39] for example, found that police response (especially arrest) could, under certain demographic conditions, dramatically reduce the incidence of criminal behavior. Additionally, Kohfeld and Sprague found that arrest "constitutes communication to criminals in general...," further supporting the notion that inputs provided by the justice system enhance or reduce the likelihood of criminal occurrences.

Few crimes can occur without a victim. Sometimes the victim is just a passive participant in the crime—as have been innocent people killed by random gunfire in drive-by shooting on the streets outside their homes. Even in such cases, however, the victim contributes his or her person to the event which thereby increases the severity of the incident (i.e., the random shooting that injures no one may still be against the law, but it is a far less serious crime than a similar incident in which somebody is killed). Sometimes, however, the victim contributes to his or her own victimization through the appearance of defenselessness (perhaps because of old age, drunkenness, disability, etc.) by failing to take appropriate defensive measures (leaving doors unlocked, forgetting to remove keys from a car's ignition, etc.), through an unwise display of wealth (flashing large-denomination bills in a public place), or simply by being in the wrong place at the proverbial wrong time (walking down a dark alley off of Times Square at 2 or 3 A.M., for example).

In a recent study of Canadian victimization, Leslie W. Kennedy and David R. Forde[40] found that violent personal victimization "...is contingent on the exposure that comes from following certain life-styles." This was especially true, they found, "for certain demographic groups, particularly young males." Victim-precipitated offenses, involving even greater victim participation in the initial stages of a criminal event, may take place when the soon-to-be victim instigates criminality in others (as in barroom fights, where the eventual victim may "ask for it" through insulting or rude behavior).

Finally, the general public contributes to the criminal event both formally and informally via a definition of particular situations and through the setting of public policy. Date rape, for example, may occur when a male concludes that his date "owes" him something for the money he has spent on her. That feeling, however inappropriate from the point of view of the victim and the justice system, probably has its roots in early learned experiences—including values communicated from television, the movies, and popular music—about the male's role under such circumstances. In other words, society, through the divergent values it places upon people, property, and behavior under particular conditions, may provide the valuative basis for some offenses. Similarly, we can identify other social roots of crime insofar as generic social conditions such as poverty, poor education, and discrimination can all be said to contribute to criminal behavior. In addition, societal economics (i.e., free enterprise in the United States), which influences the content of

Some crimes are especially difficult to understand. Susan Smith, of Union, South Carolina, confessed to drowning her two young sons Alex, 1, and Michael, 3 in October, 1994. The boys are shown in happier times in the photo on the left. *Spartan Herald Journal/Sygma and American Fast Photo/SABA Press Photos, Inc.*

the mass media (television, newspapers, popular music, etc.), and the availability of services can exercise a strong hold over behavior—criminal or otherwise.

In a recent study of the availability of medical resources (especially quality hospital emergency services), for example, William G. Doerner[41] found that serious assaults may "become" homicides where such resources are lacking, but that "homicides" can be effectively prevented via the effective utilization of capable medical technology. Hence, societal decisions on the distribution and placement of advanced medical support equipment and personnel can effectively lower homicide rates in selected geographic areas. In Doerner's words, "the causes of homicide transcend the mere social world of the combatants."[42] Additionally, the contributions society makes to the background of both offender and victim, and to the structure of the justice system, and the influences each in turn have on the general social order provide for a "feedback loop" in this vision of crime (even though the loop is not shown in our chart for fear of unnecessarily complicating it). Finally, as we will discuss in a later chapter, society contributes still further to the criminal event by defining what forms of activity are criminal.

Examined together, all the elements, experiences, and propensities brought to the criminal event by the offender, victim, society, and the justice system constitute what criminologists call situationally defined behavior (or the "situation") that surrounds the impending event. Taken in concert, these various aspects of the situation either give rise to the criminal event itself or they inhibit it.

In a cross-national survey of the situational characteristics of crime, Gary LaFree and Christopher Birbeck[43] defined the term "situation" as "the perceptive field of the individual at a given point in time." From our perspective, it is worthwhile to recognize that the situation surrounding a criminal event will be variously defined according to the perspective of the observer (whether he or she be the victim, the offender, etc.).

The causes of crime, however well documented, tell only half the criminological story. Figure 1.1 contains four boxes that hold the phrase "interpretation of the event." These boxes show that while a crime is occurring, and after it has taken place, each party to the event must make sense out of what has transpired. Such interpretations consist of cognitive, behavioral, and emotional reactions to the criminal event.

In an interesting and detailed study of the interpretive activity of criminal justice system personnel, for example, James F. Gilsinan[44] has documented what happens when callers reach the 911 dispatcher on police emergency lines. Since many prank calls, as well as calls for information, are made to 911 operators, the operator must judge the seriousness of every call that comes through. What the caller says was found to be only a small part of the informational cues that the dispatcher seeks to interpret prior to assigning the call to a particular response (or nonresponse) category. Honest calls for help may go unanswered if the operator misinterprets the call. Hence, quite early on in the criminal event, the potential exists for a crucial representative of the justice system to misinterpret important cues and conclude that no crime is taking place.

Other interpretative activities are at least as significant. The justice system, taken as a whole, must decide guilt or innocence as well as attempt to deal effectively with convicted offenders. Victims must attempt to make sense of their victimization in such a way as to allow them to testify in court (if need be) and to pick up the pieces of crime-shattered lives. The offender must come to terms with himself or herself, and decide whether to avoid prosecution (if escape, for example, is possible), accept blame, or deny responsibility. Whatever the outcome of these more narrowly focused interpretative activities, society—because of the cumulative impact of individual instances of criminal behavior—will also face tough decisions through its courts and law-making agencies. Societal-level decision making may revolve around the implementation of policies designed to stem future instances of criminal behavior, the revision of criminal codes, or the elimination of unpopular laws.

Our perspective takes a double-barreled view of crime referring to (1) the multiplicity of causes and (2) the continual interpretation and redefinition of social events and individual actors. Such a perspective has been variously termed interpretive sociology, phenomenological psychology, or symbolic interactionism, depending not only on the subject matter to which it has been applied, but to the scholarly era in which it has predominated. From this perspective, crime itself can be viewed as an emergent phenomenon—one that arises out of the complex interrelationships between victim, offender, and the social order. The advantages of a **phenomenological** perspective comes in accurately assessing and communicating the personal and social underpinnings, as well as the consequences, of crime. The chapters that follow employ the integrative perspective advocated here to analyze criminal events and to show how theoretical perspectives can be woven together into a somewhat consistent perspective on crime.

Phenomenology the study of the contents of human consciousness without regard to external conventions nor prior assumptions.

SUMMARY

At the start of this chapter crime was simply defined as a violation of the criminal law. The chapter's end recognized the complexity of crime, calling it an "emergent phenomenon." Crime was effectively redefined as a law-breaking event whose significance arises out of an intricate social nexus involving a rather wide variety of participants. As we enter the twenty-first century, contemporary criminologists face the daunting task of reconciling an extensive and diverse collection of theoretical explanations for criminal behavior. All these perspectives aim to assist in the understanding of a social phenomenon that is itself open to interpretation and runs the gamut from petty offenses to major infractions of the criminal law. At the very least, we should recognize that explanations for criminal behavior rest on shaky ground insofar as the subject matter they seek to interpret contains many different forms of behavior, each of which is subject to personal, political, and definitional vagaries.

DISCUSSION QUESTIONS

1. What is crime? What is the difference between crime and deviance? How does the notion of crime change over time? What impact does the variable nature of crime hold for criminology?
2. Do you believe that doctor-assisted suicide should be legalized? Why or why not? What do such "crimes" as doctor-assisted suicide have to tell us about the nature of the law and about crime in general?

3. Describe both the social responsibility and social problem approaches to the study of crime. How might social policy decisions vary between these two perspectives?
4. Describe the various participants in a criminal event. How does each contribute to a definition of the significance of the event?
5. What do criminologists do? Do you think you might want to become a criminologist? Why or why not?

NOTES

1. James Q. Wilson, *Thinking About Crime* (New York: Basic Books, 1983), p. 251.
2. Air date: November 22, 1993.
3. George B. Vold and Thomas J. Bernard, *Theoretical Criminology*, 3rd ed. (New York: Oxford University Press, 1986).
4. Matt Spetalnick, "No Charges to Be Filed Against Michael Jackson," Reuters wire services, September 21, 1994.
5. Ibid.
6. Richard Lacayo, "In the Reign of Fire," *Time on-line*, October 9, 1994.
7. Paul W. Tappan, "Who Is the Criminal?" in Gilbert Geis and Robert F. Meier, eds., *White Collar Crime* (New York: Free Press, 1947), p. 277.
8. Edwin Sutherland, *Principles of Criminology*, 4th ed. (New York: J. B. Lippincott, 1947).
9. Carrie Dowling, "Assisted-Suicide Law Blocked," *USA Today*, December 8, 1994, p. 3A.
10. "Elders Says Drug Legalization Could Cut Violence," Reuters wire services, December 7, 1993.
11. "Topless Standard," *Fayetteville Observer-Times*, November 14, 1991, p. 7A.
12. *The American Heritage Dictionary* on CD-ROM.
13. Sutherland, *Principles of Criminology*, p. 1.
14. Clarence Ray Jeffery, "The Historical Development of Criminology," in Herman Mannheim, ed., *Pioneers in Criminology* (Montclair, N.J., Paterson Smith, 1972), p. 458.
15. Jack P. Gibbs, "The State of Criminological Theory," *Criminology*, Vol. 25, no. 4 (November, 1987), pp. 822–823.
16. Don M. Gottfredson, "Criminological Theories: The Truth as Told by Mark Twain," in William S. Laufer and Freda Adler, eds., *Advances in Criminological Theory*, Volume 1 (New Brunswick, N.J.: Transaction, 1989), p. 1.
17. "Fanning the Fire over Beavis," *USA Today*, October 15, 1993, p. D1.
18. "Networks Turn Thumbs Down on TV-Violence Report," United Press wire services, Northeastern edition, December 17, 1993.
19. "Film Scene to Be Cut After Fatal Imitation," *USA Today*, October 20, 1993, p. 1A.
20. "Fanning the Fire over Beavis."
21. Alfred Blumstein, "Making Rationality Relevant: The American Society of Criminology 1992 Presidential Address," *Criminology*, Vol. 31, no. 1 (February 1993), p. 1.
22. Ibid.
23. "Job Worries Persist, Poll Shows," *USA Today*, December 15, 1993, p. 4A, reporting on the 1994 Battleground Survey by the Tarrance Group and Mellman-Lazarus-Lake.
24. Ibid., p. 4A.
25. *Washington Post* wire services, December 20, 1993.
26. Northwestern National Life Insurance Company, *Fear and Violence in the Workplace*, research report, October 18, 1993.
27. "Survey: Homicides at Work on the Rise,"

USA Today, October 18, 1993, p. 3B.

28. "Cab Drivers Face High Death Risk," *Fayetteville Observer-Times,* October 31, 1993, p. 8A.
29. John J. DiIulio, Jr., "A Limited War on Crime That We Can Win," *The Brookings Review,* Vol. 10, no. 4 (Fall 1992), pp. 6–11.
30. Carolyn Skorneck, "Anti-Drug Spending," Associated Press wire services, December 2, 1993.
31. "Right of Silence to Go in New British Crime Bill," Reuters wire services, December 17, 1993.
32. "Clinton—Crime," Associated Press wire services, December 9, 1993.
33. "Clinton Task Force to Act Against Violence," Reuters wire services, December 9, 1993.
34. Nat Hentoff, "Justice Blackmun Reconsiders the Death Penalty," *Washington Post* wire services, December 11, 1993.
35. "Wilson Calls for End to Inmate Rights," United Press wire services, Western edition, December 10, 1993.
36. "Denny Beating," Associated Press wire services, December 8, 1993.
37. Joan McCord, "Family Relationships, Juvenile Delinquency, and Adult Criminality," *Criminology,* Vol. 29, no. 3 (August 1991), pp. 397–417.
38. Elizabeth Candle and Sarnoff A. Mednick, "Perinatal Complications Predict Violent Offending," *Criminology,* Vol. 29, no. 3 (August 1991), pp. 519–529.
39. Carol W. Kohfeld and John Sprague, "Demography, Police Behavior, and Deterrence," *Criminology,* Vol. 28, no. 1 (February 1990), pp. 111–136.
40. Leslie W. Kennedy and David R. Forde, "Routine Activities and Crime: An Analysis of Victimization in Canada," *Criminology,* Vol. 28, no. 1 (February 1990), pp. 137–152.
41. William G. Doerner, "The Impact of Medical Resources on Criminally Induced Lethality: A Further Examination," *Criminology,* Vol. 26, no. 1 (February 1988), pp. 171–177.
42. Ibid., p. 177.
43. Gary LaFree and Christopher Birbeck, "The Neglected Situation: A Cross-National Study of the Situational Characteristics of Crime," *Criminology,* Vol. 29, no. 1 (February 1991), pp. 73–98.
44. James F. Gilsinan, "They is Clowning Tough: 911 and the Social Construction of Reality," *Criminology,* Vol. 27, no. 2 (May 1989), pp. 329–344.

MARKE
FRU
Natura
NO

C H A P T E R 2

PATTERNS OF CRIME

The statistics are staggering: a person murdered an average of every 22 minutes, a rape every four minutes, a robbery every 26 seconds. You're right to be afraid.

—*The Associated Press*[1]

First, we must recognize that most violent crimes are committed by a small percentage of criminals who too often break the laws even when they are on parole. Now those who commit crimes should be punished, and those who commit repeated violent crimes should be told when you commit a third violent crime, you will be put away and put away for good. Three strikes and you are out.

—*President Clinton, 1994 State of the Union Address*

17-CB: Gacy

IMPORTANT NAMES

Adolphe Quételet
André Michel Guerry
Thomas Robert Malthus

IMPORTANT TERMS

UCR
NCVS
negligent homicide
criminal homicide
robbery
larceny-theft
demographics
simple assault
household crimes
first-degree murder
NIBRS
serial murder
forcible rape
aggravated assault
motor vehicle theft
statistical school
Part I offenses
correlation
second-degree murder
felony murder
mass murder
clearance rate
burglary
arson
date rape
carjacking

INTRODUCTION

Ninety-four-year-old Wesley "Pop" Honeywood doesn't know much about statistics—but he is familiar with crime. Over the years Honeywood, who lives in Jacksonville, Florida, has been arrested 46 times. Five of those arrests were for felonies. Honeywood has been imprisoned on eight occasions since 1946, serving sentences in Philadelphia, Baltimore, Tampa, Orlando, and Jacksonville.

Honeywood's troubles with the law began at the close of World War II when he and a couple of friends stole a bomber and flew it over Italy for fun. After landing, Honeywood was arrested by military police, did a brief stint in jail, and received a dishonorable discharge from the Army.

In October 1994 the geriatric career criminal stood before a Florida judge, awaiting sentencing after pleading guilty to charges of armed assault and possession of a firearm by a convicted felon. The incident grew out of Honeywood's liking for grapes, which he had watched ripen in his neighbor's yard at the end of the summer. Finally, unable to resist the temptation any longer, Honeywood helped himself to bunches of the fruit. When confronted by the neighbor, Honeywood pulled a gun and threatened the man.

Because of all the crimes he's committed, Honeywood now faces sentencing as a habitual offender and could be sent to prison for sixty years. Making matters worse is the fact that Honeywood was on probation for the attempted sexual battery of a 7-year-old girl when he was arrested for the grape theft. And age hasn't mellowed him. Honeywood admits shooting a man in the buttocks in 1989, but claims self-defense. The case never went to trial.

Honeywood says he is not afraid of a prison sentence. "I can do it," he smiles. "I've been locked up a whole lot of times here, but they turn me loose every time."

Circuit Judge R. Hudson Olliff, who will soon sentence Honeywood, worries about his age and the fact that he probably won't survive a long prison stay. But, he says, "[t]he first duty is to protect the public. If he is a 94-year-old that is a danger to the public and he has to go to jail, so be it."

Honeywood, however, wishes he'd plea bargained. "I wish they would give me house arrest," he says. "I don't go nowhere, but stay home. My lawyer says he [the judge] might put me in an old folks home." Even if he goes to prison, Honeywood figures he may beat the odds. His father lived to be 113.

A HISTORY OF CRIME STATISTICS

Pop Honeywood is a statistical anomaly. Few people are involved in crime past middle age. Fewer still ever reach Honeywood's stage in life. Statistical data from the *Sourcebook of Criminal Justice Statistics*[2] show that the likelihood of crime commission declines with age. Persons 65 years of age and older, for example, commit fewer than 1% of all crimes, while the proportion of crimes committed by those over age 90 is so small that it can't be meaningfully expressed as a percentage of total crime.

While the gathering of crime statistics is a relatively new phenomenon, population statistics have been collected periodically since pre-Roman times. *Old Testament* accounts of enumerations of the Hebrews, for example, provide evidence of Middle Eastern census-taking thousands of years ago. In like manner, *The New Testament* describes how the family of Jesus had to return home to be counted during an official census—providing evidence of routine census taking during the time of Christ. The *lustrum*, which was a ceremonial purification of the entire ancient Roman population after census taking, leads historians to conclude that Roman population counts were made every five years. Centuries later, the *Doomsday Book*, created by order of William the Conqueror in 1085–1086, provided a written survey of English landowners and their property. Other evidence shows that primitive societies around the world also took periodic counts of their members. The Incas, for example, a pre-Columbian Indian empire in western South America, required successive census reports to be recorded on knotted strings called "quipas."

While census taking has occurred throughout history, inferences based upon **demographic** statistics appear to be a product of the last two hundred years. In 1798 the English economist **Thomas Robert Malthus** (1766–1834) published his *Essay on the Principle of Population as It Affects the Future Improvement of Society*, in which he described a worldwide future of warfare, crime, and starvation. The human population, Malthus predicted, would grow exponentially over the following decades or centuries, leading to a shortage of needed resources, especially food. Conflict on both the interpersonal and international levels would be the result, Malthus claimed, as individuals and groups competed for survival.

Demographics the characteristics of population groups, usually expressed in statistical form.

Adolphe Quételet and André Michel Guerry

As a direct result of Malthusian thought, investigators throughout Europe began to gather "moral statistics," or social enumerations which they thought might prove useful in measuring the degree to which crime and conflict existed in societies of the period. Such statistics were scrutinized in hopes of gauging "the moral health of nations"—a phrase commonly used throughout the period. One of the first such investigators was **André Michel Guerry,** who calculated per capita crime rates throughout various French provinces in the early 1800s.

In 1835 the Belgian astronomer and mathematician **Adolphe Quételet** (1796–1864) published a statistical analysis of crime in a number of European countries, including Belgium, France, and Holland. Quételet set for himself the goal of assessing the degree to which crime rates vary with climate, sex, and age. He noticed what is still obvious to criminal statisticians today—that crime changes with the seasons, with many violent crimes showing an increase during the hot summer months, and property crimes increasing in frequency during colder parts of the year. As a consequence of these observations, Quételet proposed what he called the "thermic law." According to thermic law, Quételet claimed, morality undergoes seasonal variation—a proposal that stimulated widespread debate in its day.[3]

The first officially published crime statistics appeared in London's *Gazette* beginning in 1828 and France's 1825 *Compte generale.* Soon comparisons (or what contemporary statisticians call correlations) began to be calculated between economic conditions and the rates of various types of crime. From a study of English statistical data covering the years 1810 to 1847, for example, Joseph Fletcher concluded that prison commitments increased as the price of wheat rose. In like fashion, the German writer Gerog von Mayr, whose data covered the years 1836 to 1861, discovered that the rate of theft increased with the price of rye in Bavaria.

The work of statisticians such as Guerry and Quételet formed the historical basis for what has been called the **statistical school** of criminology. The statistical school foreshadowed the development of both sociological criminology and the ecological school, perspectives which are discussed in considerable detail later in this book.

Statistical school a criminological perspective with roots in the early 1800s that seeks to uncover correlations between crime rates and other types of demographic data.

CRIME STATISTICS TODAY

Gathering of crime statistics has continued apace ever since crime-related data gathering began over a century ago. Crime statistics in the United States are reported in two major surveys: the **National Crime Victimization Survey (NCVS)** published yearly by the Bureau of Justice Statistics (BJS) and the Federal Bureau of Investigation's (FBI) **Uniform Crime Reports (UCR).**

NCVS (National Crime Victimization Survey) published annually by the Bureau of Justice Statistics (BJS) provides data on surveyed households which report they were affected by crime.

UCR (Uniform Crime Reports) a summation of crime statistics tallied annually by the Federal Bureau of Investigation and consisting primarily of data on crimes reported to the police and of arrests.

NCVS data appear in a number of annual reports, the most significant of which are called *Criminal Victimization in the United States* and *Crime and the Nation's Households.* FBI data take the form of the annual publication *Crime in the United States.* Numerous other surveys and reports are made available through the Bureau of Justice Statistics. Such surveys cover not only the incidence of crime and criminal activity in the United States, but extend to many other aspects of the criminal justice profession, including justice system expenditures, prisons and correctional data, probation and parole populations, jail inmate information, statistics on law enforcement agencies and personnel, and information on the activities of state and federal courts. These and other reports are generally made available free of charge to interested parties through the National Criminal Justice Reference Service (NCJRS), which is located in Rockville, Maryland.[4]

The largest single annual statistical compilation of printed data on crime and criminal justice to be found in one source is BJS's *Sourcebook of Criminal Justice Statistics* that is stocked yearly by the U.S. Government Printing Office. The *Sourcebook* consists of around eight hundred tables covering all aspects of criminal justice in the United States. Sourcebook information is a compilation of statistics from many different sources, and includes much of the data found in the aforementioned *Crime in the United States* and *Criminal Victimization in the United States.*

Other sources of crime-related and criminal justice information include the National Archive of Criminal Justice Data, operated by the Inter-university Consortium for Political and Social Research (ICPSR) at Ann Arbor, Michigan; the Justice Statistics Clearinghouse (part of BJS); the Justice Research and Statistics Association in Washington, D.C.; the Bureau of Justice Assistance Clearinghouse; the Police Executive Research Forum (PERF); the Police Foundation; the Data Resources Program of the National Criminal Justice Reference Service; and the SEARCH Group, Inc. The SEARCH Group, located in Sacramento, California, is one of a number of agencies and organizations now providing ease of access to statistical information via an on-line bulletin-board system.

This chapter will describe crime in the United States, or what some authors call "the crime picture" in America, using information derived from the latest available NCVS and UCR reports. It is important to realize at the outset, however, that the two surveys differ significantly in both purpose and methodology. A recent UCR release, for example, begins with these words: "Data users are cautioned against comparisons of crime trends presented in this report and those estimated by the National Crime Victimization Survey (NCVS), administered by the Bureau of Justice Statistics. Because of differences in methodology and crime coverage, the two programs examine the Nation's crime problem from somewhat different perspectives, and their

Crimes—especially crimes of violence—appear to be occurring with increasing frequency. Here a man with a knife threatens Washington, D.C., police outside the U.S. Supreme Court building. *Dennis Cook/AP/Wide World Photos.*

results are not strictly comparable. The definitional and procedural differences can account for many of the apparent discrepancies in results from the two programs."[5] The next few paragraphs highlight the key features of UCR and NCVS survey data.

The UCR Program

The Uniform Crime Reporting Program was begun by the FBI in 1929 in response to a national initiative undertaken by the International Association of Chiefs of Police (IACP). The IACP goal was to develop a set of uniform crime statistics for use by police agencies and policymakers throughout the country. In 1930 the U.S. Congress enacted Title 28, Section 534, of the United States Code, which authorized the attorney general of the United States to begin gathering crime information. The attorney general designated the FBI to serve as a national clearinghouse on crime

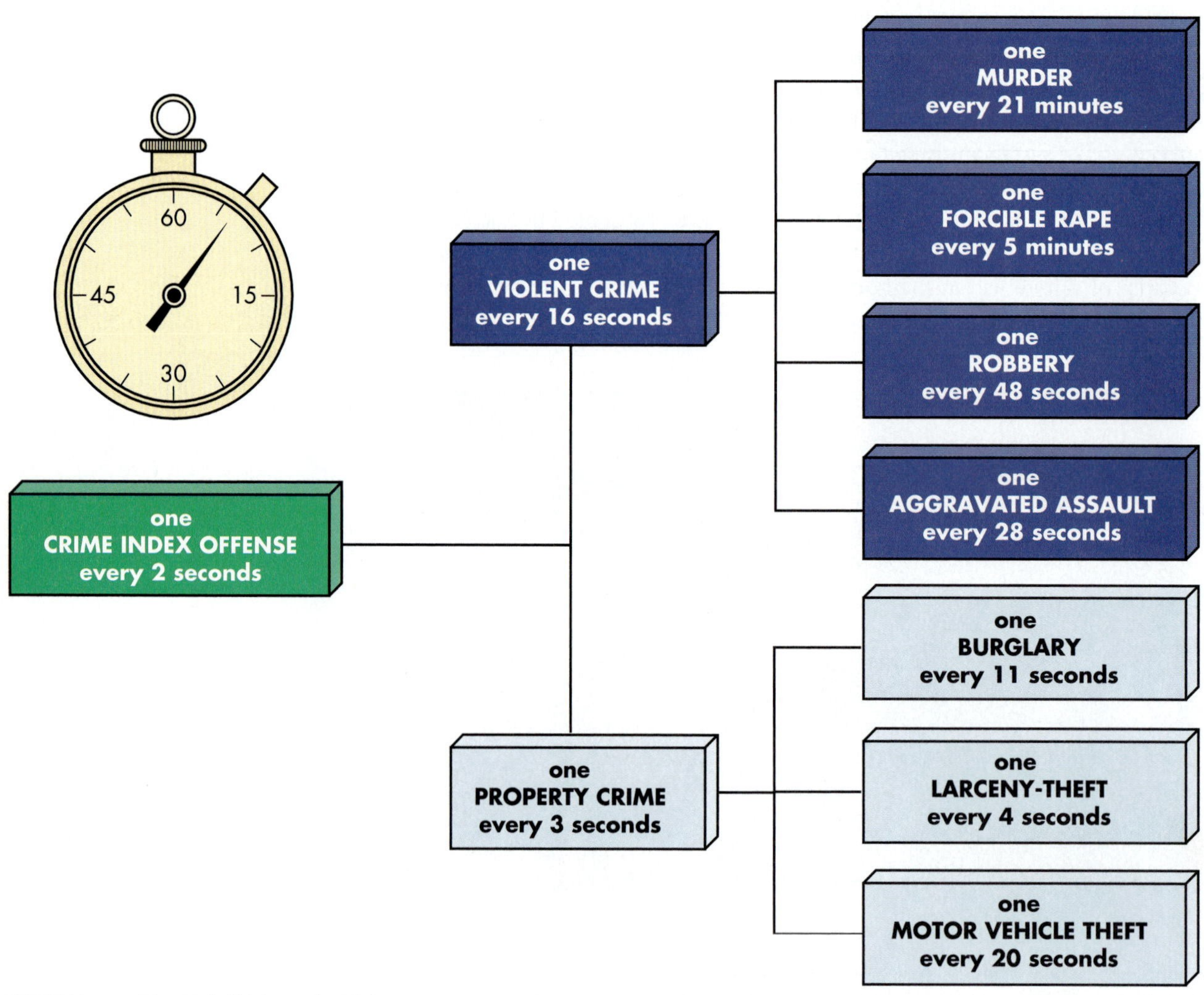

FIGURE 2.1 The FBI's "Crime Clock" for 1993. *Source*: FBI, *Crime in the United States, 1993* (Washington, D.C.: U.S. Government Printing Office 1994), p 4.

statistics, and police agencies around the country began submitting data under the UCR Program. In its initial year of operation, four hundred police departments representing cities and towns in forty-three states participated in the Program.

Initial UCR data were structured in terms of seven major offense categories: murder, rape, robbery, aggravated assault, burglary, larceny, and motor vehicle theft. These crimes, called **Part I Offenses,** when averaged together and compared to the country's population formed a "crime index." The crime index provides a crime rate that can be compared over time and from one geographic location to another. Rates of crime under the UCR Program are generally expressed as "x-number of offenses per 100,000 persons." The 1993 rate of criminal homicide, for example, was 9.5 people murdered for every 100,000 persons in the American population.

Part I offenses that group of offenses, also called "major offenses" or "index offenses," for which the UCR publishes counts of reported instances, and which consist of murder, rape, robbery, aggravated assault, burglary, larceny, auto theft, and arson.

In 1979 Congress mandated that arson be added to the list of index offenses. Unfortunately, the inclusion of arson as an eighth index offenses has made it more difficult to compare pre- and post-1979 crime indexes. Such comparisons now often require a separate tabulation whereby arson is factored out of the index.

Part I offenses are subdivided into two categories: violent personal crimes—consisting of murder, rape, robbery, and aggravated assault—and property crimes—consisting of burglary, larceny, motor vehicle theft, and arson. Part I offenses, showing the number of crimes reported to the police in 1993 are listed in Table 2.1 and diagrammatically represented in Figure 2.1, the FBI's "Crime Clock."

When the FBI issues the annual UCR, it includes information within each Part I offense category on the percentage of crimes that have been cleared. Cleared crimes are those for which an arrest has been made or for which the perpetrator is known but an arrest is not possible (as when the offender is deceased or out of the country). Cleared crimes are also referred to as "solved," although clearances as

TABLE 2.1

MAJOR CRIMES KNOWN TO THE POLICE, 1993 (UCR PART I OFFENSES)

Offense	*Number*	*Rate per 100,000*	*Clearance Rate*
Personal/Violent Crimes			
Murder	24,526	9.5	66%
Forcible rape	104,806	40.6	53
Robbery	659,757	255.8	24
Aggravated assault	1,135,099	440.1	56
Property Crimes			
Burglary	2,834,808	1,099.2	13
Larceny	7,820,909	3,032.4	20
Motor vehicle theft	1,561,047	605.3	14
Arson	82,348	—	15
U.S. total	14,140,952	5,482.9	21

Source: Federal Bureau of Investigation, *Crime in the United States, 1993* (Washington, D.C.: U.S. Government Printing Office, 1994).

counted by the FBI have nothing to do with successful in-court prosecution. Hence, those charged with a crime that is scored as "cleared" by the FBI may not yet have been adjudicated.

In official UCR terminology, a Part I offense is regarded as cleared or solved when (1) "a law enforcement agency has charged at least one person with the offense" or (2) "a suspect has been identified and located and an arrest is justified, but action is prevented by circumstances outside law enforcement control." **Clearance rates** are reported in the UCR for each Part I crime category. A clearance rate refers to the proportion of reported or discovered crime within a given offense category which is solved.

Clearance rate the proportion of reported or discovered crimes within a given offense category which are solved.

Programmatic Problems with Available Data

The most significant methodological feature of the Uniform Crime Reporting Program is indicated by its name. It is a "reporting" program. In other words, only crimes that are reported to the police (or which are discovered by them, or by someone else who then reports them) are included in the statistics compiled by the program. Unless someone complains to the police about a criminal incident, it will go unreported and will not appear in the UCR. Most complaints, of course, are made by victims.

Because UCR data are based upon *reported* crime, the program has been criticized for seriously underestimating the true incidence of criminal activity within the United States—a measurement that would also include unreported crimes. Unreported and underreported criminal activity has been called the "hidden figure" of crime. Some experts say, for example, that rape is the most underreported crime in the UCR, with four to five times as many rapes occurring each year as are reported. Reasons for not reporting a crime like rape are numerous and include (1) fear of the perpetrator; (2) shame, which may carry over from traditional attitudes about sexual behavior and a woman's role in sexual encounters; (3) fears the victim may have of not being believed, and (4) fear of further participation in the justice system, such as the possibility of the victim's being required to go to court and testify against the offender, thereby exposing herself to potentially embarrassing cross-examination and public scrutiny.

Many other crimes are underreported as well. Although rape is indeed seriously underreported (a conclusion drawn from comparison of NCVS and UCR rape statistics), the most seriously underreported crime may in fact be larceny, since the theft of small items may never make it into official police reports and may even be forgotten by victims during interviews with NCVS surveyors.

Another problem with the UCR (as well as with the NCVS) lies in the specialized definitions it employs in deciding which events should be scored as crimes, and in the difficulties this creates in assigning reported crimes to specific offense categories. UCR definitions of criminal activity rarely correspond precisely with statutory definitions of federal and state crimes, making comparisons with other state and federal crime tabulations difficult. Contrast, for example, the following four definitions of rape, one of which represents the standard UCR definition, another the NCVS definition, while a third is taken from the United States Code, and a fourth is quoted verbatim from California criminal law:

CRIME AND CRIMINAL JUSTICE INFORMATION AT YOUR FINGERTIPS

Listed here is an abbreviated directory of phone numbers, locations, and computer bulletin board numbers for some of the data-rich crime and criminal justice resources discussed in this chapter.

Bureau of Justice Statistics (BJS) Clearinghouse

Box 6000
Rockville, MD 20850
Phone: 800-732-3277

Drugs and Crime Data Center and Clearinghouse

1600 Research Boulevard
Rockville, MD 20850
Phone: 800-666-3332

Inter-university Consortium for Political and Social Research (ICPSR)

P.O. Box 1248
Ann Arbor, MI 48106
Phone: 800-999-0960
From outside the United States: 313-763-5010

Juvenile Justice Clearinghouse

1600 Research Boulevard
Rockville, MD 20850
Phone: 800-638-8736
BBS: 301-738-8895

National Criminal Justice Reference Service (NCJRS)

Box 6000
Rockville, MD 20850
Phone: 800-851-3420
From outside the United States: 301-251-5500
BBS: 301-738-8895

SEARCH-BBS

Suite 145
7311 Greenhaven Drive
Sacramento, CA 95831
BBS: 916-392-4640

Forcible Rape (UCR)

Forcible rape, as defined in the Program, is the carnal knowledge of a female forcibly and against her will. Included are rapes by force and attempts or assaults to rape. Statutory offenses (where no force is used but the victim is under the age of legal consent) are excluded.

Rape (NCVS)

Carnal knowledge through the use of force or the threat of force, including attempts. Statutory rape (without force) is excluded. Both heterosexual and homosexual rape are included.

Aggravated Sexual Abuse (U.S. Code): Title 18, Chapter 109A, Sec. 2241

(a) By force or threat. Whoever, in the special maritime and territorial jurisdiction of the United States or in a Federal prison, knowingly causes another person to engage in a sexual act—
  (1) by using force against that other person; or
  (2) by threatening or placing that other person in fear that any person will be subjected to death, serious bodily injury, or kidnapping; or attempts to so, shall be fined under this title, imprisoned for term of years or life, or both.

Rape (California Penal Code)

Rape is an act of sexual intercourse accomplished with a person not the spouse of the perpetrator, under any of the following circumstances:

(a) Where a person is incapable, because of mental disorder or development or physical disability, of giving legal consent...
(b) Where it is accomplished against a person's will by means of force, violence, duress, menace, or fear of immediate and unlawful bodily injury on the person of another.
(c) Where a person is prevented from resisting by any intoxicating or anesthetic substance, or any controlled substance...
(d) Where a person is at the time unconscious of the nature of the act...
(e) Where a person submits under the belief that the person committing the act is the victim's spouse...
(f) Where the act is accomplished against the victim's will by threatening to retaliate in the future against the victim or any other person...
(g) Where the act is accomplished against the victim's will be threatening to use the authority of a public official to incarcerate, arrest, or deport the victim or another...

As the definitions reveal, the UCR only counts as rape the forced "carnal knowledge" of a *female* and excludes homosexual rape. Even more significantly, the UCR Program counts attempts to commit rape as though the crime had actually been accomplished—even though a woman may have fought off her assailant. The NCVS, on the other hand, *does* count homosexual rape (the rape of a person by another person of the same sex) within its tally of rape statistics but, as discussed in more detail shortly, does not include rapes perpetrated on individuals under the age of 12. California law defines rape exclusively in terms of sexual intercourse, although it does not define that term other than to say that "penetration however slight" is sufficient for the crime of rape to have occurred. Likewise, the California law does not specifically exclude the rape of males from consideration for prosecution under the law, but it *does* preclude from prosecution the rape of one's spouse (although a separate California statute, entitled "Spousal Rape," does not). Federal law is the most inclusive of all, since a 1986 law against "sexual abuse" replaced previous federal rape statutes. Under the new federal statute, which avoids use of the term "rape" entirely, the crime of "sexual abuse" encompasses both hetero- and homosexual forms of rape, as well as rape within marriage, and many other forms of forced sexual activity.

Recent Changes in the UCR

Recently the UCR has undergone a number of significant changes, and more are scheduled to be implemented over the next few years as a new enhanced UCR program is phased in. The new program will revise the definitions of a number of index offenses and will also be "incident driven." "Incident driven" means that in the future the UCR program, which will officially be called the **National Incident-Based Reporting System (NIBRS)**, will "collect data on each single incident and arrest within 22 crime categories," with incident, victim, property, offender, and arrestee information being gathered whenever available. The goal of NIBRS is to make data on reported crime more useful by relating it more completely than the present system does to other available information such as victim and offender characteristics. Although the FBI began accepting crime incident data in the NIBRS format in 1989, the transition process is expected to be a slow one, perhaps taking a decade or more. According to the FBI, NIBRS will be implemented "at a pace commensurate with the resources, abilities, and limitations of the contributing law enforcement agencies."

NIBRS (National Incident-Based Reporting System) a new form of the UCR which will collect data on each single incident and arrest within 22 crime categories.

Another recent change in the UCR Program involves the collection of hate crime statistics, which was mandated by the U.S. Congress with passage of the 1990 Hate Crime Statistics Act. The law requires a five-year collection period during which the FBI will serve as a repository for data collected on crimes motivated by religious, ethnic, racial, or sexual orientation and prejudice. Hate crimes data collection began in 1990, but will end in 1995 unless the act is renewed (as is likely).

Data Gathering Under the NCVS

The NCVS differs from the UCR in one especially significant way: rather than depending upon reports of crimes to the police, the data contained in the NCVS consist of information elicited through interviews with members of randomly selected households throughout the nation. Hence, the NCVS uncovers a large number of crimes that may not have been reported, and it is therefore regarded by many researchers as a more accurate measure of the actual incidence of crime in the United States than is the UCR. NCVS data are gathered by U.S. Census Bureau personnel who survey approximately 49,000 households consisting of about

101,000 persons. Interviews are conducted at six-month intervals, with individual households rotating out of the sample every three years. New households are continually added to the sample to replace those which have been dropped.

NCVS interviewers collect individual and household victimization data from anyone 12 years old or older at residences within the sample. Questions are asked about the incidence of rape, personal robbery, aggravated and simple assault, household burglary, personal and household theft, and motor vehicle theft as they have affected household members during the past six months. Information is gathered on victims (including sex, age, race, ethnicity, marital status, income, and educational level), offenders (sex, age, race, and relationship to the victim), and crimes (time and place of occurrence, use of weapons, nature of injury, and economic consequences of the criminal activity for the victim). Questions also cover self-protective measures employed by victims, the possibility of substance abuse by offenders, and the level of previous experience victims may have had with the criminal justice system. Finally, interviewed victims are asked to describe and assess law enforcement response to victimizations that were reported to the police. Unlike the UCR, the NCVS does not measure criminal homicide, arson, or crimes against businesses (such as shoplifting, burglaries of stores, robberies of gas stations and convenience stores, and credit card and commercial fraud). Similarly, the NCVS does not attempt to uncover, nor does it report, crimes against children under 12 years of age.

The NCVS survey instrument is well designed, and data gatherers are thoroughly schooled in interviewing techniques. NCVS interviewers are trained, for example, not to inadvertently lead or "coach" respondents into supplying doubtful information, or to spend an excess amount of time making small talk with respondents. Questions used by the survey, however, are designed to elicit information about crimes that may not be in the forefront of respondents' minds. A few typical survey questions are the following:

51. Was anything stolen from you while you were away from home, for instance at work, in a theater or restaurant, or while traveling? (If "yes," how many times?)
52. (Other than any incidents you've already mentioned) was anything (else) at all stolen from you during the last 6 months? (If "yes," how many times?)
53. Did you find any evidence that someone ATTEMPTED to steal something that belonged to you? (other than any incidents already mentioned) (If "yes," how many times?)
54. Did you call the police during the last 6 months to report something that happened to YOU which you thought was a crime? (Do not count any calls made to the police concerning the incidents you have just told me about.) (If "yes," what happened?)
55. Did anything happen to YOU during the last 6 months which you thought was a crime, but did NOT report to the police? (other than incidents already mentioned) (If "yes," what happened?)

The number of victimizations counted by the NCVS for any single reported criminal occurrence is based upon the number of persons victimized by the event. Hence, a robbery may have more than one victim, and will be so reported in

NCVS data. Although this distinction is applied to personal crimes, households are treated as individual units and all household crimes are counted only once no matter how many members the household contains.

NCVS Findings

The next few sections of this chapter present both UCR and NCVS data in narrative form. Some of the more general findings from NCVS reports for the 1990s, however, reveal a number of consistent and interesting patterns. They include

- Nearly 35 million victimizations are reported to the NCVS annually.
- Approximately 23 million American households (25% of the total) report being touched by crime in any given year.
- City residents are twice as likely as rural residents to be criminally victimized.
- About one-half of all violent crimes, two-fifths of all household crimes, and slightly more than one quarter of all personal thefts are reported to the police.
- Men are more likely to be victimized than are women.
- Young people are more likely to be victimized than are older people.
- Blacks are more likely than members of any other racial group to be victimized.
- Members of lower-income families are more likely to become victims of violent crimes than are members of middle- and upper-income families.
- Young males display the greatest likelihood of violent victimization, while elderly females display the lowest.
- The chance of violent criminal victimization is much higher among young black males than among any other segment of the population.

Finally, it must be noted that victimization rates reported by the NCVS are declining in all categories except crimes of violence. Rates of criminal victimization for crimes of violence, personal theft (larceny), and **household crimes** throughout the United States for the years 1973 through 1993 are shown in Figure 2.2.[6] The decline in observed rates of victimization is especially significant since it contrasts with an otherwise heightened fear of crime, as reported in Chapter 1. Increased levels of crime fear may however, be explained by three events: (1) increases in the *absolute number* of violent crimes that have been significant (although the *rate* of such crimes has held constant due to growth in the American population); (2) increased reporting of all crimes, especially crimes of violence, which has led to the sense that crime is on the increase throughout America; and (3) an ever-growing media focus on violent crime, especially as it characterizes America's cities, and on drug abuse.

Household crimes (NCVS) attempted and completed crimes that do not involve personal confrontation (such as burglary, motor vehicle theft, and household larceny).

Increased reporting, in turn, may be the result of a growth in crime awareness. In 1973, for example, only about 33% of all crimes were reported to the police.[7] Today nearly 40% of all crimes which occur are so reported. Similarly, while only around 20% of personal thefts were reported to the police in 1973, the rate of reporting for such crimes now stands around 30%.[8]

Critique of the NCVS

Just as the UCR has been criticized for underestimating the actual incidence of criminal activity within the United States, the NCVS can be criticized for possible overreporting. No attempt is made to verify the actual occurrence of any of the crimes reported to NCVS interviewers. Hence, no measure exists as to the number of crimes falsely reported, or of the number of crimes that might be underreported in NCVS data. Although the proportion is not known, it is likely that some individuals, when approached by NCVS interviewers, may be unable to resist embellishing crime reports pertaining to their households, and may even concoct criminal incidence data for purposes of self-aggrandizement or because of attempts to please interviewers via the provision of copious amounts of data.

NCVS data-gathering efforts began in 1972. Hence, the program is much newer than the FBI's UCR Program, and comparisons of officially reported crimes with levels of self-reported victimization are unavailable for the years prior to 1973. As with the UCR, definitions of crimes measured by the NCVS do not necessarily correspond to any federal or state statutes or definitions used for other purposes—making comparisons with other state and federal crime records difficult. Complicating matters still further, recent changes in NCVS categories have resulted in the inability to easily compare NCVS findings of even a few years ago with current NCVS data.[9]

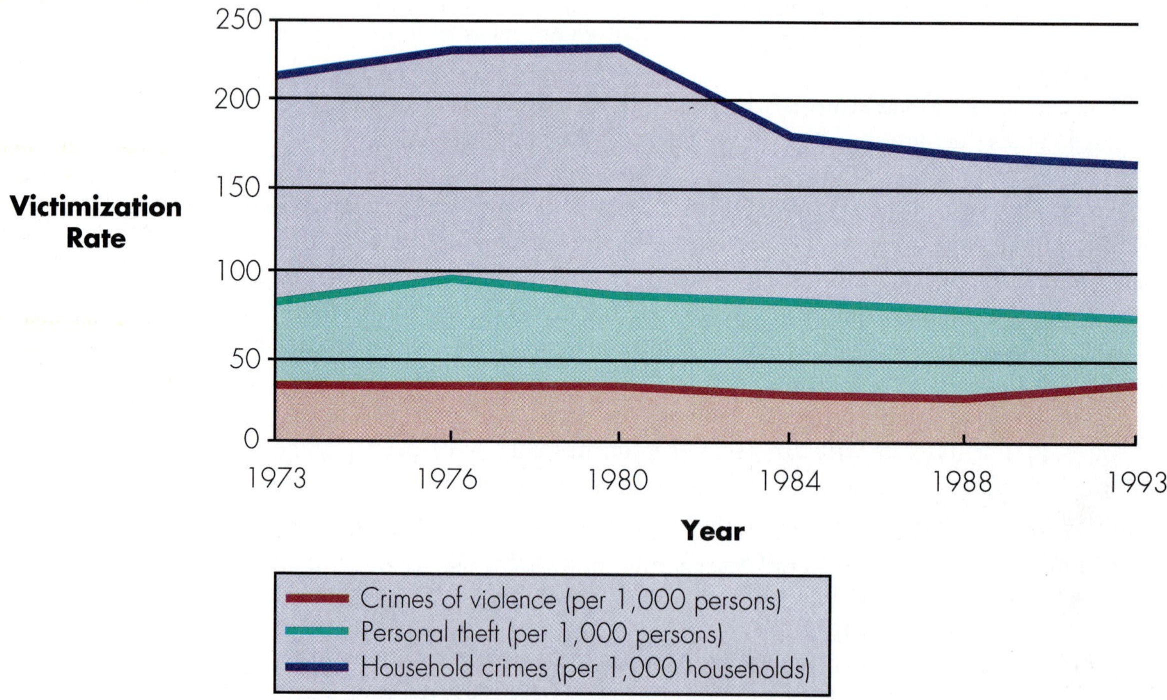

FIGURE 2.2 Rates of criminal victimization in the United States, 1973–1993. *Source*: Bureau of Justice Statistics, *Criminal Victimization in the United States* (Washington, D.C.: U.S. Department of Justice, various years).

Criminal Homicide

A few years ago, in a dispute turned violent over grades, 24-year-old Charles R. Mize, Jr., repeatedly stabbed and killed his father, a popular Georgia high school football coach, and then knifed his mother twelve times before she persuaded him to call police.[10] Mize, a student at Georgia State University, who was described as a stable, fun-loving young man by friends and neighbors, pled guilty under Georgia law to "murder with malice." As a result of his cooperation, prosecutors dropped their plans to seek the death penalty, and Mize was sentenced to life in prison plus five years. Mize's mother recovered and has indicated that, in time, she may be able to forgive her son for what he did. Charles Mize will be eligible for parole in as few as seven years.

The terms homicide and murder are often used interchangeably, although they are not the same. Homicide refers to the willful killing of one human being by another, while murder is an unlawful homicide. Some homicides, such as those committed in defense of one's self or family, may be justifiable and therefore legal. The term used by most courts and law enforcement agencies to describe murder is **criminal homicide.** In legal parlance criminal homicide means the causing of the death of another person without legal justification or excuse.

elicit examples

Criminal homicide the causing of the death of another person without legal justification or excuse. Also, the illegal killing of one human being by another.

First-degree murder criminal homicide that is planned or involves premeditation.

Second-degree murder criminal homicide which is unplanned, and which is often described as a "crime of passion."

Negligent homicide (UCR) causing death of another by recklessness or gross negligence.

Jurisdictions generally distinguish between various types of murder. Among the distinctions made are **first-degree murder,** also called premeditated murder, **second-degree murder,** and third-degree murder, or **negligent homicide.** First-degree murder differs from the other two types of murder in that it is planned. It involves what some statutes call "malice aforethought," which might become evident by someone "lying in wait" for his or her victim, but can also be proven by a murderer's simple action of going into an adjacent room to find a weapon and returning with it to kill. In effect, any activity in preparation to kill that demonstrates the passage of time, however brief, between formation of the intent to kill and the act of killing itself is technically sufficient to establish the legal requirements needed for a first-degree murder prosecution.

Second-degree murder, on the other hand, is legally regarded as a true crime of passion. It is an unlawful killing in which the intent to kill and the killing itself arise almost simultaneously. Hence, a person who kills in a fit of anger is likely to be charged with second-degree murder, as is one who is provoked into killing by insults, physical abuse, and the like. For a murder to be second degree, however, the killing must follow immediately upon the abuse. Time that elapses between abuse or insults and the murder itself allows the opportunity for thought to occur and, hence, for premeditation.

Both first- and second-degree murderers intend to kill. Third-degree murder is different. It is a term that varies in meaning between jurisdictions, but often refers to homicides that are the result of some other action which is unlawful or negligent. Hence, it is frequently called negligent homicide, negligent manslaughter, manslaughter, or involuntary manslaughter. Under negligent homicide statutes, for example, a drunk driver whose driving results in a fatal accident may be charged with third-degree murder, even though she or he had not the slightest intent to kill.

Serial murder criminal homicide that involves the killing of several victims in three or more separate events.

Mass murder the illegal killing of four or more victims at one location, within one event.

Serial murder and **mass murder** are two varieties of first-degree murder.[11] While most murderers only kill once in their lives, serial and mass murderers kill more than one person. Serial killers murder their victims over a period of time, perhaps even years. The serial killer John Wayne Gacy, for example, who was put to death in Illinois in 1994, and whose execution is described in a box in this chapter, was the highly publicized killer of thirty-three young men and boys. Gacy's sale of prison paintings to curious collectors earned him thousands of dollars.[12]

Jeffrey Dahmer, another serial killer, was convicted only a few years ago of the homosexual dismemberment slayings of 15 young men and sentenced to 936 years in prison. Dahmer was himself murdered in prison in 1994. Other serial killers of the past few years include David Berkowitz, better known as the infamous "Son of Sam" who killed young men and women in New York; Charles Manson who ordered his followers to kill 7 Californians, including famed actress Sharon Tate; Henry Lee Lucas, the Texas killer convicted of 11 murders, but linked to as many as 140 more; Ted Bundy, who killed many college-age women; and the female serial killer Aileen Carol Wuornos, charged with the murders of 6 men who picked her up as she hitchhiked through Florida. For record-keeping purposes, serial murder has been defined as criminal homicide that "involves the killing of several victims in three or more separate events."[13]

Mass murderers are different. They kill a number of people at one time. Mass murder has been defined by the Bureau of Justice Statistics as "the killing of four or more victims at one location, within one event."[14] Terrorist actions, as in the 1993 World Trade Center bombing in which five people died, sometimes result in mass murder. Robberies may result in numerous homicide victims, and revenge-seeking gunmen sometimes claim many lives. There have been many mass killings in the United States in recent years. The worst probably occurred in 1990 at the Happy Land social club in the Bronx, New York, when eighty-seven people were burned to death by an arsonist upset that his girlfriend, who worked as a hat checker at the club, had left him. Other instances of mass murder include thirty-one people killed in 1991 when a gunman smashed a pickup truck through the front window of a Kileen, Texas, cafeteria and shot lunchgoers to death; twenty-one killed at a McDonald's restaurant in San Ysidro, California, in 1984 by an out-of-work security guard named James Huberty; and thirteen killed at the University of Texas by sniper Charles Whitman who was holed up in a clock tower.

Felony murder a special class of criminal homicide whereby an offender may be charged with first-degree murder whenever his or her criminal activity results in another person's death.

Some jurisdictions have created a special category of **felony murder,** whereby an offender who commits a crime during which someone dies (or which causes someone to die) can be found guilty of first-degree murder, even though the person committing the crime had no intention of killing anyone. Bank robberies in which one of the robbers is shot to death by police, for example, or in which a bank patron succumbs to a fear-induced heart attack, may leave a surviving robber subject to the death penalty under the felony murder rule. Hence, felony murder is a special class of criminal homicide whereby an offender may be charged with first-degree murder whenever his or her criminal activity results in another person's death.

THEORY VERSUS REALITY

Serial Killer John Wayne Gacy's Execution

On May 10, 1994, serial killer John Wayne Gacy was put to death by lethal injection at Statesville Correctional Center, a maximum-security facility in Joliet, Illinois. Gacy, once known as an affable remodeling contractor, had been convicted a decade and a half earlier of the sex-linked slayings of thirty-three young men and boys. His execution was originally set for June 1980, but dozens of appeals kept him alive on death row for fourteen years.

According to prosecutors, Gacy often dressed as a clown, handcuffing his victims and looping a rope around their necks on the pretext that he was about to perform a clever stunt. Others may have participated willingly in the sexual sadism that preceded their deaths. Most ended up being horribly tortured and mutilated before dying. Bodies of some of Gacy's victims were discovered in the muddy basement crawl space of his home near O'Hare International Airport. Others were dumped into a nearby river.

As Gacy was strapped to a gurney in preparation for execution, revelers outside shouted "Kill the clown!" Others yelled, "John-nee, the devil's waiting for you!" Vendors sold $10 T-shirts bearing slogans that read "No Tears for the Clown." Death penalty opponents, however, continued to file appeals and seek clemency for Gacy right up until the time of execution. Seth Donnelly, executive director of the Illinois Coalition Against the Death Penalty, explained his group's delaying tactics this way: "The crimes for which he [Gacy] has been convicted are heinous. But, we're opposed to the death penalty as an institution, not on the basis of who may be scheduled to be executed."

Following the procedure, relatives of Gacy's victims expressed relief that he was dead. "I don't think anything he has gone through has been the smallest part of what he has put us and our families through. He got off easy," said Vito Mazzara, whose 20-year-old brother, James, was killed by Gacy. "He got a much easier death than any of his victims," said William Kunkle, who prosecuted Gacy and witnessed the execution.

According to state Corrections Director Howard Peters, Gacy's last statement was that "taking his life would not compensate for the loss of the others and that this was the state murdering him."

QUESTIONS

1. What is the difference between mass murder and serial killing? Between first- and second-degree murder? Which categories best fit Gacy? Why?

Serial killer John Wayne Gacy sometimes dressed as a clown to disarm his victims. This painting by Gacy shows his fascination with clowns. Brad Elterman/SIPA Press.

2. Why would someone like Gacy kill? What might have motivated him? How could you investigate such a question so that you could have confidence that your answers would reflect Gacy's true motivation?
3. Are you in favor of the death penalty or opposed to it? Defend your position.

References: Lindsey Tanner, "Gacy Execution," the Associated Press on-line, May 10, 1994, and "State Team Preparing for Gacy Killing," United Press on-line, Central edition, April 11, 1994.

Murder Statistics

Statistics discussed in this section are derived from the UCR, since the NCVS does not gather information on criminal homicide. UCR statistics count only the number of murders committed, not attempts to murder, since attempts are scored as aggravated assaults. Likewise, the UCR program does not count cases of negligent manslaughter among murder statistics.

According to the UCR, 24,526 murders were committed throughout the United States in 1993.[15] The 1993 rate of criminal homicide was 9.5 persons murdered for every 100,000 individuals in the American population.

Age is no barrier to murder. In 1993, for example, 272 murder victims were under the age of 1, while 467 were 75 years old or older. Ninety-four murders were committed by offenders over 75, while 2 were committed by those aged 5 to 9. Seventy-seven percent of murder victims in 1993 were male, while 51% were black (46% were white, and the remainder were of other races).

The most populous region of the country, the Southern states, accounted for the most murders—41% of the total. However, although the UCR divides the country into four regions (the Northeast, South, Midwest, and West), each region varies significantly by population. Hence cross-regional comparisons, other than rates, or changes in reported rates, must be interpreted with caution. While all regions of the country showed an increase in the murder rate of 3% from 1992 to 1993, the nation's cities showed a 10% increase. Metropolitan murder rates were twice that of rural areas—about 11 per every 100,000 city residents.

As in other recent years, the typical murder offender (arrestee) in 1993 was a young black male. Ninety-one percent of all those arrested for murder in 1993 were male, 77% were between the ages of 15 and 34 years old, and 56% were black. Significantly, although blacks make up only 13% of the American population, they account for more than half of all persons arrested for murder.

FBI statistics reveal a plethora of other information about the crime of murder. About one-half of all murder victims in 1993, for example, were either related (12%) to or acquainted (35%) with their assailants. Only 14% of murders were committed by strangers, while the relationship between killer and victim was undetermined for 39% of all reported murders.

Murder is primarily an intraracial crime. In 1993, 84% of white victims were killed by other whites, while 94% of black victims died at the hands of black killers. As in other years, handguns were the weapon of choice in most murders, with 57% of all murder victims dying of handgun-inflicted injuries. Another 5% were killed with shotguns, and 3% with rifles. Knives (or other sharp instruments) were used in 13% of murders, and blunt instruments (clubs, hammers, and so forth) in 4%. Hands, feet, and fists were listed as murder weapons in those 5% of all murder cases in which victims were kicked and punched to death.

Various circumstances lead to murder, although in 1993 arguments were the most common cause of such crime. Twenty-nine percent of all murders resulted from arguments, while 19% were the consequence of other felonious activity (such as robbery, rape, and arson). Murderous arguments may arise over sexual claims, jealousy, money, personal honor, or just about anything else that might lead to anger or bring offense.

Sixty-six percent of all reported or discovered criminal homicides in 1993 were cleared—the highest rate of clearance for any of the Index offenses. Small cities and towns (those with populations under 10,000) reported the highest clearance rates (76%), while large cities had the lowest rates of clearance (65%).

Forcible Rape

Former world heavyweight boxing champion Mike Tyson may be the most famous person to recently serve prison time for **forcible rape.** In 1991 Tyson was convicted of the hotel room rape of 18-year-old Desiree Washington and sentenced to six years in prison. Ms. Washington was participating in the 1991 Miss Black America pageant when she met Tyson and accompanied him to his room.

Forcible rape (UCR) the carnal knowledge of a female forcibly and against her will. Assaults or attempts to commit rape by force or threat of force are also included in the UCR definition; however, statutory rape (without force) and other sex offenses are excluded.

On June 13, 1994, Tyson's bid for parole was denied during a hearing before Indiana judge Patricia Gifford after Tyson refused to admit his guilt. "I do not take responsibility for raping anyone," Tyson said in response to questions raised at the hearing. "I have done no criminal conduct," he said, claiming that a sexual tryst between him and Ms. Washington was consensual.[16] "I should have been more polite. I should have walked her down the stairs and been more of a gentleman to her," Tyson told the judge. Still nonrepentant, Tyson was released from prison in March 1995.

The UCR distinguishes between three categories of rape: (1) forcible rape, (2) statutory rape, and (3) attempted forcible rape. Some jurisdictions draw a distinction between forcible rape in which a weapon is used and forcible rape in which there is no weapon. Although the UCR does not make such a distinction, it does, however, record statistics on the use of weapons associated with the crime of rape.

Date rape unlawful forced sexual intercourse with a female against her will which occurs within the context of a dating relationship.

Other types of rape include spousal rape, gang rape, **date rape,** and homosexual rape. Spousal rape, or the rape of one's spouse, is a relatively new concept, having only entered the law of many state jurisdictions in recent years. Prior to modern times it was believed that a woman entering into marriage implicitly gave her consent to sexual intercourse at the behest of her husband. In today's more enlightened times, wives may prosecute their spouses under rape statutes if their husbands force them to have nonconsensual intercourse.

Date rape, which is often defined as unlawful forced sexual intercourse with a female against her will that occurs within the context of a dating relationship, has also received much attention in recent times—although it is undoubtedly a phenomenon that has existed as long as the institution of dating. According to recent studies, date rape is much more common than previously believed. Some authors suggest that date rape may occur when a male concludes that his date "owes" him something for the money he has spent on her.[17] Many women apparently do not report the crime, and their hesitancy exists for a variety of reasons. Sometimes they feel responsible for some aspect of the social relationship which led to the rape, while in other instances they may feel some concern for the offender and not wish to have him become the target of a criminal prosecution—even one that is deserved.

Homosexual rape, while not punishable as rape in all jurisdictions, is coming to be more widely recognized. Many states and a number of foreign countries now provide for the prosecution of men who force other men to have sex with them, as especially happens in prison. In 1994 the English House of Lords, for example, passed an amendment to the British Criminal Justice Bill[18] replacing the present offense of "non-consensual buggery of men," which carries a ten-year sentence, with the crime of "male rape," which will be punishable by life imprisonment.

Although rape statutes have evolved to the point where many jurisdictions prosecute cases of homosexual rape, gender bias still characterizes most rape laws. No jurisdictions, for example, effectively prosecute husbands raped by their wives, and lesbian rape (the rape of one woman by another) is never prosecuted as such. On very rare occasions, however, a female may be charged with the rape of a male. In 1993, for example, 24-year-old Jean-Michelle Whitiak, a 24-year-old Fairfax County, Virginia, swimming coach, pled guilty to one count of statutory rape resulting from an affair with a 13-year-old boy.[19] Whitiak also admitted to having sex with two of the boy's friends.

The motivation of rapists has been the subject of frequent study. Contemporary social scientific wisdom, supported by the research of scholars such as A. Nicholas Groth,[20] holds that rape is primarily a crime of power, and that most rapists seek self-aggrandizement via the degradation of another human being. Rapists, this school of thought maintains, demean their victims in order to feel important and powerful. Hence, the rape of very elderly and physically unattractive women by virile and powerful young men can be explained as a crime of power rather than one of sex. Some scholars, however, have recently begun to cast doubt upon power as the primary motivation of rapists, returning to an emphasis on sexual gratification as the root cause of sexual assault.[21]

Rape Statistics

UCR statistics on rape include both forcible rape and attempted forcible rape. Statutory rape and other sex offenses are excluded from the count of rape crimes. In 1993 104,806 rapes were reported nationwide under the UCR program, a decrease of 3.9% over the previous year. The rate of reported forcible rape was officially put at 40.6 rapes per 100,000 persons. However, the rape rate for females is effectively twice that figure since any realistic tally of such crimes should compare the number of women raped with the number of females in the overall population (rather than to a count of the entire population, which includes males). When such a comparison is made, the rate of reported rape for women in large cities is 84 per 100,000, 76 per 100,000 for women in small towns, and 49 per 100,000 females in rural counties. The hot summer months generally show the highest rate of reported forcible rape. The year 1993 was no exception, with the month of July showing the largest number of reports.

Substantial regional variation exists in UCR statistics on forcible rape. In 1993 the highest rape rate was recorded at 88 victims per 100,000 females in the southern states, with 84 per 100,000 in the western states, 83 per 100,000 in the Midwest, and a low of 55 per 100,000 in the Northeast. Although the FBI reports that rapes in the southern part of the United States occur with almost twice the frequency of such crimes in the northeastern part of the nation, it makes no attempt to explain the observed variation.

Forcible rapes show the highest rate from among all reported crimes to be "unfounded." Unfounded crime reports are those determined by police investigation to be false. In the case of rape, false reports may be made (1) out of anger, (2) from a felt need for revenge, (3) as a tool of blackmail, (4) because of personal disappointment in the course of a love relationship, and (5) because of numerous other causes. In 1993 police departments across the country determined that 8% of forcible rape complaints were unfounded (versus a 2% average for other reported Index offenses).

In 1993, 53% of all reported forcible rapes were cleared by arrest or exceptional means, with rural and suburban county law enforcement agencies reporting slightly higher clearance rates than city law enforcement agencies. Although the nationwide number of reported rapes decreased slightly over the previous year, the proportion of clearances increased slightly (by 1%).

NCVS data paint a somewhat different picture of rape than the UCR statistics. According to the NCVS 160,000 rapes occurred in 1993 while 152,000 were attempted—giving a total rape count of 312,000 cases.[22] The NCVS calculates a rape rate of 150 per 100,000 females—a rate substantially higher than that found in the UCR.

The NCVS reports that rapes by strangers are almost twice as common as those by nonstrangers. Fifty percent of rapes involving strangers occur between 6 P.M. and midnight, while only 38% of nonstranger rape occurs during those hours. The NCVS also records the location of criminal events to include parking lots or garages, commercial buildings, school property, school buildings, apartments, yards and parks, public transportation, and so forth. Most rapes (17.9%) are described as occurring "on the street not near own or friend's home." However, rapes involving nonstrangers mostly (50%) occur within the victim's home. Only 17.2% of rapes recorded by the NCVS involved the use of weapons, although weapons were employed in 34.6% of all rapes committed by strangers.

The NCVS also collects data on self-protective measures taken by victims. Eighty percent of rape victims responding to NCVS interviewers reported the use of some type of self-protective measure. Self-protective measures included "resisting" (20.8% of all such measures reported), persuading or appeasing the offender (18.7%), running away or hiding (13%), scaring or warning the offender (13%), raising an alarm (11%), and screaming (8.9%). Only 6% of rape victims reported attacking their victimizers, while fewer than one out of 100 attacked the offender with weapons.

Most rape victims (51%) reported that self-protective measures that were taken helped the situation, although 17% felt the measures made their situation worse. Another 14% said such measures had no effect on the situation. Twenty percent of rape victims reported economic costs due to time lost from work as a result of victimization.

As mentioned earlier, NCVS data score only victimizations of household residents who are 12 years of age or older. Recent Bureau of Justice Statistics studies, however, have found that many victims of rape are quite young. A 1994 study,[23] for example, of eleven states and the District of Columbia, found that 10,000 women under the age of 18 were raped in reporting jurisdictions—about half of all the rapes that were reported in those areas. Investigators found that at least 3,800 victims were children under the age of 12. As a result of these figures, the study's authors concluded that "the rape of young girls is alarmingly commonplace." When young women and girls are raped, however, the crimes often go unreported because they frequently involve family members or friends. The survey found that although girls under the age of 18 comprise 25% percent of the nation's female population, they account for 51% of all rape victims.

Even researchers were surprised by the number of young girls who reported having been raped. As Patrick A. Langan, one of the report's authors, said, "The [finding] that one in six of the reported rapes were girls under 12 was startling. You would think that the number would have been minute. But it's not tiny….It's a substantial part of the picture."

Earlier studies of rape had found that 20% of female victims under the age of 12 had been raped by their fathers, 26% were attacked by other relatives, and 50% were assaulted by friends and acquaintances. Only 4% of rape victims under 12 were attacked by strangers, such studies found.

Robbery

Robbery (UCR) the unlawful taking or attempted taking of property that is in the immediate possession of another by force or threat of force or violence and/or by putting the victim in fear.

The crime of **robbery** is regarded as a personal crime because it is committed in the presence of the victim. Robbery is defined by the UCR Program as "the unlawful taking or attempted taking of property that is in the immediate possession of another by force or threat of force or violence and/or by putting the victim in fear." The NCVS definition is similar, and also involves attempts. Although some individuals mistakenly use the terms robbery and burglary interchangeably (as in the phrase "my house was robbed"), it should be remembered that robbery is a personal crime and that individuals are robbed, not houses (which are burglarized).[24]

A number of terms are used to describe subtypes of robbery. Highway robbery, for example, simply refers to any robbery that occurs in a public place, generally out of doors. It is also called "street robbery" by the FBI. Strong-armed robbery means that the robber or robbers were unarmed and took the victim's possessions through intimidation or brute physical force. Strong-armed robbery is often perpetrated by a group of robbers working in consort, as when a gang preys upon one or two unwary victims. The term "armed robbery" signifies that a weapon was used—most often a gun. Armed robberies usually occur when banks, service stations, convenience stores, and other commercial establishments are robbed.

Robbery Statistics

The 1993 UCR reports that 659,757 robberies came to the attention of authorities across the nation that year, meaning that the rate of robbery was 256 per every 100,000 people in the United States. Cities are the places where most robberies occur, with metropolitan areas recording a robbery rate of 312 per 100,000 inhabitants in 1993. Small towns reported a robbery rate of only 71 per 100,000, and rural areas a mere 16 per 100,000.

In 1993, according to the UCR, 38% of robberies were committed using strong-arm tactics, and firearms were the weapons of choice in 42% more. Knives were used in 10%, and a variety of other dangerous weapons in the remainder.

Robberies are most frequent in December, probably reflecting an increased need for money and other goods around the holiday season. Most robbery (about 55%) takes the form of highway robbery, while robberies of businesses account for about 22% of all such crimes. Less than 2% of robberies are bank robberies, and in 1993 10,384 bank robberies were reported. According to the FBI, the average amount lost per robbery incident in 1993 was $815, with a per incident bank robbery loss of $3,308 increasing the average.

Estimated losses due to robberies throughout the United States in 1993 totaled $538 million. However, as the FBI concludes, "[t]he impact of this violent crime on its victims cannot be measured in terms of monetary loss alone. While the object of a robbery is to obtain money or property, the crime always involves force or threat of force, and many victims suffer serious personal injury."[25] In addition to monetary loss and possible physical injury, many robbery victims suffer lasting psychological trauma.

The nationwide clearance rate for robberies reported by the UCR in 1993 was 24%. The highest clearance rate was 39% in rural counties, while the lowest rate of clearance for robberies was found in the nation's cities. Persons under the age of 18 accounted for offenders arrested in 17% of all robberies counted as cleared, while 62% of all persons apprehended for robbery were under 25 years of age. Males were the offenders in 91% of all robberies, while blacks accounted for 62% of those arrested. Thirty-six percent of arrestees were white, and the remainder were members of other racial groups.

NCVS statistics show a much higher number of robberies than UCR data. NCVS surveyors uncovered approximately 1,307,000 robberies in 1993, which the BJS report broke down as 826,000 completed and 481,000 attempted. NCVS data show that 1 in every 3 attempted or completed robberies resulted in injuries to the victim. By far the most robbery-prone segment of the population is the 12- to 15-year-old age group, and males are robbed almost twice as frequently as females. Blacks report a robbery victimization rate three times higher than that of whites, and the incidence of robbery declines as family income rises. Members of the poorest families interviewed by NCVS field researchers (those with family incomes of less than $7,500) were the most frequently robbed (11.4 per 1,000 persons), while members of families with yearly incomes above $50,000 reported the lowest incidence of robbery (3.2 per 1,000 persons). Of course, income and educational levels tend to be correlated. Hence, as the NCVS report concluded, the more educated a person is, the less their chance of being robbed.

NCVS data reveal that victims took some type of protective action in 63% of all robberies, and that "a robbery…committed by an offender who was known to the victim was significantly more likely to result in physical injury than a robbery…that was committed by a stranger."[26] Eleven percent of all robbery victims incurred medical expenses as a direct result of victimization, and 12% of all robberies resulted in victims missing time at work.

NCVS survey data reveal that only 50.1% of all robberies are reported to the police. Women are far more likely to report robberies (64%) than are men (42%), although men are only slightly more likely to resist robbery than are women.

Aggravated Assault

On May 12, 1994, rapper Luther Campbell of the group 2 Live Crew was arrested and charged in Miami, Florida, with aggravated assault for allegedly aiming a gun at a woman and threatening to kill her.[27] The woman, Tina Barnett, was variously identified as Campbell's wife or as a former live-in girlfriend. According to police spokesperson Patrick Brickman, "They were having a verbal altercation over their relationship and the altercation escalated to Mr. Campbell pointing a gun at her and saying 'I swear I will kill you and dump you in a lake somewhere.'" Campbell was later released on $7,500 bond.

Aggravated assault (UCR) the unlawful attack by one person upon another for the purpose of inflicting severe or aggravated bodily injury.

The UCR Program defines **aggravated assault** as "the unlawful attack by one person upon another for the purpose of inflicting severe or aggravated bodily injury." If a weapon is used, or if serious bodily injury requiring hospitalization results, the UCR is likely to count the offense as one of aggravated assault. The NCVS definition of aggravated assault is essentially the same, although the NCVS also reports on the crime of **simple assault**, which it defines as an "attack without a weapon resulting either in minor injury or in undetermined injury requiring less than two days of hospitalization." Hence, under both programs an assault with a deadly weapon would be scored as aggravated assault, although UCR data are far more likely to score any assault which results in hospitalization as "aggravated." Under both programs, assaults that cause serious bodily injury are also scored as aggravated assaults, even if no weapon was employed. If an assault results in death, however, the offense would become a homicide rather than an assault, for statistical reporting purposes

Simple assault (NCVS) an attack without a weapon resulting either in minor injury or in undetermined injury requiring less than two days of hospitalization.

Assault Statistics

According to the UCR, 1,135,099 aggravated assaults were reported to police agencies across the nation in 1993, producing an aggravated assault rate of 440.1 for every 100,000 people in the country. A total of 2,578,000 aggravated assaults were reported to NCVS interviewers in 1993, which translates into an aggravated assault rate of 1,220 per every 100,000 persons aged 12 or more. Rates of aggravated assault were highest in metropolitan areas and lowest in rural areas.

The greatest number of aggravated assaults are usually recorded during the hot summer months, and 1993 was no exception, with July showing the highest incidence of such crimes. When cross-regional comparisons are made (always difficult since populations vary between regions), the southern states accounted for the most aggravated assaults (40%), the western states provided 25% of the total, the midwestern region 19%, and the Northeast 16%. Assault rates, however, were higher in the West than elsewhere in the country.

During 1993, 31% of aggravated assaults reported to the police were committed with blunt objects, meaning that the offender probably grabbed whatever was at hand to commence or continue the attack. Hands, feet, and fists were used in 26% of all aggravated assaults, while firearms were employed in 25%, and knives or other cutting or stabbing instruments in 18%. Unlike some other index offenses, aggravated assault has shown a steady increase from year to year. The number of aggravated assaults reported nationwide has increased by 19% over the past five years.

Because victims often know the people who assault them, the clearance rate for aggravated assault (which stood at 56% in 1993) is relatively high. As with most crimes, city police agencies report a lower rate of clearances for aggravated assault than other law enforcement departments, while rural areas have the highest rate of clearances.

Burglary

Burglary is a property crime, although it can have tragic consequences. In January 1994, 38-year-old Paxton, Massachusetts, police chief Robert Mortell was shot in the chest and died while involved in a foot chase with burglary suspects. A small town of only 4,100 residents, Paxton is unaccustomed to violence. Chief Mortell, a husband and father of three children, who were at the time aged 7 to 12, was very popular with townspeople. "He was more than an authority figure. He was a security figure. When you lose a security figure, it sends shock waves through the community," said Joseph W. McKay, Paxton's chief selectman.[28]

Burglary (UCR) the unlawful entry of a structure to commit a felony or a theft.

The UCR defines **burglary** as "the unlawful entry of a structure to commit a felony or a theft." The definition goes on to say that "the use of force to gain entry is not required to classify an offense as burglary." Burglaries, as scored by both the NCVS and the UCR, generally fall into three subclassifications: (1) forcible entry, (2) attempted forcible entry, and (3) unlawful entry where no force is used. Forcible entries are those burglaries in which some evidence of breakage, prying, or other evidence of forceful entry is found. Hence, a broken window, a jimmied door, a loosened air-conditioning duct—all may provide evidence of forcible entry. Attempted forcible entries (i.e., attempted burglaries), are another form of burglary reported by the UCR. Attempted forcible entry also shows evidence of force, although no actual entry may have been achieved by the perpetrator. The third type of burglary, unlawful entry where no force is used, refers to the fact that some burglars enter unlocked residences uninvited, stealing items found there.

While most burglaries are, strictly speaking, property crimes, the potential for personal violence is inherent in many such crimes. Nighttime burglary, for example, which is more severely punished in some jurisdictions than daytime burglary, holds the possibility of violent confrontation between offender and homeowner. Assault, rape, and even murder may be the outcome of such encounters. On the other hand, sometimes burglars themselves are injured or killed by irate residents.

According to the laws of most jurisdictions, and UCR and NCVS definitional categories, burglary has not occurred unless it was the intent of the unlawful entrant to commit a felony or theft once inside the burglarized location. Other forms of illegal entry might simply be counted as trespass.

Burglary Statistics

The UCR recorded 2,834,808 reported burglaries in 1993, a decrease of almost 5% over the previous year. Burglary is a crime which has shown a steady decrease over the past decade, with today's burglary rate standing about 14% lower than five years ago. The UCR rate of reported burglary in 1993 was 1,099 per 100,000 inhabitants. As with most other Part I offenses, cities had the highest rate of burglary (1,182 per 100,000), while rural areas had the lowest (633 per 100,000).

Sixty-eight percent of reported burglaries in 1993 involved forcible entry, 24% were the result of unlawful entries in which no force was used, and 8% were attempts. Two out of every three reported burglaries were of residences (the remainder were commercial burglaries, or burglaries committed on government property).

The average amount lost per burglary in 1993 was set at $1,185 by the FBI, although the loss was slightly higher for residential property (on average $1,179 per incident) than for nonresidential property ($1,189 per incident). The total loss suffered by all burglary victims in 1993 was estimated at around $3.4 billion.

Ninety percent of all persons arrested for the crime of burglary in 1993 were male, 63% were under the age of 25, and 67% were white. Blacks accounted for 31% of burglary arrestees, while members of other races made up the remaining 2%.

Because burglaries are typically property crimes, the clearance rate for burglaries is quite low. Only 13% of all burglaries were cleared in 1993. As with other crimes, rural law enforcement agencies cleared a higher proportion of burglaries (16%) than city departments (13%).

In contrast to the UCR, NCVS statistics on burglary paint quite a different picture. In 1993, the NCVS reported 5,995,000 household burglaries and attempted burglaries—nearly 100% more than UCR estimates.[29] Rates of burglary were generally higher for black households than for whites, regardless of family income levels (although wealthy black families had far lower burglary rates than did low-income white families). The same was true for locality. Hence, black persons living in cities were more likely than whites to have their houses burglarized, while blacks living in rural areas were also more likely than their white neighbors to become burglary victims, although wealthy blacks in either locale were less likely than poor whites to experience burglary. NCVS data also show that the longer a respondent lives at a particular residence, the less likely that person will be to report having been burglarized. Hence, a residence of six months or less was associated with a burglary rate of 151 (per 1,000 households) versus a rate of only 38 (per 1,000 households) where those living at the reporting address had been there for 5 years or more.

CRIME AND JUSTICE—IN THE NEWS

Wanted: The True Crime Rate

Winston Churchill once said, "we have nothing to fear but fear itself." He was, of course, referring to British involvement in World War II. Americans, it seems, are now involved in a war of their own—the highly touted "war on crime." As in any war, fears run high. Some researchers, however, question whether our nationwide fear of crime is more the result of media hype and national hysteria than it is the logical consequence of any real rise in crime rates. What follows is an article written by Associated Press staffer Arlene Levinson that raises just such questions.

> If ever a mystery persisted in the annals of American crime, it's the magnitude of crime itself. Anxiety about crime grips the land but, looking at federal statistics, you

have to wonder why. The FBI reports crime is merely crawling upward. Victim surveys show crime actually falling. Yet for many people, an evening stroll, an unlocked car or going alone to the mall hint at lunacy. After tucking in their children, many parents bolt the doors, check the alarms and pat the guns under their beds goodnight.

Measuring the dimensions of crime in the United States is a statistical nightmare: This is a vast, populous country in which crime rates vary sharply, even from police precinct to neighboring police precinct. Try to draw a picture of crime besetting 250 million people and you lose the detail. Polls indicate people feel more vulnerable, to violent crime especially. This fear fuels the "three strikes, you're out" efforts occupying Congress and close to 30 states this year, the avid prison building and the pervasive unease. Are perceptions wildly out of sync with statistics? First, some numbers:

- Crime reported by police the past 20 years climbed 36 percent, FBI Uniform Crime Reports figures show. The overwhelming majority of crime reported—85 percent—was property crime. But the largest jump in any category came in the area of violent crime, which shot up 81 percent, driven mainly by juveniles with guns settling drug scores.
- The two-decade federal victims survey indicated a 29 percent drop in crime nationwide since 1975. The National Crime Victimization Survey counts one in four households visited by crime each year, down from about one in three in 1975. The survey also found the rate of violent crime basically unchanged, except for a sharp increase in teen-age and black victims.
- Last year, about 24,500 murders were reported in the United States. That's much as it's been for the past several decades.

"The best scientific evidence we have clearly shows there is no increase in crime or violent crime in the last 20 years," said William Chambliss, a sociologist at George Washington University. "The fact is, even if the crime rate was going up, the victims who were the victims remain the victims," said Chambliss, who also is a past president of the American Society of Criminology. "The most dangerous place you can go is to your home with your boyfriend or girlfriend, family members and acquaintances. They account for most of the violent crimes that take place."

Forget the statistics, you might say. Everyone knows crime is America's biggest worry nowadays. National polls show not only that, but that many people think it is increasing in their own communities—and even more think it is increasing nationally. An Associated Press poll of 1,004 Americans last month found 52 percent of men and 68 percent of women personally worried about becoming crime victims. Even among those who said there was nowhere within a mile of their homes they would be afraid to walk at night, half still worried about being victimized.

One reason crime gets the spotlight is that it's moved up on the charts, ahead of foreign crises and the economy. Crime always ranks high on polls evaluating the country's most important problems, said Tom W. Smith, director of the General Social Survey at the National Opinion Research Center, based at the University of Chicago. And with the Cold War over and the economy brightening, politicians took note of Americans' intensified outrage against crime, adding their own spin. "For good political reasons, the Congress and the president have found crime is something politically attractive to be against," Smith said.

Other influences are at work. Crime stories permeate American life—witness their popularity as a topic of news and entertainment. Last year, crime news reported on the three major television networks more than doubled, and coverage of murders tripled, compared with 1992, according to a survey by the Center for Media and Public Affairs in Washington. Another recent survey indicates this coverage rings familiar alarm bells. In a *Times Mirror* poll released April 6, sixty-three percent of respondents said the media accurately depicts the amount of crime in this country, while 29 percent said it exaggerates. Half the people surveyed also said they were very concerned about becoming a crime victim, up from 36 percent in 1988.

Some criminologists suggest another reason the fear of crime might be greater than statistics warrant is the extra attention paid to crimes occurring in unusual spots. The highway sniper, the post office massacre, the tourist mugged and killed, the bank machine holdup, gunfire in a schoolroom—these are the crimes that dominate headlines. But exceptional bloodshed doesn't even ripple the crime graph line, even though it shocks. "You only hear about a very small number [of crimes] and that is the impression that everybody carries around," said Malcolm Young, who runs The Sentencing Project in Washington, which promotes criminal justice. "We've accepted the 19,000 [other killings] or whatever threshold we don't hear about."

QUESTIONS

1. Why is it so difficult for criminologists to agree on the true rate of crime? How does our definition of crime affect the rate of measured crime?
2. Do you agree with the author of this article that the fear of crime is out of proportion to the rate of crime? How can the two be so disjointed?

Source: Arlene Levinson, "America Behind Bars—Crime, Wanted: the True Crime Rate," the *Associated Press On-line*, Northern edition, May 8, 1994. Reprinted with permission.

Larceny

Larceny-theft (UCR) the unlawful taking, carrying, leading, or riding away by stealth of property, other than a motor vehicle, from the possession or constructive possession of another, including attempts.

Larceny is another name for theft. Sometimes the word "larceny" is used by itself in published crime reports, while at other times the phrase "larceny-theft" is used. Both mean the same thing. The UCR definition of **larceny-theft** reads: "the unlawful taking, carrying, leading, or riding away by stealth of property, other than a motor vehicle, from the possession or constructive possession of another, including attempts." The NCVS definition is similar, except that it further subdivides larceny into categories of "household larceny" and "personal larceny." Crimes of larceny do not involve force, nor do those who commit larceny intentionally put their victims in fear as do robbers.

There are differences between the NCVS and UCR in the way subtypes of larceny are categorized. The UCR, for example, scores both purse snatching and pocket-picking as "larceny-theft," while the NCVS calls such crimes "personal larceny with contact." Similarly, the UCR scores shoplifting and thefts from coin operated machines as larceny, while the NCVS does not gather data on commercial thefts and so excludes all such incidents from larceny counts. With these provisos in mind, larceny data in the NCVS and UCR can be compared.

Larceny Statistics

The UCR Program counted 7,820,909 reports of larceny in 1993, for a rate of 3,032 such crimes per every 100,000 persons in the population. The larceny rate decreased slightly (2.3%) from the previous year but, as in other years, reported larcenies were most common during July and August 1993. Most items reported stolen had been taken from motor vehicles (23%), meaning that packages, money, and other goods were stolen from parked cars. Fourteen percent of all larcenies reported were of motor vehicle accessories, such as tires, "mag" wheels, cellular phones, CD-players, radar detectors, and the like. Another 13% of the total reported number of larcenies were from buildings, 15% were due to shoplifting, and 6% were of bicycles. Purse-snatching, pocket-picking, and thefts from coin-operated machines each accounted for 1% of the total number of larcenies reported to the police in 1993.

The average reported value of property stolen per larceny incident was $504 in 1993. This figure, however, is open to interpretation since reports to the police which estimate the value (in dollar terms) of stolen or destroyed property are likely to be exaggerated. Oftentimes victims hope to receive a high return from insurance companies for stolen goods (even though such hope may be unfounded), sometimes they are unsure of the value of missing items, while at other times they honestly overestimate the worth of lost goods because they do not realistically allow for depreciation. In addition, false claims are sometimes filed by persons seeking to bilk insurance companies. Hence, in instances of larceny, burglary, auto theft, and arson it is difficult to know with certainty what the true value of lost or stolen items might be.

NCVS data on larceny estimate 24,250,000 cases of larceny in 1993, with the majority (9,642,000 cases) involving the theft of items worth less than $50. NCVS estimates put the figure for larceny far above the number of thefts officially reported to the police and recorded by the UCR. NCVS trend data, however, show that all forms of larceny have been on the decline since peaking around 1978 and 1979.

Motor Vehicle Theft

Motor vehicle theft (UCR) the theft or attempted theft of a motor vehicle. This offense category includes the stealing of automobiles, trucks, busses, motorcycles, motorscooters, snowmobiles, and the like.

Motor vehicle theft is defined by the UCR simply as "the theft or attempted theft of a motor vehicle." The FBI adds that "this offense category includes the stealing of automobiles, trucks, busses, motorcycles, motorscooters, snowmobiles, etc." Excluded from the UCR count of motor vehicle theft is the stealing of vehicles such as airplanes, boats, trains, and spacecraft (which would be counted as larcenies), while the taking of a motor vehicle by a person having lawful access to that vehicle is similarly excluded. The designation of persons who have lawful access to a vehicle often includes spouses, who are sometimes reported as having stolen a vehicle owned by their marriage partners. In most jurisdictions, however, married persons effectively own most types of property jointly even though titles, deeds, receipts, and so forth may not specifically list both parties. Hence, a wife who tells her husband that he may not drive her car will not be taken seriously when she calls the police if he disobeys.

Carjacking the stealing of a car while it is occupied.

Carjacking, a much more serious crime than motor vehicle theft, involves the stealing of a car while it is occupied. Hence, although carjacking involves theft, it is akin to robbery or kidnapping. Often the theft occurs at gunpoint, and in many carjacking cases, the victim is either injured or killed. Carjacking, almost unheard of a decade ago, increased rapidly in the early 1990s when thieves targeted vehicles which could be easily sold for valuable parts.

The NCVS definition of a motor vehicle is quite concise, and reads: "an automobile, truck, motorcycle, or any other motorized vehicle legally allowed on public roads and highways." Both the NCVS and UCR include attempts in counts of motor vehicle theft. Because of the similarity of definitions, and because most motor vehicle thefts are reported for insurance purposes, NCVS and UCR statistics on motor vehicle theft are in close agreement. A total of 1,561,047 vehicles were reported stolen in 1993 by the FBI, while NCVS data estimate that 1,967,000 were illegally taken. The rate of motor vehicle theft in 1993 was 605 vehicles per 100,000 people according to the FBI, and the value of motor vehicles stolen that year totaled $7.5 billion nationwide.

August is the prime month for motor vehicle thefts, while most thefts in any given month occur in the nation's cities. As a result, the UCR calls motor vehicle theft "primarily a large-city problem."

Law enforcement agencies reported a 14% clearance rate for motor vehicle thefts nationwide in 1993, although 62% of all stolen vehicles were recovered. Hence, while many stolen vehicles were eventually returned to their rightful owners, relatively few arrests of car thieves were made.

Arson

A few years ago William Krause and Kenneth Hayward were convicted under a federal antiarson statute of burning two large wooden crosses in the yard of a home owned by a white couple who had entertained black guests over Labor Day

An arson fire. Arson causes millions of dollars worth of property damage yearly. *Lester Sloan/Woodfin Camp & Associates.*

weekend in 1989. Each was sentenced to a number of years in prison, but appealed to the U.S. Supreme Court, claiming that their cross-burning conviction violated their constitutional right of freedom of expression. In 1994, however, the Supreme Court upheld both convictions without comment.[30]

Arson (UCR) any willful or malicious burning or attempt to burn, with or without intent to defraud, a dwelling house, public building, motor vehicle or aircraft, personal property of another, etc.

The UCR defines **arson** as "any willful or malicious burning or attempt to burn, with or without intent to defraud, a dwelling house, public building, motor vehicle or aircraft, personal property of another, etc." The FBI adds that "only fires determined through investigation to have been willfully or maliciously set are classified as arsons." The NCVS does not report arson statistics.

Arson may occur for a variety of reasons. Some arsonists are thrill-seekers and set fires for the excitement it brings. Others are vandals, wanting only to accomplish a random sort of destruction. Such people, sometimes called "pyromaniacs," may suffer from psychological problems which contribute to their firesetting activities. Sometimes arson is a vengeful act, in which a former employee may strike back at an employer, or an aggrieved former spouse may attempt to settle past scores. A few arsonists are called "vanity pyromaniacs." They are persons, often in some official or responsible role, who place themselves in position to take credit for putting out fires which they secretly start. A handful of security guards, firemen, and others in similar positions of trust have been involved in this kind of behavior.

In many other instances arson is used to disguise other felonies such as murder or burglary. Buildings containing the bodies of murder victims, for example, may be burned in order to cover the evidence of homicide or to make the victim's death appear to have been caused by the fire itself. Most instances of arson, however, appear intended to defraud insurance companies into paying for property that owners no longer want but which they haven't been able to dispose of legally (through sale, transfer, etc.).

Arson Statistics

Although nearly 16,000 law enforcement agencies contributed data to the FBI for use in 1993 UCR tabulations, only 11,860 agencies forwarded any kind of arson information. Much of the arson data received by the FBI during 1993 was incomplete, consisting of less than 12 months of information or lacking in the kind of detail needed for FBI composites. Only 11,743 agencies provided complete arson information for any part of the year, while 9,146 agencies reported such data for all 12 months of 1993. Hence, UCR arson data remain incomplete. As the FBI warns, "Caution is recommended when viewing arson trend information. The percent change figures may have been influenced by improved arson reporting procedures during the collection's relatively limited timespan. It is expected that year-to-year statistical comparability will improve as collection continues."[31]

With these provisos in mind, it is safe to say that 82,348 instances of arson were reported under the UCR Program in 1993, with an average property loss per instance of around $16,616. Of the total number of arsons reported, 30% involved residences, 24% were of motor vehicles, 7% were of commercial buildings, and nearly 5% involved storage facilities of one sort or another. Public buildings were targeted by approximately 6% of all reported arsons.

Nationally, the clearance rate for arson was only 15%, with the highest rates of clearance being reported in small towns (those with populations of less than 10,000). Forty-nine percent of all arson arrests in 1993 involved juveniles—a higher percentage than for any other Index crime. Seventy-five percent of arson arrestees were white, and 85% were male.

Part II Offenses

The UCR also contains a report on arrests made by police for various crimes which are referred to as "Part II offenses." Part II offenses are generally less serious than Part I offenses, and some of them are classified as misdemeanors in many jurisdictions. Only arrests are recorded since many Part II offenses, by virtue of both their semisecret nature (some might be regarded as victimless or social order offenses) and lesser degree of seriousness, are not reported to the police—and are discovered only when an arrest occurs.

A list of Part II offenses, along with the 1993 incidence of each, is provided in Table 2.2. Total arrests for Part II offenses in 1993 were estimated at 11.9 million, with arrests for driving under the influence (1.5 million), simple assault (1.1 million), and drug abuse violations (1.1 million) leading the list. When Part I offenses are added to the total, the overall arrest rate for the United States in 1993 was measured at 5,490 arrests per 100,000 persons, with arrests of city residents (7,103 per 100,000) showing the highest rate.

TABLE 2.2

UCR PART II OFFENSES, 1993

Offense Category	*Number of Arrests*
Simple assault	1,144,900
Forgery and counterfeiting	106,900
Fraud	410,700
Embezzlement	12,900
Stolen property (receiving)	158,100
Vandalism	313,000
Weapons (carrying)	262,300
Prostitution and related offenses	97,800
Sex offenses (statutory rape, etc.)	104,100
Drug law violations	1,126,300
Gambling	17,300
Offenses against the family (nonsupport, etc.)	109,100
Driving under the influence	1,524,800
Liquor law violations	518,500
Public drunkenness	726,600
Disorderly conduct	727,000
Vagrancy	28,200
Curfew/loitering	100,200
Runaways	180,500
All other violations of state and local laws (except traffic law violations)	3,518,700
Total	11,879,000

Source: Federal Bureau of Investigation, *Crime in the United States, 1993* (Washington, D.C.: U.S. Government Printing Office, 1994).

Part II offenses reported in the UCR do not identify arrestees, and make no attempt to distinguish offenders arrested once from those who are arrested many times. Hence, some frequently arrested individuals may have contributed significantly to the overall incidence of Part II crime statistics.

Unreported Crimes

Although differences between the UCR and NCVS abound, the greatest distinction between the two has to do with the ability of the NCVS to ferret out crimes which are not reported to the police (and that therefore do not appear in UCR statistics). According to NCVS analysts, "the majority of crimes measured by the NCVS (recently) were not reported to the police."[32] More specifically, in the words of the NCVS itself:[33]

- Only 38% of all victimizations, 48% of violent victimizations, 29% of personal thefts, and 41% of all household crimes were reported to the police. In fact, household crimes and personal thefts were more likely not to be reported to the police than to be reported.
- Of the three major crime categories, violent crimes were most likely to be reported to the police, followed by household crimes. Personal thefts were the least likely crimes to be reported.
- Three out of four motor vehicle thefts were reported to the police, making this the most highly reported of crimes. Personal larcenies without contact between victim and offender and household larcenies were least likely to be reported (at 28% and 27%, respectively).
- Females were more likely to report violent victimizations to the police than were males, and there was some evidence that this was the case for crimes of theft as well.
- White victims were somewhat more likely than black victims to report thefts to the police. The reporting rates for violent crimes committed against whites and blacks were similar.
- Violent crimes committed by strangers were no more likely to be reported to the police than violent crimes committed by someone who was known to the victim.
- The youngest victims of violent crimes and thefts—those between 12 and 19 years of age—were less likely than persons in any other age group to report crimes to the police.
- Households that owned their homes were significantly more likely than those that rented to report household crimes to the police (44% versus 38%).
- Families with an annual income of $25,000 a year or more were more likely to report victimizations of their households than those earning under $10,000 a year.
- Generally, as the value of loss increased, so did the likelihood that a household crime would be reported.

Reasons for reporting and for not reporting varied somewhat by race, sex, and age. The most common reason given for reporting violent crime was to prevent future victimization by the same offender. An interest in recovering property, or in receiving insurance payments, motivated most victims of property crimes who reported their victimization to the police. The most common reasons for not reporting violent victimizations were (1) the crime was a personal or private matter (20%) or (2) the offender was unsuccessful and the crime was only attempted (17%).

THE SOCIAL DIMENSIONS OF CRIME

What Are "Social Dimensions"?

Crime does not occur in a vacuum. It involves real people—human perpetrators and victims, just like you and I. Because society defines certain personal characteristics as especially important, however, it is possible to speak of the "social dimensions of crime," that is, aspects of crime and victimization as they relate to socially significant attributes by which groups are defined, and according to which individual are assigned group membership. Socially significant attributes include things such as gender, ethnicity or race, age, income or wealth, profession, and social class or standing within society. Such personal characteristics provide criteria by which individuals can be assigned to groups such as "the rich," "the poor," "male," "female," "young," "old," "black," "white," "white-collar worker," "manual laborer," and so on.

We have already alluded briefly to the fact that both the UCR and NCVS structure the data they gather in ways which reflect socially significant characteristics. The UCR, for example, provides information on reported crimes which reveals the sex, age, and race of offenders as well as of perpetrators. NCVS statistics document the race, age, and sex of crime victims as well as the incomes of households reporting victimizations.

Correlates of Crime

Correlation a connection or association which is observed to exist between two measurable variables.

The social dimensions of crime are said by statisticians to reveal relationships or **correlations.** A correlation is simply a connection or association which is observed to exist between two things that are capable of being measured.

Correlations are of two sorts: positive and negative. If one measurement increases whenever another, with which it is correlated, does the same, then a positive correlation or positive relationship is said to exist between the two. When one measurement decreases in value as another rises, a negative or inverse correlation has been discovered. NCVS data, for example, show a negative relationship between age and victimization. As people age, victimization rates decline. Hence, while some elderly people do become crime victims, older people as a group tend to be less victimized than younger folks. UCR data, on the other hand, show a positive relationship between youth and likelihood of arrest—specifically, between young adulthood and arrest. Young adults, it appears, commit most crimes. Hence, as people age, they tend to be both less likely to be victimized as well as less likely to become involved in criminal activity.

Age and Crime

If arrest records are any guide, criminal activity is associated more with youth than with any other stage in life. Year after year the Uniform Crime Reports consistently show that young persons, from their late teens to their early and midtwenties account for the bulk of street, property, and predatory crime (i.e., Part I offenses) reported in this country. Involvement in such crimes decreases consistently, beginning around age 25. The same is true for Part II offenses, with the exception of vagrancy, public drunkenness, gambling, and certain sex crimes—where declines in criminal involvement are more likely to begin around age 30.

Although most forms of criminality may decrease with age, even old age is no bar to criminal involvement. According to UCR statistics, more than one-half million persons aged 50 or over are arrested every year throughout the country. Of those, nearly 90,000 are past the age of 65. Figure 2.3 provides a graphical comparison of persons arrested by age for all reported Part I offenses.

Recently, crimes of the elderly, or geriatric criminality, have sparked much interest among criminologists and the popular media. Movies, such as *The Over the Hill Gang,* have depicted the exploits of aged criminals. Although in the minority, real-life elderly criminals are not hard to find. The case of Edward Cook, aged 68, who still remains a fugitive, is illustrative. Cook usually works with an elderly female companion and the two are known for showing up in swank jewelry stores, posing as casually dressed tourists. The couple travel with a video camera casually slung over Cook's shoulder. Cook, however, keeps the camera running—recording security devices and showcased valuables throughout the targeted stores. Cook returns after closing hours, deactivates store alarms, and helps himself to the choicest jewels.

Why do older people commit crimes? One author explains it this way: "The reasons older people turn to crime are varied. Some people never retire—from trouble. Others find that retirement gets them into trouble. Boredom and unstructured leisure, fear of the future, frustration over limited finances, family neglect or stress—the same conditions that contribute to teenage crime—can lead seniors to commit desperate or foolish acts."[34]

Some older criminals use their age to advantage. Few people, for example, suspect older people of criminal intent. Hence, potential victims are less likely to be

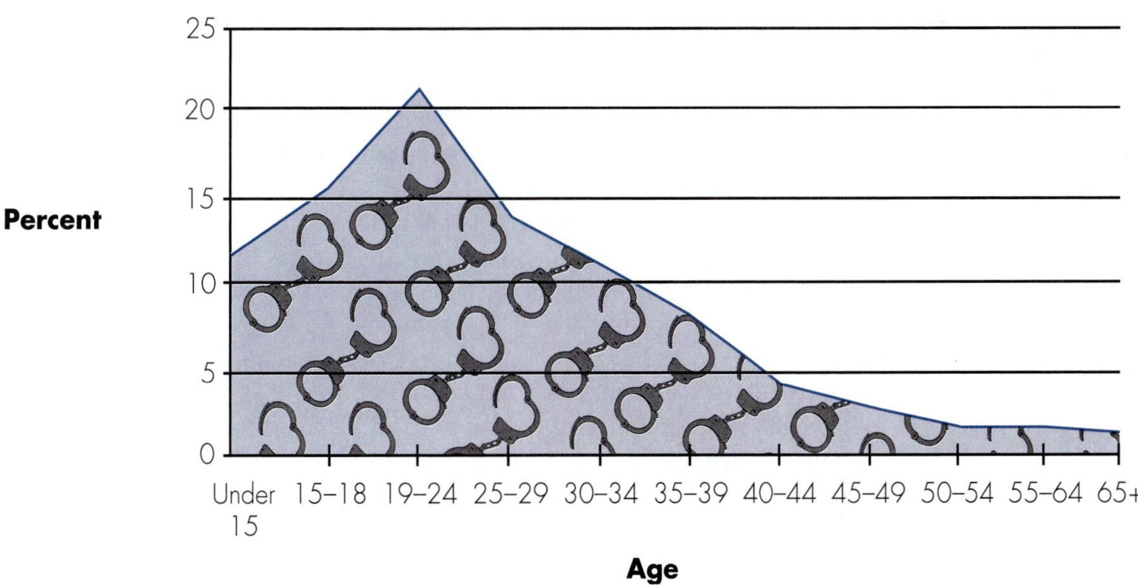

FIGURE 2.3 Arrests of Persons by Age: Part I Offenses, 1993. *Source*: Federal Bureau of Investigation, *Crime in the United States, 1993* (Washington, D.C.: U.S. Government Printing Office, 1994).

on their guard against crime in the presence of an older offender. Similarly, experience gained from previous criminality, and from life in general, can be turned into assets in the criminal arena. As the old adage goes, "knowledge is power," and while social convention holds that wisdom comes with age, so does increased criminal opportunity for those so inclined.

While street crime may be the bailiwick of the young, there are indications that older offenders are overrepresented in other forms of crime, including those that require special skills and knowledge for their commission. Many of these crimes are job related and involve fraud, deception, or business activities which are criminal. Such crimes are discussed in detail in a later chapter.

Although the elderly are less likely to be victimized than other groups, statistics show many more elderly victims than geriatric criminals. The NCVS defines "elderly" to include all persons aged 65 or older living in the United States.[35] NCVS data show that "[p]ersons age 65 or older are the least likely of all age groups in the nation to experience crime,"[36] and victimization rates among the elderly have been declining since 1974—about the time NCVS data gathering began. According to the NCVS, "[t]he rates for personal theft and household crime among the elderly in 1992 were the lowest ever recorded in the 20 year history of NCVS."[37]

Even so, 2.1 million criminal victimizations of elderly persons occurred in the United States in 1992.[38] Table 2.3 shows NCVS victimization rates for various age groups. A recent report[39] by the NCVS makes the following observations about elderly crime victims:

- The violent crime rate is nearly 16 times higher for persons under 25 than for persons over age 65 (64.6 versus 4 victimizations per 1,000 persons in each age group).
- Just as with personal crime victimizations, persons over the age of 65 are significantly less likely to become victims of all forms of household crime than members of younger age groups.
- Personal larceny with contact (purse snatching and pocket picking) is an exception. Those who are 65 or older were about as likely as those under age 65 to be victims of personal larceny with contact.
- Injured elderly victims of violent crime are more likely than younger victims to suffer a serious injury.
- Elderly violent crime victims are more likely than younger victims to face assailants who are strangers.
- Elderly victims of violent crime are almost twice as likely as younger victims to be raped, robbed, or assaulted at or near their home.
- Elderly victims less often than younger victims act to protect themselves during a violent crime.
- Elderly victims of robbery and personal theft are more likely than younger victims to report those crimes to the police.

One crime against the elderly which is often not reported is elder abuse. The physical and emotional abuse of elderly persons by family members, care-givers, and others has been called a "national tragedy,"[40] involving as it does an estimated 1.5 million cases per year. Recent hearings before the Subcommittee on Human

TABLE 2.3

NUMBER OF VICTIMIZATIONS BY AGE, 1992
(PER 1,000 PERSONS)

Age	*Violent Crime*	*Personal Theft*
12–24	64.6	112.7
25–49	27.2	71.2
50–64	8.5	38.3
65 and over	4.0	19.5

Source: U.S. Department of Justice, *Elderly Crime Victims* (Washington, D.C.: Bureau of Justice Statistics, March 1994).

Services of the House Select Committee on Aging revealed that one out of every twenty-five Americans over the age of 65 suffers from some form of abuse, neglect, or exploitation.[41] Subcommittee members also concluded that elder abuse is increasing. Unfortunately, however, cases of elder abuse rarely come to the attention of authorities. The desire shared by many elderly citizens for privacy, fear of embarrassment at having abuse at the hands of loved ones revealed, and the relatively limited ability of elderly citizens to access law enforcement services all contribute to the problem.

To address the concerns of the elderly the 1994 Violent Crime Control and Law Enforcement Act provides, under Title XXIV, "Protections for the Elderly," monies for the development of local community partnerships between senior citizen groups and law enforcement agencies designed to combat crimes against older Americans.

The act also provides monies to assist with funding a "Missing Alzheimer's Disease Patient Alert Program" which, in the words of the legislation, "shall be a locally based, proactive program to protect and locate missing patients with Alzheimer's disease and related dementias." Finally, the act increases penalties for telemarketing fraud directed against the elderly and requires criminal justice agencies to assist in providing background information on care-givers with felony convictions who are being considered for employment in nursing homes and long-term care facilities.

Gender and Crime

Gender also appears to be linked closely to criminal activity. Table 2.4 shows degree of involvement in each of the major crimes by gender. Columns in the table do not show the total number of crimes reported, but rather represent the proportion of male-female involvement in each Part I offense. For example, of all murders in this country in a given year, approximately 90% are committed by men and 10% by women.

The apparently low rate of female criminality has been explained by some as primarily due to cultural factors, including early socialization, role expectations,

Female gang members fighting. Although much female criminality has long been overlooked, criminologists are now increasingly aware of gender issues. *Copaken/Gamma-Liaison, Inc.*

and a reluctance among criminal justice officials to arrest and prosecute women. Others have assumed a biological propensity toward crime and aggression among males which may be lacking in women. While these and other issues are addressed in later chapters, it is important here to note that the rate of female criminality has changed very little over time—a fact much in contrast to assumptions made years ago by some criminologists who insisted that the degree of female involvement in crime would increase as women assumed more powerful roles in society.

Turning to victimization as it is associated with gender, women are victimized far less frequently than men in most crime categories. NCVS data show that crimes of violence reported by American women reflect victimization rates of 25.9 per 1,000 females aged 12 or older, versus 38.8 for men; while rates of personal theft among women stand at 55.9, versus 62.6 for men.

As with the population in general, the rate of female victimization for all crimes decreases with age, leading NCVS authors to conclude that (1) white women age 65 or older have the lowest violent crime rates and (2) black women age 65 or older have the lowest personal theft rates.[42]

Two significant exceptions are rape and spousal abuse. Rape is a crime of special concern to many because official reports to the police of rape have continued to increase even as reports of many other types of crimes have decreased.[43] Figure 2.4 illustrates the growth in the number of reported rape cases over the past twenty years. Recognizing some of the problems facing women today, federal policymakers—through the 1994 Violent Crime Control and Law Enforcement Act—provided more than $1 billion in funding to support a special "violence against women" initiative. The initiative:

TABLE 2.4

MALE–FEMALE INVOLVEMENT IN CRIME

UCR Index Crimes	Percentage of Arrests by Gender Males	Females
Murder and nonnegligent manslaughter	90.6%	9.4%
Rape	98.7	1.3
Robbery	91.3	8.7
Aggravated assault	84.3	15.7
Burglary	90.1	9.9
Larceny-theft	67.3	32.7
Motor vehicle theft	88.2	11.8
Arson	85.3	14.7
Average, all major crimes	80.5	19.5

Source: Federal Bureau of Investigation, *Crime in the United States, 1993* (Washington, D.C.: U.S. Government Printing Office, 1994).

- Includes funds (1) to increase and train police, prosecutors, and judges in the area of spousal abuse, (2) to encourage pro-arrest policies when abuse is encountered, (3) for victim services and victim's advocates, (4) to support battered women's shelters, (5) to fund rape education and community prevention programs, (6) to establish a national family violence hotline, and (7) to increase security in public places.
- Provides first-ever civil rights remedies for victims of felonies motivated by gender bias.
- Extends "rape shield law" protections to civil cases and to all criminal cases to bar irrelevant inquiries into a rape victim's sexual history.
- Requires all states to honor "stay-away orders" issued by courts in other states.
- Requires confidentiality for the addresses of family violence shelters and abused persons.

The 1994 act provides Crime Prevention Block Grants for the creation of battered women's shelters through a competitive funding program to be administered by the Department of Health and Human Services. It also creates supervised centers for divorced or separated parents to visit their children in "safe havens" where there is a history of risk of physical or sexual abuse.

Ethnicity and Crime

Recently, Professor Lani Guinier, of the University of Pennsylvania School of Law, was interviewed on *Think Tank*, a Public Television show. Guinier was asked by Ben Wattenberg, the program's moderator, "When we talk about crime, crime,

crime, are we really using a code for black, black, black?" Guinier responded this way: "To a great extent, yes, and I think that's a problem, not because we shouldn't deal with the disproportionate number of crimes that young black men may be committing, but because if we can't talk about race, then when we talk about crime, we're really talking about other things, and it means that we're not being honest in terms of acknowledging what the problem is and then trying to deal with it. It's a way of distancing ourselves from the real problem, which is the terrible rise in urban violence."[44]

Crimes, of course, are committed by individuals of all races. The link between crime—especially violent, street, and predatory crimes—and race, however, shows a clear and undeniable pattern. In many crime categories arrests of black offenders equal or exceed arrests of whites. In 1993, for example, 11,656 of all murder arrestees in the United States were black and 8,243 were white. While simple numbers such as these may be surprising to some, more significant still are crime rates based upon ethnicity. Such rates, which take into consideration the relative proportion of ethnic groups in the American population and calculate the extent to which criminal activity is associated with each, are very revealing. The U.S. Bureau of Census, for example, says that 12.4% of the American population consists of individuals identifying themselves as "black," while 84.1% count themselves "white." Hispanic-Americans make up most of the remainder of the population. Arrest rates by ethnicity are shown in Figure 2.5. The figure shows, for example, that while black persons are arrested for around 56% of all murders committed in a given year, the murder rate among blacks is ten times that of whites since blacks

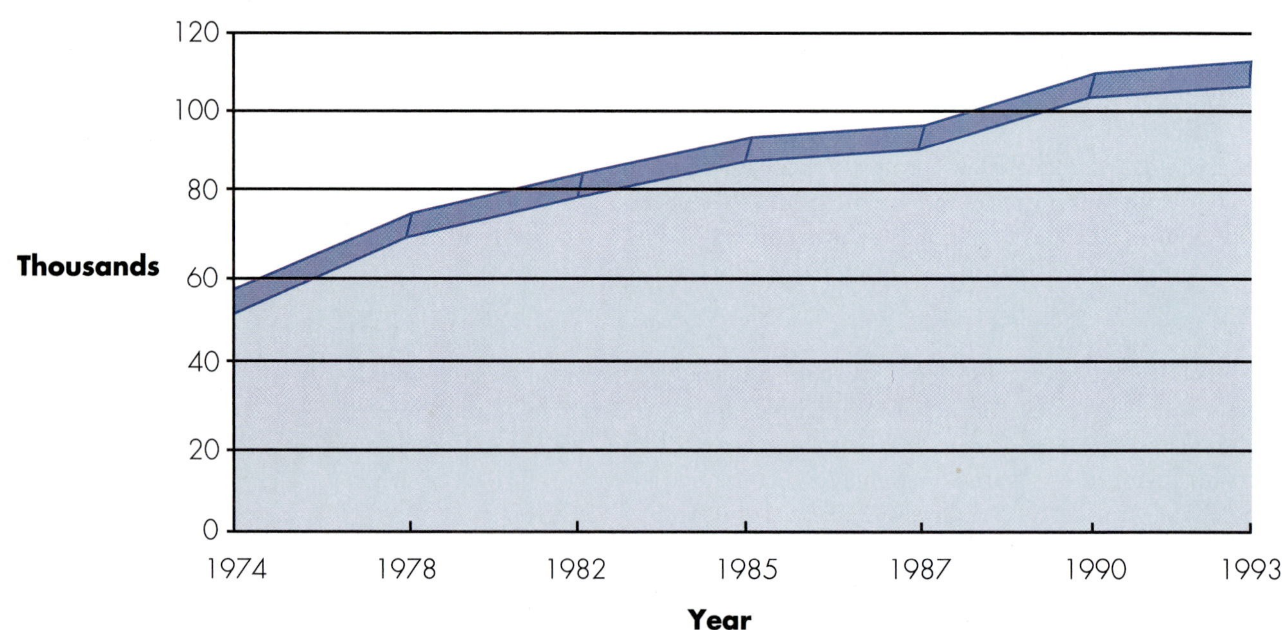

FIGURE 2.4 Female Rape (Number of Reported Cases by Year), 1974–1992. *Source*: Federal Bureau of Investigation, *Crime in the United States* (Washington, D.C.: U.S. Government Printing Office, various years).

account for only 12.4% of the population. Similar *rate* comparisons are shown in the figure for a few other crimes. The chart diagrammatically represents the yearly arrest rates (per 1,000 persons) by race that are numerically presented in Table 2.5.

Many persons today, because of personal sentiments, closely-held ideals, and what may be a misguided sense of political and social correctness, find it difficult to accept racial disparities and arrest rates in official crime reports such as those shown in Figure 2.5. Seeing statistics that point to an overrepresentation of black persons at all stages of criminal justice processing, they prefer, instead, to believe that the criminal justice system is somehow biased in its arrest, prosecution, and sentencing practices. In *The Myth of a Racist Criminal Justice System,*[45] however, William Wilbanks convincingly demonstrates that "[a]t every point from arrest to parole there is little or no evidence of an overall racial effect, in that the percentage outcomes for blacks and whites are not very different."[46] Wilbanks claims to have reviewed "all the available studies that have examined the possible existence of racial discrimination from arrest to parole." In essence, he says, "this examination of the available evidence indicates that support for the 'discrimination thesis' is sparse, inconsistent, and frequently contradictory."[47]

While American criminal justice may have been significantly racist in the past, and while some vestiges of racism may indeed remain, the system is today by-and-

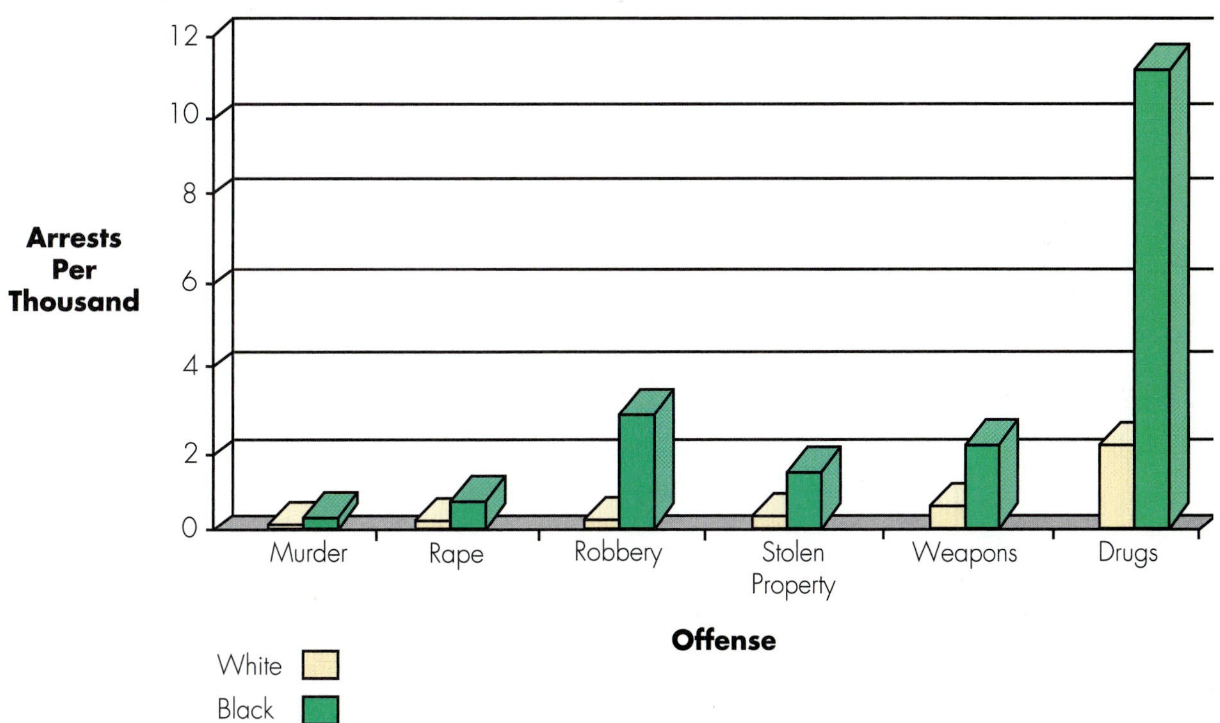

FIGURE 2.5 Arrest Rates by Ethnicity, Selected Offenses. *Source:* FBI, *Crime in the United States, 1992* (Washington, D.C.: U.S. Government Printing Office, 1994). *Note*: This figure displays population-adjusted arrest rates by ethnicity which are arrived at by calculating the number of arrests per crime category by racial group, and then computing rates based upon the relative proportion of each racial group in the American population.

TABLE 2.5

ARREST RATES BY RACE (PER 1,000 PERSONS)
SELECTED OFFENSES, 1993

	Blacks	*Whites*
Murder	0.34	0.04
Rape	0.45	0.09
Robbery	3.00	0.28
Stolen property	1.82	0.37
Weapons	2.73	0.54
Drug abuse	11.70	2.68

Source: FBI, *Crime in the United States, 1993* (Washington, D.C.: U.S. Government Printing Office, 1994).

large objective in its processing of criminal defendants, according to Wilbanks. A nonracist criminal justice system is not necessarily the result of a total absence of racism, since some individual actors within the system will inevitably act in racially biased fashion. It may be, rather, the result of a series of actions, some of which may be racially motivated, but which taken together collectively balance out. Hence, says Wilbanks, the net result is a system that is not observably racist in its results.

Wilbanks is careful to counter arguments advanced by those who continue to suggest the system is racist. He writes, for example, "...perhaps the black/white gap at arrest is a product of racial bias by the police in that the police are more likely to select and arrest black than white offenders. The best evidence on this question comes from the National Crime Survey which interviews 130,000 Americans each year about crime victimization.... The percent of offenders described by victims as being black is generally consistent with the percent of offenders who are black according to arrest figures."[48]

However, observes Wilbanks, "[t]he assertion that the criminal justice system is not racist does not address the reasons why blacks appear to offend at higher rates than whites before coming into contact with the criminal justice system....It may be," he suggests, "that racial discrimination in American society has been responsible for conditions (e.g., discrimination in employment, housing, and education) that lead to higher rates of offending by blacks, but that possibility does not bear on the question of whether the criminal justice system discriminates against blacks."[49] If such assertions are even partially correct, unpopular though they may be, then it is incumbent upon policymakers to admit and realistically assess the degree of overinvolvement in street crime that characterizes a disproportionately large segment of the black population in America today—for such an admission is the first step toward realistically addressing the problem.

African-Americans not only commit street crimes at a rate disproportionate to their representation in the population, but they are also disproportionately victimized by such crimes. One author recently asserted that "black-on-black crime is the true face of crime in America."[50] No less a figure than the American civil rights leader Jesse Jackson has identified black-on-black crime as "the most important issue of the civil rights movement today."[51]

Crime and criminal victimization have led to a heightened fear of crime among black Americans. A recent report by the Bureau of Justice Statistics, which was based upon data from the American Housing Survey (conducted by the Department of Housing and Urban Development), found that "black households are nearly three times more likely than white ones to fear crime in their neighborhoods and that black fear is growing faster than white fear...."[52] The survey shows that fear of neighborhood crime has risen almost twice as much among blacks as whites since the mid-1980s. In black central-city households, neighborhood crime was cited as resident's primary concern. Study findings are said to "mirror the incidence of violent crime, which victimizes blacks more than whites and central city residents more than those in suburbs or rural areas."[53] The BJS report noted that a separate survey of state prison inmates found that 43% were serving time for crimes committed in their own neighborhoods.

The Cost of Crime

Fear of crime and the changes it forces us to make in our lives are important aspects of the overall cost of crime. The total impact of crime on American society, however, is difficult to measure since crime can affect its victims in many ways. Some victims are physically injured and may require medical treatment or hospitalization. Others suffer the loss of valued property or are psychologically traumatized. Still others will miss time from work as they strive to repair lives shattered by crime. The Bureau of Justice Statistics, using NCVS data, attempts to measure the economic costs of crime by assessing two dimensions of total cost: the value of property lost to criminal activity and medical expenses associated with victimization. As BJS points out, however, such data are not all inclusive. "Medical costs may continue to accumulate for months or years after a victimization,"[54] says the bureau. "The victim is not specifically asked about psychological counseling, although some victims may have included this as a medical cost. Increases to insurance premiums as a result of filing claims, decreased productivity at work, moving costs incurred when moving as a result of victimization, intangible costs of pain and suffering, and other similar costs are also not included."[55]

According to BJS, victims of major crime (rape, robbery, assault, personal and household theft, burglary, and motor vehicle theft) lost $17.6 billion in direct costs in 1992. These costs included "losses from property theft or damage, cash losses, medical expenses, and amount of pay lost because of injury or activities related to...crime." Estimated economic losses for crimes recorded by the NCVS in 1992 are shown in Table 2.6.

The Bureau also notes that:

- Economic loss of some kind occurs in 71% of all personal crimes (which include rape, robbery, assault, and personal theft).
- In crimes of violence (rape, robbery, assault) economic losses occur in 23% of victimizations.

TABLE 2.6

ESTIMATED ECONOMIC LOSSES DUE TO CRIME 1992

	Average Loss per Incident	*Total Losses all Incidents*
Personal crimes	$218	$4,110,000,000
Rape	234	33,000,000
Robbery	555	680,000,000
Assault	124	649,000,000
Personal larceny	N.A.	2,748,000,000
Household crimes	914	13,536,000,000
Household larceny	221	1,750,000,000
Burglary	834	3,970,000,000
Motor vehicle theft	3,990	7,816,000,000
Mean loss, all crimes	$524	$17,646,000,000

N.A. – Not available.

Source: Patsy A. Klaus, *Bureau of Justice Statistics Crime Data Brief*, "The Costs of Crime to Victims of Crime," February 1994.

- Household crimes of burglary, theft, and motor vehicle theft involve economic loss in 91% of all victimizations.
- Lost property is not recovered in 89% of personal crimes and 85% of household crimes.
- About 31% of all victims of crimes of violence (robbery and assault) sustain some physical injury.
- For crimes of violence involving injuries in which medical expenses are known, 65% involve costs of $250 or more.
- 1.8 million victims lose 6.1 million days from work each year as a result of crime, which translates into an average of 3.4 days of lost work per victimization.

SUMMARY

Crime statistics have been gathered for at least a century and a half. While early data about crime may have been used to assess the moral health of nations, modern-day criminal statistics programs provide a fairly objective picture of crime in the United States and elsewhere. Statistics often form the basis for social policy, and innovative strategies such as the "three strikes and you're out" initiative of the Clinton administration are frequently based upon an understanding of crime provided by such information.

Today two large-scale government programs collect crime data. One, the National Crime Victimization Survey, is run by the Bureau of Justice Statistics and provides yearly reports on the criminal victimization of households and individuals. The other, the Uniform Crime Reporting Program, is administered by the Federal Bureau of Investigation and annually collects information on crimes reported to the police and on arrests throughout the country.

As we have seen, the social correlates of crime in America include age, sex, race, and social class. Although crime statistics do not tell the whole story, and there are many other forms of crime, it appears from the best information available that young black males are especially overrepresented in American street crime statistics.

Other than gender, age, and ethnicity, social class can be a significant indicator of the likelihood of criminal involvement. Suffice it here to say that crimes are committed by members of all social classes. As we will recognize in later chapters, however, since powerful classes make the laws they are both less apt to have need of breaking them and are probably more committed to preservation of the status quo. Hence, many offenders, especially those arrested for street, property, and predatory crimes, come from the lower social classes.

Some people argue that crime statistics do not justify the degree of fear Americans express about crime. Others suggest that statistics are misleading and that they do not provide a true picture of crime in America. Even though the actual incidence of crime is difficult to measure, however, crime statistics do provide us with an appreciation for the extent of the problems facing victims of crime, social policymakers, and law enforcement personnel today.

DISCUSSION QUESTIONS

1. What are the major differences between the NCVS and the UCR? Can useful comparisons be made between these two crime indices? If so, what might such comparisons consist of?
2. What is a crime *rate*? How are rates useful? How might both the NCVS and UCR make better use of rates?
3. What are the reasons victims don't report crimes to the police? Which crimes appear to be the most underreported? Why are those crimes so infrequently reported? Which crimes appear to be the most frequently reported? Why are they so often reported?
4. From a study of the incidence of crimes and crime rates discussed in this chapter do you feel that the seemingly widespread fear of crime among Americans is justified? Why or why not?
5. This chapter discusses the losses due to crime. Can you think of any ways in which "losses due to crime" might be measured other than those discussed here? If so, what might they be?
6. This chapter seems to say that black people appear to be overrepresented in many categories of criminal activity. Do you believe that the statistics cited in this chapter accurately reflect the degree of black-white involvement in crime? Why or why not? How might they be inaccurate?

NOTES

1. "Safety Fears," The Associated Press, May 20, 1994.
2. Kathleen Maguire and Ann L. Pastore, *Sourcebook of Criminal Justice Statistics, 1993* (Washington, D.C.: U.S. Government Printing Office, 1994).
3. Modern researchers have not found support for such "thermic laws," at least in the case of homicide. See, for example, Derral Cheatwood, "Is There a Season for Homicide?" *Criminology,* Vol. 26, no. 2 (May 1988), pp. 287–306.
4. NCJRS may be reached at 800-851-3420 or write to National Institute of Justice, National Criminal Justice Reference Service, Box 6000, Rockville, MD 20850.
5. Federal Bureau of Investigation, *Crime in the United States, 1992* (Washington, D.C. U.S. Government Printing Office, 1993), p. vi.
6. Recent redesign of the NCVS necessitated a recomputation of official 1993 data in terms of previously used categories.
7. Bureau of Justice Statistics, *Criminal Victimization in the United States, 1973–92 Trends* (Washington, D.C.: U.S. Department of Justice, 1994), p. 5.
8. Ibid.
9. For further information, see Ronet Bachman and Bruce Taylor, "The Measurement of Family Violence and Rape by the Redesigned National Crime Victimization Survey," *Justice Quarterly,* Vol. 11, no. 3 (September 1994); Bureau of Justice Statistics, "National Crime Victimization Survey Redesign," *BJS Fact Sheet* (October 19, 1994); and BJS, *"Questions and Answers About the Redesign"* (October 30, 1994).
10. "Son Pleads Guilty to Killing Father, Wounding Mother," United Press online, Northern edition, February 21, 1994.
11. Although, technically speaking, mass murder could be classified as second-degree murder depending upon the circumstances under which it occurs, no cases of second-degree mass murder are documented.
12. The state of Illinois later sued Gacy's estate to recoup the money made on his paintings. For additional information, see "State Wants Gacy's Money, Even If He's Dead," United Press on-line, southeast edition, May 18, 1994.
13. Bureau of Justice Statistics, *Report to the Nation on Crime and Justice,* 2nd ed. (Washington, D.C.: U.S. Government Printing Office, 1988), p. 4.
14. Ibid.
15. This and most other UCR statistics in this chapter are mostly taken from Federal Bureau of Investigation, *Crime in the United States, 1993* (Washington, D.C.: U.S. Government Printing Office, 1994).
16. Joe Gelarden, "Judge Denies Tyson's Clemency Request," Reuters wire services, June 13, 1994.
17. Frank Schmalleger and Ted Alleman, "The Collective Reality of Crime: An Integrative Approach to the Causes and Consequences of the Criminal Event," in Gregg Barak, *Varieties of Criminology: Readings from a Dynamic Discipline* (New York: Praeger Publishers, 1994).
18. "British Law Lords Recognize Male Rape," United Press on-line, Northern edition, July 12, 1994.
19. "Swim Coach Guilty of Statutory Rape," *USA Today,* August 13, 1993, p. 3A.
20. A. Nicholas Groth, *Men Who Rape: The Psychology of the Offender* (New York: Plenum Press, 1979).
21. See, for example, Frank Schmalleger and Ted Alleman, "The Collective Reality of Crime: An Integrative Approach to the Causes and Consequences of the Criminal Event."
22. This and most other NCVS data are taken from the Bureau of Justice Statistics, *Criminal Victimization in the United States, 1993* (Washington, D.C.: BJS, 1994), and Department of Justice, "Crime Rate Essentially Unchanged Last Year," BJS press release, October 30, 1994.
23. Patrick A. Langan and Caroline Wolf

Harlow, "Child Rape Victims, 1992" (Washington, D.C.: Bureau of Justice Statistics, 1994), and Pierre Thomas, "Rape of Girls Too Common, Study Finds; Half of All Victims Are Under Age 18," *The Washington Post* wire service, June 23, 1994.

24. The occupants of houses may be robbed, of course, by someone who comes to their door. Hence, household robbery is a crime distinguishable from household burglary.
25. FBI, *Crime in the United States, 1992*, p. 27.
26. BJS, *Criminal Victimization in the United States, 1990*, p. 68.
27. "Rapper Arrested," Associated Press online, Northern edition, May 17, 1994.
28. Trudy Tynan, "Chief Killed," the Associated Press on-line, February 2, 1994.
29. This is so even though the NCVS does not record burglaries of businesses or commercial properties.
30. Richard Carelli, "Scotus-Cross Burning," Associated Press on-line, March 28, 1994.
31. FBI, *Crime in the United States, 1992*, p. 54.
32. BJS, *Criminal Victimization in the United States, 1990*, p. 100.
33. Ibid., pp. 100–101.
34. Edna Buchanan, "You're Under Arrest," *New Choices for Retirement Living*, June 1994, p. 61.
35. U.S. Department of Justice, *Elderly Crime Victims* (Washington, D.C.: Bureau of Justice Statistics, March 1994).
36. Ibid.
37. Ibid.
38. For an excellent review of homicide and the elderly, see: James Alan Fox and Jack Levin, "Homicide Against the Elderly: A Research Note," *Criminology*, Vol. 29, no. 2 (May 1991), pp. 317–327.
39. U.S. Department of Justice, *Elderly Crime Victims*.
40. Mel E. Weith, "Elder Abuse: A National Tragedy," *FBI Law Enforcement Bulletin*, February 1994, pp. 24–26.
41. U.S. Congress, House Subcommittee on Human Services, Select Committee on Aging, *Elder Abuse: An Assessment of the Federal Response*, 101st Congress, 1st Session, June 7, 1989.
42. U.S. Department of Justice, *Elderly Crime Victims*, p. 4.
43. NCVS data show that the rate of rape has dropped somewhat over the past two decades even though the number of such crimes reported to the police has increased regularly. UCR data are probably more reliable than NCVS data where rape is concerned, however, because NCVS use of a redesigned questionnaire has thrown the reliability of NCVS rape data into question. In fact, for 1992, the number of rapes reported to the police (UCR data) exceeded the number of estimated rape victimizations (NCVS data) for the first time since record keeping began. See Maguire and Pastore, *Sourcebook of Criminal Justice Statistics, 1993*, Table 3.26, for additional information.
44. "For the Record," *Washington Post* wire services, March 3, 1994.
45. William Wilbanks, *The Myth of a Racist Criminal Justice System* (Monterey, CA: Brooks/Cole, 1987).
46. William Wilbanks, "The Myth of a Racist Criminal Justice System," *Criminal Justice Research Bulletin*, Vol. 3, no. 5 (Huntsville, TX: Sam Houston State University, 1987), p. 2.
47. Ibid., p. 5.
48. Ibid., p. 3.
49. Ibid., p. 2.
50. Paul Glastris and Jeannye Thornton, "A New Civil Rights Frontier: After His Own Home and Neighborhood Were Invaded by Street Punks, Jesse Jackson Dedicated Himself to Battling Black-on-Black Crime," *U.S. News & World Report*, January 17, 1994, p. 38.
51. Ibid.
52. Michael J. Sniffen, "Crime Fear," Associated Press on-line, Northern edition, June 20, 1994.
53. Ibid.
54. Patsy A. Klaus, Bureau of Justice Statistics Crime Data Brief, "The Costs of Crime to Victims of Crime," February 1994.
55. Ibid.

CHAPTER 3

RESEARCH METHODS AND THEORY DEVELOPMENT

Criminological research is most frequently concerned with the discovery of the causes of crime and the effect of various methods of treatment.

—Hermann Mannheim[1]

...criminology should be concerned with real-world applications of its research.

—Joan Petersilia, Past-President, The American Society of Criminology[2]

The cardinal principle of experimentation is that we must accept the outcome whether or not it is to our liking.

—Abraham Kaplan[3]

IMPORTANT TERMS

theory	hypothesis	research
randomization	intersubjectivity	replicability
variable	operationalization	research design
confounding effects	controlled experiments	internal validity
external validity	control group	intersubjectivity
replicability	quantitative methods	applied research
qualitative methods	data confidentiality	informed consent
pure research	primary research	secondary research
secondary analysis	survey research	descriptive statistics
inferential statistics	tests of significance	participant observation
cohort	quasi-experimental designs	

INTRODUCTION

Years ago, I taught my first criminology class at a small southern university in the heart of what was then referred to as the "Bible belt." Many of my students were devoutly religious and thoroughly churched in such hallowed concepts as "good and evil," "sin," "salvation," and "redemption." When the three and one-half month course was nearly over, and a detailed discussion of biological, psychological, and sociological theories of crime causation had ended, I decided to take a survey. I wanted to see which of the theories we had discussed most appealed to the majority of my students. On the last day of class I took a brief survey. After explaining what I was about to do, I started with the question: "How many of you think that most criminal behavior can be explained by the biological theories of crime causation we've studied?" Only one or two students raised their hands. This was a very small number, for the class, a very popular one, held 131 students and was taught in a small auditorium. "How many of you," I continued, "think psychological theories explain most crime?" Again, only a handful of students responded. "Well, then, how many of you feel sociological theories offer the best explanation for crime?" I asked. A few more hands were raised. Still, the majority of students had not voted one way or the other. Fearing that my teaching had been for naught, and not knowing what else to ask, I blurted out: "How many of you believe that 'the devil made him do it' is the best explanation for crime that we can offer?" At that, almost all the students raised their hands.

I realized then that an entire semester spent trying to communicate the best thoughts of generations of criminologists had had little impact on most students in the class. They had listened to what I had to say, they had considered each of the theories I presented, and then they had dismissed all of them out of hand as so much idle conjecture—assigning them the status of ruminations sadly out of touch with the true character of human nature and lacking in appreciation for the cosmic temper of human activity.

That class held a lesson for me greater than any which the students had learned. It taught me that criminological theory could not be fully appreciated until and unless its fundamental assumptions were comprehended. Until students could be brought to see the value of criminological theorizing, unless they could be shown why criminologists think and believe the way they do, it would be impossible to ever convince future students that the criminological enterprise was worthwhile.

This chapter, which concerns itself with criminological research methods and theory development, is my way of showing to those now embarking upon the study of criminology why modern-day criminology has both validity and purpose—that is, to show how it is applicable to social life in today's world. Were it not, criminological study would be pointless, and criminological theorizing fruitless. Happily, criminology, because it is built upon a scientific approach to the subject matter of crime, has much to offer as we attempt to grapple with the crime problems now facing us. However, for criminology to bear the fruit of which it is capable, more than mere scientific acceptance is necessary. Ultimately, to realize its true promise, criminology must become accepted as a policymaking tool, consulted by lawmakers and social planners alike, and respected for what it can tell us about both crime and its prevention.

THE SCIENCE OF CRIMINOLOGY

Over the past century, criminologists have undertaken the task of building a "scientific criminology" as distinguished from what had been the "armchair criminology" of earlier years. Armchair criminologists offered their ideas to one another as conjecture, fascinating ideas that could be debated—and sometimes were, ad nauseam. While the ruminations of armchair criminologists may have achieved a considerable degree of popular acclaim through the involvement of distinguished lecturers, the association of such ideas with celebrated bastions of higher learning, and their publication in prestigious essays, they were nonetheless unfounded in anything other than mere speculation.

The ideas of armchair criminologists followed in the intellectual tradition of Christian apologists who busied themselves with debates over questions such as how many angels could fit on the head of a pin or whether Noah had forgotten to take certain types of insects aboard the ark, but which had made the famous journey by happenstance (why, for example, would anyone take two mosquitoes?). They were the kinds of things one could probably never know with certainty, no matter how much the ideas were debated.

While it is easy to dispense of "armchair criminology" as the relaxed musings of carefree intellectuals undertaken almost as sport, it is far more difficult to agree upon the criteria necessary to move any undertaking into the realm of serious scientific endeavor. Present-day criminology is decidedly more scientific, however, than its intellectual predecessor—which means that it is amenable to objective scrutiny and systematic testing. In fact, the drive to make criminology "scientific" has been a conscious one, beginning with many of the approaches discussed in Chapter 5.

A variety of criteria have been advanced for declaring any endeavor "scientific." Among them are[4]

- The systematic collection of related facts (as in the building of a database).
- An emphasis on the availability and application of the scientific method.
- "The existence of general laws, a field for experiment or observation...and control of academic discourse by practical application."
- "The fact that it has been...accepted into the scientific tradition."
- An "emphasis on a worthwhile subject in need of independent study even if adequate techniques of study are not yet available" (as in the investigation of paranormal phenomena).

Probably all of the forgoing could be said of criminology. For one thing, criminologists do gather facts. The mere gathering of facts, however, while it might lead to a descriptive criminology, falls short of offering satisfactory explanations for crime. Hence, most contemporary criminologists are concerned with identifying relationships among the facts they observe, and with attempting to understand the many and diverse causes of crime. This emphasis on unveiling causality moves criminology beyond the merely descriptive into the realm of conjecture and theory building. A further emphasis on measurement and objectivity gives contemporary criminology its scientific flavor.

THEORY BUILDING

Ultimately, the goal of research within criminology is the construction of theories or models that allow for a better understanding of criminal behavior and which permit the development of strategies intended to address the problem of crime. A theory consists of a set of interrelated propositions which provide a relatively complete form of understanding. Hence, even if we find that crime is higher when the moon is full than at other times, we must still ask, "Why?" Is it because the light from full moons makes it possible for those interested in crime commission to see better at night? If so, then we would expect crime to be higher on full moon nights in areas where there is no cloud cover then in areas where clouds obliterate the moon's light. Likewise, cities should show less of a rise in crime during full moons than rural areas and small towns, since city lights effectively minimize the impact of the light of the moon. In any event, a complete lunar theory of crime causation would contain specific propositions about the causal nature of the phenomena involved.

There are many ways to define the word "theory." One cogent definition comes from Don M. Gottfredson, a well-known criminologist of modern times, who writes that "[t]heories consist of postulates" (i.e., assumptions), "theoretical constructs, logically derived hypotheses, and definitions. Theories," says Gottfredson, "can be improved steadily through **hypothesis** testing, examination of evidence from observations, revisions of the theory, and repetitions of the cycle, repeatedly modifying the theory in light of the evidence." [5] Another well-known methodologist describes theories this way: "...a theory is a set of related propositions that suggest why events occur in the manner that they do. The propositions that make up theories are of the same form as hypotheses: they consist of concepts and the linkages or relationships between them." [6]

Hypothesis 1. an explanation that accounts for a set of facts and that can be tested by further investigation...2. something that is taken to be true for the purpose of argument or investigation.

THE DEVIL MADE HER DO IT!

Demonic Possession Trial in Dallas

Scientific criminology generally scoffs at claims of supernatural influences in crime commission. As the story that follows shows, however, not everyone is convinced.

DALLAS—Doretha Crawford insists she and her sister didn't gouge out their sister's eyeballs with their fingers. But when a prosecutor asked her Tuesday if her sister had been possessed, she didn't hesitate.

"It wasn't her," Crawford said, describing how her sister, Myra Obasi, 30, while seemingly possessed by a demon, drove wildly, swerved toward huge trucks and tried to run off the road.

"Her whole features changed. Her eyes were big...She spoke in a man's voice. Mist came out of her mouth. Her teeth were black and scattered. It said it got her, and it was going to get us, too."

In one of the most bizarre cases in recent Texas history, Crawford and her sister, Beverly Johnson, testified in their own defense, saying they didn't blind Obasi in Dallas last March.

Instead, they insist, they fled demons for two days, prayed and sought out ministers, all trying to save their sister.

Obasi, stunning courtroom observers, said she agrees.

A Shreveport, La., schoolteacher who is now totally blind, Obasi testified in a near-whisper, crying occasionally, that she has no idea how she lost her eyeballs. But she insisted her sister's had nothing to do with it.

All three sisters were in the house of Mattye Bradfield, an elderly preacher in southern Dallas, when Obasi was horribly blinded.

But Crawford, 34, and Johnson, 35, testified that they couldn't remember the critical period—a claim prosecutor George West mocked as "stereo memory loss."

Police and prosecutors have said Obasi at first told them the sisters blinded her while trying to "beat the devil" out of her. The tale, by any measure, is a truly hellish one.

Last spring Johnson began having headaches that a doctor could not cure, according to her father, Chester Crawford. Crawford reluctantly told jurors he then took Johnson to see Benny Morgan, a practitioner of "hoodoo," a Christianized version of voodoo.

Prosecutors and police have said the diagnosis was that the family was under attack by demons. Johnson said her father told them later that one of their sisters, living in Houston, was trying to kill them. So when someone wrote the words "BLOOD ROOM" on Obasi's car last March, they fled from Arcadia, La., where the two defendants lived, to Dallas. They turned their five children over to a stranger along the way.

All three sisters say they are firm Christian believers. But prosecutors, who expect to finish the trial today, say they will convince jurors otherwise.

Both women face two to 10 years for aggravated assault.

Source: Mark Potok, "Demonic Possession Trial Has Dallas Under Its Spell, *USA Today*, September 21, 1994, p. 8A. Copyright 1994, USA Today. Reprinted with permission.

QUESTIONS

1. Do you believe that the devil plays a role in modern-day crime causation? If so, describe the nature of that role.
2. How might we research whether the devil, or some other supernatural force, is active in influencing crime rates today?

Sisters: Doretha Crawford, center, and Beverly Johnson, left, are on trial for gouging out Myra Obasi's eyes. Obasi (shown in photo on right) says her sisters had nothing to do with it. *(a) Pat sullivan/AP/Wide World Photos; (b and c) Ariane Kadoch/The Dallas Morning News.*

Theory a series of interrelated propositions that attempt to describe, explain, predict, and ultimately to control some class of events. A theory gains explanatory power from inherent logical consistency and is "tested" by how well it describes and predicts reality.

While all these definitions have something to offer, the definition of the term "theory" that we choose to use in this book combines aspects of them all. For our purposes, then, a **theory** consists of a series of interrelated propositions which attempt to describe, explain, predict, and ultimately control some class of events. Theories gain explanatory power from inherent logical consistency and are "tested" by how well they describe and predict reality. In other words, a good theory provides relatively complete understanding at the same time that it is supported by observations and stands up to continued scrutiny.

Theories serve a number of purposes. For one thing, they give meaning to observations. They explain what we see in a particular setting by relating those observations to other things already understood. Hence, a simple example of a theory of physics explains the behavior of light by saying that light has the properties of both waves and particles. Such a theory is immediately useful, for while we may have trouble conceptualizing of light's essence, we can easily grasp ideas such as "wave" and "particle," both of which we experience in everyday living.

Theories within criminology serve the same purpose as those in the physical sciences, although they are often more difficult to test. Few people, for example, can intuitively understand the motivation of "lust murderers" (a term developed by the FBI and popularized by some recent movies) or men who sexually abuse and kill women, often sadistically. Most people, after all, are not lust murderers, and therefore lack an intellectual starting point in striving to understand what goes on in the minds of those who are. Some psychiatric theories (discussed in Chapter 6) suggest that lust murderers kill because of a deep-seated hatred of women. Hate is something that most minds can grasp, and a vision of lust murder as an extreme example of the ages-old battle between the sexes provides an intellectual "handle" that many can appreciate. Hence, theory building dispenses of the old adage that "it takes one to know one," instead bringing at least the possibility of understanding within the reach of all. Note, however, that although such limited explanations as the one discussed here may provide a degree of "understanding," they must still be tested to determine whether or not they are true.

Theories provide understanding in a number of ways. Kenneth R. Hoover identifies four "uses of theory in social scientific thinking."[7] They are

- Theories provide *patterns* for the interpretation of data. Population density, for example, tends to be associated with high crime rates, and maps showing high population density tend to be closely associated with diagrams that reflect rates of crime. Hence, some theorists are quick to suggest, overcrowding increases aggression and therefore crime. "People," says Hoover, "like to think in terms of images, analogies, and patterns; this helps to simplify complex realities and to lighten the burden of thought."
- Theories *link* one study with another. Some years ago, for example, a case study of women's prisons in California found the existence of artificially constructed "families," around which women's lives centered. A similar, but later, study of a Chinese prison also found that familylike groups had been created by female inmates there—prompting some theorists to suggest that women felt a need to nurture and to be nurtured by aspects of social structure, and that they carried such a need with them into prison. The fact that cross-cultural support was found for the suggestion provided a linkage between the two studies which tended to lend further support to the suggestion itself.
- Theories supply frameworks within which concepts and variables acquire *special significance.* The death penalty, for example, while especially significant to individuals condemned to die, acquires special significance when seen as a tool employed by the powerful to keep the powerless under their control.
- Theories allow us to interpret the *larger meaning* of our findings for ourselves and for others. Hence, the death penalty has become a moral issue for many Americans today, shrouded as it is in ethical considerations and images of national identity and ultimate justice.

THE ROLE OF RESEARCH

More important than the claims made by theories and by the theorists who create them are findings of fact that either support those claims or leave them without foundation. Hence, theories, once proposed, are likely to be tested against the real world via a variety of research strategies, including experimentation and case studies.

Any theory gains credence if activity based upon it produces results in keeping with what that theory would predict. Bernard P. Cohen, a seminal thinker on the subject of social scientific theory construction, tells us that "scientific knowledge is theoretical knowledge, and the purpose of methods in science is to enable us to choose among alternative theories."[8]

Knowledge is inevitably built upon experience and observation. Hence, the crux of scientific research is data collection. Data collection occurs through a variety of techniques, including direct observation, the use of surveys and interviews, participant observation, and the analysis of existing data sets—all of which will be discussed shortly.

Research the use of standardized, systematic procedures in the search for knowledge.

Applied research scientific inquiry that is designed and carried out with practical application in mind.

Pure research research undertaken simply for the sake of advancing scientific knowledge.

Primary research research characterized by original and direct investigation.

Secondary research new evaluations of existing information that has already been collected by other researchers.

Research can be defined as the use of standardized, systematic procedures in the search for knowledge.[9] Some researchers distinguish between applied research and nonapplied or pure research. **Applied research** "consists of scientific inquiry that is designed and carried out with practical application in mind."[10] In applied research the researcher is working toward some more or less practical goal. It may be the reduction of crime, the efficient compensation of victims of crime, or an evaluation of the effectiveness of policies implemented to solve some specific aspect of the crime problem. **Pure research**, on the other hand, is undertaken simply for the sake of advancing scientific knowledge. Pure research "does not carry the promise or expectation of immediate, direct relevance."

Another type of research is called secondary research or secondary analysis, and can be distinguished from primary research.[11] **Primary research** "is characterized by original and direct investigation,"[12] while **secondary research** consists of new evaluations of existing information that has already been collected by other researchers.

Scientific research generally proceeds in stages, which can be divided conceptually among (1) problem identification, (2) the development of a research design, (3) a choice of data-gathering techniques, and (4) a review of findings, which often includes statistical analysis.

Problem Identification

Problem identification, the first step in any research, consists of the naming of a problem or choice of an issue to be studied. Topics may be selected for a variety of reasons. It may be that federal or other grant monies have suddenly become available to support studies in a specific area; perhaps the researcher has a personal interest in a particular issue and wants to learn more; maybe a professor or teacher has assigned a research project as part of the requirements for successful class completion. Whatever the reason for beginning research, however, the way in which a research problem is stated will help narrow the research focus and serve as a guide to the formulation of data-gathering strategies.

Although some criminological research undertaken today is purely descriptive, the bulk of such research is intended to explore issues of causality—especially the claims made by theories purporting to explain criminal behavior. As such, much contemporary research in criminology is involved with the testing of hypothesis.

The *American Heritage Dictionary* defines the word hypothesis in two ways:

1. "[a]n explanation that accounts for a set of facts and that can be tested by further investigation…
2. [s]omething that is taken to be true for the purpose of argument or investigation…"

Within the modern scientific tradition, a hypothesis serves both purposes. Some criminologists, as mentioned earlier, have observed what appears to be a correlation, or relationship, between phases of the moon and the rate of crime commission. Such observers might propose a hypothesis something like the following: "The moon causes crime." While this is a useful starting hypothesis, it needs to be further refined before it can be tested. Specifically, the concepts contained within the hypothesis must be translated into measurable variables. A **variable** is simply a concept which can undergo measurable changes.

Variable a concept which can undergo measurable changes.

Scientific precedent holds that only things which are measurable can be satisfactorily tested. The process of turning a simple hypothesis into one which is testable is called **operationalization**. An operationalized hypothesis is one that is stated in such a way as to facilitate measurement. It is specific in its terms and in the linkages it proposes. We might, for example, move a step further toward both measurability and specificity in our hypothesis about the relationship between the moon and crime by restating it as follows: "Rates of murder, rape, robbery, and assault rise when the moon's fullness increases, and are highest when the moon is fullest." Now we have specified what we mean by crime (i.e., murder, rape, robbery and assault), rates of which can be calculated. The degree of the moon's fullness can also be measured. Once we have operationalized a hypothesis and made the concepts it contains measurable, those concepts have, in effect, become variables.

Operationalization the process by which concepts are made measurable.

Now that the concepts within our hypothesis are measurable, we can test the hypothesis itself. That is to say, we can observe what happens to crime rates as the moon approaches fullness, as well as what happens when the moon is full, and see whether or not our observations support our hypothesis. As our dictionary definition tells us, once a hypothesis has been operationalized it is assumed to be true for purposes of testing. It is accepted, for study purposes, until observation proves it untrue, at which point it is said to be rejected. As one renowned researcher put it, "[t]he task of theory-testing…is predominantly one of rejecting inadequate hypotheses."[13]

Research Designs

Research designs structure the research process. They provide a kind of roadmap to the logic inherent in one's approach to a research problem. They also serve as guides to the systematic collection of data. **Research designs** consist of the logic and structure inherent in any particular approach to data gathering.

Research design the logic and structure inherent in an approach to data gathering.

A simple study, for example, might be designed to test the assertion that the consumption of refined white sugar promotes aggressive or violent tendencies among human males. One could imagine researchers approaching prison officials with the proposal that inmate diets should be altered to exclude all refined sugar. Under the plan cafeteria cooks would be instructed to prepare meals without the use of sugar. Noncaloric sweeteners would be substituted for sugar in recipes calling for sugar, and Kool Aid, sweetened iced tea, and carbonated beverages containing sugar would be banned. Likewise the prison "canteen" would be prohibited for selling items containing sugar for the duration of the experiment.

To determine whether the forced reduction in sugar consumption actually impacted inmates' behavior, researchers might look at the recorded frequency of aggressive incidents (sometimes called "write-ups" in prison jargon) occurring within the confines of the prison before the experiment was initiated and compare such data with similar information on such incidents following the introduction of dietary changes. A research design employing this kind of logic can be diagrammed as follows:

$$O_1 \quad X \quad O_2$$

Here "O_1" (termed a "pretest") refers to the information gathered on inmate aggressiveness prior to the introduction of dietary changes (which themselves are shown as "X," also called the "experimental intervention"), and "O_2" (termed the "posttest") signifies a second set of observations—that occurring after dietary changes have been implemented. Researchers employing a strategy of this type, which is known as a "one-group pretest-posttest" design, would likely examine differences between the two sets of observations, one made before introduction of the experimental intervention, and the other after. The difference, they might assume, would show changes in behavior resulting from changes in diet—in this case the exclusion of refined white sugar.

While this basic research design well illustrates the logic behind naive experiments, it does not lend good structure to a research undertaking since it does not eliminate other possible explanations of behavioral change. For example, during the time between the first and second observations inmates may have been exposed to some other influence which reduced their level of aggression. A new minister may have begun preaching effective sermons filled with messages of love and peace to the prison congregation; television cable service to the prison may have been disrupted, lowering the exposure inmates received to violent programming; a new warden may have taken control of the facility, relaxing prison rules and reducing tensions; a transfer or release of especially troublesome inmates, scheduled at some earlier time, may have occurred; a new program of conjugal visitation may have been initiated, creating new-found sexual outlets and reducing inmate tensions; and so on. In fact, the possibilities for rival explanations (i.e., those that rival the explanatory power of the hypothesis under study) are nearly limitless. Rival explanations such as these, called by some researchers competing hypotheses and by others **confounding effects**, make the results of any single series of observations uncertain.

Confounding effects rival explanations, also called competing hypotheses, which are threats to the internal or external validity of any research design.

Achieving Validity in Research Designs

Confounding effects, which might invalidate the results of research, are of two general types: those which affect the **internal validity** of research findings and those which limit the ability of researchers to generalize the research findings to other settings—called external validity. Often, when **external validity** is threatened researchers do not feel confident that interventions that "worked" under laboratory-like or other special conditions will still be effective when employed in the field. Hence, researchers achieving internal validity may be able to demonstrate that diets low in refined white sugar lower the number of instances of overt displays of aggressiveness in a single prison under study. They may not feel confident (for reasons discussed in the paragraphs that follow), however, that similar changes in diet, if implemented in the general nonprison population, would have a similar effect. Most researchers consider internal validity, or the certainty that experimental interventions did indeed cause the changes observed in the study group, the most vital component of any planned research. Without it, considerations of external validity become irrelevant. Factors that routinely threaten the internal validity of a design for research are said to include[14]

Internal validity the certainty that experimental interventions did indeed cause the changes observed in the study group; also the control over confounding factors which tend to invalidate the results of an experiment.

External validity the ability to generalize research findings to other settings.

- *History*: Specific events which occur between the first and second observations, which might impact measurement. The examples given in the prison study described earlier (the arrival of a new minister or new warden, etc.) are all applicable here.
- *Maturation*: Processes occurring within the respondents or subjects that operate as a result of the passage of time. Fatigue and decreases in response time due to age, are examples.
- *Testing*: The effects of taking a test upon the scores of a later testing. When respondents are measured in some way which requires them to respond, they tend to do better (i.e., their scores increase) the next time they are tested. In effect, they have learned how to take the test, or how to be measured, even though they may not have acquired more knowledge about the subject matter which the test intends to measure.
- *Instrumentation*: Changes in measuring instruments, or in survey takers, which occur as a result of time. Batteries wear down, instruments need to be recalibrated, interviewers grow tired or are replaced with others, and so on, all of which can change the nature of the observations made.
- *Statistical regression*: When respondents have been selected for study on the basis of extreme scores (as may be the case with personality inventories), later testing will tend to show a "regression toward the mean," or a return to more average scores, since some extreme scores are inevitably more the result of accident or "luck" rather than anything else.
- *Differential selection*: Built-in biases result when more than one group of subjects is involved in a study and when the groups being tested are somehow different to begin with. The random assignment of subjects to test groups greatly reduces the chances that such significant differences will exist.
- *Experimental mortality*: A differential loss of respondents from comparison groups, which may occur when more than one group is being tested (i.e., one

group loses members at a greater rate than another group, or certain kinds of members are lost from one group, but not from another).

Threats to external validity include

- *Reactive effects of testing*: A pretest might sensitize subjects in such a way that they especially respond to the experimental intervention when it is introduced. Nonpretested subjects (such as those in other locations) may not respond in the same way.
- *Self-selection*: A process whereby subjects are allowed to decide whether or not they want to participate in a study. Self-selected subjects may be much more interested in participation than others, and they may respond more readily to the experimental intervention or treatment.
- *Reactive effects of experimental arrangements*: Persons being surveyed or tested may know that they are part of an experiment and therefore react differently than if they were in more natural settings. Even if they are not aware of participating in a study, some investigative paraphernalia (such as observers, cameras, tape recorders, etc.) that may be present might change the way in which they behave.
- *Multiple-treatment interference*: Sometimes more than one study is being simultaneously conducted on the same persons or group of persons. Under such circumstances "treatments" to which subjects are exposed may interact, changing what would otherwise be the study's results. Multiple-treatment interference may also result from delayed effects, as when a current study is affected by the impact of one which has already been completed.

Experimental and Quasi-experimental Research Designs

To amass greater confidence that the changes intentionally introduced into a situation are the real cause of observed variations, it is necessary to achieve some degree of control over factors which threaten internal validity. In the physical sciences controlled experiments often provide the needed guarantees. **Controlled experiments** are those which attempt to hold conditions (other than the intentionally introduced experimental intervention) constant. In fact some researchers have defined the word "experiment" simply as controlled observation.

Controlled experiments those which attempt to hold conditions (other than the intentionally introduced experimental intervention) constant.

While constancy of conditions may be possible to achieve within laboratory settings, it is far more difficult to come by in the social world—which by its very nature is in an ongoing state of flux. Hence, while criminologists sometimes employ true experimental designs in the conduct of their research, they are more likely to find it necessary to use quasi-experimental designs or approaches to research which "are deemed worthy of use where better designs are not feasible."[15] **Quasi-experimental designs** are especially valuable when aspects of the social setting are beyond the control of the researcher. The crucial defining feature of quasi-experimental designs is that they give researchers control over *the when and to whom of measurement*, even though others decide the when and to whom of exposure to the experimental intervention.

Quasi-experimental designs approaches to research which, although less powerful than experimental designs, are deemed worthy of use where better designs are not feasible.

Sometimes, for example, legislators enact new laws intended to address some aspect of the crime problem, specifying the kinds of crime preventative measures to be employed and what segment of the population is to receive them. Midnight basketball, intended to keep young people off the streets at night, is an example of such legislatively sponsored intervention. During debate on the 1994 Violent Crime Control and Law Enforcement Act, midnight basketball became a point of contention, with senators asking whether money spent in support of such an activity would actually reduce the incidence of serious street crime in our nation's inner cities. Unfortunately, no good research data that could answer the question were available to legislators at the time. Now, however, federally funded midnight basketball programs might be studied by researchers. Hence, although criminologists were not politically situated so as to be able to enact midnight basketball legislation, they are able to study the effects of such legislation after it has been enacted.

Whether criminologists decide upon experimental or quasi-experimental designs to guide their research, they depend upon well-considered research strategies to eliminate rival explanations for the effects they observe. One relatively powerful research design, frequently employed by criminologists, is diagrammed as follows:

experimental group	O_1	X	O_2
control group	O_3		O_4

The meaning of the notation used here is similar to that of the one-shot case study design discussed earlier. This approach, however, called the "pretest-posttest control group design," gains considerable power from the addition of a second group. The second group is called a **control group**, since it is not exposed to the experimental intervention.

Control group a group of experimental subjects which, although subject to measurement and observation, are not exposed to the experimental intervention.

Critical to the success of a research design such as this is the use of randomization in the assignment of subjects to both experimental and control groups. **Randomization** is the process whereby individuals are assigned to study groups without biases or differences resulting from selection. Self-selection is not permitted (where some individuals volunteer for membership in either the experimental or control group), nor are researchers allowed to use personal judgment in assigning subjects to groups.

Randomization the process whereby individuals are assigned to study groups without biases or differences resulting from selection.

Control over potential threats to internal validity is achieved by the introduction of a properly selected control group, since it is assumed that both experimental and control groups are essentially the same to begin with, and that any threats to internal validity will affect both groups equally as the experiment progresses—effectively canceling out when final differences between the two groups are measured. If some particular historical event, for example, affects the experimental group and modifies the measurable characteristics of that group, that event should have the same impact on the control group. Hence, in the above design, when O_4 is subtracted from O_2, the remaining observable *net effects* are assumed to be attributable to the experimental intervention.

In the prison study discussed earlier, randomization would require that *all* inmates would be systematically but randomly divided into two groups. Random assignments are typically made by using a table of random numbers. In our simple study, however, something as easy as the flip of a coin should suffice. One group, the experimental group, would no longer receive refined white sugar in their diets, while the other (the control group) would continue eating as before. Since, with this one exception in diet, both groups would continue to be exposed to the same environment, it can be assumed that any other influences upon the level of violence within the prison will *cancel out* when final measurements are taken, and that measurable differences in violence between the two groups can be attributed solely to the effects of the experimental variable (in this case, of course, removal of sugar from the diet).

Techniques of Data Collection

It is the combination of (1) hypothesis building, (2) operationalization, and (3) systematic observation in the service of hypothesis testing that has made modern-day criminology scientific, and which has facilitated scientific theory building within the field. Hence, once a research problem has been identified, concepts made measurable, and a design for the conduct of the research selected, investigators must then decide upon the type of data to be gathered and the techniques of data gathering they wish to employ. Ultimately, all research depends upon the use of techniques to gather information, or data, for eventual analysis. Like research designs, which structure a researcher's approach to a problem, data-gathering strategies provide approaches to the accumulation of information needed for analysis to occur.

Social science research within a correctional setting. Inmates surveys may increase knowledge of crime causation. *Rick Friedman/Black Star.*

Many first-time researchers select data-gathering techniques on the basis of ease or simplicity. Some choose according to cost or the amount of time required by the techniques themselves. The most important question to consider, however, when beginning to gather information is *whether or not the data-gathering strategy selected will produce information in a form usable to the researcher.* The kind of information needed depends, of course, upon the questions to be answered. Surveys of public opinion as to the desirability of the death penalty, for example, cannot address issues of the punishment's effectiveness as a crime control strategy.

Four major data-gathering strategies typify research in the field of criminology:

Surveys: **Survey research** typically involves the use of questionnaires. Respondents may be interviewed in person, over the telephone, or queried via e-mail or fax. Mail surveys are very common, although they tend to have a lower response rate than other types of social surveys. The information produced through the use of questionnaires is referred to as survey data. Survey data provide the lifeblood of pollsters such as Gallup, CNN, and Roper who gather data on public opinion, voting preferences, and the like. Similarly, U.S. Census Bureau data are gathered by survey takers who are trained periodically for that purpose. Survey data also inform the National Crime Victimization Survey and result in such publications as *Crime and the Nation's Households, Criminal Victimization in the United States*, and other NCVS-related reports produced by the Bureau of Justice Statistics. Surveys have also been used in criminology to assess fear of crime, and attitudes toward the police, as well as to discover the extent of unreported crime.

Survey research a social science data-gathering technique that involves the use of questionnaires.

Case studies: Case studies are built around in-depth investigations into individual cases. The study of one (perhaps notorious) offender, scrutiny of a particular criminal organization, analysis of a prison camp, and the like may all qualify as case studies. Case studies are useful for what they can tell us to expect about other, similar, cases. If study of a street gang, for example, reveals the central role of a few leaders, then we would expect to find a similar organizational style among other gangs of the same kind.

When one individual (termed a "single subject") is the focus of a case study, the investigation may take the form of a life history. Life histories involve gathering as much historical data as possible about a given individual and his or her experiences during early socialization and adulthood. Most life histories are very subjective due to the fact that they consist primarily of recounts of events by the participants themselves. Life histories may also be gathered on groups of individuals, and similarities in life experience which are thereby discovered may provide researchers with clues to current behavior, or with points at which to begin further investigations.

Case studies, while they may suffer from high levels of subjectivity in which feelings cannot be easily separated from fact, do provide the opportunity to investigate individual cases—an element that is lacking in both survey research and participant observation.

Participant observation: **Participant observation** "involves a variety of strategies in data gathering in which the researcher observes a group by participating, to

Participant observation a variety of strategies in data gathering in which the researcher observes a group by participating, to varying degrees, in the activities of the group.

varying degrees, in the activities of the group."[16] Some participant researchers operate undercover, without revealing their identity as researchers to those whom they are studying, while others make their identity and purpose known from the outset of the research endeavor.

One of the earliest and best-known participant observers in the field of criminology was William Foote Whyte, who described his 1943 study of criminal subcultures in a slum district that he called "Cornerville" this way: "My aim was to gain an intimate view of Cornerville life. My first problem, therefore, was to establish myself as a participant in the society so that I would have a position from which to observe. I began by going to live in Cornerville, finding a room with an Italian family.... It was not enough simply to make the acquaintance of various groups of people. The sort of information that I sought required that I establish intimate social relations.... This active participation gave me something in common with them so that we had other things to talk about besides the weather. It broke down the social barriers and made it possible for me to be taken into the intimate life of the group."[17]

It is possible to distinguish between at least two additional kinds of participant observation: (1) the participant as observer and (2) the observer as complete participant. When researchers make their presence known to those whom they are observing, without attempting to influence the outcome of their observations or the activities of the group, they fit the category of participants who are observers. When they become complete participants in the group they are observing, however, researchers run the risk of influencing the group's direction. As Whyte explains it, "I made it a rule that I should try to avoid influencing the actions of the group. I wanted to observe what the men did under ordinary circumstances; I did not want to lead them into different activities."[18] Even researchers who make their presence known, however, may inadvertently influence the nature and direction of social interaction because people tend to act differently if they know they are being watched.

Another problem facing the participant observer is that of "going native," or of assuming too close an identification with the subjects or the behavior under study. Like undercover police officers who may at times be tempted to participate in the illegalities they are supposed to be monitoring, participant researchers may begin to experience feelings of kinship with their subjects. When that happens, all sense of the research perspective may be lost, and serious ethical problems can arise.

On the other hand, some researchers may feel disgust for the subjects of their research. Data gatherers with a particular dislike of drug abuse, for example, may be hard put to maintain their objectivity when working as participant observers within the drug subculture. Hence, as Frank Hagan observes, "[t]he researcher must avoid not only overidentification with the study group, but also aversion to it."[19]

Self-reporting: Another subjective data-gathering technique is one that uses self-reports to investigate aspects of a problem not otherwise amenable to study. Where official records are lacking, for example, research subjects may be asked to record and report rates of otherwise secretive behavior. Self-reports may prove especially valuable in providing checks on official reports consisting of statistical tabulations gathered through channels like police departments, hospitals, and social services agencies.

Self-reports may also be requested of subjects in survey research, and it is for that reason that self-reporting is sometimes thought of as simply another form of survey research. However, many self-reporting techniques require the maintenance of a diary or personal journal and request vigilant and ongoing observations of one's own behavior by the subject under study. Hence, sex researchers may ask subjects to maintain an ongoing record of their frequency of intercourse, the variety of sexual techniques employed, and their preference in partners—items of information which are not easy to come by through other means, or that cannot be accurately reconstructed from memory.

Self-reporting enters the realm of the purely subjective when it consists of introspection, or personal reflection. Introspective techniques, or those intended to gather data on secretive feelings and felt motivation, are often used by psychologists seeking to assess the mental status of patients. Criminologists, however, have at times used introspective techniques to categorize criminal offenders into types and to initiate the process of developing concepts more amenable to objective study.

Secondary analysis: Not all data-gathering techniques are intended to generate new information. **Secondary analysis** entails the reanalysis of existing data, that is, secondhand analysis of data that were gathered for another purpose. The secondary analysis of existing data and the use of previously acquired information describe strategies that can save researchers a considerable amount of time and expense.

Secondary analysis the reanalysis of existing data.

One important source of data for secondary analysis is the National Archive of Criminal Justice Data located in the Institute for Social Research at the University of Michigan. In the words of the U.S. Department of Justice, the Archive's sponsoring agency, "[t]he Archive continually processes the most relevant criminal justice data sets for the research community,"[20] maintaining information on victimization, various aspects of the criminal justice system and juvenile delinquency. Access to Archive data is by request, and data sets are for sale to individual researchers.

Many other important sources of existing information useful in criminological research can be found in the National's Institute of Justice's publication the *Directory of Criminal Justice Information Sources*,[21] available in a new edition every few years from NIJ. The latest edition contains a summary of information services offered, contact persons, phone numbers, addresses, a listing of publications produced, and more for 159 criminology-related information sources.

The use of secondary data rarely alerts research subjects to the fact that they (or the data they have provided) are being studied. Hence, secondary analysis, which constitutes one form of unobtrusive research, is said to be nonreactive. Although unobtrusive measures include other forms of data collection, the use of archival records in data analysis constitutes a virtual "goldmine of information waiting to be exploited."[22]

THE NATIONAL ARCHIVE OF CRIMINAL JUSTICE DATA

In 1978 the National Archive of Criminal Justice Data began operating under the joint auspices of the Bureau of Justice Statistics, an arm of the U.S. Department of Justice, and the Inter-university Consortium for Political and Social Research (ICPSR) based at the Institute for Social Research at the University of Michigan. The three goals of ICPSR are to

- Provide computer-readable data for the quantitative study of crime and the criminal justice system through the development of a central data archive that disseminates computer-readable data.
- Supply technical assistance in selecting data collections and the computer hardware and software for analyzing data efficiently and effectively.
- Offer training in quantitative methods of social science research to facilitate secondary analysis of criminal justice data.

ICPSR brings together the data collections of over 370 member colleges and universities in the United States and abroad. It also routinely receives data from BJS, NIJ, the Office for Juvenile Justice and Delinquency Prevention (OJJDP), and the FBI. As a consequence, the Consortium, which maintains the world's largest repository of computer-based research data in the area of the social sciences, has access to voluminous amounts of information. UCR and NCVS data are available through ICPSR, as is information on capital punishment, adult and juvenile correctional facilities, jails, state and federal court statistics, expenditure and employment data for the criminal justice system, and surveys of law enforcement and other criminal justice agencies.

Much of the information available through ICPSR takes the form of data sets that are ready for analysis through software packages such as the Statistical Package for the Social Sciences (SPSS) and SPSS PC-plus.

Sources: National Institute of Justice, *Data Resources Program of the National Institute of Justice* (Washington, D.C.: NIJ, 1994); and NIJ, *National Archive of Criminal Justice Data* (no date).

Intersubjectivity a scientific principle which requires that independent observers see the same thing under the same circumstances in order for observations to be regarded as valid.

Replicability (experimental) a scientific principle which holds that observations made at one time can be had again at a later time if all other conditions are the same.

Problems in Data Collection

Scientific data gathering builds upon observations of one sort or another. Observation is, of course, not unique to science. Individuals make personal observations all the time, and draw a plethora of intimate conclusions based upon what they see or hear. Scientific observation, however, generally occurs under controlled conditions, and must meet the criteria of **intersubjectivity** and **replicability**. Intersubjectivity requires that, for observations to be valid, independent observers must report seeing the same thing under the same circumstances. "Do you see what I see?" is a question that highlights the central role of intersubjectivity in scientific observation. If observers cannot agree on what they saw, then the raw data necessary for scientific analysis haven't been acquired. Replicability of observations means that, at least in the field of scientific experimentation, when the same conditions exist, the same results can be expected to follow. Hence, valid experiments can be replicated. The same observations made at one time can be had again at a later time if all other conditions are the same.

In the physical sciences replicability is easy to achieve. Water at sea level, for example, will always boil at 100 degrees Celsius. Anyone can replicate the conditions needed to test such a contention. When replicability cannot be achieved, it casts the validity of observations into doubt. Some years ago, for example, a few scientists claimed to have achieved nuclear fusion at room temperature. Their supposed accomplishment was dubbed "cold fusion" and hailed as a major breakthrough in the production of nuclear energy. When scientists elsewhere, however, attempted to replicate the conditions under which cold fusion was said to occur, they could find no evidence that the initial experimenters were correct. Replicability and intersubjectivity are critical to the scientific enterprise for, as one researcher puts it, "[s]cience rests it claim to authority upon its firm basis in observable evidence...".[23]

It is important to recognize, however, that some observations—even those which stand up to the tests of intersubjectivity and replicability—can lead to unwarranted conclusions. For example, spirit possession, an explanation for deviance that was apparently widely held in primitive times, must have appeared well validated by the positive behavioral changes which became apparent in those who submitted to the surgery called for by the theory—a craniotomy intended to release offending spirits from the head of the afflicted party. The actual cause of behavioral reformation may have been brain infections resulting from unsanitary surgical conditions, slips of the stone knife, or the intensity of pain endured by those undergoing the procedure without anesthetics. To the uncritical observer, however, the theory of spirit possession as a cause of deviance, and cranial surgery as a treatment technique, would probably appear to have been supported by the "evidence" of induced behavioral change.

Some methodologists note that "[t]heories are as much involved in the determination of fact as facts are in establishing a theory."[24] Theories are intimately involved in the process of data collection. They determine what kinds of data we choose to gather, what we look for in the data itself, and how we interpret the information we have gathered. In short, theories determine what we see, as well as what we ignore. In the late 1700s, for example, when a meteorite shower was reported to the French Academy of Sciences, observers reported that some fragments had struck the ground, causing tremendous explosions. The learned scientists of the Academy quickly dismissed these accounts, however, calling them "a superstition unworthy of these enlightened times."[25] Anyone, they said, knows that stones don't fall from the sky.

Data Analysis

Some data, once collected, are simply archived. Most data, however, are subject to some form of analysis. Data analysis generally involves the use of mathematical techniques intended to uncover correlations between variables, and to assess the likelihood that research findings can be generalized to other settings. Such techniques are called statistics, and their use in analyzing data is called statistical analysis. Some theorists, for example, posit a link between poverty and crime. Hence, we might suspect that low-income areas would be high-crime areas. Once we specify what me mean by "low income" and "crime," so that they become measurable variables, and have gathered data on income levels and the incidence of crime in various locales we are ready to begin the job of data analysis.

Statistical techniques provide tools for summarizing data. They also provide quantitative means for identifying patterns within the data, and for determining the degree of correlation that exists between variables. Statistical methods can be divided into two types: descriptive and inferential. **Descriptive statistics** are those that (1) describe, (2) summarize, or (3) highlight the relationships within the data which have been gathered. **Inferential statistics**, on the other hand, attempt to generalize findings by specifying how likely they are to be true for other populations, or in other locales.

Descriptive statistics describe, summarize, or highlight the relationships within data which have been gathered.

Inferential statistics specify how likely findings are to be true for other populations, or in other locales.

Descriptive statistics include measures of central tendency, commonly called the mean, median, and mode. The mode refers to the most frequently occurring score or value in any series of observations. If, for example, we measure the age of all juvenile offenders held in a state training facility, it may be that they range in age from 12 to 16, with 15 being the most commonly found age. Fifteen, then, would be the modal age for the population under study.

The median defines the midpoint of a data series. Half of the scores will be above the mean and the other half will be below. It may be, for example, that in our study of juveniles, we find equal numbers in each age category. The median age for those held might then be 14.

The mathematical average of all scores within a given population is referred to as the mean. The mean is the most commonly used measure of central tendency. It is calculated simply by adding together all the scores (or ages, in our example) and dividing by the total number of observations. While calculations of the mean, median, and mode will often yield similar results, such will not be the case with populations that are skewed in a particular direction. If our population of juveniles under study, for example, consisted almost entirely of 16-year-olds, then the mode for that population would inevitably be 16, while other measures of central tendency would yield somewhat lower figures.

Other descriptive statistics provide measures of the standard deviation of a population (i.e., the degree of dispersion of scores about the mean) and the degree of correlation or interdependence between variables (i.e., the extent of variation in one that can be expected to follow from a measured change in another). As discussed in Chapter 2 (where the term "correlation" is defined), while the degree of correlation may vary, the direction of correlation can also be described. We say, for example, that if one variable increases whenever another, upon which it is dependent, does the same, a positive correlation or positive relationship exists between the two. When one variable decreases in value as another rises, a negative or inverse correlation exists.

Another statistical technique, one which provides a measure of the likelihood that a study's findings are the results of chance, is commonly found in criminological literature. **Tests of significance** are designed to provide researchers with confidence that their results are in fact true, and not the result of sampling error. We may, for example, set out to measure degree of gun ownership. Let's say that the extent of gun ownership in the area under study is actually 50%. We have no way of knowing that, of course, until our study is complete. We may decide to use door-to-door surveys of randomly selected households, since cost prohibits us from canvassing all households in the study area. Even if we have made our best survey effort, however, some slight probability remains that the households that we have chosen to interview may all be populated by gun owners. Although it is very unlikely, we may, by chance, have excluded those without guns. Assuming that everyone interviewed answers truthfully, we would come away with the mistaken impression that 100% of the population in the study area is armed!

Tests of significance statistical techniques intended to provide researchers with confidence that their results are in fact true, and not the result of sampling error.

The likelihood of faulty findings increases as sample size decreases. Were we to sample only one or two households we would have little likelihood of determining the actual incidence of gun ownership. The larger the sample size, however, the greater the confidence we can have in our findings. Hence a positive correlation exists between sample size and the degree of confidence we can have in our results. Even so, in most criminological research, it is not possible to study all members of a given population, and so samples must be taken. Statistical tests of significance, expressed as a percentage, assess the likelihood that our study findings are due to chance. Hence, a study which reflects a 95% confidence level can be interpreted as having a 5% likelihood that the results it reports are mere happenstance. In effect, had the same study been conducted one hundred times, then five of those studies would yield misleading results. The problem, of course, is that it would be impossible to know which five that would be!

Quantitative Versus Qualitative Methods

In November 1994, U.S. Attorney General Janet Reno addressed researchers, criminologists, and professors gathered at the annual meeting of the American Society of Criminology in Miami, Florida. "Let's stop talking about numbers," Reno exhorted the crowd, "and start talking about crime in human terms." In her admonition Reno placed herself squarely on the side of those who feel that there has been a tendency in American criminology over the past half century to overemphasize **quantitative methods** or techniques—that is, those that produce measurable results which can be analyzed statistically. To be sure, as such critics would be quick to admit, there is a considerable degree of intellectual comfort to be

Quantitative methods research techniques which produce measurable results.

achieved in feeling that one is able to reduce complex forms of behavior and interaction to something which can be counted (as can, say, the frequency of an offense.) Intellectual comfort of this sort derives from the notion that anything which is able to be expressed in numbers must be somehow more meaningful than that which is not.

It is crucial to realize, however, that numerical expression is mostly a result of how researchers structure their approach to the subject matter and is rarely inherent in the subject matter itself. Such is especially true in the social sciences, where attitudes, feelings, behaviors, and perceptions of all sorts are subject to quantification by researchers who impose upon such subjective phenomena artificial techniques for their quantification.

One recent highly quantitative study, for example,[26] reprinted in the journal *Criminology*, reported on the relationship between personality and crime. The study found that "greater delinquent participation was associated with a personality configuration characterized by high Negative Emotionality and Weak Constraint." While it may seem easy to quantify "delinquent participation" by measuring official arrest statistics (even here, however, official statistics may not be a good measure of delinquent behavior, since many law violations go undiscovered), imagine the conceptual nightmares associated with trying to make measurable concepts such as "negative emotionality" and "weak constraint." In studies such as this, even those replete with numerical data derived through the use of carefully constructed questionnaires, questions still remain of precisely what it is that has been measured.

Not everyone who engages in social science research labors under the delusion that everything can and must be quantified. Those who do, however, are said to suffer from the mystique of quantity. As some critics point out, "[t]he failure to recognize this instrumentality of measurement makes for a kind of *mystique of quantity*; which responds to numbers as though they were repositories of occult powers.... The mystique of quantity is an exaggerated regard for the significance of measurement, just because it is quantitative, without regard either to what has been measured or to what can subsequently be done with the measure."[27] The mystique of quantity treats numbers as having intrinsic scientific value. Unfortunately, this kind of thinking been especially true in the social sciences where researchers, seeking to make clear their intellectual kinship with physical scientists, have been less than cautious in their enthusiasm for quantification.

> It is...pathetic to observe how many statistical refinements are wasted on utterly inadequate basic material.
>
> —Hermann Mannheim[28]

Qualitative methods research techniques that produce subjective results or results that are difficult to quantify.

Qualitative methods, in contrast to those that are quantitative, produce subjective results or results which are difficult to quantify. Even though their findings are not expressed numerically, qualitative methods provide yet another set of potentially useful criminological research tools. Qualitative methods are important for the insight they provide into the subjective workings of the criminal mind and the processes by which meaning is accorded to human experience. Introspection, life histories, case studies, and participant observation all contain the potential to yield highly qualitative data.[29]

Consider, for example, how the following personal account[30] of homicidal motivation conveys subjective insights into the life of a Los Angeles gang member otherwise difficult to express:

> Wearing my fresh Pendleton shirt, beige khakis, and biscuits [old men's comfort shoes, the first shoe officially dubbed "Crip shoe"], I threw on my black bomber jacket and stepped out into the warm summer night. I walked up Sixty-Ninth Street to Western Avenue and took a car at gunpoint. Still in a state of indecision, I drove toward the hospital.
>
> I intentionally drove through Sixties'hood. Actually, I was hoping to see one of them before I had made it through, and what luck did I have. There was Bank Robber, slippin' [not paying attention, not being vigilant] hard on a side street. I continued past him and turned at the next corner, parked and waited. He would walk right to me.
>
> Sitting in the car alone, waiting to push yet another enemy out of this existence, I reflected deeply about my place in this world, about things that were totally outside the grasp of my comprehension. Thoughts abounded I never knew I could conjure up. In retrospect, I can honestly say that in those moments before Bank Robber got to the car, I felt free. Free, I guess, because I had made a decision about my future.
>
> "Hey," I called out to Robber, leaning over to the passenger side, "got a light?"
>
> "Yeah," he replied, reaching into his pants pocket for a match or lighter. I never found out which.
>
> I guess he felt insecure, because he dipped his head down to window level to see who was asking for a light.
>
> "Say your prayers, muthaf...."
>
> Before he could mount a response I blasted him thrice in the chest, started the car, and drove home to watch 'Benny Hill.' Bangin' was my life. That was my decision.

An 18-year-old Los Angeles gang member. Some researchers doubt that quantitative methods can adequately assess the subjective experiences of certain kinds of offenders. *Jim Tynan/Impact Visuals Photo & Graphics, Inc.*

The passage was written by Sanyika Shakur, once known as "Monster Kody" to fellow South Central Los Angeles Crips members. Monster, named for his readiness to commit acts of brutality so extreme that they repulsed even other gang members, joined the Crips at age 11. Sent to a maximum-security prison while still in his teens, Monster learned to write, took on the name Sanyika Shakur, and joined the black nationalist New Afrikan Independence Movement. Shakur's prison-inspired autobiography, Monster, provides a soul-searching account of the life of an L.A. gang member. The purpose of the book, says Shakur, is "to allow my readers the first ever glimpse at South Central from my side of the gun, street, fence, and wall."

Although Shakur's book is a purely personal account, and may hold questions of generalizability for researchers, imagine the difficulties inherent in acquiring this kind of data through the use of survey instruments, or other traditional research techniques. Autobiographical accounts, introspection, and many forms of participant observation amount to a kind of phenomenological reporting, in which description leads to understanding, and intuition is a better guide to theory building than volumes of quantifiable data.

Some criminologists contend that qualitative data-gathering strategies represent the future of criminological research. Terming this initiative "postmodern criminology," Martin D. Schwartz and David O. Friedrichs[31] claim that central to the postmodernist approach is

1. a method that can reveal starkly how knowledge is constituted, and can uncover pretensions and contradictions of traditional scholarship in the field.
2. a highlighting of the significance of language and signs in the realm of crime and criminal justice.
3. a source of metaphors and concepts (e.g., "hyperreality") that capture elements of an emerging reality, and the new context and set of conditions in which crime occurs.

"The guiding premise here," say Schwartz and Friedrichs, "is that a postmodernist approach enables us to comprehend at a more appropriate level" than do the more traditional techniques of quantitative criminology, "our knowledge of a dynamic and complex human environment."

VALUES AND ETHICS IN THE CONDUCT OF RESEARCH

Research, especially that conducted within the social sciences, does not occur in a vacuum. Values enter into all stages of the research process, from the selection of the problem to be studied, to the choice of strategies to address it. In short, research is never entirely free from preconceptions and biases, although much can be done to limit the impact such biases have upon the results of research.

The most effective way of controlling the effects of biases is to be aware of them at the outset of the research. If, for example, a researcher knows that the project he or she is working on elicits strong personal feelings but necessitates the use of interviewers, then it would be beneficial to strive to hire interviewers who are relatively free of biases or can control the expression of their feelings. Potential data gatherers might themselves be interviewed to determine their values and the likelihood that they might be tempted to interpret the data they gather, or to report it in ways which are biased. Similarly, data gatherers who are prejudiced against subgroups of potential respondents can represent a threat to the validity of the research results. The use of such interviewers may "turn off" some respondents, perhaps through racial innuendo, personal style, mannerisms, and the like.

Of similar importance are ethical issues which, although they may not affect the validity of research results, can have a significant impact upon the lives of both researchers and research subjects. The protection of human subjects, privacy, and **data confidentiality**—in which research data are not shared outside of the research environment—are the most important ethical issues facing researchers today. **Informed consent** is a strategy used by researchers to overcome many of the ethical issues inherent in criminological research. Informed consent means that research subjects will be informed as to the nature of the research about to be conducted, their anticipated role in it, and the uses that will be made of the data they provide. Ethics may also require that data derived from personal interviews or the testing of research subjects be anonymous (not associated with the names of individual subjects) and that raw (unanalyzed) data be destroyed after a specified time interval (often at the completion of the research project).

Data confidentiality an ethical requirement of social scientific research which stipulates that research data not be shared outside of the research environment.

Informed consent an ethical requirement of social scientific research which specifies that research subjects will be informed as to the nature of the research about to be conducted, their anticipated role in it, and the uses to which the data they provide will be put.

Federal regulations require a plan for the protection of sensitive information as part of grant proposals submitted to federal agencies. The National Institute of Justice, for example, a major source of grant support for researchers in the area of criminology, has this to say:[32]

> Research that examines individuals traits and experiences plays a vital part in expanding our knowledge about criminal behavior. It is essential, however, that researchers protect subjects from needless risk of harm or embarrassment and proceed with willing and informed cooperation.
>
> NIJ requires that investigators protect information identifiable to research participants. When information is safeguarded, it is protected by statute from being used in legal proceedings: "[S]uch information and copies thereof shall be immune from legal process, and shall not, without the consent of the person furnishing such information, be admitted as evidence or used for any purpose in any action, suit, or other judicial, legislative, or administrative proceedings" (42 United States Code 3789g).

Some universities, research organizations, and government agencies have established institutional review boards tasked with examining research proposals before they are submitted to funding organizations to determine whether expectations of ethical conduct have been met. Institutional review boards often consist of other researchers with special knowledge of the kinds of ethical issues involved in criminological research.

Participant observation sometimes entails an especially thorny ethical issue. That is, should researchers themselves violate the law if their research participation appears to require it? The very nature of *participant* observation is such that researchers of adult criminal activity may at times find themselves placed in situations where they are expected to "go along with the group" in violating the law. Those researching gang activity, for example, have been asked to transmit potentially incriminating information to other gang members, to act as drug couriers, and even to commit crimes of violence to help establish territorial claims important to members of the gang. Researchers who refuse may endanger not only their research, but themselves. Compliance with the expectations of criminal groups, of course, evokes other kinds of dangers, including the danger of apprehension and prosecution for violations of the criminal law.

While the dilemma of a participant observer, especially one secretly engaged in research, is a difficult one, some of the best advice on the subject is offered by Frank E. Hagan, who says: "In self-mediating the potential conflicting roles of the criminal justice researcher, it is incumbent on the investigator to enter the setting with eyes wide open. A decision must be made beforehand on the level of commitment to the research endeavor and the analyst's ability to negotiate the likely role conflicts. Although there are no hard and fast rules... *the researcher's primary role is that of a scientist.*"[33]

Hagan also suggests that a code of ethics should guide all professional criminologists in their research undertakings. This code, says Hagan, would require the researcher to take personal responsibility to[34]

- Avoid procedures that may harm respondents.
- Honor commitments to respondents and respect reciprocity.
- Exercise objectivity and professional integrity in performing and reporting research.
- Protect confidentiality and privacy of respondents.

WRITING THE RESEARCH REPORT

After research has been completed, and data have been analyzed, findings are typically presented in the form of a report or paper in which suggestions for further study may be made. Policy issues, or strategies for addressing the problems identified by the researcher, are frequently discussed as well. Charts, graphs, and tables may be included in the body of a research report. Most reports are professional looking documents which are word-processed, grammar- and spell-checked, and laser or ink-jet printed. Some are eventually published in professional journals and a few become staples of the field—frequently cited works that serve to illustrate fundamental criminological or methodological principles.

Most research reports follow a traditional format which has developed over the years as a generally acceptable way of presenting research results. The component features of professional reports are

- *Title page*: The title page contains information about the report's authors, their institutional or professional affiliations, the date of the report and, of course, its title. Many report titles consist of a main title and a subtitle. Subtitles generally give more information about the report's subject matter. While some report titles seem all inclusive, such as

  "The Impact of Family Structure and Quality on Delinquency: A Comparative Assessment of Structural and Functional Factors"[35]

  others are relatively straightforward and to the point, such as

  "Comparing Criminal Career Models"[36]

- *Acknowledgments*: Often the author wishes to express appreciation to individuals and/or organizations that facilitated the study or without whose help the study would not have been possible. Sources of grant support, including funding agencies and foundations, individuals and organizations who either participated in the study or were themselves studied, and personnel who facilitated various aspects of the study or production of the report are all frequently acknowledged.
- *Table of contents*: Reports of any length (say, beyond ten or twelve pages) often contain a table of contents. Tables of contents help readers quickly find the material they are looking for, and provide structure to the report itself. Any good table of contents will reflect section headings within the body of the report.
- *Preface* (if desired): The purpose of a preface is to allow the author to make observations, often of a personal nature, which might not be appropriate within the body of the report. Reasons for choosing the subject of study, observations about the promise held by the field of study, and wide-ranging statements about the future of criminological research are all frequent topics of prefaces found in research reports.
- *Abstract*: An abstract is a brief (usually one paragraph) summation of the report's findings, allowing readers to gauge, without reading the entire report, whether the subject matter will be of interest to them. In this day of modern electronic information retrieval, abstracts serve the additional function of providing a quick synopsis that can readily be made available to those searching large databases containing many research articles. Reproduced here is a concise and well-written abstract from John M. Hagedorn's study entitled "Homeboys, Dope Fiends, Legits, and New Jacks" that appeared in the May 1994 issue of the journal *Criminology*.[37] Note that this abstract concludes with a one-sentence policy observation:

Milwaukee research finds that most young male adult gang members cannot be described accurately as "committed long-term participants" in the drug economy. Rather, most adult gang members are involved sporadically with drug sales, moving in and out of conventional labor markets at irregular intervals. Four types of male adult gang members are described; only one type has rejected conventional values. Despite relatively high average earnings from drug sales, most gang members would accept full-time jobs with modest wages. This suggests that severe and mandatory penalties for cocaine use and sales should be ended.

- *Introduction*: Most authors write an introductory section as part of their research report. The introduction describes the aim and purpose of the study and provides a general statement of the problem studied. It also furnishes a general conceptual framework for the remainder of the report. The introduction may outline issues related to the problem under study and which could benefit from further investigation.
- *Review of existing literature*: Most research builds upon existing knowledge and makes use of previous findings. To cite a few proverbial observations, while it is not true that "there is nothing new under the sun," when conducting research, it is also "not necessary to reinvent the wheel." In other words, the relevant works of other researchers should be discussed in any report, and the bearing previous studies have upon the present one should be explained. Sometimes researchers who are engaged in literature reviews discover that the questions they wish to study have already been answered, or that someone else has found a more concise way of stating their concerns. Hence, concept development that is merely repetitive, and even data gathering that has already been undertaken can be avoided by new investigators.
- *Description of existing situation*: Sometimes a description of the existing situation is combined with a report's introduction. If not, then it is appropriate to elaborate upon the problem under study by providing details which describe the conditions existing at the time the study was begun.
- *Statement of the hypotheses*: Research etiquette in criminology frequently requires the statement of a hypothesis to be tested. Most researchers have an idea of what they expect to find. Often they have set out to test a theory, or a proposition derived from a theory. Researchers may, for example, wish to test whether the Brady law, which limits handgun sales, has effectively met its goal of reduced deaths by firearms. Any hypothesis should be a clear and concise statement of what the study purports to test. As mentioned previously, hypotheses useful in guiding research are always operationalized, or expressed in terms that are in some way measurable. Descriptive studies, on the other hand, are not designed to prove or disprove assumptions (although they may not be free of them), and such studies might not contain hypotheses.
- *Description of the research plan*: The research design, data-gathering strategies, and plans for statistical analysis should all be described here. This section,

while it may be elaborate and lengthy, simply provides an overview of the methodology employed by the researcher, and explains how the problem was investigated and why particular research strategies were chosen.

- *Disclaimers and limitations*: Any research is subject to limitations. Shortages of money, time, personnel, and other resources impose limitations on research undertakings, as do shortcomings in statistical techniques and restrictions on the availability of data. Limitations should be honestly appraised and presented in the research report so that readers will be able to assess their impact on the results that are reported.
- *Findings or results*: Along with an overview of the research as it was actually conducted, the "findings" section provides a statement of research results. Many regard it as the heart of the report. The manner in which results are presented can be crucial for ease of understanding. Some researchers choose to employ tables containing raw numbers, when pictorial forms of representation such as charts and graphs may better facilitate comprehension. Bar charts and pie charts are probably the most commonly employed types of diagrams, although the type of data collected will determine the appropriate format for its presentation.
- *Analysis and discussion*: Once findings have been presented, they should be discussed and analyzed. Not all analysis need be of a quantitative sort. However, much of today's criminological literature is replete with statistical analyses, some of it quite sophisticated. Unfortunately, however, poorly conceptualized research cannot be helped by later analysis, no matter how sophisticated it may be. It is therefore of crucial importance to the success of any research endeavor that early planning—including conceptual development, strategies for data collection, and research designs—be undertaken with an eye toward producing data that will lend themselves to meaningful analysis after data gathering has been completed. The analysis section should also focus on whether or not the data, as analyzed, support the study's guiding hypotheses.
- *Summary and conclusions*: The summation section encapsulates the study's purpose and findings in a few paragraphs. It may also contain discussion of suggested improvements or recommended solutions to the problem studied based upon the evidence produced by the report. Policy implications are also discussed (if at all) in the conclusion of the report, since they are simply broad-based solutions to problems which have been identified.
- *Appendices*: Not all reports contain appendices. Those that do may place sample questionnaires, accompanying cover letters, concise exhibits from literature reviews, detailed statistical tables, copies of letters of support, detailed interview information, and the like near the end of the document. Appendices should only be used if they serve the purpose of further explicating the report's purpose, methods, or findings. Otherwise appendices may appear to "pad" the report and can discredit the researcher's efforts in the eyes of readers.
- *List of references*: No report is complete without a bibliography or other list of references used in planning the study and in document preparation. While all items listed in the bibliography may not be referenced within the body of the

report, source material should still be listed if it was reviewed and served some purpose in study development. Literature which was examined, for example, may have guided the researcher to other material or may have provide insights useful during the study's overall conceptual formation.

- *Endnotes*: Either endnotes or footnotes may be used to reference quoted sources or to refer readers to supporting documents. Sometimes a combination of footnotes and endnotes is employed. Endnotes, as their name implies, appear at the conclusion of a report (often after the summary but before the appendices), while footnotes are found at the bottom of the pages containing the referenced material.

Writing for Publication

Criminologists often seek to publish the results of their research in order to share them with others working in the field. The primary medium for such publication consists of refereed professional journals. Refereed journals are those which employ the services of peer reviewers to gauge the quality of the manuscripts submitted to them. While the review process can be time consuming, it is believed to result in the publication of manuscripts which make worthwhile contributions to the field of criminology and in the rejection of those of lesser quality.

Perhaps the best-known professional journals in the field of criminology today are the *American Journal of Criminal Justice, Crime and Delinquency, Crime and Social Justice,* the *Crime Control Digest, Criminal Justice and Behavior, Criminal Justice Ethics,* the *Criminal Justice Policy Review,* the *Criminal Justice Review, Criminology,* the *Journal of Contemporary Criminal Justice,* the *Journal of Crime and Justice,* the *Journal of Criminal Law and Criminology,* the *Journal of Criminal Justice Education,* the *Journal of Research in Crime and Delinquency, The Justice Professional,* and *Justice Quarterly.*

Each journal has its own requirements for manuscript submission. Some require a single copy of a manuscript; others ask for multiple copies. A few journals request manuscript files on disk along with hard copies, while still others are moving toward electronic submission via Internet. An increasing number of journals have established submission fees, usually in the $10–20 range to help defray the costs associated with the review process.

Submission etiquette within the field of criminology demands that an article be sent to only one journal at a time. Simultaneous submissions are frowned upon and create real difficulties for both authors and editors when articles are accepted by more than one publication. Given the complexities of the review and publications processes, it is probably best to write the editor of any journal to which submission is being contemplated to inquire as to that journal's particular expectations.

Most journals require that manuscripts be prepared according to a particular style. This means that citations, capitalization, footnoting, abstract, notes, headings, and subheadings are all expected to conform to the style of other articles published in the same journal. Two of the most prevalent styles are known as the

Project D.A.R.E. participants. In the real world few studies are value free. Recent studies of Project D.A.R.E. have questioned its effectiveness, but government sponsors decided not to publish the results. *Mark Burnett/Stock Boston.*

"APA style" (the style promulgated by the American Psychological Association) and the "ASA (American Sociological Association) style".

Most criminological journals, however, utilize a modification of one of these styles. When considering submitting a manuscript for publication review, it is advisable to write to the editor of the journal in question requesting a style sheet or general stylistic guidelines. Style guides are also available from the American Psychological Association[38] and the American Sociological Association, with third-party publishers making style guides available through university and special-purpose bookstores.

If a research report is not intended for publication, then other styles may be acceptable. Answers to general questions about report writing and style can be found in publications such as Strunk and White's *The Elements of Style*[39] and Mary-Claire van Leunen's *A Handbook for Scholars.*[40]

STUDY CRITICAL OF D.A.R.E. REJECTED

The interplay between politics and research is well demonstrated by the following story, which shows what can happen when research results don't support the interests of influential groups.

The federal government has decided not to publish a new study that concludes D.A.R.E., the nation's largest drug education effort, is not effective at reducing youth drug use.

The Justice Department says it rejected the federally funded study because the government disagrees with conclusions that D.A.R.E. has no statistically significant effect on drug use and was less effective than other programs.

"We're not trying to hide the study," says the National Institute of Justice's Ann Voit. "We just do not agree with one of the major findings."

D.A.R.E. spokeswoman Roberta Silverman faulted the study as "old data from old studies about a curriculum that's not taught any more." She says D.A.R.E. is now more interactive with students, who are taught D.A.R.E.'s antidrug message in just over half the USA's school systems.

D.A.R.E. has attacked the study since early results were revealed at a conference in March 1993.

"We're proud to have the support of the Department of Justice," says D.A.R.E. America executive director Glenn Levant in a statement.

The government's decision not to publish was criticized by scientists, including the head of D.A.R.E.'s scientific advisory board.

"As a scientist, I'm much happier having the data out so we can debate it," says Herb Kleber, head of the D.A.R.E. scientific board.

Tom Colthurst, head of drug studies at the University of California-San Diego, also says the study should be published. "Science loses something when this happens," he says.

D.A.R.E.—Drug Abuse Resistance Education—gets $700 million a year from the Justice Department, Education Department, local governments and private donors.

But the eleven-year-old program has been haunted by studies that have found it ineffective.

In 1991, the National Institute of Justice hired the Research Triangle Institute, a respected research firm in North Carolina, to do an extensive study of D.A.R.E., including a statistical analysis of all D.A.R.E. studies.

D.A.R.E. originally supported the study. A 1992 letter to state coordinators urged cooperation: "The review of the D.A.R.E. evaluation literature will give us ammunition to respond to critics who charge that D.A.R.E. has not proven its effectiveness."

But D.A.R.E. began to criticize the study after researchers failed to find statistical evidence that D.A.R.E. had an effect on drug use.

Research Triangle Institute researcher Susan Ennett says the report, which analyzed eight studies involving 9,300 children, is valid. It should help decide how to spend drug education money, she says.

Today, in contrast to the National Institute of Justice, the most prestigious academic journal in the field will publish the study's results. The *American Journal of Public Health* says the D.A.R.E. study passed rigorous scrutiny by its academic experts.

And it criticized D.A.R.E. for pressuring it to withdraw the study from its September issue.

"D.A.R.E. has tried to interfere with the publication of this," says the journal's Sabine Beisler. "They tried to intimidate us."

D.A.R.E.'s Silverman says she asked that the article be pulled because "we felt it was highly inappropriate for the broad study to come out before NIJ released its findings."

After learning the journal planned to publish the results, the National Institute of Justice on Thursday released a two-page summary of the study, focusing on D.A.R.E.'s popularity. It briefly mentioned D.A.R.E.'s failure to reduce drug use but gave no details.

National Institute of Justice director Jeremy Travis, a police department lawyer until last month, says he did not succumb to pressure from D.A.R.E. He says his group won't publish the report because its independent reviewers unanimously recommended against it.

But reviewer William DeJong says he never advised against publishing the study. "They may be misremembering what I said," says DeJong, a Harvard lecturer.

He says the study should have been more careful in choosing drug education programs to compare with D.A.R.E. Also, he says drug use among adolescents, some in the fifth grade, is so low it's hard to measure.

Source: Dennis Cauchon, "Study Critical of D.A.R.E. Rejected," *USA Today*, October 4, 1994, p. 2A. Copyright 1994, USA Today. Reprinted with permission.

QUESTIONS

1. Government spokespersons cited here say they "disagree with findings" of the D.A.R.E. study. How might they arrive at such a conclusion independent of other studies?
2. Do you think it would be more productive for critics to challenge a study's findings, or its methods? Why?
3. Do you believe that quality research should be published regardless of the findings it reports, or do you think that political considerations should play a role in deciding which studies will be published? Give reasons for your position.

SOCIAL POLICY AND CRIMINOLOGICAL RESEARCH

A few years ago Joan Petersilia, then-president of the American Society of Criminology, used the occasion of her 1990 presidential address to identify how research funded by the National Institute of Justice had impacted social policy. Petersilia identified five such areas. Research, she said,[41] has

1. shaped the way police respond to calls for service and how they are deployed.
2. helped to identify career criminals and has provided information about their behavior, along with suggestions on how best to deal with such people.
3. improved the ability of judges, correctional officials, and others to classify offenders and to predict recidivism.
4. provided useful information about the relationship between drug use and crime.
5. confirmed that no particular rehabilitation program "necessarily" reduces recidivism.

While research in the area of criminology may have much to offer policymakers, publicly elected officials are often either ignorant of current research or do not heed the advice of professional criminologists. Even when excellent research is available to guide policy, a realistic appraisal must recognize that criminologists are as much to blame for counterproductive policies as anyone.

As Robert Bohm explained in his 1993 presidential address to the Academy of Criminal Justice Sciences: "Besides powerful critiquing of both existing and proposed policies, many of us have the capability of producing reasoned analyses and proposals based on historical, theoretical, and cross-cultural understanding. Yet...much of our work is simply ignored because it is not politically expedient or does not serve the dominant ideology. At the same time, others among us are more than willing to do the bidding of politicians and criminal justice officials in order to feed at the trough of political largess. I don't know whether these people actually believe in what they are doing, or maybe they still believe in the myth that their work is objective or value-neutral. In either case, these apologists for the status quo legitimize and perpetuate...short-sighted, counterproductive, detrimental policies...and do a disservice to our discipline."[42]

The new "three-strikes" laws, now popular with legislatures across the country, provide an example of the kind of dilemma facing criminologists who would influence social policy on the basis of statistical evidence. Three-strikes laws require that three-time felons receive lengthy prison sentences (often life without the possibility of parole) following their third conviction.

During the first few years of the Clinton presidency, the concept of selective incapacitation, upon which "three-strikes" laws are based, was represented by what advocates called "the six percent solution." The term signified a then widely heard claim that "6 percent of America's criminals commit 70 percent of the country's violent crime." The 6% solution was incorporated into the "three strikes and you're out" philosophy advocated by President Clinton and many other democrats, and which became part of The Violent Crime Control and Law Enforcement Act of 1994. The act requires "[m]andatory life imprisonment without possibility of parole for Federal offenders with three or more convictions for serious violent felonies or drug trafficking crime."[43] Unfortunately, the 6% solution may have been nothing more than a political sham. An investigative reporter who tried recently to track down the scientific basis for the 6% claim was unable to find any valid source.[44] About the same time, Marc Mauer, assistant director of the D.C.-based Sentencing Project, told a House subcommittee: "The 6% figure is based on a misreading of well-known criminology studies conducted by Dr. Marvin Wolfgang of the University of Pennsylvania many years ago" on a **cohort** of boys born in Philadelphia in 1945 and another set born in 1958 (a study discussed in more detail later in this book). Wolfgang, said Mauer, found that 7.5% of all boys in the cohort (not 6% of the cohort's offenders) were responsible for 69% of all serious crimes committed by the group.

Cohort a group of individuals sharing certain significant social characteristics in common, such as sex, time and place of birth.

"The difference is enormous," observes William Raspberry of the *Washington Post*.[45] "Imprisoning 6% of known criminals for life," Raspberry says, "might stretch current prison capacity, but it is doable. Life sentences for 6% of young men of peak-crime age is neither doable nor thinkable."

SUMMARY

Criminology—like its sister disciplines of sociology, psychology, geography, and political science—is a social science which endeavors to apply the techniques of data collection and hypothesis testing through observation and experimentation. Successful hypothesis testing can lead to theory building, and to a more complete understanding of the nature of crime and crime causation. Although the scientific framework and its techniques have largely been inherited from the physical sciences—such as chemistry, astronomy, and physics—in which they have been well established for centuries, criminology has been accepted into the scientific tradition by all but the most hard-nosed purists. Even so, criminologists are still game to study aspects of the field which are "in need of study" even where adequate resources (funding) or techniques (for example, the complete mapping of all human chromosomes) are not yet available.

Another component of scientific criminology, the detailed description of crime and related phenomena even where meaningful hypotheses are lacking, is also very much with us. In one descriptive area alone, that of crime statistics (discussed in the Chapter 2), so much data have already been gathered that it is unlikely they will ever be effectively analyzed.

DISCUSSION QUESTIONS

1. What is a hypothesis? What does it mean to operationalize a hypothesis? Why is operationalization necessary?
2. What is a theory? Why is the task of criminological theory construction so demanding? How do we know if a theory is any good?
3. Explain experimental research. How might a good research design be diagrammed? What kinds of threats to the validity of research designs can you identify? How can such threats be controlled or eliminated?
4. List and describe the various types of data-gathering strategies discussed in this chapter. Is any one technique "better" than another? Why or why not? Under what kinds of conditions might certain types of data-gathering strategies be most appropriate?
5. What is the difference between qualitative and quantitative research? What are the advantages and disadvantages of each?

NOTES

1. Hermann Mannheim, *Comparative Criminology* (Boston: Houghton Mifflin, 1967), p. 73.
2. Joan Petersilia, "Policy Relevance and the Future of Criminology—The American Society of Criminology, 1990 Presidential Address," *Criminology*, Vol. 29, no. 1, 1991, pp. 1–15.
3. Abraham Kaplan, *The Conduct of Inquiry: Methodology for Behavioral Science* (San Francisco: Chandler, 1964), p. 145.
4. Mannheim, *Comparative Criminology*, p. 20.
5. Don M. Gottfredson, "Criminological Theories: The Truth as Told by Mark Twain," in William S. Laufer and Freda Adler, eds., *Advances in Criminological Theory*, Volume 1 (New Brunswick, N.J.: Transaction, 1989), p. 3.
6. Kenneth R. Hoover, *The Elements of Social Scientific Thinking*, 5th ed. (New York: St. Martin's, 1992).
7. Ibid., p. 35.
8. Bernard P. Cohen, *Developing Sociological Knowledge: Theory and Method*, 2nd ed. (Chicago: Nelson-Hall, 1989), p. 13.

9. Ibid., p. 71.
10. Susette M. Talarico, *Criminal Justice Research: Approaches, Problems and Policy* (Cincinnati: Anderson, 1980), p. 3.
11. For a good review of secondary research, see J. H. Laub, R. J. Sampson, and K. Kiger, "Assessing the Potential of Secondary Data Analysis: A New Look at the Glueck's Unraveling Juvenile Delinquency Data," in Kimberly L. Kempf, ed., *Measurement Issues in Criminology* (New York: Springer-Verlag, 1990), pp. 241–257.
12. Ibid., p. 3.
13. Donald T. Campbell and Julian C. Stanley, *Experimental and Quasi-Experimental Designs for Research* (Chicago: Rand McNally, 1966), p. 35.
14. As identified in Donald T. Campbell and Julian C. Stanley, *Experimental and Quasi-Experimental Designs for Research* (Chicago: Rand McNally, 1966), p. 5, from which many of the descriptions that follow are taken.
15. Ibid., p. 34.
16. Frank E. Hagan, *Research Methods in Criminal Justice and Criminology* (New York: Macmillan, 1993), p. 103.
17. William Foote Whyte, *Street Corner Society: The Social Structure of an Italian Slum* (Chicago: University of Chicago Press, 1943), pp. v–vii.
18. Ibid., p. vii.
19. Hagan, *Research Methods in Criminal Justice and Criminology*, p. 192.
20. Nicole Vanden Heuvel, *Directory of Criminal Justice Information Sources*, 8th ed. (Washington, D.C.: National Institute of Justice, 1992), p. 145.
21. Joyce Hutchinson, *Directory of Criminal Justice Information Sources*, 9th ed. (Washington, D.C.: National Institute of Justice, 1994).
22. Hagan, *Research Methods in Criminal Justice and Criminology*, p. 218.
23. Hoover, *The Elements of Social Scientific Thinking*, p. 34.
24. Kaplan, *The Conduct of Inquiry*, p. 134.
25. As reported in ibid.
26. Avshalom Caspim, Terrie E. Moffitt, Phil A. Silva, Magda Stouthamer-Loeber, Robert F. Krueger, and Pamela S. Schmutte, "Are Some People Crime-Prone? Replications of the Personality-Crime Relationship Across Countries, Genders, Races, and Methods," *Criminology*, Vol. 32, no. 2 (May 1994), pp. 163–195.
27. Kaplan, *The Conduct of Inquiry*, p. 172.
28. Mannheim, *Comparative Criminology*, p. 87.
29. Of course, as with almost anything else, qualitative data can be assigned to categories and the categories numbered. Hence qualitative data can be quantified, although the worth of such effort is subject to debate.
30. Sanyika Shakur, *Monster: The Autobiography of an L.A. Gang Member* (New York: Penguin Books, 1993), pp. 45–46.
31. Martin D. Schwartz and David O. Friedrichs, "Postmodern Thought and Criminological Discontent: New Metaphors for Understanding Violence," *Criminology*, Vol. 32, no. 2 (May 1994), pp. 221–246.
32. National Institute of Justice, 1994-95 NIJ Program Plan (Washington, D.C.: NIJ, 1993), p. 21.
33. Hagan, *Research Methods in Criminal Justice and Criminology*, pp. 31–32.
34. Ibid., p. 42.
35. Patricia Van Voorhis, Francis T. Cullin, Richard A. Mathers, and Connie Chenoweth Garner, "The Impact of Family Structure and Quality on Delinquency: A Comparative Assessment of Structural and Functional Factors" *Criminology*, Vol. 26, no. 2 (May 1988), pp. 235–261.
36. David F. Greenberg, "Comparing Criminal Career Models," *Criminology*, Vol. 30, no. 1 (February 1992), pp. 133–140.
37. John M. Hagedorn, "Homeboys, Dope Fiends, Legits, and New Jacks," *Criminology*, Vol. 32, no. 2 (May 1994), p. 197.
38. American Psychological Association, *Publication Manual of the American Psychological Association* (Washington, D.C.: APA, 1994).

39. William Strunk, Jr., and E. B. White, *The Elements of Style*, 3rd ed. (New York: Macmillan, 1979, and later editions).
40. Mary-Claire van Leunen, *A Handbook for Scholars*, rev. ed. (Oxford: Oxford University Press, 1992).
41. Joan Petersilia, "Policy Relevance and the Future of Criminology—The American Society of Criminology, 1990 Presidential Address," *Criminology*, Vol. 29, no. 1, 1991, pp. 1–15.
42. Robert M. Bohm, "On the State of Criminal Justice: 1993 Presidential Address to the Academy of Criminal Justice Sciences," *Justice Quarterly*, Vol. 10, no. 4 (December 1993), p. 537.
43. Office of the U.S. Attorney General, Memorandum, September 15, 1994.
44. William Raspberry, "Crime and the 6 Percent Solution," *Washington Post* wire services, March 14, 1994.
45. Ibid.

PART TWO

CRIME CAUSATION

The only way to get out is to die.

—Eleven-year-old Eric Norah, after attending the funeral of his classmate Robert Sandifer, killed in a gang shooting in Chicago as police sought him on murder charges.

G.pe Bossi dis.
G.pe Benaglia inc.

CHAPTER 4

THE CLASSICAL THINKERS

What we don't see is that freedom is not a concept in which people can do anything they want, be anything they can be. Freedom is about authority. Freedom is about the willingness of every single human being to cede to lawful authority a great deal of discretion about what you do.

—NYC Mayor Rudolph W. Giuliani

Nature has placed mankind under the governance of two sovereign masters, pain and pleasure.

—Jeremy Bentham[1]

The more promptly and the more closely punishment follows upon the commission of a crime, the more just and useful will it be.

—Cesare Beccaria[2]

IMPORTANT NAMES

Jean Jacques Rousseau
Thomas Hobbes
John Locke
Montesquieu
Cesare Beccaria
Jeremy Bentham
Thomas Paine
William Graham Sumner

IMPORTANT TERMS

social contract
natural law
natural rights
The Enlightenment
trephination
folkways
mores
mala in se
mala prohibita
Code of Hammurabi
Twelve Tables
common law
deterrence
hedonistic calculus
utilitarianism
Panopticon
retribution
just deserts model
specific deterrence
general deterrence
recidivism
incapacitation
Classical school
dangerousness
recidivism rate
Neoclassical criminology
capital punishment
law and order advocates
individual rights advocates

INTRODUCTION

A little over a year ago, at a conference sponsored by *The New York Post*, New York City Mayor Rudolph W. Giuliani confronted issues of crime and social responsibility head on. In his speech, Giuliani laid the crux of the crime problem at the feet of what he called the tension between personal freedoms and individual responsibilities. We mistakenly look to government and elected officials, Giuliani said, to take on responsibility for solving the problem of crime when, instead, it is each individual citizen who must become accountable for fixing what is wrong with society today. In the mayor's words, "We only see the oppressive side of authority.... What we don't see is that freedom is not a concept in which people can do anything they want, be anything they can be. Freedom is about authority. Freedom is about the willingness of every single human being to cede to lawful authority a great deal of discretion about what you do."

"The fact is," the Mayor continued, "that we're fooling people if we suggest to them the solutions to these very, very deep-seated problems are going to be found in government.... The solutions are going to be found when we figure out as a society what our families are going to be like in the next century, and how maybe they are going to be different. They are going to have to be just as solid and just as strong in teaching every single youngster their responsibility for citizenship. We're going to find the answer when schools once again train citizens.... If we don't do that, it's very hard to hold us together as a country, because it's shared values that hold us together. We're going to come through this when we realize that it's all about, ultimately, individual responsibility. That, in fact, the criminal act is about individual responsibility and the building of respect for law and ethics is also a matter of individual responsibility."

Many of the problems facing Guiliani's administration, including rampant crime, and what the Mayor sees as an overemphasis on individual rights at the expense of group responsibility, have roots that go back centuries to the time of **the Enlightenment** and to the American and French revolutions. We shall discuss that era shortly, following some additional introductory comments.

The Enlightenment also known as the Age of Reason, was a social movement which arose during the eighteenth century and which was built upon ideas such as empiricism, rationality, free will, humanism, and natural law.

MAJOR PRINCIPLES OF THE CLASSICAL SCHOOL

This brief section serves to summarize the central features of the Classical school of criminological thought. Each of the points listed in this discussion can be found elsewhere in this chapter, where they are discussed in more detail. The present cursory overview, however, is intended to provide more than a summation—it is meant to be a guide to the rest of this chapter.

Most Classical theories of crime causation make certain basic assumptions. Among them are

- Human beings are fundamentally rational, and most human behavior is the result of free will coupled with rational choice.
- Pain and pleasure are the two central determinants of human behavior.
- Punishment, a necessary evil, is sometimes required to deter law violators and to serve as an example to others who would also violate the law.
- Root principles of right and wrong are inherent in the nature of things, and cannot be denied.
- Society exists to provide benefits to individuals which they would not receive in isolation.
- When men and women band together for the protection offered by society, they forfeit some of the benefits which accrue from living in isolation.
- Certain key rights of individuals are inherent in the nature of things, and governments which contravene those rights should be disbanded.
- Crime disparages the quality of the bond that exists between individuals and society, and is therefore an immoral form of behavior.

FORERUNNERS OF CLASSICAL THOUGHT

The notion of crime as a violation of established law did not exist in the most primitive of preliterate societies. The lack of lawmaking bodies, the paucity of formal written laws, and loose social bonds precluded the concept of crime as law violation. All human societies, however, from the simplest to the most advanced, evidence their own widely held notions of right and wrong. Sociologists term such fundamental concepts of morality and propriety **mores** and **folkways.** Mores, folkways, and laws were terms used by **William Graham Sumner**[3] near the start of the twentieth century to describe the three basic forms of behavioral strictures imposed by social groups upon their members. According to Sumner, mores and

Mores behavioral proscriptions covering potentially serious violations of a group's values. Examples include strictures against murder, rape, and robbery.

Folkways time-honored ways of doing things. While folkways carry the force of tradition, their violation is unlikely to threaten the survival of the social group.

folkways govern behavior in relatively small primitive societies, while in large, complex societies, they are reinforced and formalized through written laws.

Mores consist of proscriptions covering potentially serious violations of a group's values. Murder, rape, and robbery, for example, would probably be repugnant to the mores of any social group. Folkways, on the other hand, are simply time-honored ways of doing things, and while they carry the force of tradition, their violation is less likely to threaten the survival of the social group. The fact that American men have traditionally worn little jewelry illustrates a folkway which has given way in recent years to various types of male adornment—including earrings, gold chains, and even makeup. Mores and folkways, although they may be powerful determinants of behavior are nonetheless informal, since it is only laws which, from among Sumner's trinity, have been codified into formal strictures wielded by institutions created specifically for enforcement purposes.

Mala in se acts which are thought to be wrong in and of themselves.

Mala prohibita acts which are wrong only because society says they are.

Another way of categorizing socially proscriptive rules is provided by some criminologists who divide crimes into the dual categories of ***mala in se*** and ***mala prohibita.*** Acts which are *mala in se* are said to be fundamentally wrong—regardless of the time or place in which they occur. Forcing someone to have sex against their will and the willful killing of children are sometimes given as examples of behavior thought to be *mala in se.* Those who argue for the existence of *mala in se* offenses as a useful heuristic category usually point to some fundamental rule, such as religious teachings (the Ten Commandments, the Koran, etc.), to support their belief that some acts are inherently wrong. Such a perspective assumes that uncompromisable standards for human behavior rest within the very fabric of lived experience.

helping to find out or discover, stimulating research

Mala prohibita offenses are those which are said to be wrong for the simple reason that they are prohibited. So-called "victimless" or "social order" offenses such as prostitution, gambling, drug use, and premarital sexual behavior provide examples of *mala prohibita* offenses. The status of such behaviors as *mala prohibita* is further supported by the fact that they are not necessarily crimes in every jurisdiction. Prostitution, for example, is legal in parts of Nevada, as is gambling. Gambling, mainly because of the huge revenue potential it holds, is being rapidly legalized in many areas while it remains illegal in others.

The Demonic Era

Since time began humankind has been preoccupied with what appears to be an ongoing war between good and evil. Oftentimes evil has appeared in impersonal guise, as when the great bubonic plague, also known as the Black Death, ravaged Europe and Asia in the fourteenth century, leaving as much as three quarters of the population dead in a mere span of twenty years. At other times evil has seemed to wear a human face, as when the Nazi Holocaust claimed millions of Jewish lives during World War II.

Whatever its manifestation, the very presence of evil in the world has begged for interpretation, and sage minds throughout human history have advanced many explanations for the evil conditions that individuals and social groups have from time to time been forced to suffer through. Some forms of evil, like the plague and the Holocaust, appear cosmically based—while others, including personal victimization, criminality, and singular instances of deviance—are the undeniable result of individual behavior. Cosmic-level evil has been explained by ideas as diverse as divine punishment, karma, fate, and the vengeful activities of offended gods. Early explanations of personal deviance ranged from demonic possession to spiritual influences, and temptation by fallen angels—and even led to the positing of commerce between supernatural entities such as demons, werewolves, vampires, and ghosts and human beings.

Archeologists have unearthed skeletal remains which provide evidence that some early human societies believed outlandish behavior among individuals was a consequence of spirit possession. Carefully unearthed skulls, dated by various techniques to approximately forty thousand years ago, show signs of early cranial surgery, or **trephination**, apparently intended to release evil spirits thought to be residing within the heads of offenders. Such surgical interventions were undoubtedly crude, and probably involved fermented anesthesia along with flint cutting implements.

Trephination a form of surgery, typically involving bone and especially the skull. Early instances of cranial trephination have been taken as evidence for primitive beliefs in spirit possession.

As we saw in Chapter 3, any theory gains credence if activity based upon it produces results in keeping with what that theory would predict. Hence, spirit possession, as an explanation for deviance, probably appeared well validated by positive behavioral changes in those "patients" who submitted to the surgery called for by the theory. The actual cause of such observed reformation, however, may have been brain infections resulting from unsanitary conditions, "slips" of the stone knife, or the deterrent power of the pain endured by those undergoing the procedure. Nonetheless, to the uncritical observer the theory of spirit possession as a cause of deviance, and cranial surgery as a treatment technique, might have appeared to be supported by the "evidence" of low rates of future crime.

Early Sources of the Criminal Law

The Code of Hammurabi

Modern criminal law is the result of a long evolution of legal principles. The **Code of Hammurabi** is one of the first known bodies of law to survive and be available for study today. King Hammurabi ruled the ancient city of Babylon around the year 2000 B.C. and created a legal code consisting of a set of strictures engraved on stone tablets. The Hammurabi laws were originally intended to establish property and other rights and were crucial to the continued growth of Babylon as a significant commercial center. Hammurabi law spoke to issues of theft, property ownership, sexual relationships, and interpersonal violence. As Marvin Wolfgang has observed, "In its day, 1700 B.C., the Hammurabi Code, with its emphasis on **retribution**, amounted to a brilliant advance in penal philosophy mainly because it represented an attempt to keep cruelty within bounds."[4] Prior to the Code, captured offenders often faced the most barbarous of punishments, frequently at the hands of revenge-seeking victims, no matter how minor their transgressions had been.

Code of Hammurabi an early set of laws established by the Babylonian King Hammurabi around the year 2000 B.C.

Retribution the act of taking revenge upon a criminal perpetrator.

Early Roman Law

Of considerable significance for our own legal tradition is early Roman law. Roman legions under the Emperor Claudius (10 B.C.–54 A.D.) conquered England in the mid-first century, and Roman authority over "Britannia" was further consolidated by later Roman rulers who built walls and fortifications to keep out the still-hostile Scots. Roman customs, law, and language were forced upon the English population during the succeeding three centuries under the *Pax Romana*—a peace imposed by the military might of Rome.[5]

Twelve Tables early Roman laws written around 450 B.C. which regulated family, religious, and economic life.

Early Roman law derived from the **Twelve Tables,** which were written about 450 B.C. The tables were a collection of basic rules regulating family, religious, and economic life. They appear to have been based upon common and fair practices generally accepted among early tribes which existed prior to the establishment of the Roman Republic. Unfortunately, only fragments of the tables survive today.

The best-known legal period in Roman history occurred during the reign of Emperor Justinian I (527–565 A.D.). By the end of the sixth century, the Roman Empire had declined substantially in size and influence and was near the end of its life. In what may have been an effort to preserve Roman values and traditions, Justinian undertook the laborious process of distilling Roman laws into a set of writings. The Justinian Code, as these writings came to be known, actually consisted of three lengthy legal documents: (1) the Institutes, (2) the Digest, and (3) the Code itself. Justinian's code distinguished between two major legal categories: public and private laws. Public laws dealt with the organization of the Roman state, its Senate, and governmental offices. Private law concerned itself with contracts, personal possessions, the legal status of various types of persons (citizens, free persons, slaves, freedmen, guardians, husbands and wives, and so forth), and injuries to citizens. It contained elements of both our modern civil and criminal law and influenced Western legal thought through the Middle Ages.

Common Law

Common law a body of unwritten judicial opinion originally based upon customary social practices of Anglo-Saxon society during the Middle Ages.

Common law forms the basis for much of our modern statutory and case law. It has often been called *the* major source of modern criminal law. Common law refers to a traditional body of unwritten legal precedents created through everyday practice and supported by court decisions during the Middle Ages in English society. Common law is so called because it was based upon shared traditions and standards, rather than those which varied from one locale to another. As novel situations arose and were dealt with by British justices, their declarations became the start for any similar future deliberation. These decisions generally incorporated the customs of society as it operated at the time.

Common law was given considerable legitimacy upon the official declaration that it was the law of the land by the English King Edward the Confessor (ruled 1042–1066) in the eleventh century. The authority of common law was further reinforced by the decision of William the Conqueror to use popular customs as the basis for judicial action following his subjugation of Britain in 1066 A.D.

Eventually, court decisions were recorded and made available to barristers (the English word for trial lawyers) and judges. As Howard Abadinsky wrote, "Com-

The Magna Carta, an important source of modern Western laws and legal procedure. *Bettmann.*

mon law involved the transformation of community rules into a national legal system. The controlling element (was) precedent."[6] Today common law forms the basis of many of the laws on the books in English-speaking countries around the world.

The Magna Carta

The Magna Carta (literally, "great charter") is another important source of modern laws and legal procedure. The Magna Carta was signed on June 15, 1215, by King John of England at Runnymede, under pressure from British barons who took advantage of John's military defeats at the hands of Pope Innocent III and King Philip Augustus of France. The barons demanded a pledge from the king to respect their traditional rights and forced the king to agree to be bound by law.

At the time of its signing, the Magna Carta, although sixty-three chapters in length, was little more than a feudal document[7] listing specific royal concessions. Its original purpose was to ensure feudal rights and to guarantee that the king could not encroach on the privileges claimed by land-owning barons. Additionally, the Magna Carta guaranteed the freedom of the church and ensured respect for the customs of towns. It's wording, however, was later interpreted during a judicial revolt in 1613 to support individual rights and jury trials. Sir Edward Coke, chief justice under James I, held that the Magna Carta guaranteed basic liberties for all British citizens and ruled that any acts of Parliament which contravened common law would be void. There is some evidence that this famous ruling became the basis for the rise of the U.S. Supreme Court, with its power to nullify laws enacted by Congress.[8] Similarly, one specific provision of the Magna Carta, designed originally to prohibit the king from prosecuting the barons without just cause, was expanded into the concept of "due process of law," a fundamental cornerstone of modern legal procedure. Because of these later interpretations, the Magna Carta has been called "the foundation stone of our present liberties."[9]

The Enlightenment

The Enlightenment, also called the Age of Reason, was a highly significant social movement which occurred during the eighteenth century. The Enlightenment built upon ideas developed by seventeenth-century thinkers such as Francis Bacon (1561–1626), Thomas Hobbes (1588–1679), John Locke (1632–1704), Rene Descartes (1596–1650), Jean Jacques Rousseau (1712–1778), Baruch Spinoza (1632–1677), and others. Because of their indirect contributions to Classical criminological thought, it will be worthwhile to spend a few paragraphs discussing the writings of a few of these important historical figures.

Thomas Hobbes (1588–1679)

The English philosopher Thomas Hobbes developed what many writers regard as a very negative view of human nature and social life which he described in his momentous work, *Leviathan* (1651). Hobbes described the natural state of men and women as one that is "nasty, brutish, and short." Fear of violent death, he said, forces human beings into a **social contract** with one another in order to create a state. The state, according to Hobbes demands the surrender of certain natural rights and submission to the absolute authority of a sovereign, while offering protection and succor to its citizens in return. Although the social contract concept significantly influenced many of Hobbes's contemporaries, much of his writing was condemned for assuming an overly pessimistic view of both human nature and existing governments.

Social contract the Enlightenment-era concept that human beings abandon their natural state of individual freedom in order to join together and form society. Although, in the process of forming a social contract, individuals surrender some freedoms to society as a whole, government, once formed, is obligated to assume responsibilities toward its citizens and to provide for their protection and welfare.

John Locke (1632–1704)

In 1690 the English philosopher John Locke published his *Essay Concerning Human Understanding* (1690), in which he put forth the idea that the natural human condition at birth is akin to that of a blank slate upon which interpersonal encounters and other experiences indelibly inscribe the traits of personality. In contrast to earlier thinkers, who assumed that people are born with certain innate propensities and even rudimentary intellectual concepts and ideas, Locke ascribed the bulk of adult human qualities to life experiences.

In the area of social and political thought Locke further developed the Hobbesian notion of the social contract. Locke contended that human beings, through a social contract, abandon their natural state of individual freedom and lack of interpersonal responsibility to join together and form society. Although individuals surrender some freedoms to society, government, once formed, is obligated to assume responsibilities towards its citizens and to provide for their protection and welfare. According to Locke and other writers, governments should be required to guarantee certain inalienable rights to their citizens, including rights to life, health, liberty, and possessions. A product of his times, during which the dictatorial nature of monarchies and the Roman church were being much disparaged, Locke stressed the duties which governments have toward their citizens, while paying very little attention to the flip side of the coin—the responsibilities of individuals to the societies of which they are a part. As a natural consequence of such an emphasis, Locke argued that political revolutions, under some circumstances, might become an obligation incumbent upon citizens.

Locke also developed the notion of checks and balances between divisions of government, a doctrine that was elaborated by the French jurist and political philosopher Charles Louis de Secondat **Montesquieu** (1689–1755). In his *The Spirit of Laws* (1748), Montesquieu wove Locke's notions into the concept of a separation of powers between division of government. Both ideas later found a home in the United States Constitution.

Jean Jacques Rousseau (1712–1778)

The Swiss-French philosopher and political theorist **Jean Jacques Rousseau** further advanced the notion of the social contract in his treatise of that name (*Social Contract,* 1762). According to Rousseau, human beings are basically good and fair in their natural state, but historically were corrupted by the introduction of shared concepts and joint activities such as property, agriculture, science, and commerce. As a result, the social contract emerged when civilized people agreed to establish governments and systems of education to correct the problems and inequalities brought on by the rise of civilization.

Rousseau also contributed to the notion of **natural law,** a concept originally formulated by St. Thomas Aquinas (1225–1274), Baruch Spinoza (1632–1677), and others to provide an intuitive basis for the defense of ethical principles and morality. Natural law was used by early Christian church leaders as a powerful argument in support of their interests. Submissive to the authority of the Church, secular rulers were pressed to reinforce Church doctrine in any laws they decreed. Thomas Aquinas, a well-known supporter of natural law, wrote in his *Summa Theologica* that any man-made law which contradicts natural law is corrupt in the eyes of God. Religious practice, which strongly reflected natural law conceptions, was central to the life of early British society. Hence, natural law, as it was understood at the time, was incorporated into English common law throughout the Middle Ages.

Natural law the philosophical perspective that certain immutable laws are fundamental to human nature and can be readily ascertained through reason. Man-made laws, in contrast, are said to derive from human experience and history—both of which are subject to continual change.

Rousseau agreed with earlier writers that certain immutable laws are fundamental to human nature and can be readily ascertained through reason. Man-made law, in contrast, he claimed, derives from human experience and history—both of which are subject to continual change. Hence man-made law, also termed positive law, changes from time to time, and from epoch to epoch. Rousseau expanded the concept of natural law to support emerging democratic principles, and claimed that certain fundamental human and personal rights were inalienable since they were based upon the natural order of things.

Thomas Paine (1737-1809), an important contributor to the concept of natural law. *Bettmann.*

Natural rights the rights that, according to natural law theorists, individuals retain in the face of government action and interests.

Thomas Paine (1737–1809) the English-American political theorist and author of *The Rights of Man* (1791 and 1792), defended the French Revolution, arguing that only democratic institutions could guarantee the **natural rights** of individuals. At the Second Continental Congress, Thomas Jefferson (1743–1826) and other congressional representatives—many of whom were well versed in the writings of Locke and Rousseau—built the Constitution of the United States around an understanding of natural law as they perceived it. Hence, when Jefferson wrote of inalienable rights to "life, liberty, property," he was following in the footsteps of his intellectual forebearers, and meant that such rights were the natural due of all men and women since they were inherent in the social contract between citizens and their government.

Natural law and natural rights have a long intellectual history and are with us today in a number of guises. In a recent *National Review* article[10] subtitled "If natural law does not permit us to distinguish between men and hogs, what does?" Harry V. Jaffa, director of the Claremont Institute's Center for the Study of the Natural Law, called an 1854 speech given by Abraham Lincoln "the most moving and compelling exhibition of natural-law reasoning in all political history." In that speech Lincoln argued in favor of freedom for slaves by succinctly pointing out that there is no difference between people whatever their color. In Lincoln's words: "Equal justice to the South, it is said, requires us to consent to the extending of slavery to new countries. That is to say, inasmuch as you do not object to my taking my hog to Nebraska, therefore I must not object to your taking your slave. Now, I admit this is perfectly logical, if there is no difference between hogs and Negroes." Lincoln's point, of course, was that there is a huge difference between human beings and animals by virtue of their nature, and that such a difference cannot be denied by logic.

Although the concept of natural law has waned somewhat in influence over the past two centuries, many people today still hold that the basis for various existing criminal laws can be found in immutable moral principles, or in some other identifiable aspect of the natural order. The Ten Commandments, "inborn tendencies," the idea of sin, and perceptions of various forms of order in the universe and in the social world have all provided a basis for the assertion that "natural law" exists. Modern-day advocates of natural law still claim that it comes from outside the social group and that it is knowable through some form of revelation, intuition, or prophecy.

The present debate over abortion is an example of modern-day use of natural law arguments to support both sides in the dispute. Antiabortion forces, frequently called "pro-lifers," claim that an unborn fetus is a person and that he or she is entitled to all the protection that we would give to any other living human being. Such protection, they suggest, is basic and humane and lies in the natural relationship of one human being to another, and within the relationship of a society to its children. Right-to-lifers are striving for passage of a law, or a reinterpretation of past Supreme Court precedent that would support their position. Advocates of the present law (which allows abortion upon request under certain conditions) maintain that abortion is a "right" of any pregnant woman because she is the only one who should be in control of her body. Such "pro-choice" groups also claim that the legal system must address the abortion question, but only by way of offering protection to this "natural right" of women.

Perhaps the best-known modern instance of natural law debate occurred during confirmation hearings for U.S. Supreme Court Justice Clarence Thomas. Thomas, who was confirmed in 1991, once wrote an opinion in which he argued from a natural law point of view. That opinion was later challenged by Senate Judiciary Committee members who felt that it reflected an unbending judicial attitude.

THE CLASSICAL SCHOOL

As many authors have pointed out, the Enlightenment fueled the fires of social change, leading eventually to the French and American revolutions and providing many of the intellectual underpinnings of the U.S. Constitution. The Enlightenment, one of the most powerful intellectual initiatives of the last millennium, also inspired other social movements and freed innovative thinkers from the chains of convention. As a direct consequence of Enlightenment thinking, superstitious beliefs were discarded and men and women began to be perceived, for the first time, as self-determining entities possessing a fundamental freedom of choice. Following the Enlightenment, many supernatural explanations for human behavior fell by the wayside and free will and rational thought came to be recognized as the linchpins of all significant human activity. In effect, the Enlightenment

Classical school a criminological perspective operative in the late 1700s and early 1800s that had its roots in the Enlightenment, and which held that men and women are rational beings, that crime is the result of the exercise of free will, and that punishment can be effective in reducing the incidence of crime since it negates the pleasure to be derived from crime commission.

inspired the reexamination of existing doctrines of human behavior from the point of view of rationalism.

Within criminology the Enlightenment led to the development of what we refer to as the **Classical school** of criminological thought. Crime and deviance, which had been previously explained by reference to mythological influences and spiritual shortcomings, took their place in Enlightenment thought alongside other forms of human activity as products of the exercise of free will. Once man was seen as self-determining, crime came to be explained as a particularly individualized form of evil, or moral wrongdoing fed by personal choice.

Cesare Beccaria (1738–1794)

Cesare Beccaria (whose Italian name was Cesare Bonesana, but who held the title Marchese di Beccaria) was born in Milan, Italy. The eldest of four children he was trained at Catholic schools and earned a doctor of laws degree by the time he was 20.

In 1764 Beccaria published his *Essay on Crimes and Punishment.*[11] Although the work appeared originally in Italian, it was translated in London into English in 1767. Beccaria's *Essay* consisted of forty-two short chapters covering only a few major themes. Beccaria's purpose in penning the *Essay* was not to set forth a theory of crime, but to communicate his observations on the laws and justice system of his time. In the *Essay,* Beccaria distilled the notion of the social contract into the idea that "[l]aws are the conditions under which independent and isolated men united to form a society." More than anything else, however, his writings consisted of a philosophy of punishment. Beccaria claimed, for example, that although most criminals are punished based upon an assessment of their criminal intent, they should be punished instead based upon the degree of injury they cause. The purpose of punishment, he said, should be **deterrence** rather than retribution, and punishment should be imposed to prevent offenders from committing additional crimes. Beccaria saw punishment as a tool to an end and not an end in itself, and crime prevention was more important to him than revenge.

Deterrence the prevention of crime.

In order that crimes might be prevented, Beccaria argued, adjudication and punishment should both be swift, and once punishment is decreed, it should be certain. In his words: "[t]he more promptly and the more closely punishment follows upon the commission of a crime, the more just and useful it will be." Punishment that is imposed immediately following crime commission, claimed Beccaria, is connected with the wrongfulness of the offense, both in the mind of the offender and in the minds of others who might see the punishment imposed and thereby learn of the consequences of involvement in criminal activity.

Beccaria concluded that punishment should be only severe enough to outweigh the personal benefits to be derived from crime commission. Any additional punishment, he argued, would be superfluous. Beccaria's concluding words on punishment are telling. "In order," he said, "for punishment not to be, in every instance, an act of violence of one or of many against a private citizen, it must be essentially public, prompt, necessary, the least possible in the given circumstances, proportionate to the crimes, [and] dictated by the laws."

Beccaria distinguished between three types of crimes, including those that threatened the security of the state, those which injured citizens or their property, and those that ran contrary to the social order. Punishment should fit the crime, Beccaria wrote, declaring that theft should be punished through fines, personal injury through corporeal punishment, and serious crimes against the state (such as inciting revolution) via application of the death penalty. Beccaria, however, was opposed to the death penalty in most other circumstances, seeing it as a kind of warfare waged by society against its citizens.

Beccaria condemned the torture of suspects, a practice still used in the eighteenth century, saying that it was a device which insured that weak suspects would incriminate themselves, while strong ones would be found innocent. Torture, he argued, was also unjust, since it punished individuals before they had been found guilty in a court of law. In Beccaria's words, "No man can be called guilty before a judge has sentenced him, nor can society deprive him of public protection before it has been decided that he has in fact violated the conditions under which such protection was accorded him. What right is it then, if not simply that of might, which empowers a judge to inflict punishment on a citizen while doubt still remains as to his guilt or innocence?"

Beccaria's *Essay* also touched upon a variety of other topics. He distinguished, for example, between two types of proof—that which he called perfect proof in which there was no possibility of innocence and imperfect proof, where some possibility of innocence remained. Beccaria also believed in the efficacy of a jury of one's peers, but recommended that half of any jury panel should consist of peers of the victim, while the other half should be comprised of peers of the accused. Finally, Beccaria wrote that oaths were useless in a court of law, since accused individuals will naturally deny their guilt even if they know themselves to be fully culpable.

Beccaria's ideas were widely recognized as progressive by his contemporaries. His principles were incorporated into the French penal code of 1791, and significantly influenced the justice-related activities of European leaders such as Catherine the Great of Russia, Frederick the Great of Prussia, and the Austrian Emperor Joseph II. There is evidence that Beccaria's *Essay* influenced framers of the American Constitution, and some scholars claim that the first ten amendments to the Constitution, known as the Bill of Rights, might not have existed were it not for Beccaria's emphasis on the rights of individuals in the face of state power. Perhaps more than anyone else, Beccaria is responsible for the contemporary belief that criminals have control over their behavior, that they choose to commit crimes, and that they can be deterred by the threat of punishment.

Jeremy Bentham (1748–1832)

Jeremy Bentham,[12] another founding personality of the Classical school, wrote in his *Introduction to the Principles of Morals and Legislation* (1789) that "nature has placed mankind under the governance of two sovereign masters, pain and pleasure." To reduce crime or, as Bentham put it, "to prevent the happening of mischief," the pain of crime commission must outweigh the pleasure to be derived from criminal activity. Bentham's claim rested upon his belief, spawned by Enlightenment thought, that human beings are fundamentally rational and that

Jeremy Bentham (1748-1832) whose work is closely associated with the Classical school of criminology. *Bettmann.*

criminals will weigh in their minds the pain of punishment against any pleasures thought likely to be derived from crime commission.

Bentham advocated neither extreme nor cruel punishment—only punishment sufficiently distasteful to the offender that the discomfort experienced would outweigh the pleasure to be derived from criminal activity. Generally, Bentham argued, the more serious the offense the more reward it holds for its perpetrator and, therefore, the more weighty the official response must be. "Pain and pleasure," said Bentham, "are the instruments the legislator has to work with" in controlling antisocial and criminal behavior.

Hedonistic calculus or **utilitarianism** the belief, first proposed by Jeremy Bentham, that behavior holds value to any individual undertaking it according to the amount of pleasure or pain that it can be expected to produce for that person.

Bentham's approach has been termed **hedonistic calculus** or **utilitarianism** due to its emphasis upon the worth any action holds for an individual undertaking it. As Bentham put it, "[b]y the principle of utility is meant that principle which approves or disapproves of every action whatsoever, according to the tendency which it appears to have to augment or diminish the happiness of the party whose interest is in question; or, what is the same thing...to promote or to oppose that happiness." In other words, Bentham believed that individuals could be expected to weigh, at least intuitively, the consequences of their behavior before acting so as to maximize their own pleasure and minimize pain. The value of any pleasure, or the inhibitory tendency of any pain, according to Bentham could be calculated by its intensity, duration, certainty and immediacy (or remoteness in time).

Bentham claimed that there was really nothing new in his pleasure/pain perspective. "Nor is this a novel and unwarranted, any more than it is a useless theory," he wrote. "In all this there is nothing but what the practice of mankind, wheresoever they have a clear view of their own interest, is perfectly comfortable to. An article of property, an estate in land, for instance, is valuable, on what account? On account of the pleasures of all kinds which it enables a man to produce, and what comes to the same thing the pains of all kinds which it enables him to avert." In fact, Bentham's ideas were not new, but their application to criminology was. In 1739 David Hume distilled the notion of utilitarianism into a philosophical perspective in his book *A Treatise of Human Nature*. Although Hume's central concern was not to explain crime, scholars who followed Hume observed that human behavior is typically motivated more by self interest than by anything else.

Like Beccaria, Bentham focused on the potential held by punishment to prevent crime and to act as a deterrent for those considering criminal activity. In any criminal legislation, he wrote, "[t]he evils of punishment must...be made to exceed the advantage of the offence." Bentham distinguished between eleven different kinds of punishment, as follows:

- *capital punishment* or death.
- *afflictive punishment*, which includes whipping and starvation.
- *indelible punishment* such as branding, amputation, and mutilation.
- *ignominious punishment*, such as public punishment involving use of the stocks or pillory.
- *penitential punishment*, whereby an offender might be censured by his or her community.
- *chronic punishment* such as banishment, exile, and imprisonment.
- *restrictive punishment* such as license revocation or administrative sanction.
- *compulsive punishment* which requires an offender to perform a certain action like make restitution or keep in touch with a probation officer.
- *pecuniary punishment* involving the use of fines.
- *quasi-pecuniary punishment* in which the offender is denied services which would otherwise be available to him or her.
- *characteristic punishment* like mandating that prison uniforms be worn by incarcerated offenders.

Utilitarianism is a practical philosophy, and Bentham was quite practical in his suggestions about crime prevention. Every citizen, he said, should have their first and last names tattooed on their wrists for the purpose of facilitating police identification. He also recommended creation of a centralized police force focused on crime prevention and control—a recommendation which found life in the English Metropolitan Police Act of 1829 when it established London's New Police under the direction of Sir Robert Peel.

Bentham's other major contribution to criminology was his suggestion that prisons be designed along the lines of what he called a Panopticon House. The **Panopticon,** as Bentham envisioned it, was to be a circular building with cells along the circumference, each clearly visible from a central location staffed by guards. Bentham recommended that Panopticons should be constructed near or within cities so that they might serve as examples to others of what would happen to them should they commit crimes. He also wrote that prisons should be managed by contractors who could profit from the labor of prisoners, and that the contractor should "be bound to insure the lives and safe custody of those entrusted to him." Although a Panopticon was never built in Bentham's England, French

Panopticon a prison designed by Jeremy Bentham that was to be a circular building with cells along the circumference, each clearly visible from a central location staffed by guards.

officials funded a modified version of such a prison which was eventually built at Lyons, and three prisons modeled after the Panopticon concept were constructed in the United States.

Bentham's critics have been quick to point out that punishments seem often not to work. Even punishments as severe as death appear not to have any effect upon the incidence of crimes such as murder (a point which we will discuss in greater detail later in this chapter). Such critics forget Bentham's second tenant, however, which is that for punishment to be effective, "it must be swift and certain." For any punishment to have teeth, Bentham said, it must not only mandate a certain degree of displeasure, but must follow almost immediately upon it's being decided, and there must be no way of avoiding it.

Heritage of the Classical School

The Classical school was to influence criminological thinking for a long time to come. From the French Revolution and the U.S. Constitution to today's emphasis on deterrence and crime prevention, the Classical school has molded the way in which thinkers on the subject of crime have viewed the topic for more than two hundred years. The heritage left by the Classical school is still operative today in the following five principles, each of which is a fundamental constituent of modern-day perspectives on crime and human behavior:

- *The Principle of Rationality:* Human beings have free will and the actions they undertake are the result of choice.
- *The Principle of Hedonism:* Pleasure and pain, or reward and punishment, are the major determinants of choice.
- *The Principle of Punishment:* Criminal punishment is a deterrent to unlawful behavior, and deterrence is the best justification for punishment.
- *The Human Rights Principle:* Society is made possible by individuals cooperating together. Hence, society owes to its citizens respect for their rights in the face of government action, and for their autonomy insofar as such autonomy can be secured without endangering others or menacing the greater good.
- *The Due Process Principle:* An accused should be presumed innocent until proven otherwise, and an accused should not be subject to punishment prior to guilt being lawfully established.

NEOCLASSICAL CRIMINOLOGY

Neoclassical criminology a contemporary version of Classical criminology which emphasizes deterrence and retribution with reduced emphasis on rehabilitation.

As some writers have observed "[t]here appeared to be a tentative resurgence of the Classical School in the 1970s demonstrated in part by the adoption of determinate sentencing tactics and the reduction of emphasis on rehabilitation."[13] Determinate sentencing is a strategy which mandates a specified and fixed amount of time to be served for every offense category. Under determinate sentencing schemes, for example, judges in affected jurisdictions might be required to impose a seven-year sentence on armed robbers, but only one-year sentences upon strong-arm robbers (who use no weapon). Determinate sentencing schemes build upon the twin notions of Classical thought that (1) the pleasure of a given crime can be somewhat accurately assessed, and (2) a fixed amount of punishment necessary for deterrence can be calculated and specified.

Although some writers have loudly proclaimed the death of Classical and Neoclassical thought, their demise is greatly exaggerated. Two Neoclassical schools of thought continues to exist today. The first Neoclassical school continues to build upon ideas inherent in the notion of a social contract and places an emphasis on individual rights and due process. A second takes the form of three ideas that extend well beyond the calculus of determinate sentencing. Those three ideas are (1) criminal behavior is the result of free choice; (2) criminal behavior is rewarding and crime holds a number of attractions, from sensuality to monetary gain to fame; and (3) criminal punishment is necessary for deterrence. In its modern guise this second type of classical thinking has taken the form of a **just deserts model** of criminal sentencing, with a society-wide emphasis on both deterrence and retribution as the twin goals of criminal punishment. If a person is attracted to crime and chooses to violate the law, modern Neoclassical thinkers argue, he or she *deserves* to be punished since the consequences of crime were known to the offender before the crime was committed. Moreover, the criminal *must* be punished, such thinkers propose, in order that future criminal behavior can be curtailed. It is the second school of Neoclassical thought which is now in ascendancy, and it is to that mode of thought that we turn our attention throughout much of the remainder of this chapter.

Just deserts model
the notion that criminal offenders deserve the punishment they receive at the hands of the law, and that punishments should be appropriate to the type and severity of crime committed.

NOT ALL URGING MERCY FOR TEEN FACING FLOGGING

The Classical school emphasis on punishment as a deterrent is still very much alive in contemporary America, as evidenced by the following story from *USA Today.*

Michael Fay's father pleaded Sunday for the International Red Cross to intervene. Fay's mother begged for leniency. President Clinton said the penalty outweighs the crime.

But when it comes to the case of the Dayton, Ohio, man who may be flogged—six lashes—for spray-painting cars in Singapore, some Americans have no sympathy, and have written Singapore officials to say so.

The punishment—meted out with a 4-foot-long, half-inch-thick split-bamboo rod called a rotan—is "hardly a spanking," says lawyer Theodore Simon, who represents Fay, 18.

When a prisoner is struck, "pieces of skin and flesh fly at each stroke of the rotan," says Simon. If the prisoner faints, he's revived by a doctor so the flogging can continue.

"This is mutilation, basically," says the father, George Fay of Dayton.

The elder Fay said he thinks his son's confession was coerced and he'll ask Singapore President Ong Teng Cheong for clemency. He also intends to get the International Red Cross to attend and monitor the flogging.

Michael Fay makes the "sign of the cross" before entering Singapore's High Court. *Jonathan Drake/Bettmann.*

Michael Fay was singled out because he's an American, his father says. Fay's mother, Randy Chan, with whom he lives in Singapore, has lobbied for leniency.

Also:

- A worldwide association of meeting planners is threatening to boycott Singapore unless it grants Fay clemency. "We'll hit Singapore in its pocketbook" if Fay is caned, said Troy Johnson of the Arizona-based International Society of Meeting Planners.
- Clinton has called the punishment extreme and has urged Singapore to reconsider.
- Although the sentence has outraged Fay's parents, more than 100 letters and 200 phone calls in support of the punishment have come from Americans, says Chin Hock Seng of the Singapore Embassy.
- "America should be taking lessons from Singapore on how to prevent crime. Hold the line—don't give in," said a letter from Huntington Beach, Calif.
- "Punish hooligans and enjoy the benefits of a safe, clean society!" said a writer from Fresno, Calif.
- "I urge you to...vigorously apply Singapore law to the criminal's rear end," said a writer from Silver Spring, Md.

Chicago Tribune columnist Mike Royko wrote that he had received letters "several inches high," and 99% wrote that "yes, hooray, [Fay] should be flogged."

The Dayton *Daily News,* Fay's hometown newspaper, also is getting mail in support of the flogging.

The ordeal began last month when Michael Fay pleaded guilty to a 10-day spree in which he and other foreign students spray-painted and threw eggs, bricks and flower pots at 18 cars. Fay was sentenced to four months in prison, a $2,230 fine and flogging with the split-bamboo cane.

A State Department human-rights report last year criticized caning, and Amnesty International has called it a form of torture.

Michael Fay remained in jail in Singapore, awaiting the outcome of his appeal. No date has been set for the punishment.

As most readers will recall, Fay did not receive clemency and was flogged—a punishment referred to as "caning" in Singapore. Due to American outcry over the event, however, the number of lashes he received was reduced to four. Fay then spent an additional month imprisoned in Singapore before being released and returning to the United States.

Source: Carol J. Castaneda, "Not All Urging Mercy for Teen Facing Flogging," *USA Today*, April 4, 1994, p. 3A. Copyright 1994, *USA Today*. Reprinted with permission.

QUESTIONS

1. Do you believe that corporeal punishments can be an effective response to crime? Why or why not?
2. Do you believe that the caning of Michael Fay was deserved? Why or why not?
3. Do you believe that independent nations, like Singapore, should be permitted to implement their own sense of justice without American interference? Why or why not?

Free Will in Neoclassical Thought

Representative of today's Neoclassical scholars who emphasize crime's rewards is Jack Katz, whose book *Seductions of Crime*[14] explains crime as the result of what Katz calls the "often wonderful attractions within the lived experience of criminality." Crime, Katz says, is often pleasureful for those committing it and pleasure of one sort or another is the major motivation behind crime. Sometimes, however, the kind of pleasure to be derived from crime is not immediately obvious. Unfortunately, as Katz points out in the following paragraph, few criminologists have been interested to understand just how crime *feels* to those who commit it.

> The social science literature contains only scattered evidence of what it means, feels, sounds, tastes, or looks like to commit a particular crime. Readers of research on homicide and assault do not hear the slaps and curses, see the pushes and shoves, or feel the humiliation and rage that may build toward the attack, sometimes persisting after the victim's death.... How adolescents manage to make the shoplifting or vandalism of cheap and commonplace things a thrilling experience has not been intriguing to many students of delinquency.... The description of "cold-blooded, senseless murders" has been left to writers outside the social sciences. Neither academic methods nor academic theories seem to be able to grasp...how it makes sense to them to kill when only petty cash is at stake. Sociological and psychological studies of robbery rarely focus on the distinctive attractions of robbery, even though research has now clearly documented that alternative forms of criminality are available and familiar to many career robbers....[15]

For criminal offenders, crime is indeed rewarding, Katz says. It feels good, he tells his readers. "The particular seductions and compulsions [which criminals] experience may be unique to crime," he says, "but the sense of being seduced and compelled is not. To grasp the magic in the criminal's sensuality, we must acknowledge our own." Katz describes the almost sexual attraction shoplifting held for one young offender. As the thief said, "the experience was almost orgasmic for me. There was a buildup of tension as I contemplated the danger of a forbidden act, then a rush of excitement at the moment of committing the crime, and finally a delicious sense of release."[16] Willful participation in forbidden activity, be it as simple as shoplifting or as felonious as murder, marks the offender in the minds of today's Neoclassical thinkers as a candidate for punishment.

Punishment and Neoclassical Thought

Deterrence

Specific deterrence a goal of criminal sentencing which seeks to prevent a particular offender from engaging in repeat criminality.

General deterrence a goal of criminal sentencing which seeks to prevent others from committing crimes similar to the one for which a particular offender is being sentenced.

The concept of deterrence survives into modern times with the Neoclassical thinkers. Neoclassical writers of today generally distinguish between deterrence that is specific and that which is general. **Specific deterrence** is a goal of criminal sentencing which seeks to prevent a particular offender from engaging in repeat criminality. **General deterrence** works by way of example and seeks to prevent others from committing crimes similar to the one for which a particular offender is being sentenced.

Following their Classical counterparts, modern-day advocates of deterrence frequently stress that for punishment to be an effective impediment to crime it must be swift, certain, and severe enough to outweigh the rewards which flow from criminal activity. Unfortunately, those who advocate punishment as a deterrent are often frustrated by the complexity of today's criminal justice system and the slow and circuitous manner in which cases are handled and punishments are meted out. Punishments today, even when imposed by a court, are rarely swift in their imposition. Swift punishments would follow quickly after sentencing. The wheels of modern criminal justice, however, are relatively slow to grind to a conclusion given the many delays inherent in judicial proceedings and the numerous opportunities for delay and appeal available to defense counsel. Similarly, certainty of punishment is anything but a reality. Certain punishments are those which cannot be easily avoided. However, even when punishments are ordered, they are frequently not carried out—at least not fully. In contemporary America offenders sentenced to death, for example, are unlikely to ever have their sentences finalized. For those who do, an average of nearly eight years passes between the time a sentence of death is imposed and it is carried out.[17] Death row inmates and their lawyers typically barrage any court that will hear them with a plethora of appeals designed to delay or derail the process of justice. Often they win new trials. If they are able to wait long enough, most inmates will find their sentences overturned by blanket U.S. Supreme Court rulings that find fault with some obscure aspect of a state's trial process. Those who are able to delay even longer may die of natural causes long before the machinery of the state grinds its way to a conclusion.

Recidivism the repetition of criminal behavior.

If the Neoclassicists are correct criminal punishments should, ideally, prevent a repetition of crime. Unfortunately, as high rates of contemporary **recidivism** indicate, punishments in America rarely accomplish that goal. Recidivism means, quite simply, the repetition of criminal behavior by those already involved in crime. Recidivism can also be used to measure the success of a given approach to the problem of crime. When so employed it is referred to as a **recidivism rate,** expressed as the percentage of convicted offenders who have been released from prison and who are later rearrested for a new crime, generally within five years following release. Studies show that recidivism rates are high indeed, reaching levels of 80–90% in some instances—meaning that eight or nine out of every ten criminal offenders released from confinement are rearrested for new law-breaking activity within five years of being set free. What such studies do not measure, however, are the numbers of released offenders who return to crime but who are not caught, or who return to crime later than five years after release from prison. Were such numbers available, recidivism rates would likely be higher still.

Recidivism rate the percentage of convicted offenders who have been released from prison and who are later rearrested for a new crime, generally within five years following release.

One reason why American criminal justice seems so ineffectual at preventing crime and reducing recidivism may be that the punishments provided for by contemporary criminal law are rarely applied to the majority of offenders. Statistics show that few law-breakers are ever arrested, and of those who are, fewer still are convicted of the crimes with which they have been charged. After a lengthy court process, most offenders processed by the justice system are released, fined, or placed on probation. Relatively few are sent to prison, although short of capital punishment prison is the most severe form of punishment available to authorities today. To represent this situation, criminal justice experts often utilize a diagram known as a "crime funnel." Figure 4.1 shows the crime funnel for a recent year. As a glance at the figure shows, less than 1% of criminal law violators in America can be expected to spend time in prison as punishment for their crimes.

Exacerbating the situation still further is the fact that few persons sent to prison ever serve anything close to the sentences that have been imposed on them. Many inmates serve only a small fraction of their sentences due to early release

FIGURE 4.1 The Crime Funnel. *Source*: Statistics derived from The Bureau of Justice Statistics, *Sourcebook of Criminal Justice Statistics, 1993* (Washington, D.C.: National Institute of Justice, 1994).

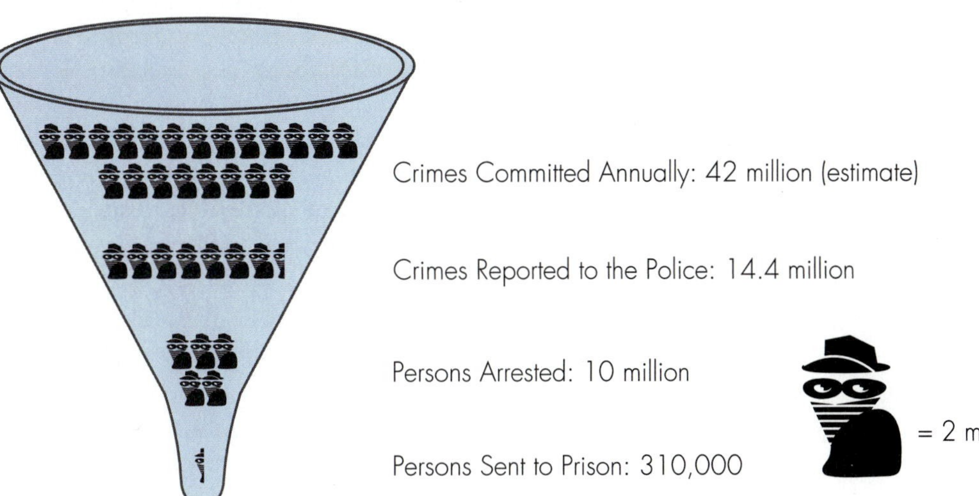

made possible by time off for good behavior, mandated reentry training, and the practical considerations necessitated by prison overcrowding.

Neoclassical perspectives are experiencing a contemporary resurgence through a new-found emphasis on the wider use of punishment as a criminal deterrent. A recent *Washington Post* article, for example, unwittingly headlined the modern-day survival of classical notions of crime and punishment when it proclaimed "Failure to Punish Misdemeanors Fuels Violence."[18] The *Post* article was reporting on the fact that more than three out of every one hundred St. Louis, Missouri, residents are victimized violently every year. In analyzing the data on St. Louis, Thomas Edsall, the article's author concluded that "the real failing of the criminal justice system is in dealing with the seemingly minor crime and deviant behavior that disrupts communities and is the first step toward violent crime."

Supporting Edsall's claims were numerous justice systems experts such as St. Louis District Attorney Dee Joyce Hayes. Hayes, reacting to the crime wave which has swept St. Louis for the past few decades, claimed that the real "fraud" in the criminal justice system is that almost "no one convicted of a misdemeanor does jail time" since the nation's prisons and jails are so overcrowded. As a result of this situation, the implication went, misdemeanants never have the opportunity to learn that criminal behavior can carry with it serious negative consequences. David Barber, Jefferson County Alabama's district attorney, believes Hayes is right. "The hammer doesn't come down on anybody until it's too late," said Barber. "We've reinforced their activity." Such thinking, frequently found among contemporary criminal justice professionals, is part of the heritage left by the Classical school.

Just Deserts

The old adages, "he got what was coming to him," or "she got her due," well summarize the thinking behind the just deserts model of criminal sentencing. Just deserts refers to the notion that criminal offenders deserve the punishment they receive at the hands of the law, and that any punishment which is imposed should be appropriate to the type and severity of crime committed. The idea of just deserts has long been a part of Western thought, dating back at least to Old Testament times. The Old Testament dictum of "an eye for an eye, and a tooth for a tooth," has been cited by many as divine justification for strict punishments. Some scholars believe, however, that in reality, the notion of "an eye for an eye" was intended to reduce the barbarism of existing penalties whereby an aggrieved party might exact the severest of punishments for only minor offenses. Even petty offenses were often punished by whipping, torture, and sometimes death.

One famous modern-day advocate of the just deserts philosophy was the Christian apologist C. S. Lewis, who wrote:

> The concept of desert is the only connecting link between punishment and justice. It is only as deserved or undeserved that a sentence can be just or unjust. I do not here contend that the question: "is it deserved?" is the only one we can reasonably ask about a punishment. We may very properly ask whether it is likely to deter others and to reform the criminal. But neither of these two last questions is a question about justice. There is no sense in talking

> about a "just deterrent" or a "just cure"—we demand of a deterrent not whether it is just but whether it will deter. We demand of a cure not whether it is just but whether it succeeds. Thus when we cease to consider what the criminal deserves and consider only what will cure him or deter others, we have tacitly removed him from the sphere of justice altogether.[19]

According to the Neoclassical perspective, doing justice ultimately comes down to an official meting out of what is deserved. Justice for an individual is

THEORY IN PERSPECTIVE

The Classical School and Neoclassical Thinkers

THE CLASSICAL SCHOOL

a criminological perspective operative in the late 1700s and early 1800s which had its roots in the Enlightenment, and which held that men and women are rational beings, that crime is the result of the exercise of free will, and that punishment can be effective in reducing the incidence of crime since it negates the pleasure to be derived from crime commission.

CLASSICAL CRIMINOLOGY. The application of Classical School principles to problems of crime and justice.

Period: 1700s-1880
Theorists: Cesare Beccaria, Jeremy Bentham, others
Concepts: Free will, deterrence through punishment, social contract, natural law, natural rights, due process, Panopticon

NEO-CLASSICAL CRIMINOLOGY, TYPE I: THE LAW AND ORDER SCHOOL. Involves modern-day application of Classical principles to problems of crime and crime control in contemporary society in the guise of "get-tough" social policies.

Period: 1970s-Present
Theorists: Jack Katz, many others
Concepts: Determinate sentencing, just deserts, specific deterrence, general deterrence

NEO-CLASSICAL CRIMINOLOGY, TYPE II: INDIVIDUAL RIGHTS ADVOCACY. Involves modern-day application of the Classical principles of due process and natural rights to problems of crime in contemporary society.

Period: 1960s-Present
Theorists: Many
Concepts: Due process, constitutional rights, incapacitation, dangerousness

nothing more nor less than what that individual deserves when all the circumstances surrounding his or her situation and behavior are taken into account.

Punishment is a central feature of both Classical and Neoclassical thought. While punishment served the ends of deterrence in Classical thought, it's role in Neoclassical thinking has been expanded. It is, for example, but a small step from the concept of just deserts to the concept of retribution. Those who advocate retribution see the primary utility of punishment in its ability to provide revenge.

Notions of just deserts and retribution are morally based. They build upon a sense of indignation at criminal behavior as well as upon the sense of righteousness inherent in Judeo-Christian notions of morality and propriety. Both philosophies of punishment turn a blind eye to the mundane and practical consequences of any particular form of punishment. Hence, advocates of the just deserts or retributive philosophies of punishment easily dismiss critics of, say, the death penalty, who frequently challenge the efficacy of court-ordered capital punishment on the basis that such sentences do little to deter others. Wider issues, including general deterrence, become irrelevant when one focuses narrowly on the emotions which crime and victimization engender in a given instance. Simply put, from the Neoclassical perspective some crimes cry out for vengeance, while others demand little more than a slap on the wrist, or an apology from the offender.

The Death Penalty

Capital punishment the legal imposition of a sentence of death upon a convicted offender. Another term for the death penalty.

Notions of deterrence, retribution, and just deserts all come together in **capital punishment.** Given the many different philosophies of punishment represented by the death penalty it is not surprising that so much disagreement exists as to the efficacy of death as a form of criminal sanction.

The extent to which the death penalty acts as a general deterrent has been widely studied. As mentioned earlier in this chapter, some researchers[20] have compared murder rates between states which have eliminated the death penalty and those which retain it, finding very little variation in the rate at which murders are committed. Others have looked at variations in murder rates over time in jurisdictions which have eliminated capital punishment, with similar results.[21] A 1988 Texas study provided a comprehensive review of capital punishment by correlating homicide rates with the rate of executions within the state between 1930 and 1986.[22] The study, which was especially important because Texas has been very active in the capital punishment arena, failed to find any support for the use of death as a deterrent. Opponents of capital punishment frequently cite studies such as these to claim that the death penalty is ineffective as a deterrent and should be abolished.

Other abolitionist rationales include claims that (1) the death penalty has, at times, been imposed on innocent people, (2) human life is sacred and state-imposed death lowers society to the same moral (or amoral) level as the individual murderer, and (3) the death penalty has been (and may still be) imposed in haphazard and discriminatory fashion.

Advocates of capital punishment generally discount each of these claims, countering with the notion that death is *deserved* by those who commit especially heinous acts, and that anything short of capital punishment under certain circumstances is an injustice in itself. Some people, the claim is made, deserve to die for what they have done. Such arguments evolve from a natural law perspective, and are based upon the notion of just deserts discussed earlier.

Many death penalty advocates are also not convinced that the sanction cannot be an effective deterrent. As with other punishments, a death penalty which is swift and certain, they point out, is likely to deter others. Modern-day capital punishment, however, does meet these requirements. In contemporary America offenders sentenced to death are unlikely to ever have their sentences finalized. For those who do, an average of nearly eight years passes between the time a sentence of death is imposed and it is carried out.[23] Even if the threat of death does not effectively deter others, advocates of capital punishment say, it will ensure that those people who are put to death will never commit another crime.

REHABILITATION ON A SMALL SCALE

Intensive Programs Save Some Youngsters

Can criminal offenders be changed if caught early enough? Does it take strict discipline to do it? As the story which follows shows, innovative programs may be demonstrating that change is possible.

Marriottsville, Md.—John Yates was 15 and abandoned by his parents when he started prowling the streets, breaking into cars and homes.

So 30 years later, he has no trouble relating to the young offenders he supervises at the Thomas O'Farrell Youth Center here.

"They're 'tough guys' but they're really kids," says Yates, called "Colonel" to 38 teen-age boys whose crimes range from drug dealing and car theft to armed robbery and assault.

Juvenile justice experts name the center as one of a number of programs that help turn criminal kids around.

Through strict regimens of education, discipline and counseling, these small, intensive facilities show that some young offenders can, indeed, be reformed.

"We've come a long way from a few years ago when the claim was 'nothing works,'" says John Wilson, acting chief of the federal Office of Juvenile Justice and Delinquency Prevention. "A lot of programs work."

Critics say those programs are all too rare—but they count O'Farrell among them.

Barry Krisberg, president of the National Council on Crime and Delinquency, declares O'Farrell "wonderful—a national model."

Not every bad kid can be saved: overall, six of 10 O'Farrell residents avoid further trouble with the law—much better than the 70% recidivism in some correction programs.

O'Farrell does not admit murderers or rapists because of an agreement with the local community.

The campus-like center is nestled in Maryland's rolling horse country. It's a far cry from traditional juvenile correctional facilities where a hundred or more young criminals may be held in aging institutional buildings.

Key to O'Farrell's program: 8-10 months of intensive counseling, schooling and discipline, followed by six months of supervision and support.

"We give them a vision...hope," says Yates, who oversees the operation of O'Farrell and two other programs.

A case in point: Neal, 17, came to O'Farrell in May after three years of crime. For him, lawbreaking began with selling crack and smoking pot.

He armed himself with a TEC-9—a semiautomatic pistol—to protect against "stick-up boys" who rob drug dealers. But he found that selling drugs "wasn't interesting enough," so he began stealing cars, too.

When that lost its thrill, Neal became an armed robber.

"It made me feel very powerful, in total control," he says. "It makes your heart pump...keeps you on the edge. I didn't care about my life anymore."

Since his arrest, Neal is trying to earn a high school equivalency diploma. He works at the center's kitchen and hopes to become an architect.

What would Neal say to people who are skeptical that criminals like him can be reformed?

"I would take them to a facility just like this one," he says. "They would see a bunch of changed young men."

Other successful programs:

- South Carolina's Family and Neighborhood Services program relies on master's degree-level therapists working with juvenile offenders and their families on a daily basis. After more than a year, only 20% of those in the program are incarcerated for some other charge, compared with 68% of juvenile offenders who are simply placed on probation.
- The Florida Environmental Institute—a program in a remote part of the Everglades and known as "The Last Chance Ranch"—exposes some of the state's most serious juvenile offenders to school, hard work and adult role models. After three years, only one-third have a new conviction.
- Alternative Rehabilitative Communities, a non-profit group that runs 10 facilities in Pennsylvania, including a secure facility for murderers and other seriously violent boys ages 15$\frac{1}{2}$ to 18. Courts often send kids to ARC as the last stop before transferring them to the adult criminal system.

ARC students follow strict schedules of classes, chores, physical exercise, and intensive counseling to root out causes of their violent acts.

Of the 13 "students" at the Chambersburg facility on a recent day, two had attempted murder; yet even with the hardest cases, ARC reports about two-thirds of students who graduate don't re-offend.

The "nasty kid who wants to take on the whole world is the one we work with best," says ARC director Dan Elby.

Heather, 16, argued with her stepfather and stabbed him four times with a kitchen knife: "He about died, but he didn't."

First she went to a detention facility where, she says, "You just watch TV." Then she came to ARC for a year where she studied, got a culinary degree and was released this month to a foster home.

Ruben, 18, came to ARC's Chambersburg facility eight months ago, after his life of drug deals and drive-by shootings ended with the wounding of an 8-year-old boy. He'll be out early next year.

Ruben says ARC taught him a sense of discipline and morality, and "to talk about my problems. Before, I just reacted."

Even in the best programs, not all juvenile offenders will reform. But rehabilitation efforts are still in the public's best interest, Wilson says.

"If all you've done is warehouse them, they're going to come out as monsters."

Frustration Setting In

USA TODAY's "Crackdown on Kids" coverage, describes a nation panicked at the rising violence of youth crime, and frustrated with a juvenile justice system that often fails either to protect or rehabilitate.

- The juvenile justice system spends $20 billion a year to arrest and jail kids—and as many as 70% commit crimes again.
- Rehabilitation programs seem costly and slow to a public panicked by ever-deadlier youth crime: In 10 years, the share of murders juveniles committed rose 125%.
- Stiff penalties have popular appeal. In a USA TODAY/CNN/Gallup Poll, 60% favor executing teen murderers. And at least 19 states plan get-tough changes in juvenile codes.
- But critics say most get-tough, punitive programs only lock up kids for a while, then send them back as more vicious, proficient criminals.

Source: Sam Vincent Meddis and Patricia Edmonds, "Rehabilitation on a Small Scale—Intensive Programs Save Some Youngsters," *USA Today*, September 29, 1994, p. 10A. Copyright 1994, *USA Today*. Reprinted with permission.

QUESTIONS

1. Can criminal offenders be changed if caught early enough?
2. Does it take strict discipline to bring about change, or will other strategies work as well? What might such other strategies be?

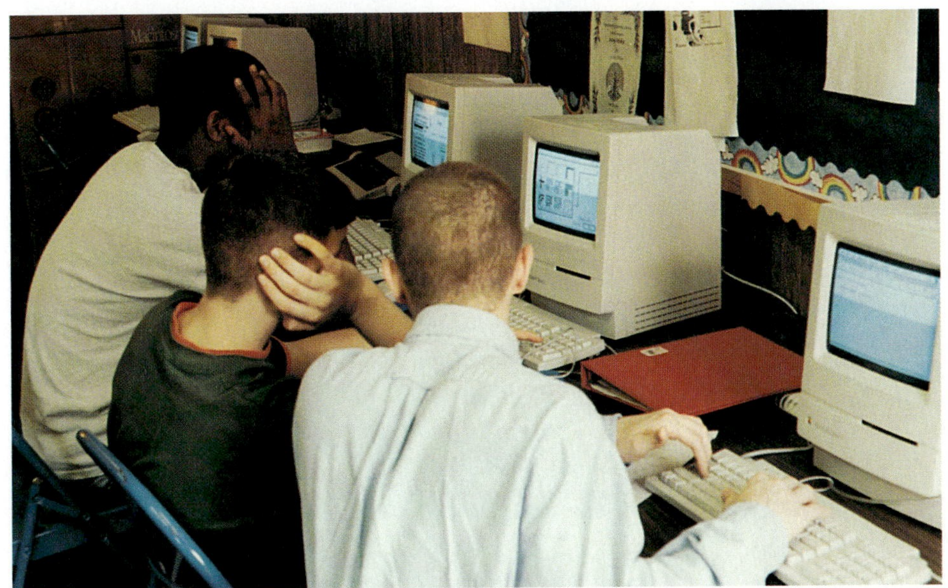

IN MARYLAND: Juvenile offenders train on computers at Thomas O'Farrell Youth Center in Marriottsville, a facility that has been successful in turning young criminals around. *Tim Dillon/USA Today.*

POLICY IMPLICATIONS OF THE CLASSICAL SCHOOL

Much of the practice of criminal justice in America today is built around a conceptual basis provided by Classical school theorists. Programs designed to prevent crime have their philosophical roots in the Classical axiom of deterrence, and punishment—in the modern guise of probation, fines, and especially imprisonment—remains a central tenant of modern-day criminal justice practice. The emphasis on punishment, however, as an appropriate response to crime, whether founded on principles of just deserts, revenge, or deterrence, has left many contemporary criminal justice initiatives foundering on overcrowded prisons and courtrooms packed into near paralysis.

There can be little denying that prisons today are dramatically overcrowded. By the beginning of 1994 the nation's state and federal prison population (excluding jails) stood at 948,881 inmates, a figure that represented an increase of 7.4% over the previous year.[24] Overcrowding in federal institutions exceeded 36%, while state prisons were between 18% and 29% over capacity depending upon the state in question. Drug offenses have accounted for almost half of the growth in prison populations since 1980, according to a Bureau of Justice Statistics report. Increases in the number of parole and probation violators returned to prison, as well as heightened rates of imprisonment for crimes such as sexual assault, robbery, aggravated assault, and burglary, explain the remainder of the increase.

According to the Bureau of Justice Statistics, the incarceration rate during 1994 was higher among black males than any other segment of the population, with young black males (those between the ages of 25 and 29) being incarcerated at a rate of 6,301 per every 100,000 similar individuals in the country[25]—meaning that in the year of the study more than 1 out of every 20 young black males in the United States was imprisoned!

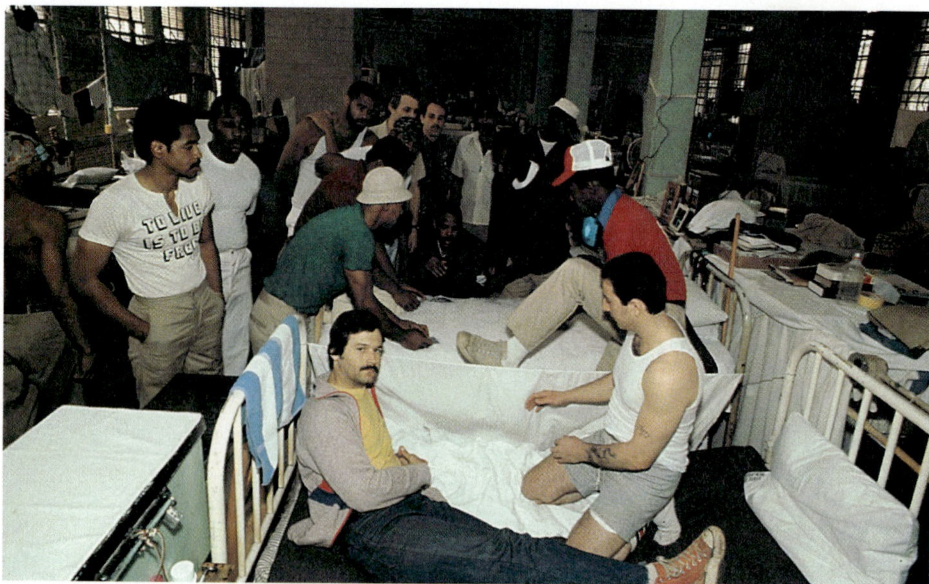

Rahway (New Jersey) State Prison. Today's "law and order" approach has led to dramatically overcrowded prisons. *J.P. Laffont/Sygma.*

Among the states, Texas had the highest incarceration rate at 553 inmates per 100,000 residents, followed by Oklahoma at 506 per 100,000, and Louisiana at 499 per 100,000. States with the largest inmate population included California, with 119,951, Texas, with 71,103, and New York, with 64,569 inmates. Figure 4.2 shows the total U.S. prison population projected through the year 2000.

The social policy position of today's Classical school heirs is complex and anything but clear. On the one hand, those heirs of the Classical school who see punishment as the central tenant of criminal justice policy believe it to be a natural and deserved consequence of criminal activity. Such thinkers call for greater prison capacity and new prison construction. They use evidence such as the crime funnel (described earlier) to argue that while punishment is theoretically an effective crime preventative, in today's society few criminals are ever effectively punished. These proponents of Neoclassical theory, often called **law and order advocates,** frequently seek stiffer criminal laws and enhanced penalties for criminal activity. They insist on the importance of individual responsibility and claim that law violators should be held unfailingly responsible for their actions. Law and order advocates generally want to ensure that sentences imposed by criminal courts are the sentences served by offenders, and they argue against reduced prison time for whatever reason. Finally, many such Neoclassical thinkers of today rally around the death penalty because they believe it is either justified as a natural consequence of specific forms of abhorrent behavior or because they believe that it

Law and order advocates those who suggest that, under certain circumstances involving criminal threats to public safety, the interests of society should take precedence over individual rights.

FIGURE 4.2 U.S. Prison Population, Historical and Projected Totals, 1960–2000. *Source*: Bureau of Justice Statistics, *Prisoners in 1993* (Annapolis Junction, MD: BJS, 1994), and "Bureau of Prisons Cites Need to Expand Prison Industries," *Criminal Justice Newsletter*, May 16, 1994, pp. 4–5.

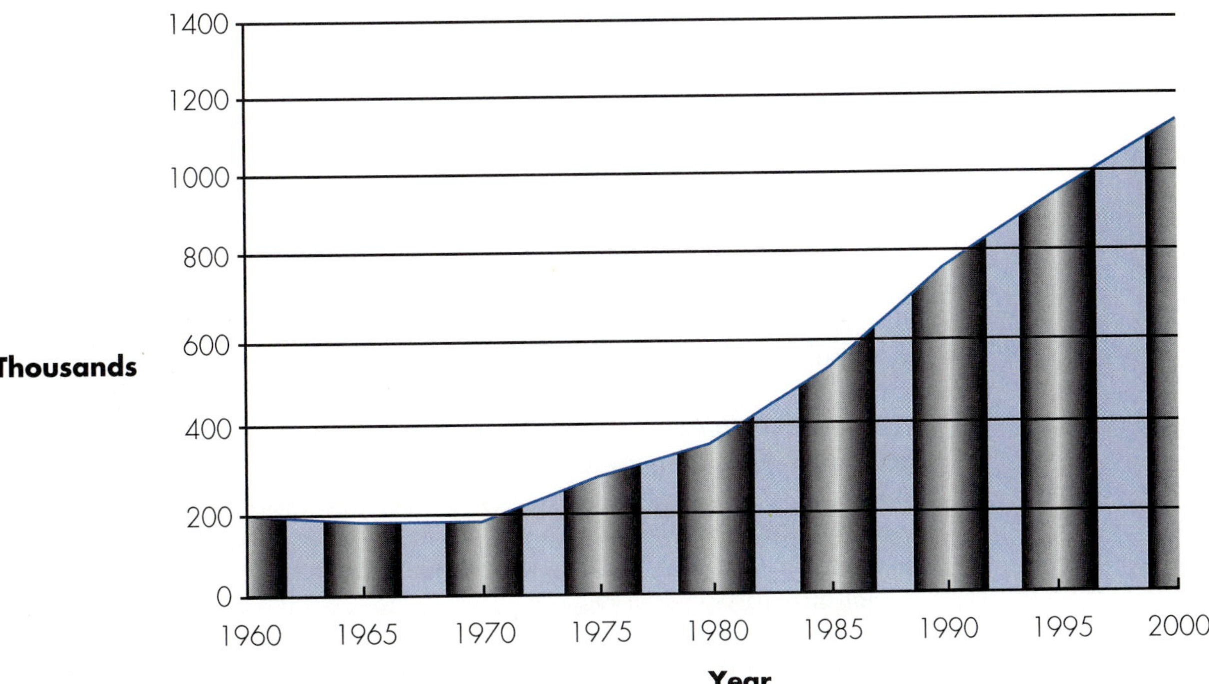

will deter others from committing similar crimes in the future. They answer critics who claim that evidence does not support a belief in capital punishment as a deterrent by pointing out that death is at least a specific deterrent, if not a general one. As previously discussed, they add that the efficacy of the death penalty as a deterrent is impossible to accurately assess since capital punishment today is so mired in procedural restrictions that it is anything but certain and swift.

Individual rights advocates those who seek to protect personal freedoms in the face of criminal prosecution.

Dangerousness the likelihood that a given individual will later harm society or others. (Dangerousness is discussed in more detail in a later chapter.)

Incapacitation the use of imprisonment or other means to reduce the likelihood that an offender will be capable of committing future offenses.

On the other hand, a second school of today's Neoclassical thinkers emphasizes individual rights, rather than punishment. **Individual rights advocates** intuitively defend the prerogatives of individuals against potential government excesses inherent in the social contract. Citing correctional overcrowding, high rates of recidivism, and increased criminal activity in many areas of society, this second school of Neoclassical thinkers points out that an increasing emphasis on imprisonment has done little to stem the tide of rising crime. They call for renewed recognition of individual rights in the face of criminal prosecution, and for reduction in the use of imprisonment as a criminal sanction—suggesting that it be employed as a kind of last resort in order to deal with only the most dangerous offenders. **Dangerousness,** or the likelihood that a given individual will later harm society or others, should be the major determining criterion for government action against the freedom of its citizens, individual rights advocates argue. Dangerousness, they suggest, should form the standard against which any need for **incapacitation** might be judged. Incapacitation, simply put, is the use of imprisonment or other means to reduce the likelihood that an offender will be capable of committing future offenses.

Proponents of modern-day incapacitation often distinguish between selective incapacitation, in which crime is controlled via the imprisonment of specific individuals and collective incapacitation whereby changes in legislation and/or sentencing patterns lead to the removal from society of entire groups of individuals judged to be dangerous. Advocates of selective incapacitation as a crime-control strategy point to studies which show that the majority of crimes are perpetrated by a small number of hard-core repeat offenders. The most famous of those studies was conducted by University of Pennsylvania professor Marvin Wolfgang and focused on 9,000 males born in Philadelphia in 1945. By the time this cohort of individuals had reached age 18, Wolfgang was able to determine that 627 "chronic recidivists" were responsible for the large majority of all serious violent crimes committed by the group. Other, more recent, studies have similarly shown that a small hard core of criminal perpetrators is probably responsible for most criminal activity in the United States.

Such thinking has led to the development of incapacitation as a modern-day treatment philosophy, and to the creation of innovative forms of incapacitation that do not require imprisonment—such as home confinement, the use of halfway houses or career training centers for convicted felons, and psychological and/or chemical treatments designed to reduce the likelihood of future crime commissions. Similarly, such thinkers argue, the decriminalization of many offenses and the enhancement of social programs designed to combat what they see as the root causes of crime—including poverty, low educational levels, a general lack of skills, and inherent or active discrimination—will lead to a much reduced incidence of crime in the future making high rates of imprisonment unnecessary.

Although both the law and order and the individual rights perspectives have much to recommend them, it appears that advocates of law and order have the upper hand in today's political arena. The country is rife with fear of crime, and calls for "get-tough-on-crime" policies are well received by most political constituencies.

Responses have not been slow in coming. In 1994 the U.S. Congress passed the Violent Crime Control and Enforcement Act, one of the most far-reaching get-tough-on-crime measures ever seen on Capitol hill. The law contains a "three-strikes-and-you're-out" provision that provides for mandatory life sentences after a third felony conviction. It also allocates massive amounts of money ($22 billion) for new prison construction and mandates long prison sentences for violent offenders and for those who use guns during the commission of crimes. Get-tough comments characteristic of many lawmakers on the eve of the bill's passage were made by Texas Republican Phil Gramm, who said, "We want ten years in prison without parole for possessing a firearm during commission of a violent crime; twenty years for discharging it. We want life imprisonment for murder, and the death penalty in aggravated cases."[26] The new law also bans many types of semiautomatic assault weapons and authorizes the hiring of twenty thousand additional police officers across the country. Typical of the current nationwide resurgence of interest in the death penalty, it expands the federal death penalty to nearly sixty offenses.

Many of today's new get-tough policies directly impact incarcerated offenders. In 1994, for example, Texas Governor Ann Richards, in a fashion characteristic of her gubernatorial counterparts across the nation, unveiled a plan to put prisoners to work on community service projects throughout the state. "We want the work done by these inmates to serve as payment to the citizens of this state," she said. "We're putting prisoners to work where it benefits our communities."[27] Richards also devised a method whereby Texas inmates would pay for all phone calls they make, with a portion of fees paid returned to the state. "Every time a prisoner makes a call home," Richards said, "he or she will be making a payment to the state." Texas Comptroller John Sharp estimated that the phone plan would generate up to $43 million in additional revenues over a five-year period, but Richards said the figure would be higher since the state is building more prisons, which will allow inmates to serve longer sentences.

Other get-tough policies include truth-in-sentencing initiatives which require judges to assess and make public the actual time an offender is likely to serve once sentenced to prison. Over the years, time off for good behavior and early release because of prison overcrowding have dramatically reduced the time a sentenced offender can be expected to spend behind bars. Last year, for example, in support of a growing national initiative, the Supreme Court for the state of New Jersey imposed a truth-in-sentencing rule on judges throughout the state, requiring them to disclose how much time a convicted defendant is likely to spend behind bars.[28] New Jersey Governor Christie Whitman had pushed for truth-in-sentencing as part of her anticrime platform.

A CRITIQUE OF CLASSICAL THEORIES

The Classical school of thought represents more a philosophy of justice than it does a theory of crime causation. As Randy Martin, Robert Mutchnick, and Timothy Austin have sagely observed, however, "[t]he true test of Beccaria's essay can be judged by the influence it has had over time on our justice system."[29] The influence of Beccaria, the Enlightenment, and Classical thinkers remains with us today in the

U.S. Constitution, get-tough approaches to crime, and an emphasis on individual rights. Martin and colleagues conclude that the Classical school "has left behind a legacy that we see in almost every aspect of our present-day justice system."[30]

Critics charge, however, that the Classical school lacks explanatory power over criminal motivation—other than to advance the simple claim that crime is the result of free will and individual choice. Such critics point out that Classical theory is bereft of meaningful explanations as to how a choice for or against criminal activity is made. Similarly, Classical theory lacks any appreciation for the deeper fonts of personal motivation, including those represented by aspects of human biology, psychology, and the social environment. Moreover, the Classical school, as originally detailed in the writings of Beccaria and Bentham, lacked any scientific basis for the claims it made. Although Neoclassical writers have advanced the scientific foundation of Classical claims (via studies such as those showing the effectiveness of particular forms of deterrence), many still defend their way of thinking by reference to philosophical ideals (such as just deserts).

In a world grown accustomed to measuring the success of an idea in terms of its measurable consequences, Neoclassical theorists are hard put to defend their philosophies. Citing the fact that boot camps prisons, for example, have not measured up to the claims of reduced recidivism touted by get-tough Neoclassical politicians, some writers have called for a return to programs already shown to work. As the pragmatic editorialist Colman McCarthy recently pointed out in an article criticizing the Clinton administration's plan to increase funding for boot camp prisons, "If helping nonviolent first offenders get their lives and values together is the goal, then the $3 billion for boot camps needs to be redirected to such proven programs as drug counseling, alternative sentences, work furloughs, literacy courses and well-supervised probation."[31]

THEORY VERSUS REALITY

Assessing Dangerousness

Dangerousness is a difficult concept to grapple with. Indicators of dangerousness have yet to be well defined in the social scientific literature, and legislators who attempt to codify any assessment of future dangerousness often find themselves frustrated. On the individual level, however, dangerousness might be more easily assessed. What follows is a description of the criteria one judge, Lois G. Forer, used in deciding whether or not an offender needed to spend a long time away from society.

I had my own criteria or guidelines—very different from those established by most states and the federal government—for deciding on a punishment. My primary concern was public safety. The most important question I asked myself was whether the offender could be deterred from committing other crimes. No one can predict with certainty who will or will not commit a crime, but there are indicators most sensible people recognize as danger signals:

- First, was this an irrational crime? If an arsonist sets a fire to collect insurance, that is a crime but also a rational act. Such a person can be deterred by being made to pay for the harm done and the costs to the fire department. However, if the arsonist sets fires just because he likes to see them, it is highly unlikely that he can be stopped from setting others, no matter how high the fine. Imprisonment is advisable even though it may be a first offense.
- Second, was there wanton cruelty? If a robber maims or slashes the victim, there is little likelihood that he can safely be left in the community. If a robber simply displays a gun but does not fire it or harm the victim, then one should consider his life history, provocation, and other circumstances in deciding whether probation is appropriate.
- Third, is this a hostile person? Was his crime one of hatred, and does he show any genuine remorse? Most rapes are acts of hostility, and the vast majority of rapists have a record of numerous sexual assaults. I remember one man who raped his mother. I gave him the maximum sentence under the law—20 years—but with good behavior, he got out fairly quickly. He immediately raped another elderly woman.
- Fourth, is this a person who knows he is doing wrong but cannot control himself? Typical of such offenders are pedophiles. One child abuser who appeared before me had already been convicted of abusing his first wife's child. I got him on the second wife's child and sentenced him to the maximum. Still, he'll get out with good behavior, and I shudder to think about the children around him when he does. This is one case in which justice is not tough enough.

By contrast, some people who have committed homicide present very little danger of further violence—although many more do. Once a young man came before me because he had taken aim at a person half a block away and then shot him in the back, killing him. Why did he do it? "I wanted to get me a body." He should never get out.

Source: Lois G. Forer, "Justice by the Numbers; Mandatory Sentencing Drove Me from the Bench," *The Washington Monthly*, April 1992, pp. 12–18. Reprinted with permission from *The Washington Monthly*. Copyright by *The Washington Monthly Company*, 1611 Connecticut Ave., N.W., Washington, D.C. 20009.

QUESTIONS

1. How are public safety and criminal punishment related?
2. Do you agree that the criteria used by Judge Forer to identify dangerousness are useful ones? Why or why not?
3. Do you think that offenders who are identified as "dangerous" should be treated differently from other offenders? If so, how?

SUMMARY

The Enlightenment proved to be a highly liberating force in the Western world. Enlightenment thinkers established many of the democratic principles that formed the conceptual foundations of the American and French revolutions. Their ideas are still very much with us today, and significantly shape our understanding of human nature and human behavior. The twin conceptual prongs around which this textbook is built—social responsibility and individual rights—both have their roots in Enlightenment thought and in the belief in free will which it engendered. Notions of deterrence as a goal of justice system intervention, and of punishment as a worthy consequence of crime, owe much of their contemporary influence to the Classical school of criminology. As we enter the twenty-first century we carry with us an intellectual heritage far older than we may realize.

DISCUSSION QUESTIONS

1. Name the various pre-Classical thinkers identified by this chapter. What ideas did each contribute to Enlightenment philosophy? What form did those ideas take in Classical criminological thought?
2. Define natural law. Do you think that natural law exists? If so, what kinds of behavior would be contravened by natural law? If not, why not?
3. What is meant by the idea of a "social contract"? How does the concept of social contract relate to natural law?
4. What were the central concepts that defined the Classical School of criminological thought? Which of those concepts are still with us today? Where do you see evidence for the survival of those concepts?
5. What are the various philosophies of punishment identified by this chapter? Which philosophy of punishment appeals most to you? Why? Which is the least attractive? Why?
6. Define recidivism. What is a recidivism rate? Why are recidivism rates so high today? What can be done to lower them?

NOTES

1. Jeremy Bentham, *An Introduction to the Principles of Morals and Legislation* (1789).
2. Cesare Beccaria, *On Crimes and Punishments*, translated by Henry Paolucci (New York: Bobbs-Merrill, 1963).
3. William Graham Sumner, *Folkways* (New York: Dover, 1906).
4. Marvin Wolfgang, "The Key Reporter," *Phi Beta Kappa*, Vol. 52, no. 1.
5. Roman influence in England had ended by 442 A.D., according to Crane Brinton, John B. Christopher, and Robert L. Wolff, *A History of Civilization*, 3rd ed., Volume 1 (Englewood Cliffs, NJ: Prentice Hall, 1967), p. 180.
6. Howard Abadinsky, *Law and Justice* (Chicago: Nelson-Hall, 1988), p. 6.

7. Edward McNall Burns, *Western Civilization*, 7th ed. (New York: W. W. Norton, 1969), p. 339.
8. Ibid., p. 533.
9. Brinton, Christopher, and Wolff, *A History of Civilization*, p. 274.
10. Harry V. Jaffa and Ernest van den Haag, "Of Men, Hogs, and Law: If Natural Law Does Not Permit Us to Distinguish Between Men and Hogs, What Does?" *National Review*, February 3, 1992, p. 40.
11. Beccaria, *On Crimes and Punishments.*
12. Bentham, *An Introduction to the Principles of Morals and Legislation.*
13. Randy Martin, Robert J. Mutchnick, and W. Timothy Austin, *Criminological Thought: Pioneers Past and Present* (New York: Macmillan, 1990), p. 18.
14. Jack Katz, *Seductions of Crime: Moral and Sensual Attractions in Doing Evil* (New York: Basic Books, 1988).
15. Ibid., p. 3.
16. Ibid., p. 71.
17. Lawrence A. Greenfeld, *Capital Punishment 1989* (Washington, D.C.: Bureau of Justice Statistics, 1990), p. 1.
18. "Failure to Punish Misdemeanors Fuels Violence," *Washington Post* wire services, April 11, 1994.
19. C. S. Lewis, "The Humanitarian Theory of Punishment," *Res Judicatae*, Vol. 6 (1953), pp. 224–225.
20. See, for example, W. C. Bailey, "Deterrence and the Death Penalty for Murders in Utah: A Time Series Analysis," *Journal of Contemporary Law*, Vol. 5, no. 1 (1978), pp. 1–20, and "An Analysis of the Deterrent Effect of the Death Penalty for Murder in California," *Southern California Law Review*, Vol. 52, no. 3 (1979), pp. 743–764.
21. See, for example, B. E. Forst, "The Deterrent Effect of Capital Punishment: A Cross-State Analysis of the 1960s," *Minnesota Law Review*, Vol. 61 (1977), pp. 743–764.
22. Scott H. Decker and Carol W. Kohfeld, "Capital Punishment and Executions in the Lone Star State: A Deterrence Study," *Criminal Justice Research Bulletin* (Criminal Justice Center, Sam Houston State University), Vol. 3, no. 12 (1988).
23. Lawrence A. Greenfeld, *Capital Punishment 1989* (Washington, D.C.: Bureau of Justice Statistics, 1990), p. 1.
24. Bureau of Justice Statistics, *Prisoners in 1993* (Annapolis Junction, MD: BJS, 1994).
25. Ibid.
26. "Senate Reaffirms Tough Stand Against Crime," Reuters wire services, May 19, 1994.
27. "Richards: Inmates Must Pay for Calls," United Press on-line, Southwest edition, June 27, 1994.
28. Thomas Martello, "Truth in Sentencing," April 26, 1994.
29. Randy Martin, Robert J. Mutchnick, and W. Timothy Austin, *Criminological Thought: Pioneers Past and Present* (New York: Macmillan, 1990), p. 17.
30. Ibid., p. 18.
31. Colman McCarthy, "Give the Boot to Boot Camps," *Washington Post* wire services, March 26, 1994.

CHAPTER 5

BIOLOGICAL ROOTS OF BEHAVIOR

The evidence is very firm that there is a genetic factor involved in crime.

—*Sarnoff A. Mednick*[1]

Investigators of the link between biology and crime find themselves caught in one of the most bitter controversies to hit the scientific community in years.

—*Time*[2]

Men have always loved to fight. If they didn't love to fight, they wouldn't be men.

—*General George S. Patton, Jr.*[3]

IMPORTANT NAMES AND CASES

- Konrad Lorenz
- Franz Joseph Gall
- Ernst Kretschmer
- Earnest A. Hooton
- Edward O. Wilson
- *Buck* v. *Bell*
- Cesare Lombroso
- C. Ray Jeffery
- William H. Sheldon
- Richard L. Dugdale
- James Q. Wilson
- Charles Darwin
- Johann Gaspar Spurzheim
- Charles Buckman Goring
- Henry H. Goddard
- Richard J. Herrnstein

IMPORTANT TERMS

- biological theories
- born criminal
- phrenology
- displastics
- testosterone
- hypoglycemia
- Juke family
- sociobiology
- aggression
- criminaloid
- cycloids
- somatotypology
- mesomorph
- supermale
- eugenics
- consititutional theories
- atavism
- positivism
- schizoids
- ectomorph
- endomorph
- monozygotic twins
- Kallikak family
- paradigm

INTRODUCTION

One of the most vicious murders Arizona has ever seen was the 1984 mutilation killing of Maude Moorman by her 36-year-old adoptive son, Robert Henry Moormann.[4] Moormann's biological mother drowned shortly after his birth in 1948, and he lived with his grandparents for a short while before being turned over to a Catholic social services agency for adoption. At age $2\frac{1}{2}$, a childless couple, Henry and Maude Moormann, adopted the boy. According to popular accounts, Maude was overly protective of her new son, leaving him ill prepared for encounters with other children. Robert became a notoriously poor student, frequently failing classes and often running away from home. At age 13 he was sent to the Sun School in Phoenix, a shelter for troubled boys, after having been accused of molesting a little girl. While home for Christmas holidays he hid a .22-caliber pistol under his pillow and shot his mother in the stomach when she sat by his bed to talk with him. The bullet lodged in her liver and surgeons feared to remove it. Though she recovered, Maude Moormann always insisted that the shooting had been an accident. Afterward, Robert was in and out of juvenile facilities for a variety of offenses—most centered on sexual maladjustment and the molestation of young females. By the time he was 18, Moormann had been arrested for accosting yet another girl and had been placed on the drug Mellaril to limit his sexual appetites.

As an adult, Moormann was finally sent to prison for kidnapping and molesting an 8-year-old neighbor girl in 1972. In 1979 he was paroled, but soon went back to prison for a parole violation. By 1984 Moorman had entered the prison's furlough program and, on January 12 of that year, was released to visit with his mother in a local motel. On that fateful night, Moormann demanded that his mother sign papers that would leave him sole heir to her estate. After she refused, Moormann beat her, tied her to the motel room bed, and suffocated her with a pillow. He then made a brief trip to a convenience store where he bought household cleansers and a variety of knives. Upon returning to the motel room he cut his mother's body into many pieces, stuffing some in a local trash dumpster and flushing her severed fingers down the toilet so that her remains couldn't be easily identified. Then he meticulously cleaned the room to hide any signs of the murder. He was arrested, however, after arousing the suspicions of a prison guard to whom he had offered a box of flesh-covered raw bones for the guard's dogs. It took a jury only two hours to convict him and he was sentenced to death.

Robert Henry Moormann was a poor physical specimen who had been judged unfit for the military draft. He had poor vision and flat feet, and suffered from low reading skills and learning disabilities. One physician, to whom he had been taken as a boy, diagnosed him as suffering from brain-stem trauma—the result of two traffic accidents in which he had been involved when young.

Did Moormann's crimes have a biological basis? Of that we may never be sure, although many biological theories have been advanced to explain criminality. Abnormalities of the brain, genetic predispositions, vitamin deficiencies, an excess of hormones such as testosterone, hypoglycemia (low blood sugar), an overabundance of neurotransmitters such as serotonin, and blood abnormalities are among the many biological explanations of crime available today.

Unfortunately, the field of criminology has been slow to give credence to biological theories of human behavior. Criminology's academic roots are firmly grounded in the social sciences. As the well-known biocriminologist **C. Ray Jeffery**, commenting on the historical development of the field, observes, "[t]he term *criminology* was given to a social science approach to crime as developed in sociology.... Sutherland's (1924) text *Criminology* was pure sociology without any biology or psychology; beginning with publication of that text, criminology was offered in sociology departments as a part of sociology separate from biology, psychology, psychiatry and law.... Many of the academicians who call themselves criminologists are sociologists."[5]

Even today, there can be little doubt that biological understandings of criminality are out of vogue. In 1992, for example, a National Institutes of Health–sponsored conference[6] that was intended to focus on the biological roots of crime was canceled after critics charged that the meeting would, by virtue of its biological focus, be racist and might intentionally exclude sociological perspectives on the subject. Dr. Peter Breggin, director of the Center for the Study of Psychiatry in Bethesda, Maryland, and leader of the opposition to the conference, argued that "[t]he primary problems that afflict human beings are not due to their bodies or brains, they are due to the environment. Redefining social problems as public health problems is exactly what was done in Nazi Germany."[7]

Unfortunately for the field of criminology, such critics fail to recognize that the advance of science has never been impeded by objective consideration of alternative points of view. Narrow-minded criticism, made before all the facts are in, while sadly characteristic of many so-called students of human behavior, does little to advance human understanding. Open inquiry requires objective consideration of all points of view, and an unbiased examination of each for their ability to shed light upon the subject under study. Hence, for an adequate consideration of biological theories as they may relate to crime and crime causation, we need to turn to literature outside of the sociological and psychological mainstream.

MAJOR PRINCIPLES OF BIOLOGICAL THEORIES

Biological theories of criminology maintain that the basic determinants of human behavior, including criminality, are constitutionally or physiologically based and often inherited.

This brief section serves to summarize the central features of **biological theories** of crime causation. Each of these points can be found elsewhere in this chapter, where they are discussed in more detail. This cursory overview, however, is intended to provide more than a summary—it is meant to be a guide to the rest of this chapter.

Biological theories of crime causation make certain fundamental assumptions. Among them are

- The brain is the organ of the mind and the locus of personality. In the words of the well-known biocriminologist Clarence Ray Jeffery, "The brain is the organ of behavior; no theory of behavior can ignore neurology and neurochemistry."[8]
- The basic determinants of human behavior, including criminal tendencies, are, to a considerable degree, constitutionally or genetically based.
- Observed gender and racial differences in rates and types of criminality may be at least partially the result of biological differences between the sexes and/or between racially distinct groups.
- The basic determinants of human behavior, including criminality, may be passed on from generation to generation. In other words, a penchant for crime may be inherited.
- Much of human conduct is fundamentally rooted in instinctive behavioral responses characteristic of biological organisms everywhere. Territoriality, condemnation of adultery, and acquisitiveness are but three examples of behavior which may be instinctual to human beings.
- The biological roots of human conduct have become increasingly disguised, as modern symbolic forms of indirect expressive behavior have replaced more primitive and direct ones.
- At least some human behavior is the result of biological propensities inherited from more primitive developmental stages in the evolutionary process. In other words, some human beings may be further along the evolutionary ladder than others, and their behavior may reflect it.
- The interplay between heredity, biology, and the social environment provides the nexus for any realistic consideration of crime causation.

BIOLOGICAL ROOTS OF HUMAN AGGRESSION

In 1966 **Konrad Lorenz** published his now-famous work, *On Aggression.*[9] It was an English language translation of a 1963 book entitled *Das Sogenannte Bose: Zur Naturgeschichte der Aggression (The Nature of Aggression)* which had originally

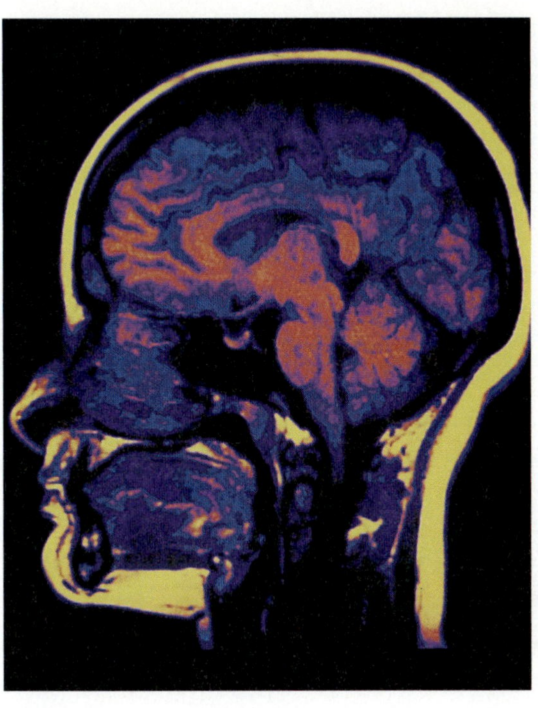

The brain is indeed "the organ of the mind" as modern researchers are continuing to discover. Here a computer-enhanced image shows areas of activity within the brain. *Scott Camazsine/Photo Researchers, Inc.*

appeared in German. In his writing, Lorenz described how aggression permeates the animal kingdom, and asked "What is the value of all this fighting?" "In nature," he said, "fighting is such an ever-present process, its behavior mechanisms and weapons are so highly developed and have so obviously arisen under the...pressure of a species-preserving function, that it is our duty to ask this...question."[10]

Lorenz accepted the evolutionary thesis of the nineteenth-century biologist **Charles Darwin** that intraspecies aggression favored the strongest and best animals in the reproductive process, but he concluded that aggression served a variety of other purposes as well. Aggression, said Lorenz, ensures an "even distribution of animals of a particular species over an inhabitable area..."[11] and provides for a defense of the species from predators. Human aggression, he claimed, meets many of the same purposes, but can take on covert forms. The drive to acquire wealth and power, for example, that was so characteristic of Western males at the time of his writing, was described by Lorenz as part of the human mating ritual whereby a man might "win" a prized woman through displays of more civilized forms of what could otherwise be understood as intraspecies aggression.

In today's enlightened times such observations may seem to many like mere foolishness. Lorenz's greatest contribution to the study of human behavior, however, may have been his claim that all human behavior is, at least to some degree, "adapted instinctive behavior." In other words, much of human conduct, according to Lorenz, is fundamentally rooted in instinctive behavioral responses characteristic of biological organisms everywhere, and present within each of us in the form of a biological inheritance from more primitive times. Even rational human thought, claimed Lorenz, derives it's motivation and direction from instinctual aspects of human biology. The highest human virtues, such as the value placed on

Charles Darwin (1809—1882), founder of modern evolutionary theory. *Julia Cameron/Bettmann.*

human life, "could not have been achieved," said Lorenz, "without an instinctive appreciation of life and death."[12]

Building upon the root functions of aggression, Lorenz concluded that much of what we today call crime is the result of overcrowded living conditions, such as those experienced by city dwellers, combined with a lack of legitimate opportunity for the effective expression of aggression. Crowding, from this perspective, increases the likelihood of aggression, while contemporary socialization simultaneously works to inhibit it. In the words of Lorenz, "...in one sense we are all psychopaths, for each of us suffers from the necessity of self-imposed control for the good of the community."[13] When people break down, said Lorenz, they become neurotic or delinquent, and crime may be the result of stresses that have been found to typically produce aggression throughout the animal kingdom.

At first blush, Lorenz's explanations, like many of the biologically based theories we will encounter in this chapter, appear more applicable to violent crime than to other forms of criminal offense. However, it is important to recognize that modern frustrations and concomitant manifestations of aggression may be symbolically, rather than directly, expressed. Hence, the stockbroker who embezzles his or her client's money, spurred on by the need to provided material goods for an overly acquisitive family, may be just as criminal as the robber who beats his victim and steals her purse to have money to buy liquor.

Early Biological Theories

Phrenology the study of the shape of the head to determine anatomical correlates of human behavior.

Numerous perspectives on criminal biology predate Lorenz's work. One of the earliest criminological anthropologists was **Franz Joseph Gall** (1758–1828). Gall hypothesized, in his theory of **phrenology** (also called craniology), that the shape

THEORY IN PERSPECTIVE

Types of Biological Theories

BIOLOGICAL THEORIES

adhere to the principle that the basic determinants of human behavior, including criminality, are constitutionally or physiologically based and inherited.

EARLY POSITIVISM. These biological approaches built upon evolutionary principles and were the first to apply scientific techniques to the study of crime and criminals. Early positivistic theories saw criminals as throwbacks to earlier evolutionary epochs.

Period: 1880s-1930
Theorists: Franz Joseph Gall, Johann Gaspar Spurzheim, Cesare Lombroso, Charles Goring, and Earnest Hooton
Concepts: Phrenology, atavism, born criminals, criminaloids

CONSTITUTIONAL THEORIES. Such biological theories explain criminality by reference to offenders' body types, inheritance, genetics, and/or external observable physical characteristics.

Period: Classical constitutional theories 1930s-1940s
Modern constitutional theories 1960s- Present
Theorists: Ernst Kretschmer, William H. Sheldon, Richard Dugdale, Arthur H. Estabrook, Henry H. Goddard
Concepts: Somatotyping, mesomorph, ectomorph, endomorph, XYY supermale, twin studies

BODY CHEMISTRY. Such biological theories utilize chemical influences, including hormones, food additives, allergies, vitamins, and other chemical substances to explain criminal behavior.

Period: 1940s-Present
Theorists: Various
Concepts: Hypoglycemia, vitamins, food allergies, seratonin, PMS, MAOA

SOCIOBIOLOGY. A theoretical perspective developed by Edward O. Wilson to include "the systematic study of the biological basis of all social behavior," which is "a branch of evolutionary biology and particularly of modern population biology."

Period: 1975-Present
Theorists: Edward O. Wilson
Concepts: Altruism, tribalism, survival of the gene pool

of the human skull was indicative of the personality and could be used to predict criminality. Gall's approach contained four themes:

- The brain is the organ of the mind.
- Particular aspects of personality are associated with specific locations in the brain.
- Portions of the brain that are well developed will cause personality characteristics associated with them to be more prominent in the individual under study, while poorly developed brain areas lead to a lack of associated personality characteristics.
- The shape of a person's skull corresponds to the shape of the underlying brain and is therefore indicative of the personality.

Gall was one of the first Western writers to firmly locate the roots of personality in the brain. Prior to his time it was thought that aspects of personality resided in various organs throughout the body—a fact reflected in linguistic anachronisms which survive into the present day (as, for example, when someone is described "as hard hearted," or as having "a lot of gall," or as thinking with some organ other than the brain). The Greek philosopher Aristotle was said to believe that the brain served no function other than to radiate excess heat from the body. Hence, Gall's perspective, although relatively primitive by today's standards, did much to advance physiological understandings of the mind-body connection in Western thought.

Although Gall never tested his theory, it was widely accepted by many of his contemporaries because it represented something of a shift away from theological perspectives prevalent at the time and a move toward scientific understanding—a trend that was well underway by the time of his writings. Phrenology also provided for systematic evaluation of suspected offenders and was intriguing for its ease of use. One of Gall's students, **Johann Gaspar Spurzheim** (1776–1853), brought phrenological theory to America and, through a series of lectures and publications on the subject, helped to spread its influence. Phrenology's prestige in America extended into the twentieth century, finding a place in classification schemes used to evaluate newly admitted prisoners. Even Arthur Conan Doyle's fictional character Sherlock Holmes was described as using phrenology to solve a number of crimes. It is still popular today among palm-readers and fortune tellers, some of whom offer phrenological "readings"—although a few states have outlawed such activities.

The Positivist School

Atavism a concept used by Cesare Lombroso to suggest that criminals are physiological throwbacks to earlier stages of human evolution. The term "atavism" is derived from the Latin term *atavus*, which means "ancestor."

One of the best-known early scientific biological theorists, the nineteenth-century Italian physician **Cesare Lombroso** (1835–1909), coined the term **atavism** to suggest that criminality was the result of primitive urges which, in modern-day human throwbacks, survived the evolutionary process. He described "the nature of the criminal" as "an atavistic being who reproduces in his person the ferocious instincts of primitive humanity and the inferior animals."[14]

At about this time, as was the case with Lorenz (discussed earlier), Charles Darwin was making a substantial impact upon the scientific world with his theory of biological evolution. Darwin proposed that human beings as well as other contemporary living organisms were the end products of a long evolutionary process governed by rules such as natural selection, survival of the fittest, and so on. Lombroso adapted elements of Darwin's theory to suggest that primitive traits survived in present-day human populations and led to heightened criminal tendencies among individuals who harbored them. Darwin himself had proposed this idea when he wrote: "[w]ith mankind some of the worst dispositions which occasionally without any assignable cause make their appearance in families, may perhaps be reversions to a savage state, from which we are not removed by very many generations."[15]

The atavistic individual, said Lombroso in his now-classic work *L'Uomo delinquente* (1876), was essentially a throwback to a more primitive biological state. According to Lombroso, such an individual, by virtue of possessing a relatively undeveloped brain, is incapable of conforming his behavior to the rules and expectations of modern complex society. Lombroso has been called the father of modern criminology because he was the first criminologist of note to employ the scientific method—particularly measurement, observation, and attempts at generalization—in his work. Other writers, more specific in their pronouncements, have referred to him as the "father of the Italian School" of criminology.

Lombroso's scientific work consisted of postmortem studies of the bodies of executed offenders, which he conducted with assistants, measuring the bodies in many different ways. The body of one such well-known criminal, named Vilella, provided Lombroso with many of his findings and reinforced his belief that most offenders were genetically predisposed toward criminality. Study of another offender, an Italian soldier whom Lombroso calls "Misdea" in his writings[16] and who "attacked and killed eight of his superior officers and comrades," supported such conclusions. The use of science and scientific techniques in the service of criminology has been termed **positivism.** C. Ray Jeffery, offering a somewhat limited definition of the term, but one which applies well to Lombroso's work, has said that "the main characteristic of Positivism is its attempt to answer the riddle of criminality by means of scientific studies of the individual offender."[17]

Positivism the application of scientific techniques to the study of crime and criminals.

Lombroso claimed to have found a wide variety of bodily features predictive of criminal behavior. Among them were exceptionally long arms, an index finger as long as the middle finger, fleshy pouches in the cheeks "like those in rodents," eyes that were either abnormally close together or too far apart, large teeth, ears which lacked lobes, prominent cheekbones, crooked noses, a large amount of body hair, protruding chin, large lips, a nonstandard number of ribs, and eyes of differing colors or hues. Lombroso went so far as to enumerate characteristics of particular types of offenders. Murderers, whom he called "habitual homicides," have, in Lombroso's words, "cold, glassy eyes, immobile and sometimes sanguine and inflamed; the nose, always large, is frequently aquiline or, rather, hooked; the jaws are strong, the cheekbones large, the hair curly, dark, and abundant; the beard is frequently thin, the canine teeth well developed and the lips delicate...."[18]

Atavism implies the notion that criminals are born that way. Lombroso was continuously reassessing his estimates of the proportion, from among all offenders, of the born criminal population. At one point he asserted that fully 90% of offenders committed crimes because of atavistic influences. He later revised the figure downward to 70%, admitting that normal individuals might be pulled into

Criminaloids a term used by Cesare Lombroso to describe occasional criminals who were pulled into criminality primarily by environmental influences.

Born criminals individuals who are born with a genetic predilection toward criminality.

lives of crime. In addition to the category of the born criminal, Lombroso described other categories of offenders, including the insane, **criminaloids,** and criminals incited by passion. The insane were said to include mental and moral degenerates, alcoholics, drug addicts, and the like. Criminaloids, also termed occasional criminals, were described as persons who were pulled into breaking the law by virtue of environmental influences. Nevertheless, most criminaloids were seen by Lombroso as exhibiting some degree of atavism and hence were said to "differ from **born criminals** in degree, not in kind." Those who became criminals by virtue of passion were said to have given in to intense emotions, including love, jealousy, hatred or an injured sense of honor.

Although he focused on physical features, Lombroso was not insensitive to behavioral indicators of criminality. In his later writings he claimed that criminals exhibited acute sight, hearing abilities that were below the norm, an insensitivity to pain, a lack of moral sensibility, cruelty, vindictiveness, impulsiveness, a love of gambling, and a tendency to be tattooed.

In 1893 Lombroso published *The Female Offender.*[19] In that book he expressed his belief that women exhibit far less anatomical variation than do men, but insisted that criminal behavior among women, as among men, derived from atavistic foundations. Lombroso saw the quintessential female offender, the prostitute, as "the genuine typical representative of criminality...."[20] Prostitutes, he said, are acting out atavistic yearnings and returning to a form of behavior characteristic of humankind's primitive past.

Evaluations of Atavism

Following in Lombroso's positivistic footsteps, around the turn of the twentieth century the English physician **Charles Buckman Goring** (1870–1919) conducted a well-controlled statistical study of Lombroso's thesis of atavism. Using newly developed but advanced mathematical techniques to measure the degree of correlation between physiological features and criminal history, Goring examined nearly three thousand inmates at Turin prison beginning in 1901 and enlisted the aid of London's Biometric Laboratory to conclude that "the whole fabric of Lombrosian doctrine, judged by the standards of science, is fundamentally unsound."[21] Goring compared the prisoners to students at Oxford and Cambridge universities, British soldiers, and noncriminal hospital patients, and published his findings in 1913 in his lengthy treatise *The English Convict: A Statistical Study.*[22] The foreword to Goring's book was written by Karl Pearson, who praised Goring for having no particular perspective of his own to advance and who could, he said, therefore objectively evaluate the ideas of others such as Lombroso.

A similar study was conducted between the years 1927–1939 by **Earnest A. Hooton,** a professor of anthropology at Harvard University. In 1939 Hooton published *Crime and the Man,*[23] in which he reported having evaluated 13,873 inmates from 10 states, comparing them along 107 physiological dimensions to 3,203 nonincarcerated individuals who formed a control group. His sample consisted of 10,953 prison inmates, 2,004 county jail prisoners, 743 criminally insane, 173 "defective delinquents," 1,227 "insane civilians," and 1,976 "sane civilians."

Hooton distinguished between regions of the country, saying that "states have favorite crimes, just as they have favorite sons." He reported finding physiological features characteristic of specific criminal types in individual states. For example, "Massachusetts criminals," he said, "are notable for thick beards, red-brown hair, dark brown, green-brown and blue-gray eyes, whites of eyes discolored with yellow or brown pigment flecks, rayed pattern of the iris of the eye, external and median folds of the upper eyelids, broad, high nasal roots and bridges, concave nasal profiles, thick nasal tips, right deflections of the nasal septum, thin integumental lips, thin upper membranous lip and thick lower lip, absence of lip seam, some...protrusion of the jaws, pointed or median chins, much dental decay but few teeth lost, small and soldered or attached ear lobes, and right facial asymmetries."[24] He went on to say that, through a sufficient degree of statistical manipulation, "[w]e finally emerge with differences between the offense groups which are not due to accidents of sampling, are not due to state variations, and are independent of differences between the ages of the offense groups. Thus, in the case of

FIGURE 5.1 Earnest A. Hooton's "Massachusetts Criminal." Reprinted by permission of the publishers from *Crime and The Man* by Earnest Albert Hooton, Cambridge Mass: Harvard University Press. Copyright © 1939 by the President and Fellows of Harvard College, renewed 1967 by Mary C. Hooton.

OLD AMERICAN CRIMINALS

Mosaic of Cranial, Facial, Metric and Morphological Features

MASSACHUSETTS

Narrowest face
Narrowest jaw
Thick beards
Broad, high nasal roots and bridges
Thick nasal tips
Right deflections of nasal septum
Concave profiles ①
External and median eyefolds ②
Small, attached ear lobes ③
Thin integumental lips ④
Membranous lips–upper thin, lower thick
Lip seams absent
Undershot jaw
Facial prognathism ⑤
Right facial asymmetry ⑥
Median chins

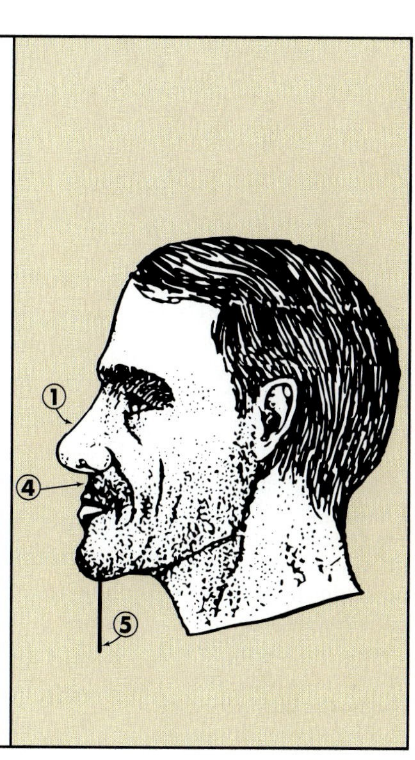

first-degree murder we find the members of that offense group deficient in persons with abundant head hair, deficient in individuals with narrow nasal bridges, presenting an excess of persons with pointed or median chins, and with compressed cheek bones."[25] He also found that first-degree murderers were more "square-shouldered" than other criminals and had larger ear lobes. From findings such as these, he was drawn to the conclusion that "crime is not an exclusively sociological phenomenon, but is also biological."[26]

In writing "it is impossible to improve and correct environment to a point at which these flawed and degenerate human beings will be able to succeed in honest social competition,"[27] Hooton made it clear that he did not believe that rehabilitation programs could have much effect upon most offenders and suggested banishing them to a remote location. Hooton concluded that criminals showed an overall physiological inferiority to the general population, and that crime was the result of "the impact of environment upon low grade human organisms."[28]

Hooton's work was quickly criticized along a number of dimensions. Stephen Schafer, the well-known contemporary criminologist, says "[t]he major criticisms were that his criminal population was not a representative sample of all criminals, that his control group was a fantastic conglomeration of noncriminal civilians...that he emphasized selected characteristics and disregarded others, that he gave no convincing evidence that the criminal's 'inferiority' was inherited, and that he failed to explore other important data that were available."[29] Perhaps even more significantly, Hooton failed to recognize that members of his noncriminal control group may, in fact, have been involved in crime but had managed to elude capture and processing by the criminal justice system. In other words, it may have been that the most successful criminals did not appear in Hooton's study group of inmates because they had eluded the law, thereby making their way into his supposedly noncriminal control group. His study may have simply demonstrated that "inferior" criminal specimens are the ones who get caught and end up in prison.

Body Types

Somatotyping the classification of human beings into types according to body build and other physical characteristics.

Cycloid a term developed by Ernst Kretschmer to describe a particular relationship between body build and personality type. The cycloid personality, which was associated with a heavy-set, soft type of body, was said to vacillate between normality and abnormality.

Another constitutional or physiological orientation which found its way into the criminological mainstream during the early and midtwentieth century was that of body types. Also called **somatotyping,** this perspective was primarily associated with the work of **Ernst Kretschmer** and **William H. Sheldon.** Kretschmer, a professor of psychiatry at the German University of Tubingen, proposed a relationship between body build and personality type and created a rather detailed "biopsychological constitutional typology." Kretschmer's somatotypology revolved around three basic mental categories: **cycloids** (also called cyclothymes), **schizoids** (or schizothymes), and **displastics**. The cycloid personality, which was associated with a heavy-set, soft type of body according to Kretschmer, vacillated between normality and abnormality. Cycloids were said to lack spontaneity and sophistication, and were thought to commit mostly nonviolent property types of offenses. Schizoids, who tended to possess athletic, muscular bodies but, according to Kretschmer, could also be thin and lean, were seen as more likely to be schizophrenic and to commit violent types of offenses. Displastics were said to be a

Endomorphs on the march. A group of would-be actors line up to audition for roles in the new movie, "Fat Chance." *Marty Lederhandler/AP/Wide World Photos.*

mixed group described as highly emotional and often unable to control themselves. Hence, they were thought to commit mostly sexual offenses and other crimes of passion.

Influenced by Kretschmer, William H. Sheldon utilized measurement techniques to connect body type with personality.[30] Sheldon felt that Kretschmer had erred in including too large an age range in his work. Therefore, he chose to limit his study to two hundred boys between the ages of 15 and 21 at the Hayden Goodwill Institute in Boston. Sheldon concluded that four basic body types characterized the entire group. Each type, described partly in words that Sheldon used, is as follows:

- The endomorph, who is soft and round and whose "digestive viscera are massive and highly developed" (i.e., the person is overweight and has a large stomach).
- The mesomorph, who is athletic and muscular and whose "somatic structures...are in the ascendancy" (i.e., the person has larger bones and considerable muscle mass).
- The ectomorph, who is thin and fragile, and who has "long, slender, poorly muscled extremities, with delicate, pipestem bones."
- The balanced type, which is of average build, being neither overweight, thin, nor exceedingly muscular.

Constitutional theories those which explain criminality by reference to offenders' body types, genetics, and/or external observable physical characteristics.

Ectomorph a body type originally described as thin and fragile, with long, slender, poorly muscled extremities, and delicate bones.

Endomorph a body type originally described as soft and round, or overwieght.

Individuals were ranked along each of the three major dimensions (the balanced type was excluded) using a seven-point scale. A score of 1-1-7, for example would indicate that a person exhibited few characteristics of endomorphology or mesomorphology, but was predominantly ectomorphic. Sheldon claimed that varying types of temperament and personalities were closely associated with each of the body types he identified. Ectomorphs were said to be cerebrotonic, or restrained, shy, and inhibited. Endomorphs were viscerotonic, or relaxed and sociable. The mesomorphic, or muscular, body type, however, he said was most likely to be associated with delinquency or somatotonia, which he described as "a predominance of muscular activity and...vigorous bodily assertiveness."

Early biological theorists such as Sheldon, Lombroso, and Gall provide an interesting footnote in the history of criminological thought. Today, however, their work is mostly relegated to dust bins of academic theorizing. Modern biological theories of crime are far more sophisticated than their early predecessors, and it is to these that we now turn.

Chemical Precursors of Crime

Recent research in the area of nutrition has produced some limited evidence that the old maximum "You are what you eat!" may contain more than a grain of truth. Biocriminology has made some significant strides in linking violent or disruptive behavior to eating habits, vitamin deficiencies, genetics, inheritance, and other conditions which impact body tissues. Studies of nutrition, endocrinology, and environmental contaminants have all contributed to advances in understanding such behavior.

Hypoglycemia a condition characterized by low blood sugar.

One of the first studies to focus on chemical imbalances in the body as a cause of crime was reported in the British medical journal *Lancet* in 1943.[31] Authors of the study linked murder to **hypoglycemia**, or low blood sugar. Low blood sugar, produced by too much insulin in the blood or by near-starvation diets, was said to reduce the mind's capacity to effectively reason, or to judge the long-term consequences of behavior. More recent studies have linked excess consumption of refined white sugar to hyperactivity and aggressiveness. Popular books such as *Sugar Blues* provide guides for individuals seeking to free themselves from the negative effects of excess sugar consumption.

To some degree even courts have accepted the notion that excess sugar consumption may be linked to crime. In the early 1980s, for example, Dan White, a former San Francisco police officer, was given a reduced sentence after his lawyers convinced the court that their defendant's consumption of massive amounts of refined white sugar had increased his excitability and lowered his ability to make reasoned decisions. White had been convicted of murdering San Francisco mayor Moscone and city councilman Harvey Milk during a dispute in the mayor's office. The night before the killings White had stayed awake, drinking Coca-Cola and eating many Twinkies.

More than ten years later, however, a well-conducted 1994 study reported in the *New England Journal of Medicine*[32] seemed to contradict the notion that sugar may lead to hyperactivity. Similarly, neither sugar nor artificial sweeteners were shown to have any link to an increase in learning disabilities. In the study, researchers at Vanderbilt University and the University of Iowa varied the diets of supposedly sugar-sensitive youngsters from ones which were high in sugar, to one that was low in sugar but contained the artificial sweetener aspartame. A third experimental diet contained very little sugar, but had added saccharin. After surveying parents, teachers, and baby-sitters and testing the study group for changes in memory, concentration and math skills, the researchers concluded "[w]e couldn't find any difference in terms of their behavior or their learning on any of the three diets."[33] Hence, to date, the evidence concerning sugar's impact on behavior is less than clear.

Allergic reactions to common foods have been reported as the cause of violence and homicide by a number of investigators.[34] Some foods, including milk, citrus fruit, chocolate, corn, wheat, and eggs, are said to produce allergic reactions in sensitive individuals, leading to a swelling of the brain and the brain stem. Involvement of the central nervous system in such allergies, it has been suggested, reduces the amount of learning which occurs during childhood, and may contribute to delinquency as well as to adult criminal behavior. Such swelling is also thought to impede the higher faculties, reducing one's sense of morality and creating conditions that support impulsive behavior.

Some studies have implicated food additives, such as the flavor enhancer monosodium glutamate, dyes, and artificial flavorings in producing criminal violence.[35] Other research[36] has found that coffee and sugar may trigger antisocial behavior. Researchers were led to these conclusions through finding that inmates consumed considerably greater amounts of coffee, sugar, and processed foods than others.[37] It is, however, unclear whether inmates drink more coffee because of boredom, or whether "excitable" personalities feel a need for the kind of stimulation available through coffee consumption. On the other hand, habitual coffee drinkers in nonprison populations have not been linked to crime, and other studies, such as that conducted by Mortimer Gross of the University of Illinois, show no link between the amount of sugar consumed by inmates and hyperactivity.[38] Nonetheless, some prison programs have been designed to limit intake of dietary stimulants through nutritional management and the substitution of artificial sweeteners for refined sugar. Vitamins have also been examined for their impact on delinquency. At least one researcher found that disruptive children consumed far less than optimal levels of vitamins B_3 and B_6 than did nonproblem youths.[39] Some researchers have suggested that the addition of these vitamins to the diets of children who were deficient in them could control unruly behavior and improve school performance.

The role of food and diet in producing criminal behavior, however, has not been well established. The American Dietetic Association and the National Council Against Health Fraud have concluded that no convincing scientific relationship between crime and diet has yet been demonstrated.[40] Both groups are becoming concerned that poor nutrition may result from programs intended to have behavioral impacts, such as those which reduce or modify diets in prisons or elsewhere.

Hormones and Criminality

Testosterone the primary male sex hormone, produced in the testes and functioning to control secondary sex characteristics and sexual drive.

Hormones have also come under scrutiny as potential behavioral determinants. The male sex hormone **testosterone,** for example, has been linked to aggression. Most studies on the subject have consistently shown an apparent relationship between high blood testosterone levels and increased aggressiveness in males. More focused studies have unveiled a direct relationship between the amount of the chemical present and the degree of violence used by sex offenders,[41] while other researchers have linked steroid abuse among body builders to destructive urges and psychosis.[42] Contemporary investigations[43] demonstrate a link between testosterone levels and aggression in teenagers, while others[44] show that adolescent problem behavior and teenage violence rise in proportion to the amount of testosterone levels in the blood of young males. In 1987, for example, a Swedish researcher, Dan Olweus,[45] reported that boys aged 15–17 showed levels of both verbal and physical aggression which correlated with the level of testosterone present in their blood. Olweus also found that boys with higher levels of testosterone "tended to be habitually more impatient and irritable than boys with lower testosterone levels." He concluded that high levels of the hormone led to increased frustration and habitual impatience and irritability.

In what may be the definitive work to date on the subject, Alan Booth and D. Wayne Osgood[46] conclude that there is a "moderately strong relationship between testosterone and adult deviance"[47] but suggest that the relationship "is largely mediated by the influence of testosterone on social integration and on prior involvement in juvenile delinquency."[48] In other words, measurably high levels of testosterone in the blood of males may have some effect on behavior, but those effects are likely to be moderated by the social environment.

Sex hormones, such as testosterone, have been linked to aggressive behavior. Testosterone also enhances secondary sexual characteristics such as body hair and muscle mass in males. *The Kobal Collection.*

A few limited studies have attempted to measure the effects of testosterone on women. Women's bodies manufacture roughly one-tenth of the amount of the hormone secreted by males. Even so, subtle changes in testosterone levels in women have been linked to changes in personality and sexual behavior.[49] Few such studies exist, however, and their findings should probably be regarded as inconclusive.

Fluctuations in the level of female hormones, however, may also bear some relationship to law violation. In 1980 a British court exonerated Christine English of charges she murdered her live-in lover, after English admittedly ran him over with her car after an argument. English's defense rested on the fact that she was suffering from premenstrual syndrome (PMS) at the time of the homicide. An expert witness, Dr. Katharina Dalton, testified at the trial that PMS had caused Ms. English to be "irritable, aggressive,...and confused, with loss of self-control."

Another case[50] involving PMS was decided in 1991 by a Fairfax, Virginia, judge who dismissed drunk-driving and other charges against a female orthopedic surgeon named Dr. Geraldine Richter. Richter allegedly kicked and cursed a Virginia state trooper and admitted to having consumed four glasses of wine after being stopped for driving erratically. A Breathalyzer test showed her blood-alcohol level to be nearly 0.13%—above the 0.10% level Virginia law set for such a violation. Charges against Dr. Richter were dismissed after a gynecologist testified on her behalf, saying that the behavior she exhibited was likely to have been due primarily to PMS.

While evidence linking PMS to violent and/or criminal behavior is far from clear, some researchers believe that a drop in serotonin levels in the female brain just prior to menstruation might explain the agitation and irritability sometimes associated with premenstrual syndrome. Serotonin has been called a "behavior-regulating chemical" and animal studies have demonstrated a link between low levels of the neurotransmitter present in the brain and aggressive behavior. Monkeys, for example, with low serotonin levels have been found more likely to bite, slap, and chase others of their kind. Low serotonin levels in humans have been linked via studies at the National Institute on Alcohol Abuse and Alcoholism to impulsive crimes. Men convicted of premeditated murder, for example, have been found to have normal serotonin levels, while those convicted of crimes of passion have lower levels.[51]

GENETICS AND CRIME

Criminal Families

Some scholars suggest that a penchant for crime may be inherited, and that criminal tendencies are genetically based. Early studies of this type often focused upon criminal families, or families that appeared to exhibit criminal tendencies from generation to generation.

In 1877 **Richard L. Dugdale** (1841–1883) published a study[52] of one such family, called the **Jukes.** Dugdale traced the Juke lineage back to a notorious character named "Max," a Dutch immigrant who arrived in New York in the early 1700s.

The Jukes a well-known "criminal family" studied by Richard L. Dugdale.

Two of Max's sons married into the notorious "Juke family of girls," six sisters, all of whom were said to be illegitimate. Max's male descendants were reputed to be vicious, while one woman, named Ada, had an especially bad reputation and came to be known as "the mother of criminals." By the time of the study, Dugdale was able to identify approximately 1,200 of Ada's descendants. Included among their numbers were 7 murderers, 60 habitual thieves, 90 or so other criminals, 50 prostitutes, and 280 paupers. Dugdale compared the crime-prone Jukes with another family, the pure-blooded progeny of Jonathan Edwards, a Puritan preacher and one-time president of Princeton University. Descendants of Edwards included American presidents and vice presidents and many successful bankers and businesspeople. None were identified from among the Edwards lineage who had run-ins with the law. In 1915 **Arthur H. Estabrook** published a follow-up to Dugdale's work, in which he identified an additional 715 Juke descendants, including 378 more prostitutes, 170 additional paupers, and 118 other criminals.

Killikak family a well known "criminal family" studied by Henry H. Goddard.

Following in the tradition of family tree researchers, **Henry H. Goddard** (1866–1957) published a study[54] of the **Kallikak** family in 1912. Goddard attempted to place the study of deviant families within an acceptable scientific framework via the provision of a kind of control group. For comparison purposes he used two branches of the same family. One branch began as the result of a sexual liaison between Martin Kallikak, a Revolutionary War soldier, and a barmaid whose name is unknown. As a result of this illegitimate union a son (Martin, Jr.) was born. After the war, Martin, Sr., returned home and married a righteous Quaker girl, and a second line of descent began. Although the second, legitimate branch, produced only a few minor deviants, the illegitimate line resulted in 262 "feebleminded" births and various other epileptic, alcoholic, and criminal descendants. The term "feebleminded," which was very much in vogue at the time of Goddard's study, was later recast as "mental retardation," while people exhibiting similar characteristics today might be referred to as mentally handicapped or mentally challenged. Since feeblemindedness appeared to occur with some predictability in Goddard's study, while criminal activity seemed to be only randomly represented among the descendants of either Kallikak line, Goddard concluded that a tendency toward feeblemindedness was inherited while criminality was not.

Eugenics the study of hereditary improvement by genetic control.

Studies such as these, which focused on inherited mental degeneration, led to the **eugenics** movement of the 1920s and early 1930s under which mentally handicapped women were frequently sterilized to prevent their bearing additional offspring. That movement was epitomized in the 1927 U.S. Supreme Court case of ***Buck* v. *Bell*,**[55] in which Justice Oliver Wendell Holmes, Jr., writing in support of a Virginia statute permitting sterilization, said "[i]t is better for all the world, if instead of waiting to execute degenerate offspring for crime, or to let them starve for their imbecility, society can prevent those persons who are manifestly unfit from continuing their kind."

The XYY "Supermale"

Recent developments in the field of human genetics have led to the study of the role of chromosomes, and sex-linked chromosomes in particular, in crime causation. The first well-known study[56] of this type was undertaken by Patricia A. Jacobs, a British researcher who, in 1965 examined 197 Scottish prisoners for chromosomal abnormalities through a relatively simple blood test known as karyotyping.[57] Twelve of the group displayed chromosomes which were unusual, and 7 were found to have an XYY chromosome. "Normal" males possess an XY chromosome structure, while "normal" females are XX. Some other unusual combinations might be XXX, wherein a female's genetic makeup contains an extra X chromosome, or XXY, also called Klinefelter's syndrome, in which a man might carry an extra X, or "female" chromosome. Klinefelter's males often are possessed of male genitalia, but are frequently sterile and evidence breast enlargement and intellectual retardation. The XYY male, however, whose incidence in the prison population was placed at around 3.5% by Jacobs, was quickly identified as potentially violent and termed a **supermale.**

Supermale a human male displaying the XYY chromosome structure.

Following introduction of the supermale notion into popular consciousness, a number of offenders attempted to offer a chromosome-based defense. In 1969, for example, Lawrence E. Hannell, who was adjudged a supermale was acquitted of murder in Australia on the grounds of insanity.[58] Such a defense, however, did not work for Richard Speck, another claimed XYY male, convicted of killing eight Chicago nursing students in 1966. It was later learned that Speck did not carry the extra Y chromosome.

24-CB

To date there have been nearly 200 studies of XYY males. Although not all researchers agree, taken as a group these studies[59] tend to show that supermales

- Are taller than the average male, often standing 6'1" or more.
- Suffer from acne or skin disorders.
- Are of less than average intelligence.
- Are over represented in prisons and mental hospitals.
- Come from families with less history of crime or mental illness.

The supermale phenomenon, also called the XYY syndrome, may have been more sensationalism than fact. There is little evidence that XYY males actually commit crimes of greater violence than do other males, although they may commit somewhat more crimes overall. A 1976 Danish study[60] of four thousand men, which found precisely that, may have helped put the issue to rest. The Danish survey, conducted of men born in Copenhagen between 1944 and 1947, also found that the incidence of XYY men was less than 1% in the general male population. Other recent researchers have similarly concluded that "studies done thus far are largely in agreement and demonstrate rather conclusively that males of the XYY type are not predictably aggressive."[61]

Chromosomes and Modern-Day Criminal Families

In 1993 Dutch criminologists caught worldwide attention with their claim that they had uncovered a specific gene with links to criminal behavior. Geneticist Han Brunner, researcher H. Hilger Ropers, and collaborators studied what media sources called "the Netherlands' most dysfunctional family."[62] Although the unnamed family displayed IQs which were nearly normal, they seemed unable to control their impulses, and often ended up being arrested for violations of the criminal law. Arrests, however, were always of men. Tracing the family back five generations, Brunner found 14 men whom he classified as genetically given to criminality. None of the females in the family displayed criminal tendencies, although they were often victimized by their crime-prone male siblings. One brother raped a sister and later stabbed a mental hospital staffer in the chest with a pitchfork. Another tried to run over his supervisor with his car. Two brothers repeatedly started fires, and were classified as arsonists. Another brother frequently crept into his sisters' rooms and forced them to undress at knifepoint.

According to Ropers and Brunner, because men have only one X chromosome they are especially vulnerable to any defective gene. Women, with two X chromosomes, have a kind of backup system in which one defective gene may be compensated for by another wholesome and correctly functioning gene carried in the second X chromosome. After a decade of study, which involved the laboratory filtering of a huge quantity of genetic material in a search for the defective gene, Ropers and Brunner announced that they had isolated the specific mutation that caused the family's criminality. The gene, they said, is one which is responsible in the body for production of an enzyme called "monoamine oxidase A" (MAOA). MAOA is crucially involved in the process by which signals are transmitted within the brain. Specifically, MAOA breaks down the chemicals serotonin and noradrenaline. Both are substances that, when found in excess in the brain, have been linked to aggressive behavior in human beings. Since men with the mutated gene don't produce the enzyme necessary to break down chemical transmitters, researchers surmise, their brains are overwhelmed with stimuli—a situation that results in uncontrollable urges and, ultimately, criminal behavior.

Twin Studies

Studies of the criminal tendencies of fraternal and identical twins provide a methodologically sophisticated technique for ferreting out the role of inheritance in crime causation. Fraternal twins (also called dizygotic or DZ twins) develop from different fertilized eggs and share only that genetic material common among siblings. Identical twins (also called **monozygotic** or MZ **twins**) develop from the same egg, and carry virtually the same genetic material.

Monozygotic (or MZ) twins as opposed to dizygotic (or DZ) twins, develop from the same egg, and carry virtually the same genetic material.

One of the first studies[63] to link MZ twins to criminality was published in the 1920s by the German physician Johannes Lange. Lange examined only 17 pairs of fraternal and 13 pairs of identical twins, but found that in 10 of the 13 identical pairs both twins were criminal, while only 2 of the 17 fraternal pairs exhibited such similarity. Lange's findings drew considerable attention, even though his sample was very small and he was unable to adequately separate environmental influences from genetic ones. The title of his book, *Verbrechen als Schicksal,* whose English translation is *Crime as Destiny,* indicates Lange's firm conviction that criminality has a strong genetic component.

TABLE 5.1

MALE AND FEMALE MURDER PERPETRATORS AS A PERCENTAGE OF ALL ARRESTS FOR HOMICIDE 1960–1993

1960		*1975*		*1980*		*1993*	
Male	*Female*	*Male*	*Female*	*Male*	*Female*	*Male*	*Female*
82.5%	17.5%	84.7%	15.3%	87.2%	12.8%	90.6%	9.4%

Source: Adapted from Federal Bureau of Investigation, *Crime in the United States*, (Washington, D.C.: U.S. Department of Justice, 1961, 1976, 1981, and 1994).

A much larger twin study[64] was conducted in 1968 by the European researchers Karl Christiansen and Sarnoff Mednick, who analyzed all twins (3,586 pairs) born on a selected group of Danish Islands between 1881 and 1910. Christiansen and Mednick found significant statistical support for the notion that criminal tendencies are inherited, and concluded that 52% of identical twins and 22% of fraternal siblings displayed the same degree of criminality within the twin pair. Such similarities remained apparent even among twins who had been separated at birth and who were raised in substantially different environments.

Male-Female Differences in Criminality

A number of writers unequivocally recognize that "the male is much more criminalistic than the female."[65] As Chapter 2 describes, with the exception of crimes such as prostitution and shoplifting, the number of crimes committed by males routinely far exceeds the number of crimes committed by females in almost any category. The data on the extent of male-female criminality show surprising regularity over time. The proportion of homicides committed by males versus females, for example, has remained more or less constant for decades (see Table 5.1). In fact, as the table shows and contrary to popular expectations, *male* perpetrators appear to be involved in an ever-larger proportion of murders over the past thirty-five years. Similarly, the proportion of men murdered by men versus the proportion of women murdered by women has continuously shown a much larger propensity for men to murder one another.

If culture exercises the major role in determining criminality, as many social scientists today suggest, then we would expect to see recognizable increases in the degree and nature of female criminality over time, especially as changes in socialization practices, cultural roles, and other ethnographic patterns increase the opportunity for women to commit what had previously been regarded as traditionally male offenses. With the exception of a few crimes, such as embezzlement, drug abuse, and liquor law violations, however, such has not been the case. While women comprise 51% of the population of the United States, they are arrested for only 13% of all violent crimes and 26% of property crimes[66]—a proportion that has remained surprisingly constant over the years since the FBI began gathering crime data more than half a century ago. Simply put, even with all of the cultural changes which have created new possibilities for women in crime, few women have taken advantage of these new found freedoms. Such apparent differences have existed not only over time, but can be seen in cross-cultural studies as well. Chapter 2 provides additional statistics of this sort.

Such findings are in contrast with the suggestions of authors such as Freda Adler, who in her 1975 book *Sisters in Crime*,[67] proposed that as women entered "nontraditional occupations" and roles, there "would be a movement toward parity with men in the commission of crime in terms of both incidence and type." Darrell Steffensmeir,[68] who studied changes in women's criminality over a twelve-year period following publication of Adler's book, found almost no evidence to support the belief that a new female criminal is emerging, or that female criminality is undergoing the kind of increase Adler might have expected. The lack of contemporary validation for Adler's thesis suggests that something else is occurring, that is, that some element other than cultural inhibition or equality of opportunity is preventing women from taking their place alongside men as equals in crime. Biological criminologists suggest that the organic correlates of gender provide the needed explanation.

In evaluating the criminality of women based upon statistics alone, however, there is always the danger of misidentifying causal factors operative in the behavior itself. While men consistently commit more murders than women, for example, we should not jump to the conclusion that this bit of evidence shows a genetic predisposition toward interpersonal violence in men which is absent in women. To do so would fail to recognize the role of other causal factors. Observable racial variation in crime rates has provided some writers with a basis for claiming that some racial groups are disproportionately violent—while simultaneously attributing such violence to a genetic basis. A look at the statistics, for example, shows that in the United States blacks are five times as likely as whites to commit murder, three times as likely to commit rape, six times as likely to rob, and twice as likely, on average, to commit any kind of crime.[69] Chapter 2 provides additional statistics of this sort.

Such statistics can be inherently misleading because—unlike the undeniable and easily observable biological differences which exist between men and women—racial groupings are defined more by convention than by genetics. In fact, some writers suggest that "pure" racial groups no longer exist, and that even historical racial distinctions were based more upon political convention than significant genetic differences.

The criminality of women (or relative lack thereof) is, in all likelihood, culturally determined to a considerable degree. Nonetheless, the consistency of data which routinely show that women are far less likely than men to be involved in most property crimes, and less likely still to commit violent crimes, requires recognition. We have already evaluated the role which testosterone may play in increasing the propensity toward violence and aggression among males. A few authors suggest that testosterone is the agent primarily responsible for male criminality, and that its relative lack in women leads them to commit fewer crimes. Some evidence supports just such a hypothesis. Studies[70] have shown, for example, that female fetuses exposed to elevated testosterone levels during gestation develop masculine characteristics, including a muscular body build and a demonstrably greater tendency toward aggression later in life. Even so, genetically based behavioral differences between males and females are so overshadowed by aspects of the social environment, including socialization, the learning of culturally prescribed roles, the expectations of others, and so on, that definitive conclusions are difficult to reach.

Sociobiology

In the introduction to his insightful article[71] summarizing sociobiology, Arthur Fisher writes "[e]very so often, in the long course of scientific progress, a new set of ideas appears, illuminating and redefining what has gone before like a flare bursting over a darkened landscape." To some, **sociobiology—**a theoretical synthesis of biology, behavior, and evolutionary ecology—brought to the scientific community by **Edward O. Wilson** in his seminal 1975 work *Sociobiology: The New Synthesis,*[72] holds the promise of just such a new paradigm. In his book, Wilson defined sociobiology as "the systematic study of the biological basis of all social behavior" and as "a branch of evolutionary biology and particularly of modern population biology." Through his entomological study of social insects, especially ants, Wilson demonstrated that particular forms of behavior could contribute to the long-term survival of the social group. Wilson focused on altruism (selfless, helping behavior) and found that, contrary to the beliefs of some evolutionary biologists, helping behavior facilitates the continuity of the gene pool found

Sociobiology the systematic study of the biological basis of all social behavior.

Sociobiologists tell us that certain traits, such as territoriality, are common to both animals and humans. *Paul Lally/Stock Boston*

among altruistic individuals. Wilson's major focus was to show that the primary determinant of behavior, including human behavior, was the need to ensure the survival and continuity of genetic material from one generation to the next. Territoriality, another primary tenant of Wilson's writings, was said to explain much of the conflict seen between and among human beings, including homicide, warfare, and other forms of aggression. In Wilson's words, "[p]art of man's problem is that his intergroup responses are still crude and primitive, and inadequate for the extended extraterritorial relationships that civilization has thrust upon him. The "unhappy result," as Wilson terms it, may be "tribalism," expressed through the contemporary proliferation of street gangs, racial tension, and the hardened encampments of survivalist and separatist groups such as David Koresh's Branch Davidians.

Wilson writes that his theory "suggests that a particularly severe form of aggressiveness should be reserved for actual or suspected adultery. In many human societies," he observes, "where sexual bonding is close and personal knowledge of the behavior of others detailed, adulterers are harshly treated. The sin," he adds, "is regarded to be even worse when offspring are produced."[73] Hence, territoriality and acquisitiveness extend, from a sociobiological perspective, to location, possessions, and even other people. Human laws are designed to protect genetically based relationships which people have with one another, their material possessions, and their claimed locations in space. Violations of these intuitive relationships result in crime, and in official reactions by the legal system.

Wilson's writing propelled researchers into a flurry of studies intended to test the validity of his assertions. One study,[74] for example, found that Indian adult male Hanuman langurs (a type of monkey) routinely killed the young offspring of females with whom they bonded whenever those offspring had been sired by other males. A Canadian study[75] of violence in the homes of adoptive children found a human parallel in the langur study, showing that stepchildren run a seventy times greater risk of being killed by their adoptive parent(s) than do children living with their natural parents. Some writers concluded that "murderous behavior, warfare, and even genocide were unavoidable correlates of genetic evolution, controlled by the same genes for territorial behavior that had been selected in primate evolution."[76] Others suggested that biological predispositions developed during earlier stages of human evolution color contemporary criminal activity. Males, for example, tend toward robbery and burglary—crimes in which men can continue to enact their "hunter instincts" developed long ago. The criminality of women, on the other hand, is more typical of "gatherers" when it involves shoplifting, simple theft, and so on.

Human behavioral predilections can be studied in a variety of ways. In the 1989 book *Evolutionary Jurisprudence*,[77] John H. Beckstrom reports upon his examination of over four hundred legal documents which, he claimed, showed support for Wilson's contentions that humans tend to act so as to preserve territorial claims, the likelihood of successful reproduction, and the continuation of their own particular genetic material. Beckstrom used legal claims and court decisions in his analysis, spanning over three hundred years of judicial activity. Other theorists have gone so far as to imply that, among human beings, there may be a gene-based tendency to experience guilt and to develop a conscience. Hence, notions of right and wrong, whether embodied in laws or in social convention, may flow from such a naturalistic origin.

As sociobiology began to receive expanded recognition from American investigators, some social scientists, believing the basic tenants of their profession to be challenged by the movement, began to treat it as "criminology's anti-discipline."[78] John Madison Memory writes, "[b]y the early 1980s sociobiology presented such a significant threat to American criminology that it could no longer be ignored."[79] Criticisms were quick to come. Memory identifies many such critiques, including charges that

- "Sociobiology...fails to convey the overwhelming significance of culture, social learning, and individual experiences in shaping the behavior of individuals and groups."
- "Sociobiology is fundamentally wrong in its depiction of the basic nature of man; there is no credible evidence of genetically based or determined tendencies to act in certain ways."
- "Sociobiology is just another empirically unsupported rationale for the authoritative labeling, stigmatization of despised, threatening, powerless minorities."
- "Man is so thoroughly different from other animal species, even other primates, that there is no rational basis for the application to man of findings from animal studies."

Many such criticisms were advanced by old guard academicians, some of whom still flourish, in an effort to prevent their own discipline's decline in influence in the face of otherwise convincing sociobiological claims. In the words of one observer, "[m]ost criminologists, like most academicians, were wedded to a **paradigm,** and wedded even to the idea of paradigm, the idea that one great problem solution can permit the explanation of nearly all the unexplained variation in the field."[80] In other words, many criminologists were committed to the idea that one theory (generally their own) could explain all that there was to know about crime and its causes. Fortunately, today many open-minded scholars are beginning to sense the growing need for a new synthesis—for a way in which to integrate the promise of biological theories such as sociobiology with other long-accepted perspectives like sociology and psychology. As a result, there is evidence that the field of criminology is now ripe for a new multicausal approach.

Paradigm an example, model, or theory.

CRIME AND HUMAN NATURE: A CONTEMPORARY SYNTHESIS

A decade ago Arnold L. Lieber[81] delivered the invited address at the annual meeting of the American Psychological Association in Denver, Colorado. Lieber used the forum to describe his research, which linked phases of the moon to fluctuations in the incidence of violence among human beings. Nights around full moons, according to Lieber, show a significant rise in crime. Although critics found this kind of research nonsensical, police officers, hospital personnel, ambulance drivers, and many late-night service providers who heard of Lieber's talk understood what he was describing. Many such individuals, in their own experience, had apparently seen validation of the "full moon thesis."

Shortly after Lieber's presentation, criminologist **James Q. Wilson** and psychologist **Richard J. Herrnstein** teamed up to write *Crime and Human Nature,*[82] a book-length treatise that reiterates many of the arguments proposed by biological criminologists over the past century. Their purpose, at least in part, was to reopen discussion of biological causes of crime. "We want to show," Herrnstein said, "that the pendulum is beginning to swing away from a totally sociological explanation of crime."[83] Their avowed goal was "not to state a case just for genetic factors, but to state a comprehensive theory of crime that draws together all the different factors that cause criminal behavior."

Constitutional factors which Wilson and Herrnstein cite as contributing to crime include[84]

- *Gender:* "Crime," the authors say, "has been predominantly male behavior."
- *Age:* "In general," they write, "the tendency to break the law declines throughout life."
- *Body Type:* "A disproportionate number of criminals," the authors say, "have a mesomorphic build."
- *Intelligence:* Criminality is said to be clearly and consistently associated with low intelligence.
- *Personality:* Criminals are typically aggressive, impulsive, and cruel, according to Wilson and Herrnstein.

While personality, behavioral problems, and intelligence may be related to environment, the authors say, "each involve some genetic inheritance." Although Wilson and Herrnstein recognize social factors in the development of personality, they suggest that constitutional factors predispose a person to specific types of behavior, and that societal reactions to such predispositions may determine, to a large degree, the form of continued behavior. Hence, the interplay between heredity, biology, and the social environment may be the key nexus in any consideration of crime causation.

POLICY ISSUES

Biological theories of crime causation present unique challenges to policy makers. According to C. Ray Jeffery, a comprehensive biologically based program of crime prevention and crime control would include

- "Pre- and postnatal care for pregnant women and their infants," to monitor and address potentially detrimental developmental conditions which could lead to heightened aggression and crime later in life.
- Monitoring of children throughout the early stages of their development to identify "early symptoms of behavioral disorder."
- Monitoring of children in their early years to reduce the risk of exposure to violence-inducing experiences such as child abuse and violence committed by other children.
- Neurological examinations, including "CAT, PETT, and MRI scans...given when the need is evident."
- Biological research, conducted in our nation's prisons and treatment facilities, which might better identify the root causes of aggression and violence. Laws that prevent the experimental use of prison subjects, the analysis of the bodies of executed prisoners, and other similar types of biological investigations must change, says Jeffery.[85]

Jeffery adds that the fundamental orientation of our legal system must change so as to acknowledge contributions of biological criminologists. Such a change would replace or supplement our current "right to punishment" doctrine with a "right to treatment" philosophy. Jeffery concludes his analysis by saying, "[i]f legal and political barriers prevent us from regarding antisocial behavior as a medical problem, and if we do not permit medical research on criminal behavior, how can we ever solve the crime problem?"[86]

The dangers of an overly large dependence on biological approaches to crime, however, raise the specter of a *1984*-type bogey man in charge of every aspect of human social life, from conception to the grave—and include the possible abortion of defective fetuses, capital punishment in lieu of rehabilitation, and enforced sterilization. Precedent for such fears can be found in cases such as *Buck* v. *Bell*,[87] discussed earlier in this chapter, in which the U.S. Supreme Court, influenced by genetically based perspectives of the times, sanctioned state-enforced sterilization statutes.

Potential links between race and crime, suggested by some researchers, are especially repugnant to many who criticize biological criminology. Ronald Walters, a political scientist at Howard University, observes, "[s]eeking the biological and genetic aspects of violence is dangerous to African-American youth.... When you consider the perception that black people have always been the violent people in this society, it is a short step from this stereotype to using this kind of research for social control."[88] According to Gary LaFree and Katheryn K. Russell, "a major reason for moving away from studies of differential crime rates by race, beginning in the 1960s, was to avoid negative associations between race and crime: blacks already were disadvantaged by the economy and the society. Thus, to imply that crime problems were more serious for blacks than for others seemed to be double victimization."[89] Yet, these same authors add, "[n]o group has suffered more than African-Americans by our failure to understand and control street crime."

While biological theories of crime may have problems, to ignore the potential contributions of biological theorists because of hypothetical policy consequences, or because of the supposed danger of racial prejudice, does a disservice to the science of criminology and denies the opportunity for compassionate and objective researchers to realistically assist in the process of crime reduction. In 1993, for example, The Youth Violence Initiative, begun under President Bush to study problem behavior among American youth, was canceled by the Clinton administration because indications were it that it might identify a disproportionate number of racial and ethnic minorities as delinquent. Such head-in-the-sand science does no one any good in the long run, although it may temporarily appease selected political constituencies.

CRITIQUES OF BIOLOGICAL THEORIES

An excellent contemporary critique of biological perspectives on crime causation is provided by Glenn D. Walters and Thomas W. White,[90] who contend that "genetic research on crime has been poorly designed, ambiguously reported, and exceedingly inadequate in addressing the relevant issues." Walters and White highlight the following specific shortcomings of studies in the area:

- Few biological studies adequately conceptualize of criminality. "Several studies," they say, "have defined criminality on the basis of a single arrest."
- Twin studies, in particular, have sometimes failed to properly establish "whether a pair of twins is monozygotic (MZ) or dizygotic (DZ)." This is because some MZ twins are not identical in appearance, and only a few twin studies have depended upon biological testing rather than a simple evaluation of appearances.
- Problems in estimating the degree of criminality among sample populations are rife in biological (and in many other) studies of criminality. Interview data are open to interpretation and existing statistical data on the past criminality of offenders are not always properly appreciated.
- Methodological problems abound in many studies which attempt to evaluate the role of genetics in crime. Walters and White mention, among other things, the lack of control or comparison groups, small sample sizes, the dropping out of subjects from study groups, biased sampling techniques, and the use of inappropriate forms of statistical analysis.
- Results obtained outside of the United States may not have applicability within this country. Twin studies conducted in Sweden and Denmark provide an example of this potential lack of generalizability.

Walters and White, nonetheless, conclude that "[g]enetic factors are undoubtedly correlated with various measures of criminality," but add that "the large number of methodological flaws and limitations in the research should make one cautious in drawing any causal inferences at this point in time."[91]

SUMMARY

Contemporary criminology has shown considerable reluctance to adapt the contributions of biological theories to an understanding of criminality. An objective understanding of any social phenomenon, however, requires clear consideration of all available evidence. Modern proponents of biological perspectives on crime and crime causation point out that the link between the social environment and human behavior is continuously mediated by the physical brain. Human activity flows from the human mind, and the mind is biologically grounded in the brain. The brain itself is apparently subject to influences from other aspects of the body, such as hormones, neurotransmitters, and the levels of various chemicals in the blood. Such realizations require only a small intellectual leap to the realization that other biological aspects of the human organism may play similar contributory roles in criminal behavior.

Unfortunately, however, for proponents of biological theories which seek to explain crime, the influence of the environment upon human behavior appears to be nearly overpowering, and studies purporting to have identified biological determinants of behavior have been thoroughly criticized on methodological and other grounds. For the time being, we must draw the conclusion that while biology provides both a context for, and specific precursors to, human behavior, biological predispositions for behavior in most instances of human interaction are routinely overshadowed by the role of volition, the mechanisms of human thought, and the undeniable influences of socialization and acculturation. Even so, any comprehensive approach to human behavior must give due recognition to the biological precursors of behavior itself.

DISCUSSION QUESTIONS

1. What are the central features of biological theories of crime? How do such theories differ from other perspectives that attempt to explain the same phenomena?
2. Why have biological approaches to crime causation been out of vogue? Do you agree or disagree with those critical of such perspectives? Why or why not?
3. What does the author of this book mean when he writes, "[o]pen inquiry requires objective consideration of all points of view, and an examination of each for their ability to shed light upon the subject under study." Do you agree or disagree with that assertion? Why?
4. What are the social policy implications of biological theories of crime? What U.S. Supreme Court case, discussed in this chapter, might presage a type of policy based upon such theories?

NOTES

1 Karen J. Winkler, "Criminals Are Born as Well as Made, Authors of Controversial Book Assert," *Chronicle of Higher Education,* January 16, 1986, p. 9.
2. Anastasia Toufexis, "Seeking the Roots of Violence," *Time,* April 19, 1993, p. 52.
3. As cited in David Jones, *History of Criminology: A Philosophical Perspective* (Westport, CT: Greenwood Press, 1986), p. 1.
4. For a detailed description of the life of Robert H. Moormann, see John C. C'Anna, "Robert Henry Moormann," *Police,* April 1992, pp. 50–54, 86–88.
5. C. Ray Jeffery, "Biological Perspectives," *Journal of Criminal Justice Education,"* Vol. 4, no. 2 (Fall 1993), pp. 292–293.
6. C. Ray Jeffery, "Genetics, Crime and the Canceled Conference," *The Criminologist,* Vol. 18, no. 1 (January/February 1993), pp. 1–8.
7. Anastasia Toufexis, "Seeking the Roots of Violence," *Time,* April 19, 1993, p. 53.
8. Jeffery, "Biological Perspectives," p. 298.
9. Konrad Lorenz, *On Aggression* (New York: Harcourt, Brace & World, 1966).
10. Ibid., p. 23.
11. Ibid., p. 38.
12. Ibid., p. 249.
13. Ibid., p. 225.
14. Cesare Lombroso, "Introduction," in Gina Lombroso-Ferrero, *Criminal Man According to the Classification of Cesare Lombroso,* 1911; reprinted Montclair, NJ, 1972 by Patterson Smith, p. xiv.
15. Charles Darwin, *Descent of Man: And Selection in Relation to Sex,* revised edition (London: John Murray, 1874), p. 137
16. Lombroso, "Introduction," in Lombroso-Ferrero, *Criminal Man According to the Classification of Cesare Lombroso,* p. xv.
17. As cited in Hermann Mannheim, *Pioneers in Criminology,* 2nd ed. (Montclair, NJ: Patterson Smith, 1972), p. 29.
18. *Della Fossetta Cerebellare Mediana in un Criminale,* Institute Lombardo di Scienze e Lettere, 1872, pp. 1058–1065, as cited and translated by Thorsten Sellin, "A New Phase of Criminal Anthropology in Italy," *The Annals of the American Academy of Political and Social Science, Modern Crime,* 525 (May 1926), p. 234.
19. The English language version appeared in 1895 as Cesare Lombroso, *The Female Offender* (New York: D. Appleton & Co., 1895).
20. Marvin Wolfgang, "Cesare Lombroso," in Hermann Mannheim, *Pioneers in Criminology,* 2nd ed. (Montclair, NJ: Patterson Smith, 1972), p. 254.
21. Charles Goring, *The English Convict: A Statistical Study* (London: His Majesty's Stationary Office, 1913). Reprinted in 1972 by Patterson Smith, Montclair, NJ, p. 15.
22. Ibid.
23. Earnest A. Hooton, *Crime and the Man* (Cambridge, MA: Harvard University Press, 1939), reprinted by Greenwood Press, Westport, CT, 1972.
24. Ibid., pp. 57–58.
25. Ibid., p. 72.
26. Ibid., p.75.
27. Ibid., p. 388.
28. Ernest A. Hooton, *The American Criminal: An Anthropological Study* (Cambridge, MA: Harvard University Press, 1939).
29. Stephen Schafer, *Theories in Criminology: Past and Present Philosophies of the Crime Problem* (New York: Random House, 1969), p. 187.
30. William H. Sheldon, *Varieties of Delinquent Youth* (New York: Harper & Brothers, 1949).
31. D. Hill and W. Sargent, "A Case of Matricide," *Lancet,* Vol. 244 (1943) pp. 526–527.
32. Nanci Hellmich, "Sweets May Not Be Cul-

prit in Hyper Kids," *USA Today*, February 3, 1994, p. 1A, reporting on a study reported in the *New England Journal of Medicine.*

33. Ibid., p. 1A.
34. See, for example, A. R. Mawson and K. J. Jacobs, "Corn Consumption, Tryptophan, and Cross National Homicide Rates," *Journal of Orthomolecular Psychiatry*, Vol. 7 (1978), pp. 227–230; and A. Hoffer, "The Relation of Crime to Nutrition," *Humanist in Canada*, Vol. 8 (1975), p. 8.
35. See, for example, C. Hawley and R. E. Buckley, "Food Dyes and Hyperkinetic Children," *Academy Therapy*, Vol. 10 (1974), pp. 27–32, and Alexander Schauss, *Diet, Crime & Delinquency* (Berkeley, CA: Parker House, 1980).
36. "Special Report: Measuring Your Life with Coffee Spoons," *Tufts University Diet & Nutrition Letter*, Vol. 2, no. 2 (April 1984), pp. 3–6.
37. See, for example, "Special Report: Does What You Eat Affect Your Mood and Actions?" *Tufts University Diet & Nutrition Letter*, Vol. 2, no. 12 (February 1985), pp. 4–6.
38. See *Tufts University Diet & Nutrition Newsletter*, Vol. 2, no. 11 (January 1985), p. 2, and "Special Report: Why Sugar Continues to Concern Nutritionists," *Tufts University Diet & Nutrition Letter*, Vol. 3, no. 3 (May 1985), pp. 3–6.
39. A. Hoffer, "Children with Learning and Behavioral Disorders," *Journal of Orthomolecular Psychiatry*, Vol. 5 (1976), p. 229.
40. "Special Report: Does What You Eat Affect Your Mood and Actions?" *Tufts University Diet & Nutrition Letter*, Vol. 2, no. 12 (February 1985), p. 4.
41. See, for example, R. T. Rada, D. R. Laws, and R. Kellner, "Plasma Testosterone Levels in the Rapist," *Psychomatic Medicine*, Vol. 38 (1976), pp. 257–268.
42. "The Insanity of Steroid Abuse," *Newsweek*, May 23, 1988, p. 75.
43. Dan Olweus, Mattsson Ake, Daisy Schalling, and Hans Low, "Testosterone, Aggression, Physical and Personality Dimensions in Normal Adolescent Males," *Psychosomatic Medicine*, Vol. 42 (1980), pp. 253–269.
44. Richard Udry, "Biosocial Models of Adolescent Problem Behaviors," *Social Biology*, Vol. 37 (1990), pp. 1–10.
45. Dan Olweus, "Testosterone and Adrenaline: Aggressive Antisocial Behavior in Normal Adolescent Males," in Sarnoff A. Mednick, Terrie E. Moffitt, and Susan A. Stack, *The Causes of Crime: New Biological Approaches* (Cambridge: Cambridge University Press, 1987), pp. 263–282.
46. Alan Booth and D. Wayne Osgood, "The Influence of Testosterone on Deviance in Adulthood: Assessing and Explaining the Relationship," *Criminology*, Vol. 31, no. 1 (1993), pp. 93–117.
47. Ibid., p. 93.
48. Ibid.
49. Richard Udry, Luther Talbert, and Naomi Morris, "Biosocial Foundations for Adolescent Female Sexuality," *Demography*, Vol. 23 (1986), pp. 217–227.
50. "Drunk Driving Charge Dismissed: PMS Cited," The *Fayetteville Observer-Times* (North Carolina), June 7, 1991, p. 3A.
51. Anastasia Toufexis, "Seeking the Roots of Violence," *Time*, April 19, 1993, pp. 52–54.
52. Richard Louis Dugdale, *The Jukes: A Study in Crime, Pauperism, Disease, and Heredity*, 3rd ed. (New York: G. P. Putnam's Sons, 1895).
53. Arthur H. Estabrook, *The Jukes in 1915* (Washington, D.C: Carnegie Institute of Washington, 1916).
54. Henry Herbert Goddard, *The Kallikak Family: A Study in the Heredity of Feeble-mindedness* (New York: Macmillan, 1912).
55. *Buck* v. *Bell*, 274 U.S. 200, 207 (1927).
56. P. A. Jacobs, M. Brunton, and M. Melville, "Aggressive Behavior, Mental Subnormality, and the XXY Male," *Nature*, Vol. 208 (1965), p. 1351.

57. Biologists often define "karyotype" as "a photomicrograph of metaphase chromosomes in a standard array." The process of karyotyping typically involves drawing a small sample of blood.
58. See David A. Jones, *History of Criminology: A Philosophical Perspective* (Westport, CT: Greenwood Press, 1986), p. 124.
59. Many of which have been summarized in J. Katz and W. Chambliss, "Biology and Crime," in J. F. Sheley, ed., *Criminology* (Belmont, CA: Wadsworth, 1991), pp. 245–272.
60. As reported by S. A. Mednick and J. Volavka, "Biology and Crime," in N. Morris and M. Tonry, *Crime and Justice: An Annual Review of Research,* Vol. 2 (Chicago: University of Chicago Press, 1980), pp. 85–158, and D. A. Andrews and James Bonta, *The Psychology of Criminal Conduct* (Cincinnati: Anderson, 1994), pp. 126–127.
61. T. Sarbin and J. Miller, "Demonism Revisited: The XYY Chromosomal Anomaly," *Issues in Criminology,* Vol. 5 (1970), p. 199.
62. Geoffrey Cowley and Carol Hallin, "The Genetics of Bad Behavior: A Study Links Violence to Heredity," *Newsweek,* November 1, 1993, p. 57.
63. Johannes Lange, *Verbrechen als Schicksal* (Leipzig: Georg Thieme, 1929).
64. Karl O. Christiansen, "A Preliminary Study of Criminality Among Twins," in Sarnoff Mednick and Karl Christiansen, eds., *Biosocial Bases of Criminal Behavior* (New York: Gardner Press, 1977).
65. C. Ray Jeffery, "Biological Perspectives," *Journal of Criminal Justice Education,* Vol. 4, no. 2 (Fall 1993), p. 300.
66. Federal Bureau of Investigation, *Crime in the United States, 1993* (Washington, D.C.: U.S. Department of Justice, 1994).
67. Freda Adler, *Sisters in Crime: The Rise of the New Female Criminal* (New York: McGraw-Hill, 1975).
68. Darrell J. Steffensmeir, "Sex Differences in Patterns of Adult Crime, 1965–1977: A Review and Assessment," *Social Forces,* Vol. 58 (1980), pp. 1098–1099.
69. Federal Bureau of Investigation, *Crime in the United States, 1991* (Washington, D.C.: U.S. Department of Justice, 1992), as computed from Table 43, "Total Arrests, Distribution by Race, 1992," p. 237.
70. See, for example, D. H. Fishbein, "The Psychobiology of Female Aggression," *Criminal Justice and Behavior,* Vol. 19 (1992), pp. 99–126.
71. Arthur Fisher, "A New Synthesis Comes of Age," *Mosaic,* Vol. 22, no. 1 (Spring 1991), pp. 2–9.
72. Edward O. Wilson, *Sociobiology: The New Synthesis* (Cambridge, MA: The Belknap Press of Harvard University Press, 1975).
73. Ibid., p. 327.
74. Sarah Blaffer Hrdy, *The Langurs of Abu: Female and Male Strategies of Reproduction* (Cambridge, MA: Harvard University Press, 1977).
75. Research by Martin Daly and Margo Wilson of McMaster University in Hamilton Canada, as reported in Arthur Fisher, "A New Synthesis II: How Different Are Humans?" *Mosaic,* Vol. 22, no. 1 (Spring 1991), p. 14.
76. Arthur Fisher, "A New Synthesis II: How Different Are Humans?" *Mosaic,* Vol. 22, no. 1 (Spring 1991), p. 11.
77. John H. Beckstrom, *Evolutionary Jurisprudence: Prospects and Limitations on the Youth of Modern Darwinism Throughout the Legal Process* (Urbana, IL: University of Illinois Press, 1989).
78. John Madison Memory, "Sociobiology and the Metamorphoses of Criminology: 1978–2000," unpublished manuscript.
79. Ibid., p. 11.
80. Ibid., p. 33.
81. See, also, Arnold. L. Lieber, *The Lunar Effect: Biological Tides and Human Emotions* (Garden City: Anchor Press, 1978).
82. James Q. Wilson and Richard J. Herrnstein, *Crime and Human Nature* (New York: Simon & Schuster, 1985).
83. Karen J. Winkler, "Criminals Are Born as Well as Made, Authors of Controversial Book Assert," *The Chronicle of Higher Education,* January 16, 1986, p. 5.
84. Ibid., p. 8.

85. Jeffery, "Biological Perspectives," p. 303.
86. Ibid.
87. *Buck* v. *Bell*, 274 U.S. 200, 207 (1927).
88. *Time*, April 19, 1993, p. 53.
89. Gary LaFree and Katheryn K. Russell, "The Argument for Studying Race and Crime," *Journal of Criminal Justice Education*, Vol. 4, no. 2 (Fall 1993), p. 279.
90. Glenn D. Walters and Thomas W. White, "Heredity and Crime: Bad Genes or Bad Research?" *Criminology*, Vol. 27, no. 3 (1989), pp. 455–485. See, also, P. A. Brennan and S. A. Mednick, "Reply to Walters and White: Heredity and Crime," *Criminology*, Vol. 28, no. 4 (November 1990), pp. 657–661.
91. Ibid., p. 478.

CHAPTER 6

PSYCHOLOGICAL AND PSYCHIATRIC FOUNDATIONS OF CRIMINAL BEHAVIOR

Question: "When you put the shotgun up against her left cheek and pulled the trigger, did you love your mother?"

Answer: "Yes."

—*Lyle Menendez, testifying at his trial on charges that he and his brother killed their parents.*[1]

Society secretly *wants* crime, *needs* crime, and gains definite satisfactions from the present mishandling of it! We condemn crime; we punish offenders for it; but we need it. The crime and punishment ritual is part of our lives!

—*Karl Menninger*[2]

IMPORTANT NAMES AND CASES

Sigmund Freud
Hervey Cleckley
B. F. Skinner
Albert Bandura
Hans Eysenck
Foucha v. *Louisiana*

IMPORTANT TERMS

correctional psychology
dangerousness
psychopath
psychopathology
psychological theories
sociopath
alloplastic adaptation
autoplastic adaptation
neurosis
psychosis
antisocial personality
asocial personality
conditioning
id
ego
superego
psychotherapy
sublimation
paranoid schizophrenic
schizophrenics
electroencephalogram (EEG)
psychiatric criminology
social learning theory
behavior theory
forensic psychiatry
psychoanalysis
Thanatos
operant behavior
reward
punishment
psychological profiling
insanity
McNaughten rule
irresistible impulse test
Durham rule
substantial capacity test
guilty but mentally ill
selective incapacitation

INTRODUCTION

On July 22, 1991 a handcuffed man flagged down a police car in suburban Milwaukee.[3] Officers soon learned that the man was Tracy Edwards, a 32-year-old city resident. The lurid story of homosexual abuse and physical attack that Edwards told led investigators to the apartment of a 31-year-old loner named Jeffrey Dahmer. Dahmer was quickly arrested, and a search of his apartment revealed the body parts of at least eleven people. In a confession to police, Dahmer told of how he had repeatedly lured men to his apartment, murdered them, and then dismembered their bodies. Soon police investigations implicated Dahmer in a ten-year killing spree which spanned several states and may have reached as far as Europe. Edwards, whom Dahmer had met in a shopping mall, explained that he went to Dahmer's apartment because, "He (Dahmer) seemed so normal."[4] Sadly, one of Dahmer's victims, a 15-year-old boy, had been earlier discovered by police dazed and bleeding—and was returned to Dahmer's apartment after officers concluded that the situation involved nothing but a dispute between homosexual lovers. Although Dahmer pleaded insane as a defense to charges of murder, an expert witness at his trial, psychiatrist Park Dietz, testified that although Dahmer suffered from various psychological disorders, he could have chosen not to kill. Comparing Dahmer's sexual desires with someone who wants money but chooses not to rob, Dietz said, "[t]he choice is exactly the same.... The freedom to make it is exactly the same."[5] In contrasting testimony, another expert witness claimed that Dahmer "had uncontrollable urges to kill and have sex with dead bodies...."[6] Dahmer was

15A - CB - Dahmer

Jeffrey Dahmer, perhaps the most infamous serial killer of the twentieth century. *Milwaukee Journal/Sipa Press.*

sentenced to fifteen consecutive life terms—one each for the murders of fifteen men[7]—but was himself murdered by another inmate in November 1994.

Murder appears to be occurring with increasing frequency throughout the United States. A few years ago, for example, Texan Donald Leroy Evans admitted killing 10-year-old Beatrice Louise Routh.[8] The young girl's homeless mother had given Evans permission to take Beatrice shopping. Soon after his capture however, Evans—a parolee—confessed to sixty killings and became a suspect in America's worst serial murder case. His arrest came one month before Aileen Wuornos, whom investigators have called the "nation's first true female serial killer," was scheduled to be tried in Florida for killing seven men who had offered her rides and two months before a gunman smashed a pickup truck through the front window of a Texas cafeteria and shot 31 lunchgoers to death. Although Wuornos, an admitted prostitute, claimed self-defense, many suggested that a long-festering hatred of men drove her to kill them.

In 1994, a case which made headlines around the world found Manassas, Virginia, housewife Lorena Bobbitt being tried on charges of malicious wounding for admittedly severing her allegedly philandering husband's penis with one stroke from a sharp kitchen knife while he slept. Bobbitt drove away with the severed organ still clutched in her fist, and threw it out of her car window onto a grassy field some distance from the couple's apartment. Rescue workers recovered the organ in a predawn search, and it was reattached during $9\frac{1}{2}$ hours of microvascular surgery.[9] In defense of her actions she later accused her husband, John, of marital rape. Although he was arrested and charged with raping his wife, a jury voted 12 to 0 to acquit him of all charges.[10]

On the morning immediately following the mutilation, Mrs. Bobbitt had told police that her husband "always [has] an orgasm and he doesn't wait for me.... I don't think it's fair, so I pulled back the sheets and I did it." The prosecutor in the case, sounding very much like a pop-psychologist, explained Mrs. Bobbitt's actions to the jury in these words, "[w]hy did she cut his penis off? Something happened...that drove her over the edge. If this was sheer jealousy, she'd have cut his throat. But what did she attack?...The very thing that wounded her."

Finally, in a very violent incident which, at the time, helped to further the interests of social responsibility advocates in pending federal crime control legislation, six people were shot to death, and another nineteen wounded aboard a Long Island, New York, commuter train near Christmastime in 1993 by Colin Ferguson, a disgruntled Jamaican immigrant. Ferguson, who moved through the train firing as many as forty shots from his semiautomatic handgun, was apparently motivated to commit mass murder by a hatred of white people, whom he blamed for numerous personal failures and other disappointments.[11] Ferguson's actions were explained by Judy Louis, a psychologist at St. John's University in New York City, as the result of a rare delusional disorder. "People who suffer from this [disorder] appear to be rational," said Louis, "except for this delusion they have. The delusion is their focal point." Louis added that people who suffer from the disorder can be difficult to detect. "They can go to the store, they can talk to people and seem perfectly rational."[12]

What motivates people to kill or maim—or to commit other, less serious offenses? How can many killers "seem so normal" before their crimes—giving no hints of the atrocities they are about to commit? Serial killer, mass murderer, sexual mutilator, even book thief—all must wrestle, before and after the criminal event, with their own personal demons. For answers to questions such as these many people turn to psychological theories. Psychologists are the pundits of the modern age of behaviorism—offering explanations rooted in determinants that lie within *individual actors.* Psychological determinants of deviant or criminal behavior may be couched in terms of exploitive personality characteristics, poor impulse control, emotional arousal, an immature personality, and so on. One contemporary source observes, "[t]he major sources of theoretical development in criminology have been—and continue to be—psychological. A theory of criminal conduct is weak indeed if uninformed by a general psychology of human behavior."[13]

What is the fundamental distinguishing feature of psychological approaches as opposed to other attempts to explain behavior? Criminologists Cathy Spatz and Hans Toch offer the following insight:[14] "...theories are psychological insofar as they focus on the individual as the unit of analysis. Thus any theory that is concerned with the behavior of individual offenders or which refers to forces or dynamics that motivate individuals to commit crimes would be considered to have a psychological component." Another writer, Curt Bartol, defines psychology as "the science of behavior and mental processes."[15] Bartol goes on to say that "[p]sychological criminology...is the science of the behavior and mental processes of the criminal." "[P]sychological criminology" says Bartol, "focuses on individual criminal behavior—how it is acquired, evoked maintained, and modified."

Psychological theories those derived from the behavioral sciences and which focus on the individual as the unit of analysis. Psychological theories place the locus of crime causation within the personality of the individual offender.

MAJOR PRINCIPLES OF PSYCHOLOGICAL THEORIES

This brief section serves to summarize the central features of **psychological theories** of crime causation. Each of these points can be found elsewhere in this chapter, where they are discussed in more detail. This cursory overview, however, is intended to provide more than a summary—it is meant to be a guide to the rest of this chapter.

Most psychological theories of crime causation make certain fundamental assumptions. Among them are

- The individual is the primary unit of analysis.
- Personality is the major motivational element within individuals, because it is the seat of drives and the source of motives.
- Crimes result from abnormal, dysfunctional, or inappropriate mental processes within the personality.
- Criminal behavior, while condemned by the social group, may be purposeful for the individual insofar as it addresses certain felt needs. Behavior can be judged "inappropriate" only when measured against external criteria purporting to establish normality.
- Normality is generally defined by social consensus—that is, what the majority of people in any social group agree is "real," appropriate, or typical.
- Defective, or abnormal, mental processes may have a variety of causes, including
  - A diseased mind.
  - Inappropriate learning or improper conditioning.
  - The emulation of inappropriate role models.
  - Adjustment to inner conflicts.

EARLY PSYCHOLOGICAL THEORIES

A twin thread wove through early psychological theories. One emphasized behavioral **conditioning,** while the other focused mostly on personality disturbances and diseases of the mind. Taken together, these two foci constituted the early field of psychological criminology. The concept of conditioned behavior was popularized through the work of the Russian physiologist Ivan Pavlov (1849–1936), whose work with dogs won him the Nobel Prize in physiology and medicine in 1904. The dogs, who salivated whenever food was presented to them, were always fed in the presence of a ringing bell. Soon, Pavlov found, the dogs would salivate, as if in preparation for eating, when the bell alone was rung—even when no food was present. Hence, salivation, an automatic response to the presence of food, could be conditioned to occur in response to some other stimulus—demonstrating that animal behavior could be predictably altered via association with external changes arising from the environment surrounding the organism.

Conditioning a psychological principle which holds that the frequency of any behavior can be increased or decreased through reward, punishment, and/or association with other stimuli.

The concept of **psychopathology,** or the diseased mind, is well summarized in the words of Nolan Lewis, who wrote during his tenure as director of the New York State Psychiatric Institute and Hospital at Columbia University during World War II that "[t]he criminal, like other people, has lived a life of instinctive drives, of desires, of wishes, of feelings, but one in which his intellect has apparently functioned less effectually as a brake upon certain trends. His constitutional makeup deviates toward the abnormal, leading him into conflicts with the laws of society and its cultural patterns."[16]

Psychopathology the study of pathological mental conditions, that is, mental illness.

The role of personality in crime causation is central to early psychological theorizing. In 1944, for example, the well-known psychiatrist David Abrahamsen wrote, "[w]hen we seek to explain the riddle of human conduct in general and of antisocial behavior in particular, the solution must be sought in the personality."[17] Psychopathological definitions of mental illness, however, have shown themselves to be sensitive to changes in cultural perspectives. In 1975, for example, the American Psychiatric Association dropped the classification of homosexuality as a mental disorder.

The Psychopathic Personality

Psychopath or sociopath
a person with a personality disorder, especially one manifested in aggressively antisocial behavior, which is often said to be the result of a poorly developed superego.

Eventually, psychologists developed the concept of a psychopathic personality. The **psychopath,** also called a **sociopath,** was viewed as perversely cruel—often without thought or feeling for his or her victims.

The concept of a psychopathic personality, which by its very definition is asocial, was fully developed by **Hervey Cleckley** in his 1964 book *The Mask of Sanity.*[18] Cleckley described the psychopath as a "moral idiot," or as one who does not feel empathy with others, even though he or she may be fully cognizant of what is objectively happening around them. The central defining characteristic of a psychopath is poverty of affect, or the inability to accurately imagine how others think and feel. Hence, it becomes possible for a psychopath to inflict pain and engage in cruelty without appreciation for the victim's suffering. Charles Manson, for example, whom some have called a psychopath, once told a television reporter, "I could take this book and beat you to death with it, and I wouldn't feel a thing. It'd be just like walking to the drugstore."

In *The Mask of Sanity* Cleckley describes numerous characteristics of the psychopathic personality. A few of them are

1. An absence of delusions, hallucinations, or other signs of psychosis.
2. The inability to feel guilt or shame.
3. Unreliability.
4. Chronic lying.
5. Superficial charm.
6. Above-average intelligence.
7. Ongoing antisocial behavior.
8. Inability to learn from experience.
9. Self-centeredness.

According to Cleckley, psychopathic indicators appear early in life, often in the teenage years. They include lying, fighting, stealing, and vandalism. Even earlier signs may be found, according to some authors, in bedwetting, cruelty to animals, sleep-walking, and fire-setting.[19]

While the terms "psychopath" and "criminal" are not synonymous, individuals manifesting many of the characteristics of a psychopathic personality are likely, sooner or later, to run afoul of the law. As one writer on the topic says, "[t]he impulsivity and aggression, the selfishness in achieving one's own immediate

Charles Manson. Manson achieved notoriety because he seemed so difficult to understand. *Bettmann.*

needs, and the disregard for society's rules and laws bring these people to the attention of the criminal justice system."[20]

The causes of psychopathology are unclear. Somatogenic causes, or those which are based upon physiological features of the human organism, are said to include a malfunctioning of the central nervous system characterized by a low state of arousal that drives the sufferer to seek excitement, and brain abnormalities that may have been present in most psychopaths since birth. Some studies show that **electroencephalograms (EEGs)** taken of psychopathic patients are frequently abnormal, reflecting "a malfunction of some...inhibitory mechanisms" that makes it unlikely the psychopath will "learn to inhibit behavior that is likely to lead to punishment."[21] It is difficult, however, to diagnose psychopathology through physiological measurements because similar EEG patterns show up in patients with other types of disorders as well. Psychogenic causes, or those rooted in early interpersonal experiences, are said to include the inability to form attachments to parents or other care-givers early in life, sudden separation from the mother during the first six months of life, and other forms of insecurity during the first few years of life. In short, a lack of love or the sensed inability to unconditionally depend upon one central loving figure (typically the mother in most psychological literature) immediately following birth is often posited as a major psychogenic factor contributing to psychopathic development. Other psychogenic causes have been identified to include deficiencies in childhood role playing, the inability to identify with one's parents during childhood and adolescence, and severe rejection by others.

Electroencephalogram (EEG) electrical measurements of brain wave activity.

Most studies of psychopaths have involved male subjects. Very little research has focused on female psychopaths, and it is believed that only a small proportion of all psychopaths are female.[22] What little research there is suggests that female psychopaths possess many of the same definitive characteristics as do their male coun-

THEORY IN PERSPECTIVE

Types of Psychological and Psychiatric Theories

PSYCHOLOGICAL AND PSYCHIATRIC THEORIES of criminology are derived from the behavioral sciences and focus on the *individual* as the unit of analysis.

PSYCHIATRIC CRIMINOLOGY, also known as **FORENSIC PSYCHIATRY.** Envisions a complex set of drives and motives operating from recesses deep within the personality to determine behavior.

Period: 1930s-Present
Theorists: Hervey Cleckley, many others
Concepts: Psychopath, sociopath, antisocial, asocial personality

PSYCHOANALYTIC CRIMINOLOGY. A psychiatric approach developed by the Austrian psychiatrist Sigmund Freud which emphasizes the role of personality in human behavior, and which sees deviant behavior as the result of dysfunctional personalities.

Period: 1920s-Present
Theorists: Sigmund Freud and others
Concepts: Id, ego, superego, sublimation, psychotherapy, Thanatos, neurosis, psychosis, schizophrenia

FRUSTRATION–AGGRESSION THEORY. Holds that frustration is a natural consequence of living and a root cause of crime. Criminal behavior can be a form of adaptation when it results in stress reduction.

Period: 1940s-Present
Theorists: J. Dollard, Albert Bandura, Richard H. Walters, S.M. Halleck
Concepts: Frustration, aggression, displacement, catharsis, alloplastic and autoplastic adaptation

SOCIAL LEARNING THEORY. A psychological perspective that says people learn how to behave by modeling themselves after others whom they have the opportunity to observe.

Period: 1950s-Present
Theorists: Albert Bandura and others
Concepts: Interpersonal aggression, modeling, disengagement

BEHAVIOR THEORY. A psychological perspective which posits that individual behavior which is rewarded will increase in frequency, while that which is punished will decrease.

Period: 1940s-Present
Theorists: B. F. Skinner and others
Concepts: Operant behavior, conditioning, stimulus-response, reward, punishment

terparts, and that they assume their psychopathic roles at similarly early ages.[23] The life-styles of female psychopaths, however, appear to emphasize sexual misconduct, including what have been described as abnormally high levels of sexual activity. Such research, however, can be misleading because cultural expectations of female sexual behavior inherent in early studies may have not always been in keeping with reality. That is, so little may have been accurately known about female sexual activity to early researchers that the behavior of females judged to be psychopaths may have actually been far closer to the norm than it was thought to be.

The terms sociopath and psychopath have fallen into professional disfavor in recent years. By 1968 the American Psychiatric Association's *Diagnostic and Statistical Manual of Mental Disorders*[24] had discontinued use of both terms, replacing them with jargon such as **antisocial** or **asocial personality**. In that year the APA manual changed to a description of the "antisocial personality" type as "individuals who are basically unsocialized and whose behavior pattern brings them repeatedly into conflicts with society. They are incapable of significant loyalty to individuals, groups, or social values. They are grossly selfish, callous, irresponsible, impulsive, and unable to feel guilt or to learn from experience and punishment. Frustration tolerance is low. They tend to blame others or offer plausible rationalization for their behavior."[25] Some recent studies,[26] which attempt to classify criminal offenders by type of mental disorder, have determined that antisocial personalities comprise 46.6% of all inmates, while schizophrenics account for 6.3%, manic-depressives another 1.6%, drug-disordered persons 18.6%, depressed individuals 8.1%, and alcohol abuse-related suffers another 33.1%. A review[27] of 20 such studies found great variation in the degree and type of disorders said to be prevalent among incarcerated offenders. The studies categorized from 0.5% to 26% of all inmates as psychotic, 2.4% to 28% as mentally subnormal, 5.6% to 70% as psychopathic, 2% to 7.9% as neurotic, and from 11% to 80% of inmates tested as suffering from mental disorders induced by alcoholism or excessive drinking. Generally, however, such studies conclude that few convicted felons are free from mental impairment of one sort or another.

Antisocial or asocial personality refers to individuals who are basically unsocialized and whose behavior brings them repeatedly into conflict with society.

Personality Types and Crime

In 1964 **Hans Eysenck,** a British psychiatrist, published *Crime and Personality,*[28] a book-length treatise, in which he explained crime as the result of fundamental personality characteristics linked to individual central nervous system characteristics. Eysenck described three personality dimensions, each with links to criminality. Psychoticism, which Eysenck said "is believed to be correlated with criminality at all stages,"[29] is defined by characteristics such as a lack of empathy, creativeness, tough-mindedness, and antisociability. Psychoticism, said Eysenck, is also frequently characterized by hallucinations and delusions. Extroverts were described as carefree, dominant, and venturesome—operating with high levels of energy. "The typical extravert," Eysenck wrote "is sociable, likes parties, has many friends, needs to have people to talk to, and does not like reading or studying by himself."[30] Neuroticism, the third of the personality characteristics Eysenck described, was said to be typical of people who are irrational, shy, moody, and emotional.

According to Eysenck, psychotics are the most likely to be criminal because they combine high degrees of emotionalism with similarly high levels of extroversion. Individuals with such characteristics, claimed Eysenck, are especially difficult to socialize and to train. Eysenck cited many studies in which children and others who harbored characteristics of psychoticism, extroversion, and neuroticism performed poorly on conditioning tests designed to measure how quickly they would respond appropriately to external stimuli. Conscience, said Eysenck, is fundamentally a conditioned reflex. Therefore, an individual who does not take well to conditioning will not fully develop a conscience and will continue to exhibit the asocial behavioral traits of a very young child.

Eysenck's approach might be termed biopsychology, since he claimed that personality traits were fundamentally dependent upon physiology—specifically upon the individual's autonomic nervous system, which Eysenck described as "underlying the behavioral trait of emotionality or neuroticism."[31] Some individuals were said to possess nervous systems that could not handle a great deal of stimulation. Such individuals, like the introvert, shun excitement and are easily trained. They rarely become criminal offenders. Those who possess nervous systems, however, which need stimulation, said Eysenck, seek excitement and are far more likely to turn to crime. As support for his thesis, Eysenck cited studies of twins showing that identical twins were much more likely than fraternal twins to perform similarly on simple behavioral tests. In particular, Eysenck quoted from the work of J. B. S. Haldane, who was reputed to be a "world-famous geneticist." Haldane, having studied the criminality of thirteen sets of identical twins, concluded, "[a]n analysis of the thirteen cases shows not the faintest evidence of freedom of the will in the ordinary sense of the word. A man of a certain constitution, put in a certain environment, will be a criminal. Taking the record of any criminal, we could predict the behavior of a monozygotic twin placed in the same environment. Crime is destiny."[32] Up to two-thirds of all behavioral variance, claimed Eysenck, could be attributed to "a strong genetic basis."

Early Psychiatric Theories

Psychiatric criminology theories derived from the medical sciences, including neurology, and which, like other psychological theories, focus on the individual as the unit of analysis. Psychiatric theories form the basis of psychiatric criminology.

Forensic psychiatry that branch of psychiatry having to do with the study of crime and criminality.

Psychological criminology, with its historically dual emphasis on (1) early forces that shape personality and (2) conditioned behavior, can be distinguished from **psychiatric criminology,** also known as **forensic psychiatry,** which envisions a complex set of drives and motives operating from hidden recesses deep within the personality to determine behavior. David Abrahamsen, a psychiatrist writing in 1944, explains crime this way: "[a]ntisocial behavior is a direct expression of an aggression or may be a direct or indirect manifestation of a distorted erotic drive." "Crime," said Abrahamsen, "may...be considered a product of a person's tendencies and the situation of the moment interacting with his mental resistance."[33] The key questions to be answered by psychiatric criminology, according to Abrahamsen, are "[w]hat creates the criminal impulse? What stimulates and gives it direction?" A later forensic psychiatrist[34] answered the question this way: "Every criminal is such by reason of unconscious forces within him...." Forensic psychiatry explains crime as caused by biological and psychological urges mediated through consciousness. Very little significance is placed upon the role of the environment external to the individual after the first few formative years of life. Psychiatric theories are derived from the medical sciences, including neurology, and, like other psychological theories, focus on the individual as the unit of analysis.

CRIMINAL BEHAVIOR AS MALADAPTION

The Psychoanalytic Perspective

Perhaps the best known psychiatrist of all time is **Sigmund Freud.** Freud coined the term **psychoanalysis** in 1896 and based an entire theory of human behavior upon it. From the point of view of psychoanalysis criminal behavior is maladaptive, or the product of inadequacies inherent in the offender's personality. Significant inadequacies may result in full-blown mental illness, which in itself can be a direct cause of crime. The psychoanalytic perspective encompasses diverse notions such as personality, neurosis, psychosis, and more specific concepts such as transference, sublimation, and repression. **Psychotherapy,** referred to in its early days as the "talking cure" because it highlighted patient-therapist communication, is the attempt to relieve patients of their mental disorders through the application of psychoanalytical principles and techniques.

According to Freud, the personality is comprised of three components, the id, the ego, and the superego as shown in Figure 6.1. The **id** is that fundamental aspect of the personality from which drives, wishes, urges, and desires emanate. Freud focused primarily on love, aggression, and sex as fundamental drives in any personality. The id is direct and singular in purpose. It operates according to the pleasure principle, seeking full and immediate gratification of its needs. Individuals, however, were said to rarely be fully aware of the urges that percolate up (occasionally into awareness) from the id, because it is a largely unconscious region of the mind. Nonetheless, from the Freudian perspective each of us carries within our id the prerequisite motivation for criminal behavior. We are, each one of us, potential murderers, sexual aggressors, and thieves—our drives and urges kept in check only by other, controlling, aspects of our personalities.

A second component of the personality, the **ego,** is primarily charged with reality testing. Freud's use of the word "ego" should not be confused with popular practice, whereby one might talk about an "inflated ego" or an "egotistical person." For Freud, the ego was primarily concerned with how objectives might be best accomplished. The ego tends to effect strategies for the individual that maximize pleasure and minimize pain. It lays out the various paths of action that can lead to wish fulfillment. The ego inherently recognizes that it may be necessary to delay gratification to achieve a more fulfilling long-term goal.

The **superego,** the last component of the personality, is much like a moral guide to right and wrong. If properly developed, it assays the ego's plans, dismissing some as morally inappropriate while accepting others as ethically viable. The id of a potential rapist, for example, might be filled with lustful drives, and his ego may develop a variety of alternative plans whereby those drives might be fulfilled,

Psychoanalysis the theory of human psychology founded by Freud on the concepts of the unconscious, resistance, repression, sexuality, and the Oedipus complex.[35]

Psychotherapy a form of psychiatric treatment based upon psychoanalytical principles and techniques.

Id the aspect of the personality from which drives, wishes, urges, and desires emanate. More formally, it is the division of the psyche associated with instinctual impulses and demands for immediate satisfaction of primitive needs.[36]

Ego the reality-testing part of the personality; also referred to as the reality principle. More formally, it is the personality component that is conscious, most immediately controls behavior, and is most in touch with external reality[37]

Superego the moral aspect of the personality; much like the conscience. More formally, it is the division of the psyche that develops by the incorporation of the perceived moral standards of the community, is mainly unconscious, and includes the conscience.[38]

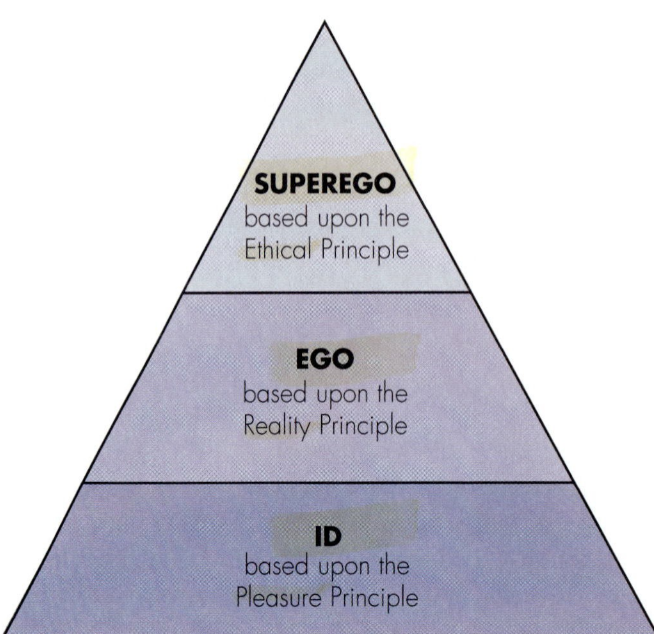

FIGURE 6.1 The Psychoanalytic Structure of Personality.

some legal and some illegal. His superego will, however, if the individual's personality is relatively well integrated and the superego is properly developed, turn the individual away from law-violating behavior based upon his sensual desires and guide the ego to select a path of action that is in keeping with social convention. When the dictates of the superego are not followed, feelings of guilt may result. The superego is one of the most misunderstood of Freudian concepts. In addition to elements of conscience, the superego also contains what Freud called the ego-ideal, which is a symbolic representation of what society values. The ego-ideal differs from the conscience in that it is less forceful in controlling behavior in the absence of the likelihood of discovery.

Although Freud wrote very little about crime per se, he did spend much of his time attempting to account for a wide variety of abnormal behavior, much of which might lead to violations of the criminal law. One way in which a person might be led into crime according to the perspective of psychoanalysis is as the result of a poorly developed superego. In the individual without a fully functional superego, the mind is left to fall back upon the ego's reality testing ability. To put it simply, the ego, operating without a moral guide, may select a path of action which, although expedient at the time, violates the law. Individuals suffering from poor superego development are likely to seek immediate gratification without giving a great deal of thought to the long-term consequences of the choices they may make in the moment.

Sublimation the psychological process whereby one aspect of consciousness comes to be symbolically substituted for another.

From the Freudian point of view, inadequate sublimation can be another cause of crime. Sublimation is the psychological process whereby one item of consciousness comes to be symbolically substituted for another. **Sublimation** is often a healthy process. Freud held that the many outstanding accomplishments of the human species have been due to sublimation, through which powerful sexual and aggressive drives are channeled into socially constructive activity. However, crime

Sigmund Freud (1856–1939), examining a manuscript in the office of his Vienna home, circa 1930. *Bettmann.*

can result from improper sublimation. According to Freud, for example, a man may hate his mother, his hatred being perhaps the faulty by-product of the striving for adult independence. He may, however, be unable to give voice to that hatred directly. Perhaps the mother is too powerful, or the experience of confronting his mother would be too embarrassing for the man. The man may act out his hatred for his mother, however, by attacking other women whom he symbolically substitutes in his mind for the mother figure. Hence, from the Freudian perspective, men who beat their wives, become rapists, sexually harass coworkers, or otherwise abuse women may be enacting feelings derived from early life experiences that they would be unable to otherwise express.

Sublimation, like many other psychoanalytical concepts, is a slippery idea. Mother hatred, for example, although a plausible explanation for acts of violence by men against women, is difficult to demonstrate, and the link between such hidden feelings and adult action is impossible to prove. Even so, should an offender be so diagnosed, it would do little good for him to deny the psychoanalytical explanation assigned to him, since doing so would only result in the professional reproach, "yes, but you have hidden knowledge of your true feelings from yourself. You are not aware of why you act the way you do!"

Freud also postulated the existence of a death instinct, which he called **Thanatos.** According to Freud, all living things, which he referred to as "animate matter" have a fundamental desire to relax back into an inanimate state, or death. Living, said Freud, takes energy and cunning. Hence death, at least at some level, is an easier choice since it releases the organism from the need for continued expenditure of energy. Thanatos was seen as contributing to many of the advances made by the human species, and as underlying a large proportion of individual accomplishments. Were it not for a wish to die, operative at some basic instinctual level, said Freud, few people would have the courage to take

Thanatos a death wish.

risks—and without the assumption of risk, precious little progress is possible in any sphere of life. The notion of an innate death wish has been used to explain why some offenders seem to behave in ways that ensure their eventual capture. Serial killers who send taunting messages to the police, terrorists who tell the media of their planned activities or take credit for public attacks, rapists who "accidentally" leave their wallets at the scene, burglars who break into occupied dwellings may all, for the most part unconsciously, be seeking to be stopped, captured, punished, and even killed.

Neurosis functional disorders of the mind or of the emotions involving anxiety, phobia, or other abnormal behavior.

From the Freudian perspective **neurosis,** a minor form of mental illness, may also lead to crime. Neurotic individuals are well in touch with reality, but may find themselves anxious, fearful of certain situations, or unable to help themselves in others. Fear of heights, for example, may be a neurosis, as may be compulsive hand-washing or eating disorders. A classic example of the compulsive neurotic can be found in the individual who uses paper towels to open doorknobs, refraining from touching the knob directly for fear of picking up germs. While such behavior may be unreasonable from the point of view of others, it is reality based (there *are* germs on doorknobs) and, for the individual demonstrating it, probably unavoidable. Most neuroses do not lead to crime. Some, however, can. A few years ago, for example, Stephen Blumberg of Des Moines, Iowa, was sentenced in federal court to nearly six years in prison and fined $200,000 for the theft of more than twenty-one thousand rare books from hundreds of libraries.[39] Blumberg, whose compulsive interest in rare books began at yard sales and with searches in trash dumpsters, may have seen himself as involved in a messianic mission to preserve recorded history. Compulsive shoplifters may also be manifesting another form of neurosis—one in which a powerful need to steal can drive even well-heeled individuals to risk arrest and jail.

The Psychotic Offender

While neurotic individuals often face only relatively minor problems in living, psychotic people, according to psychiatric definitions, are out of touch with reality in some fundamental way. They may suffer from hallucinations, delusions, or other breaks with reality. The classic psychotic thinks he is Napoleon, or sees spiders covering what others see only as a bare wall. Individuals suffering from a **psychosis** are said to be psychotic. Psychoses may be either organic, that is, caused by physical damage to, or abnormalities in, the brain, or functional, that is, those with no known physical cause. Gwynn Nettler says "[t]hought disorder is the hallmark of psychosis...people are called crazy when, at some extremity, they cannot 'think straight.'"[40] Nettler identifies three characteristics of psychotic individuals: "(1) a grossly distorted conception of reality, (2) moods, and swings of mood, that seem inappropriate to circumstance, and (3) marked inefficiency in getting along with others and caring for oneself."[41] Psychotic persons have also been classified as schizophrenic or **paranoid schizophrenic. Schizophrenics** are said to be characterized by disordered or disjointed thinking, in which the types of logical associations they make are atypical of other people. Paranoid schizophrenics suffer from delusions and hallucinations.

Psychosis a form of mental illness in which sufferers are said to be out of touch with reality.

Schizophrenics mentally ill individuals who suffer from disjointed thinking and, possibly, delusions and hallucinations.

Paranoid schizophrenics schizophrenic individuals who suffer from delusions and hallucinations.

Unfortunately, psychiatrists have not been able to agree on definitive schizophrenic criteria that would allow for convenient application of the term. One prominent psychiatrist writes of "how varying...schizophrenia may appear, ranging from no striking symptoms at all to conspicuous psychotic features.... Thus on the surface," he continues, "the schizophrenic may appear normal and, to some extent, lead a conventional life."[42] The same author later tells us "[s]chizophrenia is not a clearly defined disease.... It is characterized rather by a...kind of alteration of thinking or feeling...."[43] At the very least, then, we can safely say that schizophrenia is a disorganization of the personality. In its most extreme form, it may manifest itself by way of hallucinations, delusions, and seemingly irrational behavior.

With these caveats in mind, it is fair to say that psychoses may lead to crime in a number of ways. Following the Vietnam war, for example, a number of instances were reported in which former American soldiers suffering from a kind of battlefield psychosis killed friends and family members thinking they were Viet Cong soldiers, that is, the enemy. These men, who had been traumatized by battlefield experiences in Southeast Asia, relived their past on American streets. In other crimes committed by psychotics, thought disorders may be less obvious, or may only exist temporarily.

The Link Between Frustration and Aggression

In his early writings, Freud suggested that aggressive behavior is a response to frustration. Aggression toward others, Freud said, is a natural response to frustrating limitations imposed upon a person. The frustration-aggression thesis was later developed more fully in the writings of J. Dollard,[44] Albert Bandura, Richard H. Walters, and others. Dollard's frustration-aggression theory held that although frustration can lead to a variety of forms of behavior—including regression, sublimation, and aggressive fantasy—direct aggression toward others is its most likely consequence. Since everyone suffers some form of frustration throughout life, beginning with weaning and toilet training, Dollard argued, aggression is a natural consequence of living. Dollard pointed out, however, that aggression could be manifested in socially acceptable ways (perhaps through contact sports, military or law enforcement careers, or simple verbal attacks) and that it could be engaged in vicariously by observing others who are acting violently (as in movies, on television, through popular fiction, and so on). Dollard applied the psychoanalytical term "displacement" to the type of violence which is vented on something or someone not the source of the original frustration and suggested that satisfying one's aggressive urges via observation was a form of "catharsis."

The story of Paul Calden, a former insurance company executive, provides us with an example of frustration-aggression theory as it applies to real-life crime. In January 1993, the 33-year-old Calden, dressed in a business suit, opened fire with a 9mm semiautomatic handgun on his ex-bosses in the Island Center Cafe, a Tampa, Florida, cafeteria—killing three people and injuring two others. Calden went up to the table where the five were eating, showed them the gun, shouted "[t]his is what you get for firing me!" and pulled the trigger.[45] He had been let go from his position as an underwriter with Fireman's Fund Insurance Company in

March 1992. Calden then killed himself. Calden appears to have been acting out of frustrations born of his experience with having been fired.

Some psychologists have tried to identify what it is that causes some individuals to displace aggression or to experience it vicariously (through catharsis), while others respond violently and directly toward the immediate source of their frustrations. Andrew Henry and James Short,[46] for example, writing in the 1950s suggested that child-rearing practices are a major determining factor in such a causal nexus. Restrictive parents who both punish and love their children, said Henry and Short, will engender in their children the ability to suppress outward expressions of aggression. When one parent punishes and the other loves, or when both punish but neither show love, children can be expected to show anger directly and perhaps even immediately since they will not be threatened with the loss of love. Physical punishment, explained Henry and Short, rarely threatens the loss of love, and children so punished cannot be expected to refrain from direct displays of anger.

In 1960 Stewart Palmer[47] studied murderers and their siblings to determine the degree of frustration to which they had been exposed as children. He found that male murderers had experienced much more frustration than their brothers—in fact more than twice as many frustrating experiences, ranging from difficult births to serious illnesses, childhood beatings, severe toilet training, and negative school experiences, were reported by the murderers than by their law-abiding siblings.

CRIME AS ADAPTIVE BEHAVIOR

Some psychiatric perspectives have held that "...crime is a compromise, representing for the individual the most satisfactory method of adjustment to inner conflicts which he cannot express otherwise. Thus, his acting out the crime fulfills a certain aim or purpose."[48] One of the most pressing needs of many criminals, according to some psychologists, is the need to be punished—a need that arises, according to psychiatric theory, from a sense of guilt. Psychiatrists who suggest that the need to be punished is a motivating factor in criminal behavior are quick to point out that such a need may be a closely guarded secret, unknown even to the offender. Hence, from the psychiatric point of view, many drives, motives, and wishes are unconscious or even repressed by people who harbor them. The concept of repression holds that the human mind may choose to keep certain aspects of itself out of consciousness, possibly because of shame, self-loathing, or a simple lack of adequate introspection. The desire for punishment, however, sometimes comes to the fore. In 1993, for example, Westley Dodd was hanged to death by authorities in Washington state for the kidnap, rape, and murder of three little boys four years earlier. Dodd, who said he had molested dozens of children over the course of a decade, sought the death penalty after he was convicted—saying he deserved to die, and vowing to sue the American Civil Liberties Union (ACLU) or anyone else who sought to save him.[49]

Crime can be adaptive in other ways as well. Some psychiatrists see it as an adaptation to life's stresses. According to Seymour L. Halleck,[50] turning to crime

Westley Alan Dodd, hanged in 1993 for murdering young boys whom he molested. "People need to know it's the only thing that will stop me," he said of his execution. *Benjamin Benschneider/Seattle Times/Gamma-Liaison, Inc.*

can provide otherwise disenfranchised individuals with a sense of power and purpose. In Halleck's words, "[d]uring the planning and execution of a criminal act the offender is a free man.... The value of this brief taste of freedom cannot be overestimated. Many of the criminal's apparently unreasonable actions are efforts to find a moment of autonomy...."[51] Halleck says that crime can also provide "excellent rationalizations" for perceived inadequacies—especially for those whose lives have been failures when judged against the benchmarks of the wider society. "The criminal is able to say..., 'I could have been successful if I had not turned to crime. All my troubles have come to me because I have been bad.'"[52] Hence, crime, according to Halleck, provides "a convenient resource for denying, forgetting or ignoring...other inadequacies."

Insofar as the choice of crime reduces stresses which the individual faces by producing changes in the environment (empowerment), it is referred to as an **alloplastic adaptation.** When crime leads to stress reduction as a result of internal changes in beliefs, value systems, and so forth, it is called **autoplastic adaptation**. The offender who is able to deny responsibility for other failures by turning to crime is said to be seeking autoplastic adaptation. Since other forms of behavior may also meet many of the same needs as does crime, Halleck points out that an individual may select crime over various other behavioral alternatives only when there are no reasonably available alternatives, or when criminal behavior has inherent advantages—as might be the case under instances of economic or social oppression (i.e., individuals who are actively discriminated against may find personal and political significance in violating the laws of the oppressing society).

Alloplastic adaptation that form of adjustment which results from changes in the environment surrounding an individual.

Autoplastic adaptation that form of adjustment which results from changes within an individual.

In any case, from Halleck's point of view crime "has many advantages even when considered independently of the criminal's conscious or unconscious needs for gratification."[53] In other words, even though crime can be immediately rewarding or intensely pleasureful, says Halleck, such rewards are more "fringe benefits" than anything else. The central of significance of criminal behavior for most offenders is that it "is an action which helps one survive with dignity."[54] Halleck tells us that "[w]e cannot understand the criminal unless we appreciate that his actions are much more than an effort to find a specific gratification."[55] In the final analysis, criminal behavior is, from Halleck's point of view, a form of adjustment to stress and oppression.

Finally, we should recognize that perceptions vary, and although criminal behavior may appear to be a valid choice for some individuals who are seeking viable responses to perceived stresses and oppression, their perceptions may not be wholly accurate. In other words, misperceived stress and oppression may still lead to crime even when far simpler solutions may be found in a more realistic appraisal of one's situation.

SOCIAL LEARNING THEORY

Social learning theory a psychological perspective that says people learn how to behave by modeling themselves after others whom they have the opportunity to observe.

More recently, **Albert Bandura** has attempted to develop a comprehensive **social learning theory** of aggression. Bandura tells us that "[a] complete theory of aggression must explain how aggressive patterns are developed, what provokes people to behave aggressively, and what sustains such actions after they have been initiated."[56] Although everyone is capable of aggression, he says, "[p]eople are not born with...repertories of aggressive behavior. They must learn them." He goes on to say that, "the specific forms that aggressive behavior takes, the frequency with which it is expressed, the situation in which it is displayed, and the specific targets selected for attack are largely determined by social learning factors." According to Bandura, people learn by observing others. In some of his early work, Bandura experimented with children who observed adult role models striking inflatable cartoon characters. When the children were observed following their encounter with adult behavior, they too exhibited similarly aggressive behavior toward the models. Bandura also studied violence on television and concluded that "[t]elevision is an effective tutor. Both laboratory and controlled field studies in which young children and adolescents are repeatedly shown either violence or nonviolent fare, disclose that exposure to film violence shapes the form of aggression and typically increases interpersonal aggressiveness in everyday life." A later study,[57] by other researchers, showed that even after ten years the level of violence engaged in by young adults was directly related to the degree of violent television they had been exposed to as children.

Social learning theory also shows how people can model the behavior of others. Bandura explained modeling behavior by reference to the frequent hijacking of domestic airliners to Cuba which occurred in the United States in the late 1960s and early 1970s. Such hijackings, Bandura found, followed immediately on the heels of similar incidents in Eastern European nations under Soviet domination. American hijackings, he said, were simply modeling those in Europe, and hijackers in this country were learning from news accounts of their foreign tutors.

Aggressive behavior may be built on models. Skinhead brothers Bryan (left) and David Freeman (right) await trial with their cousin, Nelson Birdwell. The brothers are accused of killing their parents and younger brother in 1995. *Reprinted with permission from* The Morning Call, *Allentown, PA.*

Once aggressive patterns of behavior have been acquired, it becomes necessary to show how they can be activated. Aggression can be provoked, Bandura suggests, through physical assaults and verbal threats and insults, as well as by thwarting a person's hopes or obstructing his or her goal-seeking behavior. Deprivation and "adverse reductions in the conditions of life" (a lowered standard of living, the onset of disease, a spouse leaving or caught cheating, etc.) are other potential triggers of aggression. Bandura adds, however, that a human being's ability to foresee the future consequences of present behavior infuses another dimension into the activation of learned patterns of aggression. That is, aggressive behavior can be perceived as holding future benefits for individuals exhibiting it. In short, it can be seen as a means to a desired end.

Sometimes individuals become aggressive, said Bandura, because they are rewarded for doing so. The early twentieth-century American concept of a "macho"—virile and masculine—male was often associated with the expectation of substantial reward. The "macho" male was the one who won the most respect from his fellows, inevitably came away with the greatest honors (on the playing field, in school, from the community, etc.), and eventually married the most desirable woman. Whether this perception was accurate or not, it was nonetheless subscribed to by a significant proportion of American men and, for many decades, served as a guide to daily behavior.

Another form of reward can flow from aggression. Bandura called it the reduction of aversive treatment." By this he meant that simply standing up for one's self can improve the way one is treated by others. Oftentimes, for example, standing up to a bully is the most effective way of dealing with the harassment one might otherwise face. Similarly, there is an old saying that "the squeaky wheel gets the grease," and it means, quite simply, that people who are the most demanding will be recognized. Aggressive people often get what they go after.

Bandura recognized that all persons have self-regulatory mechanisms that can ameliorate the tendency toward aggression. People reward or punish themselves, Bandura said, according to internal standards they have for judging their own behavior. Hence, aggression may be inhibited in people who, for example, value religious, ethical, or moral standards of conduct such as compassion, thoughtfulness, and courtesy. Nonetheless, Bandura concluded, people who devalue aggression may still engage in it via a process he called "disengagement," whereby rationalizations are constructed which overcome internal inhibitions. Disengagement may result from (1) "attributing blame to one's victims"; (2) dehumanization through bureaucratization, automation, urbanization, and high social mobility; (3) vindication of aggressive practices by legitimate authorities; and (4) desensitization resulting from repeated exposure to aggression in any of a variety of forms.

Social learning theory has been criticized for lacking comprehensive explanatory power. How, for example, can striking differences in sibling behavior, where early childhood experiences are likely to be much the same, be explained? Similarly, why do apparent differences exist between the sexes with regard to degree and type of criminality—irrespective of social background and early learning experiences? More recent versions of social learning theory, sometimes called "cognitive social learning theory,"[58] attempt to account for such differences by hypothesizing that reflection and cognition play a significant role in interpreting what one observes, and in determining responses. Hence, few people are likely to behave precisely as others do, since they will have their own ideas about what observed behavior means and about the consequences of emulation.

Behavior theory a psychological perspective which posits that individual behavior that is rewarded will increase in frequency, while that which is punished will decrease.

Operant behavior behavior which affects the environment in such a way as to produce responses or further behavioral cues.

Reward desirable behavioral consequences likely to increase the frequency of occurrence of that behavior.

Punishment undesirable behavioral consequences likely to decrease the frequency of occurrence of that behavior.

BEHAVIOR THEORY

Behavior theory has sometimes been called the "stimulus-response approach to human behavior.... At the heart of behavior theory is the notion that behavior is determined by environmental consequences which it produces for the individual concerned."[59] When an individual's behavior results in rewards, or in the receipt of feedback which the individual, for whatever reason, regards as rewarding, then it is likely that the behavior will become more frequent. Under such circumstances the behavior in question is said to be reinforced. Conversely, when punishment follows behavior, chances are that the frequency of that type of behavior will decrease. The individual's responses are termed **operant behavior,** since behavioral choices effectively operate upon the surrounding environment to produce consequences for the behaving individual. Similarly, stimuli provided by the environment become behavioral cues, which serve to elicit conditioned responses from individuals. Responses are said to be conditioned according to the individual's past experiences, wherein behavioral consequences effectively defined some forms of behavior as desirable and others as undesirable. Behavior theory is often employed by parents seeking to control children through a series of **rewards** and **punishments.** Young children may be punished, for example, with spanking, the loss of a favored toy (at least for a period of time), a turned-off television, and so forth. Older children are often told what rules they are expected to obey, and the rewards that they can anticipate receiving from adherence to those rules, as well as the punishments that will follow if they don't.

Rewards and punishments have been further divided into four conceptual categories: (1) positive rewards, which increase the frequency of approved behavior by adding something desirable to the situation—as when a "good" child is given a toy; (2) negative rewards, which increase the frequency of approved behavior by removing something distressful from the situation—as when a "good" child is permitted to skip the morning's chores; (3) positive punishments, which decrease the frequency of unwanted behavior by adding something undesirable to the situation—as when a "bad" child is spanked; and (4) negative punishments, which decrease the frequency of unwanted behavior by removing something desirable from the situation—as when a "bad" child's candy is taken away. According to behavior theory, it is through the application of rewards and punishments that behavior is shaped.

Behavior theory differs from other psychological theories in that the major determinants of behavior are envisioned as residing in the environment surrounding the individual rather than in the individual herself. Perhaps the best-known proponent of behavior theory is Burrhus Frederic Skinner (1904–), popularly referred to as "**B. F. Skinner.**" Skinner, a former Harvard professor, rejected unobservable psychological constructs, focusing instead on patterns of responses to external rewards and stimuli. Skinner did extensive animal research involving behavioral concepts and created the notion of programmed instruction, which allows students to work at their own pace and provides immediate rewards for learning accomplishments.

While behavior theory has much to say about the reformation of criminal offenders through the imposition of punishment, the approach is equally significant for its contributions to understanding the genesis of such behavior. As one writer puts it, "it is the balance of reinforcement and punishment in an individual's learning history which will dictate the presence or absence of criminal behavior."[60] According to the behavioral model, crime results when individuals "receive tangible rewards (positive reinforcement) for engaging in delinquent and criminal behavior, particularly when no other attractive alternative is available."[61]

A little more than a year ago, for example, 15-year-old Sundahkeh "Ron" Bethune shot and killed a 26-year-old pizza delivery man who gunned his car motor as Bethune attempted to rob him. Ron, who had been dabbling in the drug trade, and who could afford high-priced clothing, jewelry, and other accouterments of apparent wealth, was looked up to by many other young people in his Morganton, North Carolina, community. When the delivery man tried to run f om Ron in front of a group of his friends, Bethune didn't see any other choice but to kill him. "I just had to show them I wasn't some little punk,"[62] he said afterward in a prison interview. Ron Bethune didn't think of the long-term consequences of his behavior on the night of the killing. All he wanted was to earn the approval of those who were watching him. The crowd's anticipated awestruck response to murder was all the reward Ron needed to pull the trigger that night. He is now serving five years for second-degree murder.

Behavior theory has been criticized for ignoring the role that cognition plays in human behavior. Martyrs, for example, persist in what may be defined by the wider society as undesirable behavior, even in the face of severe punishment—including the loss of their own lives. No degree of punishment is likely to deter a martyr who answers to some higher call. Similarly, criminals who are punished for official law violations may find that their immediate social group interprets criminal punishment as status enhancing. As an acquaintance of the author said, after being released from prison where he had served time for murder, "You woulda thought I had won a Grammy award or somethin'." Members of his community held him in awe. As he walked down the street young people would say "There goes John! You better not mess with John!" From the point of view of behavior theory, criminal punishments are in danger of losing sway over many forms of human behavior in today's diverse society. Our society's fragmented value system leads to various interpretations of criminal punishments thereby changing the significance of experiences such as arrest, conviction, and imprisonment. In times past, criminal offenders were often shunned and became social outcasts. Today, those who have been adjudicated criminal may find that their new status holds many rewards.

INSANITY AND THE LAW

Insanity[63] (psychological) persistent mental disorder or derangement.

Insanity (law) a legally established inability to understand right from wrong or to conform one's behavior to the requirements of the law.

Insanity is a defense allowable in criminal courts. A criminal defendant may be found not guilty by reason of insanity and avoid punitive sanctions even when it is clear that he or she committed a legally circumscribed act. Legal and psychiatric definitions of insanity, however, rarely coincide. In the words of the U.S. Supreme Court,[64] "It is by now well established that insanity as defined by the criminal law has no direct analog in medicine or science." "[T]he divergence between law and psychiatry," the Court has said, "is caused in part by the legal fiction represented by the words 'insanity' or 'insane,' which are a kind of lawyer's catchall and have no clinical meaning." C. Ray Jeffery[65] writes that "[t]hree concepts are confused in the insanity defense": (1) psychiatric, (2) legal, and (3) neurological understandings of mental illness. Even so, psychotic offenders are more likely than most other kinds of criminal wrongdoers to be adjudicated insane or to have their degree of criminal culpability reduced by the courts in recognition of the mental problems they face. The burden of proving a claim of "not guilty by reason of insanity," however, falls upon the defendant.[66] Just as a person is assumed to be innocent at the start of any criminal trial, so too is he or she assumed to be sane.

An individual has a right to the opportunity to prove a claim of insanity in court and cannot be forced to take medications during trial that might control the condition. In 1992, for example, the U.S. Supreme Court, in the case of *Riggins v. Nevada*,[67] held that the "forced administration of antipsychotic medication" may have impaired the accused's ability to defend himself and violated due process guarantees.

In 1984 the U.S. Congress enacted the Insanity Reform Act, spurred to action by John Hinckley's attempted assassination of then-president Reagan. Hinckley's

Insanity can be used as a defense against criminal charges. Lorena Bobbitt sobs on the witness stand before acquittal on charges she severed her husband's penis with a kitchen knife. Bobbitt claimed a kind of irresistible impulse. *Gary Hershorn/Bettmann.*

lawyers claimed that their client's history of schizophrenia left him unable to control his behavior, and Hinckley was acquitted of the criminal charges which had been brought against him. Although Hinckley was institutionalized to prevent him from harming others, his release is mandated by federal law when (and if) he recovers. In the words of the U.S. Supreme Court, "[t]he Insanity Defense Reform Act of 1984 ensures that a federal criminal defendant found not guilty by reason of insanity will not be released onto the streets."[68]

The Insanity Reform Act is especially significant for the fact that it contains a provision which permits mentally ill individuals to be held for trial in the hopes that they will recover sufficiently to permit their trial to proceed. The law allows for an initial hearing to determine the mental status of the defendant. If the defendant is found incompetent to stand trial he or she will be committed to a hospital "for such a reasonable period of time, not to exceed four months,...to determine whether there is a substantial probability that in the foreseeable future he will attain the capacity to permit the trial to proceed; and...for an additional reasonable period of time until...his mental condition is so improved that trial may proceed...."[69] The law sets no maximum period of confinement, implying only that the defendant will undergo periodic review while institutionalized "...if the court finds that there is a substantial probability that within such additional period of time he will attain the capacity to permit the trial to proceed...."

The McNaughten Rule

One of the first instances within the western legal tradition where insanity was accepted as a defense to criminal liability can be found in the case of Daniel McNaughten (also spelled "M'Naughton" and "M'Naghton"). McNaughten was accused of the 1844 killing of Edward Drummond, the secretary of British prime

INSANITY AS A DEFENSE UNDER FEDERAL LAW

Federal law permits the defense of insanity, as follows:

Sec. 17. Insanity defense

- (a) Affirmative Defense. It is an affirmative defense to a prosecution under any Federal statute that, at the time of the commission of the acts constituting the offense, the defendant, as a result of a severe mental disease or defect, was unable to appreciate the nature and quality or the wrongfulness of his acts. Mental disease or defect does not otherwise constitute a defense.
- (b) Burden of Proof. The defendant has the burden of proving the defense of insanity by clear and convincing evidence.

Source: Section 17, Public Law 99-646, November 10, 1986.

minister Sir Robert Peel. By all accounts McNaughten had intended to kill Peel, but because he was suffering from mental disorganization shot Drummond instead, mistaking him for Peel. At his trial, the defense presented information to show that McNaughten was suffering from delusions, including the belief that Peel's political party was, in some vague way, persecuting him. The court accepted his lawyer's claims and the defense of insanity was established in western law. Other jurisdictions were quick to adopt the **McNaughten rule,** as the judge's decision in the case came to be called. The McNaughten rule holds that a person cannot be held criminally responsible for their actions if at the time of the offense either (1) they did not know what they were doing, or (2) they did not know that what they were doing was wrong.

McNaughten rule a standard for judging legal insanity which requires that either an offender did not know what they were doing or that, if they did, that they did not know it was wrong.

Today the McNaughten rule is used by fifteen states when insanity is at issue in criminal cases. Critics of the McNaughten rule say that, although the notion of intent inherent within it appeals well to lawyers, "[i]t is...so alien to current concepts of human behavior that it has been vigorously attacked by psychiatrists. An obvious difficulty with the McNaughten rule is that practically everyone, regardless of the degree of his criminal disturbance, knows the nature and quality and rightness or wrongness of what he is doing."[70]

Irresistible impulse test a standard for judging legal insanity which holds that a defendant is not guilty of a criminal offense if the person, by virtue of their mental state or psychological condition, was not able to resist committing the action in question.

The Irresistible Impulse Test

The McNaughten ruling opened the floodgates for other types of insanity claims offered as defenses to charges of criminal activity. One of the more interesting of these claims is that of irresistible impulse. The **irresistible impulse test**—employed by eighteen states, some of which also follow the dictates of

McNaughten—holds that a defendant is not guilty of a criminal offense if the person, by virtue of their mental state or psychological condition, was not able to resist committing the action in question. Some years ago, for example, a television advertisement claimed that a certain brand of potato chip was so good that, once you opened the container, you couldn't eat just one. Friends of the author would test themselves by purchasing the brand in question, opening the pack, and eating a chip. They would then try and resist the temptation to have another—thereby hoping to prove the commercial wrong. While this may seem a silly exercise in self-assessment, it did prove a point. The commercial, in fact, was right most of the time. Additional chips were almost impossible to avoid for anyone who tried this experiment—especially if they kept the chips around for any length of time!

Of course, eating potato chips is not a crime, even if the chips are irresistible. However, for individuals who suffer from other types of compulsions, some of them criminal, the test may effectively measure their mettle. Even so, it is difficult for anyone to really know whether or not a given person in a particular situation was able to control their behavior or not. Kleptomania is a disorder in which an individual feels compelled to steal. Kleptomaniacs are often shoplifters, but have also been known to be unable to resist the urge to steal while visiting the homes of friends or relatives.

Scientific advances now on the horizon combine with the irresistible impulse test to open a number of intriguing possibilities. One has to do with new colognes and perfumes rumored soon to be marketed. These scents combine the usual toiletries with human pheromones—chemical substances that, at least in insect form, have been shown to produce very predictable, and apparently uncontrollable, behavior. Pheromones, which stimulate the olfactory nerves to produce specific chemicals which then target neuroreceptors in the brain, directly alter brain chemistry. Most uses of pheromones to date have been in the area of pest control, where sexual pheromones that attract specific types of male insects, for example, are released into the atmosphere to confuse the insect's mating behavior or to lure pests into a trap. Clearly at issue, should the new products be released, will be claims of uncontrollable sexual desire. Will toiletries containing human pheromones lead to instances of sexual attack? If they do, will the attackers be held blameless on claims of irresistible impulse, and what will then be the civil liability of the product makers themselves?

In 1994, Lorena Bobbitt, whose case was described earlier in this chapter, was found not guilty by virtue of temporary insanity of charges of maliciously wounding her husband by cutting off his penis with a kitchen knife. Her attorneys successfully employed the irresistible impulse defense, convincing the jury that Ms. Bobbitt acted as a result of irresistible impulse after years of "physical abuse, verbal abuse and sexual abuse" at the hands of her husband. Her attorneys maintained that, while committing the crime, she had a brief psychotic breakdown, and could not resist the impulse to maim her husband.

The Durham Rule

In 1954 Judge David Bazelon of the U.S. Court of Appeals for the District of Columbia announced a new rule in the case of Monte Durham. In the words of the court, "[t]he rule we now hold is simply that an accused is not criminally responsible if his unlawful act was the product of mental disease or mental defect." Judge Bazelon continued, defining the terms of the court's decision: "We use 'disease' in the sense of a condition which is considered capable of improving or deteriorating. We use 'defect' in the sense of a condition which is not considered capable of either improving or deteriorating and which may be congenital or the result of injury or the residual effect of a physical or mental disease."[71]

While this new rule was intended to simplify the adjudication of mentally ill offenders, it has resulted in additional confusion. Many criminal defendants suffer from mental diseases and/or defects. Some show retarded mental development, others are dyslexic, a few are afflicted with Down's syndrome, others have cerebral palsy (which may or may not meet Judge Bazelon's definition), and a vast number evidence some degree of neurosis or psychosis. The link between any of these conditions and criminal behavior in specific cases, however, is far from clear. Some people struggle with psychological handicaps or mental illnesses all their lives, never engaging in violations of the criminal law. Others, with similar conditions, are frequent law violators. The **Durham rule** provides no way of separating one group from the other.

Durham rule a standard for judging legal insanity which holds that "an accused is not criminally responsible if his unlawful act was the product of mental disease or mental defect."

Finally, some observers have noted the "danger of circularity in the Durham rule." If a person exhibits very unusual behavior during the commission of a crime, the criminal behavior itself may be taken as a sign of mental disease—automatically exonerating the offender of criminal culpability.

The Substantial Capacity Test

Substantial capacity test a standard for judging legal insanity which requires that a person lack "the mental capacity needed to understand the wrongfulness of his act, or to conform his behavior to the requirements of the law."

In the determination of insanity for purposes of criminal prosecution nineteen of the United States adhere to the **substantial capacity test**—a standard embodied in the Model Penal Code of the American Law Institute. The substantial capacity test blends elements of the McNaughten rule with the irresistible impulse standard. Insanity is said to be present when a person lacks "the mental capacity needed to understand the wrongfulness of his act, or to conform his behavior to the requirements of the law."[72] A lack of mental capacity does not require total mental incompetence, nor does it mandate that the behavior in question meet the standard of total irresistibility. The problem, however, of determining just what constitutes "substantial mental capacity," or its lack, has plagued this rule from its inception.

The Brawner Rule

The Brawner rule, created in 1972 in the case of *Brawner* v. *U.S.*,[73] is rather unique among standards of its type. This rule, in effect, leaves it up to the jury to determine what constitutes insanity. The jury is asked to decide whether or not the defendant could be justly held responsible for the criminal act with which he or she stands charged, in the face of any claims of insanity or mental incapacity. Under the Brawner rule, which has not seen wide applicability, juries are left with few rules to guide them other than their own sense of fairness.

Guilty But Insane

Frustrated by the seeming inability of criminal courts to effectively adjudicate mentally ill offenders, and by the abuse of insanity claims by offenders seeking to avoid criminal punishments, a number of states have enacted legislation permitting findings of "guilty but insane" or **"guilty but mentally ill" (GBMI).** Offenders so adjudicated are, in effect, found guilty of the criminal offense with which they are charged but, because of their prevailing mental condition, are generally sent to psychiatric hospitals for treatment rather than to prison. Once they have been declared "cured," however, such offenders can be transferred to correctional facilities to serve out their sentences.

Guilty but mentally ill (GBMI) a finding that an offender is guilty of the criminal offense with which they are charged but, because of their prevailing mental condition, they are generally sent to psychiatric hospitals for treatment rather than to prison. Once they have been declared "cured," however, such offenders can be transferred to correctional facilities to serve out their sentences.

In 1975 Michigan became the first state to pass a "guilty but mentally ill" statute, permitting a finding of GBMI. As of this writing, approximately a dozen states permit such a finding.

Federal Provisions for the Hospitalization of Individuals Found "Not Guilty by Reason of Insanity"

Federal law provides for confinement in a "suitable facility" of criminal defendants found not guilty by reason of insanity.[74] The law mandates a "psychiatric or psychological examination and report" and a hearing to be held within forty days after the not guilty verdict. If the hearing court finds that the person's release would "create a substantial risk of bodily injury to another person or serious damage of property of another due to a present mental disease or defect, the court" in the language of the statute, "shall commit the person...." To be later released, a person committed under the law "has the burden of proving by clear and convincing evidence that his release would not create a substantial risk of bodily injury to another person or serious damage of property of another due to a present mental disease or defect." The person can be discharged "[w]hen the director of the facility in which an acquitted person is hospitalized...determines that the person has recovered from his mental disease or defect to such an extent that his release, or his conditional release under a prescribed regimen of medical, psychiatric, or psychological care or treatment, would no longer create a substantial risk of bodily injury to another person or serious damage to property of another...."

The federal statute has been used as a model by many of the states. A few laws, which differ from the federal model, have been held to be unconstitutional, especially when they permit the continued confinement of offenders who have been declared "well," even though they may still be dangerous. In 1992, for example, the U.S. Supreme Court, in the case of ***Foucha* v. *Louisiana*,**[75] ordered the release of Terry Foucha who had been adjudicated "not guilty by reason of insanity" in the state of Louisiana. Although a psychiatrist later found Foucha to have overcome a drug-induced psychosis which had been present at the time of the crime, a state court ordered Foucha returned to the mental institution in which he had been committed, ruling that he was dangerous on the basis of the same doctor's testimony. The psychiatrist found that although Foucha was "in good shape" mentally, he had "an antisocial personality." Foucha's antisocial personality was described as "a condition that is not a mental disease and is untreatable." The doctor cited the fact that Foucha had been involved in several altercations at the institution, and said that he would not "feel comfortable in certifying that he would not be a danger to himself or to other people." In effect, the Supreme Court struck down a provision of the Louisiana law which made possible continued confinement of recovered persons who had once been deemed not guilty by reason of insanity, where their continued confinement was predicated solely on the basis of the belief that they might represent a continuing danger to the community.

SOCIAL POLICY AND FORENSIC PSYCHOLOGY

Psychological theories continue to evolve. For example, recent research in the field has shown a stability of aggressiveness over time. That is, children who display early disruptive or aggressive behavior have been found, through the use of studies that follow the same individuals over time,[76] likely to continue their involvement in such behavior even as adults. Some researchers have found that aggressiveness appears to stabilize over time.[77] Children who demonstrate aggressive traits early in life often evidence increasingly frequent episodes of such behavior until, finally, such behavior becomes a major component of the adolescent or adult personality. From such research it is possible to conclude that problem children are likely to become problem adults.

Dangerousness the likelihood that a given individual will later harm society or others. Dangerousness is often measured in terms of recidivism, or as the likelihood of new crime commission, or rearrest for a new crime within a five-year period following arrest or release from confinement.

Expanding research of this sort holds considerable significance for those who are attempting to assess **dangerousness,** and to identify personal characteristics which would allow for the prediction of dangerousness in individual cases. The ability to accurately predict future dangerousness is of great concern to today's policymakers. In 1993, for example, Michael Blair, a convicted child molester paroled after serving eighteen months of a ten-year prison sentence, was charged with the kidnap-slaying of young Ashley Estell, who disappeared from a soccer match in Plano, Texas. Ashley was found dead the next day.[78] Similarly, in November of that year, Anthony Cook was executed in Huntsville, Texas, for the slaying of law student Dirck VanTassel, Jr.[79] Cook killed VanTassel only thirteen days after being paroled, robbing him of his wallet, watch, and wedding ring and shooting him four times in the head. Less than a month later, in what was to be a very sad case, Richard Allen Davis, a twice-convicted kidnapper, was arrested for the kidnap-murder of 12-year-old Polly Klaas.[80] Klaas was abducted from a slumber party in her Petaluma, California, home as her mother slept in the next room. Davis had been paroled only a few months earlier after serving an eight-year prison term for a similar offense.

Can past behavior predict future behavior? Do former instances of criminality presage additional ones? Are there other, identifiable, characteristics which violent offenders might manifest that could serve as warning signs to criminal justice decision makers faced with the dilemma of whether or not to release convicted felons? This, like many other areas, is one in which criminologists are still learning. One recent study[81] found a strong relationship between childhood behavioral difficulties and later problem behavior. According to authors of the study "early antisocial behavior is the best predictor of later antisocial behavior. It appears that this rule holds even when the antisocial behavior is measured as early as the preschool period." Using children as young as 3 years old, researchers were able to predict later delinquency, leading them to conclude that "some antisocial behavioral characteristics may be components of temperament." A second study,[82] which tracked a sample of male offenders for over twenty years, found that stable, but as yet "unmeasured individual differences" account for the positive association which exists between past criminal behavior and the likelihood of future recurrence.

Prediction, however, requires more than generalities. It is one thing to say, for example, that generally speaking 70% of children who evidence aggressive behavior will similarly show violent tendencies later in life, and quite another to be able to predict which specific individuals will engage in future violations of the criminal law. **Selective incapacitation** is a policy based upon the notion of career criminality.[83] Career criminals, also termed habitual offenders, are persons who repeatedly commit violations of the criminal law. Research has shown that only a very small percentage of all offenders account for most crimes which are reported to the police. Some studies have found that as few as 8% of all offenders commit as many as sixty serious crimes each per year.[84] A recent Wisconsin study found that imprisonment of individuals determined to be career offenders saved the state about $14,000 per year per offender when the cost of imprisonment was compared to the estimated cost of new crimes. Researchers in the Wisconsin study concluded that "prison pays" and suggested that the state continue pursuing a policy of aggressive imprisonment of career offenders even in the face of escalating costs and vastly overcrowded prisons. The strategy of selective incapacitation, however, which depends upon accurately identifying potentially dangerous offenders out of existing criminal populations, has been criticized by some authors[85] for yielding a rate of "false positives" of over 60%. Potentially violent offenders are not easy to identify, even on the basis of past criminal records, and sentencing individuals to long prison terms simply because they are thought likely to commit crimes in the future would no doubt be unconstitutional.

Selective incapacitation a social policy which seeks to protect society by incarcerating those individuals deemed to be the most dangerous.

The 1984 federal Comprehensive Crime Control Act,[86] which established the U.S. Sentencing Commission, targeted career offenders. Guidelines created by the commission contain, as a central feature, a "criminal history" dimension which substantially increases the amount of punishment an offender faces based upon his or her history of law violations. The sentencing guidelines originally classified a defendant as a career offender if "(1) the defendant was at least 18 years old at the time of the...offense, (2) the...offense is a crime of violence or trafficking in a controlled substance, and (3) the defendant has at least two prior felony convictions of either a crime of violence or a controlled substance offense."[87] The definition, however, later came under fire for casting individuals with a history of minor drug trafficking into the same category as serial killers and the like.

Definitions of dangerousness are fraught with difficulty because, as some authors have pointed out, "dangerousness is not an objective quality like obesity or brown eyes, rather it is an ascribed quality like trustworthiness." Dangerousness[88] is not necessarily a personality trait which is stable or easily identifiable. Even if it were, recent studies[89] of criminal careers seem to show that involvement in crime decreases with age. Hence, as one author puts it, if "criminality declines more or less uniformly with age, then many offenders will be 'over the hill' by the time they are old enough to be plausible candidates for preventive incarceration."[90]

Correctional psychology that aspect of forensic psychology which is concerned with the diagnosis and classification of offenders, the treatment of correctional populations, and the rehabilitation of inmates and other law violators.

No discussion of social policy as it relates to the insights of criminal psychology, would be complete without mention of **correctional psychology.** Correctional psychology is concerned with the diagnosis and classification of offenders, the treatment of correctional populations, and the rehabilitation of inmates and other law violators. Perhaps the most commonly used classification instrument in correctional facilities today is the Minnesota Multiphasic Personality Inventory, better known as the MMPI. Based upon results of MMPI inventories offenders may be assigned to various security levels, differing correctional programs, or a variety of treatment programs. Psychological treatment, where it is employed, typically takes the form of individual or group counseling. Psychotherapy, guided group interaction, cognitive therapy, behavioral modification, and various forms of interpersonal therapy are representative of the range of techniques used.

Social Policy and the Psychology of Criminal Conduct

A practical synthesis of psychological approaches to criminal behavior is offered by D. A. Andrews and James Bonta in their 1994 book *The Psychology of Criminal Conduct.*[91] Andrews and Bonta prefer the term "psychology of criminal conduct," or PCC, to distinguish their point of view from what they call "the weak psychology represented in mainstream sociological criminology and clinical/forensic psychology."[92] Any useful synthesis of contemporary criminal psychology, they claim, should be fundamentally objective and empirical. They make it clear that they dislike many currently well-accepted perspectives, which they say have "placed higher value on social theory and political ideology than [on] rationality and/or respect for evidence."[93] Specifically, say Andrews and Bonta, "[t]he majority of perspectives on criminal conduct that are most favored in mainstream criminology reduce people to hypothetical fictions whose only interesting characteristics are their location in the social system. Almost without exception…," they write, "the causal significance of social location is presumed to reflect inequality in the distribution of social wealth and power." This kind of theorizing, the authors claim, "is a major preoccupation of mainstream textbook criminology, even though such a focus has failed to significantly advance understanding of criminal conduct."[94]

In *The Psychology of Criminal Conduct* Andrews and Bonta do not attempt to develop a new behavioral theory, but rather ask for the objective application of what is now understood about the psychology of crime and criminal behavior. Their book is a call for practical coalescence of what is already known of the psychology of criminal offenders. Such coalescence is possible, they say, through the application of readily available high-quality psychological findings. The authors claim, for example, that from the nearly five hundred published reports on "controlled evaluations of community and correctional interventions," it is possible to conclude that treatment reduces recidivism "to at least a mild degree." Further, a detailed consideration of published studies finds that, among other things, targeting higher-risk cases and using treatments outside of formal correctional settings which extend to an offender's family and peers are all elements of the most effective treatment strategies. Similarly, Andrews and Bonta say, along with objective measures of the success of rehabilitation programs and strategies, effective intervention and treatment services based upon the use of psychological assessment instruments which have already demonstrated their validity, empirically established risk factors that can be accurately assessed, and accurately measured community crime rates, are all ready and waiting to make a practical psychology of criminal conduct available to today's policymakers. In the words of Andrews and Bonta, "[t]here exists now an empirically defensible general psychology of criminal conduct (PCC) that is of practical value...it should speak to policy advisors, policy-makers and legislators who must come to see that...human science is not just [a] relic of a positivistic past."[95] The major remaining issue, say the authors, "on which work is only beginning, is how to make use of what works."[96]

PSYCHOLOGICAL PROFILING

During World War II psychologists and psychoanalysts were recruited by the War Department in an attempt to predict future moves enemy forces might make. Psychological and psychoanalytical techniques were applied to the study of Adolph Hitler, the Italian leader Benito Mussolini, the Japanese general and prime minister Tojo Hideki, and other Axis leaders. Such **psychological profiling** of enemy leaders may have given the Allies the edge in battlefield strategy. Hitler, probably because of his heightened sensitivity to symbols, his strong belief in fate, and his German ancestry (Freud was Austrian), became the central figure analyzed by profilers.

Psychological profiling the attempt to categorize, understand, and predict the behavior of certain types of offenders based upon behavioral clues they provide.

Today psychological profiling is used to assist criminal investigators seeking to better understand individuals wanted for serious offenses. Profilers develop a list of typical offender characteristics and other useful principles by analyzing crime scene data in conjunction with interviews and other studies of past offenders. In general, the psychological profiling of criminal offenders is based upon the belief that almost any form of conscious behavior, including each and every behavior engaged in by the offender during a criminal episode, is symptomatic of an individual's personality. Hence, the way in which a kidnapper approaches his victims, for example, the manner of attack used by a killer, and the specific sexual activities of a rapist, might all help paint a picture of the offender's motivations, personal characteristics, and likely future behavior. Sometimes psychological profiles can provide clues as to what an offender might do following an attack. Some offenders have been arrested, for example, after returning to the crime scene—a behavior typically predicted by specific behavioral clues left behind. Remorseful types can be expected to visit the victim's grave, permitting fruitful stakeouts of cemeteries.

In a well-known study[97] of lust murderers (men who kill and often mutilate victims during or following a forced sexual episode), Special Agents Robert R. Hazelwood and John E. Douglas distinguished between the organized nonsocial and the disorganized asocial types. The organized nonsocial lust murderer was described as exhibiting complete indifference to the interests of society, and as being completely self-centered. He was also said to be "methodical and cunning," as well as "fully cognizant of the criminality of his act and its impact on society."

His counterpart, the disorganized asocial lust murderer, was described this way: "The disorganized asocial lust murderer exhibits primary characteristics of societal aversion. This individual prefers his own company to that of others and would be typified as a loner. He experiences difficulty in negotiating interpersonal relationships and consequently feels rejected and lonely. He lacks the cunning of the nonsocial type and commits the crime in a more frenzied and less methodical manner. The crime is likely to be committed in close proximity to his residence or place of employment, where he feels secure and more at ease."[98]

During the 1980s the FBI led the movement to develop psychological profiling techniques through its concentration on violent sex offenders and arsonists. Today, the Behavioral Sciences Unit at the FBI Training Academy in Quantico, Virginia, continues to focus on serial killers, "lust murderers," domestic terrorists, and the like. The unit's activities were popularized a few years ago by the movie *Silence of the Lambs,* starring Jodie Foster and Anthony Hopkins, which portrayed the activities of a serial killer and enforcement activities designed to stop him. Movies, however, may lead the public to put too much stock in behavioral techniques such as psychological profiling. "It's not the magic bullet of investigations," says retired agent Robert Ressler, "[i]t's simply another tool."[99]

SUMMARY

Psychological and psychiatric theories of criminal behavior emphasize the role of individual propensities and characteristics in the genesis of criminality. Whether the emphasis is on conditioned behavior or on the psychoanalytical foundations of human conduct, such approaches ponder the wellsprings of human motivation, desire, and behavioral choice. Unfortunately, legal strictures have prevented psychology from making the kinds of courtroom contributions of which it appears capable. Even so, some theorists now consider the state of psychological criminology sufficiently advanced to allow for the development of a consistent and dependable social policy in the prediction of dangerousness and the rehabilitation of offenders. Similarly, psychological profiling may soon facilitate informed criminal investigations as well as the prevention of future crime.

DISCUSSION QUESTIONS

1. How do psychological theories of criminal behavior differ from the other types of theories presented in this book? How do the various psychological and psychiatric approaches presented in this chapter differ from one another?
2. How would the various perspectives discussed in this chapter suggest offenders might be prevented from committing additional offenses? How might they be rehabilitated?
3. How can crime be a form of adaptation to one's environment? Why would an individual choose such a form of adaptation over others that might be available?

4. What is the difference, if any, between the antisocial personality and the psychopath?
5. Which of the various standards for judging legal insanity discussed in this chapter do you find the most useful? Why?

NOTES

1. George J. Church, "Sons and Murderers," *Time*, on-line edition, October 3, 1993.
2. Karl Menninger, *The Crime of Punishment* (New York: Viking, 1968).
3. "Police Fear Killings Span 10 Years," *USA Today*, July 26, 1991, p. 3A.
4. "Mutilator 'Seemed So Normal,'" *Fayetteville Observer-Times*, July 28, 1991, p. 7A.
5. "Doctor: Dahmer Wanted to Freeze-Dry a Victim," *Fayetteville Observer-Times*, February 13, 1992, p. 7A.
6. "Psychiatrist: Dahmer Lacked Will to Stop," *Fayetteville Observer-Times*, February 4, 1992, p. 5A.
7. "Dahmer: 936 Years for 'Holocaust,'" *USA Today*, February 18, 1992, p. 1A.
8. "Drifter: I Killed 60 People," *USA Today*, August 15, 1991, p. 1A.
9. Carlos Sanchez and Marylou Tousignant, "Jury Acquits Bobbitt; Discrepancies, Lack of Evidence Cited," *Washington Post* wire services, November 11, 1993.
10. Ibid.
11. "New York Train Gunman a Walking Time Bomb," Reuters wire services, December 12, 1993.
12. Ibid.
13. D. A. Andrews and James Bonta, *The Psychology of Criminal Conduct* (Cincinnati: Anderson, 1994), p. 69.
14. Cathy Spatz Widom and Hans Toch, "The Contribution of Psychology to Criminal Justice Education," *Journal of Criminal Justice Education*, Vol. 4, no. 2 (Fall 1993), p. 253.
15. Curt R. Bartol, *Criminal Behavior: A Psychosocial Approach*, 3rd ed. (Englewood Cliffs, NJ: Prentice Hall, 1991), p. 16.
16. Nolan D.C. Lewis, "Foreword," in David Abrahamsen, *Crime and the Human Mind* (Montclair, NJ: Patterson Smith, 1969), p. vii. Originally published in 1944.
17. Ibid., p. 23.
18. Hervey M. Cleckley, *The Mask of Sanity*, 4th ed. (St. Louis, MO: C. V. Mosby, 1964).
19. Gwynn Nettler, *Killing One Another* (Cincinnati: Anderson, 1982), p. 179.
20. Albert I. Rabin, "The Antisocial Personality—Psychopathy and Sociopathy," in Hans Toch, *Psychology of Crime and Criminal Justice* (Prospect Heights, IL: Waveland, 1979), p. 330.
21. R. D. Hare, *Psychopathy: Theory and Research* (New York: John Wiley & Sons, 1970).
22. L. N. Robins, *Deviant Children Grow Up* (Baltimore: Williams and Wilkins, 1966).
23. S. B. Guze, *Criminality and Psychiatric Disorders* (New York: Oxford University Press, 1976).
24. American Psychiatric Association, *Diagnostic and Statistical Manual of Mental Disorders*, 2nd ed. (Washington: APA, 1968).
25. Ibid., p. 43.
26. S. Hodgins and G. Cote, "The Prevalence of Mental Disorders Among Penitentiary Inmates in Quebec," *Canada's Mental Health*, Vol. 38 (1990), pp. 1–4.
27. H. Prins, *Offenders, Deviants or Patients? An Introduction to the Study of Socio-forensic Problems* (London: Tavistock, 1980).
28. Hans J. Eysenck, *Crime and Personality* (Boston: Houghton Mifflin, 1964).
29. Hans J. Eysenck, "Personality and Criminality: A Dispositional Analysis," in William S. Laufer and Freda Adler, eds., *Advances in Criminology Theory*, Vol. 1 (New Brunswick, NJ: Transaction, 1989), p. 90.
30. Eysenck, *Crime and Personality*, pp. 35–36.

31. Ibid., pp. 92.
32. Ibid., p. 53, citing J. B. S. Haldane, "Foreword," to Johannes Lange, *Crime as Destiny, A Study of Criminal Twins* (London: G. Allen & Unwin, Ltd., 1931), p. 53.
33. David Abrahamsen, *Crime and the Human Mind* (Montclair, NJ: Patterson Smith, 1969), p. vii. Originally published in 1944.
34. P. Q. Roche, *The Criminal Mind: A Study of Communications Between Criminal Law and Psychiatry* (New York: Grove Press, 1958), p. 52.
35. *The American Heritage Dictionary and Electronic Thesaurus* (Boston: Houghton Mifflin, 1987).
36. Ibid.
37. Ibid.
38. Ibid.
39. "Nationline: Book Thief," *USA Today,* August 1, 1991, p. 3A.
40. Nettler, *Killing One Another,* p. 159.
41. Ibid., p. 155.
42. Abrahamsen, *Crime and the Human Mind,* p. 99.
43. Ibid., p. 100.
44. J. Dollard, L. Doob, N. Miller, O. Mowrer, and R. Sears, *Frustration and Aggression* (New Haven, CT: Yale University Press, 1939).
45. Carl Weiser, "This Is What You Get for Firing Me!" *USA Today,* January 28, 1993, p. 3A.
46. Andrew F. Henry and James F. Short, Jr., *Suicide and Homicide: Economic Sociological, and Psychological Aspects of Aggression* (Glencoe, IL: Free Press, 1954).
47. Stewart Palmer, *A Study of Murder* (New York: Crowell, 1960).
48. Abrahamsen, *Crime and the Human Mind,* p. 26.
49. Nancy Gibbs, "The Devil's Disciple," *Time,* January 11, 1993, p. 40.
50. Seymour L. Halleck, *Psychiatry and the Dilemmas of Crime: A Study of Causes, Punishment and Treatment* (Berkeley: University of California Press, 1971).
51. Ibid., p. 77.
52. Ibid., p. 78.
53. Ibid., p. 80.
54. Ibid.
55. Ibid.
56. Albert Bandura, "The Social Learning Perspective: Mechanisms of Aggression," in Toch, *Psychology of Crime and Criminal Justice,* pp. 198–236.
57. M. M. Lefkowitz, L. D. Eron, L. O. Walder, and L. R. Huesmann, "Television Violence and Child Aggression: A Follow-up Study," in G. A. Comstock and E. A. Rubinstein, eds., *Television and Social Behavior,* Volume 3 (Washington, D.C.: U.S. Government Printing Office, 1972), pp. 35–135.
58. Widom and Toch, "The Contribution of Psychology to Criminal Justice Education."
59. Ibid., p. 253.
60. C. R. Hollin, *Psychology and Crime: An Introduction to Criminological Psychology* (London: Routledge, 1989), p. 42.
61. Ibid., p. 254.
62. "15-Year-Old Killer Feared Being Called a 'Little Punk,'" *Fayetteville Observer-Times,* December 26, 1993, p. 1A.
63. *The American Heritage Dictionary and Electronic Thesaurus.*
64. *Foucha* v. *Louisiana,* no. 90-5844. Argued November 4, 1991. Decided May 18, 1992.
65. C. Ray Jeffery, *Criminology: An Interdisciplinary Approach* (Englewood Cliffs, NJ: Prentice Hall, 1990), p. 431.
66. *Leland* v. *Oregon,* 343 U.S. 790, 1952.
67. *Riggins* v. *Nevada,* no. 90-8466. Argued January 15, 1992. Decided May 18, 1992.
68. *Terrance Frank* v. *U.S.,* no. 91-8230. Decided October 13, 1992.
69. October 12, 1984, P.L. 98-473, title II, Sec. 403(a), 98 Stat. 2057.
70. Halleck, *Psychiatry and the Dilemmas of Crime,* p. 213.
71. *Durham* v. *U.S.,* 214 F.2d 862 (D.C. Cir. 1954).
72. American Law Institute, *Model Penal Code: Official Draft and Explanatory Notes* (Philadelphia: The Institute, 1985).
73. *U.S.* v. *Brawner,* 471 F.2d 969 (D.C. Cir. 1972).
74. June 25, 1948, ch. 645, 62 Stat. 855; Oct. 12, 1984, P.L. 98-473, title II, Sec. 403(a), 98 Stat. 2059; November 18, 1988, P.L. 100-690, title VII, Sec. 7043, 102 Stat. 4400.

75. *Foucha* v. *Louisiana,* 1992.
76. See, for example, D. P. Farrington, "Childhood Aggression and Adult Violence: Early Precursors and Later Life Outcomes," in D. J. Pepler and K. H. Rubin, eds., *The Development and Treatment of Childhood Aggression* (Hillsdale, NJ: Erlbaum, 1990), pp. 2–29; and R. E. Tremblay, B. Masse, D. Perron, M. LeBlanc, A. E. Schwartzman, and J. E. Ledingham, "Early Disruptive Behavior: Poor School Achievement, Delinquent Behavior and Delinquent Personality: Longitudinal Analyses," *Journal of Consulting and Clinical Psychology,* Vol. 60, no. 1, 1992, pp. 64–72.
77. R. Loeber, "Questions and Advances in the Study of Developmental Pathways," in D. Cicchetti and S. Toth, eds., *Models and Integration: Rochester Symposium on Developmental Psychopathology* (Rochester, NY: University of Rochester Press, 1991), pp. 97–115.
78. "State Probing Release of Molester Now Charged with Murder," United Press International wire services, Southwestern edition, September 24, 1993.
79. "Texas Executes Convicted Killer Who Waived Appeals," Reuters wire service, Western edition, November 10, 1993.
80. Christine Spolar, "California Town Cries as Polly Klaas Is Found; Twice-Convicted Suspect Faces Murder, Kidnapping Charges in Abduction of 12-Year-Old," *Washington Post* wire service, December 6, 1993.
81. Jennifer L. White, Terrie E. Moffitt, Felton Earls, Lee Robins, and Phil A. Silva, "How Early Can We Tell? Predictors of Childhood Conduct Disorder and Adolescent Delinquency," *Criminology,* Vol. 28, no. 4 (1990), pp. 507–528.
82. Daniel S. Nagin and David P. Farrington, "The Stability of Criminal Potential from Childhood to Adulthood," *Criminology,* Vol. 30, no. 2 (1992), pp. 235–260.
83. For one of the first and still definitive works in the area of selective incapacitation, see Peter Greenwood and Allan Abrahamse, *Selective Incapacitation* (Santa Monica, CA: Rand Corporation, 1982).
84. M. A. Peterson, H. B. Braiker, and S. M. Polich, *Who Commits Crimes?* (Cambridge: Oelgeschlager, Gunn and Hain, 1981).
85. J. Monahan, *Predicting Violent Behavior: An Assessment of Clinical Techniques* (Beverly Hills, CA: Sage, 1981).
86. The 1984 Amendment to Section 200 of title II (Sec. 200-2304) of P.L. 98-473, is popularly referred to as the "1984 Comprehensive Crime Control Act."
87. U.S. Sentencing Commission, *Federal Sentencing Guidelines Manual* (Washington, D.C.: U.S. Government Printing Office, 1987), p. 10.
88. Jill Peay, "Dangerousness—Ascription or Description," in M.P. Feldman, ed., *Developments in the Study of Criminal Behavior,* Volume 2, *Violence* (New York: John Wiley & Sons, 1982), p. 211, citing N. Walker, "Dangerous People," *International Journal of Law and Psychiatry,* Vol. 1 (1978), pp. 37–50.
89. See, for example, Michael Gottfredson and Travis Hirschi, *A General Theory of Crime* (Stanford, CA: Stanford University Press, 1990); and Travis Hirschi and Michael Gottfredson, "Age and the Explanation of Crime," *American Journal of Sociology,* Vol. 89 (1983), pp. 552–584.
90. David F. Greenberg, "Modeling Criminal Careers," *Criminology,* Vol. 29, no. 1 (1991), p. 39.
91. D. A. Andrews and James Bonta, *The Psychology of Criminal Conduct* (Cincinnati: Anderson, 1994).
92. Ibid., p. 1.
93. Ibid.
94. Ibid., pp. 20–21.
95. Ibid., p. 227.
96. Ibid., p. 236.
97. Robert R. Hazelwood and John E. Douglas, "The Lust Murderer," *FBI Law Enforcement Bulletin* (Washington: U.S. Department of Justice, April 1980).
98. Ibid.
99. Anastasia Toufexis, "Mind Games with Monsters," *Time,* May 6, 1991, pp. 68, 69.

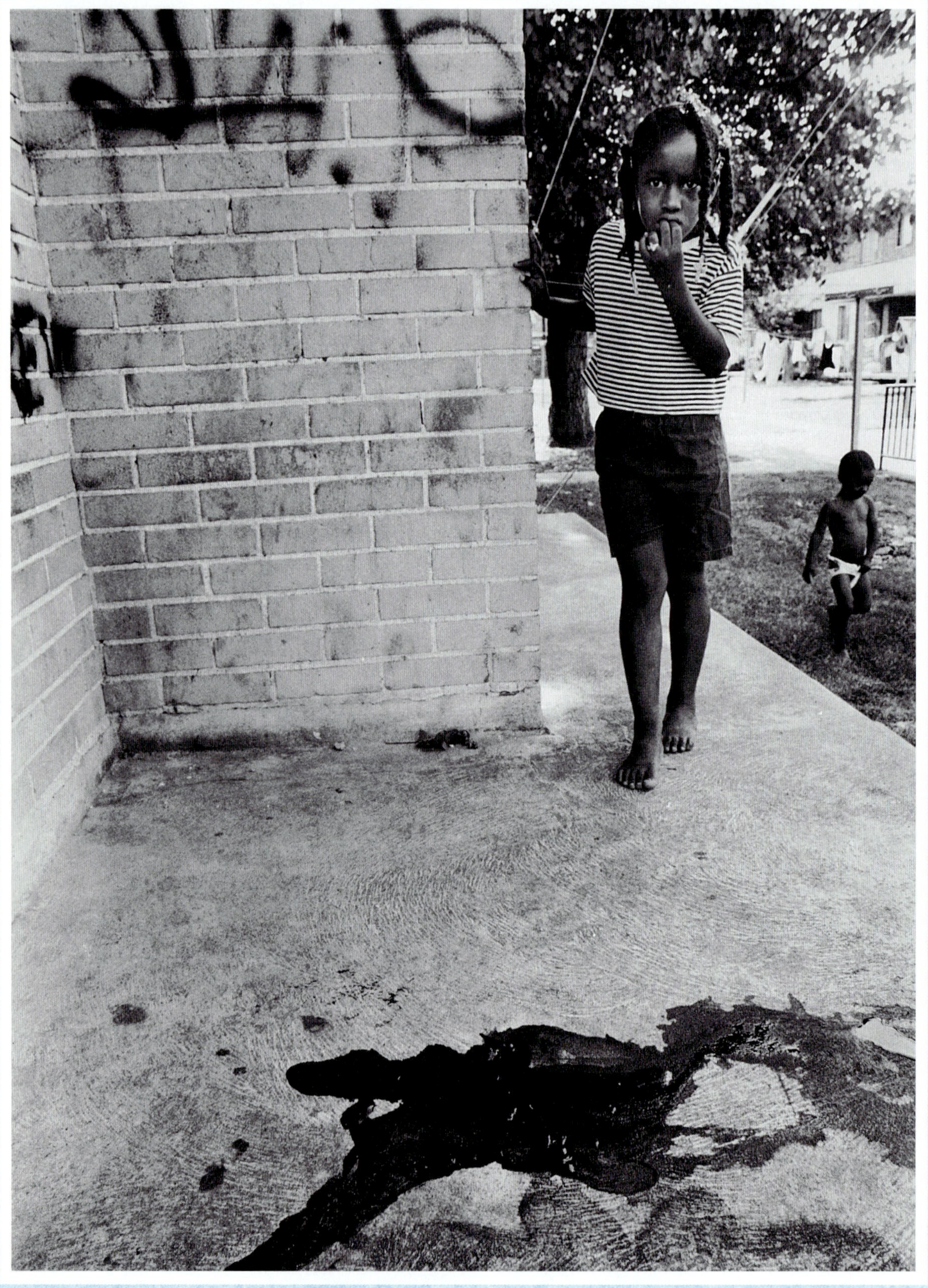

CHAPTER 7

CRIME AND THE ROLE OF THE SOCIAL ENVIRONMENT

If we would change the amount of crime in the community, we must change the community.

—Frank Tannenbaum[1]

Children *learn* to become delinquents by becoming members of groups in which delinquent conduct is already established....

—Albert K. Cohen[2]

If they don't convict those dudes of beating that man, it's gonna happen again. I know I'm gonna do everything I can to make it happen. I got a 14-shot Beretta and I ain't worried about no police or anybody else.

—Broadway Gangster Crip member "Antoine" threatening to riot, before the verdict in the 1993 federal trial of police officers charged with the beating of Rodney King.[3]

IMPORTANT NAMES

Ernest Burgess
Florian Znaniecki
Thorsten Sellin
Albert Cohen
Frederic M. Thrasher
Gresham Sykes
Marvin Wolfgang
Robert Park
Clifford Shaw
Richard Cloward
Edwin Sutherland
William Foote Whyte
David Matza
Walter Reckless
W. I. Thomas
Henry McKay
Lloyd Ohlin
Robert K. Merton
Walter B. Miller
Franco Ferracuti
Travis Hirschi

IMPORTANT TERMS

sociological theories
social pathology
ecological theory
culture conflict
anomie
subculture
focal concerns
social control theory
illegitimate opportunity structure
social structure
social disorganization
Chicago school
conduct norms
strain theory
opportunity structure
criminology of place
defensible space
techniques of neutralization
social-structural theories
subcultural theory
reaction formation
differential association
learning theory
social bond
containment
environmental criminology
control theory

INTRODUCTION

In late July 1993 a tourist traveling home to Mint Hill, North Carolina, from the state's seacoast city of Wilmington, a couple of hundred miles away, was robbed and shot while he napped during a rest period on the shoulder of state route 74. The murder, like the twenty-two others committed that year in rural Robeson County, North Carolina, would have attracted little attention outside of the local area had it not been for the fact that the dead tourist was 57-year-old James Jordan, father of Chicago Bulls basketball superstar, Michael Jordan. After Jordan was killed, his body was dumped 25 miles away in South Carolina's Gum Swamp Creek. The new red Lexus sport coupe that Jordan had been driving showed up later, apparently stripped by teenagers acquainted with the killers.

Two local 18-year-olds, Larry Demery and Daniel Green, were quickly arrested and charged with Jordan's murder. Both had long records of trouble with the law. Demery, a lanky native American with a *Guns N' Roses* tattoo on his right forearm, was out of work and on parole for check forgery at the time of the murder. In the year preceding the crime, Demery had been charged with four other felonies—ranging from armed robbery to breaking and entering.[4] In one crime attributed to Demery, the robbery of a convenience store, a 61-year-old clerk was struck on the head with a cinder block and seriously injured. When Demery was arrested in the Jordan case, police were already looking for him on four other warrants, all issued for failure to appear for trial on more than a dozen occasions.

Daniel Green's record of law violations was even more serious. In the 9th grade the semiliterate Green was suspended for assaulting the school's principal. He promptly dropped out of school. Shortly afterward, in 1991, Green was convicted of assault with intent to kill after he pled guilty to charges of beating a friend with the blunt side of an axe. The friend, Robert Ellison, 18, was in a comma for months.

A few days after the Jordan killing another murder was committed only a short distance from the spot where Jordan's stolen vehicle was recovered. It happened when U.S. Army sergeant Kenny French walked into Luigi's Italian Restaurant in Fayetteville, North Carolina, and, without warning, opened fire on the establishment's customers and staff. As he pulled the trigger, French shouted angrily about the Clinton administration's decision to admit avowed homosexuals into military ranks.[5] Killed in the fusillade were the restaurant's owner, his wife, and two customers. Seven other people were shot and injured. Until the time of the mass murder, Sergeant French, who was stationed at Fort Bragg, North Carolina, had been known to friends and former neighbors as a polite young man. French's reasons for killing were variously attributed to individualized factors, including the suicidal death of his abusive father, alcohol abuse, depression, and a discrediting family history of sexual abuse.[6]

While elements of a person's life, as in Kenny French's case, can always be identified as contributing factors in almost any crime, the motivation behind the killing of James Jordan appears to have arisen primarily from social and economic deprivation. Both Green and Demery were born into relative poverty. Both came from families lacking in educational achievement and in the basic skills needed for success in the modern world. Poverty, academic failure, and subcultural values which focused on greed and excitement dictated the direction their lives were to take—and all but insured their fateful encounter with James Jordan that sultry July afternoon.

MAJOR PRINCIPLES OF SOCIOLOGICAL THEORIES

This brief section serves to summarize the central features of sociological theories of crime causation. Each of these points can be found elsewhere in this chapter, where they are discussed in more detail. This cursory overview, however, is intended to provide more than a summary—it is meant to be a guide to the rest of this chapter.

While, as this chapter will show, those perspectives on crime causation which have been termed "sociological" are quite diverse, most such perspectives build upon certain fundamental assumptions. Among them are

- Social groups, social institutions, the arrangements of society, and social roles all provide the proper focus for criminological study.
- Group dynamics, group organization, and subgroup relationships form the causal nexus out of which crime develops.
- The structure of society, and its relative degree of organization or disorganization, are important factors contributing to the prevalence of criminal behavior.

- While it may be impossible to predict the specific behavior of a given individual, statistical estimates of group characteristics are possible to achieve. Hence, the probability that a member of a given group will engage in a specific type of crime can be estimated.

While all sociological perspectives on crime share the foregoing characteristics, particular theories may give greater or lesser weight to the following aspects of social life:

1. The clash of norms and values between variously socialized groups.
2. Socialization and the process of association between individuals.
3. The existence of subcultures and varying types of opportunities.

SOCIOLOGICAL THEORIES

Social structure the pattern of social organization and the interrelationships between institutions characteristic of a society.

Sociological theories place emphasis on the structure of society (or **social structure**), on the relationship between social institutions, and on the types of behavior which tend to characterize *groups* of people. In contrast to more individualized psychological theories, which have what is called a "micro" focus, sociological approaches utilize a "macro" perspective instead—stressing behavioral tendencies for group members, rather than attempting to predict the behavior of specific individuals.

Sociological thought has been dominant in behavioral science literature and has influenced criminological theory construction more significantly than any other perspective during the past few decades. This emphasis has probably been due, at least in part, to a widespread American concern with social problems, including civil rights, the women's movement, issues of poverty, and the decline in influence experienced by many traditional social institutions such as the family, government, organized religion, and educational institutions.

Social-structural theories explain crime by reference to various aspects of the social fabric. They emphasize relationships between social institutions and describe the types of behavior which tend to characterize *groups* of people as opposed to *individuals.*

This chapter describes various subtypes of sociological theory, including (1) ecological approaches, (2) culture conflict, (3) differential association, (4) strain theories, (5) subcultural approaches, and (6) control theories. All share some elements in common, and the classification of a theory into one subcategory or another is often more a matter of which aspects a writer chooses to emphasize rather than the result of any clear-cut definitional elements inherent in the perspectives themselves. Most of the theories in this chapter can also be termed **social-structural theories** since most explain crime by reference to various aspects of the social fabric. They name the institutional structure of society and the various formal and informal arrangements between social groups as causes of crime and deviance. Environmental influences, socialization, and traditional and accepted patterns of behavior are all used by social-structuralists to portray the criminal as a product of his or her social environment and to depict criminality as a form of acquired behavior.

Social pathology a concept that compares society to a physical organism and sees criminality as an illness.

The term **social pathology** was at times associated with early social-structural theories. Social pathology, a concept prevalent in the criminological literature of a few decades ago, was initially defined as "those human actions which run contrary to the ideals of residential stability, property ownership, sobriety, thrift, habituation to work, small business enterprise, sexual discretion, family solidarity, neighborliness, and discipline of will."[7] It meant, simply, behavior not in keeping with the prevalent norms and values of the social group. Over time, however, the concept of social pathology changed, and it came to represent the idea that aspects of society may be somehow pathological, or "sick," and may produce deviant behavior among individuals and groups who live under or are exposed to such social conditions. Social pathology has also been associated with the concept of **social disorganization,**[8] a condition said to exist when a group is faced with "social change, uneven development of culture, maladaptiveness, disharmony, conflict, and lack of consensus...."[9]

Social disorganization a condition said to exist when a group is faced with social change, uneven development of culture, maladaptiveness, disharmony, conflict, and lack of consensus.

THEORY IN PERSPECTIVE

Types of Sociological Theories

SOCIOLOGICAL THEORIES, also known as SOCIAL-STRUCTURAL APPROACHES

Emphasize relationships between social institutions and describe the types of behavior which tend to characterize *groups* of people as opposed to *individuals*.

ECOLOGICAL THEORY or **"CHICAGO SCHOOL."** Stresses the demographic and geographic aspects of groups and sees the social disorganization which characterizes delinquency areas as a major cause of criminality and of victimization.

Period: 1920s-1930s
Theorists: Robert Park, Ernest Burgess, W.I. Thomas, Florian Znaniecki, Clifford Shaw, Henry McKay
Concepts: Demographics, concentric zones, social disorganization, delinquency areas

CULTURE CONFLICT. Suggests that the root cause of crime can be found in a clash of values between variously socialized groups over what is acceptable or proper behavior.

Period: 1930s
Theorists: Thorsten Sellin and others
Concepts: Conduct norms

DIFFERENTIAL ASSOCIATION. Maintains that criminality, like any other form of behavior, is learned through a process of association with others who communicate criminal values.

Period: 1930s-1960s
Theorists: Edwin Sutherland and others
Concepts: Differential association; crime as learned; techniques of crime; commission, frequency, duration, priority, and intensity of association

SUBCULTURAL THEORY. Highlights violent and delinquent subcultures, and emphasizes the contribution made by variously socialized cultural groups to the phenomenon of crime.

Period: 1920s-Present
Theorists: Frederic M. Thrasher, William Foote Whyte, Walter B. Miller, Albert Cohen, Gresham Sykes, David Matza, Franco Ferracuti, Marvin Wolfgang, and many others
Concepts: Subculture, socialization, focal concerns, reaction formation, delinquency and drift, techniques of neutralization

STRAIN or **ANOMIE THEORY.** Posits the disjuncture between socially and subculturally sanctioned mean and goals as the cause of criminal behavior.

Period: 1930s-Present
Theorists: Robert K. Merton, Richard Cloward, Lloyd Ohlin
Concepts: Goals, means, opportunity structures, differential opportunity

SOCIAL CONTROL APPROACHES. Ask why people obey rules instead of breaking them.

Period: 1950s-Present
Theorists: Walter C. Reckless, Travis Hirschi, and others
Concepts: Inner and outer containment, soical bond

The Chicago School

Some of the earliest sociological theories to receive widespread recognition can be found in the writings of **Robert Park** and **Ernest Burgess.** In the 1920s and 1930s Park and Burgess, through their work at the University of Chicago, developed what became known as the ecological school of criminology. The ecological school highlighted the role of concentric zones throughout a city, which were envisioned much like ever-expanding circles on a target (see Figure 7.1), wherein diverse populations and behavioral characteristics predominated. In what Park and Burgess called Zone 1, or the central business zone, retail businesses and light manufacturing could typically be found. Zone 2, surrounding the city center, generally contained areas which were in transition from residential areas to business purposes. Zone 3 contained mostly working-class homes, while Zone 4 was occupied by middle-class citizens. Zone 5, consisting largely of suburbs, was called the commuter zone. Early ecological theories were formed using 1920s Chicago as a model. While their applicability to other cities or to other time periods may be questionable, such theories pointed out the tendency for criminal activity to be associated with transition zones which, because of the turmoil or social disorganization associated with them, were generally characterized by lower property values marginal individuals, and a general lack of privacy.

Park and Burgess had been strongly influenced by **W. I. Thomas** and **Florian Znaniecki** who described, in their book *The Polish Peasant in Europe and America,*[10] the problems Polish immigrants faced in the early 1900s when they left their homeland and moved to the cities of America. Thomas and Znaniecki noted how rates of crime rose among people who had been so displaced, and they hypothesized that the cause was the social disorganization which resulted from the immigrant's inability to successfully transplant guiding norms and values from the home culture into the new one.

Clifford Shaw and **Henry McKay,** other early advocates of the ecological approach, conducted empirical studies of delinquency rates in Chicago. One such study, undertaken in the late 1920s, found that the rate of delinquency among black youths "on the South Side of Chicago decreases regularly by square mile areas from 19.4% in the area adjoining the center of the city to 3.5% in the area five miles from the center of the city."[11]

Even at the height of its popularity, the ecological school recognized that American crime patterns might be different from those found elsewhere in the world, and that crime zones might exist in city areas other than those surrounding the core. Early comparisons of American, European, and Asian data, for instance, found higher crime rates at what were called the "city gates" (near-suburban areas providing access to downtown) in Europe and Asia.

The greatest contribution the ecological school made to criminological literature can be found in its claim that society, in the form of the community, wields a

Ecological theory also called the **"Chicago school"** of criminology, is a type of sociological approach which emphasizes demographics (the characteristics of population groups) and geographics (the mapped location of such groups relative to one another) and sees the social disorganization that characterizes delinquency areas as a major cause of criminality and victimization.

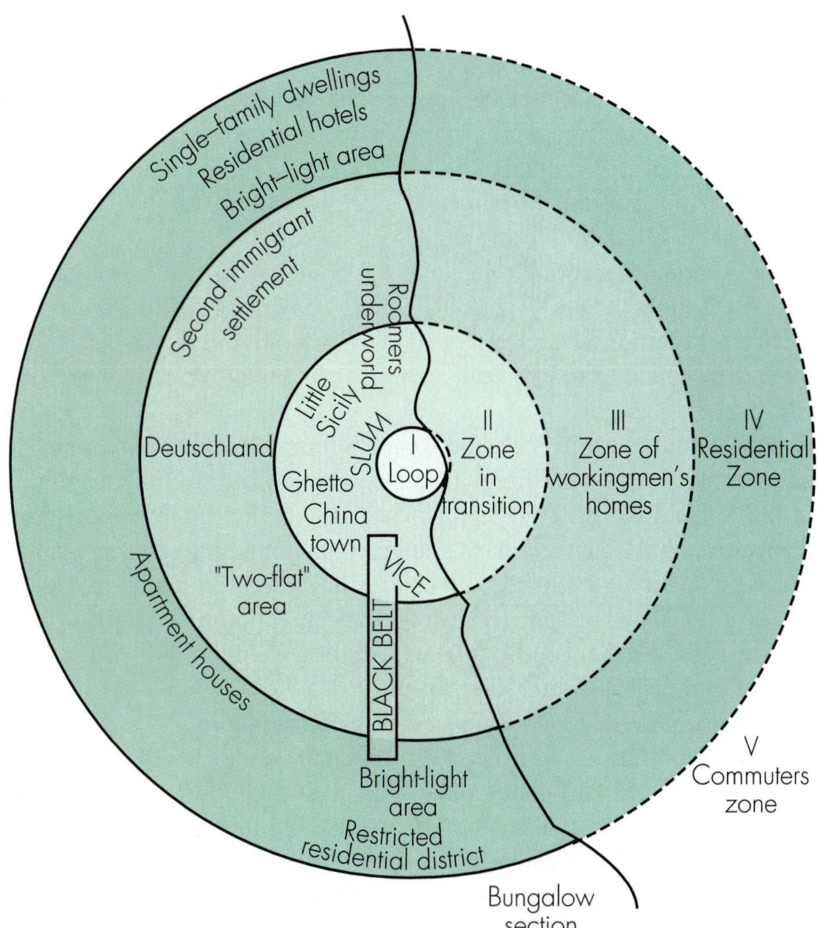

FIGURE 7.1 Chicago's Concentric Zones. *Source*: Robert E. Park, Earnest W. Burgess, and R. D. McKenzie, *The City* (Chicago: University of Chicago Press, 1925), p. 55. Copyright © University of Chicago Press. Reprinted with permission.

major influence upon human behavior.[12] Similarly, ecological theorists of the Chicago school formalized the use of two sources of information: (1) official crime and population statistics and (2) ethnographic data. Population statistics, also referred to as demographic data, combined with crime information, provided empirical material that gave scientific weight to ecological investigations. Ethnographic information, gathered in the form of life stories, or ethnographies, described the lives of city inhabitants. By comparing one set of data with the other—demographics with ethnographies—ecological investigators were able to show that life experience varied from one location to another, and that personal involvement in crime had a strong tendency to be associated with place of residence.

A Critique of the Ecological School

The ecological school, like many sociological approaches to explaining crime, has been criticized for its tendency to forget the individual. By concentrating on the role social institutions and social disorganization play in crime causation, ecological approaches rarely acknowledge the influence of individual psychology, distinctive biology, or personal choice on criminal activity. This sort of criticism was insightfully advanced by W. S. Robinson in a classic 1950 article.[13] Robinson pointed out the "problematic nature of making individual-level inferences on the basis of aggregate data."[14]

Other authors have suggested that ecological theories give too much credence to the notion that location determines crime and delinquency. The nature of any given location changes over time, and evolutions in land-use patterns, such as a movement away from home ownership and toward rental or low-income housing, for example, may seriously affect the nature of a neighborhood and the concomitant quality of social organization found there.

Similarly, rates of neighborhood crime and delinquency may be "an artifact of police decision-making practices,"[15] and bear little objective relationship to the actual degree of law violation in an area. Such police bias, should it exist, may seriously mislead researchers into categorizing certain areas as high in crime when, in fact, they may not be.

Another critique of the ecological school can be found in its seeming inability to differentiate between the condition of social disorganization and the things such a condition is said to cause. What, for example, is the difference between social disorganization and high rates of delinquency? Is not delinquency a form of the very thing said to cause it? As Stephen Pfohl has observed, early ecological writers sometimes used the incidence of delinquency as "both an example of disorganization and something caused by disorganization,"[16] making it difficult to gauge the efficacy of their explanatory approach.

Finally, many crimes occur outside of geographic areas said to be characterized by social disorganization. Murder, rape, burglary, incidents of drug use, assault, and so on, all occur in affluent "well-established" neighborhoods as well as in other parts of a community. Likewise, white-collar, computer, environmental, and other types of crime may actually occur with a greater frequency in socially well-established neighborhoods than elsewhere. Hence, the ecological approach is clearly not an adequate explanation for all crime, nor for all types of crime.

EMERGING THEORY

The Criminology of Place

Ecological approaches to crime causation have found a modern rebirth in what is now called the "criminology of place." **The criminology of place,** also called **environmental criminology,** is an emerging perspective within the contemporary body of criminological theory that emphasizes the importance of geographic location and architectural features as they are associated with the prevalence of victimization. "Hot spots" of crime, including neighborhoods, specific streets, and even individual houses and business establishments have been identified by recent writers. Lawrence Sherman, for example, tells of a study[1] which revealed that 3% of places (addresses and intersections) in Minneapolis produce 50% of all calls to the police. Crime, says Sherman, while it is relatively rare, is geographically concentrated.

Environmental criminology an emerging perspective which emphasizes the importance of geographic location and architectural features as they are associated with the prevalence of criminal victimization.

Another researcher, Rodney Stark, asks "[h]ow is it that neighborhoods can remain the site of high crime and deviance rates despite a complete turnover in their populations?...There must be something about places as such that sustains crime."[2] Stark has developed a theory of deviant neighborhoods. It consists of thirty propositions, including the following:[3]

1. "To the extent that neighborhoods are dense and poor, homes will be crowded."
2. "Where homes are more crowded there will be a greater tendency to congregate outside the home in places and circumstances that raise levels of temptation and opportunity to deviate."
3. "Where homes are more crowded, there will be lower levels of supervision of children."
4. "Reduced levels of child supervision will result in poor school achievement, with a consequent reduction in stakes in conformity and an increase in deviant behavior."
5. "Poor, dense neighborhoods tend to be mixed-use neighborhoods."
6. "Mixed use increases familiarity with and easy access to places offering the opportunity for deviance."

Even within so-called high-crime neighborhoods, however, crimes tend to be concentrated at specific locations such as street blocks or multiple-family dwellings. This kind of microlevel analysis has also shown, for example, that some units within specific apartment buildings are much more likely to be the site of criminal occurrences than others. Apartments near complex or building entrances appear to be more criminally dangerous, especially if they

Defensible space the range of mechanisms that combine to bring an environment under the control of its residents.

are not facing other buildings or apartments. Likewise, pedestrian tunnels, unattended parking lots, and convenience stores with clerks stationed in less visible areas are often targeted by criminal offenders.

The criminology of place employs the concept of **defensible space,** a term which evolved out of a conference in 1964 at Washington University in St. Louis, Missouri.[4] Defensible space has been defined as "a surrogate term for the range of mechanisms—real and symbolic barriers, strongly defined areas of influence, and improved opportunities for surveillance—that combine to bring an environment under the control of its residents."[5] The St. Louis conference, which brought criminologists, police officers, and architects face to face, focused on crime problems characteristic of public housing areas. Findings demonstrated that specific architectural changes which enhanced barriers, defined boundaries, and removed criminal opportunity could do much to reduce the risk of crime—even in the midst of high-crime neighborhoods.

The criminology of place holds that location can be as predictive of criminal activity as the life-styles of victimized individuals or the social features of victimized households. (Place has been defined by researchers as "a fixed physical environment that can be seen completely and simultaneously, at least on its surface, by one's naked eyes."[6]) Places can be criminogenic due to the routine activities associated with them. On the other hand, some places host crime because they provide the characteristics which facilitate its commission. In Sherman's study, for example, Minneapolis parks drew "flashers" because they provided "opportunities for concealment" up until the moment when the flasher struck. Changes to the parks, such as moving walkways some distance from trees and shrubbery could reduce criminal opportunity.

Recognizing the criminology of place, New York police developed a program a few years ago designed to close businesses with repeated crime problems. Called Operation Padlock, the program appeared to be successful in reducing the incidence of certain kinds of crime. However, as Sherman points out, "[n]either capital punishment of places (as in arson of crack houses) nor incapacitation of the routine activities of criminal hot spots (as in revocation of liquor licenses) seems likely to eliminate crime. But since the routine activities of places may be regulated far more easily than the routine activities of persons, a criminology of place would seem to offer substantial promise for public policy as well as theory."[7]

1 Lawrence W. Sherman, Patrick R. Gartin, and Michael E. Buerger, "Hot Spots of Predatory Crime: Routine Activities and the Criminology of Place," *Criminology*, Vol. 27, no. 1 (1989), pp. 27–55.

2. Rodney Stark, "Deviant Places: A Theory of the Ecology of Crime," *Criminology*, Vol. 25, no. 4 (1987), p. 893.

3. Ibid., pp. 895–899.

4. Oscar Newman, *Architectural Design for Crime Prevention* (Washington, D.C.: U.S. Department of Justice, 1973).

5. Oscar Newman, *Defensible Space: Crime Prevention Through Urban Design* (New York: Macmillan, 1972), p. 3.

6. "Hot Spots of Predatory Crime," p. 31.

7. Ibid., p. 49.

Culture Conflict

Fundamental to ecological criminology was the belief that zones of transition, because they tended to be in flux, harbor groups of people whose values are often at odds with those of the larger, surrounding, society. This perspective found its clearest expression in the writings of **Thorsten Sellin** in his 1938 book, *Culture Conflict and Crime.*[17] Sellin maintained that the root cause of crime could be found in different values about what is acceptable or proper behavior. According to Sellin, **conduct norms,** which provide the valuative basis for human behavior, are acquired early in life through childhood socialization. It is the clash of norms between variously socialized groups that results in crime. Because crime is a violation of laws established by legislative decree, the criminal event itself, from this point of view, is nothing other than a disagreement over what should be acceptable behavior. For some social groups, what we tend to call crime, is simply part of the landscape—something that can be expected to happen to you unless you take steps to protect yourself. From this point of view, those to whom crime happens are not so much victims as ill prepared.

Conduct norms the shared expectations of a social group relative to personal conduct.

Sellin wrote about two kinds of **culture conflict.** The first type, primary conflict, arises when a fundamental clash of cultures occurs. Sellin's classic example was that of an immigrant father who kills his daughter's lover following an "old world" tradition which demands that a family's honor be kept intact. In Sellin's words, "[a] few years ago, a Sicilian father in New Jersey killed the sixteen-year-old seducer of his daughter, expressing surprise at his arrest since he had merely defended his family honor in a traditional way. In this case…[t]he conflict was external and occurred between cultural codes or norms. We may assume that where such conflicts occur…norms of one cultural group or area migrate to

Culture conflict a sociological perspective on crime which suggests that the root cause of criminality can be found in a clash of values between variously socialized groups over what is acceptable or proper behavior.

Conflict is a pervasive part of everyday life—much of it based on a clash of values built upon subcultural differences. *John Giordano/SABA Press Photos, Inc.*

another and that such conflict will continue so long as the acculturation process has not been completed."[18]

The other type of conflict, called secondary conflict, arose, according to Sellin, when smaller cultures within the primary one clashed. So it is that middle-class values, upon which most criminal laws are based, may find fault with inner-city or lower-class norms, resulting in the social phenomenon we call "crime."

In Sellin's day prostitution and gambling provided plentiful examples of secondary conflict. Many lower-class inner-city groups accepted gambling and prostitution as a way of life—if not for individual members of those groups, then at least as forms of behavior which were rarely condemned for those choosing to participate in them. Today, drug use and abuse provide more readily understandable examples. For some segments of contemporary society drug sales have become a source of substantial income, and the conduct norms which typify such groups support at least the relative legitimacy of lives built around the drug trade. In other words, in some parts of America, drug dealing is an acceptable form of business. To those who make the laws, however, it is not. It is from the clash of these two opposing viewpoints that conflict, and crime, emerge.

Differential Association

Learning theory the general notion that crime is an acquired form of behavior, which is learned just as are many other forms of behavior.

Differential association the sociological thesis that criminality, like any other form of behavior, is learned through a process of association with others who communicate criminal values.

One of the most important perspectives on criminality was a form of **learning theory** advanced by **Edwin Sutherland** in 1939. Called **differential association,** Sutherland's thesis was that criminality is learned behavior, and that it is learned through a process of association with others who communicate criminal values and who may advocate the commission of crimes. All significant human behavior, according to Sutherland, is learned behavior, and crime, therefore, is not substantively different from any other form of behavior.

Although Sutherland died in 1950, the tenth edition of his famous book, *Criminology,* was published in 1978 under the authorship of Donald R. Cressey, a professor at the University of California at Santa Barbara. The 1978 edition of *Criminology* contained the finalized principles of differential association (which, for all practical purposes, were complete as early as 1947). Nine in number, they read as follows:

1. "Criminal behavior is learned."
2. "Criminal behavior is learned in interaction with other persons in a process of communication."
3. "The principal part of the learning of criminal behavior occurs within intimate personal groups."
4. "When criminal behavior is learned, the learning includes (a) techniques of committing the crime, which are sometimes very complicated, sometimes very simple, and (b) the specific direction of motives, drives, rationalizations, and attitudes."
5. "The specific direction of motives and drives is learned from definitions of the legal codes as favorable or unfavorable."
6. "A person becomes delinquent because of an excess of definitions favorable to violation of law over definitions unfavorable to violation of law."

7. "Differential associations may vary in frequency, duration, priority, and intensity."
8. "The process of learning criminal behavior by association with criminal and anticriminal patterns involves all of the mechanisms that are involved in any other learning."
9. "While criminal behavior is an expression of general needs and values, it is not explained by those general needs and values, since noncriminal behavior is an expression of the same needs and values."

Differential association found considerable acceptance among theorists of the midtwentieth century because it combined then-prevalent psychological and sociological principles into a coherent perspective on criminality. Crime as a form of learned behavior became the catchword of twentieth-century criminology, and biological and other perspectives were essentially abandoned by those involved in the process of theory testing.

Critique of Differential Associaion

Differential association is not without its critics. Perhaps the most potent criticism is the claim that differential association alone is not a sufficient explanation for crime. If it were, then we might expect correctional officers, for example, to become criminals by virtue of their constant and continued association with prison inmates. Similarly, wrongly imprisoned persons might be expected to turn to crime upon release from confinement. There is little evidence that either of these scenarios actually occurs. In effect, differential association does not seem to provide for free choice in individual circumstances, nor for the fact that some individuals, even when surrounded by associates who are committed to lives of crime, are still able to hold onto other, noncriminal, values.

Subcultural Theory

Inherent in the writings of the ecological school, and of Thorsten Sellin and Edwin Sutherland is the notion of **subculture.** Like the larger culture of which it is a part, a subculture is a collection of values and preferences which is communicated to subcultural participants through a process of socialization. Subcultures differ from the larger culture in that they claim the allegiance of smaller groups of people. While the wider American culture, for example, may proclaim that hard work and individuality are valuable, a particular subculture may espouse the virtues of deer hunting, male bonding, and recreational alcohol consumption. While it is fair to say that most subcultures are not at odds with the surrounding culture, some subcultures do not readily conform to the parameters of national culture. Countercultures, which tend to reject and invert the values of the surrounding culture, and criminal subcultures, which may actively espouse deviant activity, represent the other extreme.

Subculture a collection of values and preferences which is communicated to subcultural participants through a process of socialization.

Some of the earliest writings on subcultures can be found in **Frederic M. Thrasher's** 1927 book, *The Gang.*[19] Thrasher studied 1,313 gangs in Chicago. His work, while primarily descriptive in nature, led to a typology in which he described different types of gangs. In 1943, **William Foote Whyte,** drawing on

Thrasher, published Street *Corner Society.*[20] Whyte, in describing his 3-year study of the Italian slum he called "Cornerville," further developed the subcultural thesis, showing that lower-class residents of a typical slum could achieve success through the opportunities afford by slum culture—including racketeering and bookmaking.

Differential Opportunity

The link between subcultures and crime was fully articulated in the 1960s by **Richard Cloward** and **Lloyd Ohlin** in their book, *Delinquency and Opportunity.*[21] Cloward and Ohlin said a delinquent act could be "defined by two essential elements: it is behavior that violates basic norms of the society, and, when officially known, it evokes a judgment by agents of criminal justice that such norms have been violated."[22]

Cloward and Ohlin studied juvenile gangs, and observed that paths to success, which they called **opportunity structures,** were of two types: legitimate and illegitimate. Legitimate opportunity structures, they wrote, were generally available to individuals born into middle-class culture. However, participants in lower-class subcultures are often denied access to these forms of opportunities. In such cases they turn to illegitimate opportunities, which, in fact, are often seen as quite acceptable by participants in so-called "illegitimate subcultures."

Opportunity structure a path to success. Opportunity structures may be of two types: legitimate and illegitimate.

Cloward and Ohlin used the term **illegitimate opportunity structure** to describe subcultural paths to success. Where illegitimate paths to success are not already in place, alienated individuals may undertake a process of ideational evolution through which "a collective delinquent solution," or a "delinquent means of achieving success" may be decided upon by members of the gang. Because the two paths to success, legitimate and illegitimate, differ in their availability to members of society, Cloward and Ohlin's perspective has been termed *differential opportunity.*

Illegitimate opportunity structures subcultural pathways to success which are disapproved of by the wider society.

Subcultural theory a sociological perspective which emphasizes the contribution made by variously socialized cultural groups to the phenomenon of crime.

According to Cloward and Ohlin, delinquent behavior may result from the ready availability of illegitimate opportunities along with the effective replacement of the norms of the wider culture with expedient subcultural rules. Hence, delinquency and criminality may become "all right" or legitimate in the eyes of gang members, and may even form the criteria used by other subcultural participants to judge successful accomplishments. In the words of Cloward and Ohlin, "[a] delinquent subculture is one in which certain forms of delinquent activity are essential requirements for the performance of the dominant roles supported by the subculture."[23] Its "most crucial elements" are the "prescriptions, norms, or rules of conduct that define the activities required of a full-fledged member."[24] "A person attributes legitimacy to a system of rules and corresponding models of behavior," wrote Cloward and Ohlin, "when he accepts them as binding on his conduct."[25] "Delinquents have withdrawn their support from established norms and invested officially forbidden forms of conduct with a claim to legitimacy…."[26]

For Cloward and Ohlin crime and deviance were just as "normal" as any other form of behavior supported by group socialization. In their words, "deviance and conformity generally result from the same kinds of social conditions…" and "deviance ordinarily represents a search for solutions to problems of adjustment."

In their view, deviance is just as much an effort to conform, albeit to subcultural norms and expectations, as is conformity to the norms of the wider society. They added, however, that "[i]t has been our experience that most persons who participate in delinquent subcultures, if not lone offenders, are fully aware of the difference between right and wrong, between conventional behavior and rule-violating behavior. They may not care about the difference, or they may enjoy flouting the rules of the game, or they may have decided that illegitimate practices get them what they want more efficiently than legitimate practices."[27]

Cloward and Ohlin described three types of delinquent subcultures: (1) criminal subcultures, in which criminal role models are readily available for adoption by those being socialized into the subculture; (2) conflict subcultures, in which participants seek status through violence; and (3) retreatist subcultures, where drug use and withdrawal from the wider society predominate. Each subculture was thought to emerge from a larger, all encompassing, "parent" subculture of delinquent values. According to Cloward and Ohlin, delinquent subcultures had at least three identifiable features: (1) "acts of delinquency that reflect subcultural support are likely to recur with great frequency, (2) access to a successful adult criminal career sometimes results from participation in a delinquent subculture, and (3) the delinquent subculture imparts to the conduct of its members a high degree of stability and resistance to control or change."[28]

Cloward and Ohlin divided lower-class youth into four types according to their degree of commitment to middle-class values and/or material achievement. Type I youths were said to desire entry to the middle class via improvement in their economic position. Type II youths were seen as desiring entry to the middle class, but not improvement in their economic position. Type III youth were portrayed as desiring wealth without entry to the middle class. As a consequence, Type III youths were seen as the most crime prone. Type IV youth were described as dropouts who retreated from the cultural mainstream through drug and alcohol use.

Cloward and Ohlin had substantial impact on American social policy through the sponsorship of David Hackett, President John F. Kennedy's head of the newly created Committee on Juvenile Delinquency and Youth Crime. Out of the relationship between the theorists and Hackett, the Mobilization for Youth program, established under the auspices of the 1961 Juvenile Delinquency Prevention and Control Act, was begun with $12.5 million in initial funding in 1962.[29] Mobilization for Youth, a delinquency prevention program based upon Cloward and Ohlin's opportunity theory, created employment and educational opportunities for deprived youths.

Reaction Formation

Another criminologist whose work is often associated with the subcultural perspective is **Albert Cohen.** Cohen's work focused primarily on the gang behavior of delinquent youth. In Cohen's words, "[w]hen we speak of a delinquent subculture, we speak of a way of life that has somehow become traditional among certain groups in American society. These groups are the boys' gangs that flourish most conspicuously in the 'delinquency neighborhoods' of our larger American cities.

The members of these gangs grow up, some to become law-abiding citizens and others to graduate to more professional and adult forms of criminality, but the delinquent tradition is kept alive by the age-groups that succeed them."[30]

Cohen argued that youngsters from all backgrounds were generally held accountable to the norms of the wider society through a "middle-class measuring rod" of expectations related to things like school performance, language proficiency, cleanliness, punctuality, neatness, nonviolent behavior, and allegiance to other similar standards. Unfortunately, not everyone is prepared, by virtue of the circumstances surrounding their birth and subsequent socialization for effectively meeting such expectations.

In an examination of vandalism, Cohen[31] found that "nonutilitarian" delinquency, in which things of value are destroyed rather than stolen or otherwise used for financial gain, is the result of middle-class values turned upside down. Delinquent youths, argued Cohen, who are often alienated from middle-class values and life-styles through deprivation and limited opportunities, can achieve status among their subcultural peers via vandalism and other forms of delinquent behavior.

Children, especially those from deprived backgrounds, turn to delinquency, Cohen claimed, because they experience status-frustration when judged by adults and others according to middle-class standards and goals which they are unable to achieve. Since it is nearly impossible for nonmainstream children to succeed in middle-class terms they may overcome anxiety through the process of reaction formation, in which hostility toward middle-class values develops. Cohen adapted the term **reaction formation** from psychiatric perspectives, and used it to mean "the process in which a person openly rejects that which he wants, or aspires to, but cannot obtain or achieve."[32]

Reaction formation the process in which a person openly rejects that which he or she wants, or aspires to, but cannot obtain or achieve.

Cohen discovered the roots of delinquent subcultures in what he termed the collective solution to the problem of status. When youths who experience the same kind of alienation from middle-class ideals band together, a collective and independent solution is achieved and a delinquent subculture is created. Cohen wrote, "[t]he delinquent subculture, we suggest, is a way of dealing with the problems of adjustment.... These problems are chiefly status problems: certain children are denied status in the respectable society because they cannot meet the criteria of the respectable status system. The delinquent subculture deals with these problems by providing criteria of status which these children *can* meet."[33]

Cohen's approach is effectively summarized in a "theoretical scenario" offered by Donald J. Shoemaker,[34] who says that lower-class youths undergo a working-class socialization that combines lower-class values and habits with middle class success values. Lower-class youth then experience failure in school because they cannot live up to the middle class norms operative in American educational institutions. They suffer a consequent loss of self-esteem and increased feelings of rejection, leading to dropping out of school and "association with delinquent peers." Hostility and resentment toward middle-class standards grows through reaction formation. Finally, such alienated youths achieve status and a sense of improved self-worth through participation in a gang of like-minded peers. Delinquency and crime are the result.

Gangs Today

Gangs have become a major source of concern in contemporary American society. While the writings of investigators such as Cohen, Thrasher, and Cloward and Ohlin focused on the illicit activities of juvenile gangs in the nation's inner cities, most gang-related crimes of the period involved vandalism, petty theft, and battles over turf. The ethnic distinctions which gave rise to gang culture in the 1920s through the 1950s are today largely forgotten. Italian, Hungarian, Polish, and Jewish immigrants, whose children comprised many of the early gangs, have been, for the most part, successfully integrated into the society that is modern America.

Today's gang members are much more likely to be black or Hispanic, and the gangs themselves appear far more violent, drug involved, and intransigent than those studied by the early researchers. During 1992 alone Los Angeles County, California, for example, saw more than 800 gang-related homicides, and over 12,000 injuries caused by gang activities. The growth of gang killings has been staggering. In 1987 such killings in Los Angeles County totaled 387 and had risen to 420 in 1988.[35] Today the Los Angeles area is estimated to be home to over 600 different gangs.

Members of modern youth gangs generally identify with a name (such as the "Crips" and "Bloods," which are well-known Los Angeles–area gangs), a particular style of clothing, symbols, tattoos, jewelry, haircut, and hand symbols. Gangs can be big business. In addition to "traditional" criminal activities such as burglary, extortion, vandalism, and protection rackets, drug dealing has become a mainstay of many inner-city gangs. Los Angeles police estimate that at least four city gangs earn over $1 million each per week through cocaine sales.[36] The potential for huge

Los Angeles gang members under arrest. Gangs have become a major source of concern in contemporary society. *Douglas C. Pizac/AP/Wide World Photos.*

drug-based profits appears to have changed the nature of gangs themselves, making them more prone toward violence and cutthroat tactics. Gang killings, including the now-infamous drive-by shootings, have become commonplace in our nation's cities.

Rodney Dailey, a self-avowed former Boston-area drug dealer and gun-wielding gang member, says that in today's gang world, "Shoot before you get shot is the rule."[37] According to Dailey, "[t]hings that normally people would have had fistfights about can get you shot or stabbed" today. Dailey is founder of Gang Peace, an outreach group which tries to reduce gang-related violence.

Guns have become a way of life for many young gang members. As a young man named Jamaal, hanging around with friends outside Boston's Orchard Park housing project, recently put it, "We don't fight, we shoot." Police in the area describe how values among youth have changed over the past decade or two. Today they "think it's fun to pop someone," they say.

Contemporary researchers, however, are drawing some new distinctions between gangs and violence. A few years ago, G. David Curry and Irving A. Spergel, in a study[38] of Chicago communities distinguished between juvenile delinquency and gang-related homicide. They found that communities characterized by high rates of delinquency do not necessarily experience exceptionally high rates of crime or of gang-related homicides. They concluded that while gang activity may be associated with homicide, "gang homicide rates and delinquency rates are ecologically distinct community problems." Gang-related homicide, they found, seems to be well explained by classical theories of social disorganization and is especially prevalent in areas of the city characterized by in-migration and by the "settlement of new immigrant groups." In their study, high rates of juvenile delinquency seemed to correlate more with poverty, which the researchers defined as "social adaptation to chronic deprivation." According to Curry and Spergel, "[s]ocial disorganization and poverty rather than criminal organization and conspiracy may better explain the recent growth and spread of youth gangs to many parts of the country. Moreover, community organization and social opportunity in conjunction with suppression, rather than simply suppression and incapacitation, may be more effective policies in dealing with the social problem."[39]

Crime and Social Structure

Strain Theory

Anomie a social condition in which norms are uncertain or lacking.

Strain, or *anomie*, theory a sociological approach which posits a disjuncture between socially and subculturally sanctioned mean and goals as the cause of criminal behavior.

In 1938 **Robert K. Merton** offered what is now regarded as a classic statement of the causes of crime in his concept of ***anomie.*** *Anomie* is a French word meaning "normlessness" and was popularized by Emile Durkheim in his 1897 book, *Suicide.*[40] Durkheim used the term to explain how a breakdown of predictable social conditions can lead to a feeling of personal loss and dissolution.

Merton's use of the term *anomie* was somewhat different. In Merton's writings[41] *anomie* came to mean a disjunction between socially approved means to success and legitimate goals. This posited *strain* between goals and means has led to Merton's approach being called **strain theory.** Merton maintained that legitimate goals,

COLORADO HOPES TO TAKE BIG BITE OUT OF CRIME

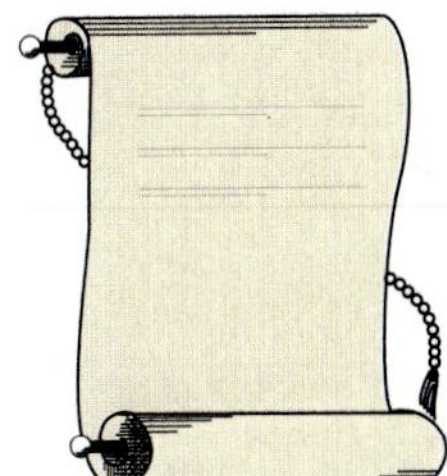

In what some observers say may become a model for the nation, the state of Colorado is hoping to reduce gang-related juvenile crime through a tough program of sanctions.

Colorado legislators on Tuesday opened a special session on gang violence, with Governor Roy Romer issuing a hard-line call to jail any juveniles arrested with guns. "The problem is kids killing kids...gangs and control of our neighborhoods...guns in the hands of children," Romer said, opening what's believed to be the USA's first special session devoted to gang violence. Romer urged legislators to tell young gun-toting thugs "we are not going to let you do this." Romer, a Democrat whose second term ends next year, called for the session on violence after a rash of shootings.

Although it was not the state's worst summer of crime statistically, residents were shocked by children being shot and random murders of adults. In May, a gang summit in Kansas City led to a truce among national gang leaders, a call for records on 15,000 police brutality cases and a federal police brutality watchdog commission. Denver police also sponsored gang summits—which brought a temporary truce and have encouraged residents to help gang leaders get out of their dangerous lifestyle.

Romer rode with police and met with mayors, prosecutors and others before establishing five key proposals:

- Jail juveniles with guns pending a detention hearing.
- Prohibit possession of a handgun by juveniles except in limited, supervised settings.
- Expedite prosecutions.
- Create a special court system for violent, gun-using and gang offenders ages 14 to 18.
- Add up to 500 detention beds for young offenders.

Tuesday, former Reagan press secretary Jim Brady, in a wheelchair since being shot in a 1981 assassination attempt, asked for "common-sense gun laws." "There are few things more important to me than the safety of America's children," Brady said.

But National Rifle Association protesters passed out leaflets saying, "There is no evidence that gun control works." The NRA bought radio ads criticizing the session, which is costing taxpayers $75,000. The session lasts through Saturday.

But a poll of Colorado adults Monday by *The Denver Post* and KCNC-TV showed 77% back the session; 82% support laws making it illegal for those under 18 to carry a handgun except for legitimate purposes.

Romer called the NRA "out of touch" and "part of the problem, not part of the solution." "They don't know Broderick Bell," he said, referring to a 6-year-old boy hit in the face by a stray bullet "They don't know Lori Ann Lowe," a teacher who was killed by gang gunfire.

Source: "Colorado Hopes to Take Big Bite Out of Crime," *USA Today*, September 8, 1993, p. 3A.

DISCUSSION QUESTIONS

1. Why does violence seem to be so prevalent among young people today? What are the root causes of such violence?
2. How can the violence be stopped?
3. Do you agree with Governor Romer that juveniles with guns should automatically be sent to detention? Why or why not?

FIGURE 7.2

GOALS AND MEANS DISJUNCTURE

	Goals	*Means*
Conformity	+	+
Innovation	+	–
Ritualism	–	+
Retreatism	–	–
Rebellion	±	±

Source: Robert K. Merton, *Social Theory and Social Structure*, 1968 enlarged edition. Copyright 1967, 1968 by Robert K. Merton. Adapted with permission of the Free Press, a division of Macmillan, Inc.

involving such things as wealth, status, and personal happiness, were generally defined as desirable for everyone. The widely acceptable means to these goals, however, including education, hard work, financial savings, and so on, were not equally available to all members of society. As a consequence, crime and deviance tended to arise where individuals felt pressed to succeed in approved terms but were not given the tools necessary for such success. In Merton's words, "[i]t's not how you play the game, it's whether you win."[42] Complicating the picture still further, Merton maintained, was the fact that not everyone accepted the legitimacy of socially approved goals. Merton diagrammed possible combinations of goals and means as shown in Figure 7.2, referring to each combination as a mode of adaptation.

The initial row in the figure signifies acceptance of the goals society holds out as legitimate for everyone, with ready availability of the means approved for achieving those goals. The mode of adaptation associated with this combination of goals and means is called conformity and typifies most middle- and upper-class individuals.

Innovation, the second form of adaptation, arises where an emphasis on approved goal achievement combines with a lack of opportunity to participate fully in socially acceptable means to success. This form of adaptation is experienced by many lower-class individuals who have been socialized to desire traditional success symbols such as expensive cars, large homes, and big bank accounts, but who do not have ready access to approved means of acquiring them, such as educational opportunity. Innovative behavioral responses, including crime, can be expected to develop when individuals find themselves so deprived. However, in Merton's words, "[p]overty as such, and consequent limitation of opportunity, are not sufficient to induce a conspicuously high rate of criminal behavior. Even the often mentioned 'poverty in the midst of plenty' will not necessarily lead to this result." It is only insofar as those who find themselves in poverty are pressured to achieve material success and the acquisition of other associated symbols of status that innovation results.

The table's third row, termed "ritualism," describes the form of behavior that arises when members of society participate in socially desirable means, but show little interest in goal achievement. A ritualist may get a good education, work everyday in an acceptable occupation, and outwardly appear to be leading a solid middle-class life-style. Yet he or she may care little for the symbols of success, choosing to live an otherwise independent life-style.

Retreatists are those who reject both the socially approved goals and means. They may become dropouts, drug abusers, or homeless or participate in alternative life-styles such as communal living. Such individuals are socially and psychologically often quite separate from the larger society around them.

Merton's last category, that of the rebel, signifies one who wishes to replace socially approved goals and means with some other system. Political radicals, revolutionaries, and anti-establishment agitators may fit into this category. Merton believed that conformity was the most common mode of adaptation prevalent in society, whereas retreatism was least common.

Since Merton's time, strain theory has undergone considerable refinement. A recent analysis of strain theory by Robert Agnew[43] found that all such theories share at least two central explanatory features. Strain theories, Agnew said, (1) focus "explicitly on negative relationships with others; relationships in which the individual is not treated as he or she wants to be treated," and (2) argue that "adolescents are pressured into delinquency by the negative affective states—most notably anger and related emotions—that often result from negative relationships." Agnew also found that strain theories generally describe three different types of negative relationships with others, or forms of "strain": (1) situations in which individuals actively prevent another person from achieving positively valued goals, (2) the intentional removal or threatened removal of something which is positively valued, or (3) the presenting or threatened presenting of negatively valued stimuli. Agnew sees the crime-producing effects of strain as cumulative and concludes that whatever form it takes, "[s]train creates a predisposition for delinquency in those cases in which it is chronic or repetitive."[44]

Critique of Anomie

Merton's strain theory, while it has much of value to say about the consequences of unequal opportunity, is probably less applicable to American society today than it was in the 1930s. That is because in the last few decades considerable effort has been made toward improving success opportunities for all Americans—regardless of ethnic heritage, race, or gender. Hence it is less likely that individuals today will find themselves without the opportunity for choice, as was the case decades ago. Even so, social programs designed to provide equal opportunity have had little impact on some apparently well-insulated segments of society where even the semblance of participating in "approved means" may be grounds for derision.

General strain theories such as those summarized by Agnew, on the other hand, may have more contemporary relevance. As Agnew realizes, opportunities may be blocked at many points in the life course, resulting in strain, frustration, and anger—all of which may produce law-violating behavior in those undergoing such experiences.

Travis Hirschi,[45] however, criticizes strain theory for its inability "to locate people suffering from discrepancy" and notes that human beings are naturally optimistic—a fact, he says, which "overrides...aspiration-expectation disjunction." Hirschi concludes that "[e]xpectations appear to affect delinquency, but they do so regardless of aspirations, and strain notions are neither consistent with nor required by the data."

Focal Concerns

In 1958 **Walter B. Miller** attempted to detail the values that drive members of lower-class subcultures into delinquent pursuits. Miller described lower-class culture as "a long established, distinctively patterned tradition with an integrity of its own." In Miller's words, "[a] large body of systematically interrelated attitudes, practices, behaviors, and values characteristic of lower-class culture are designed to support and maintain the basic features of the lower-class way of life. In areas where these differ from features of middle-class culture, action oriented to the achievement and maintenance of the lower-class system may violate norms of the middle class and be perceived as deliberately nonconforming.... This does not mean, however, that violation of the middle-class norm is the dominant component of motivation; it is a byproduct of action primarily oriented to the lower-class system."[46]

Focal concerns the key values of any culture, and especially the key values of a delinquent subculture.

In an article entitled "Lower Class Culture as a Generating Milieu of Gang Delinquency,"[47] Miller outlined what he termed the **focal concerns** of delinquent subcultures. Such concerns included trouble, toughness, smartness, excitement, fate, and autonomy. Miller concluded that subcultural crime and deviance are not the direct consequences of poverty and lack of opportunity, but emanate, rather, from specific values characteristic of such subcultures. Just as middle-class concerns with achievement, hard work, and delayed gratification lead to socially acceptable forms of success, said Miller, so too do lower-class concerns provide a path to subculturally recognized success for lower-class youth.

Miller found that trouble "is a dominant feature of lower class culture." Getting into trouble, staying out of trouble, dealing with trouble when it arises become focal points in the lives of many members of lower-class culture. Miller recognized that "getting into trouble" was not necessarily valued in and of itself, but seen as an oftentimes necessary means to valued ends. In Miller's words, "[for] men, 'trouble' frequently involves fighting or sexual adventures while drinking; for women, sexual involvement with disadvantageous consequences."[48]

Like many theorists of the time, Miller was primarily concerned with the criminality of males. The lower-class masculine concern with toughness which he identified, Miller admitted, may have been a product of the fact that many males in the groups he examined were raised in female-headed families. Miller's "toughness," then, may reflect an almost obsessive concern with masculinity as a reaction to the perceived threat of over-identification with female role models. In words that sound as applicable today as when they were written, Miller tells us, "[t]he genesis of the intense concern over 'toughness' in lower-class culture is probably related to the fact that a significant proportion of lower-class males are reared in a predominantly female household and lack a consistently present male figure with whom to identify and from whom to learn essential components of a 'male' role. Since women serve as a primary object of identification during the pre-adolescent years, the almost obsessive lower-class concern with 'masculinity' probably resembles a type of compulsive reaction-formation."[49]

Miller described "smartness" as the "capacity to outsmart, outfox, outwit, dupe, take, [or] con another or others and the concomitant capacity to avoid being outwitted, taken or duped oneself.... In its essence," said Miller, "smartness involves the capacity to achieve a valued entity—material goods, personal status—through a maximum use of mental agility and a minimum of physical effort."

Excitement was seen as a search for thrills—often necessary to overcome the boredom inherent in lower-class life-styles. Fights, gambling, picking up women, making the rounds, were all described as derivative aspects of the lower-class concern with excitement. "The quest for excitement," said Miller, "finds...its most vivid expression in the...recurrent 'night on the town'...a patterned set of activities in which alcohol, music, and sexual adventuring are major components."

Fate related to the quest for excitement, and to the concept of luck or of "being lucky." As Miller put it, "[m]any lower-class persons feel that their lives are subject to a set of forces over which they have relatively little control. These are not...supernatural forces or...organized religion...but relate more to a concept of 'destiny' or man as a pawn.... This often implicit world view is associated with a conception of the ultimate futility of directed effort toward a goal...."

Autonomy, as a focal concern, manifests itself in statements such as "I can take care of myself" or "No one's going to push me around." Autonomy produces behavioral problems from the perspective of middle-class expectations when it surfaces in work environments, public schools, or other social institutions built upon expectations of conformity.

Miller's work derived almost entirely from his study of black inner-city delinquents in the Boston, Massachusetts, area. As such, it may have less relevance to members of lower-class subcultures at other times, or in other places.

Delinquency and Drift

Members of delinquent subcultures are still, to at least some degree, participants in the larger culture that surrounds them. How is it, then, that subcultural participants may choose behavioral alternatives which seemingly negate the norms and values of the larger society? In other words, how can a person give allegiance to two seemingly different set of values at the same time?

An answer to this question was offered by **Gresham Sykes** and **David Matza** in their 1957 article "Techniques of Neutralization."[50] Sykes and Matza suggested that offenders can overcome feelings of responsibility when involved in crime commission through the use of five types of justifications. These include

1. *Denial of responsibility,* by pointing to one's background of poverty, abuse, lack of opportunity, and so on. Example: "The trouble I get into is not my fault."
2. *Denial of injury,* by explaining how insurance companies, and so on, cover losses. Claims that "everyone does it" or that the specific victim could "afford it" fall into this category. Example: "They're so rich, they'll never miss it."

3. *Denial of the victim,* or justifying the harm done by claiming that the victim, for whatever reason, deserved his or her victimization. Example: "I only beat up drunks."
4. *Condemning the condemners,* by asserting that authorities are corrupt or responsible for their own victimization. Offenders may also claim that society has made them into what they are, and must now suffer the consequences. Example: "They're worse than we are. They're all on the take."
5. *An appeal to higher loyalties,* as in defense of one's family honor, gang, girlfriend, or neighborhood. Example: "We have to protect ourselves."

In the words of Sykes and Matza, "[i]t is our argument that much delinquency is based on what is essentially an unrecognized extension of defenses to crimes, in the form of justifications for deviance that are seen as valid by the delinquent but not by the legal system or society at large."[51]

Techniques of neutralization culturally available justifications which can provide criminal offenders with the means to disavow responsibility for their behavior.

A few years later Matza went on to suggest that delinquents tended to drift into crime when they found that available **techniques of neutralization** combined with weak or ineffective values espoused by the controlling elements in society. In effect, said Matza, the delinquent "drifts between criminal and conventional action," choosing whichever is the more expedient at the time. By employing techniques of neutralization, delinquents need not be fully alienated from the larger society. When opportunities for crime present themselves, such techniques provide an effective way for overcoming feelings of guilt, and of allowing for ease of action. Matza used the phrase "soft determinism" to describe drift, saying that delinquents were neither forced to make choices because of fateful experiences early in life, nor were they entirely free to make choices unencumbered by the realities of their situation.

More recent studies have found that while "only a small percentage of adolescents generally approve of violence or express indifference to violence…[a] large percentage of adolescents…accept neutralizations justifying the use of violence in particular situations."[52] The acceptance of such justifications by many young people today is seen as supportive of high levels of adolescent violence. Studies have also found that young people who disapprove of violence but associate with delinquent peers will often use neutralization techniques as justifications for violence in which they personally engage.[53]

Violent Subcultures

In 1967 **Franco Ferracuti** and **Marvin Wolfgang** published their seminal work, *The Subculture of Violence: Toward an Integrated Theory of Criminology,*[54] which drew together many of the sociological perspectives previously advanced to explain delinquency and crime. According to some writers,[55] the work of Wolfgang and Ferracuti "was substantively different from the other subculture theories, perhaps because it was developed almost a decade after delinquent-subculture theories and criminology had developed new concerns." Ferracuti and Wolfgang's main thesis was that violence is a learned form of adaptation to certain problematic life circumstances, and that learning to be violent takes place within the con-

Violent subcultures produce violent acts. Eighteen spent cartridges lay around the body of this New Orleans murder victim. *Bryce Lankard.*

text of a subcultural milieu which emphasizes the advantages of violence over other forms of adaptation. Such subcultures are characterized by songs and stories which glorify violence, by gun ownership, and by rituals which tend to stress "macho" models. They are likely to teach that a quick and decisive response to insults is necessary to preserve one's prestige within the group. Subcultural group members have a proclivity for fighting as a means of settling disputes. Subcultures of violence both expect violence from their members, and legitimize it when it does occur. In Wolfgang's words, "the use of violence...is not necessarily viewed as illicit conduct, and the users do not have to deal with feelings of guilt about their aggression."

Wolfgang and Ferracuti based their conclusions on an analysis of data which showed substantial differences in the rate of homicides between racial groups in the Philadelphia, Pennsylvania, area. At the time of their study, nonwhite males had a homicide rate of 41.7 per 100,000, versus a homicide rate of only 3.4 for white males. Statistics on nonwhite females showed a homicide rate of 9.3 versus 0.4 for white females. Explaining these findings, Wolfgang and Ferracuti tell us: "[h]omicide is most prevalent, or the highest rates of homicide occur, among a relatively homogeneous subcultural group in any large urban community.... The value system of this group, as we are contending, constitutes a subculture of violence. From a psychological viewpoint, we might hypothesize that the greater the degree of integration of the individual into this subculture, the higher the probability that his behavior will be violent in a variety of situations."[56]

Wolfgang and Ferracuti extend their theory of subcultural violence with the following "corollary propositions":[57]

1. "No subculture can be totally different from or totally in conflict with the society of which it is a part."
2. "To establish the existence of a subculture of violence does not require that the actors sharing in these basic value elements should express violence in all situations."
3. "The potential resort or willingness to resort to violence in a variety of situations emphasizes the penetrating and diffusive character of this culture theme."
4. "The subcultural ethos of violence may be shared by all ages in a sub-society, but this ethos is most prominent in a limited age group, ranging from late adolescence to middle age."
5. "The counter-norm is nonviolence."
6. "The development of favorable attitudes toward, and the use of, violence in a subculture usually involve learned behavior and a process of differential learning, association, or identification."
7. "The use of violence in a subculture is not necessarily viewed as illicit conduct and the users therefore do not have to deal with feelings of guilt about their aggression."

Other writers have commented on geographical distinctions between violent subcultures in different parts of the United States. A body of criminological literature exists,[58] for example, which claims that certain forms of criminal violence are more acceptable in the southern United States than in northern portions of the country. Some writers have also referred to variability in the degree to which interpersonal violence has been accepted in the South over time, while others have suggested that violence in the South might be a traditional tool in the service of social order.[59] Without at least a modicum of expressive violence such as lynchings, dueling, and outright fighting, these authors suggest, southern social solidarity following the Civil War might have been seriously threatened. In short, the notion of a southern violence construct holds that an "infernal trinity of Southerner, violence and weaponry"[60] may make crimes like homicide and assault more culturally acceptable in the South than in other parts of the country.

In an interesting aside that relates to the story which opened this chapter and further illustrates how violent subcultural norms are transmitted from generation to generation, 41-year-old Virginia Demery, the mother of Larry Martin Demery, one of the men arrested and charged with killing Michael Jordan's father, was convicted on September 28, 1993, of using a shotgun in an assault upon reporters who came to her mobile home following her son's arrest. Although no one was injured in the incident, reporters who brought criminal charges against her later said that members of the news media should be able to "expect a general amount of civility when they go to interview someone." Ms. Demery gave reporters until the count of five to leave her property but the gun discharged, accidentally she claimed, at the count of two.[61]

The wider culture often recognizes, sometimes begrudgingly and sometimes matter-of-factly, a violent subculture's internal rules. Hence, when one member of such a subculture kills another, the wider society may take the killing less "seriously" than if someone outside the subculture had been killed. As a consequence of this realization, Wolfgang described what he called "wholesale" and "retail" costs for homicide, in which killings that are perceived to occur within a subculture of violence (where both the victim and perpetrator are seen as members of a violent subculture) generally result in a less harsh punishment than do killings which occur outside of the subculture. Punishments, said Wolfgang, relate to the perceived seriousness of the offense, and if members of the subculture within which a crime occurs accept the offense as part of the landscape, so, too, will members of the wider culture which imposes official sanctions on the perpetrator.

Critique of Violent Subcultures Theory

Canadian criminologist Gwynn Nettler criticizes the subculture of violence thesis by insisting that it is tautological, or circular. That is, saying that people fight because they are violent, or that "they are murderous because they live violently" does little to explain their behavior, according to Nettler. Attributing fighting to "other spheres of violence," he says, may be true, but it is fundamentally "uninformative."

The approach has also been criticized for being racist. Margaret Anderson says that "[t]he problem with this explanation is that it turns attention away from the relationship of black communities to the larger society and it recreates dominant stereotypes about blacks as violent, aggressive, and fearful. Although it may be true that rates of violence are higher in black communities, this observation does not explain the fact."[62] In sociological jargon, one might say that an observed correlation between race and violence does not necessarily provide a workable explanation for the relationship.

SOCIAL CONTROL THEORIES

Containment Theory

In the 1950s, another student of the Chicago school, **Walter C. Reckless** wrote *The Crime Problem.*[63] Reckless tackled head on the realization that most sociological theories, while conceptually enlightening, offered less than perfect predictability. That is, they lacked the ability to predict precisely which individuals, even those exposed to various "causes" of crime, would become criminal. Reckless thought that the sociological perspectives prevalent at the time offered only half of a comprehensive theoretical framework. Crime, Reckless wrote, was the consequence of social pressures to involve one's self in violations of the law, as well as of failure to resist such pressures. Reckless called his approach **containment theory,** and he compared it to a biological immune response, saying that only some people exposed to a disease actually come down with it. Sickness, like crime, Reckless avowed, results from the failure of control mechanisms—some internal to the person, and others external. In the case of sickness, external failures might include unsanitary conditions, the failure of the public health service, the lack of availability of preventative medicine or the lack of knowledge necessary to make such medicine effective. Still, disease would not result unless the individual's resistance to

Containment those aspects of the social bond which act to prevent individuals from committing crimes and keep them from engaging in deviance.

disease causing organisms was low, or unless the individual was in some other way weak or susceptible to the disease.

In the case of crime, Reckless wrote, external containment consists of "the holding power of the group." Under most circumstances, Reckless said, "[t]he society, the state, the tribe, the village, the family, and other nuclear groups are able to hold the individual within the bounds of the accepted norms and expectations." In addition to setting limits, Reckless saw society as providing individuals with meaningful roles and activities. Such roles were seen as an important factor of *external containment.*

Inner containment, said Reckless, "represents the ability of the person to follow the expected norms, to direct himself." Such ability was said to be enhanced by such things as a positive self-image, a focus on socially approved goals, personal aspirations that are in line with reality, a good tolerance for frustration, and a general adherence to the norms and values of society. A person with a positive self-concept can avoid the temptations of crime simply by thinking, "I'm not that kind of person." A focus on approved goals helps keep one on the proverbial "straight and narrow" path. "Aspirations in line with reality" are simply realistic desires. In other words, if one seriously desires to be the richest person in the world, disappointment will probably result. Even when aspirations are reasonable, however, there will be disappointing times—hence the need for a tolerance for frustration. Adherence to the norms and values of the larger society are a basic component of inner containment and a kind of capstone factor.

Reckless's containment theory is diagrammed in Figure 7.3. "Pushes toward crime" represents all those factors in an individual's background that might propel him or her into criminal behavior. They include a criminogenic background or upbringing that involves participation in a delinquent subculture, deprivation, biological propensities toward deviant behavior, and psychological maladjustment. "Pulls toward crime" signifies all the perceived rewards crime may offer, including financial gain, sexual satisfaction, and higher status. "Containment" is a stabilizing force and, if effective, blocks such pushes and pulls from leading the individual toward crime.

FIGURE 7.3 A diagrammatic representation of containment theory.

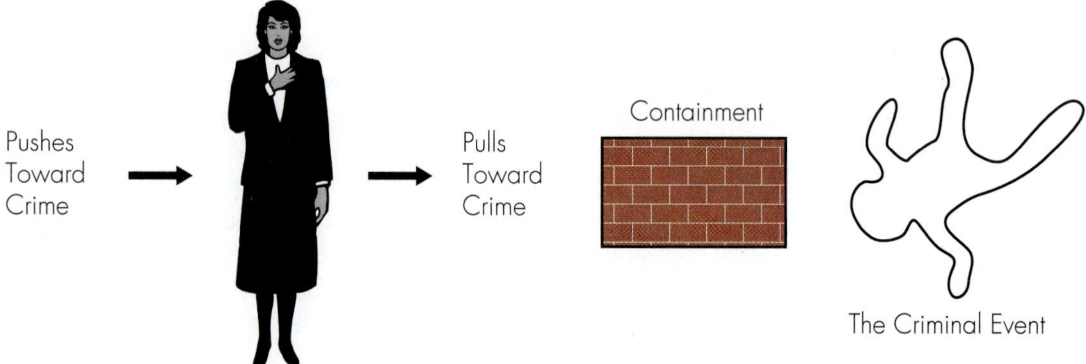

Reckless believed that inner containment was far more effective than external containment in preventing law violations. In his words, "[a]s social relations become more impersonal, as society becomes more diverse and alienated, as people participate more and more for longer periods of time away from a home base, the self becomes more and more important as a controlling agent."

Containment theory was one of the first **social control theories** to be proposed. Social control approaches argue that social institutions exercise considerable control over individuals, either directly (as in the case of external containment) or indirectly, perhaps through socialization (as in the case of inner containment). Such theories, rather than stressing causative factors in criminal behavior, ask why people obey rules instead of breaking them.

Social control theory rather than stressing causative factors in criminal behavior, asks why people actually obey rules instead of breaking them.

Social Bond Theory

Another form of **control theory** was popularized by **Travis Hirschi** in his 1969 book *Causes of Delinquency.*[64] Hirschi argued that, through successful socialization, a bond forms between individuals and the social group. When that bond is weakened or broken deviance and crime may result. Hirschi described four components of the social bond: attachment, commitment, involvement, and belief.

Control theory a perspective which holds that crime is the result of weakened bonds between the individual and society.

In his writings[65] Hirschi cites the psychopath as an example of a person whose attachment to society is nearly nonexistent. Other, relatively "normal," individuals may find their attachment to society loosened through "[t]he process of becoming alienated from others [which] often involves or is based on active interpersonal conflict. Such conflict could easily supply," says Hirschi, "a reservoir of socially derived hostility sufficient to account for the aggressiveness of those whose attachments to others have been weakened."

The second component of the **social bond**—commitment—reflects a person's investment of time and energies into, and the potential loss of rewards that he or she has already gained from, conforming behavior. In Hirschi's words, "[t]he idea, then, is that the person invests time, energy, himself, in a certain line of activity—say, getting an education, building up a business, acquiring a reputation for virtue. Whenever he considers deviant behavior, he must consider the costs of this deviant behavior, the risk he runs of losing the investment he has made in conventional behavior." For such a traditionally successful person, says Hirschi, "a ten-dollar-holdup is stupidity," because the potential for losing what has already been acquired through commitment to social norms far exceeds what stands to be gained. Recognizing that his approach applies primarily to individuals who have been successfully socialized into conventional society, Hirschi adds, "[t]he concept of commitment assumes that the organization of society is such that the interests of most persons would be endangered if they were to engage in criminal acts."

Social bond the rather intangible link between individuals and the society of which they are a part. The social bond is created through the process of socialization.

Involvement, for Hirschi, means "engrossment in conventional activities" and is similar to Reckless's concept of meaningful roles. In explaining the importance of involvement in determining conformity, Hirschi cites the colloquial saying that "idle hands are the devil's workshop." Time and energy, he says, are limited, and, if a person is busy at legitimate pursuits, he or she will have little opportunity for crime and deviance.

Belief, the last of Hirschi's four aspects of the social bond, sets his control theory apart from subcultural approaches. Hirschi says that unlike subcultural theory, "control theory assumes the existence of a common value system within the society or group whose norms are being violated...we not only assume the deviant has believed the rules, we assume he believes the rules even as he violates them." How can a person simultaneously believe it is wrong to commit a crime and still commit it? Hirschi's answer is that "[m]any persons do not have an attitude of respect toward the rules of society." That is, while they know the rules are there, they basically do not care. They invest little of their sense of self in moral standards.

POLICY IMPLICATIONS

Theoretical approaches which fault the social environment as the root cause of crime point in the direction of social action as a panacea. In the 1930s, for example, Clifford Shaw, in an effort to put his theories into practice, established the Chicago Area Project. The Chicago Area Project attempted to reduce social disorganization in slum neighborhoods through the creation of community committees. Shaw staffed committees with local residents rather than professional social workers. The Project had three broad objectives: (1) improving the physical appearance of poor neighborhoods, (2) providing recreational opportunities for youths, and (3) involving Project members directly in the lives of troubled youth through school and courtroom mediation. The program also made use of "curbside counselors," streetwise workers who could serve as positive role models for inner-city youths. Although no effective assessment programs were put into place to evaluate the Chicago Area Project during the program's tenure, Rand Corporation reviewers in 1984 provided a fifty-year review of the program declaring it "effective in reducing rates of juvenile delinquency."[66]

Similarly, Mobilization for Youth, cited earlier in this chapter as an outgrowth of Cloward and Ohlin's theory of differential opportunity, provides a bold example of the treatment implications of social-structural theories. Mobilization for Youth sought not just to provide new opportunities, but through direct social action to change the fundamental arrangements of society and thereby to address the root causes of crime and deviance. Leaders of Mobilization for Youth decided that "[w]hat was needed to overcome...formidable barriers to opportunity...was not community organization but community action" that attacked entrenched political interests. Accordingly, MFY promoted boycotts against schools, protests against welfare policies, rent strikes against 'slum landlords,' lawsuits to ensure poor people's rights, and voter registration."[67] A truly unusual government-sponsored program for its time, Mobilization for Youth was eventually disbanded amid protests that "the mandate of the President's Committee was to reduce delinquency, not to reform urban society or to try out sociological theories on American youths."[68]

A contemporary example of social intervention efforts based upon sociological theories can be had in Targeted Outreach,[69] a program now being operated by Boys and Girls Clubs of America. The Club program had its origins in the 1972 implementation of a youth development strategy based upon studies undertaken at the University of Colorado which showed that at-risk youths could be effectively diverted from the juvenile justice system through the provision of positive alternatives. Utilizing a wide referral network comprised of local schools, police departments, and various youth service agencies, Club officials work to end what they call the "inappropriate detention of juveniles." The program, in its current form, recruits at-risk youngsters—many as young at 7 years old—and diverts them into activities that are intended to promote a sense of (1) belonging, (2) competence, (3) usefulness, and (4) power. A sense of belonging is fostered through clubs that provide familiar settings where individuals are accepted. Competence and usefulness are developed through the provision of opportunities for meaningful activities which young people in the Club program can successfully undertake. Finally, Targeted Outreach provides its youthful participants with a chance to be heard and, consequently, with the opportunity to influence decisions affecting their future.

To date, Targeted Outreach has served more than 10,000 at-risk youths, although it currently operates through only three local clubs. Plans are for Targeted Outreach to eventually involve more than 1.5 million youngsters between the ages of 7 and 17.

Mobilization for Youth and Targeted Outreach both stand as examples of the kinds of programs that theorists who focus on the social environment typically seek to implement. Social programs of this sort are intended to change the cultural conditions and societal arrangements which are thought to lead people into crime.

KIDS DISOBEY, PARENTS PAY

New Laws Demand More Accountability

Huntington, W. Va.—Because her 8-year-old daughter missed 59 days of school, Eva Wilkenson is serving 100 days in jail.

Wilkenson complains that Cabell County Judge L. D. Egnor put her in jail, and her three kids in foster care, to "make an example of me." And the judge doesn't deny he'd like Wilkenson's sentence to scare others.

But what Wilkenson's case may most exemplify is the nation's growing appetite for parental accountability laws.

In a twist on the biblical axiom, these laws visit the sins of the children upon their parents. They make parents pay—with fines, community service, even jail time—for truancy, vandalism or other misbehavior of children.

Many laws have been on the books for years—100 years, in West Virginia's case. But they're being beefed up, or enforced more vigorously, because other attempts at correcting kids—and parents—don't seem to work.

Doing Time: Eva Wilkenson, serving 100 days in a Huntington, W.Va., jail after her daughter missed 59 days of school. *Michele Katz/Herald-Dispatch.*

The crackdown "is very favorably received," says Judge Michael Conese, who since January 1993 has hauled 206 parents of truants into Hamilton, Ohio, municipal court. "People know some parents aren't doing their job, and they have no tolerance."

Nationwide, a range of accountability laws have been passed or proposed:

- In Effingham, Ill., Wednesday, a county judge sentenced Tammy Campe to 12 months probation, 25 hours of community service and $150 in fines for not insisting that her two children go to school.
- In Los Angeles Tuesday night, the city council debated bringing juvenile graffiti "taggers" to court where they'd be spanked with wooden paddles by their parents. The council rejected the notion, "but the fact it was even on the agenda shows people are looking for answers," says Ronald Stephens, an expert on youth issues.
- In the Chicago suburb of Richton Park, Ill., under an ordinance passed in January, parents can be sentenced to as much as $500 in fines and 160 hours of community service—including manual labor—if their children break truancy, curfew, liquor possession and vandalism laws.
- In Honolulu, if a student misses even four hours of school, the police chief may summon parent and child to a special class—and if they don't attend, the case can go to juvenile court.
- In a dozen states, welfare payments can be docked if kids are truant.

These laws are increasingly popular because "the general public is frustrated with the vandalism, the violence, the lack of social responsibility," says Stephens, who directs

Pepperdine University's National School Safety Center. "They're going back to the primary source of control of youngsters...the parents."

In Wilkenson's case, school officials cite a 5-year record of truancy problems with her three daughters: The 8-year-old, and 14-year-old twins.

Despite repeated efforts—including getting Wilkenson to sign a contract that her daughters would attend school—officials say the girls frequently were absent, or arrived with head lice.

Early in May, Egnor took one 14-year-old away from Wilkenson after the girl missed 55 schools days, and put her in the custody of state social services. On May 11—after 59 absences for the 8-year-old, and 35 for the other 14-year-old—Egnor put those two girls in state custody, and Wilkenson in jail.

Under West Virginia's compulsory attendance law, the parent can be sentenced to up to 20 days in jail for each day of school missed by the child.

"There are some who think we're the scum of the earth for putting this lady in jail, and others who support it," says Bennie Thomas, Cabell County attendance director. "We're not out to get anybody—but we mean for kids to be at school."

When the judge sentenced her, Wilkenson says, "My heart dropped out. And when he said the kids was taken away...that's punishing me twice."

Interviewed in jail during her third week there, Wilkenson still seemed stunned: "My lawyer told me I'd never see the inside of a jail."

She acknowledges that her kids sometimes "didn't care whether they went to school." But she insists, "This will not happen ever again. My kids tell me, 'Mommy, we'll go to school every day'" if the judge lets them all go home.

Egnor says he might do that, if Wilkenson uses work-release from jail to clean her house, which her lawyer Keith Newman calls "filthy."

At a hearing June 27, Egnor will review Wilkenson's progress, and consider a request to reduce her sentence and return her kids.

Egnor had received scores of letters and calls, most supporting Wilkenson's jailing: "People are saying, 'It's about time somebody did something serious.' "

Source: Patricia Edmonds, "Kids Disobey, Parents Pay," *USA Today*, June 3, 1994, p. 3A. Copyright 1994, *USA Today*. Reprinted with permission.

DISCUSSION QUESTIONS

1 Do you believe that parents should be held responsible for the behavior of their underage children? Why or why not?
2. What do you think will be the future of parental accountability laws? Will more jurisdictions pass them? Why or why not?

CRITIQUE OF SOCIAL-STRUCTURAL THEORIES

Social-structural theories suffer from one general shortcoming that similarly affects most other perspectives on crime causation. In the words of Canadian criminologist Gwynn Nettler, "the conceptual bias of social scientists emphasizes environments—cultures and structures—as the powerful causes of differential conduct. This bias places an intellectual taboo on looking elsewhere for possible causes as, for example, in physiologies. This taboo is...strongly applied against the possibility that ethnic groups may have genetically transmitted differential physiologies that have relevance for social behavior."[70] In other words, Nettler is telling us that social scientists downplay the causative role of non-sociological factors. Since sociological theorizing has captured the lion's share of academic attention over the past few decades, the role of other causative factors in the etiology of criminal behavior stand in danger of being shortchanged.

SUMMARY

Sociological theories suggest that the causes of crime lie in the structural arrangements of society, and in the way in which social institutions communicate their values to group members. Overall, the concept of subcultures plays an especially important role in sociological theorizing, for even those perspectives which do not directly speak of organized subcultures seem to imply their existence. Additionally, sociological theories build upon the notion that crime is learned in association with others through the process of communication.

Since sociological theories look to the organization of society for their explanatory power, intervention strategies based upon them typically argue for the modification of formal or informal group processes—including the educational process and familial and work arrangements—and to the increased availability of legitimate opportunity structures. Social programs may be created under the exegesis of particular sociological theories, such as the Chicago Area Project or Mobilization for Youth.

DISCUSSION QUESTIONS

1. Do you believe ecological theories have a valid place in contemporary criminological thinking? Why or why not?
2. How, if at all, does the notion of a "criminology of place" differ from more traditional ecological theories? Do you see the criminology of place offering anything new over traditional approaches? If so, what?
3. What is a violent subculture? Why do some subcultures stress violence? How might participants in a subculture of violence be turned toward less aggressive ways?
4. Compare and contrast the theories discussed in this chapter, citing differences and similarities between and among them. How, for example, does

Reckless's notion of containment differ from Hirschi's idea of a social bond? How is it similar?

5. What policy implications do you think the theories discussed in this chapter hold? That is, what sorts of changes in society and in government policy might bring about a reduction in crime?

NOTES

1. Frank Tannenbaum, *Crime and the Community* (Boston: Ginn and Company, 1938), p. 25.
2. Albert K. Cohen, *Delinquent Boys: The Culture of the Gang* (Glencoe, IL: Free Press, 1955).
3. "L.A.: Waiting on a Razor's Edge," *Newsweek,* March 29, 1993, p. 28.
4. "Nation, Town 'Shocked' by Slaying," *USA Today,* August 18, 1993, p. 1A.
5. "Hometown Paints a Portrait of Pain," *Fayetteville Observer-Times,* August 15, 1993, p. 1A.
6. Ibid., p. 4A.
7. Edwin M. Lemert, *Social Pathology* (New York: McGraw-Hill, 1951), p. 3.
8. For an excellent contemporary review of measuring the extent of social disorganization, see Barbara D. Warner and Glenn L. Pierce, "Reexamining Social Disorganization Theory Using Calls to the Police as a Measure of Crime," *Criminology,* Vol. 31, no. 4 (November 1993), pp. 493–513.
9. Edwin M. Lemert, *Social Pathology* (New York: McGraw-Hill, 1951), p. 7
10. W. I. Thomas and Florian Znaniecki, *The Polish Peasant in Europe and America* (Boston: Gorham, 1920).
11. Clifford R. Shaw, et al., *Delinquency Areas* (Chicago: University of Chicago Press, 1929).
12. David Matza, *Becoming Deviant* (Englewood Cliffs, NJ: Prentice Hall, 1969).
13. W. S. Robinson, "Ecological Correlation and the Behavior of Individuals," *American Sociological Review,* Vol. 15, pp. 351–357.
14. Robert J. Bursik, "Social Disorganization and Theories of Crime and Delinquency: Problems and Prospects," *Criminology,* Vol. 26, no. 4 (1988), p. 519.
15. Ibid., p. 354
16. Stephen J. Pfohl, *Images of Deviance and Social Control* (New York: McGraw-Hill, 1985), p. 167.
17. Thorsten Sellin, *Culture Conflict and Crime* (New York: Social Science Research Council, 1938).
18. Ibid., p. 68.
19. Frederick M. Thrasher, *The Gang* (Chicago: University of Chicago Press, 1927).
20. William F. Whyte, *Street Corner Society: The Social Structure of an Italian Slum* (Chicago: University of Chicago Press, 1943).
21. Richard A. Cloward and Lloyd E. Ohlin, *Delinquency and Opportunity: A Theory of Delinquent Gangs* (Glencoe, IL: Free Press, 1960).
22. Ibid., p. 3.
23. Ibid., p. 7.
24. Ibid., p. 13.
25. Ibid., p. 16.
26. Ibid., p. 19.
27. Ibid., p. 37.
28. Ibid., pp. 12–13.
29. Stephen J. Pfohl, *Images of Deviance and Social Control,* pp. 224–225.
30. Cohen, *Delinquent Boys: The Culture of the Gang.*
31. Ibid., p. 13.
32. Donald J. Shoemaker, *Theories of Delinquency: An Examination of Explanations of*

Delinquent Behavior (New York: Oxford University Press, 1984), p. 102.

33. Cohen, *Delinquent Boys*, p. 121.
34. Shoemaker, *Theories of Delinquency*, p. 105.
35. *Criminal Justice Newsletter*, Vol. 19, no. 19 (October 3, 1988), p. 2.
36. Carl Rogers, "Children in Gangs," *Criminal Justice 1993–94* (Guilford, CT: Dushkin Publishing, 1993), pp. 197–199.
37. "Youths Match Power, Fear, Guns," *Fayetteville Observer-Times*, September 6, 1993, p. 2A.
38. G. David Curry and Irving A. Spergel, "Gang Homicide, Delinquency, and Community," *Criminology*, Vol. 26, no. 3 (1988), pp. 381–405.
39. Ibid., p. 401.
40. Emile Durkheim, *Suicide: A Study in Sociology* (New York: Free Press, 1897); reprinted and translated in 1951.
41. Robert K. Merton, "Social Structure and Anomie," *American Sociological Review*, Vol. 3 (October, 1938), pp. 672–682; and Robert K. Merton, *Social Theory and Social Structure*, rev. ed. (New York: Free Press, 1957).
42. Robert Merton, *Social Theory and Social Structure* (New York: Glencoe, 1957), p. 190.
43. Robert Agnew, "Foundation for a General Strain Theory of Crime and Delinquency," *Criminology*, Vol. 30 (February 1992), pp. 47–87.
44. Ibid., p. 60.
45. Travis Hirschi, "Review of Delbert S. Elliott, David Huizinga, and Suzanne S. Ageton, *Explaining Delinquency and Drug Use*" (Beverly Hills, CA: Sage, 1985), in *Criminology*, Vol. 25, no. 1 (February 1987), p. 195.
46. Walter Miller, "Lower Class Culture as a Generating Milieu of Gang Delinquency," *Journal of Social Issues*, Vol. 14, no. 3 (1958), pp. 5–19.
47. Ibid., p. 19.
48. Ibid., p. 8
49. Ibid., p. 9.
50. Gresham Sykes and David Matza, "Techniques of Neutralization: A Theory of Delinquency," *American Sociological Review*, Vol. 22 (December 1957), pp. 664–670.
51. Ibid.
52. Robert Agnew, "The Techniques of Neutralization and Violence," *Criminology*, Vol. 32, no. 4 (1994), pp. 555–580.
53. Ibid.
54. Franco Ferracuti and Marvin Wolfgang, *The Subculture of Violence: Toward an Integrated Theory of Criminology* (London: Tavistock, 1967).
55. Frank P. Williams III and Marilyn D. McShane, *Criminological Theory* (Englewood Cliffs, NJ: Prentice Hall, 1988), p. 79.
56. Ferracuti and Wolfgang, *The Subculture of Violence*, p. 151.
57. Ibid.
58. For an excellent review of the literature, see F. Frederick Hawley, "The Southern Violence Construct: A Skeleton in the Criminological Closet," paper presented at the annual meeting of the American Society of Criminology, 1988.
59. Bertram Wyatt-Brown, *Southern Honor: Ethics and Behavior in the Old South* (Oxford: Oxford University Press, 1983).
60. "The Southern Violence Construct," p. 27.
61. "Suspect's Mom Convicted of Shooting at Reporters," *The Fayetteville Observer-Times*, September 29, 1993, p. 1A.
62. Margaret Anderson, "Review Essay: Rape Theories, Myths, and Social Change," *Contemporary Crises*, Vol. 5 (1983), p. 237.
63. Walter C. Reckless, *The Crime Problem*, 4th ed. (New York: Appleton-Century-Crofts, 1967).
64. Travis Hirschi, *Causes of Delinquency* (Berkeley: University of California Press, 1969).
65. Ibid.
66. Steven Schlossman et al., *Delinquency Prevention in South Chicago: A Fifty-Year Assessment of the Chicago Area Project* (Santa Monica, CA: Rand Corporation, 1984).
67. J. Robert Lilly, Francis T. Cullen, and Richard A. Ball, *Criminological Theory: Context and Consequences* (Newbury Park, CA: Sage, 1989), p. 80.

68. Lamar T. Empey, *American Delinquency: Its Meaning and Construction* (Homewood, IL: Dorsey, 1982), p. 243.
69. Robert W. Sweet, Jr., "Preserving Families to Prevent Delinquency," *Office of Juvenile Justice and Delinquency Prevention Model Programs 1990* (Washington, D.C.: U.S. Department of Justice, April 1992).
70. Gwynn Nettler, *Killing One Another* (Cincinnati: Anderson, 1982), p. 54.

CHAPTER 8

THE MEANING OF CRIME—SOCIAL PROCESS PERSPECTIVES

It's like it ain't so much what a fellow does, but it's the way the majority of folks is looking at him when he does it.

—*William Faulkner*[1]

Plainly, it is of crucial importance that we distinguish between the meaning of the act to the actor...and its meaning to us as scientists.

—*Abraham Kaplan*[2]

Deviation is criminal only if effectively reacted to and symbolized as such.

—*Edwin M. Lemert*[3]

The stigmatized and the normal are part of each other; if one can prove vulnerable, it must be expected that the other can too.

—*Erving Goffman*[4]

IMPORTANT NAMES

Frank Tannenbaum
Erving Goffman
Hans von Hentig
Margaret Fry
Marvin E. Wolfgang
Edwin M. Lemert
Stanton Samenow
Benjamin Mendelsohn
Stephen Schafer
Stuwart Henry
Howard Becker
Samuel Yochelson
Richard Quinney
Henry Ellenberger
Dragan Milovanovic

IMPORTANT TERMS

tagging
labeling
impression management
phenomenology
victim-proneness
postcrime victimization
restitution
victim/witness assistance programs
interactionist perspectives
primary deviance
moral enterprise
discrediting information
social process theories
penal couple
VOCA
OJJDP
victim-precipitated homicide
secondary deviance
dramaturgical perspective
constitutive criminology
victimology
victimogenesis
total institutions
victim-impact statements
phenomenological criminology

INTRODUCTION

In late 1993 James Hamm found himself at the center of a vicious controversy. Hamm, a convicted murderer, had served eighteen years in prison for shooting a man in the head over a drug deal gone bad and was about to enter the Arizona State University school of law. Hamm had been paroled in June 1992 after Arizona's parole board judged him "rehabilitated." While in prison Hamm, a former divinity student, earned a bachelor's degree in sociology and had been active in Middle Ground, a prisoner rights group. While the 45-year-old Hamm worked on getting an education, students at the university were challenging his access to law school, saying that a convicted murderer didn't deserve to be admitted. Mark Killian, the Arizona Republican house speaker, claimed, "There are a lot of hard-working young people out there who could not get into law school because he did."[5] Members of the Arizona Board of Regents, which runs the state's public universities, called for a review of policies on admitting ex-convicts to the schools. Nonetheless, Hamm, who scored in the top 5% of all applicants taking the law school admissions test nationwide, seemed to hold excellent promise as a student. In Hamm's words, the controversy surrounding him "touches on feelings about crime, criminals, recidivism, the failure of the criminal justice system....[6] I'm a lightning rod for those feelings," he said.

The case of James Hamm provides an example of how society's continued reaction to what it defines as criminal behavior can change the course of an offender's life—often for the worse—even after he or she has paid his or her "dues." As one of the author's former professors liked to say, while there are plenty of ex-cons, there is no such thing as an "ex-ex-con." Or "once a con, always a con." Society, it seems, never forgets.

MAJOR PRINCIPLES OF SOCIAL PROCESS PERSPECTIVES

This brief section serves to summarize the central features of social process theories of crime causation. Each of these points can be found elsewhere in this chapter, where they are discussed in more detail. This cursory overview, however, is intended to provide more than a summary—it is meant to be a guide to the rest of this chapter.

Most social process theories of crime causation make certain fundamental assumptions. Among them are

- The nature of social reality is in flux; what we think of as social reality is a construction—specifically an artifact of socialization and social interaction.
- The meaning of events and experiences is conferred upon them by the participants in any interaction. Social actors define the situations in which they are involved.
- Meaning is derived from previous learned experiences and is conferred upon experiences in typical and recurring ways.
- Behavior is criminal insofar as others define it as such and agree to its meaning.
- Criminal behavior is variously interpreted by the offender, the victim, agents of social control, and society.
- Deviant individuals and criminal offenders achieve their status by virtue of social definition, rather than because of inborn traits.
- Continued criminal activity may be a consequence of limited opportunities for acceptable behavior which follow from the negative responses of society to those defined as criminal.
- Career offenders participate in a world-view that differs from the world-view of the conformist and which grants legitimacy to nonconformist activity.

SOCIAL PROCESS PERSPECTIVES

The theories discussed in this chapter are typically called **social process theories** because they depend upon the action (or reaction) of society to the offender (or to the victim) for their explanatory power. Social process theories emphasize the give-and-take which occurs between offender, victim, and society—and specifically between the offender and agents of formal social control such as the police,

Social process theories also known as **interactionist perspectives** emphasize the give-and-take which occurs between offender, victim, and society—and specifically between the offender and agents of formal social control such as the police, courts, and correctional organizations.

courts, and correctional organizations. Another term that is frequently applied to the perspectives outlined in this chapter is interactionist, since the notion of give-and-take implies some activity to which a response is made. A major shortcoming of the theories discussed in this chapter is that they make no real attempt to explain the genesis of criminal behavior, focusing instead on the consequences of such behavior for those undertaking it, for the victims of law-breaking behavior, and for society.

The Group Perspective: Labeling

Tagging like labeling, the process whereby an individual is negatively defined by agencies of justice.

One of the earliest descriptions of lasting societal reaction to deviance can be found in the work of **Frank Tannenbaum.** Tannenbaum's book, *Crime and the Community,* was published in 1938 and popularized the term **tagging** to explain what happens to offenders following arrest, conviction, and sentencing. Tannenbaum told his readers that crime was essentially the result of "two opposing definitions of the situation," between the delinquent and the community at large. "This conflict over the situation," he said, "is one that arises out of a divergence of values. As the problem develops, the situation gradually becomes redefined. The attitude of the community hardens definitely into a demand for suppression. There is a gradual shift from the definition of the specific acts as evil to a definition of the individual as evil, so that all his acts come to be looked upon with suspicion.... From the community's point of view, the individual who used to do bad and mischievous things has now become a bad and unredeemable human being.... The young delinquent becomes bad because he is defined as bad and because he is not believed if he is good. There is a persistent demand for consistency in character. The community cannot deal with people whom it cannot define."[7]

Tannenbaum used the phrase "dramatization of evil" to explain the process whereby an offender comes to be seen as ultimately and irrevocably "bad." After the process has been completed, Tannenbaum said, the offender "now lives in a different world. He has been tagged.... The process of making the criminal, therefore, is a process of tagging...." Once a person has been defined as bad, few legitimate opportunities remain open to him or to her. As a consequence, the offender finds that only other people who have been similarly defined by society as bad are available to associate with him or with her. This continued association with negatively defined others leads to continued crime.

Primary deviance initial deviance often undertaken in order to deal with transient problems in living.

Secondary deviance that which results from official labeling and from association with others who have been so labeled.

Using terminology developed by **Edwin M. Lemert,** it became fashionable to call an offender's initial acts of deviance **primary deviance** and continued acts of deviance, especially those resulting from forced association with other offenders, **secondary deviance.** Primary deviance, Lemert pointed out, may be undertaken to solve some immediate problem or to meet the expectations of one's subcultural group.Hence,therobberyofaconveniencestorebyacollegestudenttemporarily desperate for tuition money, while not a wise undertaking, may be the first serious criminal offense ever committed by the student. The student may well intend for it to be the last, but if arrest ensues and the student is "tagged" with the status of a

THEORY IN PERSPECTIVE

Types of Social Process Theories

SOCIAL PROCESS THEORIES also known as **INTERACTIONIST PERSPECTIVES**

Emphasize the give-and-take which occurs between offender, victim, and society–and specifically between the offender and agents of formal social control such as the police, courts, and correctional organizations.

LABELING. An interactionist perspective which sees continued crime as a consequence of limited opportunities for acceptable behavior which follow from the negative responses of society to those defined as offenders.

Period: 1938-1940 and 1960s-1980s
Theorists: Frank Tannenbaum, Edwin M. Lemert, Howard Becker, and others
Concepts: Tagging, labeling, outsiders, moral enterprise, primary and secondary deviance

DRAMATURGY. An interactionist perspective which depicts human behavior as centered around the purposeful management of impressions, and which seeks to gain explanatory power from the analysis of social performances.

Period: 1960s-Present
Theorists: Erving Goffman and others
Concepts: Total institutions, impression management, back and front regions, performances, discrediting information, stigma, spoiled identity

PHENOMENOLOGICAL CRIMINOLOGY. Details the existence of criminal reality via exploration of the world-view or mind-set characteristic of committed career offenders. (Phenomenology, as a philosophical perspective, means the study of the contents of human consciousness without regard to external convention or prior assumptions.)

Period: 1970s-Present
Theorists: Stanton Samenow, Samuel Yochelson, Stuart Henry, Dragan Milovanovic
Concepts: Phenomenological method, constitutive criminology, social construction of reality, criminal world view

VICTIMOLOGY. The study of victims and their contributory role, if any, in crime causation.

Period: 1930s-Present
Theorists: Hans von Hentig, Benjamin Mendelsohn, Henry Ellenberger, Marvin E. Wolfgang, Margaret Fry, Stephen Schafer
Concepts: Victim-proneness, penal couple, victim-precipitated homicide, victimogenesis, restitution, victim impact statements, VOCA

criminal, then secondary deviance may occur as a means of adjustment to the negative status. In Lemert's words, "[w]hen a person begins to employ his deviant behavior or a role based upon it as a means of defense, attack, or adjustment to the overt and covert problems created by the consequent societal reaction to him, his deviation is secondary."[8]

Secondary deviance becomes especially important because of the forceful role it plays in causing tagged individuals to internalize the negative labels which have been applied to them. Through such a process, labeled individuals assume the role of the deviant. According to Lemert, "[o]bjective evidences of this change will be found in the symbolic appurtenances of the new role, in clothes, speech, posture, and mannerisms, which in some cases heighten social visibility, and which in some cases serve as symbolic cues to professionalization."[9]

The name most often associated with labeling theory is that of **Howard Becker.** In 1963 Becker published *Outsiders: Studies in the Sociology of Deviance,*[10] a work in which the **labeling** perspective found its fullest development. In *Outsiders,* Becker, among other things, described the deviant subculture of jazz musicians and the process by which an individual becomes a marijuana user. His primary focus, however, was to explain how a person becomes labeled an outsider, as "a special kind of person, one who cannot be trusted to live by the rules agreed on by the group."[11] The central fact about deviance, says Becker, is that it is a social product, that "it is created by society." Society creates both deviance and the deviant person by responding to circumscribed behaviors. The person who engages in sanctioned behavior is, as part of the process, labeled a deviant. In Becker's words, "social groups create deviance by making the rules whose infraction constitutes deviance, and by applying those rules to particular people and labeling them as outsiders. From this point of view, deviance is not a quality of the act the person commits, but rather a consequence of the application by others of rules and sanctions.... The deviant is one to whom that label has been successfully applied."[12]

Labeling an interactionist perspective that sees continued crime as a consequence of limited opportunities for acceptable behavior which follow from the negative responses of society to those defined as offenders.

In developing labeling theory, Becker attempted to explain how some rules come to carry the force of law, while others have less weight or apply only within the context of marginal subcultures. His explanation centered on the concept of **moral enterprise,** a term which he employed to encompass all the efforts a particular interest group makes to have its sense of propriety embodied in law. "Rules are the products of someone's initiative," said Becker, "and we can think of the people who exhibit such enterprise as moral entrepreneurs."[13]

Moral enterprise a term which encompasses all the efforts a particular interest group makes to have its sense of propriety enacted into law.

An early example of moral enterprise can be found in the Women's Christian Temperance Union, a group devoted to the idea of prohibition. The WCTU was highly visible in its nationwide fight against alcohol, holding marches and demonstrations, closing drinking establishments, and lobbying legislators. Press coverage of the WCTU's activities swayed many politicians into believing that lawful prohibition of alcoholic beverages was inevitable, and an amendment to the U.S. Constitution soon followed—ushering in the age of prohibition. Moral enterprise is similarly used, Becker claimed, by other groups seeking to support their own interests with the weight of law. Often the group which is successful at moral enterprise does not represent a popular point of view. It is simply more effective than others at maneuvering through the formal bureaucracy that attends the creation of legislation.

Becker was especially interested in describing deviant careers—the processes by which individuals become members of deviant subcultures and take on the attributes associated with the deviant role. Becker argued that most deviance, when it first occurs, is likely to be transitory. That is, it is unlikely to occur again. However, transitory deviance can be effectively stabilized in a person's behavioral repertoire through the labeling process. Once a person is labeled "deviant," opportunities for conforming behavior are seriously reduced. Behavioral opportunities which remain open are primarily deviant ones. Hence, throughout his or her career, the budding deviant increasingly exhibits deviant behavior, not so much out of choice, but rather because his or her choices are restricted by society. Additionally, successful deviants must acquire the techniques and resources necessary to undertake the deviant act (be it drug use or bank robbery), as well as develop the mind-set characteristic of others like them. Near the completion of a deviant career, the person who has been labeled a deviant internalizes society's negative label, assumes a deviant self-concept, and is likely to become a member of a deviant subgroup. Becker says, "[a] drug addict once told me that the moment she felt she was really 'hooked' was when she realized she no longer had any friends who were not drug addicts."[14] In this way, says Becker, deviance finally becomes a "self-fulfilling prophecy." Labeling, then, is a cause of crime insofar as the actions of society in defining the rule-breaker as deviant push the person further in the direction of continued deviance.

Labeling theory contributed a number of unique ideas to the criminological literature. They include the notions that

1. Deviance is the result of social processes involving the imposition of definitions, rather than the consequence of any quality inherent in human activity itself.
2. Deviant individuals achieve their status by virtue of social definition, rather than because of inborn traits.
3. The reaction of society to deviant behavior and to actors who engage in such behavior is the major element in determining the criminality of the person and of the behavior in question.
4. Negative self-images follow from processing by the formal mechanisms of criminal justice, rather than precede delinquency.
5. Labeling by society and handling by the justice system tend to perpetuate crime and delinquency rather than reduce it.

Becker's typology of delinquents helped explain the labeling approach. It consisted of those whom he called (1) the pure deviant, (2) the falsely accused deviant, and (3) the secret deviant. The pure deviant is one who commits norm-breaking behavior and whose behavior is accurately appraised as such by society. An example might be the burglar who is caught in the act of burglary, then tried and convicted. Such a person, we might say, has gotten what they deserve. The falsely accused individual is one who, in fact, is not guilty, but is labeled deviant nonetheless. The falsely accused category in Becker's typology demonstrates the power of social definition. Innocent people sometimes end up in prison, and one can imagine that the impact of conviction and of the experiences which attend prison life can leave the falsely accused with a negative self-concept and with group associations practically indistinguishable from those of the true deviant. In effect, the life of the falsely accused is changed just as thoroughly as is the life of the pure deviant by the process of labeling. Finally, the secret deviant violates social norms, but his or her behavior is not noticed, and negative societal reactions do not follow. The secret deviant again demonstrates the power of societal reaction—in this case by the very lack of consequences.

Critique of Labeling

The labeling approach, although it successfully points to the labeling process as a reason for continued deviance and as a cause of stabilization in deviant identities, does little to explain the origin of crime and deviance. Likewise, few, if any, studies seem to support the basic tenants of the theory. Critics of labeling have pointed to its "lack of firm empirical support for the notion of secondary deviance," and "many studies have not found that delinquents or criminals have a delinquent or criminal self-image."[15]

Also, there is a lack of unequivocal empirical support for the claim that contact with the justice system is fundamentally detrimental to the personal lives of criminal perpetrators. Even if that supposition were true, however, one must ask, would it ultimately be better that offenders not be caught and forced to undergo the rigors to processing by the justice system? Although labeling theory hints that official processing makes a significant contribution to continued criminality, it seems unreasonable to expect that offenders untouched by the system would forego the rewards of future criminality.

Dramaturgy

Another interactionist approach to the study of criminology can be found in the work of **Erving Goffman.** Goffman's 1959 book, *The Presentation of Self in Everyday Life,*[16] introduced students of criminology to the concept of dramaturgy. The **dramaturgical perspective** says that individuals play a variety of nearly simultaneous social roles, such as mother, teacher, daughter, wife, and part-time real-estate agent—and that such roles must be sustained in interaction with others. Shakespeare's famous claim that "[a]ll the world's a stage, and all the men and women merely players: They have their exits and their entrances; and one man in his time plays many parts"[17] provides a good summation of Goffman's dramaturgical approach.

Dramaturgical perspective also **dramaturgy** a theoretical point of view which depicts human behavior as centered around the purposeful management of interpersonal impressions.

Goffman argued that social actors present themselves more or less effectively when acting out a particular role, and that role performances basically consist of managed impressions. Through communications, both verbal and nonverbal, social actors define the situations in which they are involved. A medical doctor, for example, may wear a lab coat, a name tag with her title emblazoned on it, carry a stethoscope and other medical accouterments, and introduce herself as "*Dr.* Smith." Each choice the doctor makes, in what she wears, says, or how she acts, is

"The Taming of the Shrew," performed in Tucson, Arizona. Some criminologists suggest that people, like actors on a stage, intentionally present themselves to others in ways calculated to produce predictable social responses. *First Image/The Image Works.*

intended to convey, according to Goffman, medical authority—and to thereby establish certain rules of interpersonal interaction, that is, to demand a certain appropriate kind of subservience from specified others, including patients, nurses, laboratory technicians, and so on. Medical doctors may, by way of their esoteric knowledge and the awe they inspire in patients and family members of patients, mystify their audiences and thereby gain compliance with their wishes, which makes their jobs easier. Criminals, through a similar process of managed impressions, and by way of the fear they engender in their victims, may likewise achieve cooperation.

Impression management
the intentional enactment of practiced behavior which is intended to convey to others one's desirable personal characteristics and social qualities.

Impression management, according to Goffman, is a complex process involving a never-ending give-and-take of information. Back regions (like dressing rooms) in which actors prepare for their roles, front regions (such as offices where furniture, degrees, and plaques are carefully placed), and personal displays of status or role occupancy, all play a role in the management of impressions. When impression management has been successful, says Goffman, dramatic realization has occurred. "Together," he says, "the participants contribute to a single overall definition of the situation which involves not so much a real agreement as to what exists but rather a real agreement as to whose claims concerning what issues will be temporarily honored."[18]

Goffman also claims that a performer can "be completely taken in by his own act," or, on the other hand, "the performer may not be taken in at all by his own routine"[19] and may not be the person he represents himself as being. When the performer is not duped, but others are, then the performance is a sham or a fraud. In such cases of misrepresentation, he says, "we may take a harsh view of performers such as confidence men who knowingly misrepresent every fact about their lives, [but] we may have some sympathy for those who have but one fatal flaw and who attempt to conceal the fact that they are, for example, ex-convicts"[20]

People in total institutions share all aspects of their lives—like these monks in a Buddhist monastery. *Eastcott/Momatiuk/Woodfin Camp & Associates.*

Discrediting information information which is inconsistent with the managed impressions being communicated in a given situation.

Deviant behavior finds its place in the dramaturgical perspective through the concept of "discreditable disclosure." Some actors, says Goffman, may find themselves discredited by the introduction of new information, especially by information they have sought to hide. When such **discrediting information** is revealed, the flow of interaction is disrupted, and the nature of the performance may be altered substantially. In an example from real life, which was made into a play and the 1993 movie *M. Butterfly,*[21] a French diplomat in China spent twenty years living with a Beijing opera singer, never knowing that "she" was really a "he." Such an interpersonal relationship must have required nothing less than heroic impression management, with the potential for discrediting information always close at hand.

Goffman would say that "[t]o be a given kind of person" requires the dramatic realization of one's claimed status. What one *is* depends upon how successful one is at acquiring the abilities necessary to convince others of one's claims. In his words, "[a] status, a position, a social place is not a material thing...it is a pattern of appropriate conduct, coherent, embellished, and well articulated...it is...something that must be enacted and portrayed, something that must be realized."[22]

Goffman's work takes on considerable relevance for criminology in his later writings, especially the book *Stigma: Notes on the Management of Spoiled Identity.*[23] In *Stigma,* Goffman advances the notion that discredited, or stigmatized, individuals differ significantly from "normals" in the way that society responds to them. "By definition...," he says, "we believe that a person with a stigma is not quite human. On this assumption we exercise varieties of discrimination, through which we effectively, if often unthinkingly, reduce his life chances. We construct a stigma-theory, an ideology to explain his inferiority and account for the danger he represents.... We tend to impute a wide range of imperfections on the basis of the original one...."[24] Stigmata (the plural of stigma) may be physical (such as birthmarks), behavioral (like theft), or ideational (such as a low rank in the proverbial "pecking order").

In *Stigma,* Goffman is primarily concerned with how "normals" and stigmatized individuals interact. At times, says Goffman, discredited individuals are known to others before they come into contact with them. When that happens, normal people approach the stigmatized with expectations of encountering further stigmatizing behavior. When discrediting information does not precede interpersonal encounters, the stigmatized individual may attempt to "pass" as normal using various techniques of concealment including aliases and misrepresentation.

According to Goffman, societal reactions, while they may forcibly create social identities, are also instrumental in the formation of group identities. When similarly discredited individuals come together in like-minded groups, they may align themselves against the larger society. In so reacting, they may justify their own deviant or criminal behavior. At the conclusion of *Stigma,* Goffman reminds us, "[t]he normal and the stigmatized are not persons, but rather perspectives. These are generated in social situations during mixed contacts by virtue of the unrealized norms that are likely to play upon the encounter."[25]

Total institutions
facilities from which individuals can rarely come and go, and in which communal life is intense and circumscribed. Individuals in total institutions tend to eat, sleep, play, learn, and worship (if at all) together.

In another book, *Asylums,*[26] Goffman describes **total institutions**—facilities from which individuals can rarely come and go, and in which communal life is intense and circumscribed. Individuals in total institutions tend to eat, sleep, play, learn, and worship (if at all) together. Military camps, seminaries, convents, prisons, rest homes, and mental hospitals are all types of asylums according to Goffman. Goffman believed that residents of total institutions bring "presenting cultures" with them to their respective facilities. In the case of prisons, for example, some inmates carry street culture into correctional facilities, while others, from different walks of life, bring a variety of other cultural baggage. However, residents, says Goffman, undergo a period of "disculturation," during which they drop aspects of the presenting culture that are not consistent with existing institutional culture—a culture they must acquire.

> A criminology of relevance...should not only be empirical, but rooted in minute understandings of the varied groundings of experience.
>
> —*Peter K. Manning*[27]

Critique of Dramaturgy

Goffman's work has been criticized as providing a set of "linked concepts"[28] rather than a consistent theoretical framework. Other critics have faulted Goffman for failing to offer suggestions for institutional change or for not proposing treatment modalities based upon his assumptions. Goffman's greatest failing may be in taking the analogy of the theater too far and convincing readers that real life is but a form of play acting. According to George Psathas, one of Goffman's critics, "[p]erforming and being are not identical."

Erving Goffman was a sociologist and one-time president of the American Sociological Association. Unfortunately for the field of criminology, Goffman said very little directly about crime and criminality. Although he made a number of analytical references to prisons in *Asylums*, Goffman's work has been given wider applicability to criminology by his followers.

Phenomenology

Phenomenology the study of the contents of human consciousness without regard to external conventions nor prior assumptions.

The phenomenological tradition within social science holds that social reality is a perceptual construct, that is, a generally agreed-upon consensus as to what people, things, places, and so on *mean*. Reality is effectively defined for each person through socialization into a pre-existing culture of agreed-upon understandings. Your understanding of these words, for example, is predicated upon your learning of the English language along with a whole host of words that carry specific meanings for you. Since you and I give words pretty much the same meanings, you can understand what is written on this page, along with what it is that I wish to convey.

Along with words, the process of socialization establishes certain things as agreed-upon facts. Most individuals successfully socialized into Western culture, for example, accept the "scientific way" of doing things, and reject explanations which are overly mystical. They believe, say, that the earth's moon congealed into orbit around the planet out of space "dust" and that its orbit is sustained by its speed, trajectory, and the mutual attraction between the earth and the moon. They tend to reject the belief, say, that the moon harbors an independent consciousness which interacts with, and influences, events on earth on a grand scale (although some people, in fact, do believe this).

Once society provides us with a language and a set of beliefs about the nature of reality, or agreed-upon facts, it has prepared us for encountering new experiences and interpreting them in patterned, fairly predicable ways. We interpret things we encounter in light of previous knowledge and experiences. Hence, the next uniformed individual I encounter who wears a badge, I will probably "grasp" (in my mind) as a police officer. My interpretation of the experience could be wrong. He or she might be an actor or actress dressed in a police uniform, a private security officer, a Halloween partygoer, or a con artist attempting to mislead me. However, my responses toward this individual are likely to depend upon my socially predicated understanding of whom it is I am dealing with. Hence, while it is generally safe to assume that uniformed individuals with badges are actually police personnel, a number of unscrupulous characters have used the full assemblage of police identifiers—including uniforms, marked cars with sirens and lights, and other accouterments—to perpetrate crimes. In a number of instances, women have been attacked and raped by such impostors after stopping their cars for what they thought were police vehicles.

For most people, the process of socialization builds the foundation necessary for successful interaction with others. It allows for understanding and provides a life rich in "meaning." Without the socially derived concepts with which we interpret the world our lives would, indeed, lack "meaning" in the phenomenological sense. Yochelson and Samenow, however, in detailed discussions with forensic, or criminal, psychiatric patients discovered that such individuals possessed a criminal mind which painted a picture of reality quite different from that generally accepted by "normal" people. A criminal way of life along with a concomitant criminal way of thinking emerged. It was as though, in effect, the committed career offender lived in a different world than the one commonly populated by "others." As other writers have observed, "[t]he criminal world attracts its members from among habitual offenders by providing a ready-made system of meaning. Criminal reality—criminals' perception of the world—is the mechanism through which life becomes comprehensible for offenders. It tells criminals who they are, who others are, which actions are significant and what they mean. In short, it endows criminal life with purpose."[29]

While phenomenological understandings can be extended to individual cases of criminality, they seem to make the most sense when used to explain the concept of crime itself. In 1970, for example, Richard Quinney published *The Social Reality of Crime* that outlined a number of propositions detailing how crime is constituted out of societal interaction. Crime, according to Quinney, is "a definition of human conduct that is created by authorized agents in a politically organized society."[30] Quinney went on to say that "criminal definitions describe behaviors that conflict with the interests of segments of society that have the power to shape public policy." He also asserted that "criminal definitions are applied by the segments of society that have the power to shape the enforcement and administration of criminal law…." In his analysis Quinney recognized that class identification is crucial in determining which individuals are likely to violate the law. "Persons in the segments of society whose behavior patterns are not represented in formulating and applying criminal definitions," he wrote, "are more likely to act in ways that will be defined as criminal than those in the segments that formulate and apply criminal definitions." Quinney summarized his understanding of crime in these words: "The social reality of crime is constructed by the formulation and application of criminal definitions, the development of behavior patterns related to criminal definitions, and the construction of criminal conceptions."

Stuart Henry and Dragan Milovanovic, two contemporary proponents of **phenomenological criminology,** use the term **constitutive criminology** to refer to the process by which human beings create "an ideology of crime that sustains it as a concrete reality."[31] "We are concerned," they write, "with the ways in which human agents actively coproduce that which they take to be crime." For Henry and Milovanovic, the idea of crime itself is a social construction, and researchers, they say, should recognize that criminals and victims are also "emergent realities." Concepts such as "crime," "criminal," "victim," and so forth are codetermined by individual actors in the crime and justice drama and by society itself which confers meaning upon human interaction through ready-made and pre-existing concepts. In fact, say these writers, crime and crime control are not "object-like entities," but social constructions. To treat them as anything else is to limit one's self to the perception of distinctions which, for all their social and cognitive power, are merely arbitrary. In short, write Henry and Milovanovic, "crime is both *in* and *of* society." Note, however, that constitutive criminology, which focuses on the social process by which crime and criminology become cultural realities, is not to be confused with constitutional criminology, a biological approach which holds that one's physical constitution plays a role in crime causation.

Phenomenological criminology sees crime as a concept created through a process of social interaction and details the existence of criminal reality via exploration of the world-view or mind-set characteristic of committed career offenders.

Constitutive criminology the process by which human beings create an ideology of crime that sustains it (the notion of crime) as a concrete reality.

Unfortunately, for those unschooled in the phenomenological tradition much of the terminology used by modern-day constitutive criminologists serves merely to obfuscate the subject matter they are dealing with. Their writings can be instructive, nonetheless. Henry and Milovanovic, for example, write "...human agents transform events that they see or experience as micro events into summary representations, or mind patterns, by relying on routine practices through which they convince themselves of having achieved the appropriate representation of these events; these are then objectified in coherent narrative constructions.... [N]o clearer example exists than the very categorization of the diversity of human conflicts and transgressions into crime, or of the multitude of variously motivated acts of personal injury into violent crime or types of violent crime...."[32] In other words, some of the things that people do are called "crimes" by virtue of a kind of mental shorthand or stereotyping that others impose upon them. Likewise, notions that "law and order" are desirable and that "crime and incivility" are displeasing are created and maintained through social agreement. Or, in the words of Henry and Milovanovic, "[f]rom the perspective of constitutive criminology, then, control institutions are the relations among human agents acting to police the conceptual distinctions among discursively constructed social structures."[33]

Although their work may be more tangential than central to the phenomenological movement in criminology, some criminologists classify the writings of **Stanton Samenow,** a clinical research psychologist, and **Samuel Yochelson,** a psychiatrist, as phenomenological criminology because these researchers employed a technique they called "phenomenologic reporting." According to Yochelson and Samenow, phenomenologic reporting is "an intense probe of a criminal's stream of thinking throughout the day."[34] Although Samenow and Yochelson could just as easily be characterized as psychological or psychiatric criminologists, we include their work here because of their insistence that career offenders participate in a criminal world-view quite different from the world-view of conformists, and because of their assertion that criminality is an attitude toward life that begins in early childhood and is unlikely to ever abate.

Samenow and Yochelson worked with the criminally insane (those found "not guilty by reason of insanity," or "NGBRI") at St. Elizabeth's Hospital in Washington, D.C., during the 1960s and early 1970s. Career offenders, according to Yochelson and Samenow, demonstrate fifty-two "errors in thinking," including[35]

1. a lack of interest in schooling
2. the belief that work is for "suckers"
3. a propensity toward chronic lying—even when there seems to be no point in it
4. early sexual activity and a "great deal of sexual thinking," accompanied by sexual immaturity and an inability to form meaningful romantic relationships
5. the ability to postpone criminal activity if threatened with negative consequences
6. a disdain for rules except when their application may benefit the criminal
7. deriving enjoyment from reckless and law violating behavior, such as vandalism

8. dropping out of normal society early in life
9. untrustworthiness, irresponsibility and a focus on the "here and now" at the expense of the future
10. boredom with routine activity and concomitant restlessness
11. a "know-it-all" attitude in many situations
12. expensive tastes, but no "responsible" understanding of the value of money
13. the tendency to steal "almost anything that is not tied down or too heavy to move"
14. a sporadic commitment to formalized religion, along with a "compartmentalization" of religion from the rest of life
15. extreme fear of pain and of physical injury, accompanied by many other fears
16. chronic anger, often toward the world in general and most everything it holds
17. hesitancy to apply the term "criminal" to themselves

According to Yochelson and Samenow, "[e]ach participant in the study had committed literally thousands of crimes, but had been apprehended very few times. From early in life, the patterns grew and grew...." Most criminals, they tell us, were already well on their way to lives of crime as children. "The criminal child," they write, "sets himself apart. He does not confide in his family, and he conceals ideas and emotional reactions. Because he lies so often and engages in forbidden activity, he is ever distrustful and suspicious of other family members."[36]

Finally, Yochelson and Samenow conclude, "the criminal is not a victim of circumstances. He makes choices early in life, regardless of his socioeconomic status, race, or parents' child-rearing practices."[37] The significance of environmental factors in the development of criminality, or in its treatment is rejected by these theorists. "Changing the environment," say Yochelson and Samenow, "does not change the man." Hence, providing new opportunities for legitimate success will not reorient the criminal, but rather will be interpreted by the career offender as providing new opportunities for the commission of additional crimes. From the point of view of Yochelson and Samenow, teaching a committed offender how to weld, as many prison re-education programs do, provides the criminal not so much with a tool for employment on the outside, as it does with a device for continued criminality—to be used for safecracking, breaking and entering, vehicle theft, and so on.

Similarly, other phenomenological writers have pointed out, "[i]f poverty and unemployment are principal sources of crime, as many sociologists suggest, then all we have to do is provide jobs and decent incomes. And yet most hardened criminals spurn conventional employment and mock those who work for a living."[38]

To change career criminals, Yochelson and Samenow argued, a total conversion of the offender's personality is required. In their own notes, dictated as their studies progressed, they observed, "I am convinced there is no helping these people unless there is a 'metamorphosis.' 'Change' is not a sufficiently descriptive term for the degree of overhauling that is necessary." After all, if crime is the result of an internally consistent world-view which characterizes career offenders to the same extent as a "normal" world-view typifies the rest of us, then it would seem no less easy a task to convert the criminal into a conformist than to move conformists toward criminality.

Critique of Phenomenology

Some critics have called phenomenological criminology nihilistic, by which they mean that, in their opinion, it offers few practical solutions to the problem of crime. In effect, they say, phenomenological approaches may challenge well-accepted concepts such as crime and justice, but offer nothing in their place. While social policies based upon phenomenological concepts in the field of criminology may be hard to come by, this kind of criticism is not entirely deserved. It will be answered, in part, in the last chapter, where phenomenological criminology is discussed further under the rubric of "peacemaking criminology."

Other criticisms may be more valid. Concepts in phenomenological criminology are difficult to test and to verify. How, for example, can sociological experiments be constructed that explore the suggested process of cultural creation which is said to give rise to stereotypical concepts such as crime and justice? The fact that phenomenological writers have couched their own ideas in terminology that is itself not easy to grasp has made theory testing all the more difficult.

When criminologists attempt to apply phenomenological principles to specific situations critiques can be even more telling. In the case of Yochelson and Samenow's "phenomenologic reporting," for example, the population under study consisted of hospitalized offenders diagnosed as mentally ill. Generalizability becomes a problem when attempting to extend theoretical findings developed from observations based upon such a population. Whether traits demonstrated by offenders diagnosed as mentally ill can be expected to characterize other criminal offenders—even career ones, is highly debatable. Another shortcoming of Yochelson and Samenow's work pertains to the relatively small number of offenders they interviewed. Additionally, since these people were all institutionalized in a Washington, D.C.–area hospital, it becomes difficult to extend findings to offenders in other parts of the country.

Victimology: The Study of the Victim

Some people are labeled "criminals" by the justice system and take on a deviant identity. Others, as a consequence of forced entanglements, come to be defined as "victims" and assume the social characteristics appropriate for that role. The process by which one comes to be victimized, the interaction between criminal and victim through which victimization occurs, and the meaning given to victimization after it has occurred all suggest that victimization can be subsumed under a social process perspective on criminality.

Just as criminals have been studied to determine what kinds of social and personal experiences they have, so, too, have criminologists advocated close scrutiny of victims. As a field of study **victimology,** or the study of victims, has closely paralleled the development of criminology. As was characteristic of the wider body of criminological theory, early victimologists stressed constitutional factors which propelled the victim toward his or her victimization. The adjudged degree of an individual's potential for victimization was termed **victim-proneness.**

Victimology the study of victims and their contributory role, if any, in crime causation.

Victim-proneness the degree of an individual's likelihood of victimization.

One of the earliest writers in the field, **Hans von Hentig,**[39] depicted crime poetically—as a duet played by two. Von Hentig appears to have been heavily

Purse snatchers in action. Victimologists suggest that some people contribute to their own victimization. *Buu-Turpin/Gamma-Liaison, Inc.*

influenced by a popular German language novel of the time, entitled *The Murdered One Is Guilty.*[40] "In a sense," says von Hentig, "the victim shapes and moulds the criminal."[41] Comparing the victim and criminal to carnivore and prey, he writes, "In a certain sense, the animals which devour and those that are devoured complement each other.... To know one we must be acquainted with the complementary partner."[42]

Von Hentig created a typology, or classificatory scheme, of victims based on what he saw as biological or situational weaknesses. Weaknesses could be physically, socially, psychologically, or environmentally based. Anything that puts the potential victim at a disadvantage relative to the criminal predator, constituting "easy prey" so to speak, found a place in his typology. His scheme consisted of the following categories:

General Classes of Victims

The young—weak by virtue of age and immaturity
The female—often less physically powerful than the male
The old—incapable of physical defense, and the object of confidence schemes
The mentally defective—unable to think clearly
Immigrants—unsure of the rules of conduct in the surrounding society
Minorities—racial prejudice may lead to victimization or unequal treatment by the agencies of justice
Dull normals—the "born victims of swindlers"

Psychological Types of Victims

The depressed—submissive by virtue of emotional condition
The acquisitive or greedy—always wanting more propels such individuals into victimization

The wanton or overly sensual—ruled by passion and thoughtlessly seeking pleasure

The lonesome—similar to the acquisitive type of victim, by virtue of wanting companionship or affection

The heartbroken—like the lonesome, if only temporarily

The tormentor—a victim who asks for it, often from his or her own family and friends

Other types included the blocked, exempted, and fighting victims. Blocked victims were those on whom the tables were turned, as in cases where the swindler becomes swindled or the attacker ends up injured. In like fashion, blackmailers often end up dead. Von Hentig also wrote of "victim areas," or parts of the country to which tourists and others with money are drawn. Similarly attracted are the criminals who prey upon them. Recent incidents involving foreign tourists in Florida were presaged by this kind of thinking. Likewise, inner-city areas rich in crime were seen as creating a special relationship between victim and criminal. Criminals in such areas were described as "deleterious mosquitoes.... [B]ut," wrote von Hentig, "they could not exist if there were no social swamps."[43]

On occasion, said von Hentig, the law creates a victim where there is none at all. The man who visits a prostitute—a willing participant in the offense of prostitution—can, from some perspectives, be classified as a victim. Likewise, the prostitute herself can fall into the category of victim, although as von Hentig says, as in cases of statutory rape, "even the gratified female is supposed to be victimized if the law does not give her consent legal strength."[44]

Finally, according to von Hentig, in some cases victim and criminal are the same. Arson, burglary, auto theft, and other property crimes in which insurance coverage is sought and false police reports filed are forms of criminal activity that typify such criminal/victims.

Von Hentig used colloquial information, pre-existing statistical data, documented individual experiences, and personal observations to support his concepts. Although he did not undertake any empirical research of his own, von Hentig's ideas helped propel the importance of the victim into the forefront of criminological thinking during the 1950s and 1960s.

Some criminologists trace the development of the field of victimology to even earlier writings, including those of **Benjamin Mendelsohn.** In 1937 Mendelsohn, a European defense attorney, published a paper[45] advocating the study of victims. Three years later Mendelsohn published *Rape in Criminology,*[46] claiming that women possess formidable natural defenses against the crime of rape (including the biologically sheltered position of sex organs, the strength of leg muscles relative to the rest of the body, and so on). He intended to provide ammunition to criminal lawyers defending clients accused of rape by pointing out certain personal characteristics (including temperament, modesty, and credibility) which made some women easier targets of rape than others.

Like von Hentig, Mendelsohn created his own classification of victim types. Mendelsohn's typology was based upon the degree of guilt that the victim brought to the criminal event. It included the following six categories:

1. The completely innocent victim. Such a person, said Mendelsohn, is an "ideal victim" in popular perception. In this category he placed persons victimized while they were unconscious, and child victims.
2. Victims with only minor guilt, and those victimized due to ignorance. Mendelsohn used the example of a woman who attempts a self-administered abortion and pays with her life.
3. The victim who is just as guilty as the offender, and the voluntary victim. Suicide committed by a couple, solicited euthanasia, and other forms of suicide were included in this category.
4. The victim more guilty than the offender. This category was described as containing persons who provoked the criminal or actively induced their own victimization.
5. The most guilty victim, or the victim "who is guilty alone." Attackers killed by would-be victims in the act of defending themselves were placed into this subgroup.
6. The imaginary victim. Here Mendelsohn allowed for the fact that some individuals file false police reports, or believe themselves to have been victimized when in fact they have not been. Senile people, mentally ill individuals, children, and others could fall into this category, he said.

Mendelsohn is generally credited with creating the term "victimology," as well as the concept of the **penal couple** which describes the relationship between victim and criminal. He also coined the term "victimal" to describe the victim counterpart of the criminal and the word "victimity" which signified the opposite of "criminality." In his writings Mendelsohn called for the development of victimology as a field of study independent from criminology. He foresaw the creation of an international institute for victimological research as part of the United Nations and called for the creation of an international society of victimology which would support its own journal (which he called the *International Review of Victimology*).

Penal couple a term which describes the relationship between victim and criminal. Also, the two individuals most involved in the criminal act—the offender and the victim.

In 1954 **Henry Ellenberger,** an American psychiatrist, introduced the concept of **victimogenesis**[47] to explain how a person can undergo life experiences that eventually place them in circumstances which contribute to their future victimization. Just as a criminal experiences events in his or her life which lead to criminality, Ellenberger said, so too, many victims undergo a process of socialization that results in less caution, a proclivity to associate with possible offenders, an increased likelihood of frequenting places associated with criminal activity, and a generally higher risk of criminal victimization.

Victimogenesis the contributory background of a victim as a result of which he or she becomes prone to victimization.

In 1957 **Marvin E. Wolfgang** popularized the term **victim-precipitated criminal homicide,** in his study[48] of murders in Philadelphia between 1948 and 1952. "[V]ictim-precipitated cases," said Wolfgang, "are those in which the victim was the first to show and use a deadly weapon, to strike a blow in an altercation—in short, the first to commence the interplay or resort to physical violence."[49] Wolfgang found that victims who brought about their own homicide were more likely than other murder victims to be black males with previous police records, especially involving assault, who were killed by stabbing in a situation where alcohol was present. Significantly, he found, many victim-precipitated homicides were committed by women, often wives. Hence, mate-killing, where threatened wives

Victim-precipitated homicides killings in which the "victim" was the first to commence the interaction or was the first to resort to physical violence.

turn the tables on their abusive husbands, seemed to typify the victim-precipitated criminal homicides Wolfgang studied.

Some years later Wolfgang, writing in consort with Thorsten Sellin,[50] introduced a typology of victims based upon victim-offender relationships. They described:

1. Primary victimization—in which an individual falls victim to crime
2. Secondary victimization—in which an impersonal agency such as a business is victimized
3. Tertiary victimization—in which the government or public order is offended, perhaps through regulatory violations
4. Mutual victimization—in which the participants in an offense willingly involve themselves, such as drug sales, gambling, and fornication
5. No victimization—a category reserved for juvenile status offenses that could not be committed by an adult, such as the buying of cigarettes by an underage person

The Dynamics of Victimization

Some authors[51] have identified a number of procedural models which can be applied to a study of the victimization process—that is, for the purpose of understanding the experience the victim undergoes during and following victimization. The "victims of crime model," developed by Bard and Sangrey,[52] says that three stages are involved in any victimization: (1) the stage of impact and disorganization, during and immediately following the criminal event; (2) recoil, during which the victim formulates psychological defenses and deals with conflicting emotions of guilt, anger, acceptance, and desire for revenge (the state of recoil is said to last from three to eight months); and (3) the reorganizational stage, during which the victim puts his or her life back together and gets on with daily living in a more or less "normal" fashion. Some victims do not successfully adapt to the victimization experience, and a maladaptive reorganizational stage may last for many years.

Another model with applicability to the victimization experience is the "disaster victim's model," originally developed to explain the coping behavior of victims of natural disasters. This model outlines four stages in the victimization process: (1) preimpact, which describes the state of the victim prior to being victimized; (2) impact, or the stage at which victimization occurs; (3) postimpact, which entails the degree and duration of personal and social disorganization that follows victimization; and (4) behavioral outcome, which describes the victim's adjustment, or lack thereof, to the victimization experience.

Finally, the model developed by Elizabeth Kubler-Ross to describe the stages dying persons go through has some applicability to the victimization process. Kubler-Ross described a five-part transitional process[53] of (1) denial, (2) anger, (3) bargaining, (4) depression, and (5) acceptance. Victims often either deny the likelihood of their own victimization or believe that "this can't be happening to me." After the victimizing event many victims feel anger, and some express rage toward their victimizers. Bargaining occurs when the victim negotiates with himself or herself as well as with family members, representatives of the criminal justice community, and social service providers over how the victimization experience should be personally interpreted and about how it should be officially handled. Acceptance occurs when the victim finally acknowledges that victimization has occurred, and he or she makes the adjustments necessary to go on with life. Of course, as in the case of other models, the Kubler-Ross model allows for maladjustment in the final phase since some victims never successfully integrate the victimization experience into their psyches in a way which avoids reduction in the quality of their lives.

> The problem of crime always gets reduced to, "What can be done about criminals?" Nobody asks, "what can be done about victims?"
>
> —*Robert Reiff*[54]

The Victim as a Social Construct

Richard Quinney, whose contribution to the field of criminology is discussed elsewhere in this volume, argues that the victim is a social construction. That is, the wording of laws, the theoretical explorations of criminologists, and the cultural and institutional arrangements of society, all contribute to defining certain social actors as criminals and others as victims. The only real difference between the two, says Quinney, is convention and, one might add, happenstance.

In a 1972 article[55] entitled "Who is the Victim," Quinney wrote, "...criminologists have tended to share a singular conception of reality.... Breaking out of the theory of reality that had dominated criminological thought, we would begin to conceive of the victims of police force, the victims of war, the victims of the 'correctional' system, the victims of state violence, the victims of oppression of any sort. Because criminologists have tended to rely on a particular theory of reality, they have excluded these victims." Fundamentally, says Quinney, the concept of victimization relates to one's notion of morality and corresponding understanding of social reality. "To argue," he writes, "that abortion is victimless is to exclude the living fetus as a victim. To regard the person who loses property as a victim is to value the sanctity of private property."

From some points of view, the victim, or at least his or her degree of victimization, is a cultural artifact. For example, potential murder victims who do not die because they receive prompt medical assistance thwart application of the term "homicide." In a recent study of the availability of medical resources (especially quality hospital emergency services), William G. Doerner[56] found that serious assaults may "become" homicides where such resources are lacking, but that "homicides" can be prevented via the effective utilization of capable medical technology. Hence, societal decisions on the distribution and placement of advanced medical support equipment and personnel can lower homicide rates in selected geographic areas. In Doerner's words, "the causes of homicide transcend the mere social world of the combatants."[57] This kind of perspective bears more than a passing relationship to the "criminology of place" discussed in a box in the previous chapter.

Critique of Victimology

Victimologists move much of the onus for criminality from the offender to the victim, claiming that the victim's behavior, appearance, physical or psychological makeup, or circumstances of birth and upbringing contribute significantly to victimization and are, at least to some degree, the cause of the criminal act itself. While some of these claims may have a certain objective reality, the current political reality of crime—that is, the perception by the majority of Americans that the nation is swamped with far too much crime and the commonly expressed feeling that offenders should be held thoroughly accountable for their actions—seems to dictate a general lack of acceptance for such victimological perspectives.

However, in an article entitled "The Art of Savage Discovery: How to Blame the Victim," William Ryan points out that most victims of commonplace property and violent crimes are members of the lower class. As a consequence, blaming the victim has become something of a popular undertaking for certain groups in society, in particular the middle and upper classes. According to Ryan, most members of the middle and upper classes sympathize with victims, but they are not about to do anything to change the all-too-prevalent conditions in society (poverty, unemployment, discrimination, and the like) which generate crime and lead to victimization. "The victim blamer," says Ryan, "is a middle-class person who is doing reasonably well in a material way; he has a good job, a good income, a good house, a good car. Basically, he likes the social system pretty much the way it is...." Such people, Ryan says, employ a two-pronged approach to the problem of crime. First, they see victims as fated to be poor, uneducated, and victimized. Second, and somewhat contradictorily, they "want to make the victims less vulnerable, send them back into battle with better weapons, thicker armor, a higher level of morale.... What weapons," he asks, "...might they have lacked when they went into battle? Job skills? Education? What armor was lacking that might have warded off their wounds? Better values? Habits of thrift and foresight? And what might have ravaged their morale? Apathy? Ignorance? Deviant lower-class culture patterns?" Because the typical middle-class victim-blamer values precisely those attributes that so many lower-class victims lack, says Ryan, he or she is apt to blame the victim for choosing to be ill-equipped to deal with the challenges of crime and of criminal victimization itself.

A History of the Victim

In early times, victims took the law into their own hands. If they were able to apprehend their victimizers, they enacted their own form of revenge and imposed some form of personal retaliation. The Code of Hammurabi (circa 1750 B.C.), one of the earliest known legal codes, required that many offenders make restitution. If the offender could not be found, however, the victim's family was duty bound to care for the needs of the victim. This early period in history has been called the "Golden Age of the Victim," since victims were not only well cared for, but also had considerable say in imposing punishments upon apprehended offenders.

Eventually, however, crimes came to be understood as offenses against society, and the victim was forgotten. By the late Middle Ages the concept of "King's Peace" had emerged, wherein all offenses were seen as violations of imperial law. It became the duty of local governments to apprehend, try, and punish offenders, effectively removing the victim from any direct involvement in judicial decision making. Victims were expected only to provide evidence of a crime and to testify against those who had offended them. Society's moral responsibility toward making victims "whole again" was forgotten, and victims as a class were moved to the periphery of the justice process. Justice for the victim was forgotten, translated instead into the notion of justice for the state.

The situation remained pretty much the same until the 1960s, when renewed interest in the plight of victims led to a resurgence of positive sentiments around the world. Such sentiments were soon translated into a flurry of laws intended to provide compensation to victims of violent crimes.

Compensation for criminal injury is not unknown throughout history. More than one hundred years ago Jeremy Bentham advocated "mandatory restitution, to be paid by a state compensation system, in cases of property crime."[58] Long before that, the Code of Hammurabi specified that

> If a man has committed robbery...that man shall be put to death. If the robber is not caught, the man who has been robbed shall formally declare what he has lost...and the city...shall replace whatever he has lost for him. If it is the life of the owner that is lost, the city or the mayor shall pay one maneth of silver to his kinfolk.

The first modern victim compensation statute was adopted by New Zealand in 1963. Known as the Criminal Injuries Compensation Act, it provided an avenue for claims to be filed by victims of certain specified violent crimes. A three-member board was empowered to make awards to victims. A year later, partially in response to a movement led by the social reformer **Margaret Fry**, Great Britain established a similar board. In 1965 California passed the first piece of American legislation intended to assist victims of crime. Simultaneously the New York city council passed a "good Samaritan" statute designed to pay up to $4,000 to persons suffering physical injuries while going to the aid of others being victimized by crime. Other states soon joined the bandwagon, and today all fifty states and the District of Columbia have passed legislation providing for monetary payments to crime victims—although legislatures have rarely funded programs at the level of received requests.

All states require applicants to meet certain eligibility requirements, and most set award maximums. A number of states set minimum loss limits (similar to "deductibles provisions" in insurance policies) and have established a "needs test," whereby only needy crime victims are eligible for compensation. Likewise, some states deny awards to family members of the offender, as in the case where a son assaults a father. In all states, payments for medical assistance, lost wages, and living expenses are commonly made. Victims who are responsible in some significant way for their own victimization are generally not reimbursed for losses under existing laws.

The concept of victim compensation rests upon at least seven philosophical underpinnings:[59]

1. Strict liability theory, which claims that compensation is due victims because the social contract between victim and society (specifically, the government) has been broken by the experience of victimization. The duty of the government, says liability theory, is to safeguard its citizens, and when safeguards fail, the injured citizen is due compensation.
2. Government negligence theory, a very selective approach, which holds that the negligent actions of government representatives, including law enforcement officers, jailers, correctional personnel, and the like should result in appropriate forms of compensation.
3. Equal protection theory, which says that compensation should serve to ameliorate imbalances in society, including the huge variation in crime risk that citizens living in different parts of the nation face.
4. Humanitarian theory, which advocates compensation because of the suffering victims undergo.
5. Social welfare theory, similar to humanitarian theory, which says that victims should be compensated if they are in need. Social welfare approaches might exclude compensatory payments to well-heeled victims, but make them available on an as-needed basis to less fortunate members of society who undergo the victimization process.
6. Crime prevention theory, which holds that compensation programs will encourage more citizens to report crime, thereby resulting in more effective law-enforcement programs.
7. Political motives theory, which says that victim compensation is in vogue with the voting public and that any politician desiring continued election will support the concept.

Although many tout the benefits of victim compensation programs, a recent study of the effectiveness of government-sponsored compensation programs in New York and New Jersey[60] found that most victims had generally negative attitudes toward the programs which were supposed to help them. According to the study, "[r]espondents were dissatisfied with delays, inconveniences, poor information, inability to participate, and the restrictive eligibility requirements. These sentiments, coupled with the large number of award applications that were denied, produced strongly negative attitudes among victims toward victim compensation."[61]

Current Directions in Victimology

Victims experience many hardships extending beyond their original victimization, including the trauma of testifying, uncertainty about their role in the justice process, lost time at work, trial delays, fear of retaliation by the defendant, and a general lack of knowledge of what is expected of them as the wheels of justice grind forward. Problems which follow from initial victimization are referred to as **postcrime victimization,** or secondary victimization. Police, employer, and spouse insensitivity can all exacerbate the difficulties crime victims face. Even hospitals which charge high fees for medical records, and social service agencies that swamp applicants in a plethora of forms, can contribute to the victim's sense of continuing victimization.

Postcrime victimization or secondary victimization, refers to problems in living that tend to follow from initial victimization.

In recent years a number of victims' assistance programs, designed to provide comfort and assistance to victims of crime, have developed across the nation. The earliest of these programs began as grass-roots movements designed to counsel victims of rape. In 1975 a national survey[62] identified only twenty-three victim's assistance programs in the United States. By 1986 the number had grown to over six hundred, and estimates today place the number of such programs at nearly one thousand. Some authors have drawn a distinction between victim service programs, which emphasize therapeutic counseling, and **victim/witness assistance programs** that provide a wide array of services.

Victim/witness assistance programs counsel victims, orient them to the justice process and provide a variety of other services such as transportation to court, child care during court appearances, and referrals to social service agencies.

Most victim/witness assistance programs, however, are small and often staffed by local volunteers. They typically counsel victims, orient them to the justice process and provide a variety of other services such as transportation to court, child care during court appearances, and referrals to social service agencies where additional assistance is needed. A recent survey[63] found that most organizations explain the court process to victims (71.2% of all organizations surveyed), make referrals to other agencies (68.4%), provide court escorts (65.2%), help victims fill out victim compensation forms (64.1%), attempt to educate the public as to the needs of victims (60.9%), advocate with employers on behalf of victims (60.3%), and provide transportation to court (59.2%).

Two large public groups, the National Organization for Victims' Assistance (NOVA) and the National Victims' Center, both located in the Washington, D.C.– area, provide leadership in victims' education, lobby the federal congress, and hold conferences and workshops designed to assist local victim/witness assistance programs.

Victims' advocates argue that a victims' bill of rights is needed to provide the same kind of fairness to victims that is routinely accorded defendants. In 1982 the President's Task Force on Victims of Crime recommended sixty-eight strategies that could be used by federal, state, and local governments to improve the plight of crime victims. Legislation based upon Task Force recommendations resulted in the Victims of Crime Act (**VOCA**), passed by Congress in 1984. VOCA established the federal Crime Victims Fund which uses moneys from fines and forfeitures collected from federal offenders to supplement state support of local victims' assistance programs and state victim compensation programs. An early study[64] of VOCA grants found that most went to single-focus groups such as rape crisis centers and battered women's shelters rather than to groups providing comprehensive victim services.

VOCA the Victims of Crime Act, passed by the U.S. Congress in 1984.

THEORY VERSUS REALITY

Victims' Bill of Rights

Victims' advocates argue that a victims' bill of rights is needed to provide the same kind of fairness to victims that is routinely accorded defendants. In 1990 the state of Arizona amended its constitution to include just such a bill. As of this writing, thirteen states have modified their constitutions in support of the rights of crime victims. Twelve others have constitutional amendments pending. Because Arizona's amendment clearly sets forth a victims' "bill of rights" it is reproduced in this box:

CONSTITUTION OF THE STATE OF ARIZONA

Article II. Declaration of Rights

Section 2.1. Victim's Bill of Rights

Section 2.1 (A) To preserve and protect victims' rights to justice and due process, a victim of crime has a right:

1. To be treated with fairness, respect, and dignity, and to be free from intimidation, harassment, or abuse, throughout the criminal justice process.
2. To be informed, upon request, when the accused or convicted person is released from custody or has escaped.
3. To be present at and, upon request, to be informed of all criminal proceedings where the defendant has the right to be present.
4. To be heard at any proceeding involving a post-arrest release decision, a negotiated plea, and sentencing.
5. To refuse an interview, deposition, or other discovery request by the defendant, the defendant's attorney, or other person acting on behalf of the defendant.
6. To confer with the prosecution, after the crime against the victim has been charged, before trial or before any disposition of the case and to be informed of the disposition.
7. To read presentence reports relating to the crime against the victim when they are available to the defendant.
8. To receive prompt restitution from the person or persons convicted of the criminal conduct that caused the victim's loss or injury.
9. To be heard at any proceeding when any post-conviction release from confinement is being considered.

10. To a speedy trial or disposition and prompt and final conclusion of the case after the conviction and sentence.
11. To have all rules governing criminal procedure and the admissibility of evidence in all criminal proceedings protect victims' rights and to have these rules be subject to amendment or repeal by the legislature to ensure the protection of these rights.
12. To be informed of victim's constitutional rights.

(B) A victim's exercise of any right granted by this section shall not be grounds for dismissing any criminal proceeding or setting aside any conviction or sentence.

(C) "Victim" means a person against whom the criminal offense has been committed or, if the person is killed or incapacitated, the person's spouse, parent, child or other lawful representative, except if the person is in custody for an offense or is the accused.

Victim-Impact Statements

One consequence of the burgeoning national victim/witness rights movement has been a call for the use of **victim-impact statements** prior to the sentencing of convicted criminal defendants. A victim-impact statement is typically a written document which describes the losses, suffering, and trauma experienced by the crime victim or by the victim's survivors. In jurisdictions where victim-impact statements are used, judges are expected to consider them in arriving at an appropriate sanction for the offender.

Victim-impact statement a written document which describes the losses, suffering, and trauma experienced by the crime victim or by the victim's survivors. In jurisdictions where victim-impact statements are used, judges are expected to consider them in arriving at an appropriate sentence for the offender.

Although the drive to mandate inclusion of victim-impact statements in sentencing decisions has gathered much momentum, their final role has yet to be decided. The Victim Task Force, commissioned by then-president Reagan shortly after he took office, recommended adoption of a change to the Sixth Amendment of the U.S. Constitution. The Task Force specifically recommended adding the words "Likewise, the victim, in every criminal prosecution shall have the right to be present and to be heard at all critical stages of judicial proceedings."[65] Although such an amendment may be long in coming, significant federal legislation has already occurred. The 1982 Victim and Witness Protection Act[66] requires victim-impact statements to be considered at federal sentencing hearings and places responsibility for their creation on federal probation officers.

Some states have gone the federal government one better. In 1984 the state of California, for example, passed legislation[67] to allow victims a right to attend and participate in sentencing and parole hearings. Approximately twenty states now have laws mandating citizen involvement in sentencing. Where written victim-impact statements are not available, courts may invite the victim to testify directly at sentencing.

The legality of victim-impact statements, while in doubt for some time, appears to have been decisively upheld by the U.S. Supreme Court in the 1991 case of *Payne* v. *Tennessee.*[68] The *Payne* case began with a 1987 double murder, in which a 28-year-old mother and her 2-year-old daughter were stabbed to death in Millington, Tennessee.[69] A second child, 3-year-old Nicholas Christopher, himself severely wounded in the incident, witnessed the deaths of his mother and young sister. In a trial following the killings, the prosecution claimed that Pervis Tyrone Payne, a 20-year-old retarded man, had killed the mother and child after the woman resisted his sexual advances. Payne was convicted of both murders. At the sentencing phase of the trial, Mary Zvolanek, Nicholas's grandmother, testified that the boy continued to cry out daily for his dead sister.

In contrast to some earlier decisions which had cast doubt upon the admissibility of victim-impact statements, the Court in the Payne case held that such statements may be appropriately used at sentencing hearings because "[v]ictim impact evidence is simply another form or method of informing the sentencing authority about the specific harm caused by the crime in question...."

Victim Restitution

Restitution a criminal sanction, in particular the payment of compensation by the offender to the victim.

The victims' movement has also spawned a rebirth of the concept of **restitution.** Restitution is punishment through imposed responsibility—in particular, the payment of compensation to the victim. Restitution encompasses the notion that criminal offenders should shoulder at least a portion of the financial obligations required to make the victim whole again. Not only does restitution help make the victim "whole" again, it places responsibility for the process back upon the offender who caused the loss of "wholeness" to begin with. Advocates of restitution, which works through court-imposed fines and garnishments, claim that, as a sentence, it benefits society by leading to an increased sense of social and individual responsibility on the part of convicted offenders.

Stephen Schafer, who wrote the book *Victimology: The Victim and His Criminal*[70] in 1968, is commonly credited with repopularizing the concept of restitution. Schafer discussed three forms of restitution: (1) compensatory fines, which are imposed in addition to other court-ordered punishments and which compensate the victim for the actual amount of loss; (2) double or treble damages, in which offenders are required, as punishment, to pay the victim back more than the amount of the original injury; and (3) restitution in lieu of other punishment, where the offender discharges any criminal responsibility by compensating the victim. In the last form of restitution, no other criminal penalties are imposed if the offender meets his or her restitution obligations.

The 1982 President's Task Force on Victims of Crime recognized the inequitable financial consequences that often follow criminal victimization with these words: "It is simply unfair that victims should have to liquidate their assets, mortgage their homes, or sacrifice their health or education or that of their children while the offender escapes responsibility for the financial hardship he has imposed. It is unjust that a victim should have to sell his car to pay bills while the offender drives to his probation appointments. The victim may be placed in a financial crisis that will last a lifetime. If one of the two must go into debt, the offender should do so."[71] The report went so far as to recommend that legislation be passed requiring restitution in all criminal cases and that mandates be estab-

THEORY VERUS REALITY

Victims' Rights Soon to Be a Part of the U.S. Constitution?

Advocates of victims' rights are seeking a modification to the Sixth Amendment to the U.S. Constitution. The amendment now reads

Amendment VI [1791]

In all criminal prosecutions, the accused shall enjoy the right to a speedy and public trial, by an impartial jury of the State and district wherein the crime shall have been committed, which district shall have been previously ascertained by law, and to be informed of the nature and cause of the accusation; to be confronted with the witnesses against him; to have compulsory process for obtaining witnesses in his favor; and to have the Assistance of Counsel for his defence.

Victims' advocates would like to add the following statement:

Likewise, the victim in every criminal prosecution shall have the right to be present and to be heard at all critical stages of judicial proceedings.

Source: The President's Task Force on Victims of Crime, *Final Report* (Washington, D.C.: U.S. Government Printing Office, 1982), p. 114.

lished requiring judges to order restitution in cases where victims have suffered financially, unless compelling reasons to the contrary could be demonstrated.

A year later, in 1983, the American Bar Association, in its *Guidelines for Fair Treatment of Crime Victims and Witnesses,* recommended that "victims of a crime involving economic loss, loss of earnings, or earning capacity should be able to expect the sentencing body to give priority consideration to restitution as a condition of probation."[72]

According to Susan Hillenbrand,[73] the change in perspective which the American system of justice underwent in the 1970s and 1980s meant that restitution was no longer seen "solely as a punitive or rehabilitative measure," but came to be understood "as a matter of justice to crime victims...." Even today, however, Hillenbrand says, efforts to evaluate restitution programs "have largely assessed outcomes in terms of correctional objectives rather than in terms of benefits to victims."[74] Nonetheless, Hillenbrand offers, "restitution need not be viewed as an all or nothing proposition for either victims or defendants in order to benefit both. The fact that the criminal justice system has goals other than restoration of crime victims should not be of concern to victims as long as their own needs are included among the goals of the system."[75]

Today restitution is widely operative in sentencing practice. The state of Texas is one of a growing number of states which utilize restitution as a major component of its statewide alternatives to prison. The Texas Residential Restitution Program operates numerous community-based centers housing selected nonviolent felony offenders who work at regular jobs in the community, pay for their support and for the support of their families, and make restitution to their victims. On the national level, the Office of Juvenile Justice and Delinquency Prevention (**OJJDP**) has developed a monetary and direct victim service program for juvenile courts called RESTTA (Restitution, Education, Specialized Training, and Technical Assistance Program). RESTTA provides local juvenile courts with the information needed to make restitution a meaningful part of the disposition process for juvenile offenders.

OJJDP the Office of Juvenile Justice and Delinquency Prevention.

Contemporary restitution programs, while typically well intended, are often mired in a number of problems. Chief among them are the difficulties associated with actually collecting restitution. Offenders are typically poor, lower class, and ill motivated to participate meaningfully in restitution programs. Overworked courts often order restitution and then do little to remedy the situation when offenders do not make their payments. In the words of Thomas C. Castellano, who conducted a 1992 survey of restitution studies, "the extant studies indicate room for concern and very little suggestion that adult restitution, particularly the mere imposition of a restitution order, achieves its desired effect on offender behavior."[76]

Policy Implications

As we have been remarking throughout this chapter, both offenders and victims are stigmatized through social processes involving the formal and informal imposition of labels. Removal of the stigmata would, at least theoretically, restore both to their precrime state.

Labeling theory, in particular, would seem to predict that reverse labeling could occur, and might offer an attractive treatment technique to counteract the effects of the labeling process. Based upon this proposition some programs have attempted to change convicts by having them participate in esteem-building workshops, developing strategies whereby correctional staff might officially accord them positive labels, and by providing them with the experience of self-enhancing public rituals such as graduation ceremonies. No such efforts have resulted in positive reports of realistic and lasting behavioral changes, nor of lowered recidivism rates. Similarly, what evidence there is seems to suggest that even equipping offenders with new identities and relocating them to new areas (as in witness protection programs) does little to change their fundamental approach to life. In like manner, phenomenological perspectives seem to hold little hope for a successful change in the world-view of career offenders. As a consequence, no individualized treatment strategies seem to be offered by either of these perspectives which might result in a realistic hope for offender rehabilitation. Imprisonment, with dangerous offenders held indefinitely, appears to be the best possible social policy that could be predicated upon the theories offered here.

Studies of victims' compensation programs discussed earlier in this chapter seem to express a common caution: such programs can be effective provided they are intelligently managed and do not further expose victims to additional secondary victimization through less than effective bureaucracy. Moreover, money may not be as important to most victims as are practical assistance and fair representation within the justice system. Hence, legislation enhancing the rights of victims and local victims' assistance programs may be the best ways of channeling energies currently existing within the burgeoning victim's movement.

SUMMARY

This chapter has discussed a seemingly wide variety of perspectives, from labeling, through dramaturgy and phenomenology, to the rebirth of the victims' assistance movement. Similarly, we have used both the terms "social process approach" and "interactionist perspective" to classify the theories found in this chapter. More fundamental to each perspective described herein, however, is the concept of "social meaning," and, were it not for existing convention, this chapter might better be titled "the search for social meaning."

When an individual offender is labeled a criminal or a deviant, the meaning which that person's presence holds for the group of which he or she is a part, as well as the personal significance of that person's life, have been inexorably changed. He or she will rarely be seen the same (in the predeviant state) again. In like fashion, when a person internalizes an acquired or imposed deviant self-conception, the meaning of his or her life changes and any future decisions he or she will make take on a new significance in light of the new self-image. Some people, as Erving Goffman points out, work diligently to create impressions that convey particular sorts of meaning to others around them.

Finally, victims often find their lives dramatically modified by the victimization experience. Things previously taken for granted, such as evening strolls through one's neighborhood, may never seem the same again (especially if the person was the victim of a mugging). Hence, while each perspective covered in this chapter looks to the interaction that occurs between individuals, and especially to interaction between criminals and victims, and sees such interaction as a process that is open to analysis, the ultimate outcome of any significant interaction is always a new experience or the reinterpretation of previous experiences—it involves, in short, the creation of new meanings.

DISCUSSION QUESTIONS

1. This chapter begins with a discussion of the labeling process. Give a few examples of the everyday imposition of positive, rather than negative, labels. Why is it so difficult to successfully impose positive labels on individuals previously labeled negatively?

2. Do you believe that Erving Goffman's dramaturgical approach, which sees the world as a stage and individuals as actors upon that stage, provides any valuable insights into human affairs? If so, what are they? Do you believe that Goffman takes his analogy too far? If so, how?
3. Explain the concept of phenomenology in your own words. How might it be applied to the study of subject matter other than that of crime and criminality? Do you agree with critics that phenomenological criminology is "nihilistic"? Why or why not?
4. Examine the victims' bill of rights presented in the box in this chapter that contains a portion Arizona's state constitution. What aspects of the "bill," if any, would you wish to see deleted or changed? Why? What might be added? Why? Could portions of the bill be made more concise? If so, how?
5. Do you favor or oppose amending the U.S. Constitution to recognize the rights of crime victims? Defend your position? This chapter discusses proposed changes to the Sixth Amendment of the U.S. Constitution that would recognize such rights. Are there any other parts of the U.S. Constitution that might also be changed to address such recognition?

NOTES

1. William Faulkner, *As I Lay Dying* (New York: Random House, 1964).
2. Abraham Kaplan, *The Conduct of Inquiry: Methodology for Behavioral Science* (San Francisco: Chandler, 1964), p. 32.
3. Edwin M. Lemert, *Social Pathology: A Systematic Approach to the Theory of Sociopathic Behavior* (New York: McGraw-Hill, 1951), p. 284.
4. Erving Goffman, *The Presentation of Self in Everyday Life* (Garden City, NY: Doubleday, 1959), p. 135.
5. "Killer's Admission to Law School Criticized," *Fayetteville Observer-Times,* September 12, 1993, p. 14A.
6. Ibid.
7. Frank Tannenbaum, *Crime and the Community* (New York: Atheneum Press, 1938), pp. 17–18.
8. *Social Pathology,* p. 76.
9. Ibid.
10. Howard Becker, *Outsiders: Studies in the Sociology of Deviance* (New York: Free Press, 1963).
11. Ibid., p. 1.
12. Ibid., p. 9.
13. Ibid., p. 147.
14. Ibid., pp. 37–38.
15. Randy Martin, Robert J. Mutchnick, and W. Timothy Austin, *Criminological Thought: Pioneers Past and Present* (New York: Macmillan, 1990), p. 368.
16. *The Presentation of Self in Everyday Life.*
17. William Shakespeare, *As You Like It* [1598–1600], Act II, Scene 7, line 139.
18. *The Presentation of Self in Everyday Life,* pp. 9–10.
19. Ibid., p. 17.
20. Ibid., p. 60.
21. "People," *USA Today,* September 13, 1993, p. 2D.
22. Ibid., p. 75.
23. Erving Goffman, *Stigma: Notes on the Management of Spoiled Identity* (Englewood Cliffs, NJ: Prentice Hall, 1963).
24. Ibid., p. 5.
25. Ibid., p. 138.
26. Erving Goffman, *Asylums: Essays on the Social Situation of Mental Patients and Other Inmates* (Garden City, NY: Anchor Books, 1961).
27. Peter K. Manning, "On the Phenomenol-

ogy of Violence," *The Criminologist*, Vol. 14, no. 4 (July/August 1989), pp. 1, 4–6, 22.

28. Laurie Taylor, "Erving Goffman," *New Society*, December 1968, p. 836.
29. Frank Schmalleger, "World of the Career Criminal," *Human Nature*, March 1979.
30. Richard Quinney, *The Social Reality of Crime* (Boston: Little Brown, 1970), p. 15.
31. Stuart Henry and Dragan Milovanovic, "Constitutive Criminology: The Maturation of Critical Theory," *Criminology*, Vol. 29, no. 2 (May 1991), p. 293.
32. Ibid., p. 302.
33. Ibid.
34. Samuel Yochelson and Stanton E. Samenow, *The Criminal Personality: A Profile for Change* (New York: Jason Aronson, 1976), p. 41.
35. Samuel Yochelson and Stanton E. Samenow, *The Criminal Personality: A Profile for Change* (New York: Jason Aronson, 1976); *The Criminal Personality: The Change Process* (New York: Jason Aronson, 1977); and *The Criminal Personality: The Drug User* (Northvale, NJ: Jason Aronson, 1986).
36. Ibid., Volume 1, p. 129.
37. Ibid., Volume 1, p. 249.
38. "World of the Career Criminal."
39. Hans von Hentig, *The Criminal and His Victim: Studies in the Sociobiology of Crime* (Archon Books, 1967), reprinted from the 1948 Yale University Press edition.
40. Stephen Schafer, *The Victim and His Criminal: A Study in Functional Responsibility* (New York: Random House, 1968).
41. Ibid., p. 384.
42. Ibid., p. 385.
43. Ibid., p. 399.
44. Ibid., p. 402.
45. Benjamin Mendelsohn, "Method to Be Used by Counsel for the Defence in the Researches Made into the Personality of the Criminal," *Revue de Droit Pénal et de Criminologie* (Brussels), Fall 1937, p. 877.
46. Benjamin Mendelsohn, *Rape in Criminology* (Rome: Giustizia Penale, 1940).
47. See Henry Ellenberger, "Relations Psychologiques entre le Criminel et sa Victime," *Revue Internationale de Criminologie et de Police Technique* (Geneva), no. 2, 1954.
48. Marvin E. Wolfgang, "Victim-Precipitated Criminal Homicide," *Journal of Criminal Law, Criminology and Police Science*, Vol. 48, no. 1 (1957), pp. 1–11.
49. Ibid.
50. Thorsten Sellin and Marvin E. Wolfgang, *The Measurement of Delinquency* (New York: John Wiley & Sons, 1964).
51. Rosa Casarez-Levison, "An Empirical Investigation of the Coping Strategies Used by Victims of Crime: Victimization Redefined," in Emilio Viano, ed., *Critical Issues in Victimology: International Perspectives* (New York: Spring, 1992).
52. M. Bard and D. Sangrey, *The Crime Victim's Book*, 2nd ed. (New York: Brunner/Mazel, 1986).
53. Elizabeth Kubler-Ross, *On Death and Dying* (New York: Macmillan, 1969).
54. Robert Reiff, *The Invisible Victim: The Criminal Justice System's Forgotten Responsibility* (New York: Basic Books, 1979), p. xi.
55. Richard Quinney, "Who Is the Victim," *Criminology*, 1972, Vol. 10, no. 2, pp. 314–323.
56. William G. Doerner, "The Impact of Medical Resources on Criminally Induced Lethality: A Further Examination," *Criminology*, Vol. 26, no. 1 (February 1988), pp. 171–177.
57. Ibid., p. 177.
58. Steven Rathgeb Smith and Susan Freinkel, *Adjusting the Balance: Federal Policy and Victim Services* (Westport, CT: Greenwood Press, 1988), p. 13.
59. Robert Elias, *Victims of the System: Crime Victims and Compensation in American Politics and Criminal Justice* (New Brunswick, NJ: Transaction, 1983), pp. 24–26.
60. Ibid.
61. Ibid., p. 245.
62. Albert R. Roberts, *Helping Crime Victims* (Newbury Park, CA: Sage, 1990).
63. Ibid., p. 31.
64. Ibid., p. 22.
65. President's Task Force on Victims of Crime, *Final Report* (Washington, D.C.: U.S. Government Printing Office, 1982).
66. P.L. 97-291.

67. Proposition 8, *California's Victims' Bill of Rights.*
68. *Payne* v. *Tennessee,* no. 90-5721 (1991).
69. "What Say Should Victims Have?" *Time,* May 27, 1991, p. 61.
70. Stephen Schafer, *The Victim and His Criminal: A Study in Functional Responsibility* (New York: Random House, 1968).
71. The President's Task Force on Victims of Crime, *Final Report* (Washington, D.C.: U.S. Government Printing Office, 1982).
72. American Bar Association, *Guidelines for Fair Treatment of Crime Victims and Witnesses* (Chicago: ABA, 1983), p. 22.
73. Susan Hillenbrand, "Restitution and Victim Rights in the 1980s," in Arthur J. Lurigio, Wesley G. Skogan, and Robert C. Davis, eds., *Victims of Crime: Problems, Policies and Programs* (Newbury Park, CA: Sage, 1990), p. 192.
74. Ibid., p. 196.
75. Ibid.
76. Thomas C. Castellano, "Assessing Restitution's Impact on Recidivism: A Review of the Evaluative Literature" in Viano, *Critical Issues in Victimology: International Perspectives,* p. 240.

P A R T T H R E E

CRIME IN THE MODERN WORLD

Our country will not truly be safe again until all Americans take personal responsibility for themselves, their families, and their communities...."

—President Clinton, commenting at the signing of the $30 billion Violent Crime Control and Law Enforcement Act of 1994. The flag-bedecked ceremony with two thousand invited guests took place on September 13, 1994, on the South Lawn of the White House

CHAPTER 9

POLITICAL REALITIES AND CRIME

Freedom in America allows us to explain our cause.

—Sheik Omar Abdel-Rahman[1]

Social stratification breeds envy. And that leads to crime…

—Natalya Lemesheva, Russian school teacher[2]

To move beyond criminal justice is to move beyond capitalism.

—Richard Quinney[3]

IMPORTANT NAMES

Roscoe Pound
Richard Quinney
Raymond J. Michalowski
Karl Marx
William Chambliss
George Vold
Austin Turk

IMPORTANT TERMS

consensus model
radical criminology
Marxist criminology
state-organized crime
pluralistic perspective
proletariat
critical criminology
bourgeoisie
conflict perspective
social class
terrorism

INTRODUCTION: POLITICS AND CRIME

Around 3 A.M. on a snowy January morning in 1994, "big Oleg" Korotaev, 44, a former champion Russian boxer, was shot in the head and died on New York City's Brighton Beach Avenue. The shot which killed Korotaev, who was among the highest ranking of Russia's new organized crime figures, could be heard all the way to Moscow's Spassky Street. That's where Russian police General Gennady F. Chebotarev runs an office charged with tracking the growing worldwide threat represented by Russia's crime bosses and the organizations they run.

Russian criminal organizations rapidly gained in power and influence during the tumultuous period of social upheaval which surrounded the demise of the Soviet government. They now have roots that reach around the globe. In this country Russian organized crime groups have been reported operating in Boston, Philadelphia, San Francisco, and Los Angeles, as well as New York. These groups—using skills first developed to dodge the bureaucracy of the old Soviet system—have become expert at forgery, medical insurance fraud, credit card scams, narcotics distribution, and contract killings.

One favorite area of activity perfected by Russian criminal organizations is that of gasoline tax fraud. FBI Director Louis Freeh estimates that "Russian émigrés involved in tax-evasion schemes in this country now control the sale of more than 50 million gallons of gasoline a month, on which $7 million in federal excise taxes is evaded."[4] The Russians set up fake fuel companies, selling gasoline at "tax-included" prices—but never paying the fuel tax to local or federal revenue offices. One such scam, which resulted in the indictment of fourteen persons in Pennsylvania and New Jersey, produced an estimated $14.8 million in illegal gains for the Russian masterminds behind the plan—who quickly fled to their native country to launder the ill-gotten gains.

Money laundering is a relatively simple undertaking in Russia. There American money is more valuable than gold, and official regulations do not require the reporting of cash transactions in any amount. New to capitalism, Russia has not yet implemented U.S.-style money-laundering laws that mandate the reporting of large cash bank transactions. Although lax Russian laws are a help, Russian gangsters are undeniably thorough. Commenting on "big Oleg's" murder, one New York detective remarked, "One thing we know is that you don't solve Russian homicides."[5]

LAW AND SOCIAL ORDER PERSPECTIVES

The rapid growth of Russian organized crime highlights the close link between crime and politics which exists not only in Russia, but throughout the world. In the old Soviet Union, for example, communism precluded the existence of certain forms of crime. People were cared for by the state, and—at least theoretically—most types of private property simply did not exist. Hence, those crimes of theft or destruction of property that took place were generally regarded as crimes against the state—the entity to which most property formally belonged. Soviet understandings of crime which characterized the period were couched in terms of communist ideology and seen as the direct result of the immoral tendency toward capitalism.

As Russian laws changed following the downfall of the Soviet system, so too did the characteristic nature of crime and criminal activity within Russian society. Not only were new *opportunities* for criminal activity created by the changing social structure, but new *categories* of criminal activity were called into being by changed laws. An understanding of the interplay between formalized law and social order is critical to any study of criminology. Three analytical perspectives that shed some light on the subject will be discussed:

- the consensus perspective
- the pluralist perspective
- the conflict perspective

The Consensus Approach

The **consensus model** of social organization is built around the notion that most members of society agree on what is right and wrong, and that the various elements of society—including institutions such as churches, schools, government agencies, and businesses—work together toward a common and shared vision of the greater good. According to **Raymond J. Michalowski,** whose excellent analytical work is used to describe each of the three major approaches discussed in this section, the consensus perspective is characterized by four principles:[6]

Consensus model an analytical perspective on social organization which holds that most members of society agree as to what is right and what is wrong, and that the various elements of society work together in unison toward a common and shared vision of the greater good.

- A belief in the existence of core values. The consensus perspective holds that commonly shared notions of right and wrong characterize the majority of society's members.
- The notion that laws reflect the collective will of the people. Law is seen as the result of a consensus, achieved through legislative action, and represents a kind of social conscience.
- The assumption that the law serves all people equally. From the consensus point of view, the law not only embodies a shared view of justice, but is itself perceived to be just in its application.

- The idea that those who violate the law represent a unique subgroup with some distinguishing features. The consensus approach holds that law violators must somehow be improperly socialized, psychologically defective, or suffer from some other lapse which leaves them unable to participate in what is otherwise widespread agreement on values and behavior.

The consensus perspective was operative in American politics and characterized social scientific thought in this country throughout much of the early 1900s. It found its greatest champion in **Roscoe Pound,** former dean of the Harvard School of Law and one of the greatest legal scholars of modern times. Pound developed the notion that the law is a tool for engineering society. The law, Pound said, meets the needs of men and women living together in society, and can be used to fashion society's characteristics and major features. Pound distilled his ideas into a set of jural postulates. Such postulates, Pound claimed, explain the existence and form of all laws insofar as laws reflect shared needs. Pound's postulates read as follows:[7]

- In civilized society men and women[8] must be able to assume that others will commit no intentional aggressions upon them.
- In civilized society men and women must be able to assume that they may control for beneficial purposes what they have discovered and appropriated to their own use, what they have created by their own labor, and what they have acquired under the existing social and economic order.
- In civilized society men and women must be able to assume that those with whom they deal in the general intercourse of society will act in good faith and hence
    1. Will make good reasonable expectations that their promises or other conduct will reasonably create.
    2. Will carry out their undertakings according to the expectations which the moral sentiment of the community attaches thereto.
    3. Will restore specifically or by equivalent what comes to them by mistake or unanticipated or (via a) not fully intended situation whereby they receive at another's expense what they could not reasonably have expected to receive under the circumstances.
- In civilized society men and women must be able to assume that those who are engaged in some course of conduct will act with due care not to cause an unreasonable risk of injury upon others.
- In civilized society men and women must be able to assume that those who maintain things likely to get out of hand or to escape and do damage will restrain them or keep them within their proper bounds.

The Pluralistic Approach

Contrary to the assumptions made by consensus thinkers, however, it has become quite plain to most observers of the contemporary social scene that not everyone agrees on what the law should say. Society today is rife with examples of conflict-

Paul Hill, sentenced to die for the murders of a Florida abortion clinic doctor and the doctor's security escort. Hill's self-righteous attitude reflects the plurality of values characteristic of society today. *Steve Mawyer/Bettmann.*

ing values and ideals. Consensus is hard to find. Modern debates center on issues such as abortion, euthanasia, the death penalty, the purpose of criminal justice agencies in a diverse society, social justice, the rights and responsibilities of minorities and other underrepresented groups, women's issues, the proper role of education, economic policy, social welfare, the function of the military in a changing world, environmental concerns, and appropriate uses of high technology. As many contemporary public forums would indicate, there exists within America today a great diversity of social groups, each with its own point of view regarding what is right and what is wrong, and each with their own agenda. Add to that the plethora of self-proclaimed individual experts busily touting their own points of view, and anything but a consensus of values seems characteristic of society today.

Such a situation is described by some writers as pluralistic. A **pluralistic perspective** mirrors the thought that a multiplicity of values and beliefs exists in any complex society, and that different social groups will each have their own set of beliefs, interests, and values. A crucial element of this perspective, however, is the assumption that although different viewpoints exist, most individuals agree on the usefulness of law as a formal means of dispute resolution. Hence, from a pluralistic perspective the law, rather than reflecting common values, exists as a peace-keeping tool that allows officials and agencies within the government to settle disputes effectively between individuals and among groups. It also assumes that whatever settlement is reached will be acceptable to all parties because of their agreement on the fundamental role of law in dispute settlement. The basic principles of the pluralist perspective include notions that[9]

Pluralistic perspective an analytical approach to social organization which holds that a multiplicity of values and beliefs exist in any complex society, but that most social actors agree on the usefulness of law as a formal means of dispute resolution.

- Society consists of many and diverse social groups. Differences in age, gender, sexual preference, ethnicity, and the like often provide the basis for much naturally occurring diversity.

- Each group has its own characteristic set of values, beliefs, and interests. Variety in gender, sexual orientation, economic status, ethnicity, and other forms of diversity produce interests which may unite like-minded individuals, but which may also place them in natural opposition to other social groups.
- There exists a general agreement on the usefulness of formalized laws as a mechanism for dispute resolution. People and groups accept the role of law in the settlement of disputes and accord decisions reached within the legal framework at least a modicum of respect.
- The legal system is value neutral. That is, the legal system is itself thought to be free of petty disputes or above the level of general contentiousness which may characterize relationships between groups.
- The legal system is concerned with the best interests of society. Legislators, judges, prosecutors, attorneys, police officers, and correctional officials are assumed to perform idealized functions that are beyond the reach of the everyday interests of self-serving groups. Hence, such official functionaries can be trusted to act in accordance with the greater good, to remain unbiased, and to maintain a value-free system for the enforcement of laws.

According to the pluralistic perspective, conflict is essentially resolved through the peace-keeping activities of unbiased government officials exercising objective legal authority.

The Conflict Perspective

Conflict perspective an analytical perspective on social organization which holds that conflict is a fundamental aspect of social life itself and can never be fully resolved.

A third point of view, the **conflict perspective,** maintains that conflict is a fundamental aspect of social life itself that can never be fully resolved. At best, according to this perspective, formal agencies of social control merely coerce the unempowered or the disenfranchised to comply with the rules established by those in power. From the conflict point of view, laws become a tool of the powerful, useful in keeping others from wresting control over important social institutions. Social order, rather than being the result of any consensus or process of dispute resolution, rests upon the exercise of power through law. Those in power must work ceaselessly to remain there, although the structure which they impose on society—including patterns of wealth building that they define as acceptable and circumstances under which they authorize the exercise of legal power and military might—gives them all the advantages they are likely to need. The conflict perspective can be described in terms of six key elements:[10]

- Society is composed of diverse social groups. As in the pluralist perspective, diversity is thought to be based upon distinctions which people hold to be significant, such as gender, sexual orientation, social class, and the like.
- Each group holds to differing definitions of right and wrong. Moralistic conceptions and behavioral standards vary from group to group.
- Conflict between groups is unavoidable. Conflict is based upon differences held to be socially significant (such as ethnicity, gender, social class, etc.) and is unavoidable because groups defined on the basis of these characteristics compete for power, wealth, and other forms of recognition.

- The fundamental nature of group conflict centers on the exercise of p power. Political power is the key to the accumulation of wealth and to o forms of power.
- Law is a tool of power and furthers the interests of those powerful enough to make it. Laws allow those in control to gain what they define (through the law) as legitimate access to scarce resources and to deny (through the law) such access to the politically disenfranchised.
- Those in power are inevitably interested in maintaining their power against those who would usurp it. The powerful strive to keep their power.

The conflict perspective was brought to criminology early in the twentieth century, but popularized by **George Vold** in 1958. Vold described social conflict as "a universal form of interaction" and said that groups are naturally in conflict as their interests and purposes "overlap, encroach on one another and (tend to) be competitive."[11] Vold also addressed the issue of social cohesion, noting that as intergroup conflict intensified, loyalty of individual members to their groups increased. "It has long been realized that conflict between groups

THEORY IN PERSPECTIVE

Law and Social Order Approaches

CONSENSUS MODEL

Holds that most members of society agree as to what is right and what is wrong, and that the various elements of society work together in unison toward a common and shared vision of the greater good.

PLURALISTIC PERSPECTIVE. Holds that a multiplicity of values and beliefs exist in any complex society, but that most social actors agree on the usefulness of law as a formal means of dispute resolution.

CONFLICT PERSPECTIVE. Holds that conflict is a fundamental aspect of social life itself and can never be fully resolved.

RADICAL CRIMINOLOGY. Holds that the causes of crime are rooted in social conditions which empower the wealthy and the politically well organized, but disenfranchise those less fortunate.

Period: 1960s-Present
Theorists: Karl Marx, Richard Quinney, William Chambliss, Raymond Michalowski
Concepts: Social class, bourgeoisie, proletariat

tends to develop and intensify the loyalty of group members to their respective groups,"[12] Vold wrote. But Vold's most succinct observation of the role conflict plays in contributing to crime was expressed in these words: "The whole political process of law making, law breaking, and law enforcement becomes a direct reflection of deep-seated and fundamental conflicts between interest groups.... Those who produce legislative majorities win control over the power," said Vold, "and dominate the policies that decide who is likely to be involved in violation of the law."[13]

In other words, from Vold's point of view, powerful groups make laws, and those laws express and protect their interests. Hence, the body of laws that characterize any society is a political statement, and crime is a political definition imposed largely upon those whose interests lie outside of that which the powerful, through the law, define as acceptable. In his writings about conflict Vold went so far as to compare the criminal with a soldier, fighting, through crime commission, for the very survival of the group whose values he or she represents. In Vold's words: "[t]he individual criminal is then viewed as essentially a soldier under conditions of warfare: his behavior may not be 'normal' or 'happy' or 'adjusted'—it is the behavior of the soldier doing what is to be done in wartime."[14] Vold's analogy, probably influenced by the proximity in time of his writing to World War II, was meant to express the idea that crime was a manifestation of denied needs and values, that is, the cultural heritage of disenfranchised groups who were powerless to enact their interests in legitimate fashion. Hence, theft becomes necessary for many poor people, especially those left unemployed or unemployable by the socially acceptable forms of wealth distribution defined by law.

"MARTYR" OR MURDERER?

Abortion Protester's Death Sentence

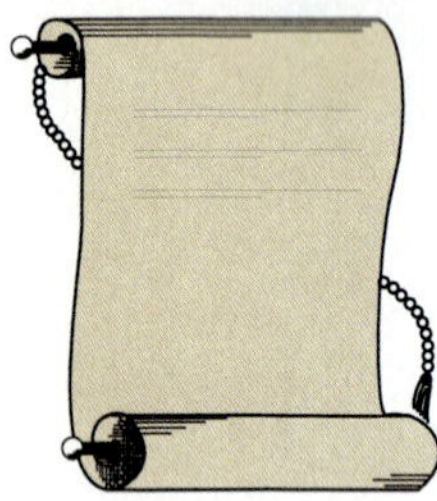

The conflict perspective seems better suited to an understanding of many contemporary social issues—among them the heated battle between "pro-lifers" and "prochoice" advocates over abortion, as the article in this box shows.

When Paul Hill used a a 12-gauge shotgun to kill an abortion clinic's doctor, abortion rights supporters—and many foes—called him a monster.

Tuesday, Hill may have graduated from monster to martyr when he was sentenced to die in Florida's electric chair for the July murders of John Bayard Britton and his escort, James Barrett, in Pensacola.

"He'll be a good poster boy for murder in the future," said David Gunn, Jr., the son of a doctor killed in 1993 by another protester.

The National Right to Life Committee denounced violence. "The murders committed by Paul Hill were deplorable and reprehensible," says President Wanda Franz.

But radical abortion-rights foes hailed Hill.

"He's a hero and a martyr in my book," says Christian Action Group's Roy McMillan of Jackson, Miss. "I believe in killing people in just wars...and there's a war in the womb."

Now, "we are going to execute someone who simply did for a stranger something every father in America would do to protect his children."

Almost from the time he joined demonstrations outside Pensacola's abortion clinics, activists watched as the articulate, soft-spoken former minister and father of three grew more fervent in his protests.

First, his fetus posters became more graphic, his shouting more intense.

"Mommy, don't let them kill me!" he cried out to women at The Ladies Center clinic.

Then, in March 1993, when another protester shot and killed abortion doctor David Gunn in Pensacola, Hill stunned the Bible Belt community by proclaiming he was part of a group that believes in "justifiable homicide" to stop abortion.

The Gunn slaying, Hill said last week on *Eye to Eye With Connie Chung*, "literally changed my life."

The double murder occurred 17 months later. Britton's wife was wounded, too.

On *Eye to Eye*, Hill said he has no regrets: "I have done something that I think the Lord is pleased with. I know...I'm going to heaven when I die."

Michael Bray, who served four years in prison in connection with the bombings of seven Washington, D.C.–area clinics, calls Hill an inspiration.

"If a martyr is one who dies for a just cause, yes," Bray said. "If he dies for doing what is good and right, yes. Therefore, I say yes."

Abortion rights activists say they're terrified such talk will provoke more violence.

"We are on red alert," says Eleanor Smeal of the Feminist Majority Foundation.

Smeal and others are urging the federal government to step up enforcement of a new law that makes it a crime to block access to clinics or threaten or harm workers. Hill also was convicted under that law.

Already, members of the new Republican-controlled Congress are considering ways to limit its scope.

"Those who commit violence ought to have federal penalties," says Rep. Chris Smith (R., N.J.). But the law goes too far, so "we're going to take a (new) look at it."

Barrett's son Bruce said Hill's sentence should send a powerful message.

"It's real important that the state showed that this kind of violence is not going to be condoned, and the only way to do that is to give the maximum penalty," he said. Hill "shot my father in the face with a shotgun. He shot Dr. Britton in the head...and he had planned to do it for a long time."

QUESTIONS

1. How is it that some people view Paul Hill as a common criminal, while others see him as a hero—even a martyr? How can otherwise law-abiding citizens condone the killing of abortion clinic workers?
2. What does the debate over abortion have to tell us about the role of law in society, and about how laws are made and enforced?
3. What other issues can you identify which are officially law violations, but which have numerous proponents?

Source: Mimi Hall "'Martyr' or Murderer? Abortion Protester's Death Sentence Ignites Debate, *USA Today*, December 7, 1994, p. 3A. Copyright 1994, *USA Today*. Reprinted with permission.

Another early conflict theorist, **Austin Turk,** said that in the search for an explanation of criminality, "one is led to investigate the tendency of laws to penalize persons whose behavior is more characteristic of the less powerful than of the more powerful and the extent to which some persons and groups can and do use legal processes and agencies to maintain and enhance their power position vis-à-vis other persons and groups."[15] In his 1969 seminal work, *Criminality and Legal Order,*[16] Turk wrote that in any attempt to explain criminality, "it is more useful to view the social order as mainly a pattern of conflict" rather than to offer explanations for crime based upon behavioral or psychological approaches. Turk, like most other conflict criminologists, saw the law as a powerful tool in the service of prominent social groups seeking continued control over others. Crime was the natural consequence of such intergroup struggle because it resulted from the definitions imposed by the laws of the powerful upon the disapproved strivings of the unempowered.

RADICAL–CRITICAL CRIMINOLOGY

Radical criminology a perspective which holds that the causes of crime are rooted in social conditions which empower the wealthy and the politically well organized, but disenfranchise those less fortunate.

Proletariat in Marxian theory, the working class.

Bourgeoisie in Marxian theory, the class of people which owns the means of production.

The conflict perspective is thoroughly entrenched in **radical criminology,** which is also diversely known as "new," "**critical**," or **Marxist criminology**. Radical criminology, which appeared on the American scene in the 1970s, has its roots in the writings of nineteenth-century social utopian thinkers. Primary among them is **Karl Marx,** whose writings on the conflicts inherent in capitalism led to the formulation of communist ideals and, many would say, to the rise of communist societies the world over.

According to Marx two fundamental social classes exist within any capitalistic society: the haves and the have nots. Marx termed these two groups the **proletariat** and the **bourgeoisie.** The proletariat encompasses the large mass of people, those who are relatively uneducated and who are without power. In short, the proletariat are the workers, while the bourgeoisie are the capitalists—the wealthy owners of the means of production (i.e., the factories, businesses, and other elements of a society's organizational infrastructure). Although Marx was German, the terms proletariat and bourgeoisie were taken from Marx's knowledge of the French language, and are in turn derived from Latin. In ancient Rome, for example, that city's lowest class was propertyless and were individually referred to as *proletarius.*

According to Marx, the proletariat, since they possessed neither capital nor the means of production such as factories, land, or natural resources, must earn their living by continuously selling their labor. The bourgeoisie, on the other hand, are the capitalist class who, by nature of their very position within society, stand opposed to the proletariat in ongoing class struggle. Marx saw such struggle between classes as inevitable to the evolution of any capitalistic society, and believed that the natural outcome of such struggle would be the overthrow of capitalistic social order and the birth of a truly classless, or communistic, society.

The tomb of Karl Marx, in Highgate cemetery, London, England. Marxist thought underpins the writings of many radical criminologists. *Rex USA Ltd.*

Radical Criminology Today

Contemporary radical criminology is the intellectual child of three important historical circumstances: (1) the ruminations of nineteenth-century social utopian thinkers referred to earlier, including Friedrich Engels, Georg Wilhelm, Friedrich Hegel, Karl Marx, George Simmel, and Max Weber; (2) the rise of conflict theory in the social sciences; and (3) the dramatic radicalization of American academia in the 1960s and 1970s.

Radical criminologists of today are considerably more sophisticated than their Marxist forebearers. Contemporary radical criminology holds that the causes of crime are rooted in social conditions which empower the wealthy and the politically well organized, but disenfranchise those less fortunate. William Chambliss, a well-known spokesperson for radical thinkers, succinctly summarizes the modern perspective in these words: "what makes the behavior of some criminal is the coercive power of the state to enforce the will of the ruling class."[17]

Central to the perspective of radical criminology is the notion of **social class.** Some authors maintain that "class is nothing but an abbreviation to describe a way of living, thinking, and feeling." For most sociologists, however, the concept of social class entails distinctions made between individuals on the basis of significant defining characteristics such as race, religion, education, profession, income, wealth, family background, housing, artistic tastes, aspirations, cultural pursuits, child-rearing habits, speech, accent and so forth. Individuals are assigned to classes

Social class distinctions made between individuals on the basis of important defining social characteristics.

by others and by themselves on the basis of characteristics which are both ascribed and achieved. Ascribed attributes are those with which a person is born, such as his or her race or gender, while achieved characteristics are acquired through personal effort or chance over the course of one's life and include things such as level of education, income, place of residence, profession, and so on.

Although Marx concerned himself with only two social classes, most social scientists today talk in terms of at least three groups: upper, middle, and lower class. Some, such as Vance Packard,[18] have distinguished between five hierarchically arranged classes (the real upper, semiupper, limited-success, working, and real lower) while further subdividing classes 'horizontally' according to ascribed characteristics such as race and religion.

Conflict theorists of the early and mid-1900s saw in the concept of social class the rudimentary ingredients of other important concepts such as authority, power, and conflict. Ralf Dahrendorf, for example, wrote that "classes are social conflict groups the determinant of which can be found in the participation in or exclusion from the exercise of authority."[19] For Dahrendorf, conflict was ubiquitous, a fundamental part of and coextensive with any society. "Not the presence but the absence of conflict is surprising and abnormal," he wrote, "and we have good reason to be suspicious if we find a society or social organization that displays no evidence of conflict. To be sure, we do not have to assume that conflict is always violent and uncontrolled...[and] we must never lose sight of the underlying assumption that conflict can be temporarily suppressed, regulated, channeled, and controlled but that neither a philosopher-king nor a modern dictator can abolish it once and for all."[20]

From Dahrendorf's perspective, it was power and authority which were most at issue between groups, and over which class conflicts arose. Dahrendorf also recognized that situations characterized by conflict are rarely static, and it is out of conflict that change arises. For Dahrendorf, change could be either destructive or constructive. Destructive change brings about a lessening of social order, whereas constructive change increases cohesiveness within society.

Two highly visible proponents of radical criminology today are **Richard Quinney** and **William Chambliss.** In 1971 Chambliss, along with Robert T. Seidman, published an intellectually renowned volume entitled *Law, Order, and Power.* Their work represented something of a bridge between earlier conflict theorists and the more radical approach of Marxists. Through its emphasis on social class, class interests, and class conflict, *Law, Order, and Power* presented a Marxist perspective stripped of any overt references to capitalism as the root cause of crime. "The more economically stratified a society becomes," Chambliss and Seidman wrote, "the more it becomes necessary for the dominant groups in the society to enforce through coercion the norms of conduct which guarantee their supremacy."[21] Chambliss and Seidman outlined their position in five propositions, as follows: [22]

- The conditions of one's life affect one's values and norms. Complex societies are composed of groups with widely different life conditions.
- Complex societies are therefore composed of highly disparate and conflicting sets of norms.

- The probability of a given group's having its particular normative system embodied in law is not distributed equally but is closely related to the political and economic position of that group.
- The higher a group's political or economic position, the greater the probability that its views will be reflected in laws.

Chambliss also believed that middle- and upper-class criminals are more apt to escape apprehension and punishment by the criminal justice system, not because they are any smarter or more capable of hiding their crimes than are lower class offenders, but because of a "very rational choice on the part of the legal system to pursue those violators that the community will reward them for pursuing and to ignore those violators who have the capability for causing trouble for the agencies."[23]

By the 1970s, however, as American academia became increasingly radicalized, Chambliss's writings assumed a much more Marxian flavor. In an article[24] published in 1975, Chambliss once again recognized the huge power gap separating the "haves" from the "have nots." Crime, he said, is created by actions of the ruling class which define as criminal undertakings and activities that contravene the interests of the rulers. At the same time, he said, members of the ruling class will inevitably be able to continue to violate the criminal law with impunity, since it is their own creation.

By 1975, the Marxian flavor of Chambliss's writing had become undeniable. He began using Marxist terminology. "[A]s capitalist societies industrialize and the gap between the bourgeoisie and the proletariat widens," he wrote, "penal law will expand in an effort to coerce the proletariat into submission."[25] For Chambliss, the economic consequences of crime within a capitalistic society were partially what perpetuated it. "[C]rime reduces surplus labor," he wrote, "by creating employment not only for the criminals but for law enforcers, welfare workers, professors of criminology, and a horde of people who live off the fact that crime exists...."[26] Socialist societies, claimed Chambliss, should reflect much lower crime rates than capitalist societies because a "less intense class struggle should reduce the forces leading to and the functions of crime."

Although Chambliss provides much of the intellectual bedrock of contemporary radical criminology, that school of thought found its most eloquent expression in the writings of Richard Quinney. In 1974 Quinney, in an attempt to challenge and change American social life for the better, set forth his six Marxist propositions for an understanding of crime. They read[27]

- American society is based on an advanced capitalist economy.
- The state is organized to serve the interests of the dominant economic class, the capitalist ruling class.
- Criminal law is an instrument of the state and ruling class to maintain and perpetuate the existing social and economic order.
- Crime control in capitalist society is accomplished through a variety of institutions and agencies established and administered by a governmental elite, representing ruling class interests, for the purpose of establishing domestic order.

- The contradictions of advanced capitalism—the disjunction between existence and essence—require that the subordinate classes remain oppressed by whatever means necessary, especially through the coercion and violence of the legal system.
- Only with the collapse of capitalist society and the creation of a new society, based on socialist principles, will there be a solution to the crime problem.

A few years later, Quinney published *Class, State, and Crime,* in which he argued that almost all crimes committed by members of the lower classes are necessary for the survival of individual members of those classes. Crimes, said Quinney—in fashion reminiscent of Vold's notion of the criminal as a soldier—are actually an attempt by the socially disenfranchised "to exist in a society where *survival* is not assured by other, collective means."[28] "Crime is inevitable under capitalist conditions," concludes Quinney, because crime is "a response to the material conditions of life." "Permanent unemployment—and the acceptance of that condition," wrote Quinney, "can result in a form of life where criminality is an appropriate and consistent response."[29] The solution offered by Quinney to the problem of crime is the development of a socialist society. "The *ultimate meaning* of crime in the development of capitalism," he writes, "is the need for a socialist society."[30]

Contemporary radical criminology attributes much of the existing propensity toward criminality to differences in social class, and in particular to those arrangements within society which maintain class differences. As Quinney puts it, "classes are an expression of the underlying forces of the capitalist mode of production...."[31] "Within the class structure of advanced capitalism," he writes, "is the dialectic that increases class struggle and the movement for socialist revolution." Table 9.1 depicts the class structure of the United States as Quinney portrayed it.

Critical Criminology

Some writers distinguish between "critical criminology" and "radical criminology," claiming that the former is simply a way of critiquing social relationships that lead to crime, while the latter constitutes a pro-active call for a radical change in social conditions in an effort to reduce or eliminate crime.

Gresham Sykes explains critical criminology this way: "it forces an inquiry into precisely how the normative content of the criminal law is internalized in different segments of society, and how norm-holding is actually related to behavior."[32] Sykes's definition, however, has been characterized as "mild" by others who bemoan the fact that "unfortunately, all of the recent alternatives to traditional criminology have been conveniently grouped under the term 'critical criminology.'"[33]

As David A. Jones puts it in his insightful *History of Criminology,* "Sometimes, it may be difficult to distinguish 'critical' from a truly Marxist criminology. One basis, advanced by Marvin Wolfgang, is that 'critical' criminology is 'more reactive than proactive,' meaning that 'critical' criminology does not aim to overthrow the 'ruling class' so much as it may criticize the way it believes such a group dominates society. On the other hand," Jones continues, "clearly, Marxism in criminology is no different from Marxism generally. It is truly proactive instead of being reactive."[34]

TABLE 9.1

CLASS STRUCTURE OF THE UNITED STATES WITH ESTIMATED PERCENTAGES OF THE ADULT POPULATION

Capitalist Class 1.5%	Owns and controls production; wields state power
Petty Bourgeoisie 18.5%	Professionals, middle management, bureaucrats
Working Class 80%	**Technical and skilled working class, 25%**
	Technical, 10%: teachers, nurses, medical technicians
	Skilled, 15%: craftsmen, clerical, sales, operatives, transport, industrial
	Unskilled working class, 55%
	Unskilled, 30%: industrial labor, service, office, sales, clerical
	Reserve army, 15%: unemployed
	Pauperized poor, 10%

Source: Richard Quinney, *Class, State, and Crime: On the Theory and Practice of Criminal Justice* (New York: David McKay, 1977), p. 77. Reprinted with permission.

Radical Criminology and Policy Issues

Some contemporary writers on radical criminology tell us that "Marxist criminology was once dismissed as a utopian perspective with no relevant policy implication except revolution. At best, revolution was considered an impractical approach to the problems at hand. Recently, however, many radicals have attempted to address the issues of what can be done under our current system."[35]

Most radical criminologists of the current genre recognize that a sudden and total reversal of existing political arrangements within the United States is highly unlikely. They have begun to focus, instead, on promoting a gradual transition to socialism and to socialized forms of government activity. These middle range policy alternatives include "equal justice in the bail system, the abolition of mandatory sentences, prosecution of corporate crimes, increased employment opportunities, and promoting community alternatives to imprisonment."[36] Likewise, programs to reduce prison overcrowding, efforts to highlight injustices within the current system, the elimination of racism and other forms of inequality in the handling of both victims and offenders, growing equality in criminal justice system employment, and the like are all frequently mentioned as midrange strategies for bringing about a justice system that is more fair and closer to the radical ideal.

Raymond Michalowski well summarizes the policy directions envisioned by today's radical criminologists when he says, "[w]e cannot be free from the crimes of the poor until there are no more poor; we cannot be free from domination of the powerful until we reduce the inequalities that make domination possible; and we cannot live in harmony with others until we begin to limit the competition for material advantage over others that alienates us from one another."[37]

Even so, few in the radical camp seem to expect to see dramatic changes in the near future. As Michael J. Lynch and W. Byron Groves put it, "[i]n the end, the criminal justice system has failed as an agent of social change because its efforts are directed at an individual as opposed to social remedies.... For these reasons, radicals suggest that we put our efforts into the creation of economic equality or employment opportunities to combat crime."[38]

Critiques of Radical Criminology

Radical criminology has been criticized for its nearly exclusive emphasis on methods of social change at the expense of well-developed theory. As *William* v. *Pelfrey* explains it, "[i]t is in the Radical School of Criminology that theory is almost totally disregarded, except as something to criticize, and radical *methods* are seen as optimum."[39]

Radical criminology can also be criticized for failing to recognize what appears to be at least a fair degree of public consensus about the nature of crime, that is, that crime is undesirable and that criminal activity is to be controlled. Were criminal activity in fact a true expression of the sentiments of the politically disenfranchised, as some radical criminologists claim, then public opinion might be expected to offer support for at least certain forms of crime. Even the sale and consumption of illicit drugs, however—a type of crime which may provide an alternative path to riches for the otherwise disenfranchised—is frequently condemned by residents of working class communities.[40]

Another effective criticism of Marxist criminology centers on the fact that Marxist thinkers appear to confuse issues of personal politics with what could otherwise be social reality. As a consequence of allowing personal values and political leanings to enter the criminological arena, Marxist criminologists have frequently appeared to sacrifice their objectivity. Jackson Toby, for example, claims that

Marxist and radical thinkers are simply building upon an "old tradition of sentimentality toward those who break social rules."[41] Such sentimentality can be easily discounted, he says when we realize that "[c]olor television sets and automobiles are stolen more often than food and blankets."[42]

Marxist criminology has been refuted by contemporary thinkers who find that it falls short in appreciating the multiplicity of problems that contribute to the problem of crime. Some years ago, for example, the astute criminologist Hermann Mannheim critiqued Marxian assumptions by showing how "subsequent developments" have shown that "Marx was wrong in thinking: (a) that there could be only two classes in a capitalist society...; (b) that...class struggle was entirely concerned with the question of private property in the means of production; (c) that the only way in which fundamental social changes could be effected was by violent social revolution; [and] (d) that all conflicts were class conflicts and all social change could be explained in terms of class conflicts...."

Mannheim went on to point out that the development of a semiskilled work force along with the advent of highly skilled and well-educated workers has led to the creation of a multiplicity of classes within contemporary capitalistic societies. The growth of such classes, said Mannheim, effectively spreads the available wealth in those societies where such workers are employed and reduces the likelihood of revolution.

Marxist criminology has also suffered a considerable loss of prestige among many would-be followers in the wake of the collapse of the former Soviet Union and its client states in Eastern Europe and other parts of the world. With the death of Marxist political organizations and their agendas, Marxist criminology seems to have lost some of its impetus. Many would argue that, in fact, the recent work of writers such as Quinney and Chambliss presaged the decline of Soviet influence and had already moved Marxist and radical criminology into new areas—effectively shedding the reigns of world communism and ending any association with its institutional embodiment in specific parts of the world. Instead, a criminology of peacemaking (discussed in Chapter 14), drawing upon an informed humanitarian awareness, is now developing out of what might otherwise be seen as the ruins of Marxist thought. It will probably not be long, however, before other radical apologists make a convincing case for a more traditional form of post-Soviet Marxist criminology.

TERRORISM

From the perspective of radical criminology, crime can be a political statement. Quinney, for example, says that "criminality is the beginning of a conscious rebellion against capitalist conditions."[43] When crime becomes a conscious and intentionally chosen response to conditions of societal oppression, then it becomes a revolutionary tool. Hence, as alluded to earlier, some thinkers not only explain crime as the result of political oppression and the inequitable distribution of wealth and power in society, but view it as a form of terrorism that is more or less consciously waged against the state by the disenfranchised.

Unfortunately for such thinkers, however, the fact is that most crimes committed today appear to victimize precisely those who are already the most victimized by existing arrangements of wealth and power, that is, the working class poor and the unemployed. Quinney recognizes this when he says, "to the extent that crime is directed against members of the working class, crime remains counterrevolutionary. Much, if not most," he says, "crime continues to victimize those who are already oppressed by capitalism...."[44] Even so, it is true that those who see themselves as actively excluded from effective participation in political decision making may turn to other means to have their voices heard. When awareness translates into alienation, conscious calls for terrorist activity may erupt.

Terrorism a violent act or an act dangerous to human life in violation of the criminal laws of the United States or of any state to intimidate or coerce a government, the civilian population, or any segment thereof, in furtherance of political or social objectives.

The FBI defines **terrorism** as "a violent act or an act dangerous to human life in violation of the criminal laws of the United States or of any state to intimidate or coerce a government, the civilian population, or any segment thereof, in furtherance of political or social objectives."[45] From the radical point of view, discussed earlier in this chapter, terrorism is simply another example of the control by state monopolies over definitions of crime. Hence, a contrasting definition of terrorism is "behaviors which menace the social, economic and political order."[46]

Regardless of definitional distinctions, both conservative and radical approaches seem to agree that "the primary distinction between violent criminal acts and terrorist acts has to do with the political motivation or ideology of the offender."[47] Hence, bombings, hostage-taking, and other similar terrorist-like acts which are undertaken for merely individual or pecuniary gain, when no political or social objectives are sought by the perpetrators, would not qualify as "terrorism" under either approach. However, as both definitions reveal, terrorists probably do not think of themselves as "criminal," preferring instead the "revolutionary" label.

Today the United States is faced with two types of terrorism: international and domestic. While the number of terrorist attacks on U.S. interests around the world has shown an overall decline in recent years (1993 was an exception), it would be a mistake to assume that international terrorism is no longer a serious threat. As one observer on the subject puts it, "[w]hile the number of terrorist attacks generally is declining, the audacity of terrorists and their choice of targets...are in some ways more alarming than ever. As long as the United States remains actively engaged in the world, as it clearly must, there will be governments and groups committed to the use of violence to attack U.S. interests and further their own political goals."[48]

According to the U.S. State Department report, *Patterns of Global Terrorism, 1993,*[49] 427 international terrorist attacks occurred around the world in 1993—an increase from the 361 incidents recorded the previous year. The main reason cited by the report for the increase was an "accelerated terror campaign perpetrated by the Kurdistan Workers Party (PKK) against Turkish interests,"[50] with most of the PKK's attacks occurring in Western Europe. State Department statisticians, however, narrowly define terrorism as "politically motivated violence involving the citizens or territory of more than one country." A more accurate measure of terrorism may be that produced by Pinkerton Risk Assessment Services which, using a much broader definition of terrorism (one that counts politically motivated violence committed inside a country by its own citizens) concludes that terrorist attacks worldwide increased to a record 5,404 in 1992.[51] Pinkerton statisticians also claims that, according to their measures, the number of people killed in worldwide terrorist attacks recently rose above 10,000 for the first time since the agency began keeping records.

As the State Department report points out, the bombing of the World Trade Center in New York City and the ensuing fire and smoke which caused six deaths and nearly one thousand injuries while leaving a five-story crater under the building, was the only externally directed terrorist incident in 1993 that claimed American lives. One year and six days after the explosion, Nidal Ayyad, Ahmad Ajaj, Mohammad Salameh, and Mahmud Abouhalima—all Islamic fundamentalists who had entered the United States from the Middle East—were convicted of all charges that the U.S. government had brought against them, including conspiracy to bomb buildings, explosive destruction of property, and assault on a federal officer. It was later discovered, however, that plotters had targeted other vital city areas, including the United Nations and the Holland and Lincoln Tunnels. Had those plots been successfully implemented, many more lives would have been lost and an untold amount of social disruption would have occurred within the northeastern United States. Also charged in the plot were Sheik Omar Abdel Rahman and many of his followers.

Devastation in downtown Oklahoma City—the result of a massive terrorist truck bomb detonated in front of the Alfred P. Murrah federal building in 1995. *David Longstreath/AP/Wide World Photos.*

The bombing of the World Trade Center may be just the beginning of a new and especially violent campaign of terrorism directed at American citizens both at home and abroad. As one terrorism expert recently put it, "The U.S. and its Arab allies are losing steadily to Islamic forces energized by several new trends in the Middle East.... It is tempting to dismiss the fundamentalists accused of bombing the World Trade Center and planning a host of other violent actions in New York as deranged fanatics, and amateurish ones at that. Yet, to do so is to ignore the fact that radical Islamists, in the U.S. and the Middle East, are pursuing an ambitious political agenda. It also is tempting to characterize the fundamentalists as a fringe group on the periphery of Middle Eastern politics, when, actually, their destabilizing activities are at the center of the region's troubles. Without illusions, Washington must recognize that the slow triumph of militant Islam in the Middle East not only will pose a major threat to the U.S.'s position in the region, but also will bring terrorism to American shores."[52]

Another expert explains it this way: "The U.S. has long been a major terrorist target, but most of the assaults on Americans and their organizations have taken place overseas. Terrorist attacks inside the U.S. have been extremely rare. There are many reasons, though, to think that may change. As the only remaining superpower, the U.S. already is the Great Satan to Islamic fundamentalists—the protector of Israel, supporter of the perceived infidel Mubarak, prime enemy of theocratic Iran. But there could well be many other groups with grievances: Bosnian Muslims who think the U.S. has abandoned them to slaughter; Kurds who think Washington has left them to the cruelties of Saddam Hussein, the Turkish government or both. Indeed, the U.S. could be a target for just about any group that feels itself aggrieved and believes the one (remaining) superpower has caused its troubles or could stop them but won't bestir itself."[53]

The April 1995 terrorist bombing of the Alfred P. Murrah federal building in downtown Oklahoma City, Oklahoma, in which more than 160 people died and hundreds more were wounded, demonstrated just how vulnerable the United States is to terrorist attack. The nine-story building, which included offices of the Social Security Administration, Drug Enforcement Administration, the Secret Service, the Bureau of Alcohol, Tobacco, and Firearms, and a day care center called "America's Kids," was devastated by the homemade bomb. The fertilizer and diesel fuel device was estimated to have weighed about 1,200 pounds. It had been left in a parked rental truck on the 5th Street side of the building. The blast left a crater 30 feet wide and 8 feet deep, and spread debris over a 10 block area. Suspects, one of whom was arrested for a traffic violation only minutes after the blast occurred, led authorities to surmise that the attack was intended to revenge the 1993 assault on David Koresh's Branch Davidian complex in Waco, Texas, which left 86 cult members dead. The Waco incident happened two years to the day before the Oklahoma City attack.

The very freedoms which allow America to serve as a model of democracy to the rest of the world have made it possible for terrorist or terrorist-affiliated groups to operate within the United States relatively unencumbered. For example, The Islamic Committee for Palestine, which some have described as a quasi-radical group with possible terrorist links, operates from a base in Tampa, Florida, from which it sponsors conferences, meetings, and speakers. Recent occasions have featured representatives of the fanatic Palestinian Islamic Jihad organization, and Sheik Abd al-Aziz Odeh, the group's spiritual leader has addressed groups there. Similarly in attendance has been Rachid al-Ghanouchi, the leader of Tunisia's outlawed al-Nahda.

Many U.S.-based terrorists may have direct links with those who control them from abroad. Others, however, may simply be motivated by a spiritual kinship with foreign ideas. Vincent Cannistraro, former head of the CIA's counterterrorism center has spoken to the issue. "What they're providing," says Cannistraro of the radical Muslim countries and their governments, "is a world vision, a means of direct participation in God's plan. That can be very appealing."[54]

Many terrorist organizations exist within other nations, however. Included among them are the Japanese Red Army, the Lebanese Hezballah, the Provisional Irish Republican Army in the United Kingdom, the Abu Nidal Organization, the ETA in Spain, Peruvian Shinning Path (*Sendero Luminoso*) guerrillas, the Palestinian Hamas, Islamic Jihad, and the Popular Front for the Liberation of Palestine-General Command. Some such organizations enjoy state sponsorship, while others do not. "Some terrorist groups that do not enjoy state sponsorship," says Timothy E. Wirth, U.S. undersecretary of state for global affairs, "have tried to develop independent means of support. Some groups have resorted to crimes such as bank robbery or extortion, while others, particularly in the Andean region, have developed close working relationships with drug dealers."

THEORY VERSUS REALITY

Domestic Terrorism Strikes University Campuses: The UNABOMber

In late 1993 the FBI announced a $1,000,000 reward for information leading to the arrest and conviction of the "UNABOMber," an as yet unidentified individual wanted in a seventeen-year-long series of fifteen unsolved bombing incidents directed against college professors and the computer and airline industries. The FBI press release follows:

> Beginning in May, 1978, a series of 15 bombing incidents have occurred across the United States for which there is no apparent explanation or motive. No person or group has been identified as the perpetrator(s) of these incidents. The explosions have taken place in seven states from Connecticut to California. As a result of these bombings, two people have been killed and 23 others injured, some grievously. There had been no incidents identified with this series of bombings since 1987. However that changed in late June, 1993, when a well known geneticist residing in Tiburon, California, and a renowned computer scientist from Yale University, New Haven, Connecticut, opened packages that had been mailed to them and both were severely injured when these packages exploded.

In the past, targets of the bomber have been associated with the computer industry, the aircraft and airline industry and universities. Eight of these devices have been mailed to specific individuals and the other seven have been placed in locations that suggest there was no specific intended victim. All but two of the explosive devices functioned as designed and exploded. All 15 crimes, dubbed "UNABOM," have had common effects: all have caused terror, grief, and fear. On September 11, 1985, Hugh Scrutton, the owner of the Rentech Computer Company, in Sacramento, California, was killed by one of these diabolic devices. In 1994, Thomas J. Mosser of New Jersey, died while opening a similar device.

In response to the June, 1993, events, the Attorney General directed that a task force of federal law enforcement agencies be re-established to urgently investigate and solve these crimes. The UNABOM Task Force, consisting of investigators from the FBI, ATF, and the U.S. Postal Inspection Service, has been operational in San Francisco and Sacramento, California, since July 12, 1993, and is dedicated exclusively to the investigation of these crimes.

Among the clues in the case are the following words in what appears to be a note possibly written by the bomber as a reminder to make a telephone call: "call Nathan R—Wed 7PM." The UNABOM Task Force believes that "Nathan R" may be associated, perhaps innocently, with the bomber and that "Nathan R" may have received a telephone call from the bomber on a Wednesday prior to the June, 1993 bombings.

The three most recent tragic bombings illustrate the senseless and tragic consequences of these crimes and demonstrate the urgent necessity of solving this case. This serial bomber will strike again. We do not know who the next victim will be. We do believe that there is someone out there who can provide the identity of the person or persons responsible for these crimes. This person may be a friend, a neighbor, or even a relative of the bomber(s).

UNABOM's chronology is as follows:

1. Northwestern University, Evanston, Illinois, May 25, 1978: A package was found in the Engineering Department parking lot at the Chicago Circle Campus of the University of Illinois. The package was addressed to an Engineering Professor at Rensselaer Polytechnic Institute in Troy, New York. The package had a return address of a Professor at Northwestern's Technological Institute. The package was returned to the addressor who turned it over to the Northwestern University Police Department because he had not sent the package. On May 26, 1978 the parcel was opened by a police officer who suffered minor injuries when the bomb detonated.
2. Northwestern University, Evanston, Illinois, May 9, 1979: A disguised explosive device that had been left in a common area in the University's Technological Institute, slightly injured a graduate student on May 9, 1979, when he attempted to open the box and it exploded.

3. Chicago, Illinois, November 15, 1979: An explosive device disguised as a parcel was mailed from Chicago for delivery to an unknown location. The bomb detonated in the cargo compartment of an airplane, forcing it to make an emergency landing at Dulles Airport. Twelve individuals were treated for smoke inhalation. The explosion destroyed the wrapping to such an extent that the addressee could not be determined.
4. Chicago, Illinois, June 10, 1980: A bomb disguised as a parcel postmarked June 8, 1980 was mailed to an airline executive at his home in Lake Forest, Illinois. The airline executive was injured in the explosion.
5. University of Utah, Salt Lake City, Utah, October 8, 1981: An explosive device was found in the hall of a classroom building and rendered safe by bomb squad personnel.
6. Vanderbilt University, Nashville, Tennessee, May 5, 1982: A wooden box containing a pipe bomb detonated on May 5, 1982, when opened by a secretary in the Computer Science Department. The secretary suffered minor injuries. The package was initially mailed from Provo, Utah, on April 23, 1982, to Pennsylvania State University and then forwarded to Vanderbilt.
7. University of California, Berkeley, California, July 2, 1982: A small metal pipe bomb was placed in a coffee break room of Cory Hall at the University's Berkeley Campus. A Professor of Electrical Engineering and Computer Science was injured when he picked up the device.
8. Auburn, Washington, May 8, 1985: A parcel bomb was mailed on May 8, 1985, to the Boeing Company, Fabrication Division. On June 13, 1985, the explosive device was discovered when employees opened it. The device was rendered safe by bomb squad personnel without injury.
9. University of California, Berkeley, California, May 15, 1985: A bomb detonated in a computer room at Cory Hall on the Berkeley Campus. A graduate student in Electrical Engineering lost partial vision in his left eye and four fingers from his right hand. The device was believed to have been placed in the room several days prior to detonation.
10. Ann Arbor, Michigan, November 15, 1985: A textbook size package was mailed to the home of a University of Michigan Professor in Ann Arbor, Michigan from Salt Lake City. On November 15, 1985, a Research Assistant suffered injuries when he opened the package. The Professor was a few feet away but was not injured.
11. Sacramento, California, December 11, 1985: Mr. Hugh Scrutton was killed outside his computer rental store when he picked up a device disguised as a road hazard left near the rear entrance to the building. Metal shrapnel from the blast ripped through Scrutton's chest and penetrated his heart.
12. Salt Lake City, Utah, February 20, 1987: On February 20, 1987, an explosive device disguised as a road hazard was left at the rear entrance to CAAMs, Inc. (computer store). The bomb exploded and injured the owner when he attempted to pick up the device.

An FBI composite sketch of the UNABOMber. *Courtesy: The FBI.*

13. Tiburon, California, June 22, 1993: On June 22, 1993, a well known geneticist received a parcel postmarked June 18, 1993, at his residence. The doctor attempted to open the package at which time it exploded severely injuring him. It has been determined that this parcel was mailed from Sacramento, California.
14. Yale University, New Haven, Connecticut, June 24, 1993: On June 24, 1993, a Professor/Computer Scientist at Yale University attempted to open a parcel that he had received at his office. This parcel exploded severely injuring him. It has been determined that this parcel was mailed from Sacramento, California on June 18, 1993.
15. North Cladwell, New Jersey, December 10, 1994: Advertising executive Thomas J. Mosser, was killed as he opened a mail bomb in the kitchen of his home.

A one million dollar reward is being offered for information that results in the identification, arrest and conviction of the person(s) responsible. Contact the UNABOM Task Force at 1 (800) 701-2662.

Source: William L. Tafoya, Ph.D., Special Agent, FBI UNABOM Task Force, San Francisco, CA, 1994.

Terrorist bombings can be costly. Here an Israeli soldier examines the aftermath of a 1994 terrorist bombing of a Tel Aviv bus. *Shaul Golan/Yedioth Aharonoth/Sygma.*

Countering the Terrorist Threat

Secretary Wirth recently testified before Congress on the growing threat of international terrorism. "Working in close consultation with the Congress," Wirth said, "successive Administrations have developed a set of principles that continue to guide us as we counter the threat posed by terrorists."[55] According to Wirth these principles dictate that the U.S. government must

Make no concessions to terrorists.

Continue to apply increasing pressure to state sponsors of terrorism.

Forcefully apply the rule of law to international terrorists.

Help other governments improve their capabilities to counter the threats posed by international terrorists.

"Our counter-terrorism strategy," testified Wirth, "has three key elements—to implement our policy of 'no concessions,' to keep pressure on state sponsors, and to apply the rule of law. These basic policies," Wirth added, "have served us well in the past, and will do so in the future..." and, said Wirth, apply "equally well to groups such as the Abu Nidal Organization, or a small and unnamed group that may come together to undertake only a single attack."

State-organized crime acts defined by law as criminal and committed by state officials in the pursuit of their job as representatives of the state.

STATE-ORGANIZED CRIME

In his 1988 presidential remarks to the American Society of Criminology, William J. Chambliss addressed the issue of what he called **state-organized crime.**[56] Chambliss characterized state-organized crime as "acts defined by law as criminal and committed by state officials in the pursuit of their job as representatives of the state."[57] Examples, said Chambliss, include a nation's "complicity in piracy, smuggling, assassinations, criminal conspiracies, acting as an accessory before or after the fact, and violating laws that limit their activities." Limits on activities would encompass such restrictions as legal regulations against spying on citizens, campaign contribution rules, the legislative earmarking of funds not to be diverted for other purposes, prohibitions against the selling of arms to belligerent nations, and statutes contravening official support for terrorism.

State-organized crime, Chambliss advised those in attendance, "does not include criminal acts that benefit only individual officeholders," including things such as the acceptance of bribes or the "illegal use of violence by the police against individuals, unless such acts...violate existing criminal law and are official policy." In his speech Chambliss gave examples of the kinds of things that *do* constitute state-organized crime. Among the activities mentioned were things as diverse as (1) the state-supported pirates who worked for France, England, and Holland against Spanish and Italian interests centuries ago; (2) America's enlistment of pirates during the War of 1812 to fend off attacks by British naval vessels; (3) French colonial profits derived from the opium trade in Indochina, which helped finance colonial governments there; (4) the use of the CIA-sponsored airline, Air America, during the Vietnam war to transport illegal opium to market in order to finance anti-Communist mountain tribes in their militant activities against the North Vietnamese army; (5) money laundering activities of U.S.-sponsored banks in Australia during the war in Southeast Asia; and (6) the plan by members of the National Security Council, the Department of Defense, and the CIA, later uncovered in Senate Hearings in 1986, to sell arms to Iran and to use money from those sales to support the activities of Contra rebels in Nicaragua.

This last example is perhaps best known to contemporary Americans, who will recall the indictment and prosecution of Lt. Colonel Oliver North and the investigations of Theodore Shackley, Thomas Clines, and Major General Richard Secord which followed from Senate suspicions that the 1985 Borland Amendment had been violated. The Borland Amendment forbade any U.S. official from assisting the Nicaraguan Contra rebels—either directly or indirectly.

Chambliss also categorizes as state-organized crime American-sponsored coups in Guatemala, Nicaragua, the Dominican Republic, and Vietnam. "[I]nvolvement in these coups," he says, "was never legally authorized." To bring his point home, Chambliss adds, "The murders, assassinations, and terrorist acts that accompany coups are criminal acts by law, both in the United States and in the country in which they take place." The DEA, the CIA, and the FBI have all been involved in such illegal clandestine activities, according to Chambliss, although they sometimes hide their involvement by establishing puppet or client organizations—such as the feared Chilean secret service (DINA) formed during the CIA-sponsored overthrow of Chilean president Salvador Allende in 1970.

Internal crimes committed by governments include things like medical experimentation on unwilling subjects, such as might have occurred following World War II when American soldiers were exposed to nuclear blasts and the dangerous fallout that followed. Experiments by the CIA involving hefty doses of LSD and other drugs on unsuspecting subjects provide yet another example of crimes committed by our own government within American borders. Finally, Chambliss cites the example of a 30-year-old FBI-run operation called CONTELPRO, which was intended to "disrupt, harass, and discredit groups that the FBI decided were in some way 'un-American.'" Targeted were the American Civil Liberties Union, representatives of the 1970s antiwar movement, militant black groups, and even organizations such as the NAACP. Chambliss calls CONTELPRO "the most flagrant violation of civil rights by federal agencies" in the nation's history, although some would argue that the internment of American civilians of Japanese descent at concentration-like camps during World War II exceeded even the FBI's harassment program in its flagrant violation of the rights of American citizens.

Many examples of state-organized crime committed by nations around the world could be given. Government-sponsored drug trade remains a major area of state-organized criminal activity. Chambliss says that "[t]oday, we see nations such as Turkey, Bolivia, Colombia, Peru, Panama, and the Bahamas encouraging the export of illegal drugs while condemning them publicly."

Although it is imperative that state-organized crime be studied, such study is fraught with difficulties including the need[58]

- To acquire reliable information on modern-day state-organized crime, which is difficult to come by since sources of such information are themselves inherently unreliable.
- For comparisons between styles of government and "political, economic, and social systems" across different historical time frames to learn why some "forms of social organization are more likely to create state-organized crime than others."
- To explore and identify parallels between state-organized criminality and the criminality of police and of other agencies of enforcement.

SUMMARY

Politics and crime are inextricably intertwined. Sometimes the actions undertaken by government officials are themselves criminal, while on other occasions governments may act to shield law violators or even assist citizens in the violation of official dictums. More significantly, however, the very action of legislative bodies in defining crime through the making of statutory law reveals the crucial nexus between social organization and the use of law as a tool of the powerful. The form of social organization endemic to a society produces a set of intergroup relationships that ultimately define which individuals and which groups are empowered to make law. Those who find themselves excluded from such important decision-making processes will either find alternative paths to success or turn to others means to empower themselves.

DISCUSSION QUESTIONS

1. Explain the difference between the consensus, pluralistic, and conflict perspectives. Which comes closest to your way of understanding society? Why?
2. What is Marxist criminology? How, if at all, does it differ from radical criminology? From critical criminology?
3. Does the Marxist perspective hold any significance for contemporary American society? Why or why not?
4. Define terrorism. Do you think that society will experience more or less terrorism in the future? How will forms of terrorism change in the future?
5. What is state-organized crime? Give examples of such crime. How can it be controlled?
6. What lessons can be learned from the April, 1995 terrorist bombing of the Alfred P. Murrah federal building in downtown Oklahoma City, Oklahoma? How likely do you believe such attacks may be in the future? How can we, as a nation, guard against them?

NOTES

1 Cited in Richard Z. Chesnoff, "Between Bombers and Believers: A Host of Radical Groups Are at Work in America," *U.S. News & World Report*, September 20, 1993 pp. 34–35.
2. Natasha Alova, "Russia-Juvenile Crime," Associated Press on-line, Northern edition, February 9, 1994.
3. Richard Quinney, *Class, State, and Crime: On the Theory and Practice of Criminal Justice* (New York: David McKay, 1977), p. 145.
4. Michael J. Sniffen, "Russian Crime," Associated Press on-line, May 24, 1994.
5. Ibid.
6. Raymond J. Michalowski, "Perspectives and Paradigm: Structuring Criminological Thought," in Robert F. Meier, ed., *Theory in Criminology* (Beverly Hills, CA: Sage, 1977), pp. 17–39.
7. Roscoe Pound, *Social Control Through the Law: The Powell Lectures* (Hamden, CT: Archon, 1968), pp. 113–114.
8. Although Pound's postulates originally made reference only to "men" we have here used the now-conventional phrase "men and women" throughout the postulates to indicate that Pound was speaking of all persons within the social group. No other changes to the original postulates have been made.
9. Adapted from Michalowski, "Perspectives and Paradigm: Structuring Criminological Thought."
10. Ibid.
11. George B. Vold, *Theoretical Criminology* (New York: Oxford University Press, 1958), p. 205.
12. Ibid., p. 206.
13. Ibid., pp. 208–209.
14. Ibid., p. 309.
15. Austin Turk, *Criminality and Legal Order* (Chicago: Rand McNally, 1969), p. vii.
16. Ibid.
17. William J. Chambliss, "Toward a Political Economy of Crime," in C. Reasons and R. Rich, *The Sociology of Law* (Toronto: Butterworth, 1978), p. 193.
18. Vance Packard, *The Status Seekers* (London: Harmondsworth, 1961).
19. Ralf Dahrendorf, *Class and Class Conflict in An Industrial Society* (Stanford, CA: Stanford University Press, 1959).
20. Ralf Dahrendorf, "Out of Utopia: Toward

a Reorientation of Sociological Analysis," *The American Journal of Sociology,* Vol. 64 (1958), pp. 115–127.

21. William Chambliss and Robert T. Seidman, *Law, Order, and Power* (Reading, MA: Addison-Wesley, 1971), p. 33.
22. Adapted from ibid., pp. 473–474.
23. William J. Chambliss, *Crime and the Legal Process* (New York: McGraw-Hill, 1969), p. 88.
24. William J. Chambliss, "Toward a Political Economy of Crime," *Theory and Society,* Vol. 2 (1975), pp. 152-153.
25. Ibid.
26. Ibid., p. 152.
27. Richard Quinney, *Critique of the Legal Order: Crime Control in Capitalist Society* (Boston: Little, Brown, 1974), p. 16.
28. Richard Quinney, *Class, State, and Crime: On the Theory and Practice of Criminal Justice* (New York: David McKay, 1977), p. 58.
29. Ibid., p. 58.
30. Ibid., p. 61.
31. Ibid., p. 65.
32. Gresham M. Sykes, "Critical Criminology," *Journal of Criminal Law and Criminology,* Vol. 65 (1974), pp. 206–213.
33. William V. Pelfrey, *The Evolution of Criminology* (Cincinnati: Anderson, 1980), p. 73.
34. David A. Jones, *History of Criminology: A Philosophical Perspective* (Westport, CT: Greenwood, 1986), p. 200.
35. Michael J. Lynch and W. Byron Groves, *A Primer in Radical Criminology,* 2nd ed. (Albany, NY: Harrow and Heston, 1989), p. 126.
36. Ibid., p. 128.
37. Raymond J. Michalowski, *Order, Law, and Crime: An Introduction to Criminology* (New York: Random House, 1985), p. 410.
38. Lynch and Groves, *A Primer in Radical Criminology,* p. 130.
39. Pelfrey, *The Evolution of Criminology,* p. 86.
40. For a good overview of critiques of radical criminology, see J. F. Galliher, "Life and Death of Liberal Criminology," *Contemporary Crisis,* Vol. 2, no. 3 (July 1978), pp. 245–263.
41. Jackson Toby, "The New Criminology Is the Old Sentimentality," *Criminology,* Vol. 16 (1979), pp. 516–526.
42. Ibid.
43. Ibid., p. 100.
44. Ibid., p. 103.
45. Federal Bureau of Investigation, Counterterrorism Section, *Terrorism in the United States, 1987* (Washington, D.C.: FBI, December 1987).
46. Lynch and Groves, *A Primer in Radical Criminology,* p. 39.
47. Ibid., p. 39.
48. Peter Flory, "Terrorism Must Continue to Be a Top Priority," *Insight on the News,* Vol. 10, no. 21, May 23, 1994, pp. 37–38.
49. U.S. Department of State, *Patterns of Global Terrorism, 1993* (Washington, D.C.: U.S. Government Printing Office, 1994).
50. Ibid.
51. As cited in George J. Church and Sophfronia Scott Gregory, "The Terror Within," *Time,* July 5, 1993, p. 22.
52. Bradford R. McGuinn, "Should We Fear Islamic Fundamentalists?" *USA Today* (magazine), Vol. 122, no. 2582 (November 1993), pp. 34–35.
53. George J. Church and Sophfronia Scott Gregory, "The Terror Within," *Time,* July 5, 1993, pp. 22–28.
54. Ibid.
55. Timothy E. Wirth, *Meeting the Challenge of International Terrorism,* U.S. Department of State Dispatch, Vol. 4, no. 29 (July 19, 1993), pp. 516–520.
56. The material in this section is taken from William J. Chambliss, "State-Organized Crime—The American Society of Criminology, 1988 Presidential Address," *Criminology,* Vol. 27, no. 2 (1989), pp. 183–208.
57. Another useful definition of state criminality is offered by Gregg Barak as "the harm illegally or legally organized and inflicted upon people by their own governments or the governments of others...." See Gregg Barak, "Crime, Criminology, and Human Rights: Toward an Understanding of State Criminality," in Gregg Barak, ed., *Varieties of Criminology: Readings from a Dynamic Discipline* (Westport, CT: Praeger, 1994), pp. 253–267.
58. "State-Organized Crime," pp. 203-204.

CHAPTER 10

WHITE-COLLAR AND ORGANIZED CRIME

More money has been stolen at the point of a fountain pen than at the point of a gun.

—*Woody Guthrie*

No longer is the criminologist a middle-class observer studying lower-class behavior. He now looks upward at the most powerful and prestigeful strata, and his ingenuity in research and theory will be tested, indeed.

—*Donald J. Newman*[1]

"Do you know what the Mafia is?"
"The what?"
"The Mafia? M-a-f-i-a?"
"I'm sorry. I don't know what you're talking about."

—*Crime boss Salvatore Moretti responding to questions during the Kefauver investigation of organized crime.*

IMPORTANT NAMES

Edwin Sutherland
Gary S. Green
James W. Coleman
Herbert Edelhertz
Travis Hirschi
Gilbert Geis
Michael Gottfredson

IMPORTANT TERMS

white-collar crime
occupational crime
Kefauver Committee
ethnic succession
organized crime
environmental crime
Mafia
omerta
RICO
asset forfeiture
corporate crime
Cosa Nostra
organized crime
money laundering

INTRODUCTION

A few years ago retiree George Salmon read an advertisement in a local newspaper calling for investors to support a new concept in wireless cable television transmissions. Wireless cable systems send television programs to homes using microwaves, and serve around 500,000 subscribers nationwide.[2] Salmon called the company's representative and was told he could make as much as a 300% return on his investment in a short time. Attracted by the promise of quick riches, Salmon sent $10,000 to Broadcast Holdings in Costa Mesa, California. Broadcast Holdings promised to develop wireless cable systems in Missouri, Tennessee, and Oregon. Two years later, however, Broadcast Holdings closed after state regulators, charging that the company was trading unregistered securities, raided its offices. In all likelihood Salmon will never see any part of his investment again.

According to a recent issue of *Worth* magazine,[3] wireless cable is the *fraud du jour*—or the scam of the day. Since 1992, says the magazine, "unscrupulous promoters have raised over $300 million in questionable deals to set up wireless systems…." Such promotions, touting other products, have been common for decades. In the 1960s and 1970s many rushed to invest in shares of fake gold mining and energy companies, spurred in part by the Arab oil embargo of 1973 which caused long "gas lines" to form in America's cities and towns. During the 1980s and early 1990s fraudulent securities dealers hawked international, telecommunications, and biomedical stocks and other sometimes worthless equities almost with impunity, advertising in some of the country's most widely read financial journals and newspapers.

Financial scandals have a long and ubiquitous history in the United States, sometimes involving government regulators themselves. In 1929, for example, the Teapot Dome scandal embroiled the administration of President Warren Harding. The scandal began in 1921, when Secretary of the Interior Albert B. Fall secretly leased naval oil reserves at Teapot Dome, Wyoming, and Elk Hills, California, to developers without asking for competitive bids. A Senate investigation later revealed that large sums of federal money had been loaned to developers without interest. Fall was eventually fined and sent to prison, and a 1927 U.S. Supreme Court decision ordered the fields restored to the U.S. government.

WHITE-COLLAR CRIME

In 1939 famed criminologist **Edwin Sutherland** defined white-collar crime during his presidential address to the American Sociological Society. **White-collar crime,** said Sutherland, consists of violations of the criminal law "committed by a person of respectability and high social status in the course of his occupation." (Today we would say "in the course of *his or her* occupation.") Many criminologists do not properly understand crime, Sutherland claimed, because they fail to recognize that the secretive violations of public and corporate trust by those in positions of authority are, in fact, just as criminal as predatory acts committed by persons of lower social standing.

White-collar crime violations of the criminal law committed by a person of respectability and high social status in the course of his or her occupation.

As Sutherland told those gathered to hear him: My thesis is that the traditional "conception(s) and explanations of crime [are] misleading and incorrect; that crime is in fact not closely correlated with poverty or with the psychopathic and sociopathic conditions associated with poverty, and that an adequate explanation of criminal behavior must proceed along quite different lines. The conventional explanations are invalid principally because they are derived from biased samples. The samples are biased in that they have not included vast areas of criminal behavior of persons not in the lower class...."[4]

The criminality of upper-class persons "has been demonstrated again and again in the investigations of land offices, railways, insurance, munitions, banking, public utilities, stock exchanges, the oil industry, real estate, reorganization committees, receiverships, bankruptcies and politics," said Sutherland.[5] For still other examples, Sutherland pointed to those he called "the robber barons" of the nineteenth century, citing Cornelius Vanderbilt's famous response to inquiries about his sometimes flagrantly illegal activities. "You don't suppose you can run a railroad in accordance with the statutes, do you?" the wealthy Vanderbilt reportedly quipped.

In a later study[6] that is still widely cited by criminologists, Sutherland reported on the frequency with which the nation's seventy largest corporations violated the law. He found that each of the corporations he studied had been sanctioned by courts or by administrative commissions, and that the typical corporation had an average of fourteen decisions against it. Ninety-eight percent of corporations are recidivists, or commit crime after crime, Sutherland said, while 90% could be called habitual criminals under the habitual offender statutes which existed at the time of his study. "Sixty of the corporations (had) decisions against them for restraint of trade, fifty-four for infringements (generally, of patents), fourty-four for unfair labor practices, twenty-seven for misrepresentation in advertising, twenty-six for (illegal) rebates, and forty-three for miscellaneous offenses,"[7] wrote

Sutherland. He also found that of the seventy largest corporations studied, "thirty were either illegal in their origin or began illegal activities immediately after their origin...." Such businesses may have been built upon price-fixing, unregulated commodities offerings, or via unlawful and clandestine negotiations with government regulators.

The only real difference between modern-day white-collar criminals and those of the past is that they are more sophisticated, Sutherland claimed. Although no hard and fast figures were available to Sutherland, he estimated that the "financial cost of white-collar crime is probably several times as great as the financial cost of all the crimes which are customarily regarded as the 'crime problem.'"[8]

Sutherland also noted that white-collar criminals are far less likely to be investigated, arrested, or prosecuted than are other types of offenders. When they are—on rare occasions—convicted, white-collar criminals are far less likely to receive active prison terms than are "common criminals." If they are sent to prison, the amount of time they are ordered to serve is far less than one would expect given the amount of damage their crimes inflict on society. The deference shown white-collar criminals, according to Sutherland is due primarily to their social standing. Many white-collar criminals are well respected in their communities, and many take part in national affairs. Few are perceived as mean spirited or even ill intentioned. Private citizens who do not fully understand business affairs sometimes assume that those charged with white-collar crimes were unwittingly caught up in obscure government regulations or that government agencies chose to make examples of a few unfortunate, but typical, businessmen or women.

Given these kinds of sentiments, criminologists felt compelled for years to address the question, "Is white-collar crime, crime?" As recently as 1987 writers on the subject were still asking, "Do persons of high standing commit crimes?"[9] Although most criminologists today would answer the question with a resounding "yes," members of the public have been far slower to accept the notion that violations of the criminal law by businesspeople share conceptual similarities with street crime. Attitudes, however, are changing as more and more headline-making charges are being filed against corporations and their representatives for illegal activities.

Examples of contemporary white-collar crime abound. The insider trading scam of stock market tycoon Ivan Boesky and the securities fraud conviction of junk bond king Michael Milken a few years ago show how fortunes can be amassed through white-collar law violations. Boesky was estimated to have netted a profit of $250 million for himself and a few close friends, while Milken paid a $600 million fine—far less than the amount he is estimated to have reaped from illegal trading.

The recent nationwide savings and loan (S&L) disaster, which some have called the "biggest white-collar crime in history," serves as another modern-day example of white-collar crime. The savings and loan fiasco was the result of years of intentional mismanagement and personal appropriation of funds by institutional executives. Although the actual amount of money lost or stolen during the scandal may never be known, it is estimated to run into the hundreds of billions of dollars. The collapse of just one such institution, Charles Keating's California-based Lincoln Savings and Loan Association, cost taxpayers—who were left to redeem the insolvent institutions—around $2.5 billion, while the collapse of Neil Bush's Silverado Banking S&L in Denver cost nearly $1 billion. Some experts say

Miami businessman David Paul shown here after his conviction on sixty-eight counts of bank fraud. Paul was chairman of south Florida's CenTrust Bank, one of the nation's largest savings and loans. *Miami Herald Publishing Co.*

that the final "bail-out" of S&Ls nationwide will cost American taxpayers $500 billion[10]—much more than has ever been stolen in all bank robberies throughout the history of our country.

Another type of white-collar crime sprang from the low interest rates characteristic of the early 1990s. Sham banking operations, often with high-sounding names and seemingly prestigious addresses, flourished—offering high interest rates and double-digit rates of return on investments held by the bank. Unfortunately such "phantom banks" as they were dubbed by the federal Comptroller of the Currency, evaporated as quickly as they were formed, leaving investors stunned and sometimes penniless. Some of the schemes involved the sale of certificates of deposit in offshore banks like those in the Caribbean; others bilked investors into buying millions of dollars of what was supposed to be newly privatized Russian stock; while still more offered the seemingly irresistible chance to earn exorbitant returns through sophisticated overseas investments. By the summer of 1994 the Federal Deposit Insurance Corporation issued a list of sixty unregulated businesses entities illegally conducting banking businesses within the United States. Canadian officials added another two hundred suspects to the list. As one expert on illegal banking operations put it, "[i]t's difficult to prosecute the criminals who run phantom banks because many times the victims are unwilling to press charges or the schemes take months to unravel...."[11]

Corporate Crime

Corporate crime
a violation of a criminal statute either by a corporate entity or by its executives, employees, or agents acting on behalf of and for the benefit of the corporation, partnership, or other form of business entity.

Corporate malfeasance, another form of white-collar crime, has been dubbed **corporate crime.** Corporate crime may be defined as "a violation of a criminal statute either by a corporate entity or by its executives, employees, or agents acting on behalf of and for the benefit of the corporation, partnership, or other form of business entity."[12] Corporate crimes come in many forms—ranging from prior knowledge about exploding gas tanks on Pinto automobiles and GM pickup trucks to price-fixing and insider securities trading. Culpability is greatest where company officials can be shown to have had advance knowledge about product defects, dangerous conditions, or illegal behavior on the part of employees.

Two of the most massive corporate liability issues in U.S. history were settled in September 1994. In one case, U.S. District Court Judge Sam Pointer gave final approval to a class action suit against makers and sellers of silicon gel breast implants.[13] The decision had taken years to reach and cleared the way for implant recipients to be paid $4.25 billion over thirty years. Of the two million American women who have had breast implants, approximately ninety thousand filed claims under the action. Women whose claims are approved could each receive between $105,000 and $1.4 million, depending on age, health, and medical condition. Claimants had argued that many of the parties involved in the manufacture and surgical implantation of the implants were aware of the dangers represented by their products but had opted to market them anyway.

In an interesting aside, which many claimed was a continuing effort to cover up critical issues in the case, Mayo Clinic researchers reported in the prestigious *New England Journal of Medicine* at the time of the implant settlement that no link could be found between implants and autoimmune and other disorders reportedly suffered by women claiming to be negatively affected by the implants. It was later revealed that financial support for the study had come from precisely those groups with the most to lose in the financial settlement. Among the contributors were the American Society of Plastic and Reconstructive Surgeons ($500,000), Plastic Surgery Education Foundation ($300,000), American Society of Aesthetic Plastic Surgeons ($210,000), Dow Corning ($500,000), and Bristol-Myers Squibb ($100,000).[14]

The second corporate liability case settled in 1994 involved Union Carbide Corporation which agreed to sell its entire remaining holdings in Union Carbide India Limited to the Indian company McLeod Russel India.[15] McLeod Russel was the highest bidder in a closed-door auction ordered by India's Supreme Court as part of the American company's punishment for a chemical leak at its storage facilities in Bhopal, India, on December 3, 1984. The Bhopal tragedy, which many claim was due to criminal negligence, caused more than three thousand deaths and disabled thousands of townspersons. Union Carbide had originally been ordered by Indian state courts to pay $81 million to the government as compensation for disaster victims. The country's Supreme Court later ordered the company to pay $470 million as final compensation. Another court then required the seizure of Union Carbide's remaining Indian assets and ordered that they be sold to the highest bidder.

Environmental crimes violations of the criminal law that, although typically committed by businesses or by business officials, may also be committed by other persons or organizational entities, and that damage some protected or otherwise significant aspect of the natural environment.

Another relatively new area of corporate and white-collar criminality is that of crimes against the environment. **Environmental crimes** are violations of the criminal law which, although typically committed by businesses or by business officials, may also be committed by other persons or organizational entities, and which damage some protected or otherwise significant aspect of the natural environment.

Whaling in violation of international conventions, for example, constitutes a form of environmental crime. So, too does intentional pollution, especially when

Crimes against the environment have recently become an area of special concern to criminologists. *J. Muir Hamilton/Stock Boston.*

state or federal law contravenes the practice. Sometimes negligence may contribute to environmental criminality, as in the case of the 1,000-foot *Valdez* supertanker owned by Exxon Corporation that ran aground off the coast of Alaska in 1989, spilling 11 million gallons of crude oil over 1,700 miles of pristine coastline. In September 1994 an Alaskan jury ordered Exxon to pay $5 billion in punitive damages to fourteen thousand people affected by the 1989 spill, and another $287 million in actual damages to commercial fishermen in the region.

Other acts against the environment violate more conventional statutes, although their environmental impact is obvious. The devastating fires set in oilfields throughout Kuwait by retreating Iraqi Army troops during the Gulf War provide an example of arson which resulted in global pollution while it negatively impacted fossil fuel reserves throughout much of the Middle East. These intentional fires, while properly classified as environmental criminality, also serve as an example of ecological terrorism since they were set for purposes of political intimidation.

The Definitional Evolution of White-Collar Crime

One early writer on white-collar crime explained, "[t]he chief criterion for a crime to be 'white-collar' is that it occurs as a part of, or a deviation from, the violator's occupational role."[17] This focus on the violator, rather than upon the offense, in deciding whether to classify a crime as "white collar" was well accepted by the 1967 Presidential Commission on Law Enforcement and Administration of Justice. In its now-classic report, *The Challenge of Crime in a Free Society,*[18] members of the commission wrote, "[t]he 'white-collar' criminal is the broker who distributes fraudulent securities, the builder who deliberately uses defective material, the corporation executive who conspires to fix prices, the legislator who peddles his influence and vote for private gain, or the banker who misappropriates funds in his keeping."

WHITE-COLLAR CRIME

The Initial Statement

At least one eminent criminologist has called the concept of white-collar crime "the most significant...development in criminology, especially since World War II...."[16] The roots of the concept go back to 1939 when Edwin Sutherland first coined the term "white-collar crime" in his presidential address to the American Sociological Society. Details of that address are discussed elsewhere in this chapter. His speech, however, concluded with the following five points:

1. White-collar criminality is real criminality, being in all cases in violation of the criminal law.
2. White-collar criminality differs from lower-class criminality principally in an implementation of the criminal law, which segregates white-collar criminals administratively from other criminals.
3. The theories of the criminologists that crime is due to poverty or to psychopathic and sociopathic conditions statistically associated with poverty are invalid because, first, they are derived from samples which are grossly biased with respect to socioeconomic status; second, they do not apply to the white-collar criminals; and third, they do not even explain the criminality of the lower class, since the factors are not related to a general process characteristic of all criminality.
4. A theory of criminal behavior that will explain both white-collar criminality and lower-class criminality is needed.
5. A hypothesis of this nature is suggested in terms of differential association and social disorganization.

Source: Edwin Sutherland, "White-Collar Criminality," *American Sociological Review*, Vol. 5 (February 1940), pp. 1–12.

Over the past few decades, however, the concept of white-collar crime has undergone considerable refinement.[19] The reason, according to the U.S. Department of Justice, is that "the focus [in cases of white-collar crime]...has shifted to the nature of the crime instead of the persons or occupations involved." The methods used to commit white-collar crime, such as the use of a computer, and the special skills and knowledge necessary for attempted law violation, have resulted in a contemporary understanding of white-collar crime that emphasizes the type of offense being committed, rather than the social standing or occupational role of the person committing it. Some of the reasons for this shift are due to changes in the work environment, and in the business world itself. Others are pragmatic. In the words of the Justice Department: "[t]he categorization of 'white-collar crime' as crime having a particular *modus operandi* [committed in a manner that utilizes deception and special knowledge of business practices and committed in a particular kind of economic environment] is of use in coordinating the resources of the appropriate agencies for purposes of investigation and prosecution."

Between the early definitions of white-collar-crime and those which came later, many other investigators refined the conceptual boundaries surrounding the term. **Herbert Edelhertz,** for example, defined white-collar-crime as any "illegal act or series of illegal acts committed by nonphysical means and by concealment or guile, to obtain money or property, to avoid the payment or loss of money or property, or to obtain business or personal advantages."[20] **Gilbert Geis,** another early writer on the subject, grappled with the notion of "upperworld crime," which he called "a label designed to call attention to the violation of a variety of criminal statutes by persons who at the moment are generally not considered, in connection with such violations, to be the 'usual' kind of underworld and/or psychologically aberrant offenders."[21] Many writers, however, were quick to realize that upperworld or white-collar crime might have its counterpart in certain forms of *blue-collar crime* committed by members of less prestigious occupational groups. Hence, the term blue-collar crime emerged as a way of classifying the law-violating behavior of persons involved in the appliance and automobile repair business, yard maintenance activities, house cleaning, and general installation services.

Finally, in an effort to bring closure to the concept of work-related crime, the term **occupational crime** emerged as a kind of catch-all category. Occupational crime can be defined as "any act punishable by law that is committed through opportunity created in the course of an occupation which is legal."[22] Occupational crimes include the job-related law violations of both white- and blue-collar workers. One of the best typologies of occupational crime to emerge in recent years is that offered by **Gary S. Green** in his book *Occupational Crime.*[23] Green identifies four categories of occupational crime:

Occupational crime
any act punishable by law which is committed through opportunity created in the course of an occupation that is legal.

- *Organizational Occupational Crime:* crimes committed for the benefit of an employing organization. In such instances only the organization or the employer benefits, not individual employees.
- *State Authority Occupational Crime:* crimes by officials through the exercise of their state-based authority. Such crime is occupation specific, and can only be committed by persons in public office or by those working for such persons.
- *Professional Occupational Crime:* crimes by professionals in their capacity as professionals. The crimes of physicians, attorneys, psychologists, and the like are included here.
- *Individual Occupational Crime:* crimes by individuals as individuals. This is a kind of "catch-all" category and includes personal income tax evasion, the theft of goods and services by employees, the filing of false expense reports, and the like.

Causes of White-Collar Crime

When Sutherland first coined the term "white-collar crime" he wrote, "a hypothesis is needed that will explain both white-collar criminality and lower-class criminality...." The answer Sutherland gave to this own challenge was that "white-collar criminality, just as other systematic criminality, is learned...." He went on to apply elements of his now-famous theory of differential association theory (discussed in Chapter 7) to white-collar crime, saying that "it is learned in direct or indirect association with those who already practice the behavior...."

Others authors have since offered similar integrative perspectives. **Travis Hirschi** and **Michael Gottfredson,** for example, in a recent issue of the journal *Criminology,* published half a century after Sutherland's initial work, wrote "[i]n this paper we outline a general theory of crime capable of organizing the facts about white-collar crime at the same time it is capable of organizing the facts about all forms of crime."[24] Their analysis of white-collar crime focuses squarely on the development of the concept itself. Hirschi and Gottfredson suggest that if we were not aware of the fact that the concept of white-collar crime arose "as a reaction to the idea that crime is concentrated in the lower class, there would be nothing to distinguish it from other" forms of crime.[25] "It may be, then," they write, "that the discovery of white-collar criminals is important only in a context in which their existence is denied by theory or policy." In other words, there may be nothing unusual about the idea of white-collar crime other than the fact that many people are loath to admit that high-status individuals commit crimes just as do those of lower status.

In fact, say Hirschi and Gottfredson, white-collar criminals are motivated by the same forces which drive other criminals: self-interest, the pursuit of pleasure, and the avoidance of pain. White-collar crimes do have some special characteristics. They are not as dangerous as other "common" forms of crime, they provide relatively large rewards, the rewards they produce may follow quickly from their commission, sanctions associated with them may be vague or only rarely imposed, and they may require only minimal effort from those with the requisite skills to engage in them.

Hirschi and Gottfredson conclude, however, that criminologists err in assuming that white-collar criminality is common, or that it is as common as the forms of criminality found among the lower classes. They reason that the personal characteristics of most white-collar workers are precisely those which we would expect to produce conformity in behavior. High educational levels, a commitment to the status quo, personal motivation to succeed, deference to others, attention to conventional appearance, and other inherent aspects of social conformity—all of which tend to characterize those who operate at the white-collar level—are not the kinds of personal characteristics associated with crime commission. "In other words," say Hirschi and Gottfredson, "selection processes inherent to the high end of the occupational structure tend to recruit people with relatively low propensity to crime."[26]

One other reason most criminologists are mistaken about the assumed high rate of white-collar criminality, Hirschi and Gottfredson tell us, is because "white-collar researchers often take organizations as the unit of analysis" and confuse the crimes committed by organizational entities with those of individuals within those organizations. Similarly, rates of white-collar offending tend to lump together the crimes of corporations with crimes committed by individual representatives of those organizations when making comparisons with the rate of criminal activity among blue-collar and other groups.

Dealing with White-Collar Crime

Certain forms of occupational crime may be easier to address than others. Individual occupational crimes may especially be subject to reduction by concerted enforcement and protective efforts, including enhanced IRS auditing programs, theft deterrent systems, and good internal financial procedures. Consumer information services can help eliminate fraudulent business practices, and increases in both victim awareness and reporting can help target both businesses and individuals responsible for various forms of white-collar or occupational crime.

However, as Donald J. Newman has observed, "[i]f white-collar crime is intrinsic to and normative within the value structure of our society, then no punishment or treatment program will effectively eradicate it."[27] Similarly, Gary S. Green points out that "[p]rofessional occupational criminals will probably continue to enjoy immunity from prosecution. Hence, they are unlikely to be deterred by sanction or threat and are unlikely to be formally disqualified by their professional organizations. They will therefore feel free and be free to continue or begin their criminal activities."[28]

In his insightful book, *The Criminal Elite: The Sociology of White-Collar Crime,*[29] **James W. Coleman** suggests four areas of reform through which white-collar crime might be effectively addressed:

- *Ethical:* Ethical reforms include such things as working to establish stronger and more persuasive codes of business ethics. Courses on ethical business might be offered in universities, and corporations could school their employees in right livelihood.
- *Enforcement:* Enforcement reforms center on the belief that white-collar criminals must be more severely punished, but also include such things as better funding for enforcement agencies dealing with white-collar crime, larger research budgets for regulatory investigators, and the insulation of enforcement personnel from undue political influence.
- *Structural:* Structural reforms "involve basic changes in corporate structure" to make white-collar crime more difficult to commit. Coleman suggests adding members of the public to corporate boards of directors; changing the process whereby corporations are chartered to include control over white-collar crime; enhancing the flow of information between businesses, the public, and administrative bodies; and the "selective nationalization of firms that have long records of criminal violations."
- *Political:* Political reforms, according to Coleman, center on eliminating campaign contributions from corporations and businesses, but also include increasing the level of fairness in determining government grants, government purchases, and government contracts. The government, says, Coleman, must also police itself. Although this includes enforcement of laws now on the books which are intended to regulate the activities of elected officials and administrative personnel, Coleman concludes that "...there is some question about how effectively the government can ever police itself."

ORGANIZED CRIME

Organized crime
the unlawful activities of the members of a highly organized, disciplined association engaged in supplying illegal goods and services, including but not limited to gambling, prostitution, loansharking, narcotics, labor racketeering, and other unlawful activities of members of such organizations.

Organized criminal groups have always existed. One of the earliest written accounts[30] of **organized crime** describes the activities of Jonathan Wild, a notorious brigand of the early 1700s. Wild was born in Wolverhampton, Staffordshire, England, in 1682 to "persons of decent character and station." Wild received a formal education, which was unusual for the times, and at age 15 was apprenticed to a buckle-maker. Married at 22, Wild left his wife and new son a year later for the excitement of nearby London. Not long after his arrival in the city, Wild was arrested for nonpayment of debts and thrown into Wood-street Compter, a prison which held both debtors and other prisoners—both male and female. During the four years he spent in prison Wild became intimate with a female inmate by the name of Mary Milliner, who was described as "one of the most abandoned prostitutes and pickpockets on the town...." Wild later said that he also used his time in prison to "learn the secrets of the criminals there under confinement." Upon release he shared a home with Milliner, calling her his wife.

Milliner ran a bar on what was then known as Cock Alley in Cripplegate, one of the most notorious parts of London. Soon the bar became a hangout for thieves and other criminals. Wild capitalized upon the situation and began purchasing all manner of stolen goods and fencing them to merchants and the general public. As one writer of the times observed, "[h]e was at first at little trouble to dispose of the articles brought to him by thieves at something less than their real value, no law existing for the punishment of the receivers of stolen goods...." However, the authorities, hearing of Wild's organized criminal activity, soon passed a law forbidding the receipt and sale of stolen goods. As a consequence, the value of stolen goods plummeted. Soon, however, Wild hit upon a way around the new law. One commentator described his solution this way: Wild called a meeting of thieves in the city and proposed "that when they made prize of anything, they should deliver it to him...saying that he would restore the goods to the owners by which means greater sums might be raised, while the thieves would remain perfectly secure from detection." It wasn't long before Wild was running the largest criminal organization in England and evading the law by returning stolen goods to their rightful owners in exchange for handsome rewards.

As he rose in both power and wealth, Wild displayed ruthless organizational skills. If a thief or burglar in Wild's gang demanded too much money or threatened to unmask the operation, Wild would have him apprehended and hanged—collecting whatever official reward had been offered for the felon's capture. As Wild's organization grew, he hired ships to transport excess inventory to France, the Netherlands, and Belgium. Soon he was trading internationally in stolen goods and living in grand style. Because of his ability to gather intelligence throughout the criminal underworld as well as in the ghettos of London, Wild gained the confidence of advisors to King George I—a relationship that kept him out of harm's way for many years. With the death of George I, however, and increasing British hostility to criminal activity, Wild was finally arrested and charged with running a criminal organization. Sentenced to hang, Wild was executed at Tyburn prison on May 24, 1725.

History of Organized Crime in the United States

Much of what most Americans traditionally think of today as organized crime—the **Mafia** or ***Cosa Nostra***—has roots which predate the establishment of the United States as a sovereign power. For hundreds of years secret societies, the products of extreme poverty, feudalism, a traditional disregard for the law, and (some would say) national temperament, have flourished in Italy.[31] During the nineteenth century the Italian *Camorra,* based in Naples, became infamous for extortion and murder. The *Camorrian* code demanded total silence, and the organization issued printed licenses to its members to kill.

Cosa Nostra (literally, "our thing") a term signifying organized crime, and one of a variety of names for the "Mafia," the "Outfit," the "Mob," the "syndicate," or the "organization."

Italian criminal organizations which migrated to the United States with the wave of European immigrants during the late nineteenth and early twentieth centuries included the Mafia and the Black Hand. The Black Hand (in Italian, *La Mano Negro*) "specialized in the intimidation of Italian immigrants,"[32] typically extorting protection monies and other valuables. The Black Hand became especially powerful in Detroit, St. Louis, Kansas City, and New Orleans.

The Mafia, with roots in Sicily, worked to become a quasi-police organization in the Italian ghetto areas of the burgeoning American cities of the industrial era—often enforcing its own set of laws or codes where official intervention was lacking. One of the first well-documented conflicts between the Mafia and American law enforcement came on March 13, 1909, when New York City police officials learned that NYPD Lieutenant Joseph Petrosino had been assassinated upon his arrival in Palermo, Italy. Petrosino had gone to Palermo to investigate allegations that Mafia bosses in New York City were importing Black Hand assassins from the "old country" to do their dirty work. He was killed as he visited the Palermo Court of Justice by a single bullet allegedly fired by Mafia boss Vito Cascio Ferro. Although Ferro was arrested and charged with the crime, local deputies provided him with an alibi, and he was never convicted.

Secret societies in Italy were all but expunged during the 1930s and early 1940s under the fascist dictator Benito Mussolini. Surviving Mafia members became vehemently antifascist, sentiments that endeared them to American and allied intelligence services during World War II. Following the war, *Mafioso* leaders resumed their traditional positions of power within Italian society, and links grew between American criminal organizations and those in Italy.

In his comprehensive book, *Organized Crime,*[33] Howard Abadinsky reports that the first mention of the Mafia in New York can be found in a *New York Times* article dated October 21, 1888. The article quotes police inspector Thomas Byrnes as saying that a murder victim named Antonio Flaccomio was "an Italian fruit dealer and a member of a secret society...." The society, said Byrnes, was called the Mafia, its members were fugitives from Sicily, an island in the south of Italy.

A Rose by Any Other Name—The *Cosa Nostra*

Other organized criminal groups, including Jewish and Irish gangs, flourished in New York City prior to the arrival of large numbers of Italian immigrants in the late 1800s. Ethnic succession has been as much a reality in organized crime as in

Much of what the public believes about organized crime comes from images such as this one of Humphrey Bogart, starring in the 1951 movie *The Enforcer. Archive Photos.*

Ethnic succession the continuing process whereby one immigrant or ethnic group succeeds another through assumption of a particular position in society.

most other aspects of American life. **Ethnic succession** refers to the continuing process whereby one immigrant or ethnic group succeeds another through assumption of a particular position in society.

Throughout the late nineteenth and early twentieth centuries, for example, Jewish gangsters like Meyer Lansky, Benjamin "Bugsy" Siegel, "Dutch" Schultz, and Lepke Buchalter ran many of the "rackets" in New York City, only to have their places taken by Italian immigrants arriving a few years later. Almost forgotten today is Arnold Rothstein, a famous Jewish gangster who was able to translate many ill-gotten gains into real estate holdings and other legitimate commercial ventures. Among those who remember, Rothstein has been called the "most important organizer and innovator"[34] among Jewish criminal operatives in turn-of-the-century New York, and the "Godfather" of organized crime in the city. Italian-American organized criminals are themselves not immune to ethnic succession, which has continued into the present day, with gangs of African-Americans, Hispanic-Americans, and Asian-Americans now running significant aspects of the drug trade and controlling other illicit activities in many parts of the country.

Even so, organized criminal activity in the United States throughout the last half-century has largely been the domain of Italian-American immigrants and their descents—especially those of Sicilian descent. As one observer notes, [i]n order to beat rival organizations, criminals of Sicilian descent reproduced the kind of illegal groups they had belonged to in the old country and employed the same rules to make them invincible."[35] Hence, it was not long before American Mafia leaders had taken over from their criminal predecessors, many of whom were either killed or forced to turn to more legitimate forms of enterprise.

As a consequence of historical events that are well documented, it is both realistic and useful to discuss American organized crime primarily in terms of Sicilian-American involvement. A few caveats must be recognized, however. For one thing, while many Sicilians who emigrated to this country either had ties to, or experience with, Mafia organizations in the "old country," most did not. Many Sicilian-Americans, in fact, emigrated to America to escape Mafia despotism at home, and most became productive members of their adopted society. Relatively few involved themselves in organized crime. Those who did created an organization known variously as the "Mafia," the "Outfit," the "Mob," ***La Cosa Nostra*** (our thing), "the syndicate," or simply "the organization." Other terms applied to Sicilian-American organized crime include "crime cartel" and "the confederation."

It is Joseph Valachi who is generally credited with popularizing the term *Cosa Nostra.* In 1963, Valachi, a member of the Genovese crime family, used the term while testifying before the McClellan Committee which was holding hearings into organized crime. Following the hearings, "Cosa Nostra" became increasingly popular both with the American press and public, and has at least partially replaced "Mafia" as the *nom de jour* of Italian-American criminal organizations.

The term "Mafia," however, is still in widespread use. Hence, in the paragraphs that follow, we will refer to Sicilian-American organized criminal groups as both Mafia and *Cosa Nostra*—terms which have been used interchangeably by police investigators, the press, the public, and government commissions over the years.

Mob informant Joseph Valachi testifying before Senate investigators in 1963. *Locs Mags (UPI)/ Bettmann.*

Prohibition and Official Corruption

By the 1920s Mafia influence extended to most American cities. But it was the advent of prohibition that gave organized crime its vital financial wherewithal. In 1919 the U.S. Congress passed the 18th Amendment to the U.S. Constitution, ushering in an age of prohibition on the manufacture, transportation, and sale of alcoholic beverages. The 18th Amendment reads as follows:

> Section 1. After one year from the ratification of this article the manufacture, sale, or transportation of intoxicating liquors within, the importation thereof into, or the exportation thereof from the United States and all territory subject to the jurisdiction thereof for beverage purposes is hereby prohibited.
>
> —*U.S. Constitution*
> *Amendment XVIII [1919]*

In many ways the advent of prohibition was a godsend for Mafia leaders. Prior to prohibition, Mafia operations in American cities were "small time," concerned mostly with gambling, protection rackets, and loansharking. Many *mafiosi*, however, also belonged to a fraternal brotherhood called *Unione Siciliana* whose members were well versed in the manufacture of low-cost high-proof untaxed alcohol,[36] an expertise which had been brought from their native country. In addition, the existing infrastructure of organized crime permitted easy and efficient entry into the running and sale of contraband liquor. As one writer explained it, "[b]y its nature, bootlegging required national (even international) organization. The liquor came from Canada or Europe, necessitating an extranational arrangement. It rode at anchor outside the territorial limits in bottoms belonging to the underworld. It had to be picked up by small craft to be smuggled ashore. The contraband had to get by the Coast Guard, Customs, and cops. The cargo had to be loaded on trucks, carried across bridges and highways, protected against hijackers, delivered to warehouses, [and] redistributed to retailers. And somewhere, somehow, there had to be collectors, bookkeepers, accountants, enforcers, personnel men, and masterminds to make the rum-running pay."[37]

Prohibition provided existing Mafia families the opportunity for accumulation of unheralded wealth. As Abadinsky puts it, "Prohibition enabled men who had been street thugs to become crime overlords."[38] Others describe it this way: "Prohibition proved to be the catalyst that established the wealth and power of modern organized crime syndicates."

The huge profits to be had from bootlegging led to the wholesale bribery of government officials and to the quick corruption of many law enforcement officers throughout the country. Nowhere was corruption more complete than in Chicago, where runners working for organized crime distributed illegal alcohol under police protection,[39] and corrupt city government officials received regular payoffs from criminal cartels.

In 1929 President Herbert Hoover appointed the National Commission on Law Observance and Enforcement, better known as the Wickersham Commission—after its chairman, George Wickersham. The Commission produced a series of fourteen reports. Three of them, *Observance and Enforcement of Prohibition, Lawlessness in Law Enforcement,* and *The Police,* either mentioned or decried the corrupting influence prohibition was having on professional law enforcement in America. Fourteen years after it had been passed, the 18th Amendment was repealed, and with it Prohibition ended.

> Section 1. The eighteenth article of amendment to the Constitution of the United States is hereby repealed.
>
> —*U.S. Constitution*
> *Amendment XXI [1933]*

Unfortunately, the heritage of Prohibition-associated corruption is still with us. Official corruption has become an institutionalized part of American life in some parts of the country. As one writer explains it, "American cities have a long history of corrupt relations between some illegal enterprises and local police or politicians. For criminal entrepreneurs, payments to politicians or police can be viewed either as normal business expenses in return for services to the enterprise or as extortionate demands that eat into the profits of the enterprise. For police and politicians, levying regular assessments on illegal entrepreneurs has provided a source of extra income as well as a way to oversee neighborhood enterprises that could not be legally controlled. Historically, oversight by local political organizations (or the police) has been the most important source of coordination for illegal enterprises in American cities."[40]

In 1967 the Task Force on Organized Crime, part of President Johnson's Commission on Law Enforcement and Administration of Justice, concluded that "[a]ll available data indicate that organized crime flourishes only where it has corrupted local officials."[41] Sometimes the roots of corruption reach far deeper. As one writer notes, "the line between organized crime and corrupt officials is often unclear, at times nonexistent.... In both Chicago and New York those who ran organized criminal activities, gambling and prostitution, were political figures and often elected officials."[42]

The Centralization of Organized Crime

The prohibition era was a tumultuous time for American organized crime. While its leaders grappled for the huge profits to be reaped from the sale of illegal alcohol, they simultaneously worked to consolidate power. Gang warfare—not unlike the drive-by shootings and execution-style slayings which now characterize inner-city youth gangs—was the order of the day.

One of the most infamous gangland wars of all time erupted in Chicago in the mid-1920s when Alphonse "Al" Capone, an up-and-coming thug, decided to make a citywide grab for power. Following a number of spectacular killings (dubbed "massacres" by the press), Capone was successful in forging a crime syndicate under which he declared himself the leader of all of Chicago's organized crime families. For a time his claim remained disputed, primarily by George 'Bugs'

Moran who had inherited the leadership of a local gang. In a bid to end competition, Capone lured Moran's men to a garage on Chicago's east side on the ruse that a truckload of bootlegged liquor was soon to arrive. Once inside the garage, Moran's men were surprised by five of Capone's executioners. Three were dressed as police officers, while the other two wore plain clothes. The uniformed men ordered the Moran gang against the garage wall, where the plain clothes killers machine-gunned them to death. The killings became known as the St. Valentine's Day massacre and established Capone as undisputed ruler of organized crime in Chicago.

Similar efforts at consolidation were being made nationwide. On April 15, 1931, influential New York City crime figure "Joe the Boss" Giuseppe Masseria was gunned down in a restaurant in the Coney Island section of Brooklyn. His killing, part of what has been called the Castellammarese War, appears to have been ordered by another of the city's bosses, Salvatore Maranzano. Following Masseria's death, Maranzano declared himself the "boss of bosses" over all of New York's crime families. Maranzano, however, soon lost favor with more "Americanized" Mafia figures, and was himself killed in September of 1931 by armed men who entered his office disguised as immigration officials.

During the next two days thirty Mafia leaders died in similar gang-ordered executions across the country. By the close of 1931, when the smoke settled and the killings stopped, the Mafia had become an integrated, coordinated criminal organization able to settle most disputes internally and capable of shielding its activities from the prying eyes of investigators. A 1939 expose written by J. Richard Davis, former attorney for one of New York's crime families, credited the centralization of control to the rise of "Charlie Lucky," also known as "Lucky Luciano" (born Charles Luciano), who "became leader of the *Unione Siciliani* in 1931.... The 'greasers' in the *Unione*," wrote Davis, "were killed off, and the organization was no longer a loose, fraternal order of Sicilian blackhanders and alcohol cookers, but rather the framework for a system of alliances which were to govern the underworld."[43] Another author described it this way: "in 1931 organized crime units across the United States formed into monopolistic corporations, and those corporations, in turn, linked themselves together in a monopolistic cartel."[44]

Following 1931, Mafia activity went underground. The Mafia's success at hiding its operations was so great that one expert was able to write, "there is a considerable body of police opinion in the United States which holds that the Mafia in America died in September 1931, on 'Purge Day.'"[45]

As the 1967 President's Commission on Law Enforcement and Administration of Justice observed, Mafia activity remained nearly invisible and investigations of Mafia operations lay dormant until the 1950s. In the words of the Commission: "[a]fter World War II there was little national interest in the problem (of organized crime) until 1950, when the U.S. Attorney General convened a national conference on organized crime."[46]

Organized crime reemerged into the national spotlight in 1951 when the federal Special Committee to Investigate Organized Crime in Interstate Commerce[47] (better known as the **Kefauver Committee,** after its chairman Estes Kefauver) reported that "a nationwide crime syndicate known as the Mafia operate(s) in many large (American) cities, and the leaders of the Mafia usually control the most lucrative rackets in their cities."[48] Although the Kefauver Committee, which interviewed hundreds of witnesses, noted that it had "found it difficult to obtain reliable data concerning the extent of Mafia operation, the nature of Mafia organization, and the way it presently operates," it was able to reach the following conclusions

- There is a nationwide crime syndicate known as the Mafia, whose tentacles are found in many large cities.
- The American Mafia has international linkages that appear most clearly in connection with the narcotics traffic.
- Mafia leaders are usually found in control of the most lucrative rackets in their cities.
- There are indications of centralized direction and control in these rackets, but leadership appears to be in a group rather than in a single individual.

Public interest in organized crime was again roused when authorities learned of a national meeting of at least seventy-five leaders of criminal cartels scheduled for November 1957. The purpose of the meeting, held at the home of Joseph Barbara in the small New York town of Apalachin, was never uncovered. Some speculate that syndicate leaders may have met to split up the empire of the recently murdered Albert Anastasia—who was himself reputed to have been a ruthless killer. Barbara, born in Castellammarese del Golfo, Italy, was boss of a northeastern Pennsylvania crime family and died two years after the meeting.

The 1957 meeting resulted in raids on Barbara's house and the arrest of many well-known organized crime figures. In 1959 Joseph Bonanno and twenty-six others were convicted of obstruction of justice for their refusal to reveal the meeting's purpose. Their convictions, however, were overturned in 1960 by the U.S. Supreme Court which, in *U.S.* v. *Bufalino*,[49] reasoned that the suspects had been arrested without probable cause.

The picture that eventually emerged from years of federal investigations into Italian-American organized criminal groups was of twenty-four crime families operating in the United States under the direction of a "commission," whose membership consisted of the bosses of the nation's most powerful families. The following, taken directly from the 1967 President's Commission report summarizes what was believed to be true of organized crime at the time of the report: "Today the core of organized crime in the United States consists of 24 groups operating as criminal cartels in large cities across the nation. Their membership is exclusively Italian, they are in frequent communication with each other, and their smooth functioning is insured by a national body of overseers.... The wealthiest and most influential core groups," the report concluded, "operate in States including New York, New Jersey, Illinois, Florida, Louisiana, Nevada, Michigan, and Rhode Island." The report placed membership in organized crime at five thousand nationwide, and said that "[e]ach of the 24 groups is known as a 'family' with membership varying from as many as 700 men to as few as 20."

Family organization was said to consist of (1) a boss, whose primary functions were described as "maintaining order and maximizing profits," (2) an underboss, who was said to collect information for the boss and to relay messages to and from him, (3) the counselor, or *consigliere,* who serves as an advisor, (4) numerous lieutenants, or *caporegime,* some of whom "serve as chiefs of operating units," and (5) solders or *soldati,* representing the lowest level of family membership, and who "operate a particular illicit enterprise" like a loansharking operation, a lottery, a smuggling operation, and the like. "Beneath the soldiers," the commission found, "are large numbers of employees and...agents who are not members of the family and not necessarily of Italian descent. These are people who do most of the actual work in the various enterprises." Unlike the family members who give them orders, "they have no buffers or other insulation from law enforcement." The structure of a typical Sicilian-American organized crime family is shown in Figure 10-1.

The President's Commission also found that organized crime members swear allegiance to a code of conduct which "stipulates that underlings should not interfere with the leaders' interests and should not seek protection from the police. They should be 'standup guys' who go to prison in order that the bosses may amass fortunes. The code gives leaders exploitative authoritarian power over everyone in the organization. Loyalty, honor, respect, absolute obedience—these are inculcated in family members through ritualistic initiation and customs within the organization, through material rewards, and through violence."[50]

The *Cosa Nostra* Today

Some writers maintain that at least twenty-four organized crime families of Sicilian-American heritage continue to operate throughout the United States today. Of these, the largest number (five) operate out of New York. They are the[51]

Luciano/Genovese Family (300–400 members)
Mineo/Gambino Family (400–500 members)
Reina/Lucchese Family (125 members)
Profaci/Colombo Family (100 members)
Bonanno Family (75 members)

Chicago is home to other influential *Cosa Nostra* families, including the Carlisi family (sometimes called the *Outfit*), while the Scarfo (run by Nicodemo "Little Nicky" Scarfo) and Stanfa organizations still operate in Philadelphia. New Orleans serves as headquarters for the Marcello gang (headed by Carlos Marcello), and organized crime in New England is controlled by Ray Patriarca, Jr., and his henchmen, while the Civella mob runs racketeering activities in Kansas City, Missouri.

The Activities of Organized Crime

The 1976 federal Task Force on Organized Crime identified five types of activity which may qualify as organized crime: (1) racketeering, (2) vice operations, (3) theft/fence rings, (4) gangs, and (5) terrorism.

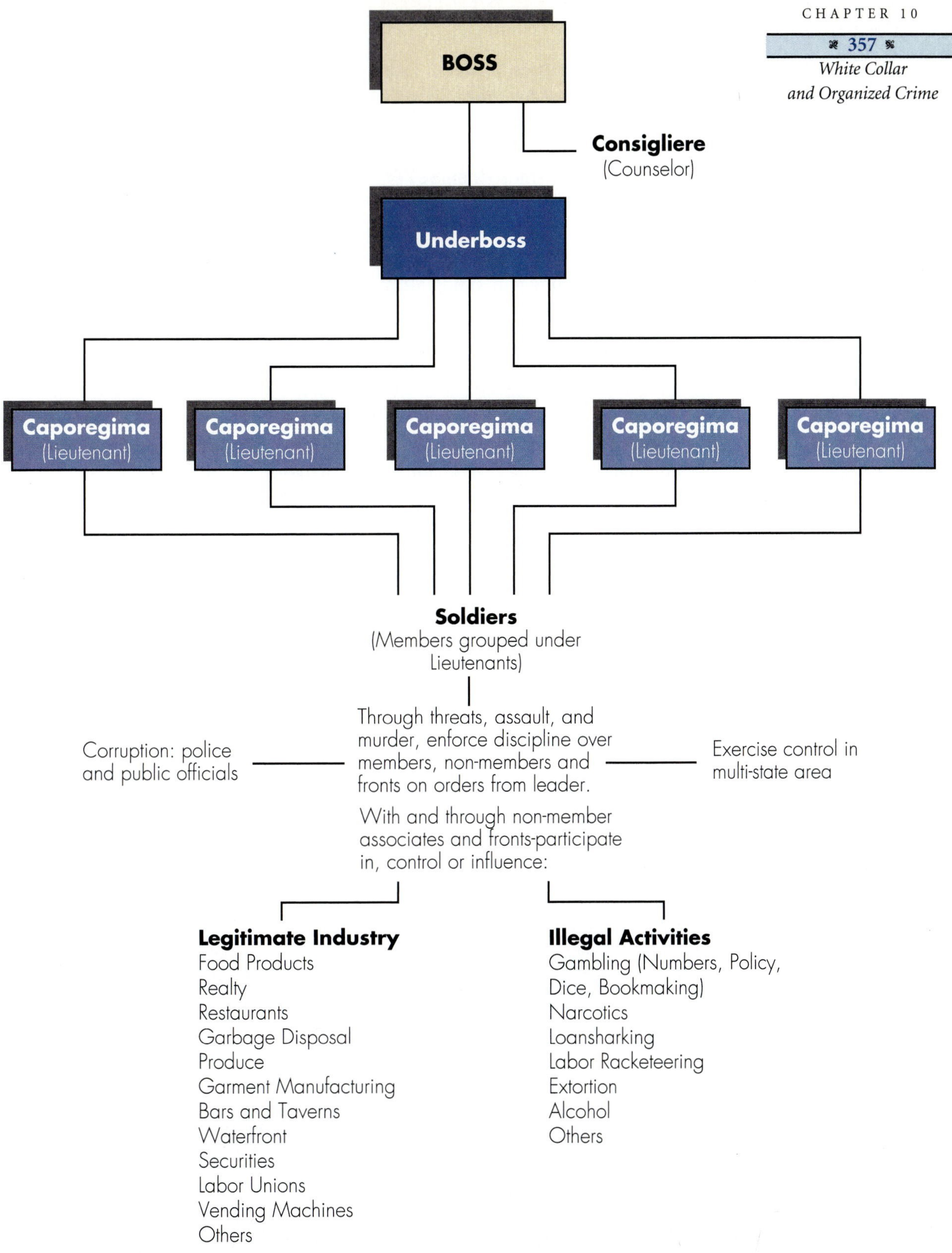

FIGURE 10.1 A Typical Organized Crime Family. *Source*: President's Commission on Law Inforcement and Administration of Justice, *The Challenge of Crime in a Free Society* (Washington, D.C.: U.S. Government Printing Office, 1967), p. 47.

Whatever its source, however, money is the centerpiece of, and primary motivation for, all organized criminal activity. Near the start of the Great Depression, the notorious Chicago gangster Al Capone achieved the distinction of being listed in the *Guiness Book of World Records* as having the highest income of any individual in a single year—more than $105 million in 1927.[52]

Things haven't changed much since Capone's day. As one expert on organized crime explains it,[53] "it is cash that dominates every aspect of the mob machines.... The mobsters' working days are spent worrying about and scheming over money, and finally, quarreling and killing for money, almost all of it derived illegitimately." The same expert gives the example of Philadelphia crime boss Nicky Scarfo, who "even considered killing his own wife, Domenica, over money when he learned that 'little by little, she had robbed him of around four hundred thousand' for her gambling sprees at Trump Plaza in Atlantic City." No amount of money seems too small for concern, and—as in much of the wider society—money often becomes a way of keeping score as to who has been the most successful at what they've done.

Throughout the past half-century Sicilian-American criminal cartels have continued to be involved in (1) the establishment and control of both legalized and illicit forms of gambling, including lotteries, bookmaking, horse-race wagering, and bets on athletic contests; (2) loansharking, which involves the lending of money at rates far higher than legally prescribed limits; (3) large-scale drug trafficking; (4) the fencing of stolen goods, including securities; (5) infiltration of legitimate businesses, including labor unions and corporations that can be used as quasi-legitimate fronts for money laundering, and so on; and (6) labor union racketeering via which legitimate businesses are intimidated through threats of strikes, walkouts and sabotage.

Anthony Accetturo (center), an alleged leader of the Lucchese crime family, celebrates after his acquittal on federal racketeering charges. The trial lasted nearly two years. *Peter Cannata/AP/Wide World Photos.*

In some states, where lotteries are now government-run, organized crime's "take" from illegal gambling has been reduced. Not to be outdone, however, Sicilian-American operatives have moved into legitimate gambling, reportedly buying stakes in casinos in Nevada, New Jersey, and elsewhere. The Flamingo Hotel, Las Vegas' first elaborate hotel-casino, was said to have been built by crime boss "Bugsy" Siegel and funded by organized crime leaders throughout the country.[54] Cleveland syndicate leader Moe Dalitz is reputed to have financed the Stardust Hotel, and federal officials claim that at least $14 million was illegally skimmed from the hotel's operations between 1973 and 1983.[55] Although New Jersey has made Herculean efforts to keep organized crime from influencing casino operation in Atlantic City, some writers point out that "Local 54 of the Hotel Employees and Restaurant Employees Union...which represents 22,000 casino hotel employees, has long been dominated by the Bruno family of Philadelphia."[56]

Organized crime is involved in many other kinds of rackets besides gambling. There is some evidence, for example, that organized crime today is becoming increasingly active in the illegal copying and distribution of copyrighted software, music, and other forms of recorded media, including videotapes, compact discs, and cassette tapes. The provision of elaborately staged videotaped pornographic productions, including "snuff movies" (in which a sex "star" is actually killed on screen), and elements of child pornography can also be traced to organized criminal activity.

Some sense of the profit derived from the activities of organized crime can be gained from official estimates of the money being collected by Nicodemo "Little Nicky" Scarfo's gang at the time of Scarfo's indictment in 1986 on charges of first-degree murder. Scarfo operated illegitimate businesses throughout Philadelphia and southern New Jersey. When he was arrested his gang was estimated to be taking in "$25,000,000 to $30,000,000 annually from illegal gambling (numbers, video poker, sports betting), and millions more from loansharking, shakedowns of drug dealers and labor union racketeering. Even bigger deals were in the making: Scarfo was preparing to control more than $200,000,000 in Philadelphia waterfront-development projects, as well as to infiltrate the union benefits plans of Atlantic City's bartenders and waitresses."[57]

The Code of Conduct

A strict code of conduct governs behavior among members of organized Sicilian-American criminal groups. This code, sometimes called *omerta* (or "manliness") is unwritten. Members are formally introduced to the code through an initiation ritual which has changed little since it was brought to American shores by Sicilian immigrants well over a hundred years ago. The code of ***omerta*** functions to concentrate power in the hands of crime bosses while ensuring their protection. As officials with one federal task force put it, "[t]hose aspects of the code which prohibit appealing to outside authorities for justice while at the same time advocating great loyalty, respect and honor are probably most essential to the concentration of power in the hands of a few and, hence to exploitation of lower-status men by their leaders."[58]

Omerta the informal, unwritten code of organized crime which demands silence and loyalty, among other things, of members.

A few years ago the FBI electronically eavesdropped on a house in Medford, Massachusetts, in which Joseph Russo, a New England *Cosa Nostra consigliere* conducted an initiation ritual for four new family members. Twenty-one men attended the candlelit ceremony. This was the first time authorities had ever captured a *Cosa Nostra* induction on tape. As each young man swore to uphold *omerta* and took a vow of silence never to betray the organization or tell its secrets, he held a burning picture of a Catholic saint and prayed: *"Come si brucia questa santa, cosi si brucera la mia anima"* (as burns this saint, so will burn my soul), a reference to the death awaiting anyone who violates the code.[59]

Another initiate described his induction into Philadelphia's Scarfo gang this way:[60] "I was driven to this million-dollar house in Philadelphia, with a big swimming pool and a big table laid out with food—shrimp, steaks, meatballs, peppers, olives, spaghetti—and about forty chairs. I was on cloud nine. Scarfo is at the head of this long table and says, 'Nick, do you know why you're here?' I said, 'No.' You're supposed to say no.... So next, he says, 'We want you to be one of us. Now, look around this table and tell me if there is anyone you have bad feelings with.' I look around and say 'no'.... So he makes a speech about how much I've done for the family and then says that I have the freedom to leave now and that I'll always be their friend. There would be no hard feelings if I didn't want to join. I said, 'No, I want to be one of you'.... Scarfo points to a gun and a knife on a table and asks if I'd use these for any of these friends around the table. Then he lights a small piece of tissue paper in my hand while I say, 'May I burn like the saints in hell if I ever betray any of my friends.' He also pricks my trigger finger. Then you go around the table and kiss everyone. Then we have a feast and then you're told the rules. In the days that follow, you go around and meet the guys who weren't at the ceremony. Then word just seems to spread everywhere you go. And everywhere you go, the respect that you receive from nonmembers is enormous."

The rules of the Scarfo family, said this inductee, included the following: "the family doesn't fool with kidnapping, counterfeit money or bonds. You can shake down or rob drug dealers, but you can't protect them, lend them money or deal drugs yourself. No fooling with a member's wife. You can't even look at another guy's wife. That's automatic death. Even hitting another member is automatic death. He can ask for your life. You're supposed to report once a week to your *capo*, unless there's a good excuse. You can't go out of town without telling him. You always have to touch base. You're also told that silence is the code and this thing comes first. It comes before your mother, your father, your sister, your brother."[61]

Federal investigators and others studying organized crime have identified seven general features characteristic of the code sworn to by family members everywhere:

- Don't be an informer. Don't "rat" on others and don't sell out.
- Be a member of the team. Be loyal to members of the organization.
- Do not interfere with the interests of others. Don't rock the boat.
- Be rational. Don't engage in battle if you can't win.
- Be a man of honor. Have class. Be independent.
- Respect women and your elders.

- Be a "stand-up" guy ("stand-up guys" take the "rap," shielding others). Keep your eyes and ears open and your mouth shut.

Like any informal unwritten code, *omerta* has many other implicit rules and is fraught with nuances fully understood only to those raised within its traditions. The code, however, imposes two clear and indisputable requirements on all family members: (1) obey your superiors, and (2) keep silent. Failure to adhere closely to either rule means death. The 1967 President's Commission report stated it this way: "The basic principle of justice in the Sicilian Mafia, as in American organized crime, is deterrence from deviation by means of the threat of certain, swift, uniform and severe punishment."

An example is provided by the recent FBI investigation focusing on New York City crime boss John Gotti (then head of the Gambino family), which yielded a wealth of secretly recorded conversations between Gotti and other organized crime figures. This is what Gotti told his underboss, Frank "Frankie Loc" Locascio, about why a subordinate had to die: "Anytime you got a partner who don't agree with us, we kill him," Gotti explained. "He didn't rob nothin'. Know why he's dying?" Gotti continued. "He's gonna die because he refused to come in when I called. He didn't do nothing else wrong."

The code of *omerta* is similar to the values found among career criminals everywhere. As one federal report put it, "there is a striking similarity between both the code of conduct and the enforcement machinery used in the confederation of organized criminals and the code of conduct and enforcement machinery which governs the behavior of prisoners."[62]

Other Organized Criminal Groups

According to Howard Abadinsky, a hallmark of true criminal organizations is that they function independently of any of their members, including their leaders, and have a continuity over time as personnel within them change. The example given by Abadinsky is of the James Gang, which dissolved with the death of its leader, Jesse James. In contrast, says Abadinsky, "[w]hen Al Capone was imprisoned fifty years later, the 'Capone Organization' continued, and in its more modern form (the 'Outfit') it continues to operate in Chicago."[63]

Although, until now, we have restricted our discussion of organized crime to Sicilian-American criminal enterprise, it is both useful and realistic to mention the existence of other organized criminal groups in the United States—each characterized by some degree of organizational continuity which is independent of its membership. Among such criminal associations are groups which have been diversely referred to as the Black Mafia, the Cuban Mafia, the Haitian Mafia, Colombian Cartels, the Russian Mafia, Asian criminals (Chinese Tongs and street gangs, Japanese Yakuza, and Vietnamese gangs), and others. Included here, as well, might be inner-city gangs (the most well known of which are probably Los Angeles' Crips and Bloods, and Chicago's Vice Lords), international drug rings, outlaw motorcycle gangs (such as the Hell's Angels and the Pagans), and other looser associations of small-time thugs, prison gangs, and drug dealers.

Noteworthy among these groups are the Latino organized bands, including Dominican, Colombian, Mexican, and Cuban importers of cocaine and other drugs. Although it is not known precisely how much cocaine has entered this country illegally, much of it has been handled by the Medellin and Cali Cartels headquartered in Colombia, South America. The Medellin and Cali Cartels consist of around thirty-five organized groups that often cooperate with one another and who have financed their own small armies for protection of both their operations and their personnel. Although recent arrests and some deaths have cut into the cartels' influence, it is believed that they are still responsible for the majority of cocaine entering the United States illegally.

While it is difficult to categorize such a diversity of groups with any consistency, it is impossible to discuss each of them in a volume of this size. Whether, however, the principle of ethnic succession (discussed earlier) will ever fully apply to organized criminal activity is open to debate—although in some American cities *Cosa Nostra* operatives have already begun to be replaced by Puerto Rican, African-American, and even Russian gangs. In part, such replacement is due to federal and state law enforcement efforts which have seriously impacted activities of the mob in some areas of the United States.

Where Sicilian-American organized criminal activity continues to flourish, however, connections with the "old country" sometime still remain. In late 1994, for example, New York City police, in conjunction with federal authorities, announced the arrest of seventy-nine suspects in New York and Italy, all charged with drug conspiracy. Drug-running activities were said to have centered on New York City's Famous Original Ray's Pizza Restaurant on Third Avenue near 43rd Street. Authorities alleged that the pizza parlor was used as a half-way point in an international drug ring whose ultimate aim was to provide cocaine to "three long-standing organized crime groups in Italy, where cocaine sells for three times what it costs in New York."[64] Among those arrested were Aniello, Francesco, and Roberto Ambrosio—brothers of Italian-American descent who ran the pizzeria.

Organized Crime and the Law

For many years American law enforcement agencies had few special weapons in the fight against organized crime. Instead, they prosecuted organized criminal operatives under statutes directed at solitary offenders, using laws such as those against theft, robbery, assault, gambling, prostitution, drug abuse, and murder. Innovative prosecutors have at times drawn upon other statutory resources in the drive to indict leaders of organized crime. On October 17, 1931, for example, Al Capone was convicted on various charges of income tax evasion after federal investigators were able to show that he had paid no taxes on an income in excess of $1 million. Laws regulating the sale of alcohol and drugs, and statutes circumscribing acts of prostitution have also been used against organized criminals, although with varying degrees of success.

The first federal legislation aimed specifically at curtailing the activities of organized crime is known as the Hobbs Act, although the term actually denotes a series of statutes that were passed beginning in 1946. In essence, the Hobbs Act made it a violation of federal law to engage in any form of criminal behavior that interferes with interstate commerce. It also criminalized interstate or foreign travel in furtherance of criminal activity, and made it a crime to use the highways, telephone, or mail in support of activities such as gambling, drug trafficking, loansharking, and other forms of racketeering.

The single most important piece of federal legislation ever passed which specifically targets the activities of organized crime is called **RICO.** RICO is an acronym for the Racketeer Influenced and Corrupt Organization statute, which was part of the federal Organized Crime Control Act of 1970. The Organized Crime Control Act defines "organized crime" as "the unlawful activities of the members of a highly organized, disciplined association engaged in supplying illegal goods and services, including but not limited to gambling, prostitution, loansharking, narcotics, labor racketeering, and other unlawful activities of members of such organizations." The RICO portion of the act sweepingly brought together under one single piece of legislation the many and diverse activities of American organized crime and made each punishable in a variety of new ways. RICO did not make racketeering itself illegal, but rather focused on the ill-gotten gains derived from such activity—specifying that it shall be unlawful for anyone involved in a *pattern* of racketeering to derive any income or proceeds from that activity. Given the continuing significance of the RICO statute, it is worthwhile to reproduce here that statute's definition of "racketeering activity." RICO defines racketeering activity to include

RICO an acronym for the Racketeer Influenced and Corrupt Organization statute, which was part of the federal Organized Crime Control Act of 1970.

> (A) any act or threat involving murder, kidnapping, gambling, arson, robbery, bribery, extortion, dealing in obscene matter, or dealing in narcotic or other dangerous drugs, which is chargeable under State law and punishable by imprisonment for more than one year;
>
> (B) any act that is indictable under any of the following provisions of title 18, United States Code: section 201 (relating to bribery), section 224 (relating to sports bribery), sections 471, 472, and 473 (relating to counterfeiting), section 659 (relating to theft from interstate shipment)...section 664 (relating to embezzlement from pension and welfare funds), sections 891-894 (relating to extortionate credit transactions), section 1029 (relating to fraud and related activity in connection with access devices), section 1084 (relating to the transmission of gambling information), section 1341 (relating to mail fraud), section 1343 (relating to wire fraud), section 1344 (relating to financial institution fraud), sections 1461-1465 (relating to obscene matter), section 1503 (relating to obstruction of justice), section 1510 (relating to obstruction of criminal investigations), section 1511 (relating to the obstruction of State or local law enforcement), section 1512 (relating to tampering with a witness, victim, or an informant), section 1513 (relating to retaliating against a witness, victim, or an informant), section 1951 (relating to interference with commerce, robbery, or extortion), section 1952 (relating to racketeering), section 1953 (relating to interstate transportation of wagering paraphernalia), section 1954 (relating to unlawful welfare fund payments), section 1955 (relating to the prohibition of illegal gambling businesses), section 1956 (relating to the laundering of monetary instruments), section 1957 (relating to engaging in monetary

Attorney General Robert Kennedy describing a link between the Teamsters and organized crime. *UPI/Bettmann.*

transactions in property derived from specified unlawful activity), section 1958 (relating to use of interstate commerce facilities in the commission of murder-for-hire), sections 2251-2252 (relating to sexual exploitation of children), sections 2312 and 2313 (relating to interstate transportation of stolen motor vehicles), sections 2314 and 2315 (relating to interstate transportation of stolen property), section 2321 (relating to trafficking in certain motor vehicles or motor vehicle parts), sections 2341-2346 (relating to trafficking in contraband cigarettes), sections 2421-24 (relating to white slave traffic),

(C) any act that is indictable under title 29, United States Code, section 186 (dealing with restrictions on payments and loans to labor organizations) or section 501(c) (relating to embezzlement from union funds),

(D) any offense involving fraud connected with a case under title 11, fraud in the sale of securities, or the felonious manufacture, importation, receiving, concealment, buying, selling, or otherwise dealing in narcotics or other dangerous drugs, punishable under any law of the United States, or

(E) any act that is indictable under the Currency and Foreign Transactions Reporting Act.

Asset forfeiture the authorized seizure of money, negotiable instruments, securities, or other things of value.

Punishments provided for under RICO include **asset forfeiture** which makes it possible for federal officials to seize the proceeds of those involved in racketeering. In the words of the statute: "Whoever violates any provision of...this chapter shall be fined...or imprisoned not more than 20 years (or for life if the violation is based on a racketeering activity for which the maximum penalty includes life imprisonment), or both, and shall forfeit to the United States, irrespective of any provision of State law...any property...derived from any proceeds that the person obtained, directly or indirectly, from racketeering activity or unlawful debt collection...." Hence, as a result of RICO, federal agents are empowered to seize the financial and other tangible fruits of organized criminal activity, including businesses, real estate, money, equities, gold and other commodities, vehicles including airplanes and boats, and just about anything else that can be shown to have been acquired through a pattern of racketeering activity.

Money Laundering

Money laundering the process of converting illegally earned assets, originating as cash, to one or more alternative forms to conceal such incriminating factors as illegal origin and true ownership.

Money laundering refers to the process by which illegal gains are disguised as legal income. A more formal definition is offered by the National Institute of Justice, which says that money laundering is "the process of converting illegally earned assets, originating as cash, to one or more alternative forms to conceal such incriminating factors as illegal origin and true ownership."[65]

Title 18, Section 1956 of the U.S. Criminal Code specifically prohibits what it calls the "laundering of monetary instruments" and defines money laundering as efforts "to conceal or disguise the nature, the location, the source, the ownership, or the control of the proceeds of specified unlawful activity...." To assist in the identification of money launderers, a provision of the 1986 federal Money Laundering Control Act requires that banks report to the government all currency transactions in excess of $10,000. This requirement is, of course, well known to high-end money launderers who routinely evade it by dealing in commodities such as gold, using foreign banks, or by making a series of smaller deposits and transfers.

Reliable official estimates of the amount of money laundered in the United States are hard to come by. A decade ago, however, the President's Commission on Organized Crime estimated that approximately $15 billion of illicit U.S. drug proceeds moved illegally every year into international financial channels.[66] Of that amount, $5 billion was thought to be taken out of the country as currency.

A few years ago, the most notorious of foreign banks set up to serve the needs of money launderers, drug dealers, terrorists, and other assorted ne'er-do-wells, was closed when banking regulators in the United States, England, and several other countries seized branch assets and arrested many of the bank's officers. *BCCI,* the Bank of Credit and Commerce, International, was chartered in Luxembourg and opened branches throughout the world, including at least one in the Bahamas—islands already known for their role in the provision of infamous "off-shore" banking services which, while trading in currencies internationally, offer customers considerable secrecy and very limited reporting requirements.

BCCI soon grew into one of the largest banks in the world, and opened offices in seventy-two countries. Its friends in America included Jimmy Carter, Washington lawyer Clifford Clark, and the powerful senator Orrin Hatch.[67]

Although there is evidence that BCCI may have provided assistance to U.S. CIA operatives, it also "served to smuggle arms to Syria, Iran, and Libya, and to launder money for the Medellin cartel and Golden Triangle drug warlord Khun Sa."[68] After repeated indictments of top officials, BCCI closed its doors in 1991. During the decade or so that it was in existence, however, it is estimated that many billions of dollars flowed through its numerous branch offices—the majority of it from drug cartels and terrorist organizations seeking to hide the source of their revenues.

In December 1993 the bipartisan President's Commission on Model State Drug Laws released its report which included a comprehensive package of forty-four model state laws designed to crack down on drug and alcohol abuse throughout the country. "Money and property are the economic lifeblood of the illegal drug industry,"[69] the report concluded, and suggested that asset forfeiture, including expedited property seizure, evictions, and strict controls on money laundering, was the best means available for fighting the problem.

If anything, however, the money laundering problem appears to be getting worse. A 1994 report by the Senate Permanent Subcommittee on Investigations found, for example, that "billions of dollars are now leaving our country every year to be put into the flow of commerce and returned to this country as laundered capital...."[70]

In that same year, however, in what many experts saw as contrary to the trend in enforcement activities needed to curb organized crime and drug trafficking, the U.S. Supreme Court made money laundering convictions harder to come by. The case involved Waldemar and Loretta Ratzlaf, high-stakes gamblers from Oregon with lines of credit at fifteen casinos in New Jersey and Nevada.[71] In 1988, in an apparent attempt to hide $160,000 in gambling losses from the IRS, the Ratzlafs went to several banks in Nevada and California and bought cashier's checks of less than $10,000 each to pay the debt. Their check purchases came under IRS scrutiny as a result of an investigation into the couple's 1986 tax return. In that year, casino records showed that the couple had engaged in large cash transactions with a number of casinos, but had reported no gambling income.

Authorities accused the Ratzlafs of "organizing financial transactions" to evade the currency-reporting requirement of the 1986 federal Money Laundering Control Act. Both Ratzlafs were convicted in federal court in Nevada on charges of conspiracy and interstate travel in aid of racketeering. Mr. Ratzlaf was sentenced to fifteen years in prison and fined $26,300, while Ms. Ratzlaf was sentenced to ten months of home detention and fined $7,900.

The couple's lawyers appealed through the 9th U.S. Circuit Court of Appeals, and finally to the U.S. Supreme Court. The Court, in a 5 to 4 decision, found in favor of the Ratzlafs, saying that federal authorities had failed to prove that the couple knew they were violating the law. The words of Justice Ruth Bader Ginsburg summarize the opinion of the majority: "Not all currency structuring serves an illegal goal.... Under the government's construction an individual would commit a felony against the United States by making cash deposits in small doses, fearful that the bank's reports would increase the likelihood of burglary, or in an endeavor to keep a former spouse unaware of his wealth."

In a separate dissenting opinion, however, Justice Harry A. Blackmun criticized the Court's majority, writing, "Waldemar Ratzlaf—to use an old phrase—will be laughing all the way to the bank." Ratzlaf, said Blackmun, "was anything but uncomprehending as he traveled from bank to bank converting his bag of cash to cashier's checks in $9,500 bundles" to pay the debt.

Policy Issues: The Control of Organized Crime

In a cogent analysis of organized crime Gary W. Potter tells us that "[t]he question of what we (should) do about organized crime is largely predicated on how we conceptualize (of) organized crime."[72] Potter criticizes current policies for focusing "almost exclusively on *criminal* aspects of organized crime." It is, says Potter, "the *organized* aspects of organized crime which offer the most useful data for formulating future policy."

To understand organized crime, and to deal effectively with it, according to Potter, we must study the social context within which it occurs. Such study reveals "that organized crime is simply an integral part of the social, political, and economic system," says Potter. Any effective attack on organized crime, therefore, would involve meeting the demands of the consumers of organized crime's products and services. Potter suggests this can be accomplished either by punishing the consumer more effectively or by educating such individuals as to the perils of their own behavior.

Fighting corruption in politics and among law enforcement personnel and administrators is another track Potter suggests in the battle against organized crime. If organized crime has been successful at least partially because it has been able to corrupt local politicians and enforcement agents, then why not work to reduce corruption at the local level, Potter asks?

Howard Abadinsky recommends four approaches to the control of organized crime, each involving changes at the policy-making level:[73]

1. Increasing the risk of involvement in organized crime by increasing the resources available to law enforcement agencies that are useful in fighting organized crime. A greater proportion of tax revenues, for example, might be moved into the fight against organized crime. The 1994 Violent Crime Control and Enforcement Act, which puts more law enforcement officers on the streets, should be helpful in freeing up others to investigate organized crime.
2. Increasing law enforcement authority so as to increase the risks of involvement in organized crime. Money laundering statues that expand the scope of law enforcement authority, racketeering laws, and forfeiture statutes all may be helpful in this regard. Abadinsky also suggests providing a special "good faith" exception "to the exclusionary rule in prosecutions involving RICO violations."[74]

Salvatore "Sammy Bull" Gravano, who admitted to nineteen murders, entered the federal witness protection program in 1995. He has been called the "most significant witness in the history of organized crime." *J. Markowitz/Sygma.*

3. Reducing the economic lure of involvement in organized crime by making legitimate opportunities more readily available. Educational programs, scholarships, job-training initiatives, and so on might all play a role in such a strategy.
4. Decreasing organized criminal opportunity through decriminalization or legalization. This last strategy is perhaps the most controversial. It would decriminalize or legalize many of the activities from which organized crime now draws income. State-run gambling and the ready availability of narcotics and other substances, now subject to widespread abuse through state-controlled facilities, provide examples of the kinds of policy changes necessary to achieve this goal.

Strict enforcement of existing laws is another option. It is a strategy that has recently been used with considerable success by a number of federal and state law enforcement operations which have targeted organized crime. In 1987, for example, Nicholas "The Crow" Caramandi agreed to testify in eleven criminal trials against organized crime figures, resulting in more than fifty-two convictions mostly in the Pennsylvania and New Jersey areas. Caramandi had bargain for lessened sentences in his own convictions on murder, racketeering, and extortion charges. A few years ago, Caramandi was released from prison and now lives far from Philadelphia, under the federal witness relocation program with a new identity and a mob-ordered sentence of death hanging over him.

One of the most spectacular mob trials in recent years was that of John Gotti, who until recently headed New York's Gambino family. Over the years Gotti had been arrested on many occasions and prosecuted at least five times for various offenses. His ability to escape conviction earned him the title "the Teflon don." That changed on April 2, 1992, when Gotti was convicted on thirteen federal charges, including murder and racketeering. Following trial, Gotti was sentenced to life in prison without possibility of parole. Gotti's major mistake appears to have been to personally participate in several executions, including that of Paul Castellano, his predecessor. Gotti and his underboss, Locascio, are now both in federal prison, while Gotti's son, John, Jr., is thought to be running the family.

Gotti's downfall came at the hands of Salvatore "Sammy Bull" Gravano, a former underboss in the Gambino family. Gravano, who admitted to nineteen murders, shared family secrets with federal investigators in return for leniency and succor through the federal witness protection program. Gravano also spent days on the witness stand testifying against his former boss. Federal prosecutor Zachary Carter later called Gravano "the most significant witness in the history of organized crime."[75]

Some say that, in the face of increased law enforcement activity, the *Cosa Nostra* is doomed. According to the FBI, most major crime families have now been decimated by enhanced investigation efforts, often supplemented by wiretaps and informant testimony. The FBI claims that a total of 1,173 *Cosa Nostra* bosses, soldiers, and associates throughout the country have been convicted during the last six years alone. Imprisoned bosses now include not only New York's John Gotti, but Los Angeles' Peter Milano and the leaders of Kansas City's Civella family. Also, a few years ago thirteen members of New England's Patriarca family were convicted of murdering Billy Grasso, one of their underbosses, and sent to prison.

Can the *Cosa Nostra* survive such pressure? Nicholas Caramandi says "yes." "It's such a bureaucracy...this thing of ours," says Caramandi. "You can't kill it.... It's the second government.... We serve needs. People come to us when they can't get justice, or to borrow money that they can't get from the bank.... It never dies. It's as powerful today as it ever was. It's just more glorified and more out in the open."[76] The Mob, says Caramandi, reaches all the way to the highest levels of political power. Survival is assured through well-placed friends in America's highest elected offices.

One expert believes that "[t]he Mafia, *Cosa Nostra,* will not be recognizable by the end of the century." John Gotti thinks otherwise. "This is gonna be *Cosa Nostra* till I die," he told his underbosses just before his arrest. "Be it an hour from now or be it tonight or a hundred years from now, it's gonna be *Cosa Nostra.*"

SUMMARY

This chapter has distinguished between white-collar and organized crime. Unfortunately, the observations made about both forms of crime, as valid and usefully descriptive as they may be, rarely rise above the level of organized conjecture. Hence, it is impossible at this point to describe a theory of white-collar crime, or a theory of organized crime, except insofar as those concepts can be ensconced within other theoretical perspectives—as was the case with Sutherland's attempt to explain white-collar crime in terms of differential association.

While both white-collar and organized crime are apparently prevalent in the United States today, and organized and white-collar criminals share similar motivations directed toward acquiring wealth and social position, there appears to be considerable variation in commitment between the two types of offenders. Organized criminals evidence a long tradition of criminal involvement, often in the form of racketeering, which is largely unknown to most white-collar offenders. Similarly, organized crime wraps its members in a kind of deviant subculture with a detailed code of conduct which affects its members throughout their life cycles. White-collar criminals, on the other hand, have typically achieved positions of power and social respectability through conformity and approved forms of achievement, and often come from cultural backgrounds that are supportive of adherence to the law. Hence, most white-collar offenders are probably drawn to criminal activity for the immediate financial rewards it offers, while organized criminals are more apt to see crime as a way of life and to condemn the conformist activity of others.

If such differences are true, then white-collar crime may be effectively prevented by strict enforcement efforts which, by their very example, serve as a strong general deterrent to other would-be offenders. Organized criminal groups, on the other hand, given their long-standing commitment to criminal activities, are unlikely to be impacted by such threats.

DISCUSSION QUESTIONS

1. What is the difference between organized crime and white-collar crime? What linkages, if any, might exist between the two?
2. What types of white-collar crime has this chapter identified? Is corporate crime a form of white-collar crime? Is occupational crime a form of white-collar crime?
3. Describe a typical organized crime family, as outlined in this chapter. Why does a crime family contain so many different "levels"?
4. What is money laundering? How might money laundering be reduced or prevented? Can you think of any strategies this chapter does not discuss for the reduction of money laundering activities in the United States? If so, what are they?
5. What strategies for combating the activities of organized crime are discussed in this chapter? Which seem best to you? Why? Can you think of any other strategies that might be effective? If so, what are they?

NOTES

1 Donald J. Newman, "White-Collar Crime: An Overview and Analysis," *Law and Contemporary Problems,* vol 23(Autumn, 1958), no. 4

2. Kathleen Murray, "The Fraud du Jour Is Wireless Cable," *Worth,* October 1994, p. 118.

3. Ibid., pp. 118–120.

4. Edwin H. Sutherland, "White-Collar Criminality," *American Sociological Review,* Vol. 5, no. 1 (February 1940), pp. 2–10.
5. Ibid.
6. Edwin H. Sutherland, "Crime of Corporations," in Albert Cohen, Alfred Lindesmith, and Karl Schuessler, eds., *The Sutherland Papers* (Bloomington: Indiana University Press, 1956), pp. 78–96.
7. Ibid.
8. Edwin H. Sutherland, "White-Collar Criminality."
9. Travis Hirschi and Michael Gottfredson, "Causes of White-Collar Crime," *Criminology,* Vol. 25, no. 4 (1987), p. 952.
10. *USA Today,* April 2, 1991, pp. B1–2.
11. Karen Gullo, "'Phantom' Banks Across the Country Bilking Investors," Associated Press, September 11, 1994.
12. Michael L. Benson, Francis T. Cullen, and William J. Maakestad, *Local Prosecutors and Corporate Crime* (Washington, D.C.: National Institute of Justice, 1993).
13. Michael Clements, "Breast Implant Pact OK'd: $4.25 Billion Is Available to Claimants," *USA Today,* September 2, 1994, p. 1A.
14. "Plastic Surgeons, Manufacturers Helped Finance Breast-Implant Study," *USA Today,* September 2, 1994, p. 10A.
15. Rahul Sharma, "Union Carbide Quits India a Decade After Bhopal," Reuters wire services, September 9, 1994.
16. Donald J. Newman, "White-Collar Crime: An Overview and Analysis," *Law and Contemporary Problems,* Vol. 23, no. 4 (Autumn 1958).
17. Ibid.
18. President's Commission on Law Enforcement and Administration of Justice, *The Challenge of Crime in a Free Society* (Washington, D.C.: U.S. Government Printing Office, 1967), p. 47.
19. For excellent reviews of the evolution of the concept of white-collar crime, see K. Schlegel and D. Weisburd, "White-Collar Crime: The Parallax View," in Kip Schlegel and David Weisburd, eds., *White-Collar Crime Reconsidered* (Boston: Northeastern University Press, 1992), pp. 3–27; and K. Schlegel and D. Weisburd, "Returning to the Mainstream: tions on Past and Future White- Crime Study," in Schlegel and Weisb *White-Collar Crime Reconsidered,* pp. 352–365.
20. Herbert Edelhertz, *The Nature, Impact and Prosecution of White-Collar Crime* (Washington, D.C.: National Institute of Law Enforcement and Criminal Justice, 1970).
21. Gilbert Geis, "Upperworld Crime," in Abraham S. Blumberg, ed., *Current Perspectives on Criminal Behavior: Original Essays on Criminology* (New York: Alfred A. Knopf, 1974).
22. Gary S. Green, *Occupational Crime* (Chicago: Nelson-Hall, 1990), p. 12.
23. Ibid., p. 16.
24. Hirschi and Gottfredson, "Causes of White-Collar Crime," p. 949.
25. Ibid., p. 951.
26. Ibid., p. 960.
27. Newman, "White-Collar Crime: An Overview and Analysis."
28. Green, *Occupational Crime,* p. 256.
29. James William Coleman, *The Criminal Elite: The Sociology of White-Collar Crime* (New York: St. Martins, 1989).
30. The details of this account are taken from Camden Pelham, *The Chronicles of Crime: The Newgate Calendar—A Series of Memoirs and Anecdotes of Notorious Characters* (London: T. Miles, 1887), pp. 57–65.
31. Much of the information in this section comes from Julian Symons, *A Pictorial History of Crime* (New York: Bonanza Books, 1966).
32. Ibid.
33. Howard Abadinsky, *Organized Crime,* 4th ed. (Chicago: Nelson-Hall, 1994).
34. Ibid., p. 112.
35. Luigi Barzini, *The Italians* (New York: Atheneum, 1965).
36. Howard Abadinsky, *Organized Crime,* 4th ed., p. 132.
37. Gus Tyler, "The Crime Corporation," in Abraham S. Blumberg, ed., *Current Perspectives on Criminal Behavior: Original Essays on Criminology* (New York: Alfred A. Knopf, 1974), p. 197, citing Hank Messick, *The Silent Syndicate* (New York:

Macmillan, 1966), pp. vii–xii.

38. Tyler, "The Crime Corporation," p. 173.
39. John Kilber, *Capone: The Life and World of Al Capone* (Greenwich, CT: Fawcett, 1971).
40. Mark H. Haller, "Illegal Enterprise: A Theoretical and Historical Interpretation," *Criminology*, Vol. 28, no. 2 (May 1990), p. 209.
41. President's Commission on Law Enforcement and Administration of Justice, *Task Force Report: Organized Crime* (Washington, D.C.: United States Government Printing Office, 1967), Appendix A.
42. Anthony E. Simpson, *The Literature of Police Corruption* (New York: The John Jay Press, 1977).
43. J. Richard Davis, "Things I Couldn't Tell Till Now," *Collier's*, August 19, 1939, p. 35.
44. Robert W. Ferguson, *The Nature of Vice Control in the Administration of Justice* (St. Paul: West, 1974), p. 379.
45. Symons, *A Pictorial History of Crime*, p. 226.
46. President's Commission on Law Enforcement and Administration of Justice, *The Challenge of Crime in a Free Society*, p. 196.
47. Special Committee to Investigate Organized Crime in Interstate Commerce, U.S. Senate, 82nd Congress, 1951.
48. President's Commission on Law Enforcement and Administration of Justice, *The Challenge of Crime in a Free Society*, p. 192, citing the Kefauver committee report.
49. *U.S.* v. *Bufalino*, 285 G.2d. 408 (1960).
50. President's Commission on Law Enforcement and Administration of Justice, *The Challenge of Crime in a Free Society*, p. 195.
51. As identified by Abadinsky in *Organized Crime*.
52. As cited by Abadinsky in ibid., pp. 186–187.
53. William Sherman, "Kingpins of the Underworld," *Cosmopolitan*, Vol. 212, no. 3 (March 1992), pp. 158–162.
54. Abadinsky, *Organized Crime*, pp. 311–312.
55. Ibid., p. 313.
56. Ibid.
57. Richard Behar, "In the Grip of Treachery," *Playboy*, Vol. 38, no. 11 (November 1991), p. 92.
58. President's Commission on Law Enforcement and Administration of Justice, *Task Force Report: Organized Crime*.
59. "Kingpins of the Underworld."
60. Behar, "In the Grip of Treachery."
61. Ibid.
62. President's Commission on Law Enforcement and Administration of Justice, *Task Force Report: Organized Crime*, p. 41.
63. Abadinsky, *Organized Crime*, p. 5.
64. Joseph B. Treaster, "In Pizza Connection II, 79 Seized in Raids in New York and Italy," *The New York Times*, September 16, 1994, p. 1A.
65. Clifford Karchmer and Douglas Ruch, "State and Local Money Laundering Control Strategies," *NIJ Research in Brief* (Washington, D.C.: NIJ, 1992), p. 1.
66. President's Commission on Organized Crime, *The Cash Connection: Organized Crime, Financial Institutions, and Money Laundering* (Washington, D.C.: U.S. Government Printing Office, 1984).
67. According to Abadinsky, *Organized Crime*, p. 427.
68. Ibid.
69. United Press on-line, Northern edition, "Presidential Commission Presents Recommendation on Drug Control," December 13, 1993.
70. Carolyn Skorneck, "Money Laundering," Associated Press on-line, Northern edition, April 7, 1994.
71. Laurie Asseo, "Scotus-Money Reporting," Associated Press on-line, Northern edition, January 11, 1994.
72. Gary W. Potter, *Criminal Organizations: Vice, Racketeering, and Politics in an American City* (Prospects Heights, IL: Waveland, 1994), p. 183.
73. Abadinsky, *Organized Crime*, p. 507.

74. Ibid., p. 508
75. "5-Year Prison Term for Mafia Turncoat," *USA Today,* September 27, 1994, p. 3A.
76. Behar, "In the Grip of Treachery."

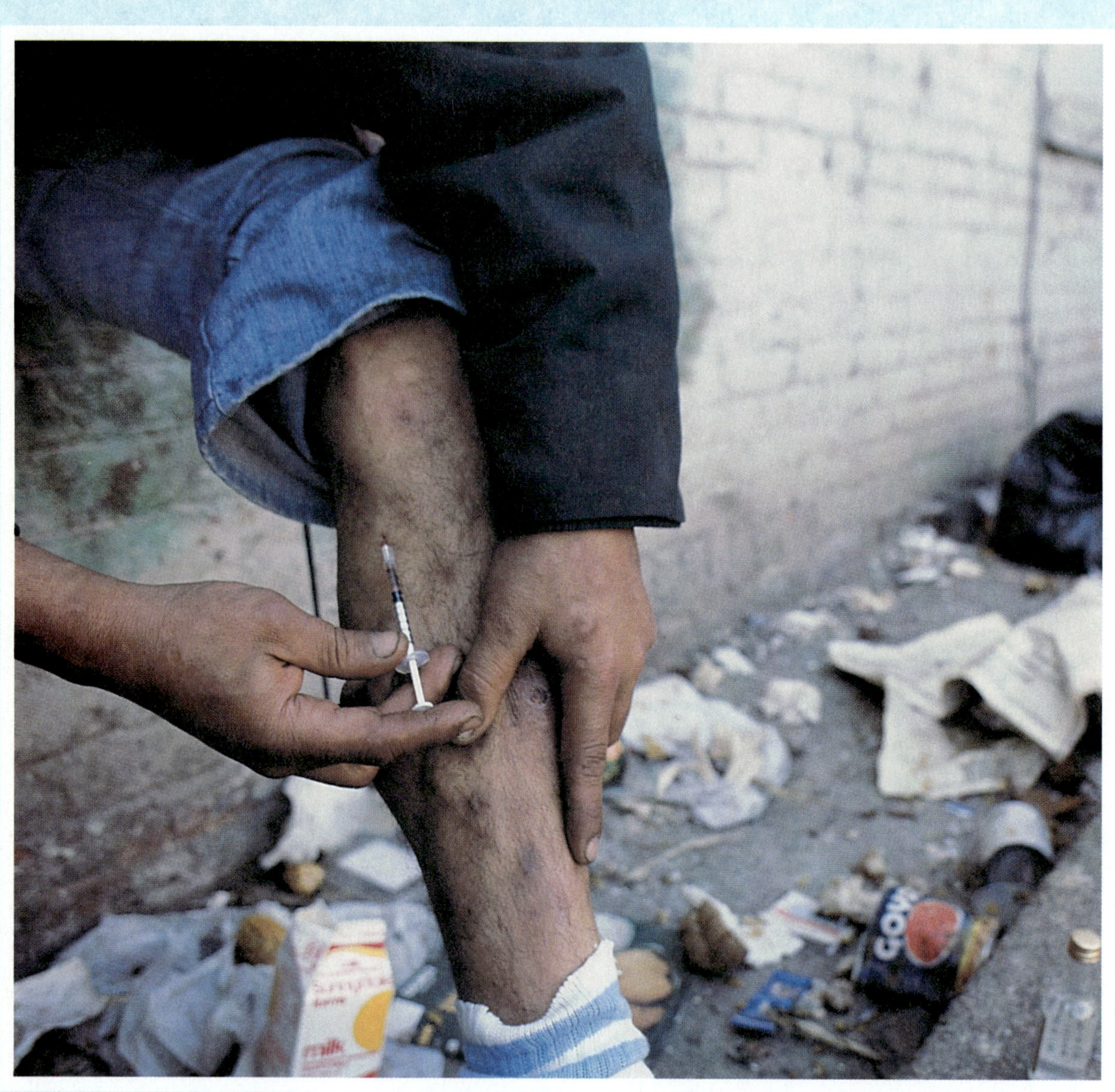

CHAPTER 11

DRUG ABUSE AND CRIME

I believe that the struggle between East and West has been replaced by the world's struggle against drugs.

—Interpol Secretary-General Raymond Kendall[1]

Drug dealers no longer count their money. They weigh it.

—A Houston, Texas, police lieutenant[2]

I don't feel that was a crime.

—Former U.S. Surgeon General Joycelyn Elders, when asked whether her son, convicted of selling cocaine to an undercover officer, might commit other crimes while free on bail.[3]

IMPORTANT TERMS

drug-defined crime	drug-related crime	dangerous drugs
pharmaceutical diversion	heroin signature program	drug trafficking
designer drugs	interdiction	asset forfeiture
legalization	decriminalization	psychoactive substances

INTRODUCTION

In mid-1994 Kevin Elders, son of former U.S. Surgeon General Joycelyn Elders, was convicted in Little Rock, Arkansas, of selling $275 worth of cocaine to an undercover police officer. The warrant for his arrest was issued a week after his mother told a National Press Club gathering that the government should consider legalizing drugs as one way of reducing the crime rate.[4] A judge rejected Elders's claim that arresting officers had sought to entrap him to expose his drug habit and embarrass his mother during Senate confirmation hearings. He was sentenced under a tough Arkansas law to ten years in prison without parole.[5]

Key testimony in the case came from a police informant, Calvin Walraven, who said that he had met Elders some years before, and that they had used drugs together several times. Walraven turned informant after being caught in a drug sting and told undercover officers that Elders had been one of his suppliers. As of this writing, Elders remains free on $10,000 bond pending appeal of his case to the Arkansas Supreme Court.

HISTORY OF DRUG ABUSE IN THE UNITED STATES

The widespread illegal use of drugs affects all segments of today's society. Sadder still is the fact that almost all forms of illicit drug use in America are associated with other forms of criminality. Drugs, and their relationship to crime provide one of the most significant policy issues of our time. Famed *Washington Monthly* columnist Paul Savoy recently reported polls showing that Americans "are so fearful about the drug-driven crime epidemic that more than half of those polled...expressed an opinion [which] favored cutting back the constitutional rights of criminal defendants and overruling Supreme Court decisions that limit police conduct in gathering evidence."[6]

The rampant and widespread use and abuse of mind- and mood-altering drugs, so commonplace in the United States today, is of relatively recent origin. Throughout the 1800s and early 1900s, the use of illegal drugs in America was mostly associated with artistic individuals and fringe groups. One hundred years ago drug abuse, as we understand it today, was almost exclusively confined to a subsegment of musicians, painters, poets, and other highly imaginative individu-

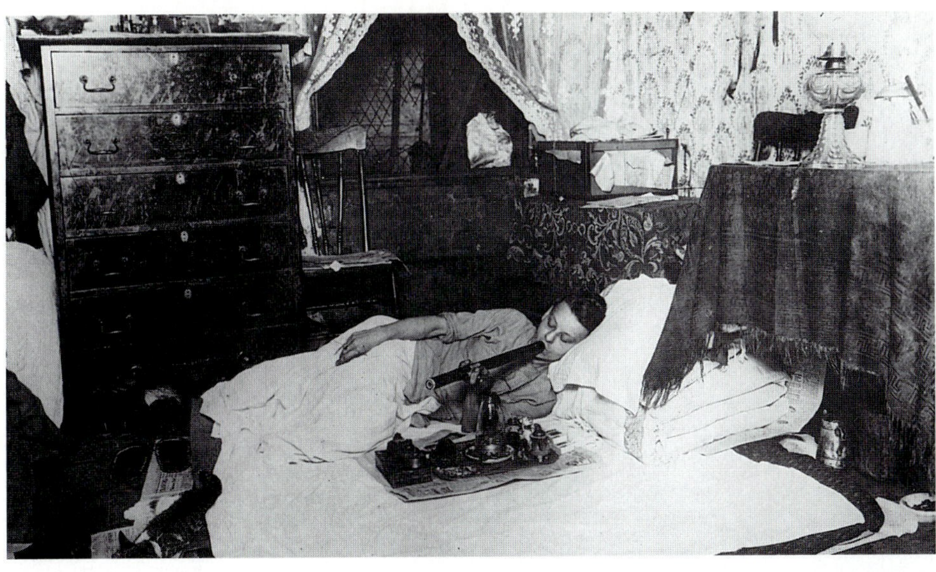

Smoker in an opium den in Chinatown, San Francisco, circa 1925. *UPI/Bettmann.*

als seeking to enhance their creativity. While it is true that medicinal elixirs of the period contained a variety of potent substances, including cocaine, alcohol, and opium, the lives of relatively few Americans were seriously affected at the time by any drug other than alcohol. One significant exception existed in the form of "opium dens" that flourished in West Coast cities and eventually made their way across the country as a result of increased Asian immigration. Some Chinese immigrants brought opium products with them and introduced other segments of the American population to opium smoking.

Psychoactive substances gained widespread acceptance during the hippie movement, a period of new-found freedoms embraced by a large number of American youths during the late 1960s and early 1970s. The movement, which was characterized by slogans such as "if it feels good, do it" and "tune in, turn on, drop out" promoted free love, personal freedom, experimentation with subjective states of consciousness, and "mind expansion." "Cheech and Chong" movies, "flower power," paisley clothes, bell-bottom jeans, long hair on men, and Eastern religions all flourished within the context of a drug-fed countercultural movement.

Psychoactive substances those which affect the mind, mental processes, or emotions.

One influential figure in the drug-inspired movement of the times was Harvard professor, Dr. Timothy Leary. Leary formed the League of Spiritual Discovery in the mid-1960s, describing it as "an orthodox, psychedelic religion that permits the use of LSD and marijuana as sacraments by League members." With the advent of the hippie era, marijuana, LSD, hashish, psyliocybin, and peyote burst upon the national scene as an ever-growing number of individuals began to view drugs as recreational substances and more and more young people identified with the tenor of the period.

It was during this time, apparently, that President Bill Clinton's experiments with marijuana took place. Clinton revealed during the 1992 presidential campaign that he had smoked marijuana as a youth, claiming that he never inhaled.

Dr. Timothy Leary, guru of the 1960s new consciousness movement, shown here in New York in 1966. *UPI/Bettmann.*

Extent of Abuse

According to the *National Household Survey on Drug Abuse*, illegal drug use in the United States—as measured by the number of people who report having used an illicit drug in the previous month—has declined steadily over the past thirteen years. Since data gathered in 1993, however, are essentially the same as those from 1992, the decline may have slowed or stopped entirely. The *Survey*, which interviews what it hopes are representative households across the nation, notes the possibility of "underreporting of drug using behavior by respondents."

In 1979, the highest year on record, 24.3 million people reported recent illegal drug use, while by 1992 the number had dropped to a low of 11.4 million.[7] It rose to 11.7 million in 1993, although the increase was not considered statistically significant.

The survey estimates that about 9 million persons currently use marijuana, with about 7 million of them using marijuana alone, the rest in combination with other drugs. Another 1.3 million persons are thought to be current users of cocaine.

If survey results are accurate, they would seem to indicate that drug abuse is now less of a problem than it was a decade ago. The largest ever estimate of marijuana use put routine users at 22.5 million in 1979, while the largest current cocaine use estimate was 5.3 million in 1985—figures far greater than those of today. Growth of the American population in the meantime gives the estimated decline even greater weight. "Compared with 1979, when 24.3 million current users represented 13.7 percent of the population age 12 and older, the 11.7 million of last year represented 5.6 percent of that population, the survey said."[8] The survey found that among the nearly 12 million current users, 1.4 million are aged 12–17; 3.8 million are 18–25; 3.2 million are 26–34; and 3.3 million are 35 and older.

Health and Human Services secretary Donna Shalala, commenting on the 1993 survey, observed that "[m]any of these remaining drug users are chronic, hard-core users, whose addictions are clearly more severe and who are more difficult to reach and more resistant to change." Lee Brown, director of the government's Office of National Drug Control Policy, said the "survey underestimates some hard-core addict populations because it excludes the homeless, prisoners, people living at colleges, active military and those in other institutions." Brown's office, for example, estimates there are 2.1 million hard-core cocaine addicts, while the survey says there are 476,000. Heroin addicts are numbered at 600,000 by Brown's office, while the survey admits its sample size is too small to offer reliable estimates.

In the occasional use area, however, survey results were less encouraging. Occasional use—defined as use in the past year but less often than monthly—of marijuana increased from 8.8 million in 1992 to 9.6 million in 1993. Occasional use of cocaine, however, declined from 3.5 million in 1992 to 3.0 million in 1993, and was also down from 8.1 million in 1985. Overall, the study found that 77 million Americans (or 37.2% of adults 12 years of age and older) have used an illegal drug at least once. Of those, 70 million have used marijuana, 23.5 million cocaine, and 18 million hallucinogens such as LSD. The survey found that reported instances of illicit drug use varied not only with age, but along racial and gender lines as well. In most categories for which data were gathered (including marijuana, cocaine, crack, inhalants, hallucinogens, stimulants, sedatives, tranquilizers, analgesics, and alcohol), males reported rates of abuse higher than that of females, while blacks reported only slightly higher rates of abuse than whites. In specific drug categories, however, there were notable differences. Black respondents, for example, were nearly three times as likely as whites, and twice as likely as Hispanics, to report the use of crack cocaine. Whites exceeded both blacks and Hispanics in reported use of inhalants, and twice as many whites as blacks reported having ever used hallucinogens. Similarly, reported illegal use of psychotherapeutic drugs (especially stimulants) was substantially greater among whites than among blacks or Hispanics, with white males showing the highest rate of such abuse. Finally, more whites (87%) than any other category (blacks, 79%; Hispanics, 77%) reported ever having used alcohol, and more whites reported having used alcohol within the past month than any other racial group.

Other significant differences were observed as well. Black males, for example, reported a rate of cocaine, crack, and marijuana use which was twice that of black females. Whites reported somewhat greater use of anabolic steroids than did other groups, and blacks reported the highest frequency of heroin abuse—with the use of needles by black males for the purpose of drug injection exceeding the frequency of reported needle use for any other category. The use of needles, which is known to spread AIDS, was highest (when rates were computed) among black males aged 26–34.

While the use of illicit drugs provides one measure of the drug problem facing our country, the ready availability of such drugs provides another. Data from the National Crime Victimization Survey[9] show that two out of three students ages 12 to

19 report ready availability of illegal drugs at their school. Students in public schools report a wider availability of drugs than do those in private schools, and students in higher grades (9 through 12) report more drugs available to them than do those in the lower grades. Similar rates of availability were reported by white students (69% of whom said drugs were available to them at school) and black students (67%), and by students living in cities (66%), suburban areas (67%), and those in rural areas (71%). The proportion of 1992 high school students reporting they could obtain drugs "fairly easily or very easily," by drug category, was as follows:

Marijuana	82.7%
Amphetamines	58.8
Cocaine powder	48.0
LSD	44.5
Barbiturates	44.0
Crack	43.5
Tranquilizers	40.9
Heroin	34.9
PCP	31.7

Other surveys show that the use of drugs among high school students may be declining. One such survey, the year-to-year results of which are shown in Figure 11.1, supports the belief that drug use among high school students peaked in 1985 and has been declining ever since. As BJS analysts note, however, "self-reports of drug use among high school seniors may underrepresent drug use among youth of that age because high school dropouts and truants are not included, and these groups may have more involvement with drugs than those who stay in school."[10]

While official statistics show a decline in self-reported illicit drug usage, they may not tell the whole story. According to the Drug Enforcement Administration, for example, the use of crack cocaine is spreading from inner-city and large urban areas to smaller cities, towns, and rural areas. The impetus for such spread is coming largely from drug trafficking organizations themselves, many of whom are beginning to experience revenue declines in existing operations. A recent DEA report found that "crack distribution and use appears to have reached the saturation point in large urban areas throughout the country.... Intensive competition during the middle-to-late 1980s," said the report, "inundated the largest consumer pools with crack.... Prices in these areas have reached levels indicative of market saturation."[11]

Costs of Abuse

The true costs of drug abuse are difficult to measure. Included among them would be measurable expenditures such as those for law enforcement activities intended to prevent drug growing, importation, and use; criminal justice case processing; drug treatment programs; money laundering; and time lost from work as a result of drug involvement. More difficult to quantify, but equally real, are other costs related to drug abuse such as sickness resulting from exposure to controlled substances; drug-related crime, the fragmentation of families and other relationships caused by illegal drug use, changes in attitudes and world-view induced among substantial segments of the American population by drug-crime fear, lost human potential, and the image of the United States on the world stage.

Acquired Immune Deficiency Syndrome (AIDS), for example, many cases of which can be traced to intravenous drug use, has proven to be a costly disease in social terms. Researchers at the Centers for Disease Control say that AIDS "is already the leading cause of death of black and Hispanic men aged 25 to 44. Preliminary data," says the CDC, "indicate AIDS has become the second-leading cause of death among black women aged 25 to 44."[12] Homicide is the second leading cause of death for black and Hispanic men in that age group. The Centers find that while there are 73 AIDS cases for every 100,000 black women, there are only 5 per 100,000 white women. Forty-seven percent of AIDS cases among minority women are traceable to intravenous drug use, while 37% appear due to heterosexual intercourse.

FIGURE 11.1 Percentage of High School Seniors Reporting Cocaine Use Within the Past Twelve Months, 1975–1993. *Source:* Lloyd D. Johnston, Patrick M. O'Malley, and Jeraid G. Bachman, "Smoking, Drinking, and Illicit Drug Use Among American Secondary School Students, College Students, and Young Adults," as reported in Bureau of Justice Statistics, *Drug and Crime Facts, 1993* (Washington, D.C.: U.S. Department of Justice, 1994), p. 26.

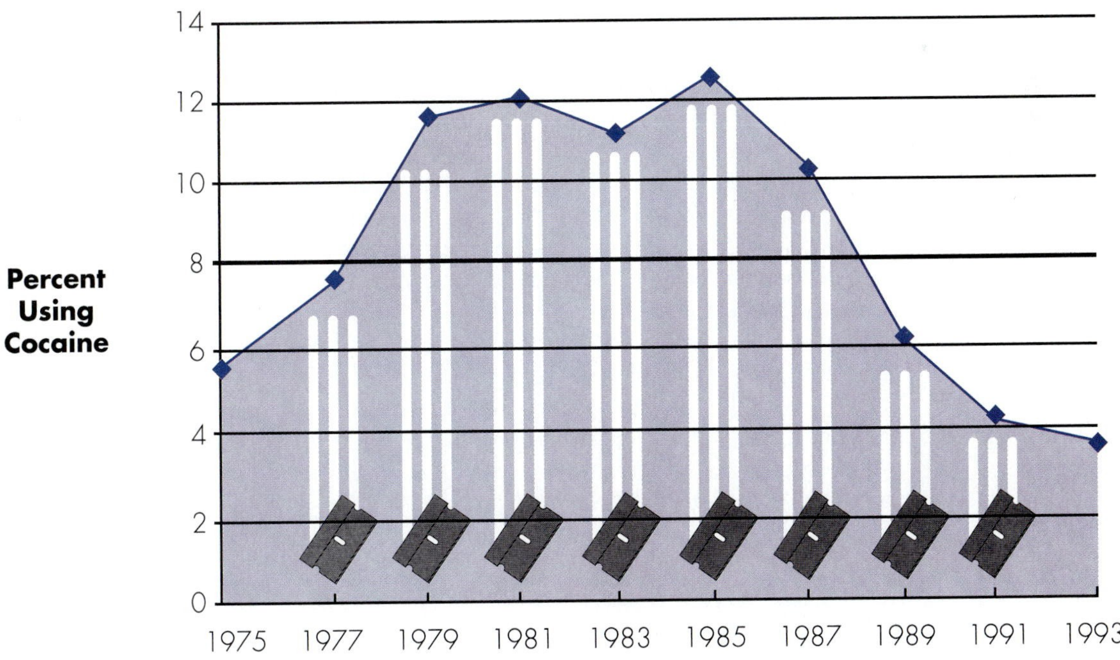

DRUG WAR CLAIMING "ENTIRE GENERATION" OF YOUNG BLACKS

Ex-Newark, N.J., police director Hubert Williams, who helped lead a government probe into last year's deadly Los Angeles riots, doesn't frighten easily.

But his voice grows grim when Williams looks at the results of a *USA Today* study that shows blacks are four times as likely as whites to be arrested for drugs.

"You'd almost have to be blind not to see the time bomb we're creating," says Williams, president of the Police Foundation, a research organization.

Williams and others say the racial disparity in drug arrests is the result of the drug war's decade-long focus on arrest and imprisonment instead of prevention and treatment.

Critics say the disparity has created a self-fulfilling cycle of police suspicion and arrest for black people.

And in communities nationwide, it has worsened festering racial tensions and fostered resentment on all sides.

"It's almost legal genocide," charges A. J. Kramer, who has a front-line view of the drug war as chief of the federal public defender office in Washington, D.C. "We're locking up an entire generation of young black Americans."

Echoes Allen Webster, president of the National Bar Association, a black lawyers' group: "It's almost like they're arresting nobody but African Americans."

Critics say part of the solution is to provide job opportunities for idle young people, especially in the inner-city; more antidrug programs; and diversion programs that get small-time users treatment, not jail.

Even some die-hard drug warriors want a change.

Detroit Judge Leonard Townsend, 57, watches with dismay as a parade of defendants, most of them black, passes through Courtroom 702. "Oh, God. Hundreds, hundreds—it's just unbelievable."

Townsend agrees the law has to "put a boot to their posteriors" when big-time dealers ask for leniency during sentencing. But almost half the cases in Detroit's criminal court involve small-time users—"victims"—Townsend calls them.

"We end up with all the little fish in the net...bogged down with cases that shouldn't be here."

Ed Dennis, former criminal division chief in the Bush Justice Department, acknowledges "some pretty deep-rooted" social problems in the inner city.

But Dennis, who is black, says the violent drug trade demanded "firm action" by police. Go ahead and spend more money on social programs, he says, "but you don't have to give up on law enforcement."

John Laux, police chief in Minneapolis, doesn't want to give up. But he concedes: "We're all trapped into this language of a 'war on drugs.'

"There's a mindset of what war means—it means guns, it means violence, it means oppression. I was certainly guilty of using that same term...and I think that sends the wrong message."

Next door in St. Paul, Police Chief William Finney says he has to scrounge for private donations for half of the money that goes to police-sponsored drug prevention programs in his city.

"For the last 12 years we suffered from people who said...'Let them eat cake,'" he says. "So we're eating cake and selling dope on the street corner."

In Berkeley, Calif., officials have already begun community policing and are working

Webster: Black lawyers' leader says, "It's almost like they're arresting nobody but African Americans."
Bob Riha/Gamma-Liaison, Inc.

on treatment and prevention programs. But assistant city manager Weldon Rucker says little can be done without a major federal effort to produce jobs and expand antidrug services.

Harriet Walden of Seattle, founder of Mothers Against Police Harassment, says it doesn't get much simpler than this: "We're filling up our jails with people who need treatment or jobs or better education."

Source: Sam Vincent, "Drug War Claiming 'Entire Generation' of Young Blacks," *USA Today*, July 27, 1993, p. 7A. Copyright 1993, *USA Today*. Reprinted with permission.

QUESTIONS

1. In this article, A. J. Kramer, chief of the federal public defender office in Washington, D.C., says, "We're locking up an entire generation of young black Americans..." because of drugs. What do you think are the root causes of such high arrest rates among young blacks today?
2. Do you believe that young black Americans are, in fact, more involved in illegal drug-related activities than other groups: On what do you base your answer?
3. Allen Webster, president of the National Bar Association, says "It's almost like they're arresting nobody but African Americans." What do you see as alternatives, if any, to the current situation? If you do see alternatives, how might they be implemented?

Tables 11.1 and 11.2 show the estimated financial and social costs of illegal drug use in the United States per year. Table 11.1 includes dollar amounts spent on systemwide efforts at drug control, and Table 11.2 lists types of costs that are much more difficult to quantify.

TABLE 11.1

DIRECT COSTS OF ILLEGAL DRUG USE

Type of Cost	*Millions*
Federal drug expenditures (1991)	$10,841
All law enforcement	7,157
Interdiction	2,028
Investigations	1,288
International	640
Prosecution	584
Corrections	1,265
Intelligence	104
State and local assistance	1,016
Regulatory compliance	31
Other law enforcement	201
Drug prevention	1,483
Drug treatment	1,752
All research and development	450
State and local drug crime expenditures	5,240
Enforcement of drug laws	2,007
Adjudication of drug law violators	123
Correction of drug law violators	3,072
State prisons	1,158
Local jails	890
Juveniles	224
Probation, pardon, and parole	677
Other corrections	122
Other criminal justice	38
Health care costs for illegal drug users (1985)	2,272
Short-stay hospitals	1,242
Specialty institutions	570
Office-based physicians	52
Support services	201
Other professional services	17
Medical care for drug-related AIDS cases	126
Support services for drug-related AIDS cases	64
Total	$18,353

Source: Bureau of Justice Statistics, *Drugs, Crime and the Justice System: A National Report from the Bureau of Justice Statistics* (Washington, D.C.: U.S. Government Printing Office, December 1992).

TABLE 11.2

INDIRECT COSTS OF ILLEGAL DRUG USE

Criminal justice expenditures on drug-related crime

- Investigating robberies, burglaries, and thefts for drug money and adjudicating and punishing the offenders
- Investigating assaults and homicides in the drug business (or by a drug user who has lost control) and adjudicating and punishing the offenders.

Health care costs

- Injuries resulting from drug-related child abuse/neglect
- Injuries from drug-related accidents
- Injuries from drug-related crime
- Other medical care for illegal drug users, including volunteer services and out-patient services, such as emergency room visits
- Resources used in non-hospital settings

Lost productivity costs

- Of drug-related accident victims
- Of drug-related crime victims
- Time away from work and homemaking to care for drug users and their dependents
- Drug-related educational problems and school dropouts
- Offenders incarcerated for drug-related or drug-defined crimes

Other costs to society

- Loss of property values due to drug-related neighborhood crime
- Property damaged or destroyed in fires, and in workplace and vehicular accidents
- Agricultural resources devoted to illegal drug cultivation/production
- Toxins introduced into public air and water supplies by drug production
- Workplace prevention programs such as drug testing and employee assistance programs
- Averting behavior by potential victims of drug-related crime
- Pain and suffering costs to illegal drug users and their families and friends

Source: Bureau of Justice Statistics, *Drugs, Crime and the Justice System: A National Report from the Bureau of Justice Statistics* (Washington, D.C.: U.S. Government Printing Office, December 1992).

TYPES OF ILLEGAL DRUGS

By convention, controlled substances are generally grouped according to both pharmacological and legal criteria into the following seven categories: stimulants, depressants, cannabis, narcotics, hallucinogens, anabolic steroids, and inhalants. A

Dangerous drugs a term used by the Drug Enforcement Administration (DEA) to refer to "broad categories or classes of controlled substances other than cocaine, opiates, and cannabis products."

separate eighth category, that of dangerous drugs, provides a kind of legal and definitional catch-all. The Drug Enforcement Administration uses the term dangerous drugs to refer to "broad categories or classes of controlled substances other than cocaine, opiates, and cannabis products."[13] Each category, along with some of the drugs it contains, is described in the paragraphs that follow.[14] Figure 11.2 summarizes the differences between drug categories.

Stimulants

Stimulants include amphetamines such as Dexedrine and Benzedrine and other drugs such as cocaine, crack, and Ice. Stimulants act as their name implies—they stimulate the central nervous system and result in higher heart rate, elevated blood pressure, and increased mental activity. Legitimate uses of stimulants include increased alertness, reduced fatigue, weight control, and topical analgesic (painkilling) action. Such drugs are used illegally, however, by those seeking to produce states of excitability and feelings of competence and power.

Cocaine, the use of which has spread rapidly through American population centers, is available in powdered form or as small "rocks" of crack. Crack cocaine, which is much less expensive than powdered cocaine, is made by mixing cocaine powder with water and baking soda or ammonia. It is usually smoked in a "crack pipe" and is named for the fact that it gives off crackling sounds when burned.

Powdered cocaine is inhaled or "snorted," but it may also be mixed with volatile chemicals and "freebased" or smoked and injected. Cocaine produces effects similar to other stimulants—euphoria, a sense of intense stimulation, psychic and physical well-being, and what may seem like boundless energy—although cocaine "highs" are generally both more intense and immediate than are those produced by other drugs. Prolonged cocaine use can cause delusions, hallucinations, weight loss, and overall physical deterioration.

Cocaine sells in Colombia, South America, for between $1,350 and $3,900 per pound and $6,600 and $11,350 (80% pure) per pound in the United States at the wholesale level. Once cut and diluted (cocaine is often mixed with sugar and other substances), the American retail price of powdered cocaine skyrockets to between $36,300 and $136,000 per pound. Crack cocaine sells for between $5 and $10 per vial, each of which contains several small "rocks." The Office of National Drug Control Policy (ONDCP) estimates that the total annual amount spent on illegal cocaine in the United States is around $18 billion.

Other stimulants include amphetamines with street names like "bennies," "speed," and "uppers." Amphetamines act to produce mental alertness and increase the ability to concentrate. They are used medically to treat narcolepsy, obesity, and some forms of brain dysfunction. They also cause talkativeness, reduce fatigue, and result in wakefulness. Abuse produces irritability, overexhaustion, and—in cases of prolonged abuse—psychosis and death from cardiac arrest.

Depressants

The depressant family includes barbiturates, sedatives, and tranquilizers with names such as Nembutal®, Seconal®, Phenobarbital®, Quaalude, Sopor, Valium®,

Librium®, Thorazine®, and Equanil®. Depressants are used legitimately to obtain release from anxiety, for the treatment of psychological problems, and as mood elevators. Illegitimate users employ such substances to produce intoxication and to counter the effects of other drugs or in the self-treatment of drug withdrawal.

Depressants are often prescribed by physicians seeking to control patients' stress-related symptoms and to induce relaxed states and even sleep. Individuals

FIGURE 11.2 Differences in Drug Categories and Characteristic Controlled Substances.

Drugs	*Federal Schedule*	*Names*	*Physical Dependency*	*Psychological Dependency*
STIMULANTS				
Cocaine	II	coke, flake, snow	Possible	High
Amphetamines	II, III	Benzedrine, Dexedrine, Ice	Possible	High
Methylphenidate	II	Ritalin	Possible	High
DEPRESSANTS				
Cloral hydrate	IV	Noctec, Somnos	Moderate	Moderate
Barbiturates	II, III, IV	Amobarbital, Phenobarbital, Secobarbital	High-Mod.	High-Mod.
Methaqualone	II	Optimil, Parest, Quaalude, Sopor	High	High
Benzodiazepines	IV	Ativan, Azene, Clonopin, Dalmane, Diazepam, Librium, Valium	Low	Low
CANNABIS				
Marijuana	I	pot, Acapulco gold, grass, reefer, weed	Unknown	Moderate
Hashish	I	hash, hash oil	Unknown	Moderate
NARCOTICS				
Opium	II, III, V	Dover's Powder, Paregoric	High	High
Morphine	II, III	Morphine, Pectoral syrup	High	High
Codeine	II, III, V	Codeine, Robitussin A-C	Moderate	Moderate
Heroin	I	Diacetylmorphine, horse, smack	High	High
Methadone	II	Dolophine, Methadone, Methadose	High	High
HALLUCINOGENS				
LSD	I	acid, microdot	None	Unknown
Mescaline, peyote	I	Mesc, buttons, cactus	None	Unknown
Amphetamine variants	I	2, 5-DMA, PMA, STP MDA, MMDA, TMA	Unknown	Unknown
Phencyclidine	II	PCP, angel dust, hog	Unknown	High
STEROIDS				
Anabolic steroids	III	Anabolin, Androlone, Durabolin, Kabolin	Low	High
INHALANTS				
Various common substances		Laughing gas, nitrous oxide, gasoline, freon toluene, amyl nitrite, butyl nitrite, acetate	Low	High

who have experienced recent traumatic events, for example, may find that the temporary use of prescribed depressants helps to alleviate the psychic distress that they would otherwise feel. If abused, however, depressants may lead to psychological dependence and to addiction.

Cannabis

The cannabis category includes marijuana, hashish, cannabis plants, sinsemilla, and hashish oil—all of which are collectively referred to as "marijuana." Marijuana is a relatively mild, nonaddictive drug with limited hallucinogenic properties. The primary active chemical in marijuana is tetrahydrocannabinol. Although legitimate uses for cannabis have not been fully recognized, some research suggests that the substance can be used in the treatment of pain, and glaucoma, and as a supplement to cancer chemotherapy—in which cannabis appears to have the ability to control the nausea associated with chemotherapy. Marijuana is used illegitimately to induce states of euphoria, gaiety, detachment, relaxation, intoxication, and focused awareness. Time distortion, increased sex drive, enhanced appetite, uncontrollable giddiness, and short-term memory loss tend to accompany its use.

Street names for marijuana include "pot," "grass," and "weed." Most marijuana is smoked in the form of dried leaves, stems, and flowers of the marijuana plant (or, more accurately, the Indian hemp plant), although processed marijuana "oil" and the cake form of hashish are also widely available. Hashish is made from resins found on the surface of the female marijuana plant and is considerably more potent than other forms of cannabis.

Most of the marijuana consumed in the United States is either grown within the country or comes from Mexico. Although one marijuana plant produces between 1 and 2 pounds of dried leaves and stems, marijuana is generally sold to consumers in 1 ounce bags. A pound of dried marijuana costs dealers between $450 and $2,700, while users pay between $25 and $200 per one ounce bag depending upon the reputed potency of the particular variety they are purchasing. Single marijuana cigarettes, sometimes called "joints" or "reefers," sell for around $1 to $5. Overall, the Office of National Drug Control Policy estimates that the total amount spent on illegal marijuana in the United States is around $9 billion annually.

Narcotics

Narcotics, including drugs such as opium, morphine, heroin, methadone, codeine, and dilaudid, have a number of legitimate uses including pain relief, antidiarrheal action, and cough suppression. Street use of these drugs is intended to induce pleasure, euphoria, a lack of concern, and general feelings of well-being. The use of narcotics produces drowsiness and relaxation, accompanied by a dreamlike state of reverie. Narcotics are thought to mimic or enhance the activity of endorphins, which are proteins produced by the brain and which control pain and influence other subjective experiences.

Heroin and morphine, which are generally sold as white powdered substances, are derived from opium and usually injected into the body, although they may also be smoked or eaten. Sometimes users inject these drugs under the skin, a practice called "skin-popping," but most addicts prefer direct intravenous injections for the strong and immediate effects produced.

One pound of 70–90% pure heroin sells in Southeast Asia for between $2,700 and $5,000. At the wholesale level in the United States the same substance brings between $40,000 and $110,000 per pound, while midlevel dealers pay up to $270,000 for that amount. Dealers, however, "cut" the drug, effectively diluting it with a variety of other substances. One writer describes it this way: "Once in the United States, heroin may be stepped on (diluted) as many as seven to ten times. What started out in some remote Asian laboratory as 99% pure heroin is cut with lactose (milk sugar, a by-product of milk processing), quinine, cornstarch, or almost any other powdery substance that will dissolve when heated...[u]ltimately, the heroin sold on the street is less than 10% pure and sometimes as little as 1% to 4% pure."[15] Street-level dealers sell diluted heroin in 0.1 gram single-dose bags for as much as $46 each, which translates into an effective retail price of more than $2 million per pound for imported heroin. The ONDCP estimates that the total amount spent on heroin in the United States is around $12 billion annually.

Although narcotics, including heroin, tend to be highly toxic when taken in large doses, frequent users build up tolerances and require larger and larger doses for the desired effects to be induced. Physical addiction may result in drug dependence, and symptoms of withdrawal may appear if the drug is not available. Withdrawal symptoms include nervousness, restlessness, severe abdominal cramps, watery eyes, nasal discharge, and—in later stages—vomiting, diarrhea, weight loss, and pain in the large muscles of the body, especially the back and legs.

Hallucinogens

Hallucinogens, which include drugs such as LSD (lysergic acid diethylamide), PCP, peyote, mescaline, psilocybin, MDA, MDMA, belladonna, and mandrake, have no official legitimate use. Street use of these drugs is intended to produce "mind expansion," hallucinations, creative mental states, and perceptual distortions—all of which have been popularly called "psychedelic experiences," or "trips."

The exact process by which hallucinogens act upon the mind is not known, and the effects of such drugs may be unpredictable. LSD "trips," for example, may produce pleasurable hallucinations and sensations, or may result in frightening experiences for the user. During such episodes uncontrollable nightmarish phantasms may appear to the user who is no longer able to distinguish external reality from his or her own subjective states.

Anabolic Steroids

Anabolic steroids include the substances nandrolene, oxandrolene, oxymetholone, and stanozolol. Steroids are used legitimately for purposes of weight gain; the treatment of arthritis, anemia, and connective tissue disorder; and in the battle against certain forms of cancer. Some body builders, professional athletes, and others, however, seeking to build body bulk and to increase strength have created a secondary market in steroids that has resulted in their ready availability through illegal channels of distribution.

Inhalants

Inhalants include a wide variety of psychotropic substances such as nitrous oxide, carbon tetrachloride, amyl nitrite, butyl nitrite, chloroform, freon, acetate, and toluene. They are highly volatile substances which generally act as central nervous system depressants. Inhalants are found in fast-drying glues, nail polish remover, room and car deodorizers, lighter fluid, paint thinner, kerosene, cleaning fluids, households sealants, and gasoline. While some of these substances, like ether, nitrous oxide, amyl nitrate, and chloroform, have legitimate medical uses, others are employed only to produce a sense of lightheadedness often described in colloquial terms as a "rush." The use of inhalants "can disturb vision, impair judgment, and reduce muscle and reflex control."[16]

Inhalants have been called "gateway drugs," or substances that initiate young people into illicit drug usage. Easy access to these chemicals is assured by the fact that few inhalants are subject to legislative control beyond simple administrative regulations. In fact, most inhalants are easily available, being found on household shelves, in hardware stores, and on the shelves of general merchandisers.

According to self-reports from members of surveyed households who are 12 years of age or older, 11.3 million Americans have used inhalants at some point in their lives, and 1.2 million report the use of such drugs within the past month.[17] Among high school seniors, only marijuana use is more widespread than the use of inhalants.[18] Eighteen percent of high school seniors report having experimented with some form of inhalant prior to graduation.

Pharmaceutical Diversion and Dangerous Drugs

Pharmaceutical diversion the process by which legitimately manufactured controlled substances are diverted for illicit use.

The **pharmaceutical diversion** and subsequent abuse of legitimately manufactured controlled substances is a major source of drug-related addictions or dependencies, medical emergencies, and deaths. Diversion occurs through illegal prescribing by physicians and illegal dispensing by pharmacists and their assistants. "Doctor shopping," the process of finding a physician who is overly liberal in the type and amount of drug prescribed and visitations to numerous physicians for the purpose of collecting large quantities of prescribed medicines are practices which exacerbate the problem. Depressants, including sedatives, tranquilizers, and antianxiety drugs (especially Xanax® and Valium®), along with stimulants and anabolic steroids constitute the types of drugs most often diverted.

A number of drugs, especially those which fall into the "designer" category, are manufactured in clandestine drug facilities, which are sometimes called "basement laboratories" because they are operated by individuals out of personal homes and apartments. As the National Institute of Justice notes, "[c]landestine laboratories range from small crude operations in sheds, bathtubs, mobile homes, boats, and motel rooms to highly sophisticated operations with professional quality laboratory glassware and equipment."[19] **Designer drugs** are so named because "they are new substances designed by slightly altering the chemical makeup of other illegal or tightly controlled drugs."[20] Designer drugs such as "Nexus," a new and reputed aphrodisiac, usually fall under the rubric "synthetic narcotic," or "synthetic hallucinogen."

Designer drugs new substances designed by slightly altering the chemical makeup of other illegal or tightly controlled drugs.

Designer drugs require the use of a number of specifically identifiable chemicals in their production. Similarly, opium, cocaine, and other naturally occurring psychoactive substances necessitate the use of chemicals in step-by-step processes that leave them ready for street-level distribution and consumption. The Chemical Diversion and Trafficking Act of 1988 (CDTA) placed the distribution of eight essential chemicals used in the production of illicit drugs, as well as twelve "precursor chemicals" (from which drugs could be made), under federal control. The CDTA also regulates the distribution of machines which can produce pharmaceutical capsules and tables. In 1994 the Domestic Chemical Diversion Control Act[21] added thirty-two other chemicals to the list, bringing the total number of drug-related chemical substances under federal control to fifty-two.

Reflecting the high social cost of drugs, fans in Seattle mourn the death of Kurt Cobain, after *Nirvana's* leader singer committed suicide. Drugs were once called "the love of Cobain's brief life."[22] *Grant M. Haller/Sygma.*

DRUG TRAFFICKING

Drug trafficking includes manufacturing, distributing, dispensing, importing, and exporting (or possession with intent to do the same) a controlled substance or a counterfeit substance.

In everyday usage the phrase "drug trafficking" can have a variety of meanings. On the one hand, it can refer to smuggling, that is, the illegal shipment of controlled substances across state and national boundaries. On the other, it can mean the sale of controlled substances. Hence, in colloquial usage, one who "trafficks" in drugs may simply sell them. Technically speaking, **drug trafficking** "includes manufacturing, distributing, dispensing, importing, and exporting (or possession with intent to do the same) a controlled substance or a counterfeit substance."[23] Federal law enforcement agencies, in their effort to reduce trafficking, focus largely on the prevention of smuggling and on the apprehension of smugglers.

Drugs like cocaine, heroin, and LSD are especially easy to smuggle, since relatively small quantities of the drugs can be adulterated with other substances to provide large amounts of illicit commodities at street level. Figure 11.3 provides a map of major cocaine trafficking routes (sometimes called "pipelines") into the United States. Most cocaine entering the United States originates in the Western hemisphere, especially in the South American nations of Colombia, Ecuador, Peru, and Bolivia. Transportation routes into the United States include (1) shipment overland from South America through Central America, (2) direct shipments to U.S. ports concealed in containers or packed with legitimate products, (3) flights into the United States via commercial airplanes or in private aircraft, and (4) airdrops to vessels waiting offshore for smuggling into the United States.

Most cocaine entering the United States is smuggled aboard maritime vessels. Fishing vessels with hidden compartments, cargo ships plying international waters, and even private submersibles have all been used in smuggling operations. In 1993, for example, Colombian authorities seized a 22-foot-long semisubmersible vessel engaged in smuggling cocaine into Puerto Rico, where it was scheduled for repackaging and shipment to the continental United States. Recent large seizures of cocaine include 5.6 metric tons discovered hidden in a cargo vessel in the port of Miami and 3.8 tons found by the U.S. Customs Service in a cargo container in Miami in 1994.[24]

Some trafficking methods are highly creative. As one DEA reports says, "[u]nusual methods of concealment encountered in 1993 included cocaine concealed in a shipment of beach towels, inside spools of industrial thread, inside cans of lard, sealed within quartz crystals, in drums of fruit pulp, in fish meal, and in avocado paste. In addition, U.S. Customs Service and U.S. Fish and Wildlife officers seized several kilograms of cocaine from within a shipment of boa constrictors. The cocaine, wrapped in condoms, had been inserted into the snakes' intestines."[25]

Heroin signature program a DEA program that identifies the geographic source area of a heroin sample through the detection of specific chemical characteristics in the sample peculiar to the source area.

The DEA tracks heroin trafficking through its **heroin signature program** (HSP), which identifies the geographic source area of a heroin sample through the laboratory detection of specific chemical characteristics in the sample which are peculiar to a source area. The signature program employs special chemical analyses to identify and measure chemical constituents of a sample of seized heroin. Results of the HSP program for 1993 showed that 68% of heroin in the United States originated in Southeast Asia, 15% in South America, 9% in Southwest Asia, and 8% in Mexico. According to the DEA, most heroin originating in Southeast Asia is produced in the Golden Triangle area comprised of Burma, Laos, and Thai-

FIGURE 11.3 Cocaine Trafficking: Major Countries of Origin and Routes of Transportation into the United States. *Source*: Bureau of Justice Statistics, *Drugs, Crime and the Justice System: A National Report* (Washington,D.C.: U.S. Government Printing Office, December, 1992), p. 47.

land. Shipments are "controlled by ethnic Chinese criminal groups…while U.S.-based ethnic Chinese traffickers with links to these international criminal groups (are) the most prolific importers and distributors of Southeast Asian heroin"[26] within the United States. HSP data for 1993 were based upon examination of over eight hundred random samples, including some obtained through undercover purchases, domestic seizures, and seizures made at U.S. ports of entry.

DRUGS AND CRIME

While the manufacture, sale, transportation, and use of controlled substances is itself criminal, drugs and crime are also linked in other ways. The person so habituated to the use of illegal drugs that they steal to support their "habit," the drug importer who kills a rival dealer, and the offender who commits a criminal act due to the stimulation provided by drugs, all provide examples of how drug abuse may be linked to other forms of criminal activity.

Drug-defined crimes violations of laws prohibiting or regulating the possession, use, or distribution of illegal drugs.

Drug-related crimes crimes in which drugs contribute to the offense (excluding violations of drug laws).

Recognizing these differences, the Bureau of Justice Statistics distinguishes between drug-defined and drug-related crimes. **Drug-defined crimes** are "violations of laws prohibiting or regulating the possession, use, or distribution of illegal drugs."[27] The costs of all drug-defined crime, says the BJS, is directly attributable to illegal drug use. **Drug-related crimes,** on the other hand, "are not violations of drug laws but are crimes in which drugs contribute to the offense." Illegal drug use, says BJS, "is related to offenses against people and property in three major ways: (1) pharmacologically drugs can induce violent behavior, (2) the cost of drugs induces some users to commit crimes to support their drug habits, [and] (3) violence often characterizes relations among participants in the drug distribution system."[28]

According to the U.S. Department of Justice, "there is extensive evidence of the strong relationship between drug use and crime." This relationship can be summarized in the following three points, each of which, the Department says, is supported "by a review of the evidence":[29]

- Drug users report greater involvement in crime and are more likely than nonusers to have criminal records.
- Persons with criminal records are much more likely than ones without criminal records to report being drug users.
- Crimes rise in number as drug use increases.

One initiative that attempts to measure the degree to which criminal offenders use controlled substances is the Drug Use Forecasting Program (DUF) of the National Institute of Justice. Begun in 1987, DUF measures drug use among persons coming into contact with the criminal justice system by tracking drug use among booked arrestees in twenty-four cities across the nation. DUF data are collected in booking facilities using trained local staff members who obtain voluntary and anonymous urine specimens and interviews from samples of booked arrestees. DUF methodologists report that volunteerism runs high, with "more than 90% of the arrestees approached agreeing to be interviewed. Approximately 80% of those interviewed provide urine specimens."[30]

Collected urine specimens are sent to a central laboratory for analysis. All specimens are analyzed for the presence of ten drugs: cocaine, opiates, marijuana, PCP, methadone, benzodiazepines (for example, Valium), methaqualone, propoxyphene (i.e., Darvon-like substances), barbiturates, and amphetamines. Tests can detect the use of most drugs within the past two to three days, while marijuana and PCP use can be detected as long as three weeks after ingestion.

Recent DUF data show that male arrestees are very likely to test positive for the presence of one or more drugs. In the most recent survey, findings ranged from a low of 47% of male arrestees in Phoenix, Arizona, who tested positive for the presence of any drug in their system, to a high of 78% of males arrestees in Philadelphia who showed the presence of at least one drug. Drug use among female arrestees ranged from a low of 44% in San Antonio to 85% in Manhattan. The average rate of detected drug use among males was approximately 60%, while it was slightly higher among females arrestees who were tested. The drug most commonly detected was cocaine, while propoxyphene, barbiturates, and methaqualone were found in relatively few (less than 3%) arrestees.

According to the NIJ "drug use among arrestees remains at high levels, especially for cocaine. In many sites," says the report, "cocaine use has shown an increase."[31] The DUF report concludes that "examination of drug use trends among arrestees across the United States clearly shows that drug use continues to be a serious problem. Although some success has been noted in decreasing drug use among the general population, DUF data indicate that these successes have not reached those persons who are coming into contact with the criminal justice system."[32]

Other information on drug use by offenders at the time of the offense comes from the NCVS, which gathers data from victims of violent crimes who are asked to report their impressions about offenders. In 1991, for example, 33% of all victims of violent crime included in the survey reported that they believed their assailants were under the influence of drugs or alcohol at the time the crime occurred. Another 46% of victims stated that they did not know whether the offender was under the influence of drugs.

Offender self-reports have also been gathered by Bureau of Justice Statistics researchers and show that, among jail inmates,[33]

- 44% used illegal drugs in the month before the offense for which they were arrested.
- 30% used illegal drugs daily in the month before the offense.
- 27% used illegal drugs at the time of the offense.
- cocaine and crack cocaine were the drugs most commonly abused by jail inmates.

Surveys of state prison inmates reveal much the same pattern. Sixty-one percent of inmates in state prisons say that they or their victims were under the influence of drugs or alcohol at the time of the offense, 50% report having been under the influence of alcohol or drugs, and 30% say their victims were under the influence of alcohol or drugs.[34] Nearly 40% of youths incarcerated in long-term state-operated facilities report having been under the influence of illegal drugs at the time of their offense.[35] When self-reports of jail and state prison inmates are evaluated to determine the proportion reporting having ever used drugs, nearly 80% of adult inmates report such use, while 83% of incarcerated juveniles say they have used drugs at some point in their lives.[36]

Surveys of drug-related crime have also been conducted in recent years. Recent interviews with adult prison inmates, for example, have determined that

24% of female inmates committed their offenses to get money to buy drugs, while 16% of male inmates say the same thing. The same surveys show that around 30% of all robberies, burglaries, and thefts are committed to obtain drug money, while 5% of murders result from such criminal activities.[37]

Illegal Drugs and Official Corruption

Sometimes the corrupting influence of drugs and drug money extends beyond street crime and street criminals. Lucrative drug profits have the potential to corrupt official agents of control as the recent Mollen Commission study of police corruption in New York City found. The Mollen Commission, headed by former Judge Milton Mollen, made its report on July 6, 1994, and found that the severity of police corruption in New York City has worsened drastically since previous investigations into the subject. According to the report, "police have crossed the line into actively engaging in criminal activity including robbery, drug dealing and even a killing."[38] It called today's corrupt police, "criminals in blue uniforms," contrasting the severity of their illegal activity with prior forms of corruption that simply involved turning a "blind eye" to crime.

Much illegal police activity was found to be drug related, with drug monies providing powerful incentives toward corruption. The report found that police officers in certain precincts banded together and regularly robbed drug dealers, sold drugs, and conducted illegal raids to confiscate additional drugs for personal gain. The commission found that "some precincts were much more prone to corruption, particularly in minority communities because of high levels of drug activ-

Vast amounts of money associated with the illegal drug trade have the potential to corrupt public officials and agents of control. *Steve Starr/ Saba Press Photos, Inc.*

Houston police remove 600 pounds of marijuana found in false tops of trucks brought from Mexico. *Gregg Smith/ Saba Press Photos, Inc.*

ity within their borders....Unlike 20 years ago, when an officer took bribes it was to turn his head away from crime. This time these (bad) cops are the criminals," Judge Mollen said, commenting on the commission's report.[39]

It is not only police officers who face the threat of corruption from the lucrative monetary rewards to be reaped from dealing drugs. In July 1994, for example, twenty District of Columbia corrections officers and employees were given stiff prison sentences after being convicted of drug smuggling activities. Even with those convictions, however, few believed that corruption in the District's prisons had been ended. U.S. District Judge Royce Lamberth, who sentenced the former officers, observed that "even as the latest prison guard drug ring was being shut down...corruption continues today as I sit in this courtroom."

SOCIAL POLICY AND DRUG ABUSE

The history of drug control policy in the United States is as interesting as it is diverse. According to some authors, "[a]lcohol prohibition marked the first legal recognition of problems emanating from substance abuse."[40] In reality, however, the 18th Amendment, which was ratified in 1919 and prohibited the manufacture, sale, and transportation of alcoholic beverages, was preceded by the Harrison Act, the first major piece of federal antidrug legislation. The Harrison Act, passed by Congress in 1914, required anyone dealing in opium, morphine, heroin, and cocaine, or their derivatives to register with the federal government and to pay a $1.00 per year tax. The act, however, only authorized the registration of physicians, pharmacists, and other medical professionals, effectively outlawing "street" use of these drugs. However, by 1920 court rulings severely curtailed the use of heroin for medical purposes, saying its prescribed use only prolonged addiction. Hence, the beginning of complete federal prohibition over at least one major drug can be traced to that time.

In 1937 passage of the Marijuana Tax Act effectively outlawed marijuana, a federal stance that was reinforced by the Boggs Act of 1951. The Boggs Act also mandated deletion of heroin from the list of medically useful substances and required its complete removal from all medicines. The 1956 Narcotic Control Act increased penalties for drug traffickers and made the sale of heroin to anyone under age 18 a capital offense.

The most comprehensive federal legislation to address controlled substances to date is the 1970 Comprehensive Drug Abuse Prevention and Control Act. Title II of that act is referred to as the Controlled Substances Act (CSA). It established five schedules that classify psychoactive drugs according to their medical use, degree of psychoactivity and adjudged potential for abuse. Table 11.3 outlines the various drug schedules under federal law. Penalties under federal law are generally more severe for possession of higher category substances (category one being the highest), but vary by amount possessed, the purpose of possession (for sale or personal use, etc.), and the offender's criminal history.

Another federal initiative, the 1988 Anti-Drug Abuse Act, proclaimed the goal of a "Drug-Free America by 1995." Although many of the act's provisions, like its preamble that contained the "drug-free" phrase, were more rhetoric than substance, the act substantially increased penalties for recreational drug users and made weapons purchases by suspected drug dealers more difficult. The law also denied federal benefits—ranging from loans (such as federal student loans) to contracts and licenses—to federal drug convicts. In 1991 steroids were added to the list of Schedule III controlled substances by congressional action.

Recent Legislation and Current Policy

The far-reaching Violent Crime Control and Law Enforcement Act of 1994 included a number of drug-related provisions. Specifically the act:

- Authorized $1 billion in Edward Byrne Memorial Formula Grant Program monies to reduce or prevent juvenile drug and gang-related activity in federally assisted, low-income housing areas.
- Authorized $1.6 billion for direct funding to localities around the country for anticrime efforts, such as drug treatment, education, and jobs, through a legislative subsection known as the Local Partnership Act.
- Allocated other drug treatment monies for the creation of state and federal programs to treat drug-addicted prisoners. The act also created a treatment schedule for all drug-addicted federal prisoners and requires drug testing of federal prisoners upon release.
- Provided $1 billion for drug court programs for nonviolent offenders with substance abuse problems. Participants will be intensively supervised, given drug treatment, and subjected to graduated sanctions—ultimately including prison terms—for failing random drug tests.
- Provided stiff new penalties for drug crimes committed by gang members and tripled penalties for using children to deal drugs near schools and playgrounds.
- Established "Drug Free Zones" by increasing penalties for drug dealing in areas near playgrounds, schoolyards, video arcades, and youth centers.

TABLE 11.3

SCHEDULED DRUGS UNDER FEDERAL LAW

Schedule	*Abuse Potential*	*Examples of Drugs Covered*	*Some of the Effects*	*Medical Use*
I	Highest	heroin, LSD, hashish, marijuana, designer drugs, methaqualone	Unpredictable effects, severe psychological or physical dependence, or death	No accepted use; some are legal for limited research use only
II	High	morphine, PCP, codeine, cocaine, methadone, Demerol, benzedrine, dexedrine	May lead to severe psychological or physical dependence	Accepted use with restrictions
III	Medium	codeine with aspirin or Tylenol, some amphetamines, anabolic steroids	May lead to moderate or low physical dependence or high psychological dependence	Accepted use
IV	Low	Darvon, Talwin, phenobarbital, Equanil miltown, Librium, diazepam	May lead to limited physical or psychological dependence	Accepted use
V	Lowest	Over-the-counter or prescription compounds with codeine, Lomatil, Robitussin A-C	May lead to limited physical or psychological dependence	Accepted use

Source: Adapted from DEA, *Drugs of Abuse*, 1989.

- Increased penalties for drug dealing near public housing projects.
- Expanded the federal death penalty to include large-scale drug trafficking and mandated life imprisonment for criminals convicted of three drug-related felonies.
- Created special penalties for drug use and drug trafficking in prison.

Throughout the years, major policy initiatives in the battle against illicit drugs have included (1) antidrug legislation and strict enforcement, (2) interdiction, (3) forfeiture, (4) crop control, and (5) antidrug education and treatment.

Current policy is much in keeping with calls for the strict enforcement of antidrug abuse laws, although much enforcement emphasis in recent years has shifted from targeting users to the arrest, prosecution, and incarceration of the distributors of controlled substances. Similar shifts have occurred among employers, some of whom no longer wait for drug-influenced behavioral problems to arise, but instead require routine drug testing as a condition of employment and retention.

In 1993 nearly 1 million persons were arrested for drug law violations throughout the United States.[41] One-third of all arrests, however, were for the sale and/or manufacture of controlled substances. While the percentage of arrests for drug distribution increased by more than 130% between 1983 and 1993, the number of arrests for drug possession increased by only about 40% during the same period. Enforcement activities within the United States also include the seizure and destruction of illegal drugs and clandestine drug laboratories. In 1993 domestic seizures of marijuana and cannabis-related substances totaled 142.9 metric tons, while 270 clandestine laboratories were seized and destroyed throughout the country. Of the total number of laboratories seized, 218 were involved in the manufacture of the stimulant methamphetamine.

Interdiction an international drug control policy which aims to stop drugs from entering the country illegally.

Interdiction is an international drug control policy which aims to stop drugs from entering the country illegally. In 1993, for example, U.S. agents arrested 232 Colombian couriers attempting to smuggle drugs into the United States aboard commercial airlines.[42] Most arrests occurred at international airports in Miami and New York. In 1994 the Federal-wide Drug Seizure System (FDSS) reported that 1993 domestic cocaine seizures totaled 111 metric tons. Foreign seizures of cocaine, most of which occurred in source countries and along trafficking routes were reported to exceed 155 metric tons of the drug. Heroin seizures in 1993 amounted to 1.4 metric tons domestically and another 23 metric tons internationally. Such amounts, however, represent mere drops in the proverbial bucket. DEA estimates of worldwide opium production, for example, exceeded 4,400 metric tons in 1994, while cocaine production in South American source countries was estimated at around 805 metric tons—most of which eventually found its way into the United States.[43]

A third strategy, crop control, has both international and domestic aspects. During 1993, for example, 4.04 million cultivated marijuana plants were seized throughout the United States, while the Colombian National Police and Colombian armed forces combined efforts to destroy cocaine fields and cocaine processing laboratories. Similarly, Mexican officials reported the eradication of 7,800 hectares of opium poppies in 1993, while Pakistan reported the destruction of 856 hectares.

Asset forfeiture the authorized seizure of money, negotiable instruments, securities, or other things of value. In federal antidrug laws: the authorization of judicial representatives to seize all moneys, negotiable instruments, securities, or other things of value furnished or intended to be furnished by any person in exchange for a controlled substance, and all proceeds traceable to such an exchange.

Forfeiture, also called **asset forfeiture**, is another strategy in the battle against illegal drugs. Forfeiture is a legal procedure that authorizes judicial representatives to seize "all moneys, negotiable instruments, securities, or other things of value furnished or intended to be furnished by any person in exchange for a controlled substance...[and] all proceeds traceable to such an exchange."[44] Unfortunately, asset forfeiture laws have at times been abused by enforcement agencies. As one writer explains it: "There have, in the past, been cases where innocent parties have had property seized and had to spend a considerable amount on lawyers' fees to get it back. Parents have had homes confiscated because children sold drugs there. Farms have been taken even though the owners were acquitted of growing marijuana on an isolated part of the property."[45] Recent U.S. Supreme Court decisions, however, now require that property owners be given notice of any pending seizures, as well as the opportunity to respond to government charges.[46] The Court has also acted to restrain seizures of property far more valuable than the proceeds of the underlying crime with which the property owner has been charged.[47]

Antidrug education and drug treatment, the final strategies we will discuss in this section, have gained significantly in popularity over the past decade. Those favoring educational attacks on the problem of drug abuse are quick to claim that other measures have not been effective in reducing the incidence of abuse. Antidrug education programs often reach targeted individuals through schools, corporations, and media campaigns. A short TV commercial of a few years ago, for example, recited the lines; "This is your brain. This is your brain on drugs," while showing a picture of an egg, followed by an egg sizzling in a frying pan. School-based programs are numerous, with many being built upon the principles developed by Project D.A.R.E. D.A.R.E., which stands for Drug Abuse Resistance Education, began as a joint effort of the Los Angeles Police Department and the Los Angeles Unified School District in 1983. D.A.R.E. uses uniformed police officers and other "experts" to explain issues of drug abuse to school-aged children and attempts to build resistance to what might otherwise be portrayed by youthful peers as attractive drug-related activities. D.A.R.E. focuses on developing competent decision-making skills, combating negative forms of peer pressure, and meaningful alternatives to drug usage.

Recent policy initiatives at the federal level have begun to once again emphasize treatment and the prevention of drug abuse through education. In 1994, for example, President Bill Clinton announced "a new national attack on drug addiction."[48] The program was aimed largely at hard-core drug users, although it also involved a three-pronged approach including (1) working with countries that produce drugs to go after kingpins, (2) destroying drug cartels, and (3) using better technology and "smarter efforts" in interdiction. In the president's words "this strategy, does more than ever before to help hard-core drug users into treatment programs where they belong."[49] The new program represented at least a partial shift away from interdiction and a movement toward greater prevention, education, and treatment. Monies budgeted for interdiction efforts under the new program were reduced by $94 million below 1994 levels. Details of the president's program included[50]

- Expansion of overall "drug demand reduction efforts," including prevention and treatment by $826.5 million, up 18.2%, to $5.4 billion.
- Increased drug prevention funds, up 28%, to $2.1 billion.
- Raising federal drug treatment funds by 14.3% to $2.9 billion.
- Increased domestic antidrug criminal justice funds by 4% to $5.9 billion.
- Increased international operations within drug-producing and transit countries by 21.7%, to $427.8 million.
- Reducing interdiction funding by 7.3%, to $1.2 billion.

Other proposals by the Clinton administration include a welfare reform plan that "would require substance abuse treatment as a condition for receiving welfare benefits."[51] Under the plan, recipients of Aid to Families with Dependent Children (AFDC) would be required to take jobs limiting their benefits to two years, and "recipients with disabilities, including severe addiction, would be temporarily deferred from work, but would be required to develop 'employability plans' that lead to work."[52]

Policy Consequences

There can be little doubt that the "war on drugs" has been a costly one. In 1991 alone, the federal government's drug control budget exceeded $10.8 billion.[53] Interdiction activities accounted for the lion's share of federal antidrug monies (28.3%), while investigations (18%) and the correctional custody of drug-convicted offenders (17.7%) were the next most expensive areas.[54] When state monies spent on the control of illegal drugs and the enforcement of drugs laws are added to funds spent on antidrug abuse education, and the personal and social costs of drug abuse identified earlier, the total cost of the war on drugs has been enormous.

The drug war has been costly in other ways as well. James Inciardi describes the current situation this way: "As an outgrowth of the U.S. 'war on drugs' during the 1980s and early 1990s, all phases of the criminal justice process have become 'drug driven.'"[55] The same could be said of the nation's system of civil justice. "Although at first blush it may seem unrelated," says writer J. Michael McWilliams, "the 'war on drugs' has had a major impact on the civil justice system at both the state and federal levels. Our courts, like all of government and commerce, are institutions of limited resources. To the extent that court resources must be diverted to deal with the enormous influx of drug prosecutions, these resources are not available to resolve civil matters.... In some jurisdictions, drug cases account for as much as two-thirds of the criminal case filings. America's major cities have been especially affected."[56] In Los Angeles, for example, three quarters of all criminal prosecutions are for drug charges or drug-related crimes.[57]

Strict enforcement has combined with a lock-em-up philosophy to produce astonishingly high rates of imprisonment for drug offenders. The proportion of federal prisoners who are drug offenders rose from 38% in 1986 to 58% in 1991 and, according to the Bureau of Prisons, stands around 62% today.[58] Part of the increase is due to congressional action that, beginning in 1986, required high mandatory minimum sentences in drug cases so that even first offenders were sentenced to long prison terms instead of probation. Today, about 70% of all first offenders in federal prisons are serving drug sentences. This is also true of 85% of illegal immigrants who are federal prisoners and 66% of female federal prisoners.[59]

Alternative Drug Policies

A number of alternative drug control policies have been tried on both state and local levels. Primary among them have been legalization and decriminalization. Both strategies are "based on the assumption that drug abuse will never be eliminated."[60] While **decriminalization** typically reduces criminal penalties associated with the personal possession of a controlled substance, **legalization** eliminates "the laws and associated criminal penalties that prohibit its production, sale, distribution, and possession."[61] Decriminalization enhances personal freedoms in the face of state control, while legalization "is aimed," in part, "at reducing the control that criminals have over the drug trade."[62] Other arguments in favor of legalization include notions that

Decriminalization (of drugs) reduces criminal penalties associated with the personal possession of a controlled substance.

Legalization (of drugs) eliminates the laws and associated criminal penalties that prohibit the production, sale, distribution, and possession of a controlled substance.

- In a free society people should be permitted to do what they want, as long as they don't harm others. Drug use is considered by many to be a "victimless crime," which harms no one other than the user. Existing drug laws, say advocates of legalization, make criminals out of otherwise law-abiding individuals.
- Keeping drugs illegal means that they will continue to be high priced. Legalizing them could greatly lower the price. The expense of illicit drugs, kept artificially high by their illegal status, encourages the commission of many drug-related crimes, such as robbery and burglary, by users seeking to feed their habits. Legalize drugs, some argue, and many other forms of crime will decline.

- Legalizing drugs would also reduce other forms of "vice," such as prostitution, pornography, and gambling, since many such offenses are also committed in an effort to obtain money to purchase high-priced drugs.
- Legalizing drugs would reduce the influence of criminal cartels now closely involved in the production, transportation, and sale of controlled substances.
- The illegal status and associated high cost of drugs indirectly victimizes others, such as the family members of drug abusers, property owners in drug-infested areas, and taxpayers who must foot the enforcement bill. Legalization would end these forms of victimization.
- Drug legalization would dramatically reduce the opportunity for official corruption which is now frequently associated with the illicit drug trade. Enforcement agents, politicians, correctional officers, and representatives of the judiciary would cease to be subject to corrupting influences dependent upon the vast financial resources available to drug trafficking cartels.
- The legalization of drugs would result in increased tax revenues, since drugs could be taxed just as alcohol and cigarettes are today.
- The legalization of drugs would allow for better control over public health issues related to drug use. The spread of AIDS, for example, caused in large part by the use of dirty needles in heroin injection, could be better controlled were sterilized needles to be made legally available. Similarly, drug quality and potency could be monitored and assured, resulting in fewer overdoses and emergency room visits by drug users now uncertain of the chemical composition of the substances they consume.

Were controlled substances to be legalized, they might still be dispensed under controlled conditions (as in liquor stores), and penalties might still accrue to those who used them injudiciously (as while driving a car).

Opponents of legalization argue that reducing official control over psychoactive substances is immoral and socially irresponsible, and would result in heightened costs to society from drug abuse. Lost time from work, drug-induced criminality (especially violence), the loss of personal self-control, and the severing of important social relationships would all accompany legalization such thinkers argue—suggesting that drug legalization would simply increase the types of problems now associated with alcohol abuse. Opponents of legalization also hold that drugs laws are enforceable, and that we are winning the war against drugs. Even if laws are not entirely enforceable is no reason to eliminate them, they say. Laws against murder and rape, for example, have not entirely eliminated such crimes, and there is no conclusive evidence that laws seriously reduce the numbers of crimes committed in any category in which intense needs or emotions are involved as motivating factors.

SUMMARY

Drug abuse has a long and varied history in American society. Policy responses to abuse have been equally diverse. Although recent statistics on drug use show some decline, a hard-core population of illicit drug users remains. Strategies to reduce the flow of illegal drugs into this country, while meeting with some success, are being increasingly supplemented with programs of education and treatment intended to reduce the demand for controlled substances. In the meantime, the potential for official corruption in the face of a lucrative drug trade remains high. Drug traffickers are now in control of vast amounts of money, leading some to suggest that only legalization can solve the secondary problems of drug-related crime, official corruption, and drug-related public health concerns.

DISCUSSION QUESTIONS

1. What are some of the costs of illicit drug usage in the United States today? Which costs can be more easily reduced than others? How would you reduce the cost of illegal drug use?
2. What is the difference between decriminalization and legalization? Should drug use remain illegal? What do you think of the arguments in favor of legalization? Those against?
3. What is the difference between drug-defined and drug-related crime? Which form of crime is more difficult to address? Why?
4. What is "asset forfeiture?" How has asset forfeiture been used in the fight against controlled substances? How have recent U.S. Supreme Court decisions limited federal asset seizures? Do you agree that such limitations were necessary? Why or why not?

NOTES

1 Melanie Goodfellow, "Interpol Head says Drugs a Threat to Democracy," Reuters wire services, October 4, 1994.
2. "Presidential Commission Presents Recommendation on Drug Control," United Press on-line, Northern edition, December 13, 1993.
3. "Perspectives," *Newsweek,* September 12, 1994, p. 19.
4. James Jefferson, "Elders—Drugs," The Associated Press on-line, July 19, 1994.
5. "Elders' Son Out on Bond Pending Appeal," United Press International on-line, Southwest edition, August 30, 1994.
6. Paul Savoy, "When Criminal Rights Go Wrong: Forget Liberal. Forget Conservative. Think Common Sense," *Washington Monthly,* Vol. 21, no. 11 (December 1989), p. 36.
7. U.S. Department of Health and Human Services, *National Household Survey on Drug Abuse* (Washington, D.C.: U.S. Government Printing Office, 1994).
8. Carolyn Skorneck, "Drug Use," The Associated Press, July 20, 1994.
9. Bureau of Justice Statistics, *Drugs and Crime Facts,* 1993 (Washington, D.C: U.S. Department of Justice, August 1994), p. 25.
10. Ibid., p. 26.
11. "Crack Reported to Be Spreading to Small Towns and Rural Areas," *Substance Abuse Letter,* July 19, 1994, p. 4.
12. Mike Cooper, "CDC Charts Impact of AIDS Among Blacks, Hispanics," Reuter's wire services, September 8, 1994.
13. National Narcotics Intelligence Consumers Committee, *The NNICC Report 1993: The Supply of Illicit Drugs to the United States* (Arlington, VA: The Drug Enforcement Administration, 1994), p. 11.

14. Most of the information in the paragraphs that follow is taken from ibid. and Bureau of Justice Statistics, *Drugs, Crime and the Justice System* (Washington, D.C.: U.S. Government Printing Office, December 1992).
15. James A. Inciardi, *The War on Drugs II* (Mountain View, CA: Mayfield, 1992), p. 69.
16. Michael D. Lyman and Gary W. Potter, *Drugs in Society: Causes, Concepts and Control* (Cincinnati: Anderson, 1991), p. 45.
17. Bureau of Justice Statistics, *Drugs, Crime and the Justice System,* p. 26.
18. Ibid., p. 27.
19. Sherry Green, "Preventing Illegal Diversion of Chemicals: A Model Statute" (Washington, D.C.: National Institute of Justice, November 1993), p. 2.
20. Ibid., p. 79.
21. Called the "Domestic Chemical Diversion Control Act of 1993," the provisions of this legislation became effective April 16, 1994.
22. Malcom Jones et al., "The Fallout of the Burnout," *Newsweek,* April 25, 1994, p. 68.
23. As defined by federal law and precedent.
24. National Narcotics Intelligence Consumers Committee, *The NNICC Report 1993.*
25. Ibid., p. 8.
26. Ibid., p. 35.
27. Bureau of Justice Statistics, *Drugs, Crime and the Justice System,* p. 2.
28. Ibid., p. 126.
29. Ibid., p. 2
30. National Institute of Justice, *Drug Use Forecasting 1992 Annual Report: Drugs and Crime in America's Cities* (Washington, D.C.: National Institute of Justice, 1993), p. 2.
31. Ibid., p. 4.
32. Ibid.
33. Bureau of Justice Statistics, *Drug and Crime Facts, 1993,* pp. 4–5.
34. Ibid., p. 6.
35. Ibid.
36. Ibid., p. 7.
37. Ibid., p. 8.
38. United Press International on-line, Northeastern edition, "Study: Bad NYC Cops 'Criminals in Blue,'" July 7, 1994.
39. Ibid.
40. Lyman and Potter, *Drugs in Society,* p. 256.
41. Federal Bureau of Investigation, *Crime in the United States, 1993* (Washington, D.C.: U.S. Government Printing Office, 1994), p. 234.
42. National Narcotics Intelligence Consumers Committee, *The NNICC Report, 1993,* p. 39.
43. Ibid., executive summary.
44. 21 U.S.C., section 881 (a) (6).
45. "Notice, Hearing and Seizure," *Washington Post* on-line, December 16, 1994.
46. *United States* v. *James Daniel Good Real Property,* 114 S. Ct. 492, 126 L. Ed. 2d 490 (1993).
47. *Austin* v. *U.S.,* 113 S. Ct. 2801, 15 L. Ed. 2d 448 (1993).
48. Juliana Gruenwald, "Clinton Unveils Anti-drug Strategy with More Money," United Press International on-line, Northeastern edition, February 9, 1994.
49. Ibid.
50. The Associated Press on-line, "Drug Strategy-Box," February 9, 1994.
51. "Required Treatment Option Included in Welfare Proposal," *Substance Abuse Letter,* July 19, 1994, p. 1.
52. Ibid.
53. Bureau of Justice Statistics, *Drugs, Crime and the Justice System,* p. 128.
54. Ibid.
55. James A. Inciardi, *Criminal Justice* (Orlando, FL: Harcourt Brace Jovanovich, 1993), p. v.
56. J. Michael McWilliams, "Setting the Record Straight: Facts About Litigation Costs and Delay," *Business Economics,* Vol. 27, no. 4 (October 1992), p. 19.
57. Ibid.
58. Bureau of Justice Statistics, *Comparing Federal and State Prison Inmates, 1991* (Washington, D.C.: U.S. Department of Justice, September 1994), and "Who Is in Federal Prison?" *The Washington Post,* October 3, 1994.
59. Ibid.
60. Lyman and Potter, *Drugs in Society,* p. 316.
61. Inciardi, *The War on Drugs II,* p. 239 (note d).
62. Lyman and Potter, *Drugs in Society,* p. 316.

SECURITY
MARC
YANKUS

CHAPTER 12

THE HIGH-TECH OFFENDER

Crime is not static. Existing patterns get displaced by new ones.

—*Georgette Bennett*[1]

As surely as the future will bring new forms of technology, it will bring new forms of crime…

—*Cynthia Manson and Charles Ardai*[2]

The rise of a new kind of economy, never before known, threatening to many, demanding rapid changes in work, life style, and habits, hurls large populations—terrified of the future—into spasms of diehard reaction. It opens cleavages that fanatics rush to fill. It arms all those dangerous minorities who live for crisis in the hopes of catapulting themselves onto the national or global stage and transporting us all into a new Dark Age.

—*Alvin Toffler*[3]

IMPORTANT TERMS

computer crime	computer abuse	computer-related crime
computer virus	computer bulletin board	federal interest computers
audit trail	hacker	phone phreak
TEMPEST	cyberspace	expert systems
the Internet	DNA fingerprinting	data encryption
Daubert standard	threat analysis	

INTRODUCTION

On August 14, 1994, famed terrorist Carlos the Jackal[4] was arrested in the African country of Sudan. Thought to be responsible for causing eighty-three deaths and more than one thousand injuries during terror campaigns in the 1970s and early 1980s, Carlos was once described as the world's most feared revolutionary. His luck ran out with the demise of world communism and the decline of state-supported terrorism.

Following arrest, Carlos was extradited to France where he faced multiple life sentences for killing two French agents in 1975. By the time of arrest, however, Carlos was already out of touch with the new world order and had fallen behind in his knowledge of terrorist tactics and technology. "Carlos is basically an anachronism," said Vincent Cannistraro, former chief of operations and analysis at the CIA's Counter Terrorism Center,[5] describing how the Jackal had been left behind by political, social, and technological advances.

CRIME AND TECHNOLOGY

Terrorism has always been linked to technology, as have other forms of criminality. The con artist who uses telephones in furtherance of a financial scam, the robber who uses a firearm and drives a getaway car, even the murderer who wields a knife—all employ at least rudimentary aspects of technology in the crimes they commit.

Technology which is taken for granted today, was at one time almost unthinkable. Telephones, for example, were created scarcely a century ago, and mass-produced automobiles are newer still. Even firearms are of relatively recent origin if one considers the entire history of humankind, and the manufacture of contemporary cutting instruments would be impossible were it not for an accumulation of technological expertise beginning with the progress in metallurgy that was made during the Iron Age.

As technology advances, it facilitates new forms of behavior. Just as we can be sure that everyday life in the future will be substantially different from life today, so too can we be certain that tomorrow's crimes will differ from those of today. In the future personal crimes of violence and traditional property crimes will undoubtedly continue to occur, while advancing technology will create new and as yet unimaginable opportunities for criminals positioned to take advantage of it and of the power such technology will afford.

A frightening preview of such possibilities can be had in events surrounding the collapse of the Soviet Union a few years ago. The resulting social disorganization in that part of the world made the acquisition of fissionable materials, which had been stolen from former Soviet stockpiles, simple for even relatively small outlaw organizations. In what has since become a nightmare for authorities throughout the world, Middle Eastern terrorist groups are known to be making forceful efforts to acquire former Soviet nuclear weapons as well as the raw materials necessary to manufacture their own bombs. There is also some evidence that nuclear weapons parts may have already been sold to wealthy international drug cartels and organized criminal groups who may now be hoarding them to use as bargaining chips against possible government prosecution. Speaking before the House of Representatives Foreign Affairs Committee in 1994, CIA Director James Woolsey warned of the possibility "that Russian organized crime groups will be able to obtain and sell nuclear weapons or weapons-grade materials as a target of opportunity. We should not rule out the prospect," Woolsey said, "that organized crime could be used as an avenue for terrorists to acquire weapons of mass destruction."[6]

Three faces of the Jackal. Carlos the Jackal, in twenty-year-old police file photos and today (center). *(left) Alain Dejean/Sygma; (middle) Sygma; (right) AP Wirephoto/AP Wide World Photos*

NUCLEAR SMUGGLING

A Bomb Waiting to Go Off

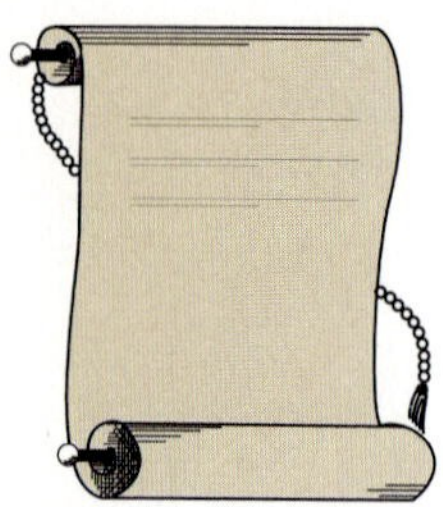

Reports of nuclear material being smuggled out of Russia are alarming U.S. officials and scientists, who say Iraq, Libya and Iran could build atomic bombs if they laid their hands on it.

"There could be enough in circulation for big trouble," says David Albright, president of the Institute for Science and International Security Studies. "But we don't know if we're seeing the tip of the iceberg or the whole thing."

"This is a matter that is serious and ought to be treated with a great deal of urgency by all governments," says State Department Spokesman Mike McCurry. U.S. officials in Moscow officially conveyed the concern on Tuesday, he said.

Germany reports more than half a pound of 87% pure plutonium 239 arrived on a flight from Moscow last week. It was confiscated by police posing as buyers willing to pay $250 million. It was the fourth, and largest, seizure of nuclear material in Germany in the past four months—all of it attributed to Russian sources by German officials.

William Potter, of the Monterey, California, Institute of International Studies, says far more material may have been smuggled than has been caught.

This latest seizure and one back in May of "superpure" material are particularly troubling, he says, because they suggest high-level complicity.

Last week's shipment was in a sophisticated package, and on the same flight as a top Russian energy official, perhaps because smugglers thought they wouldn't be carefully checked traveling with him.

Just the fact they knew his schedule "may be an indication of involvement of senior parties in the nuclear industry," said Potter, who has testified before Congress on nuclear smuggling.

"This isn't a bunch of amateurs," agrees Albright.

Russia has tons of leftover plutonium, enough for 40,000 to 50,000 nuclear bombs, and an accounting system U.S officials say is so loose tons go unaccounted for. The other former Soviet states of Belarus, Ukraine, and Khazakstan also have stockpiles.

Because only a few pounds of plutonium are needed for a bomb, U.S. officials are pressing the Russians, who publicly deny any problem, to redouble security. To a rogue nation seeking atomic weapons, creating the nuclear core is the toughest part. Usually, it takes tens of thousands of people years of work to manufacture the highly radioactive ingredients.

But John Pike of the Federation of American Scientists says a few hundred of the right people, scientists, machinists, and engineers, could quickly construct a bomb if they had the raw materials.

"It ain't going to be six guys in a garage who are going to slap this together in the back of a van," he says. But a nation like Iraq could do it he says.

The publicity surrounding the seizures may be an attempt to show smugglers that they are more likely to be caught in a "sting" than to get rich.

But with thousands of people who worked in Russia's nuclear program facing the lure of easy wealth, the task of perfectly protecting the stockpiles is formidable. And it must be near perfect.

"Even if we have a system that is 99 and $\frac{44}{100}$ths% pure...we're still talking about a few Hiroshimas between friends," Pike says.

Source: Steve Komarow, "Nuclear Smuggling: A Bomb Waiting to Go Off," *USA Today*, August 17, 1994, p. 6A.

QUESTIONS

1. Why has nuclear smuggling become a problem for international law enforcement agencies? What are the potential consequences of such smuggling?
2. What kind of policies might the United States implement which could reduce the threats represented by smuggled nuclear materials?

HIGH TECHNOLOGY AND CRIMINAL OPPORTUNITY

The coming twenty-first century has been described by some as a postindustrial information age. Information, as many now recognize, is vital to the success of any endeavor, and certain forms of information hold nearly incalculable value. Patents on new products, the chemical composition of innovative and effective drugs, corporate marketing strategies, and the financial resources of competing corporations are all forms of information whose illegitimate access might bestow unfair advantages upon unscrupulous competitors. Imagine, for example, the financial wealth and market share which would accrue to the first pharmaceutical company to patent an effective AIDS cure. Imagine, as well, the potential profitability inherent in the information describing the chemical composition of that drug—especially to a competitor who might beat the legitimate originator of the substance to the patent desk, or who might use stolen information in a later bid to challenge patents already issued.

Such a scenario is not far fetched. In 1994, for example, the huge pharmaceutical manufacturer Merck announced[7] that it would file in 1995 with the federal government and the regulatory agencies of twenty-seven other countries a request for permission to market its new medicine, Fosamax. Fosamax, a drug intended to reverse the effects of osteoporosis in postmenopausal women, was described as a corporate centerpiece in the plan to ensure Merck's leadership position among pharmaceutical manufacturers worldwide. The introduction of Fosamax to the pharmaceutical marketplace, along with ongoing clinical trials, was announced only after years of guarded negotiations and developmental research. The carefully crafted introduction was intended to ensure Merck's clear claim to ownership of the chemical compound in Fosamax, which should prove highly profitable for the company. Merck officials estimated the osteoporosis health care market in the United States alone at $10 billion annually.

High-tech criminals seeking illegitimate access to computerized information, and to the databases that contain it, have taken a number of routes. One is the path of direct access, by which office workers, or corporate spies planted as seemingly innocuous employees, violate positions of trust and use otherwise legitimate work-related entry to a company's computer resources to acquire wanted information. Such interlopers typically steal data during business hours, under the guise of normal work routines.

Another path of illegal access is sometimes called computer trespass and involves remote access to targeted machines. Anyone equipped with a home computer and a modicum of knowledge about computer modems, telecommunications, and log-on procedures has easy access to numerous computer systems across the country. Many such systems have few, if any, security procedures in place to thwart would-be invaders. In one recent case, for example, a Silicon Valley software company learned that a fired software developer had been using her telephone to enter its computers.[8] By the time she was caught, the woman had copied million of dollars worth of the company's programs. It was later learned that the stolen software had been slated for illicit transmission to collaborators in Taiwan. Had the scheme succeeded, many thousands of "pirated" copies of the software would have been distributed at great financial loss to the legitimate copyright owners. In a similar scenario, a Florida television news editor was recently arrested after moving to a new job with a different station for allegedly entering the computer of his former employer via telephone and copying researched stories.[9]

More exotic techniques used to steal data stored in computers extend to reading the electromagnetic radiation produced by such machines. Electromagnetic field (EMF) decoders, originally developed for military purposes, are capable of scanning radio-frequency emanations generated by all types of computers. Key

Coincidence or espionage? Before the dissolution of the Soviet Union, Eastern bloc scientists succeeded in building a copy of the American space shuttle, pictured here. Experts suspected that the Soviet model would not have been possible without information stolen from United States research archives. *(left) Phil Sandlin-Canapress Photo Service/AP/Wide World Photos; (right) Terry Renna-Canapress Photo Service/AP/Wide World Photos.*

stroke activity, internal chip-processed computations, disk reads, and the like can all be detected and interpreted at a distance by such sophisticated devices under favorable conditions. Computers which have been secured against such passively invasive practices are rarely found in the commercial marketplace. Those which are available to commercial organizations generally conform to a security standard developed by the United States military called **TEMPEST.**

TEMPEST a standard developed by the U.S. government which requires that electromagnetic emanations from computers designated as "secure" be below levels that would allow radio receiving equipment to "read" the data being computed.

Some criminal perpetrators intend simply to destroy or alter data without otherwise accessing or copying it. Disgruntled employees, mischievous computer **hackers,** business competitors, and others may all have varied degrees of interest in destroying the records or computer capabilities of a company.

Hacker a person who views and uses computers as objects for exploration and exploitation.

In what proved to be the first criminal prosecution of a person accused of creating a **computer virus,** Texas programmer Donald Gene Burleson was arrested in 1988 for allegedly infecting a former employer's computer with a program designed to destroy the information it contained. Since Burleson's arrest, many other would-be imitators have taken similar paths of revenge. According to Richard Baker, author of the respected *Computer Security Handbook,* "the greatest threat to your computers and data comes from inside your company, not outside. The person most likely to invade your computer," says Baker, "is not a gawky youngster in some other part of the country but an employee who is currently on your payroll."

Virus (computer) a set of computer instructions that propagates copies or versions of itself into computer programs or data when it is executed.[10]

Technically speaking, **computer crime,** which involves a wide variety of potential activities, is any violation of a federal or state computer crime statute. A recent estimate by the prestigious accounting firm Ernst & Young puts the cost of computer crime in the United States at between $3 billion and $5 billion a year.[11] According to some experts, "that may be just the beginning." As one technological visionary observes, "Our society is about to feel the impact of the first generation of children who have grown up using computers. The increasing sophistication of hackers suggests that computer crime will soon soar, as members of this new generation are tempted to commit more serious offenses."[12] Table 12.1 lists five major categories of computer crime, along with examples of each.

Computer crime any violation of a federal or state computer crime statute.

> Thou shalt not steal thy neighbor's data.
>
> —*InterLock® security devices advertisement*

While the theft or damage of information represents one area of illegitimate criminal activity, the use of technology in direct furtherance of criminal enterprise constitutes another. Illegal activity based upon advanced technologies is as varied as are the technologies themselves. Nuclear blackmail may represent the extreme technologically based criminal threat, while telephone fraud and phone "phreaking" are examples of low-end crimes that depend upon modern technology for their commission.

Phone phreaks use special dial-up access codes and other restricted technical information to avoid long-distance charges. Some are able to place calls from pay phones, while others fool telephone equipment into billing other callers. As a top telecommunications security expert explains it, "many organizations discover they have been victims of telephone fraud only after their telephone bill arrives in a carton instead of an envelop."[13]

Phone phreak a person who uses switched, dialed-access telephone services as objects for exploration and exploitation.

TABLE 12.1

CATEGORIES OF COMPUTER CRIME

Internal computer crimes
Trojan horses
Logic bombs
Trap doors
Viruses
Telecommunications crimes
Phone phreaking
Hacking
Illegal bulletin boards
Misuse of telephone systems
Computer manipulation crimes
Embezzlements
Frauds
Support of criminal enterprises
Databases to support drug distributions
Databases to support loan sharking
Databases to support illegal gambling
Databases to keep records of illegal client transactions
Money laundering
Hardware/software thefts
Software piracy
Thefts of computers
Thefts of microprocessor chips
Thefts of trade secrets

Source: Adapted from Catherine H. Conly and J. Thomas McEwen, "Computer Crime," *NIJ Reports*, January/February, 1990, p. 3.

As some companies have been surprised to learn, the responsibility for payment of stolen telephone time may rest with them. A year ago, for example, a U.S. district court ordered Jiffy Lube International, Inc., to pay AT&T $55,727 for long-distance calls made by computer hackers who had stolen the company's access codes. Judge Frank Kaufman said the law "squarely places responsibility upon a customer, such as Jiffy Lube, for all calls whether or not authorized...."[14] In effect, Judge Kaufman sent a message to corporations nationwide that they can be held responsible for ensuring the security of their telephone services.

A new form of phone phreaking emerged only a year or two ago. It involves the electronic theft of cellular telephone numbers and access codes. Thieves armed with simple mail-order scanners and low-end computers can "literally grab a caller's phone number and identification number out of the air."[15] Say experts, "Those numbers are [then] used to program computer chips, which are placed inside other cellular phones—or 'clones'—so the long-distance calls appear on the victim's bill."[16] Such high-profile figures as New York Mayor Rudolph Giuliani and his police commissioner have been among recent victims of cellular phone piracy.

Other types of crime may be perpetrated using the telephone. The federal Violent Crime Control and Law Enforcement Act of 1994, for example, made it illegal to use interstate telephone lines in furtherance of telemarketing fraud, and also expanded federal jurisdiction to cover cases of insurance fraud and frauds committed against the elderly even when such crimes do not involve use of the mail or telephone.

$50 MILLION PHONE BILL TIED TO STOLEN CARDS

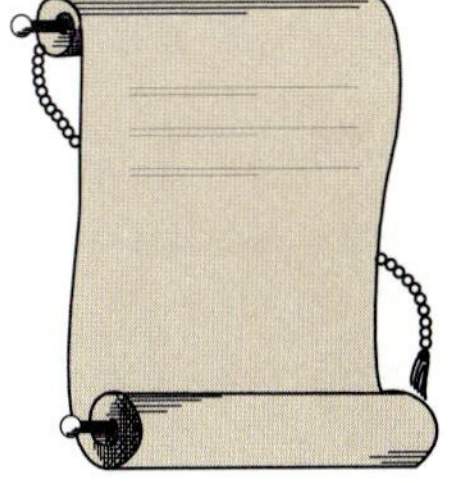

An MCI employee has been charged with running up a $50 million bill using other customers' long-distance calling cards.

MCI said Monday that Ivy James Lay, a switch technician in Cary, N.C., was arrested last week by the Secret Service. He's free on bond.

The company says more than 60,000 calling card numbers were stolen in what may be the largest and most sophisticated case of phone fraud yet uncovered, says MCI spokeswoman Leslie Aun. Customers will not be charged.

The Secret Service says Lay designed computer software to divert and hold calling card numbers from a variety of carriers—including MCI, Sprint and AT&T—that route calls through MCI equipment. Those numbers were sold to computer hackers in the United States and Europe who resold them to other users.

MCI and AT&T suspected fraud last spring, Aun says. The companies called the Secret Service after identifying Lay as a suspect.

"If suddenly 50 calls show up in a 15-minute period to a Third World country that you haven't called before, we're going to suspect something...especially if all those calls are from a pay phone in New York City," Aun says.

Fraud costs the long-distance industry $2 billion to $5 billion annually, Aun says.

Secret Service agents served warrants last week against alleged co-conspirators in Los Angeles, Seattle, Philadelphia, Minneapolis and Chicago.

Max Louarn, 22, of Palma de Mallorca, Spain, was also charged with conspiracy.

Source: Shelly Reese, "$50 Million Phone Bill Tied to Stolen Cards," *USA Today*, October 4, 1994, p. 1A. Copyright 1994, *USA Today*. Reprinted with permission

QUESTIONS

1. The theft of telephone credit cards, or calling card numbers, represents a kind of crime which would not have been possible even a few decades ago. What other new forms of crime have grown out of recent advances in technology?
2. How might telephone calling card security be improved?

Technology and Criminal Mischief

Not all computer crime is committed for financial gain. Some types of computer crime, including the creation and transmission of destructive computer viruses, "worms," and other malicious forms of programming code, might better be classified as criminal mischief. Perhaps not surprisingly, these types of activities are typically associated with young technologically sophisticated male miscreants, seeking a kind of clandestine recognition from their computer-literate peers. Computer crimes committed by youthful and idealistic offenders may represent a new form of juvenile delinquency—one aimed at expressing dissatisfaction with the status quo. As one security expert put it, "kids in the '90s will be like kids in the '60s—they are going to care about social issues, and that caring is going to rub off onto the computer business. A lot of establishment computers are going to get trashed, as kids find a cause and express their concern with non-violent electronic protest."[17]

Viruses have already shown signs of becoming effective terroristlike tools in the hands of young disaffected technonerds intent on attacking or destroying existing social institutions. A computer virus is simply a computer program that is designed to secretly invade computer systems and to modify either the way in which they operate or alter the information they store. Other types of destructive programs are logic bombs, worms, and Trojan horse routines. Distinctions between such programs are based largely either on the way in which they infect targeted machines or on the way in which they behave once they have managed to find their way into a computer. Table 12.2 lists a few of the better-known computer viruses.

Viruses may spread from one machine to another via modem (when files are downloaded), through networks or direct links (such as that provided by popular programs like LapLink Pro), and through the exchange of floppy disks, CD-ROM discs, or magnetic backup media. Contrary to popular belief, viruses can only be hidden inside of executable computer software or in the so-called "boot sectors" of floppy or hard disks. Hence, at least as of this writing, it is impossible for a virus to be hidden inside of text or document files—although coming changes in some proprietary forms of document files may soon provide new targets of opportunity for virus writers.

Perhaps the most insidious forms of destructive programming making the rounds of the computer world today are polymorphic viruses. A polymorphic virus is one which uses advanced encryption techniques to assemble varied (yet entirely operational) clones of itself. Hence, polymorphic viruses have the ability to alter themselves once they have infected a computer. This strategy is effective in circumventing most security devices that depend upon scanning techniques to recognize viral signatures. Simply put, when viruses change they can no longer be recognized. In typical leapfrog fashion, where crime fighting techniques are overtaken and surpassed by new technologies favoring law breakers and then later gain ascendancy again, polymorphic viruses have—over the last few years—largely rendered signature-based antivirus scanning technologies obsolete. Unfortunately, although many hardware devices and software products now on the market offer some degree of virus protection to individual and commercial users, new viruses

TABLE 12.2
COMPUTER VIRUSES

Hundreds of computer viruses have been identified. Viruses come in many varieties, and are often given interesting names. The names of a few are shown below:

Anthrax	Disk Killer	Jerusalem
Armageddon	Enigma	Kamikaze
Bandit	Friday 13th	Lucifer
Black Monday	Fu Manchu	Michaelangelo
Brain	Gotcha	Stealth
Chaos	Holocaust	Ping Pong-B
Dark Avenger	Invader	Stoned

are constantly being created which may soon have the ability to circumvent all security procedures now in place. The only fully effective technique for avoiding viral contamination is the complete and total isolation of computer equipment—a strategy as unlikely to be maintained as it is to be implemented.

Computer Crime and the Law

In the early years of computer-based information systems, states often tried to prosecute unauthorized computer access under preexisting property crime statutes, including burglary and larceny laws. Unfortunately, since the actual carrying off of a computer is quite different from simply making a copy of some of the information it contains or altering such information, juries frequently could not understand the applicability of such laws to high-tech crimes, and offenders were often exonerated. As a result, all states and the federal government developed computer crime statutes specifically applicable to invasive activities aimed at illegally accessing stored information. Federal statutes of relevance to crimes committed with or against computer equipment and software include (1) the Computer Fraud and Abuse Act of 1984 and its amendments—especially Section 290001 of Title XXIX of the Violent Crime Control and Law Enforcement Act of 1994 that is known as the "Computer Abuse Amendments Act of 1994," (2) the Electronic Communications Privacy Act of 1986, (3) the National Stolen Property Act, (4) the Federally Protected Property Act, and (5) the Federal Wiretap Act of 1968.

Federal laws protect mostly equipment defined as **federal interest computers,** which includes machines owned by the federal government or a financial institution, or those that are accessed across state lines without prior authorization. The U.S. Criminal Code, title 18, section 1030(a), defines as criminal the intentional unauthorized access to a computer used exclusively by the federal government or any other computer used by the government when such conduct affects the government's use. The same statute also defines as criminal the intentional and unau-

Federal interest computers those that are the property of the federal government, that belong to financial institutions, or that are accessed across state lines without authorization.

thorized access to two or more computers in different states and conduct that alters or destroys information and causes loss to one or more parties in excess of $1,000.[18] Punishment specified under federal law is a maximum sentence of five years, and a fine of up to $250,000 upon conviction. The Computer Abuse Amendments Act of 1994, however, adds the provision that "[a]ny person who suffers damage or loss by reason of a violation of [this] section...may maintain a civil action against the violator to obtain compensatory damages and injunctive relief or other equitable relief." The 1994 provision is intended to support civil actions in federal court against computer criminals by those suffering monetary losses as a result of computer crimes.

The computer crime laws of individual states are not modeled after federal legislation. As a result they contain great variation. Texas law, for example, distinguishes between only two areas of illegal use of a computer: "harmful access" and "breach of computer security." A "breach of security" occurs when an individual simply uses a computer or gains unauthorized "access to data stored or maintained by a computer without the effective consent of the owner or licensee of the data [when] the actor knows that there exists a computer security system intended to prevent him from gaining access" to the computer or the data it contains. "Harmful access" is defined under Texas law as unauthorized computer use (without the consent of the owner) when "the actor knows that there exists a computer security system intended to prevent him from making that use of the computer." Harmful access only occurs, however, when, in the words of the Texas statute, the offender

1. damages, alters, or destroys a computer, computer program or software, computer system, data, or computer network.
2. causes a computer to interrupt or impair a government operation, public communication, public transportation, or public service providing water or gas.
3. uses a computer to tamper with government, medical, or educational records, or receive or use records that were not intended for public dissemination, or gain an advantage over business competitors.
4. obtains information from or introduces false information into a computer system to damage or enhance the data or credit records of a person.
5. causes a computer to remove, alter, erase, or copy a negotiable instrument; inserts or introduces a computer virus into a computer program.

Under Texas law, the lack of a well-publicized security system becomes an open invitation for anyone seeking to invade the computer systems of others—for whatever purpose. If a theft of data takes place, no crime has occurred unless a security system was in place and efforts to secure the system were visible to the perpetrator. According to the laws of the state of Texas, however, "a person commits an offense if the person intentionally or knowingly gives a password, identifying code, personal identification number, debit card number, bank account number, or other confidential information about a computer security system to another person without the effective consent of the person employing the computer security system to restrict the use of a computer or to restrict access to data stored or maintained by a computer."

In contrast to Texas, Virginia specifically defines computer crime according to the following categories: "theft of computer services," "computer invasion of privacy," "computer trespass," "computer fraud," and "personal trespass by computer" (via which physical injury accrues to someone by virtue of unauthorized access to a computer, as may happen in the case of disruption of utility services). The laws of two other states, Colorado and Wisconsin, are shown in separate boxes in this chapter. The Colorado statute, as can be easily seen, is quite succinct, while Wisconsin's is very detailed.

Because innovative uses are continuously being found for computers and computerized equipment, it may be that some future illegitimate activities employing such equipment will not be adequately covered by existing law. For that reason some experts distinguish among computer crime (defined earlier), **computer-related crime,** and **computer abuse. Computer-related crime** may be defined as "any illegal act for which knowledge of computer technology is involved for its investigation, perpetration, or prosecution," while computer abuse is said to be "any incident without color of right associated with computer technology in which a victim suffered or could have suffered loss and/or a perpetrator by intention made or could have made gain."[19]

Computer abuse any incident without color of right associated with computer technology in which a victim suffered or could have suffered loss and/or a perpetrator by intention made or could have made gain.

Computer-related crime any illegal act for which knowledge of computer technology is involved for its investigation, perpetration, or prosecution.

COLORADO REVISED STATUTES

Title 18. Criminal Code
Article 5.5. Computer Crime
C.R.S. 18-5.5-102 (1990)
18-5.5-102. Computer Crime

(1) Any person who knowingly uses any computer, computer system, computer network, or any part thereof for the purpose of devising or executing any scheme or artifice to defraud; obtaining money, property, or services by means of false or fraudulent pretenses, representations, or promises; using the property or services of another without authorization; or committing theft commits computer crime.

(2) Any person who knowingly and without authorization uses, alters, damages, or destroys any computer, computer system, or computer network described in section 18-5.5-101 or any computer software, program, documentation, or data contained in such computer, computer system, or computer network commits computer crime.

WHAT IS A COMPUTER CRIME?

The Wisconsin Computer Crime Law

There is a considerable difference between the physical theft of computer equipment and the theft through copying of information stored in computers. The Wisconsin state computer crime statute, which makes a good attempt at distinguishing between these two types of offenses, is excerpted here. The statute is also notable for the fact that it recognizes a wide range of activities as possible forms of computer crime.

State of Wisconsin
Criminal Statutes
Chapter 293, Laws of 1981
943.70 Computer Crimes

(2) Offenses Against Computer Data and Programs.

(a) Whoever willfully, knowingly and without authorization does any of the following may be penalized as provided in paragraph (b):

1. Modifies data, computer programs or supporting documentation.
2. Destroys data, computer programs or supporting documentation.
3. Accesses data, computer programs or supporting documentation.
4. Takes possession of data, computer programs or supporting documentation.
5. Copies data, computer programs or supporting documentation.
6. Discloses restricted access codes or other restricted access information to unauthorized persons.

(b) Whoever violates this subsection is guilty of:

1. A Class A misdemeanor unless subd. 2, 3 or 4 applies.
2. A Class E felony if the offense is committed to defraud or to obtain property.
3. A Class D felony if the damage is greater than $2,500 or if it causes an interruption or impairment of governmental operations or public communication, of transportation or of a supply of water, gas, or other public service.
4. A Class C felony if the offense creates a situation of unreasonable risk and high probability of death or great bodily harm to another.

(3) Offenses Against Computers, Computer Equipment or Supplies.

(a) Whoever willingly, knowingly and without authorization does any of the following may be penalized as provided in paragraph (b):

1. Modifies computer equipment or supplies that are used or intended to be used in a computer, computer system or computer network.

2. Destroys, uses, takes or damages a computer, computer system, computer, network or equipment or supplies used or intended to be used in a computer, computer system, or computer network.

(b) Whoever violates this subsection is guilty of:

1. A Class A misdemeanor unless sub. 2, 3 or 4 applies.
2. A Class E felony if the offense is committed to defraud or obtain property.
3. A Class D felony if the damage to the computer, computer system, computer network, equipment or supplies is greater than $2,500.
4. A Class C felony if the offense creates a situation of unreasonable risk and high probability of death or great bodily harm to another.

Penalties for Infractions

939.50(3) Penalties for felonies are as follows:

(a) For a Class A felony, life imprisonment.
(b) For a Class B felony, imprisonment not to exceed 20 years.
(c) For a Class C felony, a fine not to exceed $10,000 or imprisonment not to exceed 10 years, or both.
(d) For a Class D felony, a fine not to exceed $10,000 or imprisonment not to exceed 5 years, or both.
(e) For a Class E felony, a fine not to exceed $10,000 or imprisonment not to exceed 2 years, or both.

939.51(3) Penalties for misdemeanors are as follows:

(a) For a Class A misdemeanor, a fine not to exceed $10,000 or imprisonment not to exceed 9 months, or both.
(b) For a Class B misdemeanor, a fine not to exceed $1,000 or imprisonment not to exceed 90 days, or both.
(c) For a Class C misdemeanor, a fine not to exceed $500 or imprisonment not to exceed 30 days, or both.

A PROFILE OF COMPUTER CRIMINALS

Computer criminals are often drawn from the ranks of hackers—a term defined earlier in this chapter. Hackers and hacker identities are a product of **cyberspace,** that quasi-etheric realm where computer technology and human psychology meet. Cyberspace exists only within electronic networks, and is the place where computers and human beings interact with one another. For many hackers, cyberspace provides the opportunity for impersonal interpersonal contact, technological challenges, and game playing. Fantasy role-playing games are well developed within cyberspace and may engross many "wave riders," who appear to prefer what in technological parlance is called "virtual reality" to the external physical and

Cyberspace the computer-created matrix of virtual possibilities, including on-line services, wherein human beings interact with each other and with technology itself.

Robert T. Morris, Jr., inventor of the infamous "internet worm," leaving a New York federal court. *Michael J. Okoniawski/AP/Wide World Photos.*

social worlds that surrounds them. As one writer puts it, "cyberspace is hacker heaven."[20]

Literature that glorifies cyberspace and the people who inhabit it is called cyberpunk. An understanding of cyberpunk literature is crucial for those wanting to gain an appreciation for how hackers think. According to Paul Saffo of the Institute for the Future in Menlo Park, California, "anyone trying to make sense of computing in the 1990s should add some cyberpunk books to their reading lists."[21] "Cyberpunk," says Saffo, "may become the counterculture movement" of the future. He adds that, "the cyberpunk trend is likely to be matched by an increase in the number of cyber-outlaws penetrating networks for criminal ends." Young, idealistic, and immature, hackers of this genre typically take on pseudonyms by which they can be identified by other hackers, but which also provide at least the illusion of anonymity. Names like Phiber Optik, Acid Phreak, Knight Lightning, Time Lord, Nightcrawler, and Dark Angel are just a few of the many pseudonyms that are either now in use or that have been used by hackers in recent years. A psychological and social profile of today's hackers is provided in a box in this chapter.

Some of the most infamous computer hackers of recent years, those comprising the Atlanta-based "Legion of Doom," fit the hacker profile well. A few years ago, three Legion members were sentenced to prison terms of fourteen to twenty-one months and ordered to pay $233,000 each in restitution to BellSouth Corporation for breaking into its computer systems and stealing confidential data. Following expiration of their jail time, some Legion members found themselves sought after by high-tech employers seeking to exploit their skills in the development of proprietary computer security systems. Other "legionnaires" formed a company called Comsec Data Security to help provide private business with the expertise necessary to fend off electronic intrusions.

THEORY VERSUS REALITY

The Computer Hacker

A Psychological and Social Profile

Computer hackers generally share the following social and personal characteristics:

1. Young: often 14–19 years of age.
2. Intelligent: IQ probably over 120, with the ability to articulate well.
3. "Nerdy": socializes poorly with peers, but may have close friends among like-minded fellows.
4. "WASP"-like: likely to be white, Protestant, and from a middle or upper-middle class background.
5. Fond of gadgets, especially computer-related hardware.
6. Academic Performer: likely to perform well on individual academic assignments, like tests and term papers. Unlikely to perform well on group assignments.
7. Self-perceived Hero:

   Sees self as empowering human-kind via an abstract victory over the "machine."

   Sees self as assisting humanity via participation in the fight against dehumanizing organizations (i.e., may seek to "liberate" information in the belief that information should be freely shared by all).

8. Counter-Culture Participant: has likely read, or is familiar with the following books:

   William Gibson's *Neuromancer*

   John Brunner's *Shockwave Rider*

   William Gibson's *Count Zero*

   William Gibson's *Mona Lisa Overdrive*

   Clifford Stoll's *The Cuckoo's Egg*

   Melissa Scott's *Trouble and Her Friends*

9. Self-descriptions include feelings of boredom and apathy.
10. Favorite activities include computer games and/or other games emphasizing a fantasy world (i.e., Dungeons and Dragons).

11. Membership in a thrill-seeking subcultural group of computer hackers, usually taking on the name of a fantasy world character. Communicates to various other members of subculture via a computer bulletin board or via direct computer linkages.
12. Feelings experienced when accessing a secure computer system are often referred to in terms of drug-taking and sexual activity ("getting high," "orgasmic," "the big thrill," etc.).

Source: Adapted with permission from Robert W. Taylor, "Computer Crime," in C. R. Swanson, N. C. Chamelin, and L. Territo, *Criminal Investigation* (New York: Random House, 1991).

The History and Nature of Hacking

Some authors[22] have suggested that computer hacking began with creation of the interstate phone system and direct distance dialing (DDD) implemented by AT&T in the late 1950s. Early switching devices used audible tones that were easily duplicated by electronics hobbyists, and "blue boxes" capable of emulating such tones quickly entered the illicit marketplace.

While phone phreaking has been practiced for more than forty years, a form of illegal telephone access that has recently come to the fore is voice-mail hacking. Private voice-mailboxes used for storing verbal messages have become the targets of corporate raiders and young vandals alike. In a recent case, two teenaged New York city brothers caused an estimated $2.4 million in lost business by gaining illegal access to the New Hampshire–based International Data Group's voice-mail system. The brothers were angry at not having received a poster promised with their magazine subscription. Security experts at the company first thought that the mailboxes were malfunctioning, but were alerted to the intentional disruptions by obscene outgoing messages planted by the brothers that greeted unsuspecting callers.[23]

Voice-mail fraud, another form of telephone crime, involves schemes in which mailbox access codes are shared in such a way that callers to 800 numbers can leave messages for one another in voice-mailboxes, thereby avoiding personal long-distance charges.[24] Companies which provide access to voice-mail systems through 800 numbers often learn of the need for access code security only after they find themselves the victims of such schemes.

While the hacker life-style may have begun with phone phreaking, phone phreaks represent only one type of hacker. Hackers can be distinguished both on the basis of purpose and method of operation. Such categorization, however, is merely descriptive. Other, more useful, distinctions can be made on the basis of personality and life-style. Some experts[25] have suggested that hackers can be classified according to psychological characteristics into the following groups:

- *Pioneers:* individuals who are fascinated by the evolving technology of telecommunications and explore it without knowing exactly what they were going to find. Few hard-core criminals are found among this group.

Mark Abene (left), known in hacker circles as Phiber Optik. Abene was sent to federal prison in 1994 for "computer intrusion" involving machines owned by Southwestern Bell Telephone Company. Computer hacker Kevin Mitnick (right), arrested in 1995 following the alleged theft of thousands of credit-card numbers from NETCOM, an Internet service provider. According to some "Mitnick represents our worst fears about what hackers can do." *(left) Robert Maass/SIPA Press; (right) Bob Jordan/AP/Wide World Photos.*

TECHNOLOGICAL ATTRACTION

The attraction computer hacking holds is well captured in this passage by Melissa Scott in her new cyberpunk adventure novel, *Trouble and Her Friends:*

> Trouble's on the net tonight, riding the high data like a cowboy, the plains of light stark around her. The data flows and writhes like grass in the virtual wind. IC(E)—Intrusion Countermeasures (Electronic)—rises to either side, prohibiting the nodes, and the old urge returns.... She can almost taste what lies behind that barrier, files and codes turned to candy-color shapes good enough to eat, and remembers the sweet-sour tang, the glorious greed of gorging on the good bits, sorting them in an eye-blink by taste and smell, faster and more sure than anyone else in the business...."

Source: Melissa Scott, *Trouble and Her Friends* (Garden City, NJ: Science Fiction Book Club, 1994).

- *Scamps:* hackers with a sense of fun. They intend no overt harm.
- *Explorers:* hackers who are motivated by their delight in the discoveries associated with breaking into new computer systems. The farther away such systems are geographically from the hacker's physical location, or the more secure such systems are, the more excitement associated with breaking into them.
- *Game players:* those who enjoy defeating software or system copy protection and who seek systems with games to play. Hacking itself becomes a game for this sort of hacker.
- *Vandals:* malicious hackers who deliberately cause damage with no apparent gain for themselves. The 414 Gang in Milwaukee, for example, which broke into the Sloan-Kettering Cancer Institute's computers and wiped out patients' records provides an example of this type of hacker.
- *Addicts:* classic computer "nerds" who are literally addicted to hacking and to computer technology. They may also be addicted to illicit drugs, as some hacker bulletin board systems post information on drugs as well as on modems, passwords, and vulnerable systems.

Psychologist Percy Black contends that there may be an underlying theme in all cases of hacking. It is, he says, "the search for a feeling of power, possibly stemming from a deep-seated sense of powerlessness."[26] Hence, hacking may serve as compensation for feelings of personal inferiority. By challenging the machine, and by winning against machine culture, hackers go through a kind of right of passage into adulthood whereby they prove themselves capable of success.

Since most hackers are young adolescent males, however (see Figure 12.1), it may be important to realize, as one expert on hackers, says, "Their other favorite risky business is the time-honored adolescent sport of trespassing. They insist on going where they don't belong. But then teen-age boys have been proceeding uninvited since the dawn of human puberty. It seems hard-wired. The only innovation is in the new form of the forbidden zone and the means of getting in it...."[27]

> The ease with which electronic impulses can be manipulated, modified and erased is hostile to a deliberate legal system.
>
> —*Anne W. Branscomb*[28]

Unfortunately, however, not all computer hackers are "just" kids trying their hand at beating technological challenges. As Garry M. Jenkins, assistant director of the U.S. Secret Service, put it around the time of Operation Sun Devil (a joint two-year undercover operation of Secret Service and local and state law enforcement personnel, along with the private security operatives of AT&T, PacBell, BellSouth, MCI, U.S. Sprint, NYNEX, and others), "Recently, we have witnessed an alarming number of young people who, for a variety of sociological and psychological reasons, have become attached to their computers and are exploiting their potential in a criminal manner. Often, a progression of criminal activity occurs that involves telecommunications fraud (free long-distance phone calls), unauthorized access to other computers (whether for profit, fascination, ego, or the intellectual challenge), credit card fraud (cash advances and unauthorized purchases of goods), and then moves on to other destructive activities like computer viruses.... Our experience shows that many computer hacker suspects are no longer misguided teenagers mischievously playing games with their computers in their bedrooms. Some are now high-tech computer operators using computers to engage in unlawful conduct."[29]

Not all high-tech crimes are committed using computer technology. Many technologically sophisticated professional criminals operate today, some of whom use the diverse fruits of high technology in the furtherance of serious criminal activity. The theft of money is a major area of such activity. A couple of years ago, for example, technologically sophisticated thieves in New York City rolled a fake automatic teller machine (ATM) into the local Buckland Hills shopping mall. Although the machine did not dispense money, it did record the information contained on the magnetic strips of legitimate banking cards inserted by would-be customers. Personal information numbers (PINs) which the customers entered were also recorded. Armed with the necessary codes for legitimate accounts, the thieves then fabricated their own cards and used them to withdraw thousands of dollars worth of cash from ATM machines across the city.

Although most people probably think of money as dollar bills, money today is really only information—information stored in a computer network, possibly located within the physical confines of a bank, but more likely existing as bits and

FIGURE 12.1 Ages of computer crime defendants at time of arrest. *Source*: National Council on Crime and Delinquency, as reported in Larry Coutourie, "The Computer Criminal: An Investigative Assessment," *The FBI Law Enforcement Bulletin*, September, 1989, p. 21.

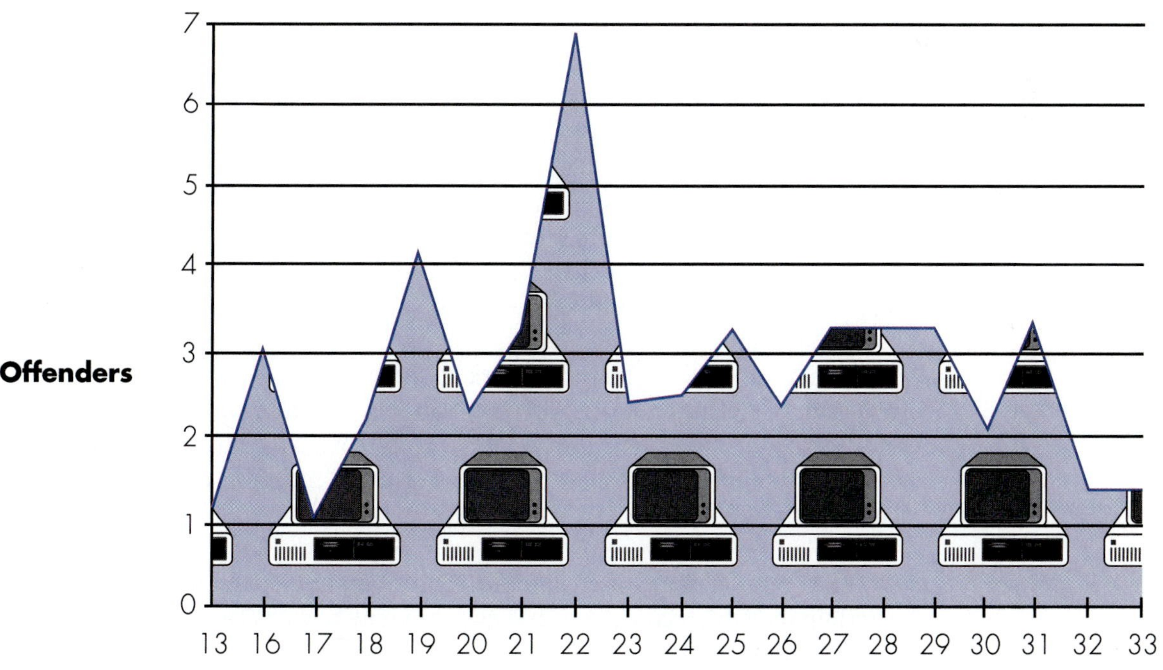

bytes of data on some service provider's machines. The typical financial customer gives little thought to the fact that very little "real" money is held by his or her bank, brokerage house, mutual fund, or commodities dealer. Nor does he or she often consider the threats to his or her financial well-being by activities such as electronic theft or the sabotage of existing accounts. Unfortunately, however, the threat is very real. Computer criminals equipped with enough information, or able to ferret out the data they need, can quickly and easily send vast amounts of money anywhere in the world.

Although billions of dollars worth of electronic transactions occur every day, no reliable estimates exist as to the losses suffered in such transactions due to the activities of technologically aware criminal perpetrators. Accurate estimates are lacking largely because sophisticated high-tech thieves are so effective at eluding apprehension, and even detection, that reliable loss figures are impossible to come by.

Bulletin board system (BBS) a computer accessible by telephone used like a bulletin board to leave messages and files for other users.

Computer **bulletin board systems (BBS)** can also facilitate criminal activity. In 1993 U.S. Customs Service agents involved in Operation Longarm, carried out raids in eighteen different states on child pornographers and suspected pedophiles using names taken from a pedophile board. According to the Customs Service, the computerized transmission of illegal pornography among pedophiles is rapidly becoming more popular than smutty magazines.[30]

Other computer bulletin boards may serve as illicit drug information exchange centers, and even a few may be run by organized criminal groups. As one expert tells it, "some BBS's are being infiltrated by organized crime syndicates because of the potential for selling stolen computer components, blackmail, and narcotics distribution. Pirate [illegal boards, or those that make copyrighted software freely available] BBS operators have been known to threaten the lives of undercover investigators who have infiltrated their systems."[31]

Computer Crime as a Form of White-Collar Crime

White-collar crime is discussed in detail in Chapter 9. It is important here, however, to recognize that a number of contemporary analysts believe that computer crime may be nothing other than a new form of white-collar crime. Some suggest that it is white-collar crime *par excellence*—that is, the ultimate expression of white-collar crime.

In what may be the definitive work to date on high-technology professional crime, Donn B. Parker, author of the National Institute of Justice's *Computer Crime: Criminal Justice Research Manual,*[32] compares white-collar criminals with computer criminals. Both share what Parker calls "common criminal behavior-related issues," such as

- Both types of acts are often committed through nonviolent means, although certain industrial, consumer, and environment-related crimes have life-threatening consequences.
- Access to computers or computer storage media, through employment-related knowledge or technical skills, is often needed.

- These acts generally involve information manipulations that either directly or indirectly create profits or losses.
- These crimes can be committed by an individual, several individuals working in collusion, and/or organizations, with the victims in the latter case ranging from individual clients, customers, or employees or other organizations.

According to Parker, computer crime and white-collar crime share other similarities, including

- These crimes are often difficult to detect, with discovery quite often started by accident or customer complaint rather than as the result of direct investigation.
- The general public views many of these acts as less serious than crimes involving physical violence.
- These crimes cost individuals, organizations, and society large amounts of resources.
- Prevention of these crimes requires a combination of legal, technical, managerial, security, and audit-monitoring controls.

THE INFORMATION SUPERHIGHWAY AND DATA SECURITY

There is much talk today about an "information superhighway" that is about to be constructed with federal tax dollars, and which will soon put information of all kinds at the fingertips of anyone with a computer, a modem, and a little technical knowledge. While funding details and the exact structure of the information superhighway remain a bit uncertain, the notion of such a data thoroughfare is closely intertwined with future expectations for our society and for the world as a whole. The historical development of the United States, which has long been a world leader in technology, was greatly facilitated by the development of railroads, river traffic, roads, and interstate highways. In short, transportation and the ability to move goods and people did much to build America and to assure its place of prominence in the world.

As we enter the twenty-first century, America has begun to leave behind its industrial roots and is moving toward becoming a service-oriented information-rich society. John Naisbitt, author of *Megatrends,* explains it this way: "the transition from an industrial to an information society does not mean manufacturing will cease to exist or become unimportant. Did farming end with the industrial era? Ninety percent of us produced 100 percent of the food in the agricultural era; now 3 percent of us produce 100 percent.... In the information age, the focus of manufacturing will shift from the physical to more intellectual functions on which the physical depends."[33]

While goods and materials will always need to be created, transported, and distributed, it is information that will form the lifeblood of the coming world order. Information, many pundits believe, will be the most valuable resource of the new age, comparable to—and even exceeding—the value which natural resources such as oil, gas, coal, and gold held over the past few centuries. As Naisbitt puts it, "information is an economic entity because it costs something to produce and because people are willing to pay for it."[34] Nations that are able to effectively manage valuable information, and which can make it accessible to their citizens, will find enhanced productivity and greater wealth as a reward.

One of the most vocal proponents of the information superhighway is Vice President Al Gore. Following his election to the U.S. Senate in 1984, Gore worked tirelessly to ensure that a high-speed fiber-optic computer network would be built throughout the nation, providing the backbone for future information development. Before becoming vice president, Gore was chairman of the Senate's Subcommittee on Science, Technology, and Space. Almost single-handedly he conceived of and authored the High Performance Computing Act of 1990, which lays the groundwork for federal government support of the data superhighway. During his fight to win the legislation's passage, Gore drew an effective contrast between modern telecommunications and the invention of the printing press centuries ago. "Gutenberg's invention," he said, "which so empowered Jefferson and his colleagues in their fight for democracy, seems to pale before the rise of electronic communications and innovations, from the telegraph to television, to the microprocessor and the emergence of a new computerized world—an information age."[35]

The Internet the world's largest computer network.

The highly touted information superhighway is a visionary way of moving data quickly, as well as a way of making information accessible to masses of citizens who can use it productively. Some suggest that the information superhighway already exists in the form of the Internet. The **Internet,** which is the world's largest computer network, had its beginnings a couple of decades ago with the linkage of military and scientific computer facilities already existing on the Arpnet and Milnet. Today the Internet consists of a vast resource of tens of thousands of computers around the world that are all tied together.

The Internet currently provides for electronic mail, "mailing lists," news groups, databases, and file transfer capability. Although Internet access has traditionally been restricted to commercial users, researchers, and university personnel, access to the Internet is now rapidly widening. Many commercial service providers such as America On Line, CompuServe, and Prodigy offer Internet gateways, and a large number of startup firms are beginning to provide Internet access to anyone able to pay minimal monthly fees. Tools such as GOPHER, WAIS (wide area information server), WWW (world wide web) browsers, ftp (file transfer protocol), and software with names like Veronica and Mosaic make it possible to search the tremendous amount of information on the Internet and to retrieve items of interest.

Unfortunately, as the Internet has grown, it too has been targeted by hackers and computer criminals, some of whom have introduced rogue computer programs into the network's machines. In 1988, for example, the infamous Internet "worm" written by Cornell University graduate student Robert T. Morris, Jr., circulated through computers connected to the Internet, effectively disabling many of them. Morris was later arrested and sentenced in 1990 to four hundred hours of community service and three years probation. He was also fined $10,000.

TECHNOLOGY IN THE FIGHT AGAINST CRIME

Technology is a double-edged sword. On the one hand, it arms evil-doers with potent new weapons of crime commission, while on the other it provides police agencies and criminal justice personnel with powerful tools useful in the battle against crime. Law enforcement capabilities and criminally useful or evasive technologies commonly leapfrog one another. Consider, for example, the relatively simple case of traffic radar, which has gone through an elaborate technological evolution from early "always-on" units through trigger-operated radar devices to today's sophisticated laser speed measuring apparatus. Each change was an attempt by enforcement agencies to keep a step ahead of increasingly sophisticated radar detection devices marketed to drivers everywhere. Although cutting-edge laser speed units are invisible to most radar detectors, laser radar detectors *do* exist. Their usefulness, however, is open to debate since they generally alert the speeding driver too late to respond. On the other hand, radar jamming devices are now being increasingly used by people apparently intent on breaking speed limit laws, and laser jammers may soon be sold. Not to be outdone, suppliers to enforcement agencies have created radar-detector detectors which are used by authorities in states where radar detectors have been outlawed.[36]

Other than traffic radar, some of the most potent technology in law enforcement service today includes computer databases of known offenders, machine-based

Less than lethal weapons are undergoing review by law enforcement agencies nationwide. Here a test dummy is incapacitated by polyester slime. *Sandia National Laboratories.*

expert systems, cellular communications, electronic eavesdropping, DNA analysis, and less than lethal weapons. Recent advances, for example, in transponder-based automated vehicle location (AVL) systems now use patrol car–based transmitters in tandem with orbiting satellites to pinpoint police vehicle locations to within 50 feet. Dispatchers making use of such information can better allocate resources available on a given shift and are able to substantially reduce police response times in crisis situations. Similarly, chip-based transponders are now being installed in private vehicles to deter thieves and to help trace stolen automobiles.

Computer-aided dispatch (CAD) systems, representing yet another area of advanced crime-fighting technology, are becoming increasingly sophisticated. In jurisdictions where CAD systems function, police dispatchers are prompted by computers for important information which allows them to distinguish one place from another (such as the location of a particular McDonald's restaurant) within a city. CAD computers can also quickly provide information about how often officers have been called to a given site and tell responding officers what they might expect to find based upon past calls from that location. As one writer[37] enticingly puts it, "Imagine this response from a 911 call-taker: 'Yes, Ms. Smith, we are aware that beer-drinking youths at the corner of Hollywood and Vine have been a problem over the past six weeks, and in fact, we've responded seven times to requests to disperse them. As soon as one of our patrol cars frees up on a robbery call, I'll be sure that it goes over to disperse the group. And by the way, we are unaware of any serious crimes that can be attributed to these youths. But please feel free to call us immediately if you observe any criminal activities.'" The same software that facilitates such a response will routinely inform responding officers about police experience with the suspects, provide background checks as a matter of course, tell whether or not they are likely to find registered guns at the address, and relay information about outstanding warrants on anyone who lives there. It can also inform dispatchers when responding officers do not call back after a statistically determined period of time for that type of call—alerting them to potential threats to officer safety.

As new technologies are developed, their potential usefulness in law enforcement activities is evaluated by the FBI, the National Institute of Justice (NIJ), and other agencies. NIJ's Technology Assessment Program (TAP) focuses on four areas of advancing technology: (1) protective equipment, such as "bulletproof" vests and other body armor; (2) forensic sciences, including the applicability of advances in DNA technology; (3) transportation and weapons, such as electronic "stun guns" and other new less than lethal weapons; and (4) communications and electronics, including computer security, electronic eavesdropping, and so on. Other groups, such as the National Computer Security Association (NCSA), the American Cryptography Association (ACA), and the American Society for Industrial Security (ASIS), bring more specialized high-technology expertise to the private security and public law enforcement professions.

DNA fingerprinting or **profiling** the use of biological residue found at the scene of a crime for genetic comparisons in aiding the identification of criminal suspects.

DNA Fingerprinting

DNA profiling or, as it is commonly called, **DNA fingerprinting,** received much media attention during the widely publicized preliminary hearing and trial of

Former football superstar O.J. Simpson. DNA evidence proved crucial in Simpson's double-murder trial. *LAPD.*

former media superstar and gridiron great O. J. Simpson in 1995. In that case, DNA evidence appeared to show that Simpson, who was accused of the murders of his wife and of a male friend who was visiting her, was present at the crime scene around the time of the killings.

A person's genetic code is contained in their DNA (deoxyribonucleic acid), whose composition is unique to each individual except in the case of identical twins. DNA samples can be taken from blood, hair, semen, saliva, or even small flakes of skin left at the scene of a crime. In cases of rape, for example, semen or pubic hairs left behind by the perpetrator and removed from the victim or gathered at the scene can provide the DNA evidence necessary for identifying a suspect. In cases of murder, victims sometimes fight with their attackers, retaining small bits of the killer's skin under their fingernails—thereby providing a tissue sample useful in DNA analysis.

After processing, DNA profiles appear like bar codes on X-ray images. A small difference in such codes can exonerate a suspect in the eyes of expert analysts—or provide nearly irrefutable evidence of guilt.

DNA evidence is long lasting, with even fossilized DNA now being used to reconstruct genetic maps of long-extinct plant and animal species. Although DNA analysis is theoretically possible using only a single cell, most reputable DNA laboratories require a considerably greater quantity of material to conduct an effective analysis. That, however, may soon change. Using a technique called polymerase chain-reaction technology, a Nobel Prize–winning technique, minute strands of DNA can be effectively amplified so that even the identity of a person taking a single puff from a cigarette can be accurately established. Although the cost and complexity of such enhancement are still prohibitive, technological advances are expected to bring the technique within the range of forensic analysts within a decade.

The National Research Council calls, DNA profiling "a highly reliable forensic tool,"[38] while admitting that it is not infallible. Although obvious differences in scrutinized DNA samples can easily eliminate a suspect, testing provides less certainty when positive identification is claimed. Human error in conducting the tests is perhaps the greatest threat to reliable results. As of this writing, at least twenty states and the federal government generally accept DNA evidence in criminal trials. Other jurisdictions, including California, are less clear in their recognition of DNA testing, and trial judges in those states may off-handedly exclude the use of such evidence when experts disagree as to its validity.

In 1993 the U.S. Supreme Court, in the case of *Daubert* v. *Merrell Dow Pharmaceuticals, Inc.*,[39] concluded that the results of DNA testing can be acceptable in criminal trials so long as the techniques employed meet the test for admission of scientific evidence published under the *Federal Rules of Evidence.* Those rules generally allow the use of evidence that has "any tendency to make the existence of any fact that is of consequence...more probable or less probable than it would be without the evidence." The Court said that the following factors may be used to determine whether any form of scientific evidence is reliable:

- It has been subject to testing.
- It has been subject to peer review.
- Known or potential rates of error can be determined.
- There are standards controlling application of the techniques involved.

***Daubert* standard** a test of scientific acceptability applicable to the gathering of evidence in criminal cases.

In setting the ***Daubert* standard,** the Court held that DNA testing conducted at the FBI's crime laboratory "easily meets" the necessary criteria for scientific acceptability. *Daubert* provides a significant easing of the rules for the admissibility of scientific evidence in federal courts, as it supersedes the much stricter *Frye* standard established by the Court in 1923. In *Frye* v. *United States,*[40] the Court held that expert opinion based on a scientific technique is inadmissible unless the technique is "generally accepted" as reliable in the scientific community.

One observer, discussing the general quality of DNA identification methods, notes: "the challenges today are no longer technical; instead they lie in taking the technology and building a meaningful legal infrastructure around it."[41] In other words, it appears to be only a matter of time until DNA evidence will be widely accepted throughout jurisdictions nationwide. Once that occurs, it is likely that DNA databases, similar in purpose to now widely used fingerprint archives, will be established in individual states and at the national level. Today approximately half a dozen states and the federal government (through the FBI laboratory) have begun building digitized forensic DNA databases. FBI crime laboratory director John W. Hicks notes, "We're doing about 2,500 profiles a year right now....In a few years, it should be in the tens of thousands."[42] Although at this point there has been no coordination between the federally funded multibillion-dollar Human Genome Initiative and forensic DNA programs, future collaboration between the two could lead to truly explosive growth in the use of human DNA in criminal case processing.

In 1995 British police, operating under the aegis of a new nationwide crime bill, became the first national police force in the world to begin routine collection of DNA samples from anyone involved in a "recordable" offense (a serious crime).[43] As scientific techniques continue to be refined it appears likely that genetic profiling will become one of the most significant crime-fighting technologies of the twenty-first century. In the words of one forensics expert, "genetic profiling—the use of biotechnology to identify the unique characteristics of an individual's DNA—is about to become as prevalent as the Breathalyzer and more important than the fingerprint."[44]

Computers as Crime-Fighting Tools

The widespread use of computers and computer applications in a diversity of professions has been one of the most far-reaching social phenomena of recent years. Computers are now used to keep records of every imaginable sort, from point-of-sale contacts to inventory maintenance and production schedules. Even organized criminal groups have been known to use computers to record criminal transactions. Computers assist in the design of new technologies and aid in the assignment of resources to problem areas. Police departments, prisons, and courts now commonly employ computer software to schedule facilities and personnel; to keep track of defendants, witnesses, and cases; and to keep account of budgetary matters.

Computers also connect people. The world's largest computer network, the Internet, now contains a number of law- and law enforcement–oriented news groups and also provides access to United Nations and worldwide crime data through its link to the United Nations Criminal Justice Information Network. Other computer services, such as CompuServe and America On Line, provide access to security information and to software useful in law enforcement administration. Specialized computer bulletin boards like the Society of Police Futurists International's toll-free on-line service, the International Association of Chiefs of Police NET, and the SEARCH Group's dial-up file server all link law enforcement professionals and criminologists throughout the country.

Other innovative computer technologies facilitate the work of enforcement agents. Among them are automated fingerprint identification systems called AFIS (often with interstate and even international links), computerized crime scene simulations and reenactments, expert systems, and on-line clearinghouses containing data on criminal activity and on offenders. AFIS, a technology developed some years ago by Hewlett-Packard and Cogent Systems, allows investigators to complete in a matter of minutes what would otherwise consume weeks or months of work manually matching a suspect's fingerprints against stored records. AFIS computers are able to compare and eliminate from consideration twelve hundred fingerprints per second, leading to the identification of a suspect in a short time. New "Live-Scan" technology, developed jointly by IBM and Identix, allows for the easy inkless digitizing of fingerprints from live suspects. In like manner, the Bureau of Alcohol, Tobacco, and Firearms' (ATF) new Bulletproof software takes a 360-degree picture of a bullet's ballistic characteristics and then compares it with others stored in a database to isolate a small universe of potential matches.

Once crime-related information or profiles of criminal offenders have been generated they are typically stored in a database and often made accessible to law enforcement agencies at other sites. Some of today's most widely used on-line criminal information services are the FBI's National Crime Information Center (NCIC), the Violent Criminal Apprehension Program (VICAP), and METAPOL—an information-sharing network run by the Police Executive Research Forum (PERF). Other specialized database programs now track inner-city gang activity and gang membership, contain information on known sexual predators, and describe missing children.

One leader in the development of law enforcement services is the Criminal Justice Information Services Division (CJISD) of the FBI. CJISD was created in 1993 to provide state-of-the-art information services to the justice community and to assist in the future development of such services. One contemporary law-enforcement oriented software program, called COPS (for criminal offender profiling system), allows for the desktop integration of digitized mug shots, videotaped images, computerized fingerprint data, and text-based information such as criminal records—all in one automated file folder.

PC Radios provide another high-tech weapon in the war on crime. These devices—which are essentially combinations of laptop computers and police radios—were initially tested by the Baltimore, Maryland, police department. Mobile data terminals placed in police cars are proving very useful in the apprehension of both traffic violators and other, more serious offenders. Officers use PC radios to (1) obtain motor vehicle information, (2) get detailed information when answering a call, and (3) report incidents either by saving data on disk or by transmitting it to other locations, such as police headquarters. PC Radios have also helped befuddle drug dealers who themselves routinely use police scanners to keep abreast of enforcement activities. The digitized transmissions of such devices consist of machine code that cannot be easily read by drug dealers or other criminals trying to outguess the police.

Expert systems computer hardware and software that attempt to duplicate the decision-making processes used by skilled investigators in the analysis of evidence and in the recognition of patterns which such evidence might represent.

Forensic **expert systems,** representing yet another computerized law enforcement technology, deploy machine-based artificial intelligence to draw conclusions and make recommendations to investigators and others interested in solving problems related to crime and its commission. Expert systems, developed by professional "knowledge engineers" who work with "knowledge bases" and computer software called "inference engines," attempt to duplicate the decision-making processes used by skilled investigators in the analysis of evidence and in the recognition of patterns which such evidence might represent. One such system is currently being perfected by the FBI's National Center for the Analysis of Violent Crime (NCAVC). The NCAVC expert system attempts to profile serial killers by matching clues left at a crime scene with individual personality characteristics. While the NCAVC system is becoming increasingly sophisticated, it has not yet replaced human investigators. As one FBI developer puts it, "there is certainly no possibility that the system we are devising will ever replace skilled human profilers. Rather, the system will function as a profiler's assistant or consultant."[45]

Finally, a number of specialized computer software programs such as ImAger, which is produced by Face Software, Inc., and Compusketch, a product of Visatex Corporation, assist police artists in rendering composite images of suspects and missing victims.

COMBATING COMPUTER CRIME

In 1982, sales of information security products to private companies and government agencies totaled $51 million. By 1992 the figure had exceeded $220 million, and recent estimates are that $425 million will be spent on the protection of critical information in 1997 alone.[46]

Gadgets, however, are not enough. Any effective program intended to secure a company or business operation against the threat of high-tech crime must be built upon a realistic **threat analysis.** Threat analysis, sometimes also called risk analysis, involves a complete and thorough assessment of the kinds of perils facing an organization. Some risks, such as floods, tornadoes, hurricanes, and earthquakes, arise from natural events and are often unpredictable. Others, including fire, electrical outages, and disruptions in public services, may be of human origin—but equally difficult to presage. Theft, employee sabotage, and terrorist attacks constitute yet another category of risk—those brought about by intentional human intervention. Responses to unpredictable threats can, nonetheless, be planned and strategies for dealing with almost any kind of risk can be implemented. Unless and until an organization adequately assesses the threats to its continuing operation, however, it will be unable to formulate a plan to effectively deal with such risks. Hence, threat analysis is a must for businesses and other organizations preparing to meet the many diverse challenges of today's world.

Threat analysis (or risk analysis) involves a complete and thorough assessment of the kinds of perils facing an organization.

Once specific threats have been identified, strategies tailored to dealing with them can be introduced. For example, one powerful tool useful in identifying instances of computer crime whenever they occur is the audit trail. Properly defined, an **audit trail** is "a sequential record of system activities that enables auditors to reconstruct, review, and examine the sequence of states and activities surrounding each event in one or more related transactions from inception to output of final results back to inception."[47] In other words, audit trails, which (once implemented) are recorded in some form of computer memory, trace and record the activities of computer operators and facilitate the apprehension of computer criminals.

Audit trail a sequential record of computer system activities that enables auditors to reconstruct, review, and examine the sequence of states and activities surrounding each event in one or more related transactions from inception to output of final results back to inception.

Unfortunately, although most large companies and financial institutions have fairly extensive computer security programs, few small business, schools, hospitals, and individuals have any real understanding of the need for security in the use of their computers. "What is surprising about computer crime," says computer security expert Kenneth Rosenblatt, "is how little is being done to deter it: industry will not beef up security, the police are not equipped to catch electronic thieves, and judges do not hand down the kind of sentences that will impress would-be computer criminals. New strategies are urgently needed."[48]

Police Investigation of Computer Crime

Unfortunately, even with new laws to back them up, few police departments are prepared with either the time or qualified personnel to effectively investigate crimes committed by computer criminals. When it comes to computer crime investigations, one technology expert concludes, "[p]olice departments are simply unsuited to the task."[49] Although specialized computer crime units have been created in some jurisdictions, they are often poorly funded and seriously understaffed. Los Angeles, California; Philadelphia, Pennsylvania; and Baltimore, Maryland, now field such units, as do the Illinois State Police, the Tarrant County, Texas, District Attorney's Office, the Arizona State Attorney General's Office, and the Santa Clara County (California) District Attorney's Office.

Most police departments, however, have no specialized computer crime units. Nor do they have personnel skilled in the investigation of such crimes. Most officers know little about tracing the activities of computer criminals, and some police investigators find it difficult to understand how a crime can actually have occurred when nothing at the scene appears to be missing or damaged. Horror stories of botched police investigations are plentiful and include tales of officers standing by while high-tech offenders perform seemingly innocuous activities that destroy evidence, of seized floppy disks allowed to bake in the sun on the dashboards of police vehicles, and of the loss of evidence stored on magnetic media due to exposure to police clipboards and evidence lockers containing magnets.

Police departments also sometimes intentionally avoid computer crime investigations because they may be complex and demanding. The amount of time and money spent on computer crime investigations, it is often felt, could better be spent elsewhere. It is not unusual for computer crime investigations to cross state lines and to involve a number of telecommunications companies and other services. Additionally, investigators who spend a lot of time on crimes involving computers tend not to be promoted as readily as their more glamorous counterparts in homicide and property crime divisions, and personnel who are truly skilled in computer applications are apt to take jobs with private industries where pay scales are far higher than in police work. As a consequence of these considerations and others, many police departments and the investigators who staff them frequently accord computer crime a low priority, focusing instead on highly visible offenses such as murder and rape, and seeing computer crime victims as too wealthy to be seriously impacted by the crimes they experience.

One expert summed up the situation this way: "Because computer crime is too much for traditional law enforcement to handle, the bulk of computer offenses go unpunished. Probably fewer than 250 cases have been prosecuted in the United States during the past decade. At this rate, prosecutions are too rare to deter computer crime. If an offender is convicted, the usual penalties are also not much of a deterrent."[50]

Dealing with Computer Criminals

While any effective policy for dealing with computer and high-tech crime must recognize the issues associated with personal freedoms and individual rights in the information age, a second aspect of effective policy necessarily relates to crime control. How can high-tech criminals be deterred? If they succeed in committing criminal acts, how can they be reformed? Kenneth Rosenblatt,[51] who focused on computer crimes during his work as a California district attorney, suggests three sanctions that he feels would be especially effective in deterring high-tech offenders:

1. confiscating equipment used to commit a computer crime
2. limiting the offender's use of computers
3. restricting the offender's freedom to accept jobs involving computers

Such penalties, says Rosenblatt, could be supplemented by a few days or weeks in a county jail—with longer periods of incarceration applicable in serious cases. "In my experience," Rosenblatt adds, "one of the best ways to hurt computer offenders, especially young hackers, is to take away their toys."

POLICY ISSUES

Personal Freedoms in the Information Age

The continued development of telecommunications resources has led not only to concerns about security and data integrity, but to an expanding interest in privacy, free speech, and personal freedoms as well. While the Constitution guarantees each of us in its 1st and 4th Amendments freedom of speech and security in our "persons, houses, papers, and effects, against unreasonable searches and seizures," it is understandably silent on the subject of electronic documents and on advanced forms of communication facilitated by technologies which did not exist at the time of the Constitutional Convention.

Within the context of contemporary society we are left to ask, "What is paper? What is speech?" Do electronic communications qualify for protection under the 1st Amendment, as does the spoken word? In an era when most houses are wired for telephone usage, and many support data links that extend well beyond voice capabilities, it becomes necessary to ask what constitutes one's "home" or one's "speech." What, exactly, is "speech"? Does electronic mail qualify as speech? Where does the concept of a "home" begin and end for purposes of constitutional guarantees? Do activities within the home that can be accessed from without (as when a computer BBS is run out of a home) fall under the same constitutional guarantees as a private conversation held within the physical confines of a house?

These and questions like them will be debated for years to come. In 1990, however, concerned individuals banded together to form the Electronic Frontier Foundation (EFF), a citizens' group funded by private contributions that set for itself the task of actively assisting in refining notions of privacy and legality as they relate to telecommunications and other computer-based media. In the Foundation's own words: "The Electronic Frontier Foundation (EFF) was founded in July of 1990 to ensure that the principles embodied in the Constitution and the Bill of Rights are protected as new communications technologies emerge. From the beginning, EFF has worked to shape our nation's communications infrastructure and the policies that govern it in order to maintain and enhance First Amendment, privacy and other democratic values. We believe that our overriding public goal must be the creation of Electronic Democracy...."[52] As Mitch Kapor, EFF cofounder, and president of Lotus Development Corporation explained it, "It is becoming increasingly obvious that the rate of technology advancement in communications is far outpacing the establishment of appropriate cultural, legal and political frameworks to handle the issues that are arising...."

The EFF, which also supports litigation in the public interest, has been an active supporter of the Palo Alto, California–based public advocacy group Computer Professionals for Social Responsibility (CPSR). CPSR maintains a "Computing and Civil Liberties Project" much in keeping with EFF's purpose. Initial EFF litigation focused on a request for full federal government disclosure of information regarding the seizure of Jackson Games computer equipment. Jackson Games, an Austin, Texas–based game manufacturer, was a target in the Secret Service's Operation Sun Devil. In a second action, the Foundation sought *amicus curiae* (friend of the court) status in a federal case against Craig Neidorf, a 20-year-old University of Missouri student who had been editor of the electronic newsletter *Phrack World News*.

PRESS RELEASE ANNOUNCING THE FORMATION OF THE ELECTRONIC FRONTIER FOUNDATION

In 1990 the Electronic Frontier Foundation came into being. What follows are excerpts from the original press release announcing formation of the EFF.

FOR IMMEDIATE RELEASE

NEW FOUNDATION ESTABLISHED TO ENCOURAGE COMPUTER-BASED COMMUNICATIONS POLICIES

Washington, D.C., July 10, 1990—Mitchell D. Kapor, founder of Lotus Development Corporation and ON Technology, today announced that he, along with colleague John Perry Barlow, has established a foundation to address social and legal issues arising from the impact on society of the increasingly pervasive use of computers as a means of communication and information distribution. The Electronic Frontier Foundation (EFF) will support and engage in public education on current and future developments in computer-based and telecommunications media. In addition, it will support litigation in the public interest to preserve, protect and extend First Amendment rights within the realm of computing and telecommunications technology.

Initial funding for the Foundation comes from private contributions by Kapor and Steve Wozniak, co-founder of Apple Computer, Inc. The Foundation expects to actively raise contributions from a wide constituency.

Source: The Electronic Frontier Foundation.

WHAT THE FUTURE HOLDS

Data encryption methods used to encode computerized information.

New technologies will continue to give rise to new forms of crime, and novel forms of criminality will engender innovative enforcement efforts. Although it is impossible to discuss every possible answer to crimes which take advantage of high-technology for their commission, **data encryption** can serve as an example of the types of techniques which may find widespread use in the twenty-first century and beyond. Data encryption is the process by which information is encoded, making it unreadable to all but its intended recipients.

Vice President Al Gore has described the potential held by data encryption technologies in these words: "Encryption is a law and order issue since it can be used by criminals to thwart wiretaps and avoid detection and prosecution. It also has huge strategic value. Encryption technology and cryptoanalysis turned the tide in the Pacific and elsewhere during World War II."[53]

Many forms of encryption are now in use. Most can be "broken" through the use of supercomputers tasked with uncovering the codes upon which they are built. The latest advance in encryption technology, however, exists in the form of a hardware/software combination commonly referred to as the "clipper chip." Clipper (referred to by government agencies as "Key Escrow Encryption") is a powerful encryption technology that scrambles communications, making them unintelligible to all but their intended recipients. To date, Clipper encryption has never been compromised, and even the most powerful supercomputers have been unable to decode Clipper-encrypted documents.

Most government agencies support continued development and implementation of clipper technology and are promoting it for use by private citizens and businesses. Plans now call for government agencies, and the government alone, to hold the electronic "key" needed to decode clipper messages. The key would be separated into two pieces so that unauthorized snooping by government agents could be avoided. The "pieces" necessary for decryption would be joined with appropriate legal authority and used to decode suspected communications of a criminal nature.

According to U.S. Attorney General Janet Reno, if the proposed plan is implemented, encryption key components "will be released to government agencies for decrypting communications subject to lawful wiretaps."[54] In a recent press release Reno said, "Key Escrow Encryption strikes an excellent balance between protection of communications privacy and protection of society. It permits the use in commercial telecommunications products of chips that provide extremely strong encryption, but can be decrypted, when necessary, by government agencies conducting legally authorized wiretaps."[55]

Steps necessary for the decryption process to be initiated by government agents have been described by the Department of Justice as follows: "When an authorized government agency encounters suspected key-escrow encryption, a written request will have to be submitted to the two escrow agents. The request will, among other things, have to identify the responsible agency and the individuals involved; certify that the agency is involved in a lawfully authorized wiretap; specify the wiretap's source of authorization and its duration; and specify the serial number of the key-escrow encryption chip being used. In every case, an attorney involved in the investigation will have to provide the escrow agents assurance that a validly authorized wiretap is being conducted. Upon receipt of a proper request, the escrow agents will transmit their respective key components to the appropriate agency. The components will be combined within a decrypt device, which only then will be able to decrypt communications protected by key-escrow encryption. When the wiretap authorization ends, the device's ability to decrypt communications using that particular chip will also be ended."[56]

Because clipper technology is so powerful, and due to the fact that, under the proposed plan only government agencies propose holding the needed decryption keys, some critics fear that important information may be kept from the public by government officials bent on secrecy—so thoroughly encrypted that its very existence might be unknown. Under such circumstances, they say, the Freedom of Information Act would lose its power, and government agencies could enter an electronic underground inaccessible to the public and without the need for public accounting. In an interesting article entitled "Jackboots on the Infobahn" published by *Wired* magazine, John Perry Barlow, a cofounder of the EFF, notes that the clipper chip has been called "a last ditch attempt by the United States, the last great power from the old Industrial Era, to establish imperial control over cyberspace."

> We live in the Space Age, but we've left our cops in the Iron Age.... Our kids play with more sophisticated electronic toys than the crude implements we give most of our police officers.... I don't see why we can give our military brilliant, 20th century technology to fight wars overseas but can't do the same thing for our police, who are fighting a war at home—the war against violence on our streets.[57]
>
> —*Rep. Charles E. Schumer (D., N.Y.)*
> Chairman of the House Judiciary
> Subcommittee on Crime

SUMMARY

High-technology crimes hold the potential to vastly change our understanding of crime. Illegal wire transfers of huge asset stores, nuclear subterfuge, and computer crime are all emerging as novel forms of criminal enterprise. Some forms of high-technology crime hold dangers never before imagined. Nuclear terrorism, for example, holds the potential to destroy more property and to claim more human lives than decades of traditional criminal activity.

The very nature of contemporary society dictates that crimes exploiting high technology will always be with us. It can only be hoped that enforcement technologies continue to keep abreast of technologies that serve criminal purposes. Unfortunately, however, no one is able to realistically assess even the current extent of high-technology crime, let alone accurately imagine the form future high-tech crimes will take.

Efforts to control high-technology crime open a Pandora's box of issues related to individual rights in the face of criminal investigation and prosecution. Such issues extend from free speech considerations to guarantees of technological privacy in the midst of digital interconnectedness. As we enter the twenty-first century, it is incumbent upon us to strike an acceptable balance between constitutional guarantees to continued freedom of access to legitimate activities based upon high technology, and enforcement initiatives which can deal effectively with the massive threat high-technology crimes represent.

DISCUSSION QUESTIONS

1. What is the difference between high-technology crime and traditional forms of criminal activity? Will the high-technology crimes of today continue to be the high-technology crimes of tomorrow? Why or why not?
2. What forms of high-technology crime can you imagine that this chapter has not discussed? Describe each briefly.
3. Do you believe that high-technology crimes will eventually surpass the abilities of enforcement agents to prevent or solve them? Why or why not?
4. What different kinds of high-tech offenders can you imagine? How best might each type be dealt with? Give reasons for your answers.

NOTES

1 Georgette Bennett, *Crimewarps: The Future of Crime in America* (New York: Anchor, 1987), p. xiii.
2. Cynthia Manson and Charles Ardai, *Future Crime: An Anthology of the Shape of Crime to Come* (New York: Donald I. Fine, 1992), p. ix.
3. Alvin Toffler, *Powershift: Knowledge, Wealth, and Violence at the Edge of the 21st Century* (New York: Bantam, 1990), p. 255.
4. Carlos was given the name Ilich Ramirez Sanchez when he was born in Venezuela on October 12, 1949.
5. "Infamous Killer Now Old, Desperate," *USA Today*, August 16, 1994, p. 1A.
6. Robert Green, "CIA Warns of Nuclear Threat from Russian Gangs," Reuters wire service on-line, June 27, 1994.
7. Merck and Co., Inc., *Interim Report for the Period Ended June 30, 1994*, p. 4.
8. Kenneth Rosenblatt, "Deterring Computer Crime," *Technology Review*, Vol. 93, no. 2 (February/March 1990), pp. 34–41.
9. Ibid.
10. This and most other definitions related to computer crime in this chapter are taken from Donn B. Parker, *Computer Crime: Criminal Justice Resource Manual* (Washington, D.C.: National Institute of Justice, 1989).
11. Rosenblatt, "Deterring Computer Crime."
12. Ibid.
13. Stephen R. Purdy, "Protecting Your Telephone Systems Against Dial-Tone Thieves," *Infosecurity News*, July/August 1993, p. 43.
14. "Out Slicked," *Infosecurity News*, July/August 1993, p. 11.
15. Paul Keegan, "High Tech Pirates Collecting Phone Calls," *USA Today*, September 23, 1994, p. 4A.
16. Ibid.
17. Paul Saffo, "Desperately Seeking Cyberspace," *Personal Computing*, May 1989, p. 248.
18. As described in M. Gemiganni, "Viruses and Computer Law," *Communications of the ACM*, Vol. 32 (June 1989), p. 669.

19. Parker, *Computer Crime: Criminal Justice Resource Manual.*
20. Saffo, "Desperately Seeking Cyberspace," p. 247.
21. Ibid.
22. J. Bloombecker, "A Security Manager's Guide to Hacking," *DATAPRO Reports on Information Security,* Report #IS35-450-101, 1986.
23. Marc Robins, "Case of the Ticked-Off Teens," *Infosecurity News,* July/August 1993, p. 48.
24. For more information, see Ronald R. Thrasher, "Voice-Mail Fraud," *FBI Law Enforcement Bulletin,* July 1994, pp. 1–4.
25. J. Maxfield, "Computer Bulletin Boards and the Hacker Problem," *EDPACS, the Electric Data Processing Audit, Control and Security Newsletter* (Arlington, VA: Automation Training Center, October 1985).
26. Percy Black, personal communication, 1991. As cited in M. E. Kabay, "Computer Crime: Hackers" (undated electronic manuscript).
27. John Perry Barlow, "Crime and Puzzlement: in Advance of the Law on the Electronic Frontier," *Whole Earth Review,* Fall 1990, p. 44.
28. Anne W. Branscomb, "Common Law for the Electronic Frontier," *Scientific American,* September 1991.
29. As cited in Barlow, "Crime and Puzzlement."
30. "Computer Porn," *Time,* March 15, 1993, p. 22.
31. Maxfield, "Computer Bulletin Boards and the Hacker Problem."
32. Parker, *Computer Crime: Criminal Justice Resource Manual.*
33. John Naisbitt, *Megatrends: Ten New Directions Transforming Our Lives* (New York: Warner Books, 1982), p. 36.
34. Ibid.
35. Al Gore, "Infrastructure for the Global Village," *Scientific American,* September 1991, p. 150.
36. For insight into how security techniques often lag behind the abilities of criminal perpetrators in the high-technology arena, see James A. Fagin, "Computer Crime: A Technology Gap," *International Journal of Comparative and Applied Criminal Justice,* Vol. 15, nos. 1 and 2 (Spring/Fall 1991), pp. 285–297.
37. Richard Larson, "The New Crime Stoppers: State-of-the Art Computer Technology Promises a Return to Neighborhood-Oriented Policing," *Technology Review,* Vol. 92, no. 8 (November/December 1989), p. 26.
38. Michael Schrage, "Today, It Takes a Scientist to Catch a Thief," *Washington Post* on-line, March 18, 1994.
39. *Daubert* v. *Merrell Dow Pharmaceuticals, Inc.,* 113 S. Ct. 2786 (June 28, 1993).
40. *Frye* v. *United States,* 54 App. D.C. 46, 47, 293 F. 1013, 1014 (1923).
41. Schrage, "Today, It Takes a Scientist to Catch a Thief."
42. Ibid.
43. "British Police to Use DNA to Catch Burglars," Reuters wire service, June 16, 1994.
44. Schrage, "Today, It Takes a Scientist to Catch a Thief."
45. Roland Reboussin, "An Expert System Designed to Profile Murderers," in Frank Schmalleger, *Computers in Criminal Justice: Issues and Applications* (Bristol, IN: Wyndham Hall Press, 1990), p. 239.
46. "Increased Spending for Security," *Infosecurity News,* July/August 1993, p. 11.
47. Don B. Parker, *Computer Crime,* p. xiii.
48. Kenneth Rosenblatt, "Deterring Computer Crime," *Technology Review,* February/March 1990, Vol. 93, no. 2, p. 34-41.
49. Ibid.
50. Ibid.
51. Ibid.
52. EFF statement of purpose, from the EFF forum on CompuServe, as of August 22, 1994.
53. The White House, Office of the Vice President, "Statement of the Vice President," February 4, 1994.
54. Department of Justice press release, "Attorney General Makes Key Escrow Encryption Announcements," February 4, 1994.
55. Ibid.
56. Ibid.
57. Taken from Marcy Gordon, "Hi-Tech for Cops," the Associated Press on-line, Northern edition, July 22, 1994.

PART FOUR

RESPONDING TO CRIMINAL BEHAVIOR

...we cannot predict with any confidence that in the more benign post-scarcity environment of future societies humans will become more like angels and less like beasts.

—Bernard Gendron[1]

Crime is...an ever-present condition, even as sickness, disease, and death. It is perennial as spring and as recurrent as winter.

—Frank Tannenbaum[2]

CHAPTER 13

CRIMINOLOGY AND SOCIAL POLICY

A mortal battle for the national conscience is being waged as I write and you read. The jousting...will determine what we, in the future, will label as "crime" and how we react to it.

—*Georgette Bennett*[3]

Fundamentally, our capacity to extinguish criminality and lawlessness lies in the moral training and moral stature of our people.

--*President Herbert Hoover*[4]

The horrific events in Oklahoma City...show the high price we pay for our Liberties.

—*Senator Orrin Hatch (referring to the 1995 terrorist bombing there)*[5]

IMPORTANT TERMS

public policy	three strikes	habitual offender statutes
deterrence strategy	nurturant strategy	social epidemiology
Kriminalpolitik	LEAA	protection/avoidance strategy

IMPORTANT LAWS AND GROUPS

Wickersham Commission
Omnibus Crime Control and Safe Streets Act of 1967
National Advisory Commission on Criminal Justice Standards and Goals
Comprehensive Crime Control Act of 1984
Anti-Drug Abuse Act of 1988
Brady Handgun Violence Prevention Act of 1993
Violent Crime Control and Law Enforcement Act of 1994

INTRODUCTION

In the study of crime, as in many other areas, life often imitates art. As this book goes to press rapper Snoop Doggy Dogg awaits trial on first-degree murder charges stemming from the November 1993 slaying of Phillip Woldermariam. Woldermariam, thought to be a member of the Venice Shoreline Crips, was shot twice in the back after meeting with Snoop. The alleged triggerman was Snoop's bodyguard. Snoop's particular brand of music, "gangsta rap," is immensely popular. His 1993 album, *Doggy Style*, climbed to the top of the charts as soon as it was released. On the other hand, gangsta rap and "hip hop" music have caught the attention of many who claim the lyrics promote antisocial and violent behavior.

Snoop is not the only gangsta rapper to run afoul of the law. Shortly before Snoop's arrest, hit musician Tupac Shakur, well-known for his starring role in the movie *Poetic Justice*, was charged with shooting two off-duty Atlanta police officers after a concert at Clark Atlanta University.[6] A few weeks later, Shakur was accused of a variety of sexual crimes, including forcible sodomy and unlawful imprisonment—charges stemming from an incident in which Shakur allegedly held a 20-year-old woman down in a room at New York City's Parker Meridien Hotel while she was sexually attacked.[7] Although he was convicted on three lesser counts of sexual abuse in that case,[8] a 1994 Los Angeles jury found Shakur guilty of assault and battery in an attack on his former film director, Allen Hughes.[9] In a violent footnote to the New York incident, Shakur was shot and hospitalized in an apparent robbery attempt while awaiting sentencing.[10]

About the same time Flavor Flav (William Drayton), a singer with the group Public Enemy, was arrested for firing a .38-caliber pistol at a neighbor. By the time of Flav's arrest, Ice-T's song *Cop Killer* had been blamed in the 1992 shooting deaths of two Las Vegas police officers who were ambushed and killed by four juveniles. The juveniles continued to sing *Cop Killer* lyrics following their arrest.[11] *Body Count*, the Time-Warner album on which *Cop Killer* appears, was shipped to stores in a miniature body bag.

Rapper Snoop Doggy Dogg in criminal court. Some claim that violent themes in "ghetto rap" lead to crime. *Pool/Starr/SABA Press Photos, Inc.*

A year later, rapper Dr. Dre (a.k.a. Andre Young) directed an 18-minute video of a Snoop performance called *Murder Was the Case.* Dre said he wanted to package it with Oliver Stone's *Natural Born Killers.*[12] *Murder* and *Killers* were both quickly criticized by law enforcement organizations, parents' groups, and black leaders decrying the lyrics of gangsta music.[13] The Reverend Arthur L. Cribbs, Jr., a black minister writing in a national editorial, called gangsta rap "nothing but modern-day violence and vulgarity wrapped and packaged in blackface."[14] Cribbs claimed the music "would not be widespread if white megarecord companies did not put filth on sale for big dollars." Soon, radio stations began banning violent rap music. WBLS-FM in New York and KACE-FM in Los Angeles announced that they would no longer play rap songs that encouraged violence, KPWR-FM in Los Angeles masked offensive words, and WCKZ-FM in Charlotte limited gangsta rap to late-night hours.

But whether gangsta rap is indeed a cause of crime, as some claim, or merely a quasi-poetic rendering of the social conditions characteristic of many inner-city American communities today, is less than clear. Snoop, who was born with the name Calvin Broadus in Long Beach, California, in 1971, and others like him have profited mightily by selling images of urban violence to mainstream youth. As a result of highly lucrative album sales, Snoop had no problem posting a $1 million bond following his arrest. The real problems, some claim, are outside rap music, not within it. Gangsta rap supporters suggest that rap may be the wake-up call needed to end black-on-black violence, which now seems out of control, and that by raising public awareness, it may do more to reduce violence than any government-sponsored program could do.

FEDERAL ANTICRIME INITIATIVES

A number of public interest groups and influential politicians—among them, the National Political Congress of Black Women, U.S. Attorney General Janet Reno, and Senator Carol Moseley-Braun—are calling for congressional investigations into the possible behavioral consequences of rap music, hoping that lawmakers will enact some sort of legislative control over the airing of offensive lyrics.[15] Should Congress undertake to control the potentially crime-inspiring effects of rap music, its action will be just one of the latest in a long series of federal government initiatives in the war against crime. **Public policy,** also called social policy, can be defined as "a course of action that government takes in an effort to solve a problem or to achieve an end."[16] Analysts of public policy have observed that policies undergo five stages in their development:[17]

Public policy a course of action that government takes in an effort to solve a problem or to achieve an end.

- identification of the problem
- agenda setting or the prioritization of problems
- policy formation
- program implementation
- program evaluation and reassessment

The Hoover Administration

Although the development of policies to combat crime and the conditions which cause it have traditionally been primarily the responsibility of state and local governments in the United States, crime control became a part of the federal approach to social problems in the United States more than half a century ago. In the foreword to James D. Calder's *The Origins and Development of Federal Crime Control Policy,*[18] George H. Nash writes: "While all complicated social policies and institutional arrangements have many roots...the decisive movement in the development of comprehensive federal crime control was the period between 1929 and 1933, the presidency of Herbert Hoover." Calder puts it even more succinctly. "The administration of Herbert Clark Hoover, thirty-first president of the United States," he writes, "marks the origins of federal crime-control policy."[19] Calder argues that a trilogy of factors combined to usher in an era of federal crime-control policies: "the proliferating stress on the judicial system" associated mostly with Prohibition; "the emergence of new perspectives in law, sociology, and criminology, and the rise of academically-trained social scientists eager to apply their knowledge to reform of the legal system," and "the election in 1928 of a president committed to reform and receptive to the approaches of the activist social scientists."[20] Other events of the era, including the sensational kidnapping of young Charles Augustus Lindbergh, Jr., better known as "the Lindbergh baby"; the rapid rise in influence of organized crime; the visibility of gang warfare; media coverage of notorious criminals; and the effects of the depression on crime rates everywhere, all necessitated serious and decisive anticrime action by the Hoover administration.

In 1929 Max Lowenthal, a Hoover administration insider, called crime and its control, "the dominant issue before the American people."[21] The opening words of Hoover's inaugural address focused the first order of business for the new administration upon "The failure of our system of criminal justice." Hoover observed that "crime had increased...and confidence in the system of criminal justice had decreased."[22] When Hoover assumed office, Calder observes, "[t]he popular belief was that crime had increased and governments at all levels had become less able to control its growth."[23] During his campaign for the presidency Hoover promised, if elected, to initiate a scientific study of crime and law enforcement. The promise was fulfilled with the 1929 appointment of George Woodard Wickersham to chair Hoover's Commission on Law Observance and Enforcement. Wickersham, a lawyer with an outstanding professional reputation, had been U.S. attorney general during the Taft administration. Wickersham's views coincided with Hoover's in many policy areas, and the two men were in constant communication during the Wickersham Commission hearings.

The Hoover administration developed policy initiatives in the areas of police, courts, and corrections. Interest centered on[24]

- developing "objectives to improve justice system practices and to reinstate law's role in civilized governance" (which was the mandate of the Wickersham Commission).
- exploring the extent to which "Prohibition was the basis for general disrespect of the law."
- investigating the extent to which deadly force was a necessary or reasonable law enforcement tool (an issue which arose after a number of innocent citizens were killed by federal and state enforcement agents determined to stop fleeing Prohibition law violators).
- controlling the illegal manufacture, sale, and importation of heroin, morphine, and opium.
- development of a system of reliable information gathering, including crime statistics, which could be used in the further development of crime-fighting policies.
- codification of federal law enforcement activities, including the elimination of overlapping law enforcement activities by different agencies.
- increasing professionalism among the federal judiciary, especially through the removal and replacement of incompetent or corrupt government prosecutors.
- streamlining the federal court system, improving court procedures, and ending the massive congestion then found in federal courtrooms across the country.
- combating organized crime and reducing its influence throughout America.
- reforming the system of federal prisons so that it might not only punish, but reform and provide a visible sense of deterrence to others contemplating criminal activity.
- elimination of abusive and unprofessional prison management.
- reducing prison overcrowding and decreasing idleness among prisoners.

Development of federal criminal justice policy during the Hoover administration era made use of "the services of the best experts in the country"—men and women like August Vollmer, former chief of police in Berkeley, California; Roscoe Pound, dean of the Harvard Law School; Henry W. Anderson, president of the Virginia Bar Association; Ada L. Comstock, president of Radcliffe College; Mabel Willebrandt, a highly visible Prohibition supporter; Sanford Bates, director of the Federal Bureau of Prisons; Frank J. Loesch, a judge and Chicago antigang leader; and many other policy leaders and critical thinkers of the times.

Unfortunately, however, policymaking groups, most notably the Wickersham Commission, did not include broad representation of blacks or other racial and ethnic minorities. Although some citizens expressed concerns that "blacks had endured more than a century of police abuse, rigged court rooms, and harsh prison treatment and that they were overrepresented in crime statistics for reasons that demanded inquiry,"[25] Hoover decided that the appointment of ethnic minorities to policymaking groups solely for the purpose of including them "would violate his principle of having no special interests represented"[26] and might produce less than objective results.

Nonetheless, the Hoover era set the tone for federal criminal justice policies that were to follow—a tone already identified in the October 1929 preliminary report of the Wickersham Commission which said: "We found that with huge investments in plant and personnel and with great operating costs, the country has been proceeding largely in a haphazard manner, without any inventory of the available facts, without commensurate research for checking a great social evil, without the application of the principles that have been so successful in some of the professions, in many businesses and in the social sciences."[27]

Many Hoover-era reforms eventually proved themselves effective. As James D. Calder observes, "Hoover's administration was the first to give formal policy attention to federal prisons and prisoners. Under his leadership, prison administration, historically ignored, was transformed from an antiquated and rawly inadequate collection of penitentiaries into a model system."[28] Other reforms were also well received. Prison expansion got underway, activities of the federal parole board were streamlined and centralized, and new federal district court standards were introduced reducing the high cost of repeated and redundant appeals which had been clogging the nation's courts.

Federal Policy Since World War II

By the end of World War II the nation basked in the glow of economic expansion as industrial production, greatly enhanced by the demands of war, turned to peaceful purposes. Unfortunately, however, domestic tranquillity was about to be disrupted by the baby-boom generation, who were themselves an offshoot of the enthusiasm which accompanied the end of the war. Baby boomers, born in the decade following 1945, contributed significantly to rising crime rates around 1960 as they began to reach their early teen years. Rising rates made crime and its control an important political issue during the presidency of John F. Kennedy (1961–1963). The Kennedy administration expanded federal crime-control policies to address juvenile crime and the rights of indigent defendants to be afforded counsel. Under the direction of Robert Kennedy, U.S. attorney general during his brother's administration, federal anticrime efforts also focused on combating organized crime—which was seen as a crime-control issue that transcended state boundaries.

After Kennedy was assassinated in 1963, Lyndon Baines Johnson was sworn in as the thirty-sixth president of the United States—serving until 1969. Although Barry Goldwater had highlighted issues of crime and violence during the 1964 presidential campaign, Johnson capitalized on them, playing to rising crime fears identified by pollsters at the time. The President's Commission on Law Enforcement and Administration of Justice was established by Johnson and formed part of his drive toward building what he called "The Great Society." Johnson's charge to the commission consisted partially of these words: "The problem of crime brings us together. Even as we join in common action, we know there can be no instant victory. Ancient evils do not yield to easy conquest. We cannot limit our efforts to enemies we can see. We must, with equal resolve, seek out new knowledge, new techniques, and new understanding."[29]

The Commission's report, *The Challenge of Crime in a Free Society*, which was issued in February 1967, laid the groundwork for many anticrime initiatives which were to follow. True to its Democratic roots, the Commission saw crime as the inevitable result of poverty, unemployment, low educational levels, and other social and economic disadvantages. It proposed legislation, eventually passed in the form of the Omnibus Crime Control and Safe Streets Act of 1967, to "eliminate the social conditions that bring about crime." Title I of the Safe Streets Act established the Law Enforcement Assistance Administration (**LEAA**), with the mandate of providing technical and financial assistance to the states for the purpose of improving and strengthening law enforcement activities at the local level. The **LEAA** (Law Enforcement Assistance Administration) spent hundreds of millions of dollars before it was disbanded.

LEAA an acronym for the Law Enforcement Assistance Administration, which was established under Title I of the Omnibus Crime Control and Safe Streets Act of 1967.

At the time of the commission's 1967 report, crime was far less a reality than it is today. Although fear of crime was widespread in the late 1960s, the crime rate was less than a third of what it is now. Carjackings, crack cocaine, drive-by shootings, metal detectors in schools, mass murder, drug cartels, and gang warfare with automatic weapons were unheard of. Even so, as the crime rate rose, personal security became a major concern of the American public. It was during this period that the nation's "war on crime" took on its modern tenor.

While the true cause of rising crime rates that characterized the period from 1960 to 1975 may never be known, many possibilities have been suggested—ranging from maturing baby boomers (discussed earlier) to the dissolution of institutions of social control such as the family, churches, and schools. Whatever the reason, it soon became clear that federal crime-control policies were no match for the underlying social forces fueling the rapid rise in crime.

When Richard Milhous Nixon became president of the United States in 1969, federal efforts at crime control took on a decidedly Republican cast. Nixon "sought all out war on crime, frequently with little concern for the accused. In his efforts to get criminals out of circulation, Nixon advocated mandatory minimum sentences, fewer pretrial releases for multiple offenders, generally heavier penalties, and selection of judges who were strict on crime."[30] As the nation's law enforcers, courts and correctional systems became hopelessly overworked, high rates of recidivism were cited as the basis for an emerging new "lock-'em-up" policy which emphasized retribution and deterrence by example. The war on crime turned increasingly conservative and calls for swift and certain penalties, accompanied by increased punishments including the reduction or abolition of parole and early release, were made into law. Nixon also commissioned the National Advisory Commission on Criminal Justice Standards and Goals in 1971. In its reports, the

Commission called for improved police-community relations and enhanced communications between criminal justice agencies.

During the Reagan administration (1981–1988) two new fronts in the "war on crime" emerged. One, which some writers have called a "war on criminals," meant that less and less attention would be paid to the root causes of crime, and more and more attention would be devoted to holding individual offenders responsible for their crimes. In support of this first front, Congress passed the Comprehensive Crime Control Act of 1984, a far-reaching law that mandated new sentencing guidelines, eliminated parole at the federal level, limited the use of the insanity defense, and increased penalties associated with drug dealing. Typical of Republican approaches to the problem of crime, Reagan insisted that, "[c]hoosing a career in crime is not the result of poverty or of an unhappy childhood or of a misunderstood adolescence; it's the result of a conscious, willful, selfish choice made by some who consider themselves above the law, who seek to exploit the hard work and, sometimes, the very lives of their fellow citizens."[31]

The second front in the Reagan administration's war on crime focused on drugs and their relationship to criminal activity. Some analysts claim that drug control provided the single most important issue on Reagan's crime-control agenda. Reagan believed that drugs contributed, both directly and indirectly, to much of the nation's crime problem. He was strongly opposed to the legalization or decriminalization of controlled substances, and in 1985 persuaded Congress to pass legislation criminalizing the manufacture, distribution, and possession of designer drugs. Under Reagan's leadership, Congress passed the Omnibus Anti-Drug Abuse Act of 1988 which substantially increased penalties for recreational drug users and created a new cabinet-level position to coordinate the drug-fighting efforts of the federal government. The position, dubbed by the press the "Drug Czar," was initially filled by William Bennett (a Bush appointee) who brought federal antidrug efforts to national attention when he declared Washington, D.C., a "drug zone" in 1989. "Drug zone" designation made the city, and others like it, eligible for federal drug-fighting assistance.

CRIME-CONTROL PHILOSOPHIES

The contemporary situation is the cumulative result of all these historical initiatives. Today's policy approach to crime control is twin pronged. One prong, that of crime control, defines crime as an issue of individual responsibility. The other, which is being cast in the guise of a public health agenda, sees criminals as victims of a kind of rampant social pathology that has turned them into offenders. In Chapter 1 we termed the first prong the "social responsibility perspective," while the second approach was called the "social problems perspective."

Social epidemiology the study of social epidemics and diseases of the social order.

Those who portray crime as the result of poor social conditions stress the need for improvements in the American infrastructure and continue to battle for an expansion of educational and employment opportunities for the disenfranchised. One new aspect of the social problems approach is its recasting in terms of **social epidemiology.** In terminology akin to the old social pathology approach of the

Prison weight-lifting bans, popular in some states, reflect a growing frustration with unsuccessful crime-control policies. *Steve Lehman/SABA Press Photos, Inc.*

Chicago school, some contemporary politicians and criminologists view crime and the conditions that create it in terms of a disease model. "Epidemiology" refers to the study of epidemics and diseases. "Social epidemiology" has come to mean the study of social epidemics and diseases of the social order. Hence, the social epidemiological approach holds that crime arises from festering conditions which promote social ills, and that individuals caught in an environment within which crime may be communicated display symptoms of this disease and suffer from its maladies. Crime becomes an illness, a social malady, but one which can be cured if the necessary resources could be dedicated to its treatment and eradication. Recognizing that crime and violence have reached epidemic proportions, such thinkers advance solutions based upon what is, in effect, a public health model. Crime as a disease becomes a new kind of social problem—one which shifts responsibility for law violations away from individuals "afflicted" with criminality and toward the society that is ultimately responsible for their control.

As a consequence of continued frustration at being unable to end the ongoing avalanche of American crime, however, and due to a lack of proven programs for assuring the rehabilitation of criminal offenders, the social responsibility perspective is now in ascendancy. Policies at both the state and federal level are more and more focused on strict enforcement of existing laws and on strict punishments. Prisons are being built apace, while tough legislation which will fill even more prisons is being passed at a feverish pitch. Americans, fed up with both crime and with the fear it engenders, are pushing their political representatives for creation of conservative policy tools to deal with it.

Reflecting such get-tough on crime attitudes, lawmakers in 1995 targeted what they saw as "soft" prisons—institutions where inmates spend their days lifting weights, watching television, reading newspapers, going to the dining hall, and living in air-conditioned relaxation. In some states, legislators—citing the 1993 Lucasville, Ohio, prison riot in which inmates threatened guards with barbells—introduced legislation designed to limit the leisure activities of inmates. Others argued that prisoners should not have the opportunity to build strength while in prison only to victimize innocent people once released. Prisoners, on the other hand, were opposed to the lawmakers' new-found conservative fervor. Harvey Garlotte, a convicted murderer serving a life sentence in the South Mississippi Correctional Facility, watched guards as they began to confiscate previously permitted private TV sets. "If they're going to take the TVs and all," Garlotte said, "things are going to blow apart."[32]

Types of Crime-Control Strategies

The dichotomous values which underlie modern-day policymaking reflect fundamental differences in philosophical and political orientations. Even so, the range of effective crime-control alternatives available to reformers of any political bent is limited to three types of strategies. These three strategies, identified by Bryan Vila,[33] one of the most seminal contemporary analysts of contemporary public policy, differ in terms of "strategic focus." That is, they are distinguishable from one another "by whether they attempt to block opportunities for crime, alter the outcome of conscious or unconscious decision-making that precedes a criminal act, or alter the broad strategic style with which people approach many aspects of their lives."[34] The three strategies are

- Protection/avoidance strategies
- Deterrence strategies
- Nurturant strategies

Which crime control policies work are the subject of considerable debate. Here, meditators affiliated with Maharishi International University work to lower crime in Washington, D.C. Later research showed a statistically significant reduction in D.C. area crime rates during the meditative session.

Protection/avoidance strategies "attempt to reduce criminal opportunities by changing people's routine activities or by incapacitating convicted offenders via incarceration or electronic monitoring devices."[35] Such strategies may also harden targets through the use of architectural design, crime prevention programs such as neighborhood watch, and increased policing.

Deterrence strategies "attempt to diminish motivation for crime by increasing the perceived certainty, severity, or celerity of penalties."[36] New and tougher laws, quicker trial court processing, and faster imposition of sentences are all deterrence strategies.

Nurturant strategies "attempt to forestall development of criminality by improving early life experiences and channeling child and adolescent development" into desirable directions. Nurturant strategies include increased infant and maternal health care, child care for the working poor, training in parenting skills, enhanced public education, and better programs to reduce the number of unwanted pregnancies.

Protection/avoidance strategy a crime-control strategy which attempts to reduce criminal opportunities by changing people's routine activities or by incapacitating convicted offenders via incarceration or electronic monitoring devices.

Deterrence strategy a crime-control strategy which attempts to diminish motivation for crime by increasing the perceived certainty, severity, or celerity of penalties.

Nurturant strategy a crime-control strategy that attempts to forestall development of criminality by improving early life experiences and channeling child and adolescent development into desirable directions.

RECENT FEDERAL POLICY INITIATIVES

The Brady Law

One result of the growing conservative push which characterized the late 1980s and early 1990s was the Brady Handgun Violence Prevention Act of 1993. The Brady law, which is primarily a protection/avoidance strategy, was the last act passed by Congress in 1993. It was signed into law by President Clinton on November 30 of that year. The law was named after former President Ronald Reagan's White House press secretary, Jim Brady, who was shot in the head during John Hinckley's 1981 attempted assassination of Reagan. Brady, although seriously injured and impaired for life, survived.

The purpose of the Brady law is to "provide for a waiting period before the purchase of a handgun and for the establishment of a national instant criminal background check system to be contacted by firearms dealers before the transfer of any firearm."[37] Under the law, firearms dealers must register with the federal government and are required to notify law enforcement officials of all handgun purchase applications. Law enforcement officers are then required to check the backgrounds of applicants and to disapprove purchase of handguns by (1) individuals under indictment for, or convicted in any court of, a crime punishable by imprisonment for a term exceeding one year; (2) fugitives from justice; (3) unlawful users of or those addicted to any controlled substance; (4) those adjudicated as mentally defective, or persons who have been committed to a mental institution; (5) illegal aliens, or those who are in the United States unlawfully; (6) persons who have not been discharged from the Armed Forces under honorable conditions; and (7) "a person who, having been a citizen of the United States, has renounced such citizenship." Gun dealers not abiding by the provisions of the law may have their licenses suspended or revoked and may be fined up to $5,000 per illegal transaction. Thirty-four states and territories must comply with the new law, but

Handgun victim James Brady sits to the right of President Clinton as the Brady Bill is signed into law. Much recent anticrime policy in the United States has focused on gun control. *Gary Hershorn/Reuter/Bettmann.*

the District of Columbia and twenty states are exempt from the law's provisions because they have more stringent laws or similar measures already in effect.

A national "instant" background check system, also approved by the law, has only recently been funded and is not yet fully operational. Under the law states are to receive $200 million in federal assistance to improve criminal record keeping, eventually leading to a nationwide computerized system for instant checking of records. The five-day waiting period will be phased out, but only after the national system is fully operational.

In an effort to reduce firearm theft, especially during the interstate shipment of weapons, the Brady law also requires that "No common or contract carrier shall require or cause any label, tag, or other written notice to be placed on the outside of any package, luggage, or other container that such package, luggage, or other container contains a firearm."

Proponents of the Brady law believed that the widespread and ready availability of guns throughout the United States was a significant factor contributing to the crime problem. Statistics seem to support that view. A 1994 report by the Bureau of Justice Statistics, for example, found that the number of crimes committed with handguns in 1992 approached 1 million and occurred at a record rate. Handguns were used in an ever-growing percentage of violent crimes, and handgun use was up, while overall nonfatal violent crimes dropped in 1992. According to the report, 917,500 nonfatal crimes were committed with handguns in 1992, 50% above the average for the previous five years. In addition, there were 13,200 handgun homicides in 1992, 24% above the five-year average. Handguns were used in 55.6% of the year's 23,760 murders, and offenders armed with handguns committed 1 in every 8 nonfatal violent crimes, including rape, robbery, and assault. The Bureau found that young black males comprised the group most victimized by handgun crime. There were 39.7 handgun crimes for every 1,000 black males age 16–19 in the U.S. population—four times the rate for young white males. Other findings were that offenders fired their weapons in 17% of all nonfatal handgun crimes, missing the victim four out of five times, and about 21,000 victims were wounded by handguns in 1992. The report also notes that, on average, 340,000 firearms are stolen each year.

Opponents of the Brady law, however, are not convinced it will reduce crime. As Rep. Harold Volkmer (D., Mo.) said at the time the bill was being debated in the Senate: "A waiting period imposes a burden on those who obey the law. Getting criminals off the street is the only way to solve the crime problem. It is ludicrous to think that tougher gun laws will stop criminals." The National Association of Chiefs of Police also went on record as opposing the Brady law. "We wonder if the standing ovation for Jim Brady would have been so resounding if all those present realized that the Brady handgun-control law can be expected to backfire by leading to a rise in crime as understaffed, overworked law enforcement agencies are forced to devote millions of hours away from patrols and crime solving to conduct background checks, mostly on law-abiding citizens," said Dennis Martin, president of the NACP.[38] The strongest and most vocal opposition to handgun control, however, comes from the National Rifle Association (NRA), which claims the Brady law and other measures like it are unconstitutional. In 1994 the NRA announced a plan that it said would help local law enforcement officials file suits challenging the Brady handgun control law. NRA spokesman Bill McIntyre said the lawsuits "are on the way in a variety of states...,"[39] and NRA legislative counsel Richard Gardiner explained that the lobbying group will not be the plaintiff in legal actions, but will instead pay for attorneys to represent law enforcement officers opposed to the legislation.

In January 1994 25-year-old Philip Toth became the first person formally accused of violating the Brady law.[40] Toth was charged in U.S. District Court in Cedar Rapids, Iowa, with stealing guns from a licensed firearms dealer, now a federal offense under the law. In April of that same year John Arnold, a Fort Walton Beach, Florida, gun dealer became the first person convicted under the law.[41] He had been charged with stealing five guns from the Gulf Breeze, Florida, Pistol Parlor in January 1994.

Other gun law changes may be in the works. Following passage of the Brady law, President Clinton said that he was intrigued by an idea raised by New York City Mayor Rudolph Giuliani, "calling for either the federal government or the states to establish gun licensing and training systems for potential gun owners, similar to current licensing requirements for motorists."

The Violent Crime Control and Law Enforcement Act of 1994

Another direct result of get-tough crime-control attitudes is the Violent Crime Control and Law Enforcement Act of 1994. At first blush, the act, which was passed by Congress in response to increasingly hard-nosed voter sentiment about crime, appears primarily representative of a deterrence strategy, although it also contains elements of the protection/avoidance approach. Conservative critics of the new law, however, which was passed by a Democratic-controlled Congress under the leadership of a Democratic president, claim that it is really a liberal agenda in disguise and that its funding of social programs in the fight against crime move it in the direction of nurturant strategies. In fact, the law tries to be all things and attempts to address the needs of a wide diversity of political constituencies. As a result, it embodies aspects of all three types of crime-control strategies identified earlier.

The 1994 law was billed as one of the most sweeping pieces of federal anticrime legislation of all time and provided massive funding for increased law enforcement and correctional resources, including $30.2 billion over six years for crime reduction efforts through the Violent Crime Reduction Trust Fund. Savings from the president's reductions in the federal work force, as calculated by the Congressional Budget Office—and locked in by reductions in federal budget caps—are expected to fund the more than $30 billion in crime bill initiatives.

Under the act, state and local law enforcement agencies are slated to receive $10.8 billion, including (1) $8.8 billion to put 100,000 police officers on the streets in community policing programs; (2) $245 million for rural anticrime and antidrug efforts; (3) $130 million for technical automation grants for law enforcement agencies; and (4) $200 million for college scholarships for students who agree to serve as police officers and for scholarships for in-service officers.

Another $2.6 billion is slated to go to enhance the activities of federal enforcement agencies, including $250 million to the FBI, $150 million to the DEA, $1.2 billion to the Immigration and Naturalization Service and Border Patrol, $50 million to United States Attorneys, $550 million to the Treasury Department, $200 million to the Justice Department, and $200 million to federal courts.

Prisons across the nation are scheduled to receive $9.7 billion, including (1) $7.9 billion in grants to the states to build and operate prisons and incarceration alternatives such as boot camps to ensure that additional prison cells will be available to put—and keep—violent offenders behind bars and (2) $1.8 billion to states for costs of incarcerating criminal illegal aliens.

Another $6.1 billion is earmarked for crime prevention efforts, including (1) $90 million to create an interagency Ounce of Prevention Council to coordinate new and existing crime prevention programs; (2) $567 million for after-school, weekend, and summer "safe haven" programs to provide children with positive activities and alternatives; (3) $243 million to provide in-school assistance to at-risk children, including education, mentoring, and other programs; (4) $1.6 billion to fight violence against women; (5) $1.6 billion for direct funding to localities around the country for anticrime efforts, such as drug treatment, education, and jobs under a portion of the bill called the Local Partnership Act; (6) $626 million for model crime prevention programs targeted at high-crime neighborhoods; (7) $270 million for lines of credit to community development corporations to stimulate business and employment opportunities for low-income, unemployed, and underemployed individuals; and (8) $383 million for drug treatment programs for state ($270 million) and federal ($113 million) prisoners.

Another $377 million is earmarked for a new Local Crime Prevention Block Grant program to be distributed to local governments to be used as local needs dictate for, among other things, (1) antigang programs, (2) midnight sports leagues to give at-risk youth nightly alternatives to the streets, (3) to establish boys and girls clubs in low-income housing communities and to encourage police officers to live in those communities, (4) to create partnerships between senior citizen groups and law enforcement to combat crimes against elderly Americans, (5) to create partnerships between law enforcement and social service agencies to fight crimes against children, and (6) to create supervised centers for divorced or separated parents to visit their children in "safe havens" when there is a history of risk of physical or sexual abuse.

Drug courts that target nonviolent offenders with substance abuse problems are funded to the tune of $1 billion. Participants in such programs will be intensively supervised, given drug treatment, and subjected to graduated sanctions—ultimately including prison terms—for failing random drug tests.

The bill also increases control over firearms including (1) a ban on the manufacture of nineteen military-style assault weapons; (2) prohibiting the sale or transfer of a gun to a juvenile and possession of a gun by a juvenile; (3) prohibiting gun sales to, and possession by, persons subject to family violence restraining orders; and (4) strengthening federal licensing standards for firearms dealers.

Likewise, the bill targets gangs and youth violence by (1) providing new, stiff penalties for violent and drug crimes committed by gangs; (2) tripling penalties for using children to deal drugs near schools and playgrounds; and (3) enhancing penalties for all crimes using children and for recruiting and encouraging children to commit a crime.

The law also (1) creates drug-free zones by increasing penalties for drug dealing near playgrounds, schoolyards, public housing projects, video arcades, and youth centers; (2) authorizes adult treatment of 13-year-olds charged with the most violent of crimes (murder, attempted murder, aggravated assault, armed robbery, and rape); (3) enhances federal penalties for acts of terrorism; (4) expands the federal death penalty to cover about sixty offenses, including terrorism, murdering a law enforcement officer, large-scale drug trafficking, drive-by shootings, and carjacking in which death occurs; (5) mandates life imprisonment for criminals convicted of three violent felonies or drug offenses (the famous "three strikes and you're out" provision); and (6) increases or creates new penalties for over seventy criminal offenses, primarily covering violent crimes, drug trafficking, and gun crimes such as drive-by shootings, the use of semiautomatic weapons, drug use and drug trafficking in prison, the possession of guns and explosives by convicts, sex offenses and assaults against children, crimes against the elderly, interstate gun trafficking, aggravated sexual abuse, gun smuggling, arson, hate crimes, and drunk driving.

In response to the complaints of state governments that the federal government is not taking seriously its responsibility to oversee the nation's borders and stem the flow of illegal immigrants, the law designates $1.2 billion for immigration enforcement, including (1) a new summary procedure to speed deportation of aliens who have been convicted of crimes; (2) increased penalties for smuggling aliens and for document fraud; and (3) monies for new border patrol agents, asylum reform, and other immigration enforcement activities.

In the area of victims rights, the bill (1) allows victims of violent and sex crimes to speak at the sentencing of their assailants, (2) requires sex offenders and child molesters to pay restitution to their victims, and (3) prohibits diversion of victims' funds to other federal programs.

Finally, the 1994 legislation increases federal criminal penalties for various types of fraud, including (1) telemarketing fraud targeted at senior citizens and multiple victims, (2) computer crime offenses, (3) a new federal offense of major fraud by insurance companies against their policyholders, and (4) credit card offenses.

For all its flamboyance, however, the Violent Crime Control and Law Enforcement Act of 1994 may eventually prove to be more rhetoric than substance. Funding for the crime-control measures enacted with the legislation, some of which are not intended to take effect until near the turn of the century, is anything but firm, and the November 1994 Republican landslide in congressional and gubernatorial elections puts such funding even more in doubt.

As this book goes to press, a Republican anti-crime package has passed the House of Representatives. The new bill would authorize $10 billion in community block grants, and permit local authorities the choice of spending money on programs to either fight or prevent crime. Such block grants would replace the 1994 Violent Crime Control and Law Enforcement Act's authorization of federal expenditures to hire 100,000 new police officers over six years, and would almost entirely eliminate billions in funding which was scheduled under the 1994 law for crime-prevention programs. The only crime-prevention measures left intact from the 1994 law would be $1.6 billion for a program to curb violence against women and $383 million for drug treatment for federal and state prisoners.

The Republican-sponsored bill would also provide $10.5 billion for prison construction over the five years, but it would limit which states could get the money. Half of all planned expenditures would be allotted to "truth in sentencing" states which imprison violent criminals for at least 85 percent of their sentences. The other half would go to states that are increasing the incarceration rate of violent criminals as measured by the proportion of violent offenders sent to prison and by the length of time they serve.

The new bill would also streamline deportation of criminal aliens and earmark $650 million a year to reimburse states for the costs of incarcerating such individuals. It would likewise eliminate $1 billion previously slated to be spent on drug courts, or special-purpose courts which are intended to divert some nonviolent drug offenders away from the criminal justice system at an early stage in their case processing.

A central feature of the proposed law, which is called the Victim Restitution Bill, would require convicted offenders to pay full restitution to their victims. Lawful compensation would include costs for actual damages suffered, and expenses incurred by a victim during trial, such as lost income, child care, and transportation to and from court.

What many criminal justice officials see as the most important feature of the new bill would be its planned expansion of the "good faith" exception to the exclusionary rule. Under the proposed law, evidence which is seized improperly by the police could still be considered in court if officers who seized the evidence did so in good faith—that is, under the "objectively reasonable belief" that they were acting lawfully.

CRIME FIGHTING: WHAT WORKS

Eugene H. Methvin

If you were America's anticrime czar, with full powers to invest $30 billion to make our cities safe again, where would you put it? This year, Congress chose to divide the money three ways. It spent $13.5 billion to hire more cops, $9.8 billion to build more prisons, boot camps and "alternate facilities," and $6.9 billion for "prevention" programs ranging from "self-esteem" classes to "gang resistance education" and a "Junior Officers in Training" program for high schoolers.

If America's bureaucracies knew how to target "prevention" dollars, crime would not be a national issue. We have spent literally trillions on programs like those Congress prescribed.

How about investing in cops?

In 1992, the U.S. had 534,000. They made fewer than 4 million felony arrests, and only 381,500 convicted felons landed in prison. Thus, the average cop is lucky to get a single serious felon locked away each year. The cops waste enormous time and money chasing the same criminals, collaring them, processing them and sitting in court—only to see them go free for one reason or another.

It costs an estimated $75,000 to put a single cop on the streets in high-crime districts, but only about $17,000 a year to keep a convicted criminal behind bars. Thus we can keep four career criminals locked up for the price of one cop on the street, and prevent far more crime.

Studying locales as diverse as London, Copenhagen, Philadelphia, Dayton, Racine, Phoenix, and Utah, criminologists have demonstrated that each year's crop of young males contains a tiny and stable minority of serious habitual offenders who commit well over half of the violent and serious crime.

A pioneering study of all 31,436 men born in Copenhagen in the years between 1944 and 1947 found that just 0.6%, offenders, committed 43.4% of the violent crime.

In our own country, the National Youth Survey followed 1,725 juveniles of both sexes aged 11 to 17, carefully selected to represent all U.S. youngsters, for fifteen years. Just thirty-two became high-rate offenders and multiple drug users. This tiny fraction, about 4% of the males, accounted for half of all the serious crimes committed by the entire group. They committed thirty to forty violent crimes and hundreds of lesser crimes, year after year, on into adulthood.

Violence has escalated in recent years not because the number of criminals has grown but chiefly because this tiny fraction of high-rate offenders has increased both the frequency and intensity of their violence.

Consider a recent study, reported in the fall 1994 edition of the *Journal of Criminology*, that followed 6,310 California prisoners released in 1962 and 1963. They were selected to represent all 25,000 California inmates at the time. These were bad hombres: 56% had been in prison before, and 44% were in for violent offenses, burglary or robbery.

Over the next 26 years, these convicts were arrested 30,464 times. Moreover, since criminologists know criminal repeaters get away with a dozen or more crimes per arrest, these 6,310 convicts undoubtedly contributed over a quarter-million crimes to California's crime rate.

For the 4,897 who were rearrested, 54.4% of the charges involved nuisance offenses, such as parole violations, drunk driving, disorderly conduct, gambling and drug possession or use. But the group also scored arrests for 10,000 serious crimes.

What if, instead of sending these career criminals on repeated trips through the revolving door, we had simply "locked 'em up and thrown away the key" in 1962?

To have kept all 6,310 in prison for 26 years would have cost California something like $1.3 billion. As it was, they cost the state a good chunk of that amount anyway—on investigation, prosecution and incarceration for their subsequent crimes.

A rough guess for California's taxpayers' net out-of-pocket costs for that "extra" law enforcement activity would be half the $1.3 billion. So the added cost to prevent almost 10,000 serious crimes—including 184 homicides, 2,084 assaults, 126 kidnappings, 144 rapes, 2,756 burglaries, 655 auto thefts, and 1,193 robberies would be well under a billion—a real bargain.

So where would you invest to cut crime in America: "prevention," cops, or prisons?

Source: Reprinted with permission of *Investor's Business Daily*, Guest Editorial. Eugene H. Methvin, "Crime Fighting: What Works?" November 2, 1994, p. A2.

"Three-Strikes" Legislation

Three-strikes a provision of some criminal statutes which mandates life imprisionment for criminals convicted of three violent felonies or serious drug offenses.

One of the most interesting as well as controversial aspects of the Violent Crime Control and Law Enforcement Act of 1994 is its "three-strikes" provision. The three-strikes provision, a deterrence strategy, reads as follows:

> Mandatory life imprisonment:
>
> Notwithstanding any other provision of law, a person who is convicted in a court of the United States of a serious violent felony shall be sentenced to life imprisonment if—
>
> (A) the person has been convicted (and those convictions have become final) on separate prior occasions in a court of the United States or of a State of—

(i) 2 or more serious violent felonies; or

(ii) one or more serious violent felonies and one or more serious drug offenses; and

(B) each serious violent felony or serious drug offense used as a basis for sentencing under this subsection, other than the first, was committed after the defendant's conviction of the preceding serious violent felony or serious drug offense.

On November 3, 1994, Thomas Lee Farmer, 42, of Des Moines, Iowa, became the first person charged under the federal "three-strikes" law.[42] Farmer, who had three previous convictions for murder, robbery, and conspiracy to commit murder dating back to 1971, was accused of trying to rob a Waterloo, Iowa, grocery store at gunpoint. If convicted, Farmer will receive a mandatory life prison term.

Three-strikes laws are part of a new nationwide initiative intended to keep repeat offenders behind bars. Nationally, many states are in the process of adopting "three-strikes laws" which are a kind of **habitual offender statute.** Such laws generally require that offenders who are convicted of three or more serious crimes be sentenced to a lengthy prison term (often life behind bars) following their third conviction. While "three-strikes" laws may be new, habitual offender statutes are not, and thirty-five states already have some form of habitual offender statute on the books. One of the first states to pass an habitual offender statute was Illinois. The Illinois law, which was enacted in 1978, covers only violent offenses. It sounds, however, like a "three-strikes" law since it mandates a life sentence without parole for people convicted of their third so-called "class X" felony. Fewer than one hundred offenders are currently serving sentences under the Illinois habitual offender statute.

Habitual offender statutes laws intended to keep repeat criminal offenders behind bars. Lately these laws have gained new attention under the rubric of "three strikes and you're out."

Other states have recently joined the "get tough on crime" bandwagon, with Georgia, for example, passing a two-strikes law in 1994. Georgia's law, one of the stiffest in the nation, requires that murderers and persons convicted of a second violent felony be sentenced to life in prison without parole.

Unfortunately, "get-tough" policies may not provide the solution those who advocate them seek. In an excellent analysis of crime-control policy,[43] Bryan Vila presents research findings which tend to show that nurturant strategies—those which attempt to get at the root causes of crime, and that address child welfare needs—are more effective than others in the long run. "We know full well that the most serious and intractable types of crime have their roots in the very child welfare problems that are neglected as we trash through one ineffective war on crime after another," says Vila. "[P]olitical support for nurturant programs might be obtainable," he says, "if we could reverse the vicious cycle of media sensationalism, short-sighted policy, and public impatience that encourages ineffective 'quick fixes' for crime."[44]

CAN WE SOLVE THE PROBLEM OF CRIME?

In 1956 the European writer H. Bianchi[45] emphasized what he saw as the difference between criminology and what he termed *Kriminalpolitik.* Criminology, said Bianchi, should be considered a "metascience" or "a science of wider scope (than that of criminal law, jurisprudence, criminal justice, or corrections) whose terminology can be used to clarify the conceptions of its subdisciplines. Far from being a mere auxiliary to the criminal law," said Bianchi, "it is therefore superior to it."[46]

For Bianchi, and other writers of the time, the concept of *Kriminalpolitik* referred to the political handling of crime, or—as we might say today—a criminology-based social policy. Bianchi believed that if criminology were to remain pure, it could not afford to sully its hands, so to speak, with political concerns. Today, however, the image esteemed by criminologists and the expectations they hold for their discipline are quite different than they were in Bianchi's time. Many criminologists expect to work hand-in-hand with politicians and policymakers, forging crime-control agendas based upon scientific knowledge and criminological theorizing. Some would say that this change in attitude represents a maturation of the discipline of criminology.

Whether effective crime-control policies can ever be implemented, however, is another question. A number of critics argue that only drastic policy-level changes can address the real issues that underlie high rates of crime and criminal activity. Drug legalization, the elimination of guns throughout America, nightly curfews, and close control of media violence, say such reformers, may be necessary before crime can be curbed. "Reforms that substantially will lower the crime rate are

The American voting public is "fed up" with crime, a fact symbolized by this drawing. A child's grief expressed through art—"The man will be kill for killing my dad.... The man was not caught," the young artist writes. Illustration by Pilar Martin.

unlikely because of cultural taboos," says Lawrence Friedman, a Stanford University law professor and author of the book *Crime and Punishment in American History.* According to Friedman, "[i]f you add up all the taboos we have—against legalization of drugs, real gun control, paying taxes for social programs we might at least try—it's hard not to come to the conclusion that there isn't much we can do about crime."[47] Many existing taboos, say such thinkers, are rooted in citizens' demands for individual freedoms. "At one time in South Korea," says Friedman, "they had an absolute curfew between midnight and 5 A.M. The police kept everyone off the streets. It was as hard on burglars as other citizens and very effective at squelching crime. But most Americans would consider that an unacceptable inroad on their personal lives."

Complicating the picture further is the fact that numerous interest groups, each with their own agenda, are clamoring to be heard by policymakers. As Robert D. Pursley puts it, "[o]ur nation's efforts to deal with crime remind us that crime, among other things, is a highly political issue that has been transformed into a racially volatile subject. This issue provides an excellent window into political policymaking. Opposing ideological lines have divided our efforts to develop comprehensive anticrime programs. Deep fissures in our social fabric have contributed to conflicting attitudes about crime and its control."[48]

Racial divisiveness has created one of those fissures. Pursley writes: "Our anticrime programs and studies of traditional street crimes, especially those involving violence, show that such crimes are disproportionately the acts of young African-American males. So long as black men commit violent crimes as a rate that is six to eight times higher than that found among whites and three to four times higher than that among Latino males, race and crime will be threads of the same cloth. These facts have become unpopular and certainly not politically correct to discuss in certain circles, but they remain facts. No attempt to silence those who raise such issues by denouncing them as 'racists' can conceal these statistics."[49]

Pursley is telling us, in effect, that for some groups in some locales, violations of the criminal law are simply part of the landscape. Among certain segments of the American population crime may be an accepted way of doing business and criminal activity, even when discovered, might not necessarily be stigmatizing. Moreover, those who commit crimes may hold positions of prestige or highly visible public offices when their constituencies fail to condemn illicit behavior. Ultimately they may even serve as role models to youngsters—albeit dubious ones. Although such a perspective is undoubtedly a minority point of view, it seriously impacts the ability of policymakers to establish consistent policies in the battle against crime.

A symbol of the divisiveness that today characterizes public attitudes toward crime was the November 1994 election of Marion Barry, a convicted drug felon and former federal inmate, to head the government of Washington, D.C. In 1990 Barry, who had been D.C. mayor for twelve years, was videotaped smoking crack cocaine during an FBI sting operation, convicted of illegal drug use, and sent to prison. A mere five years later, following release from federal prison, he was once again heading the government of our nation's capitol—reelected at a time when the federal government and many of the states were moving toward ultraconservative crime-control policies. Significantly, during the election Barry vowed that he would not submit to random drug tests if elected.

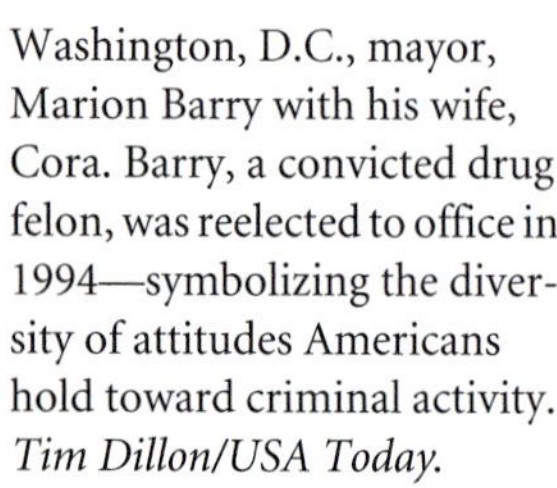

Washington, D.C., mayor, Marion Barry with his wife, Cora. Barry, a convicted drug felon, was reelected to office in 1994—symbolizing the diversity of attitudes Americans hold toward criminal activity. *Tim Dillon/USA Today.*

When all the political crime-fighting rhetoric has ended, and all the dollars have been spent, some expect that crime will still be with us. Many analysts of the contemporary scene see all crime-control policies, especially those at the federal level, as largely symbolic. As Nancy E. Marion explains, "No one could effectively argue that the federal government under any modern president has successfully reduced the amount of criminal activity in the United States. The FBI reports yearly that crime has not gone down, but only continues to increase. Further, the number of people using drugs has not gone down. Therefore, it can be said that the federal government is not making any progress in their fight against crime."[50]

Why is this so? According to Marion it is because, "many of the policies supported by the federal government may in actuality be symbolic gestures to appease the public rather than attempts to reduce crime. One reason for the presence of symbolic policies…is simply that the federal government cannot reduce crime—it is not within the government's capacity to do so."[51] Marion says that congressional power is fragmented through the influence of special interest groups, and as a result, the potential of crime-control initiatives is effectively dispersed by the time any legislation is enacted. In addition, says Marion, the American political system is decidedly shortsighted, focusing only on issues that are likely to win elections. Similarly, due to changes in incumbents (often every two to four years), it is impossible to establish consistent crime-control policies. While a Democratic president may hold office for four years, for example, it is likely that a Republican president will take office with the next elections—while in the meantime a nearly continuous shuffling of cabinet members, senators, representatives, U.S. Supreme Court justices, agency heads, federal judges and so on is occurring. Similar changes at the state level assure constant modification of laws, enforcement practices, and criminal sanctions. Without a consistent, long-term, national, and interstate approach to crime fighting, Marion suggests, crime can never be effectively reduced.

Even consistent policies may be inaccurately targeted. As one author explains it, "[o]ne reason we cannot stop crime in the United States is because many elements of the crime problem we believe to be true simply are not. Because of the way crime is presented in the media, crime events 'become distorted and are given unprecedented social consideration.' These myths help to sustain our views of crime, criminals, and the system as a whole."[52] Part of the mythology of crime, some claim, is belief in criminological theories of limited usefulness. Another problem flows from our inability to effectively conceptualize the crime itself. Laws may merely reflect moral conceptions of the political majority. Both morality and law are subject to change, making it difficult to accurately define crime. A final difficulty is one of accurately measuring the extent of crime. Although exhaustive efforts have been made toward achieving accuracy in measurement, experts are still unable to say with certainty what the true rate of crime is in the United States. Hence, as critics of contemporary crime-fighting policies point out, if we do not fully understand what crime is, or what causes it, how can we create an effective policy for controlling it?

BLACKS LAUNCH AN 'OFFENSIVE' AGAINST CRIME

WASHINGTON—Some of the nation's top black politicians, entertainers and civil rights leaders launched a new crusade over the weekend: a "moral offensive" on violence and black-on-black crime.

"There is no quick fix—but there is a fix," Jesse Jackson declared amid rousing applause during a three-day anticrime conference.

Law enforcement officials, exasperated over the continuing carnage on U.S. streets, say the unprecedented summit could be just the right step.

"It can have a significant impact," said Chuck Wexler, director of the Police Executive Research Forum, an association of big-city police officials. "What could be more important than for the civil rights community to recognize the safety of people in poor areas is really at crisis proportions?"

Anticrime summits are planned for other cities, culminating in a youth march to the White House on April 4, the day Martin Luther King Jr. was assassinated.

"We shall turn Dr. King's crucifixion date into a resurrection," vowed Jackson, whose National Rainbow Coalition sponsored the conference.

Others attending included actor Bill Cosby, movie producer Spike Lee, Attorney General Janet Reno and [then]-U.S. Surgeon General Joycelyn Elders.

Wexler hailed the conference as a way to change the perception that crime-fighting is primarily the responsibility of police, courts and prisons.

"They tend to be institutions that become involved after the problem," he said. "This problem will always be bigger than these institutions."

Many at the summit called it a watershed event in the battle against crime and violence.

"This is the first meaningful and measurable blow to deal with the problem," said Rep. Kweisi Mfume (D., Md.) of the Congressional Black Caucus.

In addition to calling for more government attention to poverty and urban problems, conference participants also called for more personal responsibility within the black community—including a return to traditional values.

Under some proposals that emerged, church-based programs across the nation would

ANTI-CRIME: Former Washington Mayor Sharon Pratt Kelly, the Rainbow Coalition's Jesse Jackson, HUD Secretary Henry Cisneros and Rep. Kweisi Mfume, from left, attend the conference. Said Jackson: "We are in desperate need of a spiritual, moral and ethical revival." *Matt Mendelsohn/USA Today.*

mentor 100,000 black youngsters annually; black colleges would provide academic courses for prison inmates.

And parents were encouraged to become more involved in their children's schooling.

"We have been doing too little, too late," said Elders. "Our children are dying."

As many conferees noted, black bloodshed often comes at the hands of other blacks. While blacks make up less than 13% of the population, they account for nearly 50% of homicide victims, and most of their assailants are black.

Gun control was another major theme, with civil rights activist Al Sharpton promoting criminal penalties for manufacturers whose guns end up on the underground market.

"A lot of the research suggests the increased killings [are] because of the lethality of weapons," said Barry Krisberg of the National Council on Crime and Delinquency. Guns were used in more than 68% of 1992 homicides, up from less than 61% in 1988.

The combination of guns, violence and the entertainment media also came under fire at the summit for creating what was called an explosive situation in the inner cities.

Gangsta rap, for example, with its lyrics about rape and murder, perpetuates violence against black women and glorifies crime, said C. Delores Tucker of the National Political Congress of Black Women.

Tucker said she was at the summit "to put the nation on notice" that her group would conduct a major campaign against the rap music industry.

Whatever their key concern, many at the summit said it was emotionally energizing.

"Everybody knows what they have to do when they go back to their communities, back to the schools," said Natalie Durham of Upper Marlboro, Maryland. "They just can't sit down and read the paper...and complain."

Rashid Jabri of Peace in the Hood, a Cleveland group that fights gang violence, said the summit's true test is later.

Similar gatherings should take place in neighborhood centers, not posh hotels like the Washington Hilton, said Jabri: "Hold them on the street corners where young people are getting murdered."

Study estimates crime costs at $202 billion a year

Crime may not pay, but it can exact a high price. A single crime can cost $41,000 in physical and psychological medical treatment, according to the journal Health Affairs in the first effort to calculate the economic effect of violent crime on such a large scale.

The tab for all crimes in a single year: $202 billion. Gunshot wounds account for 10% of the total cost.

The economic toll should prod lawmakers to find some way to curb the epidemic of violence, authors of the studies say. Their recommendations: gun control, education.

"These are preventable injuries," says Wendy Max of the University of California-San Francisco. "They represent a real potential savings of health dollars."

The pair of studies shows:

- Homicide is the most costly crime because it deprives society the rest of the victim's life contributions.
- Rape had triple the effect of assault or robbery in terms of a victim's diminished quality of life.
- Psychological costs of violent crimes, from counseling to lost quality of life, "dwarf" the physical costs.

QUESTIONS

1. What is the extent of black-on-black violence described by this article? What do you think are the root causes of such violence?
2. Black leaders cited in this article called for "more government attention to poverty... and urban problems... more personal responsibility within the black community... and a return to traditional values." Which of these solutions do you think is most likely to be effective at reducing black-on-black violence? Why?

Source: Sam Vincent Meddis, "Black's Launch an 'Offensive' Against Crime," *USA Today*, January 10, 1994, p. 8A. Copyright 1994, *USA Today*. Reprinted with permission.

SUMMARY

While crime has always been a part of American society, comprehensive efforts at crime control, at least at the federal level, originated during the depression years of the twentieth century. Efforts to reduce crime, however, while well intentioned, are fraught with political uncertainties resting largely upon fundamental disagreements within American society itself as to the sources of crime and the most appropriate means for combating it. Bryan Vila, whose work we have cited throughout this chapter, summarizes the contemporary situation this way: "Lack of a unified criminological framework has fostered shortsighted, inconsistent, and ineffective crime-control policies. Theoretical ambiguity made it easier for policymakers to base their decisions on politics rather than science. Lacking a reasonable complete and coherent explanation of the causes of crime, they have been free to shift the focus of crime-control efforts back and forth from individual-level to macro-level causes as the political pendulum swung from right to left. This erratic approach hindered crime-control efforts and fed the desperate belief that the problem of crime is intractable."[53]

Although answers to the crime problem appear to face formidable obstacles, all may not be lost. Fundamental social changes, including the development of high moral values through education, the elimination (or significant reduction) of poverty, increased opportunities for success at all levels, and decriminalization of certain offenses may all be combined someday into a workable strategy for the management of criminal activity within the United States. In any event, major inroads into the crime problem cannot be made until American society, and especially those parts of it which are now accepting of criminal activity and the conditions that produce it, undergo a fundamental change in orientation.

DISCUSSION QUESTIONS

1. What are the two major policy approaches discussed in this chapter. What are the major differences between the two? With which do you most closely identify? Why?
2. What are the three types of crime-control strategies this chapter describes? Which comes closest to your own philosophy? Why?
3. Explain the social epidemiological approach to reducing crime. In your opinion is the approach worthwhile? Why or why not?
4. If you were in charge of government crime reduction efforts, what steps would you take to control crime in the United States? Why would you choose those?

NOTES

1 Bernard Gendron, *Technology and the Human Condition* (New York: St. Martins, 1977), p. 255.
2. Frank Tannenbaum, "Foreword," in Henry Elmer Barnes and Negley K. Teeters, *New Horizons in Criminology* (Englewood Cliffs, NJ: Prentice Hall, 1943), p. v.
3. Georgette Bennett, *Crimewarps: The Future of Crime in America* (Garden City, NY: Anchor/Doubleday, 1987), p. xix
4. James D. Calder, *The Origins and Development of Federal Crime Control Policy* (Westport, CT: Praeger, 1993), p. 211.
5. Chairman of Senate Judiciary Committee, commenting on the 1995 bombing of the Alfred P. Murrah Federal Building.
6. "Shootin' Up the Charts," *Time,* November 15, 1993, p. 81. The charges were eventually dropped.
7. "Rapper Charged in Sodomy on Woman," *Fayetteville Observer-Times,* November 20, 1993, p. 5A.
8. Samuel Maull, "Shakur Trial," The Associated Press on-line, December 2, 1994.
9. James T. Jones IV, "Real-Life Woes Beset Actor/Rapper," *USA Today,* February 11, 1994, p. 2A.
10. Ibid.
11. Dennis R. Martin, "The Music of Murder," *ACJS Today,* November/December 1993, pp. 1, 3, 20.
12. Kendall Hamilton and Allison Samuels, "Dr. Dre's New 'Hood: Hollywood," *Newsweek,* August 22, 1994, p. 45.
13. See, for example, Elizabeth Snead, "Dogg's 'Murder' Video has Plenty of Bite," *USA Today,* October 13, 1994.
14. Arthur L. Cribbs, Jr., "Gangsta Rappers Sing White Racists' Tune," *USA Today,* December 27, 1993, p. 9A.

15. Some authors also hold that the nature and frequency with which crime stories appear in other popular media, such as newspapers, may influence the rate of criminal activity in society. For a thorough analysis of newspaper crime data, see H. L. Marsh, "Comparative Analysis of Crime Coverage in Newspapers in the United States and Other Countries from 1960–1989: A Review of the Literature," *Journal of Criminal Justice,* Vol. 19, no. 1 (1991), pp. 67–79.
16. James E. Anderson, *Public Policymaking: An Introduction* (Boston: Houghton Mifflin, 1990).
17. Nancy E. Marion, *A History of Federal Crime Control Initiatives, 1960–1993* (Westport: Praeger, 1994), p. 3. For a more detailed analysis of the process by which crime control policies are created, see Paul Rock, "The Opening Stages of Criminal Justice Policy Making," *The British Journal of Criminology,* Vol. 35, no. 1 (Winter 1995).
18. Calder, *The Origins and Development of Federal Crime Control Policy.*
19. Ibid., p. 1.
20. Ibid., pp. ix–x.
21. Ibid., p. 85.
22. Ibid., p. 5.
23. Ibid., p. 6.
24. Ibid., various pages.
25. Ibid., p. 83.
26. Ibid.
27. Ibid., citing the Commission, p. 102.
28. Ibid., p. 157.
29. The President's Commission on Law Enforcement and Administration of Justice, *The Challenge of Crime in a Free Society* (Washington, D.C.: U.S. Government Printing Office, 1967), p. xii.
30. Steven A. Shull, *Domestic Policy Formation: Presidential-Congressional Partnership?* (Westport, CT: Greenwood, Press, 1983), p. 41.
31. "Remarks at the Annual Conference of the National Sheriff's Association in Hartford, Connecticut," *Public Papers of the President* (June 20, 1984), pp. 884–888.
32. Richard Stratton, "Even Prisoners Must Have Hope," *Newsweek,* October 17, 1994, p. 90.
33. Bryan Vila, "A General Paradigm for Understanding Criminal Behavior: Extending Evolutionary Ecological Theory," *Criminology,* Vol. 32, no. 3 (August 1994), pp. 311–359.
34. Bryan Vila, "Could We Break the Crime Control Paradox?" paper presented at the annual meeting of the American Society of Criminology, Miami, Florida, November 1994.
35. Ibid., p. 337.
36. Ibid.
37. 103rd Congress, H.R. 1025 ("The Brady Bill"), January 5, 1993, p. 1.
38. "Police Group Unhappy with Focus on Crime," United Press on-line, Northern edition, January 26, 1994.
39. Michael Kirkland, "NRA Says It Will Help to Challenge Brady Gun Control," United Press International on line, Southwest edition, February 28, 1994.
40. "Iowa Man Believed First to Be Charged Under Brady Bill," United Press International on-line, Northern edition, January 11, 1994.
41. "Brady-First Conviction," The Associated Press on-line, Northern edition, April 14, 1994.
42. "Nationline: Three Strikes Law," *USA Today,* November 4, 1994, p. 3A.
43. Vila, "Could We Break the Crime Control Paradox?"
44. Ibid., abstract.
45. H. Bianchi, *Position and Subject-Matter of Criminology* (Amsterdam: 1956).
46. Hermann Mannheim, *Comparative Criminology* (New York: Houghton Mifflin, 1965), p. 18.
47. "Can Anything Really Be Done?" *USA Today* (magazine), Vol. 122, no. 2587 (April 1994), p. 6.
48. Robert D. Pursley, *Introduction to Criminal Justice,* 6th ed. (New York: Macmillan, 1991), p. 677.
49. Ibid.
50. Marion, *A History of Federal Crime Control Initiatives, 1960–1993,* p. 250.
51. Ibid., p. 244.
52. Ibid., p. 249.
53. Vila, "Could We Break the Crime Control Paradox?" p. 3.

DELTA CITY
THE FUTURE HAS A SILVER LINING.

CHAPTER 14

FUTURE DIRECTIONS IN CRIMINOLOGY

I seriously doubt that this country has the will to address...its crime problems...We could in theory make justice swifter and more certain, but we will not. We could vastly improve the way in which our streets are policed, but some of us won't pay for it and the rest of us won't tolerate it...We could alter the way in which at-risk children experience the first few years of life, but the opponents of this...are numerous and the bureaucratic problems enormous. Meanwhile, just beyond the horizon, there lurks a cloud that the winds will soon bring over us. By the end of this decade there will be a million more people between the ages of fourteen and seventeen...This extra million will be half male. Six percent of them will become high rate, repeat offenders—thirty thousand more young muggers, killers and thieves than we have now. Get ready.

—James Q. Wilson[1]

As we go forth into the future a world of crime as yet unknown awaits us.

—Cynthia Manson and Charles Ardai[2]

IMPORTANT NAMES

Georgette Bennett	William Tafoya	Gene Stephens
Richter H. Moore, Jr.	Larry Cohen	Marcus Felson
Ronald Clarke	Derek Cornish	Freda Adler
Rita J. Simon	Kathleen Daly	Meda Chesney-Lind
John Hagan	Harold E. Pepinsky	Richard Quinney
Walter DeKeseredy	Jock Young	

IMPORTANT TERMS

futurist	future criminology	futures research
environmental scanning	scenario writing	strategic assessment
life-style theory	routine activities theory	situational choice theory
rational choice theory	displacement	target hardening
power-control theory	feminist criminology	peacemaking criminology
realist criminology	restorative justice	deconstructionist theories
postmodern criminology	peace model	participatory justice

INTRODUCTION TO THE FUTURE

Futurist one who studies the future.

Future criminology the study of likely futures as they impinge on crime and its control.

Emile Durkheim once observed that crime and deviance are a natural part of any social world. While the form of criminal activity varies with the nature of society, it is unlikely that any human future will be free of crime. People who study the future are called **futurists**, while futurist criminologists try to imagine how crime will appear in both the near and distant future. **Future criminology** is the study of likely futures as they relate to crime and its control.

From our point of view in the present there are multiple futures, each of which is more or less probable and each of which may or may not come to pass. Another way of putting it is that the future contains an almost limitless number of possibilities, any of which might unfold but only a few of which actually will. The task of the futurist is to effectively distinguish between these impending possibilities, assessing the likelihood of each, and making more or less realistic forecasts based upon such assessments.

Some assumptions about the future, such as estimates of future world populations, can be based upon existing and highly credible public or private statistics and mathematical analyses of trends. Others, however, are much more intuitive and result from the integration of a wide range of diverse materials derived from many different sources. As one futurist explains it, "Before we can plan the future, we must make some assumptions about what that future will be like.... Assumptions about the future are not like assumptions in a geometry exercise. They are not abstract statements from which consequences can be derived with mathematical precision. But we need to make some assumptions about the future in order to plan it, prepare for it, and prevent undesired events from happening."[3]

Best known among groups that study the future is the World Future Society, which publishes *The Futurist*, a journal of well-considered essays about probable futures. Individual futurists who have become well known to the general public include Alvin Toffler, author of the trilogy of futurist titles *Future Shock*,[4] *Powershift*,[5] and the *Third Wave*;[6] John Naisbitt, author of *Megatrends: Ten New Directions Transforming our Lives*,[7] and Peter F. Drucker—who has written many books with futuristic themes, among them *Managing for the Future*, and *Post-Capitalist Society*. Within criminology the Society of Police Futurists International (PFI) represents the cutting edge of research into future crime-control policy. PFI evolved from a conference of approximately 250 educators and practitioners representing most states and 20 different nations that was held at the FBI's National Academy in Quantico, Virginia, in 1991. PFI members apply the principles of **futures research** to gain an understanding of the world as it is likely to be in the future.[8]

Futures research a multidisciplinary branch of operations research whose principal aim is to facilitate long-range planning based on (1) forecasting from the past supported by mathematical models, (2) cross-disciplinary treatment of its subject matter, (3) systematic use of expert judgment, and (4) a systems-analytical approach to its problems.

Futures research has been described as "a multidisciplinary branch of operations research" whose principle aim "is to facilitate long-range planning based on (1) forecasting from the past supported by mathematical models, (2) cross-disciplinary treatment of its subject matter, (3) systematic use of expert judgment, and (4) a systems-analytical approach to its problems."[9] In the words of PFI founder **William Tafoya**, "[f]utures research offers both the philosophy and the methodological tools to analyze, forecast, and plan in ways rarely seen" in crime-control planning. "Guided by insight, imagination, and innovation, a new perspective awaits criminal justice professionals willing to attempt creative new approaches to dealing with crime and criminals."[10]

Central to futures research are the techniques of environmental scanning, scenario writing, and strategic assessment.[11] **Environmental scanning** "is a systematic effort to identify in an elemental way future developments (trends or events) that could plausibly occur over the time horizon of interest"[12] and that might impact one's area of concern. In other words, it is impossible to predict the future without having some sense of what is happening now, especially where important trends are concerned. **Scenario writing** builds upon environmental scanning by attempting to assess the likelihood of a variety of possible outcomes once important trends have been identified. Scenario writing develops a list of possible futures and assigns each a degree of probability or likelihood. **Strategic assessment** provides an appreciation of the risks and opportunities facing those who plan for the future.

Environmental scanning a systematic effort to identify in an elemental way future developments (trends or events) that could plausibly occur over the time horizon of interest, and that might impact one's area of concern.

Scenario writing a technique intended to predict future outcomes, and which builds upon environmental scanning by attempting to assess the likelihood of a variety of possible outcomes once important trends have been identified.

Strategic assessment a technique which assesses the risks and opportunities facing those who plan for the future.

A comprehensive futures research approach, for example, might identify an important trend that shows well-to-do middle- and upper-class citizens fleeing cities and suburbs for the safety of enclosed residential enclaves surrounded by secure perimeters and patrolled by paid private security personnel. A number of likely scenarios could then be envisioned, including a further decline in America's cities as the monied classes abandon them, continued growth of street and property crimes in metropolitan areas, and rampant victimization of the urban working poor. While crime-control strategies might be developed to counter the imagined threat to cities, a number of risks must be considered in any planning. A serious decline in the value of the dollar, for example, such as has been recently experienced, may cause gated communities to unravel and create a shortfall of tax dollars that would be needed to pay for enhanced policing in cities. The influx of new and large immigrant populations, who are likely to add to the burgeoning number of inner-city dwellers, could add another new dimension to overall crime-control planning.

Issues like these have been the concern of a number of outstanding thinkers in the field of criminology. Futurists who have made their mark on criminology include Georgette Bennett, Gene Stephens, William "Bill" Tafoya, and Richter H. Moore, Jr. Their work, along with other emerging theoretical explanations for crime and new suggestions for crime-control policy, is discussed in this chapter.

FUTURE CRIMES

Murder, rape, robbery, and other types of "everyday" crime which have become mainstays of contemporary criminological analysis will continue to occur in the future, to be sure, but other new and emergent forms of criminality will grow in frequency and number. Recently, for example, Joseph F. Coates, president of the future-oriented "think tank" of Coates & Jarratt, predicted that by the year 2025, "Socially significant crime—that is, the crimes that have the widest negative effects—in the advanced nations will be increasingly economic and computer based. Examples include disruption of business, theft, introduction of maliciously false information, and tampering with medical records, air traffic control, or national-security systems."[13] Another futurist predicts that "[t]he top guns of twenty-first-century criminal organizations will be educated, highly sophisticated, computer-literate individuals who can wield state-of-the-art information technology to the best advantage—for themselves and for their organizations."[14]

A female officer calls her base. Community policing, a strategy by which law enforcement officials stay in close touch with citizens, holds great hope for the future. *Sidney/The Image Works.*

In a wide-ranging overview of future crimes **Richter H. Moore, Jr.,** paints a picture of future criminality that includes many dimensions. We are already seeing elements of what Moore predicts: "computer hackers are changing bank records, credit accounts and reports, criminal-history files, and educational, medical, and even military records."[15] Identity manipulation, says Moore, will be a nexus of future criminality. "By the twenty-first century," he writes, "genetic-based records will include a birth-to-death dossier of a person and will be the method of criminal identification." As the human genome project proceeds apace, the complete mapping of human DNA comes closer to reality. Already the U.S. military is using genetic testing to provide unique identification codes to each of its soldiers. In the event of war, such codes will allow for the identification of human remains from as little as a single cell. DNA coding, unique to each of us, may soon form the basis for nearly foolproof identification technologies which will take the science of personal identification far beyond fingerprinting, blood-type matching, or photography. The science of bioengineering, however, which is now undergoing clinical trials in the treatment of various forms of disease, may soon be clandestinely employed for the illegal modification of human DNA, with the goal of effectively altering a person's identity. It is but one more step by which the theft of computer-based genetic identification records could make it possible for one person to effectively imitate another in our future society.

Moore describes many other crimes of the future. "By the next century," he says, "criminal organizations will be able to afford their own satellites." Drug trafficking and money laundering operations could be coordinated via satellite communications, couriers and shipments could be tracked, and satellite surveillance could provide alerts of enforcement activity. Likewise, says Moore, "[p]rostitution rings will use modern technology to coordinate global activities," and children and fetuses may "become subject to unlawful trafficking." The illegal disposal of toxic materials, an activity which organized crime has already explored, may become even more profitable for criminal entrepreneurs as more and more hazardous substances are produced in the face of ever-tighter controls. The supply of nuclear materials and military-quality armaments to "private armies...terrorists, hate groups, questionable regimes, independent crime groups, and individual criminals" will be a fact of life in the next century, as will the infiltration of governments and financial institutions by sophisticated criminals whose activities are supported by large illegally acquired fortunes.

Another writer, **Georgette Bennett,** whose seminal book *Crimewarps*[16] was published in 1987 and helped establish the study of criminal futures as a purposeful endeavor, says that American society is about to experience major changes in both what society considers criminal and in who future offenders will be. Some areas of coming change that Bennett predicts are

- The decline of street crime, such as robbery and assault.
- An increase in white-collar crimes, especially high-technology crimes.
- Increasing female involvement in crime.
- Increased crime commission among the elderly.
- A shift in high crime rates from the "Frost Belt" to the "Sun Belt."
- Safer cities, with increasing criminal activity in small towns and rural areas.

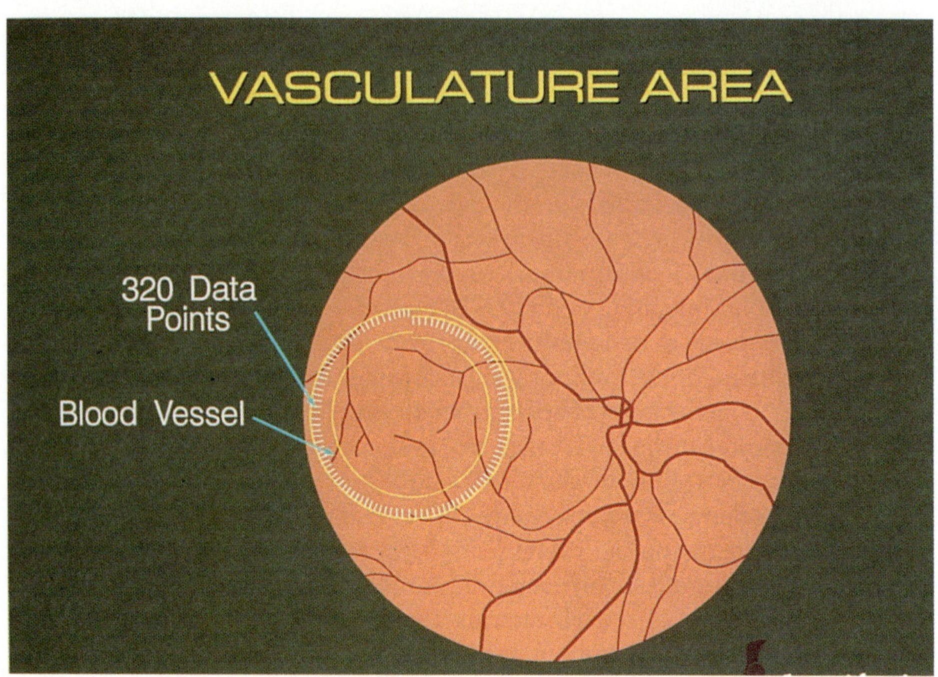

Diagram of a retinal image used for identification purposes. The security of sensitive sites and the accurate identification of personnel are being increasingly served by advanced technologies such as retinal imaging. *Courtesy Eye Dentify, Inc.*

THE NEW CRIMINOLOGIES

Along with futures research, new and emerging criminological theories provide a picture of what criminology will be like in the years and decades to come. In an intriguing article entitled "Explaining Crime in the Year 2010,"[17] L. Edward Wells suggests that "[w]hen it comes to explaining crime, we seem to have an embarrassment of riches but a poverty of results." In other words, while many explanations for criminal behavior have come and gone, "none has proven noticeably more effective in explaining, predicting, or controlling crime." That may be about to change, says Wells. Contemporary criminological theorizing is interdisciplinary and conservative in its approach to crime causation, and major changes in the premises upon which criminological theories are built are unlikely without significant ideological shifts or changes in basic components of the social structure such as the economy, the political system, or the family. Significant social change, however, can bring about the need for new theoretical formulations, says Wells. "Legal events in the 1960s and 1970s," for example, "changed abortion from a criminal act to a routine medical procedure...."[18] Similarly, an aversion to even minor forms of physical force may now be leading to a redefinition of crimes like child abuse, spousal abuse, elder abuse, and sexual aggression. Hence, our very understanding of criminal violence may be undergoing a fundamental modification that will require a concomitant change in our attempts to theorize about its causes.

Wells sees similar possibilities for theoretical change about to be introduced by advances in scientific knowledge. Should the human genome project, for example, yield definitive evidence that some forms of aggression and violence are biologically grounded, it will provide the basis for an entirely new and emergent group of biological explanations for at least certain forms of criminal activity.

Wells makes a number of specific predictions about the future of criminological theorizing. Among them, he predicts that future explanations of crime will be[19]

1. more eclectic than past theories, and less tied to a single theoretical tradition or discipline.
2. more comparative and less confined to a single society or single dominant group within society.
3. predominantly *individualistic* rather than collective, and *voluntaristic* rather than deterministic.
4. more applied and pragmatic in orientation.
5. more oriented toward explaining white-collar crime.
6. reflective of a renewed appreciation for the biological foundations of human behavior and will assign more theoretical substance to biological and medical factors.

Unfortunately, from around 1960 until 1985 criminology suffered through a few "black decades" in which theory building fell by the wayside as a generation of criminologists trained in quantitative analysis repeatedly tested existing ideas at the expense of developing new ones. In the 1980s, however, a new and dynamic era of theory building was unleashed. Frank P. Williams and Marilyn D. McShane explain: "[a]s if the restraints on theory building had created a pent-up demand, criminologists began exploring new theoretical constructs during the 1980s. Slowly at first, and then with great rapidity, theoretical efforts began to emerge."[20]

Others have suggested that new and developing theoretical approaches are largely the result of postmodernist thought, and that most such theories can be lumped together under the rubric **postmodern criminology.** Postmodern social thought, which developed primarily in Europe after World War II, holds that some Western societies have entered a new age characterized less by an emphasis upon industrialization and material production, and more by a concern with ideas and individual needs. Hence, the new American "information society" with its drift toward quasi-socialism which is so characteristic of post-industrial societies, rampant mass consumption, and overall technological sophistication lead such thinkers to classify it as one of the first truly post-modern societies to emerge in the world. Postmodern criminology applies understandings of social change inherent in postmodern philosophy to criminological theorizing and to issues of crime control. This book, at least in part, is a postmodernist work in that it describes not only historical criminology, but focuses in some detail upon new forms of crime brought about by social changes which occurred following World War II. In particular, Chapter 12, with its detailed descriptions of high-technology crime, along with the current chapter's futurist orientation provide a true postmodernist focus.

Postmodern criminology a brand of criminology that developed following World War II and which builds upon the tenants inherent in postmodern social thought.

Postmodern criminology is not a single theory, but rather a group of new and emerging criminological perspectives that are all characterized by the tone of postmodernism. Simply put, postmodern criminology builds upon the feeling that past criminological approaches have failed to realistically assess the true causes of crime and have failed to offer workable solutions for crime control—or if they have, that such theories and solutions may have been appropriate at one time, but

Deconstructionist theories emerging approaches which challenge existing criminological perspectives to debunk them, and which work toward replacing them with concepts more applicable to the postmodern era.

Rational choice theory a criminological perspective which holds that criminality is the result of conscious choice.

Routine activities theory or life-style theory, is a brand of rational choice theory which suggests that life-styles contribute significantly to both the volume and type of crime found in any society.

Situational choice theory a brand of rational choice theory which views criminal behavior as a function of choices and decisions made within a context of situational constraints and opportunities.

that they are no longer applicable to the modern era. Hence, much postmodern criminology is deconstructionist, and such theories are sometimes called **deconstructionist theories.** Deconstructionist approaches challenge—often quite effectively—existing criminological perspectives to debunk them and work toward replacing them with approaches more relevant to the postmodern era. Postmodern perspectives, none of which have yet developed fully enough to be called "theories," are now leading in some fascinating new directions. A few such approaches are discussed in the pages that follow.

Rational Choice Theory

Rational choice theory, a product of the 1980s, was a natural outgrowth of the realization that no existing criminological theory "contained an assumption of a rational, thinking individual."[21] Rational choice theory built upon the assumptions of economists, many of whom view human behavior—including that which is criminal—as the result of conscious choice. **Rational choice theory** is noteworthy for its emphasis upon the rational and adaptive aspects of criminal offending, rather than upon what other approaches might view as pathological aspects of the criminal event.

Two varieties of rational choice theory can be identified. One, which builds upon an emerging emphasis on victimization, is called **life-style theory** or **routine activities theory.** A second, in which criminal behavior is viewed "as a function of choices and decisions made within a context of situational constraints and opportunities,"[22] is called **situational choice theory.**

Routine activities theory was convincingly proposed by **Larry Cohen** and **Marcus Felson** in 1979,[23] who suggested that life-styles contribute significantly to both the volume and type of crime found in any society. According to Cohen and Felson crime is likely to occur when a motivated offender and a suitable victim come together in the absence of preventative measures. Hence, "the risk of criminal victimization varies dramatically among the circumstances and locations in which people place themselves and their property."[24] For example, a person who routinely uses an automated teller machine late at night in an isolated location is far more likely to be preyed upon by robbers than is someone who stays home after dark. Life-styles that contribute to criminal opportunities are likely to result in crime because they increase the risk of potential victimization.[25] Although noncriminal life-styles at a given point in the life course are partly the result of unavoidable social roles and assigned social positions, those who participate in a given life-style make rational decisions about specific behaviors (such as going to a given automatic teller machine at a certain time). The same is true of criminal life-styles. Hence, the meshing of choices made by both victims and criminals contribute significantly to both the frequency and type of criminal activity observed in society.

In a later work,[26] Felson suggested that a number of "situational insights" might combine to elicit a criminal response from individual actors enmeshed in a highly varied social world. Felson pointed out that "individuals vary greatly in their behavior from one situation to another" and said that criminality might flow from temptation, bad company, idleness, or provocation. Convenience stores, for example, create temptations toward theft when they display their merchandise within easy reach of customers. Other authors[27] have defined the term "situation" to mean "the perceptive field of the individual at a given point in time" and have suggested that it "can be described in terms of who is there, what is going on, and where it is taking place."

Situational choice theory, largely an extension of the rational choice perspective, suggests that the probability of criminal activity can be reduced by changing the features of a given social situation. **Ronald Clarke** and **Derek Cornish,** collaborators in the development of the situational choice perspective, analyze the choice-structuring properties of a potentially criminal situation. They define choice-structuring properties as "the constellation of opportunities, costs, and benefits attaching to particular kinds of crime."[28] Clarke and Cornish suggest the use of situational strategies such as, "cheque guarantee cards, the control of alcohol sales at football matches, supervision of children's play on public housing estates, vandal resistant materials and designs, 'defensible space' architecture, improved lighting, closed-circuit television surveillance,"[29] and the like, as effective crime-preventative additions to specific situations—all of which might lower the likelihood of criminal victimization in given instances.

In brief, rational choice theorists concentrate on "the decision-making process of offenders confronted with specific contexts" and have shifted "the focus of the effort to prevent crime...from broad social programs to target hardening, environmental design or any impediment that would persuade a motivated offender from offending."[30]

Rational choice theory is a modern version of classical deterrence theories, most of which focused on utility, or the balance between pleasure and pain, as the primary determinant or preventative of criminal behavior in everyday life. In its modern formulation, however, less emphasis is placed upon emotionality, and more upon rationality and cognition. Some rational choice theorists have gone so far as to distinguish among the types of choices offenders make as they move toward criminal involvement. Involvement decisions have been described as "multistage" and are said to "include the initial decision to engage in criminal activity as well as subsequent decisions to continue one's involvement or to desist."[31] Event decisions, on the other hand, relate to particular instances of criminal opportunity such as the decision to rob a particular person or to let them pass. Event decisions, in contrast to involvement decisions which may take months or even years to arrive at, are usually made very quickly.

Critique of Rational Choice Theory

Rational choice theory has been criticized for its overemphasis on individual choice and its relative disregard for the social and economic inequality of persons and groups. Likewise, rational choice theory seems to assume that everyone is equally capable of making rational decisions when, in fact, such is probably not the case. Some individuals are more logical than others by virtue of temperament, personality, or socialization, while still others are emotional, "hot-headed," and unthinking. Empirical studies of rational choice theory have added scant support

Displacement a shift of criminal activity from one spatial location to another.

Target hardening the reduction in criminal opportunity, generally through the use of physical barriers, architectural design, and enhanced security measures, of a particular location.

Feminist criminology a developing intellectual approach which emphasizes gender issues in the subject matter of criminology.

for the perspective's underlying assumptions, tending to show instead that criminal offenders are often unrealistic in their appraisals of the relative risks and rewards facing them.[32] Similarly, rational choice theories seem to disregard individual psychology and morality by their emphasis on external situations. Moral individuals, when faced with criminal opportunity, may reign in their desires and turn their backs on temptation.

The emphasis of rational choice theory upon changing aspects of the immediate situation to reduce crime has been criticized for resulting in the **displacement** of crime from one area to another. **Target hardening,** a key crime prevention strategy among rational choice theorists, has led to criminal offenders finding new targets of opportunity in other areas.[33]

Feminist Theory

As some have observed, "women have been virtually invisible in criminological analysis until recently and much theorizing has proceeded as though criminality is restricted to men."[34] Others put it this way: "criminological theory assumes a woman is like a man."[35] Recently, however, advances in feminist theory have been applied to criminology, resulting in what some have called a **feminist criminology.**

Early works in the field included **Freda Adler's** *Sisters in Crime*[36] and **Rita J. Simon's** *Women and Crime.*[37] Both books were published in 1975, and in them the authors attempted to explain existing divergences in crime rates between men and women as due primarily to socialization rather than biology. Women, claimed these authors, were taught to believe in personal limitations, faced reduced socioeconomic opportunities and, as a result, suffered from lowered aspirations. As gender equality increased, they said, it could be expected that male and female criminality would take on similar characteristics. As Chapter 2 points out, however, such has not been the case to date, and the approach of Adler and Simon has not been validated by observations surrounding increased gender equality over the past few decades.

While early feminist theorizing may not have born the fruit that some anticipated, it has led to a heightened awareness of gender issues within criminology. Two of the most insightful contemporary proponents of the usefulness of applying feminist thinking to criminological analysis are **Kathleen Daly** and **Meda Chesney-Lind.** Daly and Chesney-Lind have identified the following five elements of feminist thought that "distinguish it from other types of social and political thought:"[38]

1. Gender is not a natural fact but a complex social, historical, and cultural product; it is related to, but not simply derived from, biological sex difference and reproductive capacities.
2. Gender and gender relations order social life and social institutions in fundamental ways.
3. Gender relations and constructs of masculinity and femininity are not symmetrical but are based on an organizing principle of men's superiority and social and political-economic dominance over women.

4. Systems of knowledge reflect men's views of the natural and social world; the production of knowledge is gendered.
5. Women should be at the center of intellectual inquiry, not peripheral, invisible, or appendages to men.

In a similar, but more recent, analysis of feminist criminology, Susan Caulfield and Nancy Wonders describe "five major contributions that have been made by feminist scholarship and practice"[39] to criminological thinking: (1) a focus on gender as a central organizing principle of contemporary life, (2) the importance of power in shaping social relationships, (3) a heightened sensitivity to the way in which social context helps shape human relationships, (4) the recognition that social reality must be understood as a process, and the development of research methods which take this into account, and (5) a commitment to social change as a crucial part of feminist scholarship and practice. As is the case with most feminist writing in the area of criminology today, Caulfield and Wonders hold that these five contributions of feminist scholarship "can help to guide research and practice within criminology...."

Feminism is a way of seeing the world—it is not strictly a sexual orientation. To be a feminist is to "combine a female mental perspective with a sensitivity for those social issues that influence primarily women."[40] Central to understanding feminist thought in both its historical as well as its contemporary modes is the realization that feminism views gender in terms of power relationships. In other words, according to feminist approaches, men have traditionally held much more power in society than have women. Male dominance has long been reflected in the patriarchal structure of Western society, a structure which has excluded women from much decision making in socially significant areas. Sexist attitudes—deeply ingrained notions of male superiority—have perpetuated inequality between the sexes. The consequences of sexism and of the unequal gender-based distribution of power have been far reaching, affecting fundamental aspects of social roles and personal expectation at all levels.

Various schools of feminist thought exist, with liberal and radical feminism envisioning a power-based and traditional domination of women's bodies and minds by men throughout history. Radical feminism depicts men as fundamentally brutish, aggressive, and violent and sees men as controlling women through sexuality by taking advantage of women's biological dependency during child-bearing years and their inherent lack of physical strength relative to men. Liberal feminists, while they want the same gender equality that other feminists do, lay the blame for present inequalities on the development within culture and society of "separate and distinct spheres of influence and traditional attitudes about the appropriate role of men and women...."[41] Socialist feminists, who provide a third perspective, see gender oppression as a consequence of the economic structure of society and as a natural outgrowth of capitalist forms of social organization. Egalitarian societies, from the socialist point of view, would be built around socialist or Marxist principles. A fourth and complementary feminist perspective has been identified by Sally Simpson who refers to it as an alternative framework developed by "women of color."[42] In Simpson's words, "[t]he alternative frameworks developed by women of color heighten feminism's sensitivity to the complex interplay of gender, class, and race oppression."

Power-control theory a perspective which holds that the distribution of crime and delinquency within society is to some degree founded upon the consequences which power relationships within the wider society hold for domestic settings, and for the everyday relationships between men, women, and children within the context of family life.

John Hagan built upon defining features of power relationships in his book *Structural Criminology*,[43] in which he pointed out that power relationships which exist in the wider society are effectively "brought home" to domestic settings and are reflected in everyday relationships between men, women, and children within the context of family life. Hagan's approach has been termed **power-control theory,** and it is one which suggests that "family class structure shapes the social reproduction of gender relations, and in turn the social distribution of delinquency."[44]

While some theories have been built upon feminist notions, Daly and Chesney-Lind, in an analysis which transcends radical rhetoric, suggest that feminist thought is more important for the way it informs and challenges existing criminology than for the new theories it offers. Much current feminist thought within criminology emphasizes the need for gender-awareness. Theories of crime causation and prevention, it is suggested, must include women, and more research on gender-related issues in the field is badly needed. Additionally, say Daly and Chesney-Lind, "criminologists should begin to appreciate that their discipline and its questions are a product of white, economically privileged men's experiences"[45] and that rates of female criminality, which are lower than those of males, may highlight the fact that criminal behavior is not as "normal" as once thought. Because modern-day criminological perspectives were mostly developed by white middle-class males, the propositions and theories they advance fail to take into consideration women's "ways of knowing."[46] Hence, the fundamental challenge poised by feminist criminology is: Do existing theories of crime causation apply as well to women as they do to men? Or, as Daly and Chesney-Lind put it, given the current situation in theory development, "do theories of men's crime apply to women?"[47]

Aileen Wuornos, accused female serial killer. Although some women are moving into areas of traditional male criminality, the number of women committing most forms of crime is still far lower than that of men. *Daytona Beach News/Sygma.*

Other feminists have analyzed the process by which laws are created and legislation passed, and have concluded that modern-day statutes frequently represent characteristically masculine modes of thought. Such analysts have concluded that existing criminal laws are overly rational and hierarchically structured, reflecting traditionally male ways of organizing the social world.[48] Such statutes, some analysts suggest, need to be replaced by, or complemented with, "a system of justice based upon what are the specifically feminine principles of care, connection and community."[49]

In the area of social policy, feminist thinkers have pointed to the need for increased controls over men's violence toward women, the creation of alternatives (to supplement the home and traditional family structures) for women facing abuse, and the protection of children. They have also questioned the role of government, culture, and the mass media in promulgating pornography, prostitution, and rape and have generally portrayed ongoing crimes against women as characteristic of continuing traditions in which women are undervalued and controlled. Many radical feminists have suggested the replacement of men with women in positions of power, especially within justice system and government organizations, while others have noted that replacement still would not address needed changes in the structure of the system itself which is gender biased due to years of male domination. Centrists, on the other hand, suggest a more balanced approach, believing that individuals of both genders have much to contribute to a workable justice system.

Critique of Feminist Theory

In the area of theoretical development feminist criminology has yet to live up to its promise. Throughout the late 1970s and 1980s few comprehensive feminist theories of crime were proposed as feminist criminology focused instead on descriptive studies of female involvement in crime.[50] While such data gathering may have laid the groundwork for theory building which is yet to come, few descriptive studies attempted to link their findings to existing feminist theory in any comprehensive way. Theory development suffered again in the late 1980s and early 1990s as an increased concern with women's victimization, especially the victimization of women at the hands of men, led to further descriptive studies with a somewhat different focus. Male violence against women was seen as adding support to the central tenant of feminist criminology that the relationship between the sexes is primarily characterized by the exercise of power (or lack thereof). Such singularity of focus, however, did not make for broad theory building. As one writer explains the current state of feminist criminology, "[f]eminist theory is a theory in formation."[51] To date, feminist researchers have continued to amass descriptive studies, while feminist analysis has hardly advanced beyond a framework for the "deconstruction"[52] of existing theories—that is, for their re-evaluation in light of feminist insights. A fair assessment of the current situation would probably conclude that the greatest contributions of feminist thought to criminological theory building are yet to come.

Feminist criminology has faced criticism from many other directions. As mentioned previously, predicted increases in female crime rates have failed to materialize as social opportunities available to both genders have become more balanced. Similarly, other thinkers have pointed to fundamental flaws in feminist thought, asking questions such as, "If men have more power than women, then why are so many more men arrested?"[53] Where studies do exist,[54] gender disparities in arrest are rarely found, nor do sentencing practices seem to favor women.[55] The "chivalry" hypothesis of many years ago, under which it was proposed that women are apt to be treated more leniently by the justice system because of their gender, appears no longer operative today.[56]

Some critics even argue that a feminist criminology is impossible. Daly and Chesney-Lind, for example, agree that while feminist thought may inform criminology, "a feminist criminology cannot exist because neither feminism nor criminology is a unified set of principles and practices."[57] In other words, according to these authors, a criminology built solely on feminist principles is unlikely because neither feminist thought nor criminology meet the strict requirements of formal theory building. Even with such a caveat in mind, however, it should still be possible to construct a gender-aware criminology, that is, one which is informed by issues of gender and that takes into consideration the concerns of feminist writers. A "feminist-oriented criminology," say Caulfield and Wonders, is one that will transgress traditional criminology. "This transgression, or 'going beyond boundaries,'" they write, "must occur at a number of levels across a number of areas covered within criminology"[58] and will eventually move us toward a more just world.

Peacemaking Criminology

Peacemaking criminology a perspective which holds that crime-control agencies and the citizens they serve should work together to alleviate social problems and human suffering and thus reduce crime.

Throughout much of history formal agencies of social control, especially the police, officials of the courts, and correctional personnel have been seen as pitted against criminal perpetrators and would-be wrong-doers. Crime control has been traditionally depicted in terms of a kind of epic struggle in which diametrically opposed antagonists continuously engage one another, but in which only one side can emerge as victorious. Recently, however, a new point of view, **peacemaking criminology,** has come to the fore. Criminology as peacemaking has its roots in Christian and Eastern philosophies, and advances the notion that social control agencies and the citizens they serve should work together to alleviate social problems and human suffering and thus reduce crime.[59] Peacemaking criminology, which includes the notion of "service," has also been called "compassionate criminology" and suggests that "[c]ompassion, wisdom, and love are essential for understanding the suffering of which we are all a part and for practicing a criminology of nonviolence."[60]

Peacemaking criminology is a very new undertaking, having been popularized by the works of **Harold E. Pepinsky**[61] and **Richard Quinney**[62] beginning in 1986. Both Pepinsky and Quinney restate the problem of crime control from one of "how to stop crime" to one of "how to make peace" within society and between citizens and criminal justice agencies. Peacemaking criminology draws attention to many issues, among them (1) the perpetuation of violence through the continuation of social policies based upon dominant forms of criminological theory, (2) the role of education in peacemaking, (3) "commonsense theories of crime," (4)

A homeless man in New York City. Peacemaking criminology holds that the alleviation of social problems and the reduction of human suffering will lead to a truly just world, and thus reduce crime. *Susan Tannenbaum/Impact Visuals Photo & Graphics, Inc.*

crime control as human rights enforcement, and (5) conflict resolution within community settings.[63]

Commonsense theories of crime are derived from everyday experience and beliefs and are characteristic of the person-in-the-street. Unfortunately, say peacemaking criminologists, fanciful commonsense theories all too often provide the basis for criminological investigations, which in turn offer support for the naive theories themselves. One commonsense theory criticized by peacemaking criminologists is the "black-male-as-savage theory"[64] which holds that African-American men are far more crime prone than their white counterparts. Such a perspective, frequently given added credence by official interpretations of criminal incidence data, only increases the crime-control problem by further distancing black Americans from government-sponsored crime-control policies. A genuine concern for the problems facing all citizens, say peacemaking criminologists, would more effectively serve the ends of crime-control.

Richard Quinney and John Wildeman well summarize the underpinnings of peacemaking criminology with these words: "(1) thought of the Western rational mode is conditional, limiting knowledge primarily to what is already known; (2) each life is a spiritual journey into the unknown and the unknowable, beyond the ego-centered self; (3) human existence is characterized by suffering; crime is suffering; and the sources of suffering are within each of us; (4) through love and compassion, beyond the ego-centered self, we can end suffering and live in peace, personally and collectively; (5) crime can be ended only with the ending of suffering, only when there is peace and social justice; and (6) understanding, service, justice—all these—flow naturally from love and compassion, from mindful attention to the reality of all that is, here and now. A criminology of peacemaking—a nonviolent criminology of compassion and service—seeks to end suffering and thereby eliminate crime."[65]

Elsewhere Quinney writes: "A society of meanness, competition, greed, and injustice is created by minds that are greedy, selfish, fearful, hateful, and crave power over others. Suffering on the social level can be ended only with the ending of suffering on the personal level. Wisdom brings the awareness that divisions between people and groups are not between the bad and the good or between the criminal and the noncriminal. Wisdom teaches interbeing. We must become one with all who suffer from lives of crime and from the sources that produce crime. Public policy must then flow from this wisdom."[66]

Other recent contributors to the peacemaking movement include Bo Lozoff, Michael Braswell, and Clemmons Bartollas. In *Inner Corrections,*[67] Lozoff and Braswell claim that "[w]e are fully aware by now that the criminal justice system in this country is founded on violence. It is a system which assumes that violence can be overcome by violence, evil by evil. Criminal justice at home and warfare abroad are of the same principle of violence. This principle sadly dominates much of our criminology." *Inner Corrections,* which is really a compilation of previous works on compassion and prison experience, provides meditative techniques and prayers for those seeking to become more compassionate, and includes a number of letters from convicts which demonstrate the philosophy the book contains.

In another recent work entitled "Correctional Treatment, Peacemaking, and the New Age Movement,"[68] Bartollas and Braswell apply New Age principles to correctional treatment. "Most offenders suffered abusive and deprived childhoods," they write. "Treatment that focuses on the inner child and such qualities as forgiveness and self-esteem could benefit offenders. Some New Age teachings tempered by the ancient spiritual traditions may offer offenders the hope they can create a future that brings greater fulfillment than their past. This changed future may include growing out of the fear of victimization, becoming more positive and open to possibilities, viewing one's self with more confidence and humility, understanding the futility of violence, and attaining emotional and financial sufficiency."[69]

In a fundamental sense, peacemaking criminologists exhort their colleagues to transcend personal dichotomies to end the political and ideological divisiveness that separates people. "If we ourselves cannot know peace...how will our acts disarm hatred and violence?"[70] they ask. Lozoff and Braswell express the same sentiments this way: "Human transformation takes place as we change our social, economic and political structure. And the message is clear: without peace within us and in our actions, there can be no peace in our results. Peace is the way."[71]

Critique of Peacemaking Criminology

Peacemaking criminology has been criticized as being naive and utopian, as well as for failing to recognize the realities of crime control and law enforcement. Few victims, for example, would expect to gain much during the victimization process from attempting to make peace with their victimizers (although such strategies do occasionally work). Such criticisms, however, may be improperly directed at a level of analysis which peacemaking criminologists have not assumed. In other words, peacemaking criminology, while it involves work with individual offenders, envisions positive change on the societal and institutional level and does not suggest to victims that they attempt to effect personal changes in offenders.

Realist Criminology

Realist criminology an emerging perspective which insists upon a pragmatic assessment of crime and associated problems.

Realist criminology, another recent addition to the criminological landscape, is a natural outgrowth of practical concerns with street crime, the fear of crime, and everyday victimization. Realist criminology insists upon a pragmatic assessment of crime and associated problems in everyday terms—that is, terms which are understandable to those people most often affected by crime: victims and their families, offenders, and criminal justice personnel. The test insisted upon by realist criminology is not whether a particular perspective on crime control or an explanation of crime causation complies with rigorous academic criteria, but whether or not the perspective speaks meaningful to those faced with crime on a daily basis. As one contemporary source puts it, "for realists crime is no less harmful to its victims because of its socially constructed origins."[72]

Realist criminology takes two forms: left realism and right realism. Left realism, also called radical realism or critical realism, builds upon many of the concepts inherent in radical and Marxist criminology, while simultaneously claiming greater relevancy than either of its two parent perspectives. Left realism also tends to distance itself from some of the more visionary claims of early radical and Marxist theory. Left realism appears to have developed simultaneously in the United States and England.[73] Daniel J. Curran and Claire M. Renzetti portray left realism as a natural consequence of increasingly conservative attitudes toward crime and criminals in both Europe and North America. "Though not successful in converting many radicals to the right," they write, "this new conservatism did lead a number of radical criminologists to temper their views a bit and to take what some might call a less romanticized look at street crime."[74]

Some authors credit **Walter DeKeseredy**[75] with popularizing left realist notions in North America, while **Jock Young**[76] is identified as a major source of left realist writings in England. Prior to the writings of DeKeseredy and Young radical criminology, with its emphasis upon the crime-inducing consequences of existing power structures, tended to portray the ruling class as the "real criminals" and saw street criminals as social rebels who were acting out of felt deprivation. In contrast, DeKeseredy and Young were successful in refocusing leftist theories onto the serious consequences of street crime and upon the crimes of the lower classes. A central tenant of left realism is the claim that radical ideas must be translated into realistic social policies if contemporary criminology is to have any practical relevance. The major goal of left realism is to achieve "a fair and orderly society" through a practical emphasis on social justice.[77]

Right realism, on the other hand, appeals to those committed to existing power relationships within society. According to criminologist David Nelken, "[r]ight realism arose in the United States as a political strategy for addressing the urban decay and underclass produced by the very conservative forces with which it identifies."[78] It is a way of thinking "oriented to all right-thinking people who believe that the criminal law institution is there to protect their persons and property through strong measures of general deterrence, specific deterrence and incapacitation."[79] In other words, right realism is a criminological perspective that appeals to conservative, propertied, and powerful segments of the population.

Critique of Realist Criminology

Realist criminology has been convincingly criticized for representing more of an ideological emphasis than a theory. As Don C. Gibbons explains, "left realism can best be described as a general perspective centered on injunctions to 'take crime seriously' and to 'take crime control seriously' rather than as a well-developed criminological perspective."[80] Realist criminologists appear to build upon preexisting theoretical frameworks, but rarely offer new propositions or hypotheses that are testable. They do, however, frequently suggest crime-control approaches which are in keeping with the needs of the victimized. Policies promulgated by left realists understandably include an emphasis upon community policing, neighborhood justice centers, and dispute resolution mechanisms, while right realists are more punitive in their policy suggestions. Beirne and Messerschmidt summarize the situation this way: "what left realists have essentially accomplished is an attempt to theorize about conventional crime realistically while simultaneously developing a 'radical law and order' program for curbing such behavior."[81]

Theory Integration

The field of criminology today is rife with a wide variety of theoretical explanations. Some are old, others are new. Many are complex, while a few are straightforward. Each theoretical approach, however, while it may provide part of the explanation for why crime occurs or offer a portion of the answer to the question of how to control crime, is limited. It may apply to only a certain type of offender, it may explain only a particular form of crime, or it may derive from only one philosophical or theoretical base.

Some have called the contemporary situation an embarrassment of riches, while others have compared it to the old fable of many blind men trying to understand an elephant—each "sees" only a small part of the overall picture. As a consequence, an emphasis on theory integration, with the ultimate goal of developing a unified theory of crime causation and prevention, began to emerge in the 1980s. Advocates of theory integration suggest that initial attempts at blending the propositions of different perspectives should begin at the level characteristic of those theories. In other words, theoretical approaches concerned with analyzing crime at the individual level (often called micro-level theories) might be integrated at the same time that sociological, political, and economic explanations (called macro-level theories) are woven together. Finally, cross-level integration might be attempted.[82]

Other criminologists have developed rudimentary metatheories or theories about theories and the theorizing process, which they suggest may help to meld existing theories together. Some metatheoreticians, however, have expressed the concern that we may integrate theories without first properly examining their worth and that, as a consequence, we may be left with highly elaborate integrated theories that are worthless.[83]

Unfortunately for advocates of integration, however, there seems "to be a consensus that there are too many problems for successful integration to take place...."[84] The reasons why successful integration can never occur, say Frank P. Williams and Marilyn McShane,[85] are (1) "crime is a very complex phenomenon," often determined and defined by whimsical legislative action and powerful interests; (2) "theories attempt to explain different pieces of the crime puzzle" and cannot be made to address all of its aspects; and (3) theories are "embedded in the assumptions we make about human nature and the way the world functions," and we all make different assumptions.

Einstadter and Henry summarize efforts at theoretical integration in criminology with these words: "The plain fact is that integrated theorizing does not lead to a more comprehensive understanding of crime or criminal etiology. Not only does the approach leave gaps between integrated theories, through which vital nuggets of the total reality of criminological explanation slip, but by presenting a range of theories as an integrated package, it tricks us into believing that a comprehensive coverage of criminological theory has been achieved."[86]

"Vital nuggets" of the reality of crime and justice can be found in approaches like feminist criminology and black criminology, and advocates of theoretical integration are hard put to counter the ongoing development of such focused approaches. Some forms of feminist criminology, for example, even though they offer instructive insights, represent exclusive viewpoints which actively seek dismissal of much existing criminological thought—not integration with it. Similarly, other authors have advocated development of a black criminology to represent the experiences and felt needs of African-Americans and black criminologists.[87] Facing these developments, some feel that fragmentation of criminological theory, not integration, is the rule today.

Such critiques, however, may be overly harsh. One mistake made by advocates of theoretical integration is to assume that *all* existing theories must somehow be embraced and subsumed under *one* encompassing theoretical umbrella. A better strategy may be to work toward a multiple-theory approach that seeks the integration of only a few theories at a time. Multiple-theory formulations may provide the building blocks of larger and more comprehensive integrated theories of the future.

Sometimes a single organizing concept can help blend multiple perspectives. Less than a year ago, for example, Francis T. Cullen, in an incoming presidential address to the Academy of Criminal Justice Sciences, identified the concept of social support as a potential "organizing concept for criminology."[88] "In short," said Cullen, "my thesis is that both across nations and across communities, crime rates vary inversely with the level of social support." "America," he said, "has higher rates of serious crime than other industrialized nations because it is a less supportive society." The idea of social support, said Cullen, is inherent in many criminological perspectives even though few theorists use the term directly. Cullen pointed to the ecological theories of the Chicago school, in which gangs were said to replace ineffectual families, as early examples of the social support thesis. Other research, including that on child abuse, ethnographic studies of the "truly disadvantaged," and studies of welfare which show that "governmental assistance to the poor tends to lessen violent crime," all add credence to the social support thesis, said Cullen. Because the concept of social support is capable of linking so many studies and so many other perspectives it may truly hold value as an organizing or integrative concept in the field of criminology.

Cullen suggested that a "social support paradigm"—one which holds that "social support [whether] delivered through government social programs, communities, social networks, families, interpersonal relations, or agents of the criminal justice system...reduces criminal involvement"—can serve not only as a useful integrative tool, but "can provide grounds for creating a more supportive 'Good Society.'" Specifically, Cullen maintained "the provision of social supports reduces criminogenic strains, fosters effective parenting and a nurturing family life, supplies the human and social capital needed to desist from crime, creates opportunities for prosocial modeling, strengthens efforts at informal and formal control, and reduces opportunities for victimization." Nonetheless, Cullen admits that an integrative theory of social support is a long way off. "Research must discern which of these hunches have merit," he says, "and to what degree."

While we may not yet be able to see the practical promise of theoretical integration, work in the area has just begun. The door to this area will doubtlessly remain open a while longer.

POLICIES OF THE FUTURE

In a recent article, the eminent writer George F. Cole raised the question: "How can lawmakers, police, courts, and corrections begin to plan for the eventualities that lie ahead?" Cole concluded that "[i]t is essential that policy makers be given the best evidence as to prospects for future developments pertaining to the justice system and the broader socioeconomic and political context within which it will operate. Not all uncertainties about the future can be removed, but systematic and insightful exploration of the range of possibilities can provide a sounder basis for planning and a useful perspective on priorities for innovation."[89] Cole identified a number of "drivers," or significant changes likely to occur over the next 25 years, which he says "are likely to impact the crime and justice environment by the year 2010." The list he created is shown in Table 14.1.

The significance of many of the factors listed in Table 14.1 for crime-control planners can be clearly seen in the writings of **Gene Stephens.** Stephens, one of the best known futurists to focus on crime in the past decade, observes that "[c]rime is increasing worldwide, and there is every reason to believe the trend will continue through the 1990s and into the early years of the twenty-first century."[90] In particular, observes Stephens, street crimes are escalating in formerly communist countries throughout Eastern Europe, and in other European nations such as those in Scandinavia and the United Kingdom. According to Stephens, the United States was one of the first nations to experience a rapid rise in criminality because, in many ways, it was the most advanced nation on the globe. The United States is a

TABLE 14.1

LIST OF DRIVERS LIKELY TO IMPACT THE CRIME AND JUSTICE ENVIRONMENT BY THE YEAR 2010

Demography

1. Overall U.S. population increases to 300,000,000.
2. Proportion of Americans older than age 40 grows from 37% to 45%.
3. Minorities increase to 26% of the population.
4. The flow of legal immigrants, increasingly from Latin America and Asia, continues at a rate of about 750,000 per year.
5. Advancing technology and a changing economy result in a disproportionate impact on less skilled, lower socioeconomic groups.

Economics

1. Restructuring of the economy continues with disruptions in some mature industrial sectors, rapid growth in the high technology and service fields, and some outflow of jobs and capital to other nations.
2. The federal budget deficit improves, but only slowly, so funding for domestic programs remains tight.
3. Economies of the nations of the former Soviet Union remain unstable.
4. Checks and credit cards assume a larger portion of consumer monetary transactions.
5. Real growth in output and income generally is slow but steady.

Technology

1. Copying technologies advance rapidly.
2. Automation of financial transactions increase.
3. Miniaturization of computers gives patrol officers instant access to crime information files.
4. Scientists discover a chemical that has the ability to break the physical dependence on drugs from which addicts suffer.
5. Gains in laser and fiber-optic technologies revolutionize organizations.

Crime Factors

1. The war on drugs of the 1990s has been cut back as cocaine use declines and law enforcement proves costly.
2. Participation of women in criminal activity increases as their societal role is redefined.
3. Handguns continue to be owned by a significant portion of the population.
4. Incarceration rates stabilize as construction of costly new prisons declines. There is an expansion of the use of probation and intermediate sanctions.
5. Disposal of nuclear and toxic wastes becomes a major organized crime activity.

Source: George F. Cole, "Criminal Justice in the Twenty-First Century: The Role of Futures Research," in John Klofas and Stan Stojkovic, eds., *Crime and Justice in the Year 2010* (Belmont, CA: Wadsworth, 1995), pp. 4–5.

highly diverse, multicultural, industrialized, and democratic society which strongly supports individual freedoms and has fostered a strong sense of personal independence among its citizens.

Multiculturalism and heterogeneity, says Stephens, increase *anomie*, and previously isolated and homogeneous societies such as Japan, Denmark, China, and Greece are now facing growing cultural diversity due to international migration, the expansion of new social ideals, and increased foreign commerce. "Heterogeneity in societies will be the rule in the twenty-first century," says Stephens, "and failure to recognize and plan for such diversity can lead to serious crime problems, especially in emerging multicultural societies."[91] Stephens's thesis is best summarized in this passage from his work: "The connection between crime and culture cannot be overemphasized: There are high-crime and low-crime cultures around the world. In the years ahead, many low-crime cultures may become high-crime cultures because of changing world demographics and politicoeconomic systems. In general, heterogeneous populations in which people have lots of political freedom (democracy) and lots of economic choice (capitalism) are prime candidates for crime unless a good socialization system is created and maintained."[92]

Homogeneous nations, in which citizens share similar backgrounds, life experiences, and values, produce citizens who are generally capable of complying with the wishes of the majority and legislate controls over behavior which are not difficult for most citizens to comply with. In such societies a tradition of discipline, a belief in the laws, and acceptance of personal responsibility are typically the norm.

Diverse societies, on the other hand, suffer from constant internal conflict, with much of that conflict focused on acceptable ways of living and working. Heterogeneous societies tend to place a strong emphasis on individualism, and disagreement about the law and social norms is rife. Characteristic of such cultures is the fact that law-breakers tend to deny responsibility, "and violators go to great lengths to avoid capture and conviction." To highlight the difference between homogeneous and heterogeneous societies, Stephens points to the fact that in some highly homogeneous cultures, such as Japan, those who break norms will often punish themselves, even if their transgressions are not publicly discovered. Such self-punishing behavior would be almost unthinkable in an advanced heterogeneous society such as the United States. As Stephens explains it, "Some nations, such as the United States, face pervasive *anomie* due to their lack of restraints on human desires."[93]

Heterogeneity can arise in any number of ways, even within a society which had previously been relatively homogenous. One source of increasing and important differences in American society today, for example, has been the growth of a technological culture which has produced two separate and distinct groups—the technologically capable and those who are incapable of utilizing modern technology. To these two groups we might add a third: the technologically aware, or those who realize the importance of technology but who, for whatever reason—be it age, lack of education, poverty, or other life circumstances—have not yet acquired the skills necessary to participate fully in what our highly technological society has to offer. In Stephens's words: "More people are turning to street crime and violence because they find themselves unprepared, educationally or emotionally, to cope with the requirements for success in the new era."[94]

Another reason why crime rates are high—and growing—in increasingly heterogeneous societies, according to Stephens, is that such societies often display a lack of consistent child-care philosophies and child-rearing methods. "In some societies," says Stephens, "parents are seen as primarily responsible for their children, but all citizens share in that responsibility, since everyone's welfare is affected by the proper socialization of each child." In others, children are viewed as the parents' property, and little is expected of parents other than that they be biologically capable of reproducing. No requirements are set in such societies for parental knowledge, skills, income, education, and so on. Stephens describes child-rearing practices in such societies as "helter-skelter, catch-as-catch-can child care...." Lacking child-rearing standards in which the majority of members of society can meaningfully participate, heterogeneous societies tend to produce adults who are irresponsible and who do not adhere to legal or other standards of behavior.

According to Stephens, future crimes will be plentiful, with countries around the world experiencing explosive growth in their crime rates. "The United States," he says, "was the first industrialized, democratic, heterogeneous nation and thus the first to face the crime problems associated with *anomie*."[95] Now, however, other nations are undergoing increased modernization, with many entering the post-modern era previously occupied solely by the United States. "[W]e can theorize," says Stephens, "that crime will be a growth industry in many countries as they find themselves gripped by the same social forces that have long affected the United States."[96]

Other authors have similarly attempted to describe crime-control issues that may face future policymakers.[97] Richter H. Moore, Jr., for example, identifies the following seven issues that are likely to concern crime-control planners in the near future:[98]

- *New Criminal Groups:* According to Moore, "groups such as Colombian drug cartels, Jamaican posses, Vietnamese gangs, various Chinese groups, and Los Angeles black street gangs are now a much bigger concern than the Mafia," and the criminal activity and influence of these new groups is growing rapidly. Traditional law enforcement responses, such as those developed to deal with Italian-American "Mafia" organizations, may be inappropriate in the face of the new challenges these groups represent.
- *Language Barriers:* According to Moore, "U.S. law-enforcement officials now find themselves hampered by a lack of understanding about the language and culture of some of the new criminal groups" operating in America. Cuban, Mexican, Colombian, Japanese, and Chinese criminals and criminal organizations are becoming commonplace, and such groups are increasingly involved in international communications and travel.
- *Distrust by Ethnic Communities:* Recent immigrant groups have been slow to assimilate into American culture and society. As a consequence, many of these groups hold strongly to native identities, distancing themselves from formal agencies of social control such as the police. As Moore points out, "[i]n many

of their countries of origin, new immigrants see police as corrupt, self-serving individuals, a viewpoint often not without foundation." A distrust of police and government representatives is nearly instinctual for members of such groups, making the work of law enforcement within the context of immigrant communities challenging and often difficult.

- *Greater Reliance on Community Involvement:* Moore observes that "[d]ue to the increasing costs of electronic surveillance, informant programs, undercover operations, and witness-protection programs, police are now encouraging community members to become more involved in their own security." The involvement of private citizens in the battle against crime may be the only realistic solution to the problem. Neighborhood watch groups, the use of community volunteers within criminal justice organizations, along with other neighborhood self-help programs such as school and church-based education all suggest the future of neighborhood-based crime-control policy.
- *Regulating the Marketplace:* Moore advises that decriminalization and legalization will become of increasingly greater concern to future legislators who will focus on "regulating the marketplace" for criminal activities such as gambling, drug trafficking, and prostitution.
- *Reducing Public Demand:* Similarly, according to Moore, future crime control policies will aim to reduce involvement in criminal activity "through better education" and other policies that will, over the long term, lower the demand for drugs and other illegal services.
- *Increased Treatment:* Although in contrast with many of today's "get-tough" policies, Moore sees a greater emphasis in the future on the treatment of all forms of criminality, including drug abuse, gambling, rape, and other lawbreaking behaviors.

Peace model an approach to crime control which focuses on effective ways for developing a shared consensus on critical issues that have the potential to seriously affect the quality of life.

Postmodernism suggests that effective crime control in any future heterogeneous society can best be achieved by the adoption of a **peace model** based upon cooperation rather than retribution. The peace model of crime control, having emerged largely from the themes embodied in peacemaking criminology, focuses on effective ways for developing a shared consensus on critical issues that have the potential to seriously affect the quality of life. Such issues include major crimes like murder and rape, but in future societies will also extend to property rights, rights to the use of new technologies, the ownership of information, and the like. Relatively minor issues, including sexual preference, nonviolent sexual deviance, gambling, drug use, noise, simple child custody claims, and publicly offensive behavior, will be dealt with fairly, but in ways that require few resources beyond those immediately available in the community.

Alternative dispute resolution mechanisms will be necessary in any future heterogeneous society because burgeoning disagreements about everyday issues will overwhelm the ability of existing resources such as the courts and police to deal with them.[99] Mediation programs, such as modern-day dispute resolution centers and neighborhood justice centers can be expected to expand in number, and to be characterized by cooperative efforts to reach dispute resolution, rather than by adversarial-like proceedings now characteristic of most American courts. Dispute resolution programs are based upon the principle of **participatory justice,** in which all parties to a dispute accept a kind of binding arbitration by neutral parties. Now operating in over two hundred areas throughout the country, dispute resolution centers often utilize administrative hearings and ombudsmen and are staffed by volunteers who work to resolve disputes without assigning blame.

Participatory justice a relatively informal type of criminal justice case processing which makes use of local community resources rather than requiring traditional forms of official intervention.

The Community Dispute Settlement Program which began in Philadelphia, Pennsylvania, in the 1970s was one of the earliest of modern-day community mediation programs in the country and has been well-studied.[100] Mediation in America, however, has a long and varied history. For many years Native American tribes have routinely employed dispute resolution mechanisms in dealing with behavioral problems and even crime. Perhaps the best-known dispute settlement mechanism among Native Americans today is the Navajo Peacemaker Court, which serves as an adjunct to the tribal court.[101] A box in this chapter describes a form of alternative dispute resolution used by the Tlingit tribal elders' council in Klawock, Alaska, in a recent case.

Miami's "drug court," a local-area judicial initiative, provides an example of another kind of dispute resolution program. The drug court program, which began in 1989, diverts nonviolent drug users from the traditional path of streets to court to jail, and is one of the first of its kind in the nation. Officially called the Dade County Diversion and Treatment Program, the drug court "channels almost all nonviolent defendants arrested on drug possession charges into an innovative court-operated rehabilitation program as an alternative to prosecution.... [T]he program expands on the traditional concept of diversion to provide a year or more of treatment and case management services that include counseling, acupuncture, fellowship meetings, education courses, and vocational services along with strict monitoring through periodic urine tests and court appearances. Defendants who succeed in the program have their criminal cases dismissed."[102] Drug court processing appears to be successful at reducing the incidence of repeat offenses, does not result in a criminal record for those who complete the program, and offers drug-dependent offenders a second chance at gaining control over substance abuse problems.

Many alternative dispute resolution strategies are really a form of **restorative justice.** Postmodern writers describe restorative justice as "a new system based on remedies and restoration rather than on prison, punishment and victim neglect."[103] They see it as "a system rooted in the concept of a caring community" and hope that it will lead to social and economic justice and increased concern and respect for both victims and victimizers in the not-too-distant future.

Restorative justice a postmodern perspective which stresses remedies and restoration rather than prison, punishment, and victim neglect.

Alternative dispute resolution strategies are not without their critics who charge that such programs are often staffed by poorly qualified individuals who are ill prepared to mediate disputes effectively. Nonetheless, as case processing expenses continue to rise, and as minor cases continue to flood justice system agencies, we can expect that an emphasis on alternative means of dispute resolution will continue.

ALASKAN TEENS' PRISON MAY BE THE GREAT OUTDOORS

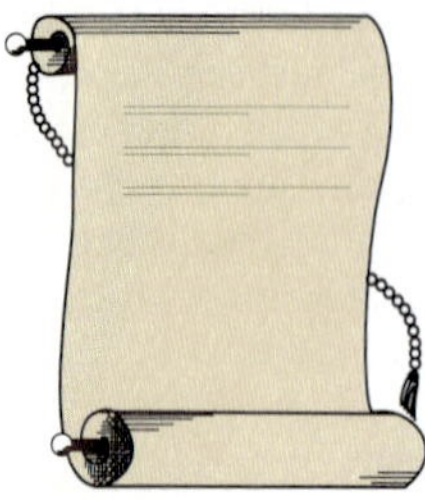

EVERETT, Wash.—Two young robbers are hoping a judge will give them an unusual deal today: replacing their prison sentences with punishment prescribed by their elders—banishment.

The Native Alaska teen-agers face three to five years in prison for attacking a pizza delivery man with a baseball bat and robbing him of the pizza, $40, and a beeper last summer.

But the Tlingit tribal elders' council in Klawock, Alaska, wants the cousins, who were visiting relatives when the attack occurred, returned home for punishment under tribal law. The elders are offering to banish Adrian Guthrie and Simon Roberts, both 17, to remote islands for a year.

They would get help building shelters and basic tools for hunting and fishing so they could sustain themselves.

"This is not a test of endurance. It's a purification rite—a place for lots of inner self-reflection," says Rudy James, who represents the elders.

Snohomish County Superior Court Judge James Allendoerfer today is expected to decide whether to stand by an earlier decision to release the youths to the elders. But deputy prosecutor Michael Magee is objecting. He questions how the teens would be supervised.

Few Native American tribes have banished members recently, and arrangements with state courts are rare.

"It's unusual, but in tribal jurisdiction there is an emphasis on alternatives to incarceration," says Joe Myers, executive director of the National Indian Justice Center.

The teens prefer the old ways: "Out in the woods, nice and quiet, you could think about all the things you did...and become a better person," Roberts says.

Allendoerfer has asked the elders for more details about the punishment period. The elders promise to check on the teens regularly, but it isn't clear if the teens would have access to emergency help. The banishment islands—among hundreds along Alaska's coast—are to be kept secret so the youths will remain isolated.

Defense attorney Thomas Cox says the elders' offer is their best hope: "If they go to prison, their behavior will be reinforced. Prison is a college for criminals."

The teens, in Snohomish County Jail almost a year, were charged as adults because of the brutality of the attack. It was their first offense.

The elders are offering to build a duplex for the victim, Tim Whittlesey, 25, who suffered severe head injuries and permanent hearing loss. It would provide him with housing and rental income.

In the youths' hometown, the 600 tribal members are split over the plans. The elders, a traditional group appointed by tribal families, kept the arrangements secret from the elected Klawock Cooperative Association, a federally recognized governing group.

The association isn't objecting. President Roseann Demmert doesn't like "what may happen to the boys in prison...but I worry about them being placed on an island and whether they will survive."

Ron Guthrie says his stepson, Adrian, isn't prepared, and he wants two weeks to teach him more wilderness skills.

"For a little while, he can survive. But he needs to know a lot more," Guthrie says.

Even if banished, the teens wouldn't be off the hook. They would return to Allendoerfer's courtroom March 15, 1996, when the judge would decide whether they must still serve prison time.

Tribal elder Theodore Roberts, 72, isn't worrying about that now. He just wants his grandson Simon back.

Tlingit Eskimo boys Adrian Guthrie (rear with glasses) and Simon Roberts (left center) are turned over to tribal judge Rudy James. *Michael O'Leary Photography.*

"I will be grateful to that judge as long as I have breath," Roberts says. "I'm ashamed of what happened, but I don't want him to go to the penitentiary."

Source: Deeann Glamser, "Alaskan Teens' Prison May Be the Great Outdoors," *USA Today*, August 12, 1994, p. 13A. Copyright 1994, *USA Today*. Reprinted with permission.

DISCUSSION QUESTIONS

1. Does banishment seem like an acceptable alternative punishment for the crimes committed by the Tlingit Eskimo boys described in this article? Why or why not?
2. What other alternative forms of punishment can you think of which might be useful in dealing with these boys? With other kinds of offenders?

SUMMARY

For all but the most astute, the future is difficult to presage. It is safe to assume, however, that the future will differ from the past, and that important differences in any future criminology will involve issues of theory formulation and crime-control policy. We can get some hint of what is to come by examining postmodern approaches which, while tending toward increased realism in their view of crime and criminal behavior, generally advocate humane alternatives to traditional crime-control agendas. Some have termed such postmodern policies "restorative justice" and have suggested that crime-control programs of the near future must take into account both the suffering of victims as well as the inequities within society which promulgate criminality. Others, however, have complained that "postmodernism does not provide any practical guidance on policy. At most," such critics say, "it offers a basis for exposing possible pretenses and illusions in the pursuit of a just policy."[104] Postmodern criminology, because of its emphasis on deconstructionism, has also been criticized "for not valuing anything, and for a belief that 'anything goes.'"[105]

But those who perceive postmodern criminology as shortsighted fail to recognize that a new social order requires a new way of understanding it. As some writers point out, "[i]t is still too early to evaluate the impact of postmodernism on criminology. Yet its influence is being felt in the increased questioning of traditional criminological concepts."[106] If early signs are any indication, postmodern criminology, combined with the traditional approaches of the past, appears to offer the best hope for coping with crime and for developing a truly just society in the twenty-first century.

DISCUSSION QUESTIONS

1. Do you believe it is possible to know the future? What techniques are identified in this chapter for assessing possible futures? Which do you think holds the most promise? Why?
2. What have been the major contributions of feminist thinking to the field of criminology? Do you believe that a "feminist criminology" is possible? Why or why not?
3. What do we mean by the word "deconstructionist" in the context of new criminological approaches to crime explanation? Why do some authors say that feminist criminology is "deconstructionist?"
4. Describe the emerging theoretical approaches outlined in this chapter. Which appeals the most to you? Why?
5. Describe peacemaking criminology. What are its central tenants? Do you believe that peacemaking criminology is realistic? Why or why not?
6. What is postmodernism? How has postmodernism affected criminology? What predictions for the future can we make based upon an understanding of postmodernist approaches?

NOTES

1. James Q. Wilson, "Crime and Public Policy," in James Q. Wilson and Joan Petersilia, *Crime* (San Francisco: Institute for Contemporary Studies, 1995), p. 507.
2. Cynthia Manson and Charles Ardai (eds.), *Future Crimes* (New York: Donald I. Fine, 1992), p. x.
3. Joseph F. Coates, "The Highly Probable Future: 83 Assumptions About the Year 2025," *The Futurist,* Vol. 28, no. 4 (July/August 1994), p. 51.
4. Alvin Toffler, *Future Shock* (New York: Random House, 1970).
5. Alvin Toffler, *Powershift: Knowledge,*

Wealth, and Violence at the Edge of the 21st Century (New York: Bantam Books, 1990).
6. Alvin Toffler, *The Third Wave* (New York: Bantam Books, 1981).
7. John Naisbitt, *Megatrends: Ten New Directions Transforming Our Lives* (New York: Warner Books, 1982).
8. Although this chapter cannot cover all future aspects of the criminal justice system, readers are referred to C. J. Swank, "Police in the 21st Century: Hypotheses for the Future," *International Journal of Comparative and Applied Criminal Justice,* Vol. 17, nos. 1 and 2 (Spring/Fall 1993), pp. 107–120, for an excellent analysis of policing in the future.
9. Society of Police Futurists International, "PFI: The Future of Policing" (brochure), no date.
10. William L. Tafoya, "Futures Research: Implications for Criminal Investigations," in James N. Gilbert, ed., *Criminal Investigation: Essays and Cases* (Columbus, OH: Charles E. Merrill, 1990), p. 214.
11. As identified by George F. Cole, "Criminal Justice in the Twenty-First Century: The Role of Futures Research," in John Klofas and Stan Stojkovic, eds., *Crime and Justice in the Year 2010* (Belmont, CA: Wadsworth, 1995).
12. Ibid.
13. Ibid.
14. Richter H. Moore, Jr., "Wiseguys: Smarter Criminals and Smarter Crime in the 21st Century," *The Futurist,* Vol. 28, no. 5 (September/October 1994), p. 33.
15. Ibid.
16. Georgette Bennett, *Crimewarps: The Future of Crime in America* (Garden City, NY: Anchor/Doubleday, 1987).
17. L. Edward Wells, "Explaining Crime in the Year 2010," in Klofas and Stojkovic, *Crime and Justice in the Year 2010,* pp. 36–61.
18. Ibid., pp. 48–49.
19. Ibid., pp. 54–57.
20. Frank P. Williams III and Marilyn D. McShane, *Criminological Theory,* 2nd ed. (Englewood Cliffs, NJ: Prentice Hall, 1994), p. 257.
21. Ibid., p. 221.
22. Ronald V. Clarke and Derek B. Cornish, eds., *Crime Control in Britain: A Review of Police and Research* (Albany: State University of New York Press), p. 8.
23. L. E. Cohen and Marcus Felson, "Social Change and Crime Rate Trends: A Routine Activity Approach," *American Sociological Review,* Vol. 44, no. 4 (August 1979), pp. 588–608. Also, see Marcus Felson and L. E. Cohen, "Human Ecology and Crime: A Routine Activity Approach," *Human Ecology,* Vol. 8, no. 4 (1980), pp. 389–406; and Marcus Felson, "Linking Criminal Choices, Routine Activities, Informal Control, and Criminal Outcomes," in Derek B. Cornish and Ronald V. Clarke, eds., *The Reasoning Criminal: Rational Choice Perspectives on Offending* (New York: Springer-Verlag, 1986), pp. 119–128.
24. Lawrence E. Cohen and Marcus Felson, "Social Change and Crime Rate Trends: A Routine Activities Approach," *American Sociological Review,* Vol. 44, no. 4 (1979), p. 595.
25. For a test of routine activities theory as an explanation for victimization in the workplace, see John D. Wooldredge, Francis T. Cullen, and Edward J. Latessa, "Victimization in the Workplace: A Test of Routine Activities Theory," *Justice Quarterly,* Vol. 9, no. 2 (June 1992), pp. 325–335.
26. Marcus Felson, *Crime and Everyday Life: Insight and Implications for Society* (Thousand Oaks, CA: Pine Forge Press, 1994).
27. Gary LaFree and Christopher Birkbeck, "The Neglected Situation: A Cross-National Study of the Situational Characteristics of Crime," *Criminology,* Vol. 29, no. 1 (February 1991), p. 75.
28. See Derek B. Cornish and Ronald V. Clarke, "Understanding Crime Displacement: An Application of Rational Choice Theory," *Criminology,* Vol. 25, no. 4 (November 1987), p. 933.
29. Clarke and Cornish, *Crime Control in Britain: A Review of Police and Research,* p. 48.
30. Werner Einstadter and Stuart Henry, *Criminological Theory: An Analysis of Its*

Underlying Assumptions (Fort Worth: Harcourt Brace, 1995), p. 70.

31. Daniel J. Curran and Claire M. Renzetti, *Theories of Crime* (Boston: Allyn & Bacon, 1994), p. 18.
32. Kenneth D. Tunnell, "Choosing Crime: Close Your Eyes and Take Your Chances," *Justice Quarterly*, Vol. 7 (1990), pp. 673–690.
33. For a good summation of target hardening, see Ronald V. Clarke, *Situational Crime Prevention* (New York: Harrow and Heston, 1992).
34. Don C. Gibbons, *Talking About Crime and Criminals: Problems and Issues in Theory Development in Criminology* (Englewood Cliffs, NJ: Prentice Hall, 1994), p. 165, citing Loraine Gelsthorpe and Alison Morris, "Feminism and Criminology in Britain," *British Journal of Criminology*, Spring 1988, pp. 93–110.
35. Sally S. Simpson, "Feminist Theory, Crime and Justice," *Criminology*, Vol. 27, no. 4 (1989), p. 605.
36. Freda Adler, *Sisters in Crime: The Rise of the New Female Criminal* (New York: McGraw-Hill, 1975).
37. Rita J. Simon, *Women and Crime* (Lexington, MA: Lexington Books, 1975).
38. Kathleen Daly and Meda Chesney-Lind, "Feminism and Criminology," *Justice Quarterly*, Vol. 5, no. 5 (December 1988), pp. 497–535.
39. Susan Caulfield and Nancy Wonders, "Gender and Justice: Feminist Contributions to Criminology," in Gregg Barak, ed., *Varieties of Criminology: Readings from a Dynamic Discipline* (Westport, CT: Praeger, 1994), pp. 213–229.
40. Roslyn Muraskin and Ted Alleman, *It's a Crime: Women and Justice* (Englewood Cliffs, NJ: Prentice Hall, 1993), p. 1.
41. Carol Pateman, "Feminist Critiques of the Public/Private Dichotomy," in Anne Phillips, ed., *Feminism and Equality* (Oxford: Basil Blackwell, 1987).
42. Simpson, "Feminist Theory, Crime and Justice."
43. John Hagan, *Structural Criminology* (New Brunswick, NJ: Rutgers University Press, 1989), p. 130.
44. Ibid.
45. Daly and Chesney-Lind, "Feminism and Criminology," p. 506.
46. Ibid.
47. Ibid., p. 514.
48. For an intriguing analysis of how existing laws tend to criminalize women and their reproductive activities, see Susan O. Reed, "The Criminalization of Pregnancy: Drugs, Alcohol, and AIDS," in Muraskin and Alleman, *It's a Crime: Women and Justice*, pp. 92–117; and Drew Humphries, "Mothers and Children, Drugs and Crack: Reactions to Maternal Drug Dependency," in Muraskin and Alleman, *It's a Crime: Women and Justice*, pp. 131–145.
49. Dawn H. Currie, "Feminist Encounters with Postmodernism: Exploring the Impasse of the Debates on Patriarchy and Law," *Canadian Journal of Women and the Law*, Vol. 5, no. 1 (1992), p. 10.
50. Such studies are still ongoing and continue to add to the descriptive literature of feminist criminology. See, for example, Deborah R. Baskin and Ira Sommers, "Female Initiation into Violent Street Crime," *Justice Quarterly*, Vol. 10, no. 4 (December 1993), pp. 559–583; Scott Decker, Richard Wright, Allison Redfern, and Dietrich Smith, "A Woman's Place Is in the Home: Females and Residential Burglary," *Justice Quarterly*, Vol. 10, no. 1 (March 1993), pp. 143–162; and Jill L. Rosenbaum, "The Female Delinquent: Another Look at the Role of the Family," in Muraskin and Alleman, *It's a Crime: Women and Justice*, pp. 399–420.
51. Ronald L. Akers, *Criminological Theories: Introduction and Evaluation* (Los Angeles: Roxbury, 1994), p. 39.
52. For additional insight into the notion of "deconstruction" as it applies to feminist thought within criminology, see Carol Smart, *Feminism and the Power of Law* (New York: Routledge, 1989).
53. Daly and Chesney-Lind, "Feminism and Criminology," p. 512.
54. See, for example, Darrell J. Steffensmeier and Emile Andersen Allan, "Sex Disparities in Arrests by Residence, Race, and Age: An Assessment of the Gender Con-

vergence/Crime Hypothesis," *Justice Quarterly,* Vol. 5, no. 1 (March 1988), pp. 53–80.

55. Darrell Steffensmeier, John Kramer, and Cathy Streifel, "Gender and Imprisonment Decisions," *Criminology,* Vol. 31, no. 3 (August 1993), pp. 411–446. Gender-based differences, however, have been discovered in some instances of probation- and parole-related decision making. See Edna Erez, "Gender, Rehabilitation, and Probation Decisions," *Criminology,* Vol. 27, no. 2 (1989), pp. 307–327, and Edna Erez, "Dangerous Men, Evil Women: Gender and Parole Decision-Making," *Justice Quarterly,* Vol. 9, no. 1 (March 1992), pp. 106–126.
56. See, for example, Kathleen Daly, "Neither Conflict nor Labeling nor Paternalism Will Suffice: Intersections of Race, Ethnicity, Gender, and Family in Criminal Court Decisions," *Crime and Delinquency,* Vol. 35, no. 1 (January 1989), pp. 136–168.
57. Citing Allison Morris, *Women, Crime and Criminal Justice* (New York: Blackwell, 1987).
58. Caulfield and Wonders, "Gender and Justice: Feminist Contributions to Criminology," p. 229.
59. For examples of how this might be accomplished, see F. H. Knopp, "Community Solutions to Sexual Violence: Feminist/Abolitionist Perspectives," in *Criminology as Peacemaking* (Bloomington: Indiana University Press), pp. 181–193; and S. Caringella-MacDonald, and D. Humphries, "Sexual Assault, Women, and the Community: Organizing to Prevent Sexual Violence," *Criminology as Peacemaking,* pp. 98–113.
60. Richard Quinney, "Life of Crime: Criminology and Public Policy as Peacemaking," *Journal of Crime and Justice,* Vol. 16, no. 2 (1993), pp. 3–9.
61. See, for example, Harold E. Pepinsky, "This Can't Be Peace: A Pessimist Looks at Punishment," in W. B. Groves and G. Newman, eds., *Punishment and Privilege* (Albany: Harrow and Heston: 1986); Harold E. Pepinsky, "Violence as Unresponsiveness: Toward a New Conception of Crime," *Justice Quarterly,* Vol. 5 (1988), pp. 539–563; and Pepinsky and Quinney, *Criminology as Peacemaking.*
62. See, for example, Richard Quinney, "Crime, Suffering, Service: Toward a Criminology of Peacemaking," *Quest,* Vol. 1 (1988), pp. 66–75; Richard Quinney, "The Theory and Practice of Peacemaking in the Development of Radical Criminology," *Critical Criminologist,* Vol. 1, no. 5 (1989), p. 5; and Richard Quinney and John Wildeman, *The Problem of Crime: A Peace and Social Justice Perspective,* 3rd ed. (Mayfield, CA: Mountain View Press, 1991)—originally published as *The Problem of Crime: A Critical Introduction to Criminology* (New York: Bantam, 1977).
63. All these themes are addressed, for example, in Pepinsky and Quinney, *Criminology as Peacemaking.*
64. For a good discussion of this "theory," see John F. Galliher, "Willie Horton: Fact, Faith, and Commonsense Theory of Crime," in ibid., pp. 245–250.
65. Quinney and Wildeman, *The Problem of Crime: A Peace and Social Justice Perspective,* pp. vii–viii.
66. Richard Quinney, "Life of Crime: Criminology and Public Policy as Peacemaking," *Journal of Crime and Justice,* vol. 16, no. 2 (1993), abstract.
67. Bo Lozoff and Michael Braswell, *Inner Corrections: Finding Peace and Peace Making* (Cincinnati: Anderson, 1989).
68. Clemmons Bartollas and Michael Braswell, "Correctional Treatment, Peacemaking, and the New Age Movement," *Journal of Crime and Justice,* Vol. 16, no. 2 (1993), pp. 43–58.
69. Ibid.
70. Ram Dass and P. Gorman, *How Can I Help? Stories and Reflections on Service* (New York: Alfred A. Knopf, 1985), p. 165; as cited in *The Problem of Crime: A Peace and Social Justice Perspective,* 3rd ed., p. 116.
71. Lozoff and Braswell, *Inner Corrections,* p. vii.

72. Einstadter and Henry, *Criminological Theory: An Analysis of Its Underlying Assumptions*, p. 233.
73. For an excellent review of critical realism within a Canadian context, see John Lowman and Brian D. MacLean, eds., *Realist Criminology: Crime Control and Policing in the 1990s* (Toronto: University of Toronto Press, 1994).
74. Daniel J. Curran and Claire M. Renzetti, *Theories of Crime* (Boston: Allyn & Bacon, 1994), p. 283.
75. See M. D. Schwartz and W. S. DeKeseredy, "Left Realist Criminology: Strengths, Weaknesses, and the Feminist Critique." *Crime, Law, and Social Change*, Vol. 15, no. 1 (January 1991), pp. 51–72; W. S. DeKeseredy and B. D. MacLean, "Exploring the Gender, Race, and Class Dimensions of Victimization: A Left Realist Critique of the Canadian Urban Victimization Survey," *International Journal of Offender Therapy and Comparative Criminology*, Vol. 35, no. 2 (Summer 1991), pp. 143–161; and W. S. DeKeseredy and M. D. Schwartz, "British and U.S. Left Realism: A Critical Comparison," *International Journal of Offender Therapy and Comparative Criminology*, Vol. 35, no. 3 (Fall 1991), pp. 248–262.
76. See Jock Young, "The Failure of Criminology: The Need for a Radical Realism," in R. Matthews and J. Young (eds.) *Confronting Crime* (Beverly Hills, CA: Sage, 1986), pp. 4–30; Jock Young, "The Tasks of a Realist Criminology," *Contemporary Crisis*, Vol. 11, no. 4, (1987) pp. 337–356; and "Radical Criminology in Britain: The Emergence of a Competing Paradigm," *British Journal of Criminology*, Vol. 28, (1988), pp. 159–183.
77. Roger Matthews and Jock Young, "Reflections on Realism," in Jock Young and Roger Matthews, eds., *Rethinking Criminology: The Realist Debate* (Newbury Park, CA: Sage, 1992).
78. David Nelken, ed., *The Futures of Criminology* (Thousand Oaks, CA: Sage, 1994), p. 91.
79. Ibid.
80. Don C. Gibbons, *Talking About Crime and Criminals: Problems and Issues in Theory Development in Criminology*, (Englewood Cliffs, NJ: Prentice Hall, 1994), p. 170.
81. Piers Bierne and James W. Messerschmidt, *Criminology* (New York: Harcourt Brace Jovanovich, 1991), p. 501.
82. For a more detailed discussion of theory integration, see Stephen F. Messner, Marvin D. Krohn, and Allan A. Liska, eds., *Theoretical Integration in the Study of Deviance and Crime: Problems and Prospects* (Albany: State University of New York Press), p. 1989.
83. Joan McCord, "Theory, Pseudotheory, and Metatheory," in W. S. Laufer and F. Adler, eds., *Advances in Criminological Theory*, Volume 1 (New Brunswick, NJ: Transaction, 1989), pp. 127–145.
84. Williams and McShane, *Criminological Theory*, p. 265.
85. Ibid., pp. 266–267.
86. Einstadter and Henry, *Criminological Theory: An Analysis of Its Underlying Assumptions*, p. 309.
87. See, for example, Katheryn K. Russell, "Development of a Black Criminology and the Role of the Black Criminologist," *Justice Quarterly*, Vol. 9, no. 4 (December 1992), pp. 668–683.
88. Francis T. Cullen, "Social Support as an Organizing Concept for Criminology: Presidential Address to the Academy of Criminal Justice Sciences," Justice Quarterly, Vol.11, no. 4, (December 1994), p. 527–559.
89. Cole, "Criminal Justice in the Twenty-First Century: The Role of Futures Research," pp. 4–5.
90. Gene Stephens, "The Global Crime Wave," *The Futurist*, Vol. 28, no. 4 (July/August 1994), pp. 22–29.
91. Ibid.
92. Ibid.
93. Ibid.
94. Ibid.
95. Ibid.
96. Ibid.
97. For an interesting and alternative view of the future—one that evaluates what might happen if the insight provided by feminist perspectives on crime were implement-

ed—see M. Kay Harris, "Moving Into the New Millennium: Toward a Feminist Vision of Justice," in Pepinsky and Quinney, *Criminology as Peacemaking.*

98. Richter H. Moore, Jr., "Wiseguys: Smarter Criminals and Smarter Crime in the 21st Century," *The Futurist,* Sept.-Oct. 1994, Vol. 28, no. 5, p. 33.
99. For a good overview of such programs, see Thomas E. Carbonneau, *Alternative Dispute Resolution: Melting the Lances and Dismounting the Steeds* (Chicago: University of Illinois Press, 1989).
100. See, for example, J. E. Beer, *Peacemaking in Your Neighborhood: Reflections on an Experiment in Community Mediation* (Philadelphia: New Society Publishers, 1986), and J. Beer, E. Steif, and C. Walker, *Peacemaking in Your Neighborhood: Mediator's Handbook* (Philadelphia: Friends Mediation Service, 1987).
101. For an excellent review of alternative dispute mechanisms among Native American groups, see D. LeResche, "Native American Perspectives on Peacemaking," *Mediation Quarterly,* Vol. 10, no. 4 (Summer 1993).
102. Peter Finn and Andrea K. Newlyn, "Miami's 'Drug Court': A Different Approach" (Washington, D.C.: National Institute of Justice, June 1993), p. 2.
103. Fay Honey Knopp, "Community Solutions to Sexual Violence: Feminist-Abolitionist Perspectives," in Pepinsky and Quinney, *Criminology as Peacemaking,* p. 183.
104. Martin D. Schwartz and David O. Friedrichs, "Postmodern Thought and Criminological Discontent: New Metaphors for Understanding Violence," *Criminology,* Vol. 32, no. 2 (1994), p. 237.
105. Williams and McShane, *Criminological Theory,* p. 280.
106. Ibid., p. 297.

GLOSSARY

Administrative law regulates many daily business activities, and violations of such regulations generally result in warnings or fines, depending upon their adjudged severity.

Age of Reason. See **Enlightenment.**

Aggravated assault (UCR) the unlawful attack by one person upon another for the purpose of inflicting severe or aggravated bodily injury. See also **simple assault.**

Alloplastic adaptation that form of adjustment which results from changes in the environment surrounding an individual.

Anomie a social condition in which norms are uncertain or lacking.

Antisocial or **Asocial personality** refers to individuals who are basically unsocialized and whose behavior pattern brings them repeatedly into conflict with society.

Applied research scientific inquiry that is designed and carried out with practical application in mind.

Arson any willful or malicious burning or attempt to burn, with or without intent to defraud, a dwelling house, public building, motor vehicle or aircraft, personal property of another, and so on.

Asocial personality. See **Antisocial personality.**

Assault. See **aggravated assault** or **simple assault.**

Asset forfeiture the authorized seizure of money, negotiable instruments, securities, or other things of value. In federal anti-drug laws: the authorization of judicial representatives to seize all moneys, negotiable instruments, securities, or other things of value furnished or intended to be furnished by any person in exchange for a controlled substance, and all proceeds traceable to such an exchange.

Atavism a concept used by Cesare Lombroso to suggest that criminals are physiological throwbacks to earlier stages of human evolution. The term "atavism" is derived from the Latin term *atavus*, which means "ancestor."

Audit trail a sequential record of computer system activities that enables auditors to reconstruct, review, and examine the sequence of states and activities surrounding each event in one or more related transactions from inception to output of final results back to inception.

Autoplastic adaptation that form of adjustment which results from changes within an individual.

Behavior theory an approach to understanding human activity which holds that behavior is determined by consequences it produces for the individual.

Biological theories of criminology maintain that the basic determinants of human behavior, including criminality, are constitutionally or physiologically based and often inherited.

Born criminals individuals who are born with a genetic predilection toward criminality.

Bourgeoisie in Marxian theory, the class of people which owns the means of production.

Bulletin board system (BBS) a computer accessible by telephone used like a bulletin board to leave messages and files for other users.

Burglary I. By the narrowest and oldest definition: the trespassory breaking and entering of the dwelling house of another in the night-time with the intent to commit a felony. II. The unlawful entry of any fixed structure, vehicle or vessel used for regular residence, industry or business, with or without force, with intent to commit a felony or larceny.

Burglary (UCR) the unlawful entry of a structure to commit a felony or a theft.

Chicago School. See **ecological theory.**

Capital punishment the legal imposition of a sentence of death upon a convicted offender. Another term for the death penalty.

Carjacking the stealing of a car while it is occupied.

Civil law that body of laws which regulates arrangements between individuals, such as contracts and claims to property.

Classical School a criminological perspective operative in the late 1700s and early 1800s which had its roots in the Enlightenment, and which held that men and women are rational beings, that crime is the result of the exercise of free will, and that punishment can be effective in reducing the incidence of crime since it negates the pleasure to be derived from crime commission.

Clearance rate the proportion of reported or discovered crimes within a given offense category which are solved.

Code of Hammurabi an early set of laws established by the Babylonian King Hammurabi around the year 2000 B.C.

Cohort a group of individuals sharing certain significant social characteristics in common, such as sex, time, and place of birth.

Common law a body of unwritten judicial opinion originally based upon customary social practices of Anglo-Saxon society during the Middle Ages.

Computer abuse any incident without color of right associated with computer technology in which a victim suffered or could have suffered loss and/or a perpetrator by intention made or could have made gain.[1]

Computer bulletin board see **bulletin board system (BBS).**

Computer crime any violation of a computer crime statute.

Computer-related crime any illegal act for which knowledge of computer technology is involved for its investigation, perpetration, or prosecution.

Computer virus a set of computer instructions that propagates copies or versions of itself into computer programs or data when it is executed.

Conditioning a psychological principle which holds that the frequency of any behavior can be increased or decreased through reward, punishment, and/or association with other stimuli.

Conduct norms the shared expectations of a social group relative to personal conduct.

Confidentiality. See **data confidentiality.**

Conflict perspective an analytical perspective on social organization which holds that conflict is a fundamental aspect of social life itself and can never be fully resolved.

Confounding effects rival explanations, also called competing hypotheses, which are threats to the internal or external validity of any research design.

Consensus model an analytical perspective on social organization which holds that most members of society agree as to what is right and what is wrong, and that the various elements of society work together in unison toward a common and shared vision of the greater good.

Constitutional theories those which explain criminality by reference to offenders' body types, inheritance, genetics, and/or external observable physical characteristics.

Constitutive criminology the process by which human beings create an ideology of crime that sustains it (the notion of crime) as a concrete reality.

Containment those aspects of the social bond which act to prevent individuals from committing crimes and keep them from engaging in deviance.

Control group a group of experimental subjects which, although the subject of measurement and observation, are not exposed to the experimental intervention.

Control theory a perspective which holds that crime is the result of weakened bonds between the individual and society.

Controlled experiments those which attempt to hold conditions (other than the intentionally introduced experimental intervention) constant.

Corporate crime a violation of a criminal statute either by a corporate entity or by its executives, employees, or agents acting on behalf of and for the benefit of the corporation, partnership, or other form of business entity.[2]

Correctional psychology that aspect of forensic psychology which is concerned with the diagnosis and classification of offenders, the treatment of correctional populations, and the rehabilitation of inmates and other law violators.

Correlation A causal, complementary, or reciprocal relationship between two measurable variables. See also **Statistical correlation.**

Cosa Nostra (literally, "our thing") a term signifying organized crime, and one of a variety of names for the "Mafia," the "Outfit," the "Mob," the "syndicate," or "the organization."

Crime behavior in violation of the criminal laws of a state, the federal government, or a local jurisdiction which has the power to make such laws.

Criminal homicide the causing of the death of another person without legal justification or excuse. Also, the illegal killing of one human being by another.

Criminal homicide (UCR) the name of the UCR category which includes and is limited to all offenses of causing the death of another person without justification or excuse.

Criminal justice the scientific study of crime, the criminal law, and components of the criminal justice system, including the police, courts, and corrections.

Criminal justice system the various agencies of "justice," especially police, courts, and corrections, whose goal it is to apprehend, convict, punish, and rehabilitate law violators.

Criminal law that body of law which regulates those actions which have the potential to harm interests of the state or the federal government.

Criminaloids a term used by Cesare Lombroso to describe occasional criminals who were pulled into criminality primarily by environmental influences.

Criminologist one who is trained in the field of criminology. Also, one who studies crime, criminals, and criminal behavior.

Criminology the scientific study of crime and criminal behavior, including their form, causes, legal aspects and control.

Criminology of place. See **environmental criminology**.

Critical criminology. See **radical criminology**.

Culture conflict a sociological perspective on crime which suggests that the root cause of criminality can be found in a clash of values between variously socialized groups over what is acceptable or proper behavior.

Cyberspace the computer-created matrix of virtual possibilities, including on-line services, wherein human beings interact with each other and with technology itself.

Cycloid a term developed by Ernst Kretschmer to describe a particular relationship between body build and personality type. The cycloid personality, which was associated with a heavy-set, soft type of body, was said to vacillate between normality and abnormality.

DNA fingerprinting (or **profiling**) the use of biological residue found at the scene of a crime for genetic comparisons in aiding the identification of criminal suspects.

Dangerous drugs a term used by the Drug Enforcement Administration (DEA) to refer to "broad categories or classes of controlled substances other than cocaine, opiates, and cannabis products." Amphetamines, methamphetamines, PCP (phencyclidine), LSD, methcathinone, and "designer drugs" are all considered "dangerous drugs."

Dangerousness the likelihood that a given individual will later harm society or others. Dangerousness is often measured in terms of **recidivism**, or as the likelihood of additional crime commission within a five year period following arrest or release from confinement.

Data confidentiality an ethical requirement of social scientific research which stipulates that research data not be shared outside of the research environment.

Data encryption methods used to encode computerized information.

Date rape unlawful forced sexual intercourse with a female against her will which occurs within the context of a dating relationship

***Daubert* standard** a test of scientific acceptability applicable to the gathering of evidence in criminal cases.

Deconstructionist theories emerging approaches which challenge existing criminological perspectives to debunk them, and which work toward replacing them with concepts more applicable to the post-modern era. Deconstructionist theories are generally post-modernist approaches, none of which have yet developed fully enough to actually deserve the name "theory."

Decriminalization (of drugs) reduces criminal penalties associated with the personal possession of a controlled substance.

Defensible space the range of mechanisms that combine to bring an environment under the control of its residents.

Demography the study of the characteristics of population groups (**demographics** the characteristics of such groups usually expressed in statistical fashion).

Designer drugs "new substances designed by slightly altering the chemical makeup of other illegal or tightly controlled drugs."[3]

Descriptive statistics describe, summarize, or highlight the relationships within data which have been gathered.

Deterrence the prevention of crime. See also **general deterrence** and **specific deterrence.**

Deterrence strategy a crime control strategy which attempts "to diminish motivation for crime by increasing the perceived certainty, severity, or celerity of penalties."[4]

Deviance behavior which violates social norms or which is statistically different from the "average."

Differential association the sociological thesis that criminality, like any other form of behavior, is learned through a process of association with others who communicate criminal values.

Discrediting information information which is inconsistent with the managed impressions being communicated in a given situation.

Displacement a shift of criminal activity from one spatial location to another.

Dramaturgical perspective (also **dramaturgy**) a theoretical point of view which depicts human behavior as centered around the purposeful management of interpersonal impressions.

Drug-defined crimes violations of laws prohibiting or regulating the possession, use, or distribution of illegal drugs.

Drug-related crimes crimes in which drugs contribute to the offense (excluding violations of drug laws).

Drug trafficking. See **trafficking.**

Durham rule a standard for judging legal insanity which holds that "an accused is not criminally responsible if his unlawful act was the product of mental disease or mental defect."

Ecological theory, also commonly called the "Chicago School" of criminology, is a type of sociological approach which emphasizes demographics (the characteristics of population groups) and geographics (the mapped location of such groups relative to one another) and sees the social disorganization which characterizes delinquency areas as a major cause of criminality and victimization.

Ectomorph a body type originally described as thin and fragile, with long, slender, poorly muscled extremities, and delicate bones.

Ego the reality-testing part of the personality; also referred to as the reality principle. More formally, the personality component that is conscious, most immediately controls behavior, and is most in touch with external reality.[5]

Electroencephalogram (EEG) electrical measurements of brain wave activity.

Encryption. See **Data encryption.**

Endomorph a body type originally described as soft and round, or overweight.

Enlightenment (the), also known as the Age of Reason. A social movement which arose during the 18th century, and built upon ideas such as empiricism, rationality, free will, humanism, and natural law.

Environmental crimes violations of the criminal law which, although typically committed by businesses or by business officials, may also be committed by other persons or organizational entities, and which damage some protected or otherwise significant aspect of the natural environment.

Environmental criminology an emerging perspective which emphasizes the importance of geographic location and architectural features as they are associated with the prevalence of criminal victimization. (Note: as the term has been understood to date, environmental criminology is *not* the study of environmental crime, but rather a perspective which stresses how crime varies from place to place.)

Environmental scanning "a systematic effort to identify in an elemental way future developments (trends or events) that could plausibly occur over the time horizon of interest,"[6] and that might impact one's area of concern.

Ethnic succession the continuing process whereby one immigrant or ethnic group succeeds another through assumption of a particular position in society.

Eugenics the study of hereditary improvement by genetic control.

Experiment. See **controlled experiments** or **quasi-experimental design.**

Expert systems computer hardware and software which attempt to duplicate the decision-making processes used by skilled investigators in the analysis of evidence and in the recognition of patterns which such evidence might represent.

External validity the ability to generalize research findings to other settings.

Federal interest computers those that are the property of the federal government, those that belong to financial institutions, or are accessed across state lines without authorization.

Felony murder a special class of criminal homicide whereby an offender may be charged with first-degree murder whenever his or her criminal activity results in another person's death.

Feminist criminology a developing intellectual approach which emphasizes gender issues in the subject matter of criminology.

First degree murder criminal homicide which is planned or involves premeditation.

Focal concerns the key values of any culture, and especially the key values of a delinquent subculture.

Folkways are time-honored ways of doing things. While they carry the force of tradition, their violation is unlikely to threaten the survival of the group. See also **mores.**

Forcible rape as defined in the UCR Program, is the carnal knowledge of a female forcibly and against her will. Assaults or attempts to commit rape by force or threat of force are also included in the UCR definition; however, statutory rape (without force) and other sex offenses are excluded.

Forensic psychiatry that branch of psychiatry having to do with the study of crime and criminality.

Forfeiture. See **Asset forfeiture.**

Frustration-aggression theory holds that frustration, which is a natural consequence of living, is a root cause of crime. Criminal behavior can be a form of adaptation when it results in stress reduction.

Future criminology the study of likely futures as they impinge on crime and its control.

Futures research "a multidisciplinary branch of operations research" whose principle aim "is to facilitate long-range planning based on 1. forecasting from the past supported by mathematical models; 2. cross-disciplinary treatment of its subject matter; 3. systematic use of expert judgment, and; 4. a systems-analytical approach to its problems."[7]

Futurist one who studies the future.

General deterrence a goal of criminal sentencing which seeks to prevent others from committing crimes similar to the one for which a particular offender is being sentenced.

Guilty but mentally ill (GBMI) a finding that an offender is guilty of the criminal offense with which they are charged but, because of their prevailing mental condition, they are generally sent to psychiatric hospitals for treatment rather than to prison. Once they have been declared "cured," however, such offenders can be transferred to correctional facilities to serve out their sentences.

Habitual offender statutes laws intended to keep repeat criminal offenders behind bars. These laws sometimes come under the rubric of "three strikes and you're out."

Hacker a person who views and uses computers as objects for exploration and exploitation.

Hedonistic calculus or **utilitarianism** the belief, first proposed by Jeremy Bentham, that behavior holds value to any individual undertaking it according to the amount of pleasure or pain that it can be expected to produce for that person.

Heroin signature program a DEA program that identifies the geographic source area of a heroin sample through the detection of specific chemical characteristics in the sample peculiar to the source area.

Homicide. See **Criminal homicide.**

Hypoglycemia a condition characterized by low blood sugar.

Hypothesis 1. [a]n explanation that accounts for a set of facts and that can be tested by further investigation..., 2. [s]omething that is taken to be true for the purpose of argument or investigation.[8]

Id the aspect of the personality from which drives, wishes, urges, and desires emanate. More formally, the division of the psyche associated with instinctual impulses and demands for immediate satisfaction of primitive needs.[9]

Illegitimate opportunity structures subcultural pathways to success which are disapproved of by the wider society.

Impression management the intentional enactment of practiced behavior which is intended to convey to others one's desirable personal characteristics and social qualities.

Incapacitation the use of imprisonment or other means to reduce the likelihood that an offender will be capable of committing future offenses.

Individual rights advocates those who seek to protect personal freedoms in the face of criminal prosecution.

Inferential statistics specify how likely findings are to be true for other populations, or in other locales.

Informed consent an ethical requirement of social scientific research which specifies that research subjects will be informed as to the nature of the research about to be conducted, their anticipated role in it, and the uses to which the data they provide will be put.

Insanity (law) a legally established inability to understand right from wrong, or to conform one's behavior to the requirements of the law.

Insanity (psychological) persistent mental disorder or derangement.[10]

Interactionist perspectives. See **social process theories.**

Interdiction an international drug control policy which aims to stop drugs from entering the country illegally.

Internal validity the certainty that experimental interventions did indeed cause the changes observed in the study group; also the control over confounding factors which tend to invalidate the results of an experiment.

Internet (the) the world's largest computer network.

Intersubjectivity a scientific principle which requires that independent observers see the same thing under the same circumstances for observations to be regarded as valid.

Irresistible impulse test a standard for judging legal insanity which holds that a defendant is not guilty of a criminal offense if the person, by virtue of their mental state or psychological condition, was not able to resist committing the action in question.

Juke family a well-known "criminal family" studied by Richard L. Dugdale.

Just deserts the notion that criminal offenders deserve the punishment they receive at the hands of the law, and that punishments should be appropriate to the type and severity of crime committed.

Kallikak family a well known "criminal family" studied by Henry H. Goddard.

Kriminalpolitik the political handling of crime, or a criminology-based social policy.

Labeling an interactionist perspective which sees continued crime as a consequence of limited opportunities for acceptable behavior which follow from the negative responses of society to those defined as offenders.

Larceny the unlawful taking or attempted taking of property other than a motor vehicle from the possession of another, by stealth, without force and without deceit, with intent to permanently deprive the owner of the property.

Larceny-theft (UCR) the unlawful taking, carrying, leading, or riding away by stealth of property, other than a motor vehicle, from the possession or constructive possession of another, including attempts.

Law and order advocates those who suggest that, under certain circumstances involving criminal threats to public safety, the interests of society should take precedence over individual rights.

LEAA an acronym for the Law Enforcement Assistance Administration, which was established under Title I of the Omnibus Crime Control and Safe Streets Act of 1967.

Learning theory the general notion that crime is an acquired form of behavior.

Legalization (of drugs) eliminates the laws and associated criminal penalties that prohibit the production, sale, distribution, and possession of a controlled substance.

Life-style theory. See r**outine activities theory**.

McNaughten rule a standard for judging legal insanity which requires that either an offender did not know what he or she were doing, or that, if he or she did, that he or she did not know it was wrong.

Mafia. See ***Cosa Nostra.***

Mala in se acts which are thought to be wrong in and of themselves.

Mala prohibita acts which are wrong only because society says they are.

Marxist criminology. See **radical criminology**.

Mass murder the illegal killing of four or more victims at one location, within one event.

Money laundering the process of converting illegally earned assets, originating as cash, to one or more alternative forms to conceal such incriminating factors as illegal origin and true ownership.[11]

Monozyotic (or MZ) **twins**, as opposed to dizygotic (or DZ) twins, develop from the same egg, and carry virtually the same genetic material.

Moral enterprise a term which encompasses all the efforts a particular interest group makes to have its sense of propriety enacted into law.

Mores are behavioral proscriptions covering potentially serious violations of a group's values, and would probably include strictures against murder, rape, and robbery. See also **folkways.**

Motor vehicle theft (**UCR**) the theft or attempted theft of a motor vehicle. This offense category includes the stealing of automobiles, trucks, buses, motorcycles, motorscooters, snowmobiles, and so on.

National Crime Victimization Survey (NCVS) conducted annually by the Bureau of Justice Statistics (BJS) and provides data on surveyed households which report they were affected by crime.

Natural law the philosophical perspective that certain immutable laws are fundamental to human nature and can be readily ascertained through reason. Man-made laws, in contrast, are said to derive from human experience and history—both of which are subject to continual change.

Natural rights the rights which, according to natural law theorists, individuals retain in the face of government action and interests.

Negligent homicide (UCR) in Uniform Crime Reports terminology, causing death of another by recklessness or gross negligence.

Neoclassical criminology a contemporary version of Classical criminology which emphasizes deterrence and retribution with reduced emphasis on rehabilitation.

Neurosis functional disorders of the mind or of the emotions involving anxiety, phobia, or other abnormal behavior.

NIBRS the National Incident-Based Reporting System, a new form of the UCR that will collect data on each single incident and arrest within twenty-two crime categories.

Nurturant strategy a crime control strategy which attempts "to forestall development of criminality by improving early life experiences and channeling child and adolescent development"[12] into desirable directions.

Occupational crime any act punishable by law which is committed through opportunity created in the course of an occupation that is legal.[13]

OJJDP the Office of Juvenile Justice and Delinquency Prevention.

Omerta the informal, unwritten code of organized crime which demands silence and loyalty, among other things, of family members.

Operant behavior behavior which affects the environment in such a way as to produce responses or further behavioral cues.

Operationalization the process by which concepts are made measurable.

Opportunity structure a path to success. Opportunity structures may be of two types: legitimate and illegitimate.

Organized crime the unlawful activities of the members of a highly organized, disciplined association engaged in supplying illegal goods and services, including but not limited to gambling, prostitution, loansharking, narcotics, labor racketeering, and other unlawful activities of members of such organizations.[14]

Panopticon a prison designed by Jeremy Bentham which was to be a circular building with cells along the circumference, each clearly visible from a central location staffed by guards.

Paradigm an example, model, or theory.

Paranoid schizophrenics schizophrenic individuals who suffer from delusions and hallucinations.

Part I offenses that group of offenses, also called "major offenses" or "index offenses," for which the UCR publishes counts of reported instances, and which consist of murder, rape, robbery, aggravated assault, burglary, larceny, auto theft, and arson.

Participant observation a variety of strategies in data gathering in which the researcher observes a group by participating, to varying degrees, in the activities of the group.[15]

Participatory justice a relatively informal type of criminal justice case processing which makes use of local community resources rather than requiring traditional forms of official intervention.

Peace model an approach to crime control which focuses on effective ways for developing a shared consensus on critical issues which have the potential to seriously affect the quality of life.

Peacemaking criminology a perspective which holds that crime-control agencies and the citizens they serve should work together to alleviate social problems and human suffering and thus reduce crime.

Penal couple a term which describes the relationship between victim and criminal. Also, the two individuals most involved in the criminal act—the offender and the victim.

Pharmaceutical diversion the process by which legitimately-manufactured controlled substances are diverted for illicit use.

Phenomenological criminology sees crime as a concept created through a process of social interaction, and details the existence of criminal reality via exploration of the world-view or mind-set characteristic of committed career offenders.

Phenomenology the study of the contents of human consciousness without regard to external conventions nor prior assumptions.

Phrenology the study of the shape of the head to determine anatomical correlates of human behavior.

Phone phreak a person who uses switched, dialed-access telephone services as objects for exploration and exploitation.

Pluralistic perspective an analytical approach to social organization which holds that a multiplicity of values and beliefs exist in any complex society, but that most social actors agree on the usefulness of law as a formal means of dispute resolution.

Positivism the application of scientific techniques to the study of crime and criminals.

Post-crime victimization or **secondary victimization** refers to problems in living which tend to follow from initial victimization.

Post-modern criminology a brand of criminology which developed following World War II, and which builds upon the tenants inherent in postmodern social thought.

Power-control theory a perspective which holds that the distribution of crime and delinquency within society is to some degree founded upon the consequences which power relationships within the wider society hold for domestic settings, and for the everyday relationships between men, women, and children within the context of family life.

Primary deviance initial deviance often undertaken to deal with transient problems in living.

Primary research research characterized by original and direct investigation.

Proletariat in Marxian theory, the working class.

Protection/avoidance strategy a crime-control strategy which attempts "to reduce criminal opportunities by changing people's routine activities or by incapacitating convicted offenders via incarceration or electronic monitoring devices."[16]

Psychiatric criminology. See **forensic psychiatry**.

Psychiatric theories those derived from the medical sciences, including neurology, and which, like other psychological theories, focus on the individual as the unit of analysis.

Psychoactive substances those which affect the mind, mental processes, or emotions.

Psychoanalysis the theory of human psychology founded by Freud on the concepts of the unconscious, resistance, repression, sexuality, and the Oedipus complex.[17]

Psychoanalytic criminology is a psychiatric approach developed by the Austrian psychiatrist Sigmund Freud which emphasizes the role of personality in human behavior, and which sees deviant behavior as the result of dysfunctional personalities.

Psychological profiling the attempt to categorize, understand, and predict, the behavior of certain types of offenders based upon behavioral clues they provide.

Psychological theories those derived from the behavioral sciences and which focus on the individual as the unit of analysis. Psychological theories place the locus of crime causation within the personality of the individual offender.

Psychopath or **sociopath** a person with a personality disorder, especially one manifested in aggressively antisocial behavior, which is often said to be the result of a poorly developed superego.

Psychopathology the study of pathological mental conditions, that is, mental illness.

Psychosis a form of mental illness in which sufferers are said to be out of touch with reality.

Psychotherapy a form of psychiatric treatment based upon psychoanalytical principles and techniques.

Public policy a course of action that government takes in an effort to solve a problem or to achieve an end.

Punishment undesirable behavioral consequences likely to decrease the frequency of occurrence of that behavior.

Pure research research undertaken simply for the sake of advancing scientific knowledge.

Qualitative methods research techniques which produce results which are difficult to quantify.

Quantitative methods research techniques which produce measurable results.

Quasi-experimental designs approaches to research which, although less powerful than experimental designs, are deemed worthy of use where better designs are not feasible.

Radical criminology a perspective which holds that the causes of crime are rooted in social conditions which empower the wealthy and the politically well organized, but disenfranchise those less fortunate. Also called **Marxist** or **critical criminology**.

Randomization the process whereby individuals are assigned to study groups without biases or differences resulting from selection.

Rape (NCVS) carnal knowledge through the use of force or the threat of force, including attempts. Statutory rape (without force) is excluded. Both heterosexual and homosexual rape are included.

Rape (UCR). See **Forcible rape.**

Rational choice theory a criminological perspective which holds that criminality is the result of conscious choice.

Reaction formation the process in which a person openly rejects that which he or she wants, or aspires to, but cannot obtain or achieve.

Realist criminology an emerging perspective which insists upon a pragmatic assessment of crime and associated problems.

Recidivism the repetition of criminal behavior.

Recidivism rate the percentage of convicted offenders who have been released from prison and who are later rearrested for a new crime, generally within five years following release.

Replicability (experimental) a scientific principle which holds that the same observations made at one time can be had again at a later time if all other conditions are the same.

Research the use of standardized, systematic procedures in the search for knowledge.[18]

Research design the logic and structure inherent in an approach to data-gathering.

Restitution a criminal sanction, in particular the payment of compensation by the offender to the victim.

Restorative justice a post-modern perspective which stresses "remedies and restoration rather than prison, punishment and victim neglect."[19]

Retribution the act of taking revenge upon a criminal perpetrator.

Reward desirable behavioral consequences likely to increase the frequency of occurrence of that behavior.

RICO an acronym for the "Racketeer Influenced and Corrupt Organization" statute, which was part of the federal Organized Crime Control Act of 1970.

Robbery (**UCR**) the unlawful taking or attempted taking of property that is in the immediate possession of another by force or threat of force or violence and/or by putting the victim in fear.

Routine activities theory or **life-style theory**) a brand of rational choice theory which suggests that life-styles contribute significantly to both the volume and type of crime found in any society.

Scenario writing a technique intended to predict future outcomes, and which builds upon environmental scanning by attempting to assess the likelihood of a variety of possible outcomes once important trends have been identified.

Schizophrenics mentally ill individuals who suffer from disjointed thinking and, possibly, delusions and hallucinations.

Second-degree murder criminal homicide which is unplanned, and which is often described as a "crime of passion."

Secondary analysis the reanalysis of existing data.

Secondary deviance that which results from official labeling and from association with others who have been so labeled.

Secondary research new evaluations of existing information which has already been collected by other researchers.

Selective incapacitation a social policy which seeks to protect society by incarcerating those individuals deemed to be the most dangerous.

Serial murder criminal homicide which involves the killing of several victims in three or more separate events.

Simple assault (NCVS) an attack without a weapon resulting either in minor injury or in undetermined injury requiring less than two days of hospitalization.

Situational choice theory a brand of rational choice theory which views criminal behavior "as a function of choices and decisions made within a context of situational constraints and opportunities."[20]

Social bond the rather intangible link between individuals and the society that they are a part. The social bond is created through the process of socialization.

Social class distinctions made between individuals on the basis of important defining social characteristics.

Social contract the Enlightenment-era concept that human beings abandon their natural state of individual freedom to join together and form society. Although, in the process of forming a social contract, individuals surrender some freedoms to society as a whole, government, once formed, is obligated to assume responsibilities toward its citizens and to provide for their protection and welfare.

Social control theory rather than stressing causative factors in criminal behavior, this perspective asks why people obey rules instead of breaking them.

Social disorganization a condition said to exist when a group is faced with social change, uneven development of culture, maladaptiveness, disharmony, conflict, and lack of consensus.

Social epidemiology the study of social epidemics and diseases of the social order.

Social learning theory a psychological perspective that says people learn how to behave by modeling themselves after others whom they have the opportunity to observe.

Social pathology a concept which compares society to a physical organism and sees criminality as an illness.

Social policies government initiatives, programs, and plans intended to address problems in society. The "War on Crime," for example, is a kind of generic (large-scale) social policy—one consisting of many smaller programs.

Social problems perspective the belief that crime is a manifestation of underlying social problems, such as poverty, discrimination, pervasive family violence, inadequate socialization practices, and the breakdown of traditional social institutions.

Social process theories, also known as **interactionist perspectives**, emphasize the give-and-take which occurs between offender, victim, and society—and specifically between the offender and agents of formal social control such as the police, courts, and correctional organizations.

Social relativity the notion that social events are differently interpreted according to the cultural experiences and personal interests of the initiator, the observer, or the recipient of that behavior.

Social responsibility perspective a viewpoint which holds that individuals are fundamentally responsible for their own behavior, and which maintains that they choose crime over other, more law-abiding, courses of action.

Social-structural theories explain crime by reference to various aspects of the social fabric. They emphasize relationships between social institutions, and describe the types of behavior which tend to characterize *groups* of people as opposed to *individuals.*

Social structure the pattern of social organization and the interrelationships between institutions characteristic of a society.

Sociobiology "the systematic study of the biological basis of all social behavior."[21]

Sociopath. See **psychopath.**

Somatotyping the classification of human beings into types according to body build and other physical characteristics.

Specific deterrence a goal of criminal sentencing which seeks to prevent a particular offender from engaging in repeat criminality.

State-organized crime acts defined by law as criminal and committed by state officials in the pursuit of their job as representatives of the state.[22]

Statistical correlation the simultaneous increase or decrease in value of two numerically valued random variables.[23]

Statistical school a criminological perspective with roots in the early 1800s which seeks to uncover correlations between crime rates and other types of demographic data.

Strain theory or ***anomie* theory** a sociological approach which posits a disjuncture between socially and subculturally sanctioned means and goals as the cause of criminal behavior.

Strategic assessment a technique which assesses the risks and opportunities facing those who plan for the future.

Subcultural theory a sociological perspective which emphasizes the contribution made by variously socialized cultural groups to the phenomenon of crime.

Subculture a collection of values and preferences which is communicated to subcultural participants through a process of socialization.

Sublimation the psychological process whereby one aspect of consciousness comes to be symbolically substituted for another.

Substantial capacity test a standard for judging legal insanity which requires that a person lack "the mental capacity needed to understand the wrongfulness of his act, or to conform his behavior to the requirements of the law."

Superego the moral aspect of the personality; much like the conscience. More formally, the division of the psyche that develops by the incorporation of the perceived moral standards of the community, is mainly unconscious, and includes the conscience.[24]

Supermale a human male displaying the XYY chromosome structure.

Survey research a social science data-gathering technique which involves the use of questionnaires.

Tagging like labeling, the process whereby an individual is negatively defined by agencies of justice.

Target hardening the reduction in criminal opportunity, generally through the use of physical barriers, architectural design, and enhanced security measures, of a particular location.

Techniques of neutralization culturally available justifications which can provide criminal offenders with the means to disavow responsibility for their behavior.

TEMPEST a standard developed by the U.S. government that requires that electromagnetic emanations from computers designated as "secure" be below levels that would allow radio receiving equipment to "read" the data being computed.

Terrorism a violent act or an act dangerous to human life in violation of the criminal laws of the United States or of any state to intimidate or coerce a government, the civilian population, or any segment thereof, in furtherance of political or social objectives.[25]

Testosterone the primary male sex hormone, produced in the testes and functioning to control secondary sex characteristics and sexual drive.

Tests of significance statistical techniques intended to provide researchers with confidence that their results are in fact true, and not the result of sampling error.

Thanatos a death wish.

Theory a series of interrelated propositions that attempt to describe, explain, predict, and ultimately to control some class of events. A theory gains explanatory power from inherent logical consistency, and is "tested" by how well it describes and predicts reality.

Threat analysis or **risk analysis** involves a complete and thorough assessment of the kinds of perils facing an organization.

Three-strikes a provision of some criminal statutes which mandates life imprisonment for criminals convicted of three violent felonies or serious drug offenses.

Total institutions facilities from which individuals can rarely come and go, and in which communal life is intense and circumscribed. Individuals in total institutions tend to eat, sleep, play, learn, and worship (if at all) together.

Trafficking includes manufacturing, distributing, dispensing, importing, and exporting (or possession with intent to do the same) a controlled substance or a counterfeit substance.[26]

Trephination a form of surgery, typically involving bone and especially the skull. Early instances of cranial trephination have been taken as evidence for primitive beliefs in spirit possession.

Twelve Tables early Roman laws written around 450 B.C. which regulated family, religious and economic life.

Uni-causal having one cause. Theories which are uni-causal posit only one source for all that they attempt to explain.

Uniform Crime Reports (UCR) a summation of crime statistics tallied annually by the Federal Bureau of Investigation (FBI) and consisting primarily of data on crimes reported to the police and of arrests.

Utilitarianism. See **hedonistic calculus.**

Variable a concept which can undergo measurable changes.

Victim impact statement a written document which describes the losses, suffering, and trauma experienced by the crime victim or by the victim's survivors. In jurisdictions where victim impact statements are used, judges are expected to consider them in arriving at an appropriate sentence for the offender.

Victim-precipitated homicides killings in which the "victim" was the first to commence the interaction or was the first to resort to physical violence.

Victim-proneness the degree of an individual's likelihood of victimization.

Victim-witness assistance programs counsel victims, orient them to the justice process, and provide a variety of other services such as transportation to court, child care during court appearances, and referrals to social service agencies.

Victimization rate (NCVS) a measure of the occurrence of victimizations among a specified population group. For personal crimes, this is based on the number of victimizations per 1,000 residents age 12 or older. For household crimes, the victimization rates are calculated using the number of incidents per 1,000 households.

Victimogenesis the contributory background of a victim as a result of which he or she becomes prone to victimization.

Victimology the study of victims and their contributory role, if any, in crime causation.

Virus (computer) a set of computer instructions that propagates copies or versions of itself into computer programs or data when it is executed.

VOCA the Victims of Crime Act, passed by the U.S. Congress in 1984.

White-collar crime violations of the criminal law committed by a person of respectability and high social status in the course of his or her occupation.

NOTES

1. This and other computer crime-related terms are generally taken from Donn B. parker, *Computer Crime: Criminal Justice Resource Manual* (Washington, D.C.: National Institute of Justice, 1989).
2. Michael L. Benson, Francis T. Cullen, and William J. Maakestad, *Local Prosecutors and Corporate Crime* (Washington, D.C.: National Institute of Justice, 1993).
3. James A. Inciardi, *The War on Drugs II* (Mountain View, CA: Mayfield, 1992), p. 79.
4. Bryan Vila, "A General Paradigm for Understanding Criminal Behavior: Extending Evolutionary Ecological Theory," Criminology, Vol. 32, no. 3 (August 1994), p. 311–359.
5. *The American Heritage Dictionary and Electronic Thesaurus* (Boston: Houghton Mifflin, 1987).
6. George F. Cole, "Criminal Justice in the Twenty-First Century: The Role of Futures Research," in John Klofas and Stan Stojkovic (eds.), *Crime and Justice in the Year 2010* (Belmont, CA: Wadsworth, 1995).
7. Society of Police Futurists International, *PFI: The Future of Policing* (brochure), no date.
8. *The American Heritage Dictionary and Electronic Thesaurus* on CD-ROM (text copyrighted, 1987 by the Houghton Mifflin Company).
9. Ibid.
10. Ibid.
11. Clifford Karchmer and Douglas Ruch, "State and Local Money Laundering Control Strategies," *NIJ Research in Brief* (Washington, D.C.: NIJ, 1992), p.1.
12. Bryan Vila, "A General Paradigm for Understanding Criminal Behavior: Extending Evolutionary Ecological Theory."
13. Gary S. Green, Occupational Crime (Chicago: Nelson-Hall, 1990), p.12.
14. The Omnibus Crime Control Act of 1970.
15. Frank E. Hagan, *Research Methods in Criminal Justice and Criminology* (New York: Macmillan, 1993), p. 103.
16. Bryan Vila, "A General Paradigm for Understanding Criminal Behavior: Extending Evolutionary Ecological Theory."
17. *The American Heritage Dictionary and Electronic Thesaurus.*
18. Abraham Kaplan, *The Conduct of Inquiry: Methodology for Behavioral Science* (San Francisco: Chandler, 1964), p. 71.
19. Fay Honey Knopp, "Community Solutions to Sexual Violence: Feminist-Abolitionist Perspectives," in Harold Pepinsky and Richard Quinney, eds., *Criminology as Peacemaking* (Bloomington: Indiana University Press, 1991), p. 183.
20. Ronald V. Clarke and Derek B. Cornish, eds., *Crime Control in Britain: A Review of Police and Research* (Albany: SUNY Press), p. 8.
21. Edward O. Wilson, *Sociobiology: The New Synthesis* (Cambridge: The Belknap Press of Harvard University Press, 1975).
22. William J. Chambliss, "State-Organized Crime—The American Society of Criminology, 1988 Presidential Address," *Criminology*, Vol. 27, no. 2 (1989), pp. 183–208.
23. *The American Heritage Dictionary and Electronic Thesaurus.*
24. Ibid.
25. Federal Bureau of Investigation, Counterterrorism Section, *Terrorism in the United States, 1987* (Washington, D.C.: FBI, December 1987).
26. Bureau of Justice Statistics, *Drugs, Crime and the Justice System* (Washington, D.C.: U.S. Department of Justice, December 1992), p. 181.

INDEXES

SUBJECT INDEX

E

F

G

T

NAME INDEX

Y

Z